"Composed in the style of the great medieval *catenae*, this new anthology of patristic commentary on Holy Scripture, conveniently arranged by chapter and verse, will be a valuable resource for prayer, study and proclamation. By calling attention to the rich Christian heritage preceding the separations between East and West and between Protestant and Catholic, this series will perform a major service to the cause of ecumenism."

AVERY CARDINAL DULLES, S.J.
Laurence J. McGinley Professor of Religion and Society
Fordham University

"The initial cry of the Reformation was *ad fontes*—back to the sources! The Ancient Christian Commentary on Scripture is a marvelous tool for the recovery of biblical wisdom in today's church. Not just another scholarly project, the ACCS is a major resource for the renewal of preaching, theology and Christian devotion."

TIMOTHY GEORGE
Dean, Beeson Divinity School, Samford University

"Modern church members often do not realize that they are participants in the vast company of the communion of saints that reaches far back into the past and that will continue into the future, until the kingdom comes. This Commentary should help them begin to see themselves as participants in that redeemed community."

ELIZABETH ACHTEMEIER
Union Professor Emerita of Bible and Homiletics
Union Theological Seminary in Virginia

"Contemporary pastors do not stand alone. We are not the first generation of preachers to wrestle with the challenges of communicating the gospel. The Ancient Christian Commentary on Scripture puts us in conversation with our colleagues from the past, that great cloud of witnesses who preceded us in this vocation. This Commentary enables us to receive their deep spiritual insights, their encouragement and guidance for present-day interpretation and preaching of the Word. What a wonderful addition to any pastor's library!"

WILLIAM H. WILLIMON
Dean of the Chapel and Professor of Christian Ministry
Duke University

"Here is a nonpareil series which reclaims the Bible as the book of the church by making accessible to earnest readers of the twenty-first century the classrooms of Clement of Alexandria and Didymus the Blind, the study and lecture hall of Origen, the cathedrae of Chrysostom and Augustine, the scriptorium of Jerome in his Bethlehem monastery."

GEORGE LAWLESS
Augustinian Patristic Institute and Gregorian University, Rome

"We are pleased to witness publication of the
Ancient Christian Commentary on Scripture. It is most beneficial for us to learn
how the ancient Christians, especially the saints of the church
who proved through their lives their devotion to God and his Word, interpreted
Scripture. Let us heed the witness of those who have gone before us in the faith."

Metropolitan Theodosius
Primate, Orthodox Church in America

"Across Christendom there has emerged a widespread interest
in early Christianity, both at the popular and scholarly level. . . .
Christians of all traditions stand to benefit from this project, especially clergy
and those who study the Bible. Moreover, it will allow us to see how our traditions are
both rooted in the scriptural interpretations of the church fathers while at
the same time seeing how we have developed new perspectives."

Alberto Ferreiro
Professor of History, Seattle Pacific University

"The Ancient Christian Commentary on Scripture fills a long overdue need for scholars and
students of the church fathers. . . . Such information will be of immeasurable
worth to those of us who have felt inundated by contemporary interpreters and novel theories
of the biblical text. We welcome some 'new' insight from the
ancient authors in the early centuries of the church."

H. Wayne House
Professor of Theology and Law
Trinity University School of Law

Chronological snobbery—the assumption that our ancestors working without benefit of
computers have nothing to teach us—is exposed as nonsense by this magnificent
new series. Surfeited with knowledge but starved of wisdom, many of us are
more than ready to sit at table with our ancestors and listen to their holy
conversations on Scripture. I know I am.

Eugene H. Peterson
Professor Emeritus of Spiritual Theology
Regent College

"Few publishing projects have encouraged me as much as the recently announced Ancient Christian Commentary on Scripture with Dr. Thomas Oden serving as general editor.... How is it that so many of us who are dedicated to serve the Lord received seminary educations which omitted familiarity with such incredible students of the Scriptures as St. John Chrysostom, St. Athanasius the Great and St. John of Damascus? I am greatly anticipating the publication of this Commentary."

FR. PETER E. GILLQUIST
Director, Department of Missions and Evangelism
Antiochian Orthodox Christian Archdiocese of North America

"The Scriptures have been read with love and attention for nearly two thousand years, and listening to the voice of believers from previous centuries opens us to unexpected insight and deepened faith. Those who studied Scripture in the centuries closest to its writing, the centuries during and following persecution and martyrdom, speak with particular authority. The Ancient Christian Commentary on Scripture will bring to life the truth that we are invisibly surrounded by a 'great cloud of witnesses.'"

FREDERICA MATHEWES-GREEN
Commentator, National Public Radio

"For those who think that church history began around 1941 when their pastor was born, this Commentary will be a great surprise. Christians throughout the centuries have read the biblical text, nursed their spirits with it and then applied it to their lives. These commentaries reflect that the witness of the Holy Spirit was present in his church throughout the centuries. As a result, we can profit by allowing the ancient Christians to speak to us today."

HADDON ROBINSON
Harold John Ockenga Distinguished Professor of Preaching
Gordon-Conwell Theological Seminary

"All who are interested in the interpretation of the Bible will welcome the forthcoming multivolume series Ancient Christian Commentary on Scripture. Here the insights of scores of early church fathers will be assembled and made readily available for significant passages throughout the Bible and the Apocrypha. It is hard to think of a more worthy ecumenical project to be undertaken by the publisher."

BRUCE M. METZGER
Professor of New Testament, Emeritus
Princeton Theological Seminary

ANCIENT CHRISTIAN
COMMENTARY ON SCRIPTURE

OLD TESTAMENT

III

EXODUS, LEVITICUS, NUMBERS, DEUTERONOMY

EDITED BY

JOSEPH T. LIENHARD, S.J.

IN COLLABORATION WITH
RONNIE J. ROMBS

GENERAL EDITOR
THOMAS C. ODEN

InterVarsity Press
Downers Grove, Illinois

InterVarsity Press
P.O. Box 1400, Downers Grove, IL 60515-1426
World Wide Web: www.ivpress.com
E-mail: mail@ivpress.com

InterVarsity Press® is the book-publishing division of InterVarsity Christian Fellowship/USA®, a student movement active on campus at hundreds of universities, colleges and schools of nursing in the United States of America, and a member movement of the International Fellowship of Evangelical Students. For information about local and regional activities, write Public Relations Dept., InterVarsity Christian Fellowship/USA, 6400 Schroeder Rd., P.O. Box 7895, Madison, WI 53707-7895.

Scripture quotations, unless otherwise noted, are from the Revised Standard Version of the Bible, copyright 1946, 1952, 1971 by the Division of Christian Education of the National Council of the Churches of Christ in the U.S.A., and are used by permission.

Pericopal headings have been adapted from the New American Bible. Copyright © 1970 Confraternity of Christian Doctrine, Inc., Washington, D.C. Used with permission. All rights reserved. No part of the New American Bible may be reproduced by any means without permission in writing from the copyright owner.

Selected excerpts from Ancient Christian Writers: The Works of the Fathers in Translation. Copyright 1946-. Used by permission of Paulist Press, www.paulistpress.com.

Selected excerpts from Fathers of the Church: A New Translation. Copyright 1947-. Used by permission of The Catholic University of America Press.

Selected excerpts from Bede: On the Tabernacle, translated with notes and introduction by Arthur G. Holder. Copyright 1994. Used by permission of Liverpool University Press.

Selected excerpts from The Works of Saint Augustine: A Translation for the 21st Century. Copyright 1990-. Used by permission of the Augustinian Heritage Institute.

Cover photograph: Scala/Art Resource, New York. View of the apse. S. Vitale, Ravenna, Italy.

Spine photograph: Byzantine collection, Dumbarton Oaks, Washington, D.C. Pendant cross (gold and enamel). Constantinople, late sixth century.

ISBN 0-8308-1473-6

Printed in the United States of America ∞

Library of Congress Cataloging-in-Publication Data

Exodus, Leviticus, Numbers, Deuteronomy/edited by Joseph T. Lienhard.

    p. cm.—(Ancient Christian commentary on Scripture. Old Testament; 3)

  Includes bibliographical references (p.) and indexes.

  ISBN 0-8308-1473-6 (cloth: alk. paper)

  1. Bible. O.T. Exodus–Commentaries. 2. Bible. O.T. Leviticus—Commentaries. 3. Bible. O.T. Numbers—Commentaries. 4. Bible. O.T. Deuteronomy—Commentaries. 5. Bible. O.T. Pentateuch—Hermeneutics—History—Early church, ca. 30-600. I. Lienhard, Joseph T. II. Series

  BS1225.3 .E96 2001

  222'.1077—dc21

                                      2001024408

| 25 | 24 | 23 | 22 | 21 | 20 | 19 | 18 | 17 | 16 | 15 | 14 | 13 | 12 | 11 | 10 | 9 | 8 | 7 | 6 | 5 | 4 | 3 | 2 | 1 |
| 22 | 21 | 20 | 19 | 18 | 17 | 16 | 15 | 14 | 13 | 12 | 11 | 10 | 09 | 08 | 07 | 06 | 05 | 04 | 03 | 02 | 01 | | | |

Contents

General Introduction

The Ancient Christian Commentary on Scripture has as its goal the revitalization of Christian teaching based on classical Christian exegesis, the intensified study of Scripture by lay persons who wish to think with the early church about the canonical text, and the stimulation of Christian historical, biblical, theological and pastoral scholars toward further inquiry into scriptural interpretation by ancient Christian writers.

The time frame of these documents spans seven centuries of exegesis, from Clement of Rome to John of Damascus, from the end of the New Testament era to A.D. 750, including the Venerable Bede.

Lay readers are asking how they might study sacred texts under the instruction of the great minds of the ancient church. This commentary has been intentionally prepared for a general lay audience of non-professionals who study the Bible regularly and who earnestly wish to have classic Christian observation on the text readily available to them. The series is targeted to anyone who wants to reflect and meditate with the early church about the plain sense, theological wisdom and moral meaning of particular Scripture texts.

A commentary dedicated to allowing ancient Christian exegetes to speak for themselves will refrain from the temptation to fixate endlessly upon contemporary criticism. Rather, it will stand ready to provide textual resources from a distinguished history of exegesis that has remained massively inaccessible and shockingly disregarded during the last century. We seek to make available to our present-day audiences the multicultural, multilingual, transgenerational resources of the early ecumenical Christian tradition.

Preaching at the end of the first millennium focused primarily on the text of Scripture as understood by the earlier esteemed tradition of comment, largely converging on those writers that best reflected classic Christian consensual thinking. Preaching at the end of the second millennium has reversed that pattern. It has so forgotten most of these classic comments that they are vexing to find anywhere, and even when located they are often available only in archaic editions and inadequate translations. The preached word in our time has remained largely bereft of previously influential patristic inspiration. Recent scholarship has so focused attention upon post-Enlightenment historical and literary methods that it has left this longing largely unattended and unserviced.

This series provides the pastor, exegete, student and lay reader with convenient means to see what Athanasius or John Chrysostom or the desert fathers and mothers had to say about a particular text for preaching, for study and for meditation. There is an emerging awareness among Catholic, Protestant and Orthodox laity that vital biblical preaching and spiritual formation need deeper grounding beyond the scope of the historical-critical orientations that have governed biblical studies in our day.

Hence this work is directed toward a much broader audience than the highly technical and specialized scholarly field of patristic studies. The audience is not limited to the university scholar concentrating on the study of the history of the transmission of the text or to those with highly focused philological interests in textual morphology or historical-critical issues. Though these are crucial concerns for specialists, they are not the paramount interest of this series.

This work is a Christian Talmud. The Talmud is a Jewish collection of rabbinic arguments and comments on the Mishnah, which epitomized the laws of the Torah. The Talmud originated in approximately the same period that the patristic writers were commenting on texts of the Christian tradition. Christians from the late patristic age through the medieval period had documents analogous to the Jewish Talmud and Midrash (Jewish commentaries) available to them in the *glossa ordinaria* and catena traditions, two forms of compiling extracts of patristic exegesis. In Talmudic fashion the sacred text of Christian Scripture was thus clarified and interpreted by the classic commentators.

The Ancient Christian Commentary on Scripture has venerable antecedents in medieval exegesis of both eastern and western traditions, as well as in the Reformation tradition. It offers for the first time in this century the earliest Christian comments and reflections on the Old and New Testaments to a modern audience. Intrinsically an ecumenical project, this series is designed to serve Protestant, Catholic and Orthodox lay, pastoral and scholarly audiences.

In cases where Greek, Latin, Syriac and Coptic texts have remained untranslated into English, we provide new translations. Wherever current English translations are already well rendered, they will be utilized, but if necessary their language will be brought up to date. We seek to present fresh dynamic equivalency translations of long-neglected texts which historically have been regarded as authoritative models of biblical interpretation.

These foundational sources are finding their way into many public libraries and into the core book collections of many pastors and lay persons. It is our intent and the publisher's commitment to keep the whole series in print for many years to come.

Thomas C. Oden
General Editor

A Guide to Using This Commentary

Several features have been incorporated into the design of this commentary. The following comments are intended to assist readers in making full use of this volume.

Pericopes of Scripture

The scriptural text has been divided into pericopes, or passages, usually several verses in length. Each of these pericopes is given a heading, which appears at the beginning of the pericope. For example, the first pericope in the commentary on Exodus is "1:1-7 The Israelites in Egypt." This heading is followed by the Scripture passage quoted in the Revised Standard Version (RSV) across the full width of the page. The Scripture passage is provided for the convenience of readers, but it is also in keeping with medieval patristic commentaries, in which the citations of the Fathers were arranged around the text of Scripture.

Overviews

Following each pericope of text is an overview of the patristic comments on that pericope. The format of this overview varies within the volumes of this series, depending on the requirements of the specific book of Scripture. The function of the overview is to provide a brief summary of all the comments to follow. It tracks a reasonably cohesive thread of argument among patristic comments, even though they are derived from diverse sources and generations. Thus the summaries do not proceed chronologically or by verse sequence. Rather they seek to rehearse the overall course of the patristic comment on that pericope.

We do not assume that the commentators themselves anticipated or expressed a formally received cohesive argument but rather that the various arguments tend to flow in a plausible, recognizable pattern. Modern readers can thus glimpse aspects of continuity in the flow of diverse exegetical traditions representing various generations and geographical locations.

Topical Headings

An abundance of varied patristic comment is available for each pericope of these letters. For this reason we have broken the pericopes into two levels. First is the verse with its topical heading. The patristic comments are then focused on aspects of each verse, with topical headings summarizing the essence of the patristic comment by evoking a key phrase, metaphor or idea. This feature provides a bridge by which modern readers can enter into the heart of the patristic comment.

Identifying the Patristic Texts

Following the topical heading of each section of comment, the name of the patristic commentator is given. An English translation of the patristic comment is then provided. This is immediately followed by the title of the patristic work and the textual reference—either by book, section and subsection or by book-and-verse references.

The Footnotes

Readers who wish to pursue a deeper investigation of the patristic works cited in this commentary will find the footnotes especially valuable. A footnote number directs the reader to the notes at the bottom of the right-hand column, where in addition to other notations (clarifications or biblical cross references) one will find information on English translations (where available) and standard original-language editions of the work cited. An abbreviated citation (normally citing the book, volume and page number) of the work is provided except in cases where a line-by-line commentary is being quoted, in which case the biblical references will lead directly to the selection. A key to the abbreviations is provided on pages xv-xvi. Where there is any serious ambiguity or textual problem in the selection, we have tried to reflect the best available textual tradition.

For the convenience of computer database users the digital database references are provided to either the Thesaurus Linguae Graecae (Greek texts) or to the Cetedoc (Latin texts) in the bibliography found on pages 361-72.

Abbreviations

ACW	Ancient Christian Writers: The Works of the Fathers in Translation. Mahwah, N.J.: Paulist, 1946-.
ANF	A. Roberts and J. Donaldson, eds. Ante-Nicene Fathers. 10 vols. Buffalo, N.Y.: Christian Literature, 1885-1896. Reprint, Grand Rapids, Mich.: Eerdmans, 1951-1956; Reprint, Peabody, Mass.: Hendrickson, 1994.
CAA	Bede the Venerable. *Commentary on the Acts of the Apostles.* Translated by L. T. Martin. Kalamazoo, Mich.: Cistercian Publications, 1989.
CCL	Corpus Christianorum. Series Latina. Turnhout, Belgium: Brepols, 1953-.
CGSL	Cyril of Alexandria. *Commentary on the Gospel of St. Luke.* Translated by R. Payne Smith. Studion Publishers, Inc., 1983.
COP	John Chrysostom. *Six Books on the Priesthood.* Translated by Graham Neville. Crestwood, N.Y.: St. Vladimir's Seminary Press, 1977.
CS	Cistercian Studies. Kalamazoo, Mich.: Cistercian Publications, 1973-.
CSEL	Corpus Scriptorum Ecclesiasticorum Latinorum. Vienna, 1866-.
CWS	Classics of Western Spirituality: A Library of the Great Spiritual Masters. Mahwah, N.J.: Paulist, 1978-. These volumes are not numbered. Numbers in the text refer to page numbers in the volume for the appropriate author cited.
FC	Fathers of the Church: A New Translation. Washington, D.C.: Catholic University of America Press, 1947-.
GCS	Die griechischen christlichen Schriftsteller der ersten Jahrhunderte. Berlin: Akademie-Verlag, 1897-.
GNLM	A. J. Malherbe and E. Ferguson, trans. *Gregory of Nyssa: The Life of Moses.* CWS. New York: Paulist, 1978.
GNTIP	Ronald E. Heine, trans. *Gregory of Nyssa's Treatise on the Inscriptions of the Psalms.* Oxford Early Christian Studies. Oxford: Clarendon Press, 1995.
HOG	Bede the Venerable. *Homilies on the Gospels.* Translated by L. T. Martin and D. Hurst. 2 vols. Kalamazoo, Mich.: Cistercian Publications, 1990.
HOP	Ephrem the Syrian. *Hymns on Paradise.* Translated by S. Brock. Crestwood, N.Y.: St. Vladimir's Seminary Press, 1990.
IWG	Macarius. *Intoxicated with God: The Fifty Spiritual Homilies of Macarius.* Translated by George A. Maloney. Denville, N.J.: Dimension, 1978.
JSSS 2	C. McCarthy, trans. and ed. *Saint Ephrem's Commentary on Tatian's Diatessaron: An English Translation of Chester Beatty Syriac MS 709. Journal of Semitic Studies* Supplement 2. Oxford: Oxford University Press for the University of Manchester, 1993.
LCC	J. Baillie et al., eds. The Library of Christian Classics. 26 vols. Philadelphia: Westminster Press, 1953-1966.

NPNF	P. Schaff et al., eds. *A Select Library of the Nicene and Post-Nicene Fathers of the Christian Church*. 2 series (14 vols. each). Buffalo, N.Y.: Christian Literature, 1887-1894; Reprint, Grand Rapids, Mich.: Eerdmans, 1952-1956; Reprint, Peabody, Mass.: Hendrickson, 1994.
OCC	Origen. *Contra Celsum*. Translated with an Introduction and Notes by Henry Chadwick. Cambridge: Cambridge University Press, 1953.
ODI	St. John of Damascus. *On the Divine Image*. Translated by David Anderson. Crestwood, N.Y.: St. Vladimir's Seminary Press, 1980.
OEM	Rowan A. Green, trans. *Origen: An Exhortation to Martyrdom, Prayer and Selected Works*. The Classics of Western Spirituality. New York: Paulist, 1979.
OFP	Origen. *On First Principles*. Translated by G. W. Butterworth. London: SPCK, 1936; Reprint, Gloucester, Mass.: Peter Smith, 1973.
PDCW	Colm Luibheid, trans. *Pseudo-Dionysius: The Complete Works*. The Classics of Western Spirituality. New York: Paulist, 1987.
PG	J.-P. Migne, ed. *Patrologiae Cursus Completus, Series Graeca*. 166 vols. Paris: Migne, 1857-1886.
PL	J.-P. Migne, ed. *Patrologiae Cursus Completus, Series Latina*. 221 vols. Paris: Migne, 1844-1864.
PMFSH	George A. Maloney, S.J., trans. and ed. *Pseudo-Macarius: The Fifty Spiritual Homilies and the Great Letter*. The Classics of Western Spirituality. New York: Paulist, 1992.
POG	Eusebius. *The Proof of the Gospel*. Translated by W. J. Ferrar. London: SPCK, 1920; Reprint, Grand Rapids, Mich.: Baker, 1981.
SNTD	Symeon the New Theologian. *The Discourses*. Translated by C. J. de Catanzaro. Classics of Western Spirituality: A Library of the Great Spiritual Masters. Mahwah, N.J.: Paulist, 1980.
TTH	G. Clark, M. Gibson and M. Whitby, eds. *Translated Texts for Historians*. Liverpool: Liverpool University Press, 1985-.
WSA	J. E. Rotelle, ed. *Works of St. Augustine: A Translation for the Twenty-First Century*. Hyde Park, N.Y.: New City Press, 1995.

Introduction to Exodus Through Deuteronomy

From the first day of its existence, on the first Easter morning, the Christian church had a Bible—that is, the Jewish Scriptures.[1] But Christians did not read these Scriptures the way the Jews did; they read them in light of what God had done in Jesus the Christ. Hence Scripture was never to have, for Christians, the absolute authority the Torah had for Jews. Christ was to be the Christians' final authority.[2]

The earliest Christians, who were converted Jews, found confirmation of their new faith in these Scriptures.[3] The first chapters of the Gospel according to Matthew, for example, or the narrative of Jesus' passion and death in the Gospel according to John, quote the Old Testament again and again, with words such as "so that the Scripture might be fulfilled."

Yet this Bible was not without its problems for Christians. They found in it dozens of verses that they took as prophecies of Christ, even of single events in his life. But these verses were only a tiny portion of that Bible. Much of it they considered irrelevant to them, especially the great bodies of ritual law in the Pentateuch. Other parts they found valuable: the Psalms quickly became a Christian prayer book; the historical narratives offered inspiring models of virtue and its rewards or of wrongdoing and its punishment; the wisdom literature was useful for teaching morality to pagans who wanted to convert to Christianity; and the prophets often condemned Jewish formalism, as Jesus had done.

But the problem that the Bible posed was not yet solved. To what extent was it God's Word for the new church? Paul had warned the Christians against falling back into Jewish ways, so some of this Bible, at least, was not to be taken literally.

Three basic approaches to the Jewish Scriptures were open to the early Christians. Either the Scriptures were law, or they were prophecy, or they were irrelevant. Paul himself faced up to the problem of the Scriptures most radically: the Scriptures were indeed law, God's law, and as such were good. But the law was temporary and had been superseded by Christ and by the order of grace. The epistle to the Hebrews represents a similar pattern: what was repeated and therefore imperfect in the Old Covenant is fulfilled and accomplished definitively in Christ. The Gospels of Matthew and John, in contrast, and other early Christian writings such as Justin's *First Apology*, understood the Old Testament as prophecy. The third possibility, that the Jewish Scriptures were virtually irrelevant to Christianity, is foreshadowed

---

[1] For these opening pages see Hans von Campenhausen, *The Formation of the Christian Bible*, trans. J. A. Baker (Philadelphia: Fortress, 1972), esp. chap. 3, "The Crisis of the Old Testament Canon in the Second Century."

[2] St. Augustine beautifully expresses the conditional authority of the Scriptures for Christians when, writing of the vision of God, he says, "When that day is at hand, the prophet will not be read to us, the book of the apostle will not be opened, we shall not require the testimony of John, we shall have no need of the gospel itself. All Scriptures will be taken out of the way, those Scriptures that in the night of this world burned like lamps so that we might not remain in darkness." *Tractates on the Gospel of John* 35.9.

[3] The study of early Christian exegesis is best viewed in relation with rabbinic exegesis of the same period. Christian scholars are increasingly studying rabbinic exegesis, even as Jewish scholars are increasingly studying patristic exegesis. This volume offers the prospect not only of enhancing comparative studies of Jewish and Christian exegesis of this period but also, and perhaps more so, providing new resources for Jewish-Christian dialogue.

in several books of the New Testament in which "the Scripture" is never quoted and is evident in writers like Ignatius of Antioch.

In the late first and early second centuries, a reversal took place in Christians' attitude to the Scriptures. The first Christians, Jewish converts, had already accepted the Scriptures and then found in them confirmation of their faith in Christ. Later Christians, converts from paganism, first accepted faith in Christ and then confronted the mysterious and often baffling Scriptures. This encounter eventually led to a crisis, and a crisis precisely of interpretation.

The two most radical solutions to this crisis of interpretation are found in Marcion of Sinope and in the *Epistle of Barnabas*, both datable roughly to around the year 140.

Marcion read the Scriptures literally and only literally. Every word of them, he held, was literally true and only literally true. The God they portrayed was so ignorant that he had to ask Adam, "Where are you?" This God was so fickle that he first forbade Moses to make graven images and then told him to make an image of a serpent. He was indecisive; a mere human being like Moses could talk him into changing his mind. The Scripture even attested that God could repent. This God could be vicious, too, and order dreadful slaughters even of women and infants. Marcion drew the only conclusion that was for him possible: these Scriptures had to be thrown out of the church, for they were unworthy of the Father of Jesus Christ, the God of love.

The author of the *Epistle of Barnabas* did the opposite: he read the Jewish Scriptures only figuratively and concluded that the Jews had never understood them. The covenant, he theorized, had been valid only from the time Moses received the commandments on Sinai until he reached the bottom of the mountain and smashed the tablets. Then a wicked angel came to the Jews and persuaded them to take the Scriptures literally.

Effectively, Marcion read the Bible only literally and threw it out of the church; Barnabas read the Bible only figuratively and took it away from the synagogue.

But the church expelled Marcion and did not accept Barnabas. Thus it decided to retain the Jewish Scriptures as its own, with the understanding that those Scriptures had in some way a double sense. They were literally true: God did show his face to the patriarchs and speak through the prophets; God did indeed make a covenant with Israel. But Christ provided the Christians with a new key to understanding the old Scriptures, and the literal sense could not be the only sense. Read in the light of Christ, the old Scriptures revealed something more profound.

Irenaeus of Lyons was the first to work out a theory of how the Old and New Testaments were related. By his time, about 190, it was clear that the church would indeed have a New Testament—that is, a collection of sacred books written by Christians and equal in authority to the Jewish Scriptures, which could now be called the Old Testament (although Irenaeus did not use that term). Irenaeus saw all of saving history as an ellipse with two foci, Adam and Christ. The two Testaments yielded one great picture: a beginning in Adam, a fall from grace and a new beginning or recapitulation in Christ.

Thus the theory was in place. But the church still lacked a practical instrument, namely, a Christian commentary on the Old Testament, book by book. Hippolytus of Rome, who died in 235, was among the first to try to fill the gap. His commentary on Daniel, which is extant, is the oldest surviving Christian commentary on any book of the Old Testament. He wrote some other commentaries, which are mostly lost; perhaps they were not very useful.

The man who assured the Old Testament its permanent place in the Christian church was Origen (c. 185-254). He did this by writing an enormous body of commentary and hundreds of homilies on almost every book of the Old Testament. From Origen's time on, the principles of Christian exegesis of the Old Testament were established, and a library of commentaries and homilies soon existed and could be consulted. Many interpreters later disagreed with Origen or even rejected his methods. Yet it is probably impossible to overestimate his influence on the history of exegesis in the church. The greater part of Origen's work is lost, so it is not always possible—especially in Greek authors—to discern his influence. Much of what does survive, survives in Latin translations. Ambrose and Jerome, among many others, depended heavily on Origen, sometimes so heavily that their explanations of the Scripture were little more than translations of Origen.

Thus, with Irenaeus and Origen, both theory and practice were established. The Jewish Scriptures were also to be the Christian Old Testament, and their full meaning was to be seen only in the light shed by Christ. This act of faith—and an act of faith it was—is enshrined in the Creed of Constantinople (381), in which Christians confess that "on the third day he rose again, according to the Scriptures," and further that the Holy Spirit "spoke through the prophets." This latter phrase enshrines the church's final rejection of Marcionism and its affirmation that the one Holy Spirit of God spoke with one voice in both Testaments.

Theory and practice were established, but a great task lay ahead. The church needed to ponder God's Word, in faith and in hope, and come to an ever fuller understanding of what indeed the Holy Spirit had said through the prophets.

The Text of the Old Testament

When the Fathers of the church—at least those who spoke Greek and Latin—read the Old Testament, they read it in translation. The Greek translation is called the Septuagint (LXX). The name comes from the legend that seventy elders translated (as Jewish versions have it) the Torah or (as Christian versions have it) the whole Old Testament from Hebrew into Greek. In the course of the third and second centuries B.C., unknown Jewish translators did indeed render the Scriptures from Hebrew into Greek, in the first great translation project in history. In doing so they also transferred their Scriptures into a different thought world. Concrete Hebrew expressions became abstract Greek concepts. One of the most fateful—or perhaps providential—translations was that of Exodus 3:14, where the translators rendered the Hebrew equivalent of "I am who I am" as "I am he who is" and thus opened the way for Greek speculation on "being" to be predicated of God. But the translation made a crucial change: while the Greeks spoke of being in the neuter, the Jewish translators used the masculine gender, implying that while Being was all the Greeks said it was, it was also what the Greeks could never have imagined, namely, a person.

Thus the Bible of the early church is preeminently the Septuagint, and Fathers like Augustine considered the Hebrew text and the Septuagint equally inspired. There are exceptions, of course, and the Fathers knew of other Greek versions, too, also produced by Jews. For after the Christians accepted the

Septuagint as their Bible, the Jews came to reject it as too free. The Babylonian Talmud comments, "It happened that five elders translated the Pentateuch into Greek for King Ptolemy. That day was as hard for Israel as the day the calf was made, because the Pentateuch could not be translated properly."[4] Thereupon Jewish scholars made at least three other translations into Greek, each of them more literal than the Septuagint, and one at least so literal as to be nearly unintelligible.[5]

If the Septuagint is an uneven collection of the work of different translators, the so-called Old Latin translation is even more complex. From the later second century on, Latin-speaking Christians began to translate the Septuagint—piecemeal, mostly—into Latin. Some of these translators had not mastered Greek perfectly, and a few had not quite mastered Latin. Yet much of Latin commentary on the Scripture, up to the fifth century, was based on the Old Latin, a translation—or better a collection of many translations—of the Septuagint into Latin.

Latin-speaking Christians themselves acknowledged the problem, and around 384 St. Jerome undertook a revision of the Latin Bible. What he produced—part of it fresh translation from Hebrew and Greek, part of it revisions of older translations, other parts never touched by him—became known as the Vulgate. Only gradually, from the late fourth century until the ninth, did the Vulgate replace the Old Latin as the standard Bible in the Latin-speaking West.

Meanwhile the Jews preserved the Hebrew text of the Bible. Some time between the fifth and the ninth centuries, the Masoretes established a definitive Hebrew text, the one on which modern translations such as the Revised Standard Version (RSV) are based. But to say that the Masoretic text (MT) is always preferable to the Septuagint is too simplistic and even erroneous. The Septuagint demonstrates, first of all, how ancient Jews understood the Hebrew text of the Bible. In some cases the Septuagint represents an older or more primitive version of a book than does the Masoretic text. A glance through the footnotes in the Revised Standard Version shows that the Masoretic text contains more than a few problematic passages, and the Revised Standard Version restores the text from the Greek or other versions.

Practically, for this volume of the Ancient Christian Commentary on Scripture, the conclusion is this: when the Fathers of the church commented on the Bible, they all but invariably commented on the Septuagint in Greek or the Old Latin or Vulgate in Latin. In a few cases they are closer to the Hebrew than the Revised Standard Version is; in all cases they are commenting on their Bible and should be accepted as doing precisely that.

Ancient Commentaries on Exodus, Leviticus, Numbers and Deuteronomy

The Fathers of the church commented on the Bible in the course of almost all their writings; it is difficult to find a patristic work that does not contain some citation of Scripture or some comment on it.

Among the literary genres that dealt specifically with the Scriptures, homilies and commentaries were the most common, the former the product of the pulpit, the latter the product of the study. Another genre used in the explication of the Bible, already familiar to Greek philosophers, was the ques-

---

[4]*Massekhet Soferim* 1:7.

[5]They are the versions of Aquila, Symmachus and Theodotion, most of which survive only in fragments, except for Theodotion's version of Daniel.

tion-and-response format.[6] The number of Fathers who wrote the equivalent of running commentaries on one or more books of the Pentateuch is small. And even in these cases, what they wrote was not precisely like modern commentaries. Concretely, patristic works on the Pentateuch survive from seven authors, four Latin and three Greek. These works are, almost of necessity, uneven in their treatment of the text. A thick book of patristic comments on Exodus 12 could be collected with little difficulty. In contrast, chapters that list names or consist only of detailed ritual law received little or no comment from the Fathers. The unevenness of the Fathers' comments is necessarily reflected in this volume.

First among all the commentators on the Pentateuch was Origen. He wrote a commentary on Genesis in thirteen books, but this work is lost. He also preached on all the books of the Pentateuch, but his homilies on Deuteronomy are lost. From Origen we have sixteen homilies on Genesis, thirteen on Exodus, sixteen on Leviticus and twenty-eight on Numbers, all in Rufinus of Aquileia's Latin translation. Origen preached his homilies in the course of liturgies of reading and preaching intended for catechumens. A relatively long portion of a book would be read, the equivalent of two or three modern chapters, and Origen would comment on a few points from that reading, with the goal of instructing his hearers in the Christian faith and urging them to live upright lives. By far the most spectacular among these homilies is the twenty-seventh homily on Numbers, in which Origen interprets the forty-two stopping places of the Israelites in the desert as the forty-two stages of growth in the spiritual life, based on the etymologies, real or imagined, of the Hebrew place names.

The next commentator on these books is Augustine of Hippo (354-430). Around the year 419, he made an intense study of the Heptateuch, the first seven books of the Bible. Two works of his report the results of this study. *Seven Books of Expressions on the Heptateuch*[7] is a running list of phrases that seemed to Augustine to contain Hebrew or Greek idioms—that is, phrases from the Latin Bible that were ungrammatical or unidiomatic. Augustine also compared several Latin codices of the Heptateuch and reported differences among them. In *Seven Books of Expressions* he offers short explanations of the problems. He found 213 problems in Genesis, 160 in Exodus, 62 in Leviticus, 127 in Numbers, 78 in Deuteronomy, 31 in Joshua and 64 in Judges. The second work is titled *Questions on the Heptateuch*.[8] In this work Augustine raises and tries to solve problems of concordance and morality that occurred to him as he read the text. The result is in one sense fascinating and even edifying: that in 419 Augustine, who had just finished his great work *On the Trinity* and was engaged in the fierce battles of the Pelagian controversy, should take time to work his way carefully through the text of the Heptateuch is little short of amazing. To describe his effort gives some sense of the scope of the work: he has 173 questions on Genesis, 177 on Exodus, 94 on Leviticus, 65 on Numbers, 57 on Deuteronomy, 30 on Joshua and 55 on Judges. Most of his comments are about a paragraph long, but at the end of his questions on Exodus Augustine has an essay on the tabernacle that extends for more than twenty pages. But the work is in some ways rather disappointing. It has the character of a preliminary study rather than a finished commentary. About

---

[6]On this genre see the magisterial survey by Gustave Bardy, "La Littérature Patristique des 'Quaestiones et Responsiones' sur l'Écriture Sainte," *Revue Biblique* 41 (1932): 210-36, 341-69, 515-37; 42 (1933): 14-30, 211-29, 328-52.
[7]Critical edition in CCL 33:381-465.
[8]Critical edition in CCL 33:1-377.

thirty passages of the *Questions on the Heptateuch* are translated here to give readers a sense of the tenor of the work; but for the readers of this series, what Augustine writes in his *Questions on the Heptateuch* is not among the most helpful of the Fathers' comments.

Another great work of commentary was compiled by Paterius (d. 604), the secretary of Gregory the Great (c. 540-604; pope 590-604). At Gregory's request Paterius compiled a collection of excerpts from Gregory's writings, especially from the enormous *Moral Interpretation of Job,* and arranged them as a running commentary on the Scriptures.[9] His commentary has thirty-eight columns on Genesis, thirty-two on Exodus, ten on Leviticus, fourteen on Numbers and twelve on Deuteronomy. For the most part, the comments are pastoral and moral and often give practical advice to the clergy on how to carry out their duties. About forty passages from Paterius are translated here. They are accompanied by references to the works of Gregory from which Paterius excerpted the passages. But Paterius exercised a certain freedom in his composition, so that the work may be considered almost as much Paterius's as Gregory's.

Isidore of Seville (c. 560-636) is often called the last of the Latin fathers. He was a collector and compiler rather than an original writer. Isidore composed a work entitled *Expositions of the Mystical Sacraments* or, more descriptively, *Questions on the Old Testament.*[10] In this work he treats the Pentateuch, along with Joshua, Judges, Kings, Ezra and Nehemiah and Maccabees. Isidore compiled not a running commentary on the Scriptures but rather collections of comments on significant topics. The work is quite uneven. In the case of the book of Numbers, for example, all Isidore does is quote paragraphs from Origen's twenty-seventh homily on that book. Some excerpts from Isidore are included here, in particular his chapter on the ten plagues of Egypt; in a few cases he is excerpting Gregory the Great, and those are noted.

In the Greek East, Origen did not find a successor until the fifth century, when Cyril of Alexandria (c. 370-444) produced two great works on the Pentateuch. The first is *On Adoration and Worship in Spirit and in Truth* in seventeen books.[11] The work is cast as a dialogue between Cyril and Palladius, although Palladius does little more than agree admiringly with Cyril every few paragraphs. Cyril's point is to show that the Mosaic law, which Israel observed according to the flesh, is to be observed by Christians according to the spirit. Cyril treats much of the Pentateuch, but not in order. The New Testament basis for Cyril's interpretation of the Old Testament is the Gospel according to John and the epistle to the Hebrews. Typically Cyril teaches that the tabernacle of the Old Testament is realized in the Christian church and its institutions, the priests and sacrifices of the Old Testament are realized in the priesthood of the New Covenant, and the laws of clean and unclean apply now to purity of heart and life. The work is a thesaurus of allegorical and moral truths but of little use for excerpting in a work like this one. Cyril's other great work on the Pentateuch, in thirteen books, is titled *Glaphyra* or *Elegant Comments.*[12] Cyril's comments take the form of extended essays on selected topics rather than running commentary. Following a pattern that is typical of the Fathers, his greatest interest is Genesis (seven books) and then Exodus (three books); Leviticus, Numbers and Deuteronomy are each treated in one book. Cyril offers a persistently christological interpretation

---

[9]PL 79:685-1136.
[10]PL 83:207-424.
[11]PG 68:133-1126.
[12]PG 69:13-678.

of the Old Testament. But here too, the essay style makes the *Glaphyra* difficult to excerpt.

Theodoret of Cyr (c. 393-c. 466) composed a running commentary on the Octateuch in the question-and-response format,[13] one of the last works he composed. Theodoret, who belonged to the Antiochene school, preferred the literal sense and incorporates little allegory into his comments. The work has 110 questions and answers on Genesis, 72 on Exodus, 38 on Leviticus, 51 on Numbers and 46 on Deuteronomy. Theodoret has been drawn on here for comment on passages where commentary is otherwise lacking, especially in Numbers and Leviticus.

Procopius of Gaza[14] (c. 475-c. 538) composed a *Catena on the Octateuch*.[15] A catena (the word, which is Latin, means "chain"—that is, passages linked together) made no pretense to originality.[16] It was rather a running commentary composed of quotations from other authors, much like the Ancient Christian Commentary on Scripture itself. Procopius's work was probably the first catena on the Scripture composed by a Christian. The Greek text has been only partially edited and printed; the full work is available only in Latin.[17] The present state of the text is poor: a sixteenth-century Latin translation of a Greek text that was not always clearly understood. Four passages have been included here, on chapters for which little else was available. But this catena, and catenas in general, need a good deal of work and are generally not well understood.

Most of the excerpts in this volume, however, are not drawn from running commentaries by the Fathers but from their doctrinal treatises, their pastoral writings, their letters and all the other genres they used. What is offered here cannot pretend to be any more than a sampling—I hope a representative one—of all that the Fathers had to say about the latter four books of the Pentateuch.

Education and Exegesis in the Fathers

Often, when the exegesis of the Fathers is discussed, the first categories used are "literal" and "allegorical," and the latter is rejected almost immediately as the work of fantasy or even as untrue to the meaning of the Bible.

---

[13]*Questions on the Octateuch* (PG 80:77-857).

[14]Information on Procopius is not easy to find. The following is useful: J. Van den Gheyn, "Procope de Gaza," *Dictionnaire de la Bible* (Paris: Létouzeyet Ané, 1912), 5:686-89.

[15]PG 87:511-992. The excerpts on Ruth are lost.

[16]Study of the catenae is notoriously difficult. The best studies by far were made by Robert Devreesse, especially the following: "Chaines Exégétiques grecques," *Dictionnaire de la Bible*, Supplément 1 (Paris: Létouzeyet Ané, 1928), pp. 1084-1233; "Anciens commentateurs Grecs sur l'Octateuque," *Revue Biblique* 44 (1935): 166-91; 45 (1936): 201-20, 364-84; and *Les Anciens commentateurs Grecs de l'Octateuche et des Rois*, Studi e Testi 201 (Vatican City: Biblioteca Apotolica Vaticana, 1959).

[17]One sign of the relative lack of interest in patristic exegesis is the state of the texts discussed here. The homilies of Origen on Genesis, Exodus, Leviticus and Numbers have fared best; they were published in a critical edition early in the twentieth century (in the series Griechische christliche Schriftsteller in Berlin), and the homilies on Exodus and Leviticus are available in good English translations. Augustine's two works on the Heptateuch have been edited critically (in the series Corpus Christianorum) but never translated into English. The last edition of Paterius's excerpts from Gregory the Great was made in the eighteenth century; the *Clavis Patrum Latinorum* announces that a new edition is in preparation. Isidore of Seville's *Questions on the Old Testament* is also available only in Migne's *Patrology*. The Greek texts are, if anything, in poorer condition. Cyril of Alexandria's *On Adoration and Worship* and *Glaphyra* were last edited in 1638 and 1636, respectively. The text of Theodoret of Cyr's *Questions on the Octateuch* in Migne's *Patrology* reprints an edition made from a single twelfth-century manuscript; happily, the *Clavis Patrum Graecorum* announces the preparation of a new edition. Procopius of Gaza's *Catena on the Octateuch* is the least accessible of all these works. Only part of the Greek text has been printed; the remaining parts can be read only in a Latin translation made in the sixteenth century. Needless to say, none of these latter works has been translated into English.

But "literal" and "allegorical" are not particularly helpful categories in understanding the way the Fathers read the Bible. Anyone who begins with such an understanding will find this volume frustrating, even useless. On page after page, a reader will discover one of the Fathers making surprising, startling and often puzzling statements about the Bible. Yet what they say makes good sense if one understands two things: first, that their way of reading the Bible grew out of the sort of education they received, and then, that they were convinced, in faith, that every sentence in the Bible, rightly understood, had something important to say to the Christian reader.

The Bible was a puzzling text. But before they even opened the Bible, ancient Christians already had a method for dealing with a puzzling text, a method they had learned in the course of their literary education.

Both Greeks and Romans had national epics, Homer's *Iliad* and *Odyssey* for the Greeks, Vergil's *Aeneid* for Latin speakers. Homer—to concentrate on the Greek side—posed serious problems for readers in the Hellenistic age and later. Some words, constructions and allusions in the text made no sense, for Homer's Greek was six or seven hundred years old and often only imperfectly understood. Then too, some of the narratives were anything but ennobling. Philosophers had developed a highly spiritual and idealized notion of God, but schoolboys read of Olympian gods and goddesses who were fallible, contentious and often scandalous in their behavior. How could this national epic be held up as an ideal, even a religious ideal?

In other words, teachers faced two problems: understanding the text and interpreting it. The teachers of grammar in the Roman Empire developed a method for dealing with the great literary epics of their culture.[18] The grammarian carried out his work in four operations: textual criticism or emendation, reading, explanation (in Greek, *exēgēsis*) and judgment. Christian exegetes followed the first three. They could not follow the fourth, for God was their judge, and they could not pass judgment on his Word.

Emendation. The fact that written texts were copied by hand meant that they were in a state of constant flux. Hence the reader's first task was to make sure that his copy of a text was as correct as possible. He would try to compare his copy with other copies and note the discrepancies. Of course, the reader then had to decide which text was correct, and he might thereby preserve old errors or introduce new ones.

Among the pagans, the occasion for the development of the science of textual criticism was the study of Homer. Readers were tempted to change unfamiliar or unintelligible words to words that were more easily understood—a risky undertaking at best. The development of a scientific philological method and of principles for criticizing and explaining a text was the work of two librarians at Alexandria, Aristophanes of Byzantium (librarian after c. 195 B.C.), and Aristarchus of Samothrace (217-145 B.C.). They represent the analogists, grammarians who located the principle of textual criticism in the regularity of language: in the same grammatical situation the same form will recur. Aristophanes preferred to

---

[18]For what follows see Rolf Gögler, *Zur Theologie des biblischen Wortes bei Origenes* (Düsseldorf: Patmos, 1963), 39-59. See also Joseph T. Lienhard, *The Bible, the Church and Authority: The History and Theology of the New Testament Canon* (Collegeville, Minn.: Liturgical Press, 1995); "Reading the Bible and Learning to Read: The Influence of Education on Augustine's Exegesis," *Augustinian Studies* 27 (1996): 7-25; and "Origen and the Crisis of the Old Testament in the Early Church," *Pro Ecclesia* 9 (2000): 355-66.

conserve rather than to emend texts.

Christians would discover remarkably similar problems in the Septuagint: words that were incomprehensible, constructions that were ungrammatical, statements that seemed unworthy of God. But such problems were not to be solved by changing the text. Origen, for example, was following the principles of the Alexandrian grammarians when he criticized the Gnostic commentator Heracleon for doing violence to the text of the Gospel according to John by adding or deleting words and changing the text arbitrarily.[19] He also noted different readings and differences among copies.[20] At times he used the Hebrew text to decide between Greek readings. At Jeremiah 15:10, for example, he writes that most copies have "to help" but the best ones have "to owe," which agrees with the Hebrew,[21] and he adds that one may not ignore the Hebrew reading but should also explain the traditional reading in church. In the New Testament, Origen decides against the nearly unanimous reading at John 1:28, "Bethany," and for "Betharaba," as the place on the Jordan where John baptized, for several reasons. One was geographical: he could not find a Bethany beyond the Jordan. Another was what he had heard when he traveled in that region. And the third was etymological: "Betharaba," which he says means house of preparation, better explains John's activity there.

Reading. After extensive textual criticism, the pupil was ready to read the text. Reading in antiquity was no easy task, since no space was left between words; the reader had to collocate the syllables correctly to have the text make sense. Moreover, all reading was done aloud; the reader could hear himself and perceive mistakes. Reading aloud meant that the text was read slowly, and after a few readings the student had the text nearly memorized. Those who read the Scriptures aloud in the churches needed education and practice.

Explanation. Explanation (*exēgēsis*) was the most difficult part of the grammarian's task. Aristarchus saw it as a way to "save the text." Besides a philological explanation, a national poet like Homer also needed an apologetic treatment. The same could apply to the Scriptures. Origen wrote, "If the discrepancy is not solved, [many] dismiss . . . the Gospels as not true, or not written by a divine spirit, or not successfully recorded."[22] Plato had taught that the philologist must also be a philosopher.[23] So when Eusebius reports that even as a child Origen asked his father about the deeper sense of the Scripture,[24] he may not be reporting a pious legend but reflecting the education the boy had already received.

Aristarchus and the other grammarians had several strategies for saving the text. Some were philological, others philosophical.

For one, Aristarchus formulated the principle that in interpreting Homer, no narrow historical or scientific criteria were to be used to judge single statements. He asserted rather that the poet had subordinated single elements to a larger goal of composition. Thus Homer might contain discrepancies on single points, but such discrepancies served a larger truth. Following this principle, Origen could assert his

---

[19]*Commentary on John* 2.14; 13.11; 13.17.
[20]*Commentary on Matthew* 15.14.
[21]*Homilies on Jeremiah* 14.3; cf. 15.5. In Greek the two words are quite similar.
[22]*Commentary on John* 10.2.10 (FC 80:256).
[23]*Republic* 9.582E; *Theataetus* 146A.
[24]*History of the Church* 6.2.9.

belief that "[the Evangelists'] intention was to speak the truth spiritually and materially at the same time where that was possible but, where it was not possible in both ways, to prefer the spiritual to the material. The spiritual truth is often preserved in material falsehood, so to speak."[25]

In the days before dictionaries, the grammarian, as exegete, would also compile lists of words in two columns: in one column, words in his text that were difficult or unusual; in the other column, the meaning of the words. Jerome wrote extensively on the Hebrew background of the Old Testament. Two works of his, *Hebrew Questions on Genesis*[26] and *Interpretation of Hebrew Names*,[27] are particularly noteworthy. The study of etymology was also cultivated, and Origen, Augustine and other Fathers often appealed to etymology as a way to explain the text.

Another principle that Aristarchus formulated was called "the person speaking." When an exegete explained a word, he had to take note of who had spoken it. Origen would ask in whose name a psalm had been spoken.[28] A prophet could speak "in God's person."[29] One must distinguish between the voice of John the Baptizer and that of John the Evangelist.[30] When the Redeemer speaks a psalm, its words acquire a different meaning.[31] The person can even speak from a unique situation; the Savior speaks Psalm 21 at the time of his passion.[32] If Christ speaks in Moses and the prophets and in the whole of the Scriptures, then the Scriptures can be understood only in the spirit of Christ—that is, in the spirit of him who speaks them.[33]

From the principle of "the person speaking" Aristarchus developed the crown of all his exegetical axioms, the principle that a writer is to be interpreted out of himself. In its classical formulation, the principle is "to explain Homer from Homer." Origen regularly employed this principle in his exegesis. The Bible should be interpreted by the Bible: that is, an obscure word or expression should be explained by studying other passages in the Bible that use that word or expression. Origen writes that when he uses the principle, he is following Jesus' command, "Search the Scriptures!"[34] The Fathers often quote verse after verse from Scripture to clarify a single word that they are investigating. Therefore Origen writes: "[The exegete] to the utmost of his power must trace out from the use of similar expressions the meaning scattered everywhere throughout the Scriptures."[35]

Origen also extends Aristarchus's axiom to another dimension: to explain Scripture from Scripture also means to interpret the Old Testament from the New and the New from the Old. That both Testaments form a unity is, for Origen, a theological principle. He writes, "One must compare passages, not only from the New but also from the Old Testament."[36] The "must" expresses a theological principle;

---

[25] *Commentary on John* 10.5.20 (FC 80:259); see also OFP 4.3.5.
[26] CCL 72:1-56.
[27] CCL 72:57-161.
[28] *Commentary on John* 6.39; 10.34.
[29] *Commentary on John* 1.23; frag. 23; *Homilies on Genesis* 14.1.
[30] *Commentary on John* 2.35; cf. 6.24.
[31] *Commentary on John* 19.16.
[32] *Commentary on John* 32.23.
[33] OFP 4.2.3; *Commentary on Matthew* 15.30; 17.13.
[34] Jn 5:39.
[35] OFP 4.3.5.
[36] *Commentary on John*, frag. 1.

"compare" describes a philological method.

Judgment. Pagan grammarians ended their lessons with a judgment passed on the work that had been read: on its beauty, nobility or moral value. Christians could not judge the Scripture, for they could not judge God's Word. Or—to put it more precisely—they could not pass judgment on the truth that the Scripture contained, even if they could acknowledge that the expression was defective.

Thus the Fathers were led to ask whether it is possible to distinguish between the words of the Scripture and their meaning. The question had arisen as early as Plato. His dialogue, the *Cratylus*, treated the much-discussed question, whether language names things according to their nature or merely by convention. Plato concludes that the word is a sign, made of symbols and letters, for a thing[37] and grants that words have an objective validity even though they are inadequate in expressing their objects. Origen agrees; words are types, figures, forms.[38] Augustine too developed a philosophy of language and meaning as he studied the Scriptures.[39]

Plato's theory rests on the supposition of a knowledge of reality that precedes language, namely, of the forms or ideas. For the Fathers, faith fulfills this function. For faith enables us to foreknow that reality in which the words of Holy Scripture are true. Faith is the light that shines upon the words of Scripture, keeps them from being misinterpreted and gives us certainty about their true meaning. Exegesis without faith cannot lead one to the true meaning of the Scripture; the words are only analogies, and unbelievers cannot recognize what is foreign to their lives.

Eventually there evolved two tendencies that differed in their explanations of how the words of Scripture are related to its meaning. Often called the Alexandrian and Antiochene schools, they are distinguished, respectively, as practitioners of allegorical exegesis and literal interpretation. But these categories are not particularly useful descriptions of the real dynamics of their reading. It is true that Origen, the church's first great exegete, was also one of the most enthusiastic practitioners of spiritual exegesis in all its forms. After Origen, one can discern a slow but general drift, at least in some schools, away from such flamboyant interpretation. But both Alexandrians and Antiochenes understood that an exclusively literal interpretation is impossible, if only because the Old Testament required a christological hermeneutic. This much might be said safely: for Alexandrians the words were a sort of veil that hid the true meaning. The exegete had to see behind the veil to the reality it concealed. For the Antiochenes, who spoke of contemplation (*theōria*) rather than allegory, the words themselves contained the deeper truth and, when they were properly understood, could be made to glow with meaning from within.

Principles of Patristic Exegesis

The Fathers of the church based their exegesis on affirmations made in faith about the Bible. For the Fathers, understanding the Scriptures is a grace and a gift for which the interpreter needs to pray.[40] "Methodology," quotes Henri de Lubac, "is a modern invention. In the first centuries of the Church,

---

[37]*Cratylus* 433B.
[38]OFP 4.2.2; *Homilies on Joshua* 2.3.
[39]See especially his *On the Teacher* and *On Christian Doctrine*.
[40]See Origen *Homilies on Genesis* 12.1; *Homilies on Exodus* 9.2.

those who explained the Scriptures entrusted themselves to the inspiration of the Holy Spirit, without concerning themselves with a preplanned methodology."[41]

Moreover, the point of departure for much of patristic exegesis of the Old Testament is the Fathers' belief that the Old Testament is wholly a prophecy of Christ; or, inversely, that Christ is the key to understanding the Old Testament.[42]

The real author of the Scriptures is the Holy Spirit, and the Holy Spirit is one. Hence the Holy Scriptures, taken together, must teach one truth. And further, if the Holy Spirit is their author, the Scriptures can never be trite or superficial. Origen writes, for example, "For what does it help me, I who have come to hear what the Holy Spirit teaches the human race, if I hear that 'Abraham was standing under a tree'?"[43] or "[The apostle's] purpose is that we might learn how to treat other passages, and especially those in which the historical narrative appears to reveal nothing worthy of the divine law,"[44] or, "And certainly if, as some think, the text of the divine Scripture was composed carelessly and awkwardly, it could have been said that Abraham went down to Egypt to dwell there because the famine prevailed over him."[45]

And finally the Fathers believed that the Scriptures, rightly understood, spoke to them, and to them in their quest for Christian holiness. Hence the modern historical-critical method would have made little sense to them. Historical criticism locates the meaning of the text so firmly in the singular past event that any application of the text to the present—especially one made in faith—is necessarily seen as a kind of departure from certainty and hence at best suspect. The Fathers thought just the opposite. The simple narrative of a past event is of no use to us (see below, Origen on Numbers 33:2). The question the Fathers ask repeatedly is, How does this passage speak to me and help me?

Moreover, exegesis for the Fathers was a fascinating undertaking, one filled with mysteries, surprises and even puzzles to be solved. Origen passed on a wonderful image that he learned from the rabbi who taught him Hebrew: the Scripture is like a great house that has many, many rooms. All the rooms are locked. At each locked door there is a key, but it is not the key to that door. The scholar's task is to match the keys to their doors. And this is a great labor.[46]

Yet the Fathers resolutely began with the "letter" of the Scripture, the words of the Bible before any application of interpretative tools, even of figures of speech. Thus the fact that honey and oil never flowed from a rock is a problem (see comment on Deuteronomy 32:13). Or, if Moses and Aaron caused all the water of Egypt to turn to blood, how did Pharaoh's magicians find water that they could turn to blood? (see comment on Exodus 7:22). The master of spiritual exegesis, Origen, warns his readers at one point that not every detail of Scripture has an allegorical sense (see comment on Exodus 25:10).

The Fathers also appealed to archaeological evidence for the literal truth of the Scriptures. Thus they

---

[41]Henri de Lubac, quoting J. Brisson, in *Geist aus der Geschichte: Das Schriftverständnis des Origenes*, trans. Hans Urs von Balthasar (Einsiedeln, Switzerland: Johannes Verlag, 1968), p. 171 n. 9.

[42]2 Cor 3:4-18 is crucial to this conviction.

[43]*Homilies on Genesis* 4.3.

[44]*Homilies on Genesis* 7.2.

[45]*Homilies on Genesis* 16.3.

[46]Fragment on Ps 1 in *Philocalia* 2.3.

said that the ruts from the Egyptians' chariots could still be seen on the shores of the Red Sea (see comments on Exodus 14:25) or the graves of the rebellious Israelites were still to be seen in the wilderness of Sinai (see comment on Numbers 11:34). A word in the Septuagint version of Exodus led the Fathers to say that Moses invented the art of writing and taught it to the Phoenicians (see comment on Exodus 2:12).

The Fathers also had philological resources. Latin speakers could appeal to the Greek text, and Origen and Jerome (among others) appealed to the Hebrew. *Pascha* is a Hebrew word, but its Greek equivalent is also significant (see Augustine on Exodus 12:11). Origen can compare the Septuagint and Hebrew texts (see comment on Exodus 4:10). Augustine clarified the gender of a Latin pronoun by consulting the Greek text (see comment on Exodus 4:24). Eusebius quotes the non-Septuagintal translation of Aquila (see comment on Exodus 6:3). Jerome learnedly corrects the Greek from the Hebrew (see comment on Exodus 8:21).

Yet the Fathers' real interest was Christianity and Christian doctrine. The best way to put it, perhaps, is that things and events in the Old Testament reminded them of Christian truths and realities. Such a process of reminding had already begun in the New Testament. Examples will be found throughout this volume. Water reminded them of baptism; bread or manna reminded them of the Eucharist; rock or stone reminded them of Christ; wood or a staff reminded them of the cross; a thorn bush reminded them of the crown of thorns and of the thorns and thistles of Genesis 3.

Moreover, the Fathers regularly find presages of the great doctrines of Christian faith—the Trinity and the two natures of the one Christ—in the Old Testament. With regard to the Trinity, they have two distinct ways of interpreting the Old Testament. For many earlier Greek fathers, well represented here by Eusebius, all theophanies of the Old Testament were theophanies of the Son, for the Son is the way God communicates with us. Eusebius retains the subordinationism of much of pre-Nicene theology. For Augustine, by contrast, most theophanies are manifestations of the Trinity, and what human eyes see is not the Trinity itself but a material form temporarily created to be seen by human eyes. In Augustine, all elements of subordinationism and the inclination to tritheism have been banished.

In regard to the person of Christ, any pair of things, one of which is exalted and the other lowly, may remind the Fathers of the two natures of Christ. Examples abound throughout the volume; the two goats of the Day of Atonement are only one example.

Stranger to modern taste is the Fathers' fascination with names, numbers and etymologies. But the Fathers thoroughly enjoyed the Bible, and their interest in numbers was in some ways akin to modern enjoyment of crossword puzzles.

Readers of this volume will be struck, for example, with the frequency with which Joshua is identified with Jesus, made easy by the fact that both names were spelled the same in Greek. The assumption, of course, was that the Holy Spirit had something to tell us when this name was invoked.

Fascination with numbers was almost universal. To give only a few examples: the number one reminded the Fathers of God, two of the two Testaments or the two great commandments, three of the Trinity, four of the Gospels, five of the senses or the books of the law, ten of the commandments, twelve of the apostles, forty of fasting and Lent, fifty of Pentecost and the Holy Spirit, seventy or seventy-two of the Lord's disciples, and so on.

Besides Origen's etymological exegesis of the forty-two stopping places in the desert, etymologies will be found frequently here. Many are correct; others are wrong or simply fantastic. Notable is the bizarre etymology of the Greek word *hagios* ("holy") as being from *a* ("not") and *gē* ("earth"), or "not of the earth" (see comment on Leviticus 11:44).

The anthropomorphisms of the Hebrew Scriptures posed a serious problem for Christian exegetes. Their educated pagan Greek contemporaries had evolved a highly abstract and impersonal notion of God. When they heard that the Scriptures spoke of God as having body parts, emotions and even changes of heart, their reaction was either rejection or ridicule. Hence the Fathers regularly needed to explain references to God's arm or hand or foot or to his anger or wrath. A particularly difficult passage was the one in which Scripture says that God hardened Pharaoh's heart, since it seemed to suppress free choice, which was one of the basic assumptions of Christian anthropology, and to teach a kind of determinism or fatalism. The third book of Origen's *On First Principles,* which is the first philosophical treatise written on free choice, is based on an exegesis of this text from Exodus.

Much of the Fathers' exegesis of the Old Testament is guided by texts quoted in or alluded to in the New Testament. Their writings continue the polemic against Jewish formalism already found in the New Testament. In many other cases, their interests were practical: moral lessons about sin and repentance, exhortations to good order in the church, contrast between the Old Testament and the New.

The entry into the world of the Fathers can be both fascinating and frustrating. To explain adequately the significance of the texts quoted here would require much more than this brief introduction; it would take another volume the same size as this one—and would probably still be inadequate. But perhaps it is best to let the Fathers speak for themselves, for we stand on the shoulders of giants, and to presume to speak for them would be presumptuous indeed.

Final Notes

In assembling this modern-day catena, I have had a great deal of help. The staff of the Ancient Christian Commentary on Scripture Project supplied me with abundant digitally researched materials, and especially with photocopies of relevant passages in English translations. Without this help, the task could not have been accomplished. I express my particular gratitude to Thomas C. Oden, who invited me to prepare this volume.

Following normal academic procedure, I have respected the original form of the many texts I excerpted from other translations. The only exceptions have been the following. The spelling of words has been conformed to the style in use in the United States. Outdated punctuation has been changed. Some words, especially pronouns whose antecedent is God, have been lowercased in conformity with modern style. Biblical names in Septuagint or Vulgate spelling have been changed to the spelling found in the Revised Standard Version. And the older English second person singular forms—*thou, thy, thine* and *thee,* and the inflected verbs used with these forms—have been changed to the modern you forms. This acknowledgment should suffice; these changes are not noted at each place they were made.

Most of the work on this volume was done at Boston College during the academic year 1999-2000, while I was privileged to be the Joseph Gregory McCarthy Visiting Professor in the department of theology there. I happily thank Dr. Eugene McCarthy, who along with his wife, Maureen (who died in the fall of 1999), endowed the chair in memory of their son and thereby made the composition of this book much easier and probably possible.

It is also my privilege to thank Ronnie J. Rombs, a Ph.D. candidate at Fordham University, who served as my assistant during the year at Boston College. He did much of the data entry for this volume, but also far more than that. His knowledge of patristic resources enabled him to check the accuracy of virtually every entry, standardize the method of citation and—again and again—pick up inconsistencies and blunders. Besides this, he drafted the translations of the passages taken from Ambrose's letters as well as of some passages from Augustine's *Questions on the Heptateuch*. We spent two semesters working together on this volume. One of the small delights of this project was deciding, as we neared the end of drafting it, that we would find a few dozen more excerpts, so that the number of passages cited here from the Fathers would be one thousand. For the sake of both justice and friendship, and with acknowledgment of the patience of his wife, Kathryn, I am pleased to include Ronnie J. Rombs's name on the title page of this volume.

Joseph T. Lienhard, S.J.
Fordham University
Bronx, New York
June 2000
Solemnity of the Sacred Heart

Exodus

1:1-7 JACOB'S DESCENDANTS IN EGYPT

¹*These are the names of the sons of Israel who came to Egypt with Jacob, each with his household:* ²*Reuben, Simeon, Levi, and Judah,* ³*Issachar, Zebulun, and Benjamin,* ⁴*Dan and Naphtali, Gad and Asher.* ⁵*All the offspring of Jacob were seventy persons;** *Joseph was already in Egypt.* ⁶*Then Joseph died, and all his brothers, and all that generation.* ⁷*But the descendants of Israel were fruitful and increased greatly; they multiplied and grew exceedingly strong; so that the land was filled with them.*

*LXX Seventy five souls

OVERVIEW: "Soul" designates the better part of a person and hence the whole person. The figure used is synecdoche, in which a part stands for the whole. The Hebrew name Joseph means "increase" (CASSIODORUS). The people of Israel increased greatly only after Joseph's death, just as Christians increased greatly in number only after Christ's redeeming death (CAESARIUS OF ARLES).

1:5 Jacob's Offspring Were Seventy Persons

SOUL MEANS PERSON. CASSIODORUS: Scripture often substitutes "souls" for men, as in Exodus: "There went down to Egypt seventy-five souls."[1] The whole man is to be understood from his better part. EXPOSITION OF THE PSALMS 33.23.[2]

AN EXAMPLE OF SYNECDOCHE. CASSIODORUS: The expression "their souls" must be interpreted as meaning the men whom he is known to have slain in that calamity. The words of Exodus attest that the soul stands for the whole person, as we have said: "So all the souls that came out

of Jacob's thigh were seventy."[3] This expression is the result of the figure of *synecdoche*, which signifies the whole from the part. EXPOSITION OF THE PSALMS 77.50.[4]

THE MEANING OF THE NAME JOSEPH. CASSIODORUS: Joseph means "increase"; the interpretation of this name is testimony to the Hebrew people who came out of the land of Egypt in increased numbers. EXPOSITION OF THE PSALMS 80.6.[5]

1:7 The Descendants of Israel Were Fruitful

JOSEPH IS A TYPE OF CHRIST. CAESARIUS OF ARLES: We have heard in the lesson which was read, dearly beloved, that "when Joseph was dead, the Israelites were exceedingly fruitful and prolific, and they sprang up like grass."[6] What does this mean, brethren? As long as Joseph

---

[1]Ex 1:5. The LXX reads "seventy-five souls" here. [2]ACW 51:334. [3]Ex 1:5. [4]ACW 52:268. [5]ACW 52:295-96. [6]Ex 1:6-7.

lived the children of Israel are not recorded to have increased or multiplied very much, but after he died they are said to have sprung up like the grass. Surely they should have increased and multiplied more when they were under the patronage and protection of Joseph. These words were prefigured in that Joseph, dearly beloved; but in our Joseph, that is, in Christ the Lord, they were fulfilled in truth. Before our Joseph died, that is, before he was crucified, few people believed in him, but after he died and rose again throughout the world the Israelites, that is, the Christian people, increased and multiplied. Thus even the Lord himself says in the Gospel: "Unless the grain of wheat falls into the ground and dies, it remains alone. But if it dies, it brings forth much fruit."[7] After the precious grain of wheat died and was buried through the passion, from that one grain a harvest of the church sprang up throughout the world. Not as formerly was "God renowned in Judah" alone, nor is "his great name" worshiped only "in Israel"; but "from the rising of the sun unto the going down"[8] his name is praised. Sermon 94.1.[9]

---

[7]Jn 12:24. [8]Ps 76:1; 113:3. [9]FC 47:61.

1:8-14 THE OPPRESSION

[8]*Now there arose a new king over Egypt, who did not know Joseph. . . . And the Egyptians were in dread of the people of Israel.* [13]*So they made the people of Israel serve with rigor,* [14]*and made their lives bitter with hard service, in mortar and brick, and in all kinds of work in the field; in all their work they made them serve with rigor.*

Overview: Pharaoh's heart was like mud, and the Sun of justice hardened it; the same Sun enlightened the people of Israel. Egypt means "darkness." Like the children of Israel, we too are in error and darkness until God's Word comes to us (Origen). Mortar and brick are the signs of the bondage of this life; through death we pass over to the land of promise (Gregory of Nazianzus). Mortar and brick signify earthly desires; Christ brings us to rest from our labors (Augustine).

1:14 In Mortar and Brick

Pharaoh's Heart of Clay Hardened. Origen: Perhaps it is in this sense that God is said to have hardened the heart of Pharaoh, because the substance of his heart was obviously such as to elicit from the Sun of justice not his illumination but his power to harden and to scorch. That no doubt was the reason why this same Pharaoh afflicted the life of the Hebrews with hard work and wore them out with clay and bricks. And certainly the works that he devised came from a heart as miry and muddy! And as the visible sun contracts and hardens the substance of clay, so with the same rays by which he enlightened the people of Israel and by means of those rays' same properties the Sun of justice hardened the heart of Pharaoh that harbored muddy devices. Commentary on the Song of Songs 2.2.[1]

---

[1]ACW 26:111*.

LUSTS AND DESIRES. ORIGEN: When the children of Israel were in Egypt, they were afflicted with mortar and brick[2] for the works of Pharaoh the king until they cried out in their groaning to the Lord.[3] And he heard their cry and sent his word to them by Moses and led them out of Egypt. When we were also in Egypt, I mean in the errors of this world and in the darkness of ignorance, we then did the works of the devil in lusts and desires of the flesh. But the Lord had pity on our affliction and sent the Word, his only begotten Son, to deliver us from ignorance of our error and to lead us to the light of divine law. HOMILIES ON NUMBERS 27.2.[4]

PASSOVER TO THE LAND OF PROMISE. GREGORY OF NAZIANZUS: I have already lived through many paschs, which was the fruit of a long life. But now I desire a purer pasch: to depart from this Egypt, the heavy and dark

Egypt of this life, and to be freed from the clay and bricks that held us in bondage[5] and to pass over to the land of promise.[6] LETTER 120.[7]

SERVING THE DEVIL. AUGUSTINE: We have been led out of Egypt where we were serving the devil as a pharaoh, where we were doing works of clay amid earthly desires, and we were laboring much in them. For Christ cried out to us, as if we were making bricks, "Come to me, all you who labor and are burdened."[8] Led out of here, we were led over through baptism as through the Red Sea—red for this reason, because consecrated by the blood of Christ—when all our enemies who were assailing us were dead, that is, when our sins have been wiped out. TRACTATE ON THE GOSPEL OF JOHN 28.9.[9]

---

[2]Ex 1:14. [3]Ex 2:23. [4]CWS 249*. [5]Ex 1:14. [6]Heb 11:9. [7]GCS 90. [8]Mt 11:28. [9]FC 88:11.

1:15-22 COMMAND TO THE MIDWIVES

[15]*Then the king of Egypt said to the Hebrew midwives, one of whom was named Shiphrah and the other Puah,* [16]*"When you serve as midwife to the Hebrew women, and see them upon the birthstool, if it is a son, you shall kill him; but if it is a daughter, she shall live."* [17]*But the midwives feared God, and did not do as the king of Egypt commanded them, but let the male children live.* [18]*So the king of Egypt called the midwives, and said to them, "Why have you done this, and let the male children live?"* [19]*The midwives said to Pharaoh, "Because the Hebrew women are not like the Egyptian women; for they are vigorous and are delivered before the midwife comes to them."* [20]*So God dealt well with the midwives; and the people multiplied and grew very strong.* [21]*And because the midwives feared God he gave them families.* [22]*Then Pharaoh commanded all his people, "Every son that is born to the Hebrews[a] you shall cast into the Nile, but you shall let every daughter live."*

a *Sam Gk Tg: Heb lacks* to the Hebrews

OVERVIEW: The devil, symbolized by Pharaoh, tries to destroy what is rational in us and to

flood the soul with passions (METHODIUS). The midwives did lie, but in this case a lie might be tolerated. The midwives' lie came not from malice but from kindness; yet their lie may not be praised (Augustine). The souls of the just do not depend on secular learning but bring forth their fruits spontaneously (Ambrose). God rewards not deception but benevolence (Augustine). God gave the Israelites families because they feared him (Jerome). In God's plan, the Egyptians drowned in the very waters in which Pharaoh wanted to drown the infant boys of the Israelites (Ephrem). In God's providence, Moses was reared in the royal palace and prepared to deliver Israel (Chrysostom).

1:16-19 *Pharaoh and the Midwives*

Reason Destroyed by Passion. Methodius: Thus too it has been said that the Pharaoh of Egypt was a type of the devil, in that he cruelly ordered the males to be cast into the Nile and permitted the females to live. So too the devil, ruling over the great Egypt of the world "from Adam unto Moses,"[1] made an effort to carry off and destroy the male and rational offspring of the soul in the flood of the passions, while he takes delight in seeing the carnal and sensual offspring increase and multiply. Banquet of the Ten Virgins 4.2.[2]

Did the Midwives Lie? Augustine: On the midwives' lie, by which they deceived Pharaoh and kept him from killing the Israelite males when they were born: The midwives said that Hebrew women did not give birth as Egyptian women did. It is usual to ask whether such lies have been approved by divine authority. Scripture says that God favored the midwives. It is unclear whether God, in his mercy, pardoned the lie or judged that the lie itself deserved a reward. For the midwives did one thing by letting the infant boys live and another by lying to Pharaoh. In letting them live they performed a work of mercy; but they used that lie for their own ends, to keep Pharaoh from harming the infants. This act could be the occasion not for

praise but for pardon. It does not seem to me that the authority to lie has been given to those of whom it is said, "And a lie has not been found in their mouths."[3] For if the lives of certain people, being far below the level of the saints' lives, include these sins of lying, these people are living in accord with their natural abilities, especially if they do not yet know that they should expect heavenly gifts but busy themselves with earthly things. As for those who live in such a way that their conversation, as the apostle says, is in heaven,[4] I do not think that they should regulate the style of their speech, insofar as it affects speaking the truth and avoiding falsehood, on the example of the midwives. But we should consider this question more carefully, on account of the other examples that are found in Scripture. Questions on Exodus 1.[5]

Lying Not Justified. Augustine: Many lies indeed seem to be for someone's safety or advantage, spoken not in malice but in kindness: such was that of those midwives in Exodus, who gave a false report to Pharaoh, to the end that the infants of the children of Israel might not be slain. But even these are praised not for the fact but for the disposition shown; since those who only lie in this way will attain in time to a freedom from all lying. Explanation of the Psalms 5.7.[6]

The Souls of the Just. Ambrose: Indeed, in regard to other Hebrew women you find it written that the Hebrew women give birth before the midwives arrive. This is so because the souls of the just do not wait upon branches of learning arranged according to kinds of knowledge, nor do they require assistance in parturition, but they bring forth their offspring spontaneously and anticipate the expected time. Flight from the World 8.47.[7]

---

[1]Rom 5:14. [2]ACW 27:76. [3]Rev 14:5. [4]Phil 3:20. [5]CCL 33:70. [6]NPNF 1 8:12 [7]FC 65:317.

1:21-22 *God and the Midwives*

GOD REWARDED THE MIDWIVES. AUGUSTINE: As for its being written that God dealt well with the Hebrew midwives and with Rahab the harlot of Jericho,[8] he did not deal well with them because they lied but because they were merciful to the men of God. And so it was not their deception that was rewarded but their benevolence; the benignity of their intention, not the iniquity of their invention. ON LYING 15.32.[9]

WE MUST FEAR GOD. JEROME: Because they feared God, they built up houses. Without the fear of God, a house cannot be built. If then with the fear of God houses were built by those who had not committed sin but rather did their building at God's pleasure, we who have been captured, what must we do? Listen, sinner; we must fear God, indeed, to avoid sin; but after shipwreck there is the second plank of repentance. "When the house was being built after captivity."[10] "When the house was being built," not "was built," for repentance is without limit. To the just man who has died, repentance naturally is rendered superfluous. Whenever there is sin, always there is remorse of conscience. Hence the psalmist says was "being built." While time lasts, the door is always open to repentance, for however long you shall live, as long as you live, you will fall into sin. HOMILY 72.[11]

IRONY IN GOD'S PROVIDENCE. EPHREM THE SYRIAN: Just as Pharaoh was drowned in those very waters in which he had drowned the infants, so too David removed Goliath's head with that very sword with which he had destroyed many.[12] Moses divided the waters through the symbol of the cross,[13] while David laid Goliath low through the symbol of the stone. Our Lord condemned Satan by the word of his mouth when the latter was tempting him. Pharaoh was drowned by the waters with which he had drowned [others]. COMMENTARY ON TATIAN'S DIATESSARON 12.[14]

GOD'S PROVIDENCE. CHRYSOSTOM: And that you may learn this—Pharaoh commanded the infants to be cast into the river. Unless the infants had been cast forth, Moses would not have been saved, he would not have been brought up in the palace. When he was safe, he was not in honor; when he was exposed, then he was in honor. But God did this to show his riches of resource and contrivance. HOMILIES ON ACTS 54, AT ACTS 20:17.[15]

---

[8]Josh 2; 6:25. [9]FC 16:165. [10]Ps 96 title LXX. [11]FC 57:107-8. [12]1 Sam 17:1-51. [13]Ex 14:16. [14]JSSS 2 89-90. [15]NPNF 1 11:321-22.

2:1-10 BIRTH AND ADOPTION OF MOSES

[1]Now a man from the house of Levi went and took to wife a daughter of Levi. [2]The woman conceived and bore a son; and when she saw that he was a goodly child, she hid him three months. [3]And when she could hide him no longer she took for him a basket made of bulrushes, and daubed it with bitumen and pitch; and she put the child in it and placed it among the reeds at the river's brink. . . . [10]And the child grew, and she brought him to Pharaoh's daughter, and

he became her son; and she named him Moses,[b] for she said, "Because I drew him out[c] of the water."

b *Heb* Mosheh c *Heb* mashah

OVERVIEW: A devout midwife and mother saved Moses from death (PRUDENTIUS).

2:3 A Basket of Reeds

A HYMN TO MOSES' MOTHER AND THE MIDWIFE. PRUDENTIUS:

> Thus Moses in a former age
> Escaped proud Pharaoh's foolish law,
> And as the savior of his race
> Prefigured Christ who was to come.

> A cruel edict had been passed
> Forbidding Hebrew mothers all,
> When sons were born to them, to rear
> These virile pledges of their love.
> Devoutly scornful of the king,
> A zealous midwife found a way
> To hide her charge and keep him safe
> For future glory and renown.

HYMNS FOR EVERY DAY 12.141-52.[1]

[1]FC 43:90.

2:11-22 MOSES' FLIGHT TO MIDIAN

[11]*One day, when Moses had grown up, he went out to his people and looked on their burdens; and he saw an Egyptian beating a Hebrew, one of his people.* [12]*He looked this way and that, and seeing no one he killed the Egyptian and hid him in the sand.* [13]*When he went out the next day, behold, two Hebrews were struggling together; and he said to the man that did the wrong, "Why do you strike your fellow?"* [14]*He answered, "Who made you a prince and a judge over us? Do you mean to kill me as you killed the Egyptian?" Then Moses was afraid, and thought, "Surely the thing is known."* [15]*When Pharaoh heard of it, he sought to kill Moses.*

But Moses fled from Pharaoh, and stayed in the land of Midian....

OVERVIEW: Moses is the subject of great praise. One writer reports that Moses invented the art of writing and that the Phoenicians learned it from the Hebrews (CLEMENT OF ALEXANDRIA). Even before God revealed himself to him, Moses avoided sin, executed justice and for forty years contemplated the mysteries of creation (BASIL). It was more important for Moses to slay wickedness and love of luxury in himself (AMBROSE). Moses' slaying the Egyptian raises a serious moral question (AUGUS-

TINE). In answer to the Hebrew's question, it was knowledge that made Moses a ruler over his people. In all his actions Moses was motivated by faith (CHRYSOSTOM). Moses fled to escape defilement. Moses became a prophet and was enabled to deliver his people from affliction (AMBROSE).

2:12 Moses Killed the Egyptian

PRAISE OF MOSES' WISDOM. CLEMENT OF

Alexandria: Eupolemus in his work *On the Kings of Judea* says that Moses was the first sage and the first person to transmit to the Jews the science of writing, which passed from the Jews to the Phoenicians and from the Phoenicians to the Greeks. When he reached the age of manhood he developed his practical wisdom, being zealous for his national, ancestral educational traditions, to the point of striking down and killing an Egyptian who was unjustly attacking a Hebrew. The mystics say that he eliminated the Egyptian simply by speaking, as later in Acts Peter is said to have killed by his words those who had kept for themselves part of the price of the land and had told lies.[1] Stromateis 1.153.4-154.1.[2]

Moses' Character. Basil the Great: He who hated the pomp of royalty returned to the lowly state of his own race. He preferred to suffer affliction with the people of God rather than to have the fleeting enjoyment of sin. He who, possessing naturally a love for justice, on one occasion even before the government of the people was entrusted to him was seen inflicting on the wicked punishment to the extent of death because of his natural hatred of villainy. He was banished by those to whom he had been a benefactor. He gladly left the uproar of the Egyptians and went to Ethiopia and, spending there all his time apart from others, devoted himself for forty entire years to the contemplation of creation. Exegetic Homilies 1.1.[3]

Moses Purified. Ambrose: Moses slew an Egyptian and became a fugitive from the land of Egypt so as to avoid the king of that land. But he would not have slain the Egyptian if he had not first destroyed in himself the Egypt of spiritual wickedness and had not relinquished the luxuries and honors of the king's palace. Cain and Abel 2.4.14.[4]

Was Moses' Deed Praiseworthy? Augustine: Concerning Moses' deed, when he killed

the Egyptian to defend his brethren, we have treated the point adequately in the book that we wrote against Faustus on the lives of the patriarchs.[5] The question was whether his role in that deed was praiseworthy, insofar as he admitted his sin, just as the richness of the earth, even before useful seeds are planted, is often praised for a growth of plants, even if they are useless. Or perhaps the deed itself should be justified. But to do so does not seem right, for up to that point Moses had no legitimate authority—neither authority that he received from God nor authority ordained by human society. But still, as Stephen says in the Acts of the Apostles, Moses thought that his brethren understood that God would bring them salvation through him,[6] so that by this testimony it appeared that Moses could dare to do this because he was already called by God to act. (But Scripture is silent on this point.) Questions on Exodus 2.[7]

2:14 Who Made You a Ruler?

Knowledge Gave Moses the Right to Rule. Chrysostom: Wherefore also very foolishly did that Hebrew say to him, "Who made you a ruler and a judge over us?" What do you say? You see the actions and doubt of the title? Just as if one seeing a physician using the knife excellently well and succoring that limb in the body which was diseased, should say, "Who made you a physician and ordered you to use a knife?" "It is my art, my good sir, and your own ailment." So too did his knowledge make him (i.e., Moses) what he claimed to be. For ruling is an art, not merely a dignity, and an art above all arts. Homilies on 2 Corinthians 15.4.[8]

Moses' Fear Enabled Him to Escape. Chrysostom: "By faith he forsook Egypt not

---

[1]Acts 5:1-11. [2]FC 85:137. [3]FC 46:4. [4]FC 42:415*. [5]*Against Faustus, a Manichaean* 22:70, 90. [6]Acts 7:25. [7]CCL 33:70-71. [8]NPNF 1 12:352*.

fearing the wrath of the king; for he endured as seeing him who is invisible."[9] What do you say? That he did not fear? And yet the Scripture says that when he heard, he "was afraid," and for this cause provided for safety by flight, and stole away and secretly withdrew himself. And afterwards he was exceedingly afraid. Observe the expressions with care: he said, "not fearing the wrath of the king" with reference to his presenting himself again. For it would have been [the part] of one who was afraid not to undertake again to defend his championship or to have any hand in the matter. That he did however again undertake it was [the part] of one who committed all to God. For he did not say, "He is seeking me and is busy [in the search], and I cannot bear again to engage in this matter."

So even his flight was [an act of] faith. Why then did he not remain? [you say]. That he might not cast himself into a foreseen danger. For this finally would have been tempting [God]: to leap into the midst of dangers and say, "Let us see whether God will save me." And this the devil said to Christ, "Cast yourself down."[10]

Do you see that it is a diabolical thing to throw ourselves into danger without cause and for no purpose and to make trial of God, whether he will save us? Homilies on Hebrews 26.5.[11]

2:15 Moses Fled from Pharaoh

Flight to Avoid Defilement. Ambrose: Thus did Moses flee from the face of Pharaoh, so that the royal palace would not defile him or royal power ensnare him. Indeed, he valued reproach for Christ as more precious than the riches of Egypt. Flight from the World 4.4.18.[12]

A Prophet to Liberate His People. Ambrose: Moses went out from Egypt and was made a prophet and sent back to the people that he might free their souls from the land of affliction. The Prayer of Job and David 4.4.14.[13]

---

[9]Heb 11:27. [10]Mt 4:6. [11]NPNF 1 14:484*. [12]FC 65:296. [13]FC 65:399.

2:23-25 SUFFERING OF THE PEOPLE OF ISRAEL

[23]*In the course of those many days the king of Egypt died. And the people of Israel groaned under their bondage, and cried out for help, and their cry under bondage came up to God.* [24]*And God heard their groaning, and God remembered his covenant with Abraham, with Isaac, and with Jacob.* [25]*And God saw the people of Israel, and God knew their condition.*

Overview: The Hebrews groaned as they carried out the works of Egypt and thereby received grace (Ambrose).

2:23 The People Groaned in Bondage

In the Service of an Unjust King. Am-

brose: Hence the Hebrews, who groaned in the works of Egypt, attained the grace of the just, and those "who ate bread with mourning and fear" were supplied with spiritual good.[1] The Egyptians, on the other hand, who in their ser-

---

[1]Tob 2:5; 1 Cor 10:3.

vice to a detestable king carried out such works with joy, received no favor. On Paradise 15.75.[2]

2:24 God Heard Their Groaning

See Origen on Exodus 1:14.

[2]FC 42:355.

3:1-6 THE BURNING BUSH

[1]Now Moses was keeping the flock of his father-in-law, Jethro, the priest of Midian; and he led his flock to the west side of the wilderness, and came to Horeb, the mountain of God. [2]And the angel of the Lord appeared to him in a flame of fire out of the midst of a bush; and he looked, and lo, the bush was burning, yet it was not consumed. [3]And Moses said, "I will turn aside and see this great sight, why the bush is not burnt." [4]When the Lord saw that he turned aside to see, God called to him out of the bush, "Moses, Moses!" And he said, "Here am I." [5]Then he said, "Do not come near; put off your shoes from your feet, for the place on which you are standing is holy ground." [6]And he said, "I am the God of your father, the God of Abraham, the God of Isaac, and the God of Jacob." And Moses hid his face, for he was afraid to look at God.

Overview: Moses rejected the honors of Egypt and chose to live in hardship (Ephrem). The Fathers often asked who the angel of the Lord was. The angel of the Lord is God himself: an angel when he is seen, the Lord when he is heard (Hilary of Poitiers). The one who appeared in the burning bush was God the Word. The unharmed bush anticipated the body that the Son assumed (Prudentius). It was the Trinity who appeared to Moses; the angel is created properties that God assumed temporarily to make himself visible to Moses (Augustine). The vision is called an angel when it speaks externally but Lord when it touches the hearer's heart (Paterius). The thorn bush has its counterpart in Christ's crown of thorns (Clement of Alexandria). The angel represents an appearance; the one who speaks is God himself (Eusebius). The lowly thorn bush became the symbol of the living God (Ephrem).

The thorn bush is the result of the punishment for sin; "thorns and thistles will the earth bring forth," God had said. The fire is the Holy Spirit; the thorns are the Jews (Caesarius of Arles). When Moses says, "I will turn aside," he means that he will rise to a higher life (Origen). To turn aside is to reject the passing pleasures of this world (Ambrose) or to leave vice behind (Jerome). Moses left behind the love of the world and turned to heavenly things (Gregory the Great).

The thorn bush represents what is lowest in us; yet God can enlighten even that (Ambrose). It is unclear whether the Lord spoke directly to Moses or through an angel (Augustine). God calls Moses to a great vocation, but the highest call was to love (Peter Chrysologus).

Why did God command Moses to take off his shoes? He was to trample the Egyptians with his bare feet (Ephrem). Shoes represent what is corporeal and worldly in us. Jesus too commanded his disciples not to wear sandals when they went out to preach. Elsewhere in the Gospels Jesus tells his disciples to wear sandals (Ambrose). Shoes are the skins of dead animals; Moses is commanded to abandon dead works (Augustine). Sandals represent the garment of the flesh (Ambrose). Nothing dead, like leather, is to come between humans and God (Gregory of Nazianzus). To remove one's shoes is to be freed from passion (Evagrius).

The only way to stand on holy ground is by faith (Ambrose). Moses' vision of the burning bush was the contemplation of invisible things (Gregory of Nyssa). The truly holy ground is the body of Christ, which sanctifies everything it touches (Caesarius of Arles). The burning bush is an image of Mary, the God-bearer (*Theotokos*), since she bore Christ without losing her virginity (John of Damascus).

Scripture gives God many names (Aphrahat). The three patriarchs represent the three stages of spiritual knowledge. God is not only the God of the patriarchs but also the God of all. The Holy Spirit can be called the spirit of Elijah and the spirit of Isaiah (Origen). As Jesus said, God is the God of the living, and hence the patriarchs must be living too (Aphrahat).

God is named under different aspects: his authority and his government, or before and after the incarnation. The three persons each have proper names (Gregory of Nazianzus). The three patriarchs are singled out because they represent a great mystery (Augustine). Jesus used this passage to demonstrate the truth of the resurrection (Cyril of Alexandria).

3:1 *Moses Kept the Flock*

Moses Rejected Honor. Ephrem the Syrian:
Moses in Egypt
    was held in great honor:
Pharaoh's daughter called him her own son
    —yet rejecting this,

he chose to be just a shepherd,
    living in hardship.
Hymns on Paradise 6.[1]

3:2 *The Angel of the Lord Appeared to Moses*

The Angel Was God. Hilary of Poitiers: The vision and the voice are in the one place, nor is anyone else heard except the one who is seen. He who is an angel of God when he is seen is the same one who is the Lord when he is heard, but he himself who is the Lord when he is heard is recognized as the God of Abraham, Isaac and Jacob. When he is called the angel of God, it is revealed that this is not his true nature and that he is not alone, for he is the angel of God. When he is called the Lord and God, he is proclaimed as possessing the glory and name of his own nature. Accordingly you have in an angel who appeared in the bush him who is also the Lord and God. On the Trinity 4.32.[2]

The Power of God's Word Shown in the Burning Bush. Prudentius:
It was the Word, breathed from the Father's
    mouth,
Who of the Virgin took a mortal frame.
The human form that not yet in the flesh
Appeared to Moses wore a brow like ours,
Since God, who would by power of the Word
Assume a body, made the face the same.
Flames rose and seemed to burn the thorny
    bush.
God moved amid the branches set with
    spines,
And tresses of the flames swayed harmlessly,
That he might shadow forth his Son's descent
Into our thorny members sin infests
With teeming briers and fills with bitter
    woes.
For tainted at its root that noxious shrub
Had sprouted from its baneful sap a crop
Of evil shoots beset with many thorns.

---

[1]*HOP* 177. [2]*FC* 25:120.

The sterile branches suddenly grew bright
As God enkindled with his mighty power
The leafy boughs, nor harmed the tangled
    briers.
He touched the scarlet berries, blood-red
    fruits,
And grazed the twigs that grew from deadly
    wood,
Shed by the tortured bush with cruel pangs.
THE DIVINITY OF CHRIST 49-70.[3]

WHAT DOES SCRIPTURE MEAN BY THE ANGEL OF THE LORD? AUGUSTINE: And here he is first called the angel of the Lord and then God. Is the angel then the God of Abraham, the God of Isaac and the God of Jacob? Therefore he may be rightly understood to be the Savior himself of whom the apostle says, "Whose are the fathers, and from whom is Christ according to the flesh, who is over all things, God blessed forever."[4] Hence even here he, who is the God blessed over all things forever, is not unreasonably understood to be himself the God of Abraham, the God of Isaac and the God of Jacob. But why was he previously called the angel of the Lord when he appeared in the flame of fire from the bush? Was it because he was one of many angels but by a dispensation represented the person of his Lord? Or was something belonging to a creature assumed which might appear visibly for the task at hand and from which words might be uttered in an audible way, whereby the presence of the Lord would also become known to the bodily senses of man, as circumstances required, by means of a creature made subject to him? For if he was one of the angels, who can readily affirm whether the person given him to announce was that of the Son, or of the Holy Spirit, or of God the Father or of the Trinity itself altogether, who is the one and only God, in order that he might say, "I am the God of Abraham, the God of Isaac and the God of Jacob"?

For we cannot say that the God of Abraham, the God of Isaac and the God of Jacob is the Son of God and not the Father. Nor will anyone dare to deny that either the Holy Spirit or the Trinity itself, which we believe and understand to be the one God, is the God of Abraham, the God of Isaac and the God of Jacob. For he who is not God is not the God of those fathers. Moreover . . . not only the Father is God, as all, even the heretics, admit, but the Son also, which willingly or not they are forced to confess, for the apostle says, "who is, over all things, God blessed forever," and the Holy Spirit as well. The same apostle declares, "Therefore glorify God in your body," when he had previously stated, "Do you not know that your bodies are the temple of the Holy Spirit in you, whom you have from God?"[5] And these three are one God, as the sound Catholic faith believes. It is not sufficiently clear which person in the Trinity that angel represented, assuming that he was one of the rest of the angels, and whether it was any person and not that of the Trinity itself. THE TRINITY 2.13.23.[6]

INTERIOR AND EXTERIOR SPEAKING. PATERIUS: What does this mean? The vision that is said to have appeared to Moses in the desert is sometimes called an angel, sometimes the Lord. It means this: he is called angel when he served by speaking externally, and Lord, because he ruled within and produced the conditions needed for speaking. For when the speaker is ruled from within, he is called both angel because of his service and Lord because of his inspiration. EXPOSITION OF THE OLD AND NEW TESTAMENT, EXODUS 7.[7]

THE THORN BUSH AND THE CROWN OF THORNS. CLEMENT OF ALEXANDRIA: When the almighty Lord of the universe began to legislate through the Word and decided to make his power visible to Moses, he sent Moses a divine vision

---

[3]FC 52:7. [4]Rom 9:5. [5]1 Cor 6:19-20. [6]FC 45:78-79. [7]PL 79:725, citing Gregory the Great *Moral Interpretation of Job* preface 1.3.

with the appearance of light, in the burning bush. Now a bramble bush is full of thorns. So too when the Word was concluding his legislation and his stay among men as their Lord, again he permitted himself to be crowned with thorns as a mystic symbol. Returning to the place from which he had descended, the Word renewed that by which he had first come, appearing first in the bush of thorns and later being surrounded with thorns that he might show that all was the work of the same one power. He is one, and his Father is one, the eternal beginning and end. CHRIST THE EDUCATOR 2.8.75.[8]

ANGELS ARE SEEN; GOD IS HEARD. EUSEBIUS: And when an angel appears to Moses, Holy Scripture also makes it plain, saying, "The angel of the Lord appeared to him in a flame of fire in a bush." But when it refers to the actual being who replies, it calls him God and Lord and no longer an angel. It is equally clear in its distinction between the angel and the Lord in the account of what happened at the Red Sea.[9] PROOF OF THE GOSPEL 5.11.238.[10]

THE MYSTERY OF GOD. EPHREM THE SYRIAN: The bush which was unsuitable even as an image of dead gods was able to depict within itself the mystery of the living God. Moses, this is a sign to you: as you saw God dwelling in the midst of fire, by fire must you serve the God who dwells in the fire. COMMENTARY ON EXODUS 3.2.[11]

THE FLAMES REPRESENT THE HOLY SPIRIT. CAESARIUS OF ARLES: It was not without reason, beloved brethren, nor without the signification of some mystery that there was a flame in the bush: "And the bush was not consumed." Indeed, the bush was a genus of thorns. What the earth has produced for sinful man cannot be put in any kind of praise, for it was first said to man when he sinned: "Thorns and thistles shall the earth bring forth to you."[12] The fact that the bush was not burned, that is, was not seized by

the flames, is understood to signify no good. In the flame is recognized the Holy Ghost; in the bush and thorns is represented the hard, haughty Jewish people. SERMON 96.1.[13]

3:3 I Will Turn Aside

TO ASCEND TO A HIGHER LIFE. ORIGEN: When Moses had seen the bush burning and not being consumed he was astonished at the sight and said, "I will cross over and see this sight." He certainly also did not mean that he was about to cross over some earthly space, or to ascend mountains or to descend the steep sides of valleys. The vision was near him, in his countenance and in his eyes. But he says, "I will cross over," that he might show that he, reminded forcefully by the heavenly vision, ought to ascend to a higher life and cross over to better things than those in which he was. HOMILIES ON GENESIS 12.2.[14]

REJECTING WORLDLY PLEASURES. AMBROSE: Moses, too, passing by things of this world, saw a great sight and said, "I will turn aside and see this great sight," for had he been held by the fleeting pleasures of this world he would not have seen so great a mystery. CONCERNING REPENTANCE 1.14.74.[15]

TO ESCAPE FROM VICE. JEROME: Moses says, "I must go over to look at this remarkable sight." If he does not go over, that is, if he does not escape all vice, he cannot behold the great marvel. HOMILIES ON THE PSALMS 51.[16]

MOSES SOUGHT HIGHER THINGS. GREGORY THE GREAT: When Moses sought the glory of contemplation on high, he said, "I will pass over and see this vision." For unless he had withdrawn the footsteps of his heart from love of the world, he would never have been able to under-

---

[8]FC 23:158. [9]Ex 14:19. [10]POG 1:256. [11]FC 91:232. [12]Gen 3:18. [13]FC 47:69. [14]FC 71:178. [15]NPNF 2 10:341. [16]FC 48:372.

stand heavenly things. MORAL INTERPRETATION OF JOB 15.57.68.[17]

3:4 God Called to Moses Out of the Bush

THE INTERPRETATION OF THE THORN BUSH. AMBROSE: Why should we despair that God should speak in men, who spoke in the thorn bush? God did not despise the bush. Would that he might also give light to my thorns. Perhaps some may wonder that there is some light even in our thorns. Some of our thorns will not burn. There will be some whose shoes shall be put off their feet at the sound of my voice, that the steps of the mind may be freed from bodily hindrances. CONCERNING VIRGINS 1.1.2.[18]

WHO SPOKE TO MOSES? AUGUSTINE: Was the Lord speaking through an angel? Or was the Lord that angel who has been called the "angel of great counsel"[19] and is understood to be Christ? For Scripture said above, "the angel of the Lord appeared to him."[20] QUESTIONS ON EXODUS 3.[21]

WHAT GOD'S CALL MEANT FOR MOSES. PETER CHRYSOLOGUS: This is why he summons Moses by his fatherly voice, addresses him with paternal love and invites him to be the liberator of his people. Why should I say more? He makes him a god; he sets him up as a god[22] before Pharaoh. He makes him a god, fortifies him with signs, arms him with virtues, wins wars through mere commands, grants to him as a soldier victory gained by a mere word. By his orders he concedes him a triumph and leads him through all the crowns of virtues to his own friendship, gives him an opportunity to share in his heavenly kingdom and allows him to be a legislator. However, Moses received all this that he might love—that at length he might be so inflamed with the love of God that he would burn with it himself and encourage others to have it too. SERMON 147.[23]

3:5 Put Off Your Shoes

WHY MOSES WAS FRIGHTENED. EPHREM THE SYRIAN: "Remove your sandals" and go trample the Egyptians. See, it is thirty years past the time of their picking. Up to this point, Moses proceeded without fear. But when he saw a sight that was more than his eyes [could bear], he hid his face out of fear of looking at God the way he looked at the angel. COMMENTARY ON EXODUS 3.1.[24]

LEAVING THE WORLD BEHIND. AMBROSE: For it is said to Moses when he was desiring to draw nearer: "Put off your shoes from your feet," how much more must we free the feet of our soul from the bonds of the body and clear our steps from all connection with this world. CONCERNING REPENTANCE 2.11.107.[25]

BEAUTIFUL FOR PREACHING THE GOSPEL. AMBROSE: Pass by like Moses, that you may see the God of Abraham and of Isaac and of Jacob and that you may see a great vision. This is a great vision, but if you wish to see it, remove the sandals from your feet, remove every bond of iniquity, remove the bonds of the world, leave behind the sandals which are earthly. Likewise Jesus sent the apostles without sandals, without money, gold and silver,[26] so that they would not carry earthly things with them. For the man who seeks the good is praised not for his sandals but for the swiftness and grace of his feet, as Scripture says, "How beautiful are the feet of those who preach the gospel of peace, of those who bring glad tidings of good things!"[27] Therefore remove the sandals from your feet, that they may be beautiful for preaching the gospel. FLIGHT FROM THE WORLD 5.25.[28]

---

[17]CCL 143A:792-93 [18]NPNF 2 10:363*. [19]Is 9:6. [20]Ex 3:2. [21]CCL 33:71. [22]On the use of "gods" see Ps 82:6; Jn 10:34. [23]FC 17:245. [24]FC 91:231. [25]NPNF 2 10:358-59. [26]Mk 6:8-9; Mt 10:9-10; Lk 9:3. [27]Rom 10:15; Is 52:7. [28]FC 65:300-301.

TO WALK IN THE SPIRIT. AMBROSE: Such was Moses, to whom it was said, "Remove the sandals from your feet," so that when he was about to call the people to the kingdom of God he might first put aside the garments of the flesh and might walk with his spirit and the footstep of his mind naked. ISAAC, OR THE SOUL 4.16.[29]

SHOES REPRESENT WHAT IS DEAD. GREGORY OF NAZIANZUS: And as to shoes, let him who is about to touch the holy land which the feet of God have trodden, put them off, as Moses did upon the mount, that he may bring there nothing dead; nothing to come between man and God. ORATION 45.19.[30]

TO BE FREE OF PASSION. EVAGRIUS: If Moses, when he attempted to draw near the burning bush, was prohibited until he should remove the shoes from his feet, how should you not free yourself of every thought that is colored by passion seeing that you wish to see One who is beyond every thought and perception? CHAPTERS ON PRAYER 4.[31]

DEAD WORKS. AUGUSTINE: What are the shoes? Well, what *are* the shoes we wear? Leather from dead animals. The hides of dead animals are what we protect our feet with. So what are we being ordered to do? To give up dead works. This is symbolically what he instructs Moses to do in his honor, when the Lord says to him, "Take off your shoes. For the place you are standing in is holy ground." There's no holier ground than the church of God, is there? So as we stand in it let us take off our shoes, let us give up dead works. SERMON 101.7.[32]

TO BE FIRM IN THE FAITH. AMBROSE: Stand firm in your hearts lest someone should overtake you or anyone would overturn you. The apostle taught us what it means to stand—that is, what was said to Moses: "The place upon which you stand is holy ground." Now no one stands except the one who stands by faith, he who is firmly fixed by the determination of his heart. LETTER 14 EXTRA COLL. (63).41.[33]

THE HEIGHTS OF CONTEMPLATION. GREGORY OF NYSSA: He willingly shook off his royal dignity like so much dust which is stripped off by the stomping of the feet.[34] He banished himself from human society for forty years and lived alone, focusing steadfastly in undistracted solitude on the contemplation of invisible things.[35] After this he was illuminated by the inexpressible light[36] and freed the lower part of his soul from the dead garment made of skin. ON THE INSCRIPTIONS OF THE PSALMS 1.7.52.[37]

HOLY GROUND MEANS THE BODY OF JESUS CHRIST. CAESARIUS OF ARLES: Finally see what the Lord said to Moses and Joshua: "Remove the strap of your shoe, for the place where you stand is holy ground." Can this be understood according to the letter, beloved brethren? How could that ground upon which they trod be holy, since doubtless it was like the rest of the earth? However, notice carefully what was said: "For the place whereon you stand is holy ground." That is to say, Christ, whose figure you bear and of whom you seem to be a type, is holy ground. True holy ground is the body of our Lord Jesus Christ through whom everything heavenly and earthly is sanctified. SERMON 96.4.[38]

AN IMAGE OF MARY, THE THEOTOKOS.[39] JOHN OF DAMASCUS: The burning bush was an image of God's mother, and when Moses was about to approach it, God said, "Do not come near; put off your shoes from your feet, for the place on which you are standing is holy ground." Now if the ground where Moses saw an image of the Theotokos is holy ground, how much more holy

---

[29]FC 65:21. [30]NPNF 2 7:430. [31]CS 4:56. [32]*WSA* 3 4:68. [33]CSEL 82 3:256-57. [34]Heb 11:24-26. [35]Heb 11:27. [36]Acts 7:30. [37]*GNTIP* 101. [38]FC 47:72. [39]Greek term meaning "God-bearer" or "mother of God."

is the image itself? Not only is it holy, I daresay, but the holy of holies. ON DIVINE IMAGES 20.[40]

3:6 The God of the Patriarchs

THE NAMES OF GOD IN HEBREW. APHRAHAT: For the name of Divinity is given for the highest honor in the world, and with whomsoever God is well pleased, he applies it to him. But however, the names of God are many and are venerable, as he delivered his names to Moses, saying to him, "I am the God of your fathers, the God of Abraham and the God of Isaac and the God of Jacob. This is my name forever, and this is my memorial unto generations." And he called his name "Ahiyah ashar Ahiyah,"[41] "El Shaddai" and "Adonai Sabaoth."[42] By these names God is called. The great and honorable name of Godhead he withheld not from his righteous ones; even as, though he is the great king, without grudging he applied the great and honorable name of kingship to men who are his creatures. DEMONSTRATIONS 17.5.[43]

See also AUGUSTINE AND HILARY ON EXODUS 3:2.

MORAL PHILOSOPHY, NATURAL PHILOSOPHY AND CONTEMPLATION. ORIGEN: For Abraham sets forth moral philosophy through obedience; his obedience was indeed so great, his adherence to orders so strict that when he heard the command "Go forth out of your country, and from your kindred, and out of your father's house" he did not delay but did as he was told forthwith. And he did even more than that: on hearing that he was to sacrifice his son, he does not hesitate but complies with the command and, to give an example to those who should come after of the obedience in which moral philosophy consists, "he spared not his only son."[44] Isaac also is an exponent of natural philosophy when he digs wells and searches out the roots of things. And Jacob practices the inspective science in that he earned his name of Israel from his contempla-tion of the things of God, and saw the camps of heaven and beheld the house of God and the angel's paths—the ladders reaching up from earth to heaven. COMMENTARY ON THE SONG OF SONGS, PROLOGUE 3.[45]

GOD IS THE GOD OF ALL. ORIGEN: God has been recorded indeed to be the God "of Abraham, and the God of Isaac and the God of Jacob." He indeed who wishes the light to belong to none other than men (because it is said, "The life was the light of men")[46] will think, according to this analogy, that the God of Abraham and the God of Isaac and the God of Jacob is the God of no one except these three fathers alone. But he is at least also the God of Elijah,[47] and, as Judith says, the God of her father Simeon,[48] and he is God of the Hebrews.[49] Wherefore, according to the analogy, if nothing prevents him from being the God of others also, nothing prevents the light of men from also being the light of other creatures besides men. COMMENTARY ON THE GOSPEL OF JOHN 2.143.[50]

GOD BECOMES OUR GOD. ORIGEN: If the God of the universe, having been made familiar to the saints, becomes their God, the being named the God of Abraham and the God of Isaac and the God of Jacob, by how much more will it be possible for the Holy Spirit, having been made familiar to the prophets, to be called their spirit, that the Spirit might thus be said to be the spirit of Elijah and the spirit of Isaiah? COMMENTARY ON THE GOSPEL OF JOHN 6.68.[51]

GOD IS THE GOD OF THE LIVING. APHRAHAT: And when the holy One called Moses from the bush he said thus to him: "I am the God of Abraham, of Isaac and of Jacob." When Death heard this utterance, he trembled and feared and was

---

[40]*ODI* 65. [41]Hebrew for "I am who I am." [42]Gen 17:1; Ex 3:14; Jer 32:18. [43]NPNF 2 13:388. [44]Gen 22:16. [45]ACW 26:44-45. [46]Jn 1:4. [47]2 Kings 2:14. [48]Jdt 9:2. [49]Ex 3:18; 5:3; 9:1, 13; 10:3. [50]FC 80:132. [51]FC 80:187.

terrified and perturbed and knew that he had not become king forever over the children of Adam. From the hour that he heard God saying to Moses, "I am the God of Abraham, of Isaac and of Jacob," Death [struck] his hands together, for he learned that God is king of the dead and of the living and that it is appointed to the children of Adam to come forth from his darkness and arise with their bodies. And observe that our Redeemer Jesus also, when he repeated this utterance to the Sadducees, when they were disputing with him about the resurrection of the dead, thus said, "God is not [God] of the dead, for all are alive unto him."[52] DEMONSTRATIONS 22.2.[53]

ON THE NAMES OF GOD. GREGORY OF NAZIANZUS: Of the other titles, some are evidently names of his authority, others of his government of the world, and of this viewed under a twofold aspect: the one before, the other in, the incarnation. For instance, the Almighty, the King of Glory, or of the Ages, or of the Powers, or of the Beloved or of Kings. Or again, the Lord of Sabaoth, that is, of hosts, or of powers or of lords;[54] these are clearly titles belonging to his authority. But the God either of salvation or of vengeance, or of peace, or of righteousness, or of Abraham, Isaac and Jacob, and of all the spiritual Israel that sees God[55]—these belong to his government. For since we are governed by these three things, the fear of punishment, the hope of salvation and of glory besides, and the practice of the virtues by which these are attained, the name of the God of vengeance governs fear, and that of the God of salvation our hope, and that of the God of virtues our practice; that whoever attains to any of these may, as carrying God in himself, press on yet more unto perfection and to that affinity which arises out of virtues. Now these are names common to the Godhead, but the proper name of the unoriginate is "Father," and that of the unoriginately begotten is "Son" and that of the unbegottenly proceeding or going forth is "the Holy Ghost." THEOLOGICAL ORATION 4.19.[56]

THE MEANING OF THE THREE PATRIARCHS. AUGUSTINE: God gives witness and says, "I am the God of Abraham, the God of Isaac and the God of Jacob." Were there not other patriarchs? Was not Noah a holy man before these, who alone in the whole human race together with his whole house deserved to be delivered from the flood, in whom and in his sons the church is represented? They escape the flood, with wood carrying them.[57] And then afterwards [come] the great men whom we know, whom Holy Scripture commends, Moses faithful in all his house.[58] And those three are named, as if they alone were deserving of him: "I am the God of Abraham, the God of Isaac and the God of Jacob; this is my name forever."

An enormous mystery! The Lord has the power to open both our mouths and your hearts that we may be able to speak as he has deigned to reveal and that you may be able to grasp as it is advantageous to you.

Therefore those patriarchs are three: Abraham, Isaac and Jacob. You already know that the sons of Jacob were twelve and from them are the people of Israel because Jacob himself is Israel and the people of Israel are the twelve tribes belonging to the twelve sons of Israel. Abraham, Isaac and Jacob, three fathers and one people. Three fathers, as it were, in the beginning of the people; three fathers in whom the people was prefigured. And the earlier people itself [is] the present people. For in the people of the Jews the people of the Christians was prefigured. There a figure, here the truth; there a shadow, here the body, as the apostle says, "Now these things happened to them in figure."[59] It is the apostle's voice, and he says, "They were written for us, upon whom the end of the world has come."[60]

---

[52]Lk 20:38. [53]NPNF 2 13:402. [54]See, e.g., Ps 24:7; 1 Tim 1:17; 6:15. [55]Gen 32:28, 30; "Israel" means "he sees God." [56]LCC 3:190. In this passage, one of the most famous in all his writings, Gregory distinguishes the three persons of the Trinity by their relationship of origin and distinguishes the origin of the Holy Spirit from that of the Son as "procession" from "begetting." [57]Gen 7:7. [58]Num 12:7; Heb 3:2. [59]1 Cor 10:11. [60]1 Cor 10:11.

Let your mind return to Abraham, Isaac and Jacob. In those three we find free women giving birth and bondwomen giving birth. We find there the progeny of free women; we find there also the progeny of bondwomen. The bondwoman signifies nothing good. "Cast out the bondwoman," [Scripture] says, "and her son; for the son of the bondwoman will not be heir with the son of the free woman."[61] The apostle mentions this;[62] and in these two sons of Abraham the apostle says was a figure of the two Testaments, Old and New. To the Old Testament belong the lovers of temporal things, the lovers of the world; to the New Testament belong the lovers of eternal life. Therefore that Jerusalem on earth was a shadow of the heavenly Jerusalem, the mother of us all, which is in heaven. And these are the apostle's words. And about that city from which we are sojourners you know many things, you have already heard many things. Now we find something remarkable in these births, that is, in these offspring, in these procreations of free women and bondwomen, namely, four types of men. And in these four types of men is comprised the figure of the Christian people,[63] so that what was said in regard to these three is not astonishing: "I am the God of Abraham, the God of Isaac and the God of Jacob." TRACTATE ON THE GOSPEL OF JOHN 11.7.2-8.2.[64]

JESUS QUOTED GOD'S WORDS. CYRIL OF ALEXANDRIA: But the Savior also demonstrated the great ignorance of the Sadducees by bringing forward their own hierophant Moses, who was well and clearly acquainted with the resurrection of the dead. For he has set before us God, he says, as saying in the bush, "I am the God of Abraham, and the God of Isaac and the God of Jacob." But of whom is he God, if, according to their argument, these have ceased to live? For he is the God of the living; and therefore certainly and altogether they will rise, when his almighty right hand brings them thereunto; and not them only but also all who are upon the earth. HOMILIES ON THE GOSPEL OF LUKE 136.[65]

---

[61]Gen 21:10. [62]Gal 4:21-31. [63]The four types of men refer to Abraham, Isaac, Jacob/Israel and the sons of Jacob/Israel. [64]FC 79:16-18. [65]CGSL 542-43.

3:7-22 THE CALL OF MOSES

[7]Then the LORD said, "I have seen the affliction of my people who are in Egypt, and have heard their cry because of their taskmasters; I know their sufferings, [8]and I have come down to deliver them out of the hand of the Egyptians, and to bring them up out of that land to a good and broad land, a land flowing with milk and honey, to the place of the Canaanites, the Hittites, the Amorites, the Perizzites, the Hivites, and the Jebusites. [9]And now, behold, the cry of the people of Israel has come to me, and I have seen the oppression with which the Egyptians oppress them. [10]Come, I will send you to Pharaoh that you may bring forth my people, the sons of Israel, out of Egypt." But Moses said to God, "Who am I?" . . .

[13]Then Moses said to God, "If I come to the people of Israel and say to them, 'The God of your fathers has sent me to you,' and they ask me, 'What is his name?' what shall I say to

*them?" *¹⁴*God said to Moses, "I am who I am."ᵉ* And he said, "Say this to the people of Israel, 'I am has sent me to you.'" ¹⁵God also said to Moses, "Say this to the people of Israel, 'The Lord,ᶠ the God of your fathers, the God of Abraham, the God of Isaac, and the God of Jacob, has sent me to you': this is my name for ever, and thus I am to be remembered throughout all generations. . . . ¹⁹I know that the king of Egypt will not let you go unless compelled by a mighty hand.ᵍ ²⁰So I will stretch out my hand and smite Egypt with all the wonders which I will do in it; after that he will let you go. ²¹And I will give this people favor in the sight of the Egyptians; and when you go, you shall not go empty, ²²but each woman shall ask of her neighbor, and of her who sojourns in her house, jewelry of silver and of gold, and clothing, and you shall put them on your sons and on your daughters; thus you shall despoil the Egyptians."*

e *Or* I am what I am *or* I will be what I will be   f *The word* LORD *when spelled with capital letters, stands for the divine name,* YHWH, *which is here connected with the verb* hayah, *to be*   g *Gk Vg: Heb* no, not by a mighty hand   *LXX *I am he who is*

Overview: Joshua, whose name is also Jesus, and not Moses, was to lead the second people, the Christians, into the land of promise (Tertullian). Should milk and honey be taken literally? Milk and honey is less a physical desription of Palestine than a reference to the works of grace and the kingdom of heaven (Augustine). There are different senses of "cry": a cry of debauchery and a cry for help (Augustine).

Moses was a modest man (Ephrem). The name that God reveals to Moses as his own is one of the great mysteries of the Old Testament. It is fit for the contemplation of God and of his nature. The Fathers offered many interpretations of the name. God the Father, as existence, is the source of all being, while all that is rational participates in the Son (Origen). God, as eternal being, imparts existence to all else that exists (Eusebius). God is the one First Principle (Pseudo-Athanasius). The Greek name for God may derive from "to run" or "to blaze" (Gregory of Nazianzus). God exists eternally without beginning or end, in everlasting eternity (Hilary of Poitiers, Ambrose). This name applies to Christ too (Ambrose). Only the Trinity is absolute being (Jerome). "I am who I am" cannot be grasped (Augustine). For God to exist means that he is immutable, unchangeable. To be truly is to be unchange-

able. All things that exist derive their existence and goodness from God. Moses' insight into God's being was far superior to anything Plato ever wrote. The name "I am who I am" properly describes God's essence. To be is to be eternally present, with no past or future (Augustine). Only the Trinity is by nature unchangeable (Fulgentius). The present tense denotes eternity. God does not derive his existence from anyone else; hence he alone exists in the fullest sense (Cassiodorus).

He who is, is without beginning or end (Chrysostom). The appearance in the burning bush was a theophany of the Son. God is Lord because he rules over all, beholds all things and is feared by all (Ambrose). When God calls himself the God of Abraham, he implies that he is immutable in himself, but the Son can take on mutable flesh (Augustine). God knows that Pharaoh will not let the people go. His foreknowledge manifests his divinity, and yet he allows people the freedom to repent (Clement of Alexandria).

Why could the Hebrew women take things from the Egyptians? Was it stealing? It might appear to be so, but Moses had to obey God's command (Augustine). The silver and gold of the Egyptians were the arrears for the wages that the Egyptians owed the Israelites (Tertullian). God's command to deceive the Egyptians must have been just. The Egyptians were in one sense deceived by the Hebrews, but God used the Hebrews to punish the Egyptians (Augustine).

3:8 A Land Flowing with Milk and Honey

Joshua Leads the People into Eternal Life. Tertullian: . . . Jesus Christ was to introduce the second people (which is composed of us nations, lingering deserted in the world previously) into the land of promise, "flowing with milk and honey" (that is, into the possession of eternal life, than which nothing is sweeter). This had to come about not through Moses (that is, not through the law's discipline) but through Joshua (that is, through the new law's grace), after our circumcision with "a knife of rock"[1] (that is, with Christ's precepts, for Christ is in many ways and figures predicted as a rock).[2] Therefore the man who was being prepared to act as an image of this sacrament was inaugurated under the figure of the Lord's name, even so as to be named Jesus.[3] Answer to the Jews 9.22.[4]

A Literal Description? Augustine: I ask whether we should take the land flowing with milk and honey spiritually, since, according to the proper sense, this phrase does not describe the land that was being given to the people of Israel. Or is it a figure of speech that is used to praise the richness and sweetness of the land? Questions on Exodus 4.[5]

Grace and the Kingdom. Augustine: Indeed, unless that land which was styled the land that flowed with milk and honey signified something great, through which, as by a visible token, he was leading those who understood his wondrous works to invisible grace and the kingdom of heaven, they could not be blamed for scorning that land, whose temporal kingdom we also ought to esteem as nothing, that we may love that Jerusalem which is free, the mother of us all,[6] which is in heaven, and truly to be desired. Explanation of the Psalms 106 (107).20.[7]

3:9 The Cry of the Israelites

Different Senses of Clamor. Augustine: Clamor: not like the clamor of the Sodomites,[8] which signified iniquity without fear or shame. Questions on Exodus 5.[9]

3:11 Who Am I That I Should Go to Pharaoh?

Moses' Modesty. Ephrem the Syrian: Moses said, "Who am I to go before Pharaoh?" Although I have a royal title, I will not be received by him. And now that I do the work of a simple shepherd, who will allow me to go before Pharaoh? And even if I were let in, what importance would he see in me to believe my words? Commentary on Exodus 3.3.[10]

3:14 I Am Who I Am

Everything Receives Its Being from the Father. Origen: That the activity of the Father and the Son is to be found both in saints and in sinners is clear from the fact that all rational beings are partakers of the word of God, that is, of reason, and so have implanted within them some seeds, as it were, of wisdom and righteousness, which is Christ. And all things that exist derive their share of being from him who truly exists, who said through Moses, "I am that I am"; which participation in God the Father extends to all, both righteous and sinners, rational and irrational creatures and absolutely everything that exists. On First Principles 1.3.6.[11]

---

[1]Josh 5:2. [2]1 Cor 10:4. [3]That is, Joshua. [4]ANF 3:163. [5]CCL 33:71. [6]Gal 4:26. [7]NPNF 1 8:529. [8]Gen 18:20. [9]CCL 33:71. [10]FC 91:232. [11]OFP 34-35.

God Is the Only Cause of Existence.
Eusebius: Everything that has ever existed or now exists derives its being from the One, the only existent and preexistent being, who also said, "I am the existent." . . . As the only being and the eternal being, he is himself the cause of existence to all those to whom he has imparted existence from himself by his will and his power and gives existence to all things and their powers and forms, richly and ungrudgingly from himself. Proof of the Gospel 4.1.[12]

The One God Is One First Principle.
Pseudo-Athanasius: As there is one Beginning and therefore one God, so one is that Essence and Subsistence which indeed and truly and really is. It is this One who said "I am that I am," and not two, that there be not two Beginnings; and from the One, a Son in nature and truth, is its own Word, its Wisdom, its Power, and inseparable from it. Fourth Oration Against the Arians 1.[13]

Meanings of the Name God. Gregory of Nazianzus: As far then as we can reach, "He who is" and "God" are the special names of his essence; and of these especially "He who is," not only because when he spoke to Moses in the mount, and Moses asked what his name was, this was what he called himself, bidding him say to the people, "I am has sent me," but also because we find that this name is the more strictly appropriate. For the name *theos* ["God"], even if, as those who are skillful in these matters say, it were derived from *theein* ["to run"] or from *aithein* ["to blaze"], from continual motion, and because he consumes evil conditions of things (from which fact he is also called a consuming fire)[14] would still be one of the relative names and not an absolute one, as again is the case with "Lord," which also is called a name of God. "I am the Lord your God," he says, "that is my name;" and "The Lord is his name."[15] But we are inquiring into a nature whose being is absolute and not [into being] bound up with something else. But being is in its proper sense peculiar to God and belongs to him entirely, and it is not limited or cut short by any before or after, for indeed in him there is no past or future. Theological Oration 4.18.[16]

To Be Is Most Characteristic of God.
Hilary of Poitiers: While therefore I was giving serious thought to these and many other similar problems, I chanced upon those books which according to Jewish tradition were written by Moses and the prophets. In them I found the testimony of God the Creator about himself expressed in the following manner: "I am who I am," and again, "Thus shall you say to the children of Israel: He who is, has sent me to you." I was filled with admiration at such a clear definition of God, which spoke of the incomprehensible nature in language most suitable to our human understanding. It is known that there is nothing more characteristic of God than to be, because that itself which is does not belong to those things which will one day end or to those which had a beginning. But that which combines eternity with the power of unending happiness could never not have been, nor is it possible that one day it will not be, because what is divine is not liable to destruction, nor does it have a beginning. And since the eternity of God will not be untrue to itself in anything, he has revealed to us in a fitting manner this fact alone, that he is, in order to render testimony to his everlasting eternity. On the Trinity 1.5.[17]

Christ, Who Always Is. Ambrose: Christ therefore is and always is; for he who is, always is. And Christ always is, of whom Moses says, "He that is has sent me." On the Christian Faith 5.1.26.[18]

---

[12]POG 1:164. [13]NPNF 2 4:433. [14]Deut 4:24; Heb 12:29. [15]Ex 20:2, 15:3; Is 42:8. [16]LCC 3:189-90. [17]FC 25:6. [18]NPNF 2 10:287.

Eternal Being. Ambrose: The Lord said, "I am who I am." You will say, "He who is sent me." This is the true name of God: always to exist. Letter 55(8).8.[19]

Only God's Nature Is Uncreated. Jerome: There is one nature of God and one only; and this, and this alone, truly is. For absolute being is derived from no other source but is all its own. All things besides, that is, all things created, although they appear to be, soon are not. For there was a time when they were not, and that which once was not may again cease to be. God alone who is eternal, that is to say, who has no beginning, really deserves to be called an essence. Therefore also he says of him, "I am has sent me." As the angels, the sky, the earth, the seas all existed at the time, it must have been as the absolute being that God claimed for himself that name of essence, which apparently was common to all. But because his nature alone is perfect and because in the three persons there subsists but one Godhead, which truly is and is one nature, whoever in the name of religion declares that there are in the Godhead three elements, three hypostases, that is, or essences, is striving really to predicate three natures of God. Letter 15.4.[20]

"I Am Who I Am" Cannot Be Understood. Augustine: Perhaps it was hard even for Moses himself, as it is much also for us, and much more for us, to understand what was said, "I am who I am" and "He who is has sent me to you." And if by chance Moses understood, when would they to whom he was being sent understand? Therefore the Lord put aside what man could not grasp and added what he could grasp. For he added and said, "I am the God of Abraham, and the God of Isaac and the God of Jacob." This you can grasp. But what mind can grasp, "I am who I am"? Tractate on the Gospel of John 38.8.3.[21]

God Abides Forever. Augustine: But now

the Lord speaks to Moses—you know all this, and I won't keep you longer on it, for lack of time—"I am who I am; he who is sent me." When he asked God's name, you see, this is what was said: "I am who I am. And you shall say to the children of Israel, he who is sent me to you." What's this all about? O God, O Lord of ours, what are you called? "I am called He is," he said. What does it mean, I am called He is? "That I abide forever, that I cannot change." Things which change are not, because they do not last. What is, abides. But whatever changes was something and will be something; yet you cannot say it is, because it is changeable. So the unchangeableness of God was prepared to suggest itself by this phrase "I am who I am." Sermon 6.4.[22]

Truly to Be Is to Be Unchangeable. Augustine: Magnificently and divinely, therefore, our God said to his servant: "I am that I am," and "You shall say to the children of Israel, He who is sent me to you." For he truly is because he is unchangeable. For every change makes what was not, to be. Therefore he truly is, who is unchangeable; but all other things that were made by him have received being from him each in its own measure. On the Nature of the Good 19.[23]

Existence and Goodness Derive from God. Augustine: He is the first and greatest existence, who is utterly unchangeable and who could say most perfectly, "I am who I am, and you shall say to them, "He who is has sent me to you." As a result, the other things which exist could not exist except by him, and these things are good insofar as they have received the ability to be. On Christian Teaching 1.32.35.[24]

Moses Is Far Superior to Plato. Augustine: Then too Plato's definition of a philosopher—one who loves God—contains an idea

---

[19]CSEL 82 2:80.   [20]NPNF 2 6:19.   [21]FC 88:111.   [22]*WSA* 3 1:228-29.   [23]NPNF 1 4:354-55.   [24]FC 2:52-53.

which shines forth everywhere in Scripture. But the most palpable proof to my mind that he was conversant with the sacred books is this, that when Moses, informed by an angel that God wished him to deliver the Hebrews from Egypt, questioned the angel concerning the name of the one who had sent him, the answer received was this: "I am who I am. Thus shall you say to the children of Israel: he who is has sent me to you," as though, in comparison with him who, being immutable, truly is, all mutable things are as if they were not. Now Plato had a passionate perception of this truth and was never tired of teaching it. Yet I doubt whether this idea can be found in any of the works of Plato's predecessors except in the text "I am who I am, and you shall say to them, he who is has sent me to you." CITY OF GOD 8.11.[25]

DESCRIBING GOD'S ESSENCE. AUGUSTINE: But God is without doubt a substance, or perhaps essence would be a better term, which the Greeks call *ousia*. For just as wisdom is so called from being wise and knowledge is so called from knowing, so essence is so called from being [esse]. And who possesses being in a higher degree than he, who said to his servant Moses, "I am who I am" and "He who is has sent me to you." But all other things that are called essences or substances are susceptible of accidents, by which a change, whether great or small, is brought about in them. But there can be no accidents of this kind in God. Therefore only the essence of God, or the essence which God is, is unchangeable. THE TRINITY 5.2.3.[26]

NO PAST OR FUTURE IN GOD. AUGUSTINE: For although that immutable and ineffable nature does not admit of *was* and *will be* but only *is* (for it truly *is*, because it cannot be changed), and therefore it was proper for him to say, "I am who I am" and "You will say to the children of Israel, 'He who is has sent me to you,'" nevertheless, on account of the changeableness of the times in which our mortality and our changeableness are involved, we do not falsely say *was* and *will be* and *is*. Was, in past ages; is, in present ones; will be, in future ones. Was, because he was never lacking; will be, because he will never be lacking; is, because he always is. TRACTATE ON THE GOSPEL OF JOHN 99.5.2.[27]

ONLY GOD IS UNCHANGEABLE. FULGENTIUS: Hold most firmly and never doubt that the holy Trinity, the only true God, just as it is eternal, is likewise the only one by nature unchangeable. He indicates this when he says to his servant Moses, "I am which I am." TO PETER ON THE FAITH 9.50.[28]

GOD'S EXISTENCE IS WHOLLY PRESENT. CASSIODORUS: So in Genesis [sic] he bade Moses say of himself, "Go and say to the children of Israel, I am who I am. He who is has sent me to you." So he wanted his eternity to be denoted by the present tense. This use of present time ("today") is acknowledged to be peculiar to the divine Scriptures in the sense of perpetuity. EXPOSITION OF THE PSALMS 2.8.[29]

GOD ALONE IS RIGHTLY SAID TO BE. CASSIODORUS: The phrase "I am" belongs to the divinity. It does not change with time but is always there and remains eternal. So the reply to Moses was "I am who I am" and again "He who is has sent me." But we must first investigate why God alone claims this term which denotes essence for himself. When it was spoken, there were angels, heavenly creatures and all earthly creatures as were decreed to exist. But because he is the only uncreated and eternal nature which did not begin in time and subsists as one divinity in three persons, God alone is rightly said to be, for he needs no one for his existence but ever abides by the strength of his own power. In it there is another mystery: a single

---

[25]FC 14:41-42. [26]FC 45:177. [27]FC 90:224. [28]FC 95:92. [29]ACW 51:62.

syllable, *sum* ("I am"), is embraced by three letters, so we are taught that the holy Trinity is one God. Exposition of the Psalms 49.7.[30]

God's Name Designates His Eternity.
Chrysostom: Moreover, do you wish to learn about his eternity? Listen to what Moses said about the Father. When he had inquired what he should answer if he should be asked by the Egyptians who it was that had sent him, he was bidden to say, "He who is sent me." Now the words "he who is" mean that he exists always and is without beginning and that he really exists and exists as Lord and Master. Homilies on the Gospel of John 15.[31]

Theophanies of the Son. Ambrose: This is the God of Abraham, the God of Isaac, the God of Jacob, who appeared to Moses in the bush, concerning whom Moses says, "He who is has sent me." It was not the Father who spoke to Moses in the bush, or in the desert, but the Son. On the Christian Faith 1.13.83.[32]

3:15 The God of Your Ancestors

To Rule All or to See All. Ambrose: For God and Lord is a name of majesty, a name of power, even as God himself says, "The Lord is my name," and as in another place the prophet declares, "The Lord almighty is his name."[33] He is God, therefore, and Lord, either because his rule is over all or because he beholds all things and is feared by all without exception. On the Christian Faith 1.1.7.[34]

The Meaning of God's Two Names.
Augustine: What does it mean then that later on he gave himself another name, where it says, "And the Lord said to Moses, I am the God of Abraham, the God of Isaac and the God of Jacob: this is my name forever"? How is it that there I am called this name that shows "I am," and lo and behold here is another name: "I am the God of Abraham, the God of Isaac and the

God of Jacob"? It means that while God is indeed unchangeable, he has done everything out of mercy, and so the Son of God himself was prepared to take on changeable flesh and thereby to come to man's rescue while remaining what he is as the Word of God. Thus he who is clothed himself with mortal flesh, so that it could truly be said, "I am the God of Abraham, the God of Isaac and the God of Jacob." Sermon 6.5.[35]

3:19-22 Despoiling the Egyptians

Opportunity for Repentance. Clement of Alexandria: He said to Moses, "Go and speak to Pharaoh, that he may let my people go, but I know that he will not let them go. . . ." He manifests his divinity by foreseeing what is to happen and also his love for man by offering to the free will of man an opportunity to repent. Christ the Educator 1.9.76.[36]

A Servant's Duty. Augustine: Whether then the reason was what I have said, or whether in the secret appointment of God there was some unknown reason for his telling the people by Moses to borrow things from the Egyptians and to take them away with them, this remains certain. This was said for some good reason and Moses could not lawfully have done otherwise than God told him, leaving to God the reason of the command, while the servant's duty is to obey. Against Faustus, a Manichaean 22.71.[37]

Just Wages. Tertullian: The Egyptians put in a claim on the Hebrews for these gold and silver vessels. The Hebrews assert a counterclaim, alleging that by the bond of their respective fathers, attested by the written engagement of both parties, there were due to them the arrears

---

[30]ACW 51:484. [31]FC 33:146. [32]NPNF 2 10:215. [33]Is 42:8. The Vulgate has "I am the Lord; this is my name." [34]NPNF 2 10:202. [35]*WSA* 3 1:229. [36]FC 23:68. [37]NPNF 1 4:299-300.

of that laborious slavery of theirs for the bricks they had so painfully made and the cities and palaces which they had built. AGAINST MAR- CION 2.20.2.[38]

DESPOILING WAS JUST. AUGUSTINE: The Lord commanded the Hebrews through Moses to take gold and silver vessels and garments from the Egyptians, and he added, "And you will despoil them." The judgment implied in this command cannot be unjust. For it is a commandment of God. It was not to be judged but obeyed. For God knew how just his command was. It pertains to the servant obediently to do what was com- manded. QUESTIONS ON EXODUS 6.[39]

WERE THE EGYPTIANS DECEIVED? AUGUS- TINE: Accordingly on the one hand the Egyp- tians deserved being deceived, and on the other the people of Israel were then situated at such a level of morality, because of the age of the human race, that it would not be unworthy of them to deceive an enemy. It therefore came about that God commanded them (or, rather, permitted them because of their desire) to ask of the Egyptians gold and silver implements which these seekers of a kingdom as yet earthly were gazing upon longingly, even though they were not going to return them, and to take them as if they were going to return them. God did not want to be unjust in the matter of the reward for such lengthy hardship and labor—a reward adapted to the level of such souls; nor did he want to be unjust in the matter of the punish- ments of the Egyptians, whom appropriately enough he caused to lose what they were under obligation to pay. And so God is not a deceiver. ON EIGHTY-THREE VARIED QUESTIONS 53.2.[40]

---

[38]ANF 3:313. [39]CCL 33:71. [40]FC 70:93.

4:1-9 CONFIRMATION OF MOSES' MISSION

[1]Then Moses answered, "But behold, they will not believe me or listen to my voice, for they will say, 'The LORD did not appear to you.'" [2]The LORD said to him, "What is that in your hand?" He said, "A rod." [3]And he said, "Cast it on the ground." So he cast it on the ground, and it became a serpent; and Moses fled from it. [4]But the LORD said to Moses, "Put out your hand, and take it by the tail"—so he put out his hand and caught it, and it became a rod in his hand—[5]"that they may believe that the LORD, the God of their fathers, the God of Abraham, the God of Isaac, and the God of Jacob, has appeared to you." [6]Again, the LORD said to him, "Put your hand into your bosom." And he put his hand into his bosom; and when he took it out, behold, his hand was leprous, as white as snow. [7]Then God said, "Put your hand back into your bosom." So he put his hand back into his bosom; and when he took it out, behold, it was restored like the rest of his flesh.

OVERVIEW: Moses' rod represents the kingdom. The snake represents mortality, for death came through a snake, but healing also came by a ser- pent, which was the sign of Christ (AUGUSTINE).

24

Moses' staff prefigures the cross of Christ (CAE-SARIUS OF ARLES). Three signs—serpent, hand and blood—denote God's threefold power (TER-TULLIAN). The bosom of Moses is the interpretation of Scripture, in which the letter kills but the spirit gives life (ORIGEN). Moses' hand—once leprous, then restored—reminds us of Christ's eternal existence and his incarnation (AMBROSE). The restoration of Moses' hand foretells the salvation of the Jews (CASSIODORUS).

4:2-3 A Rod Became a Serpent

THE SIGNS OF THE ROD AND THE SNAKE. AUGUSTINE: Let me try to explain, as far as the Lord enables me to, what these signs mean. The rod stands for the kingdom, the snake for mortality; it was by the snake that man was given death to drink. The Lord was prepared to take this death to himself. So when the rod came down to earth it had the form of a snake, because the kingdom of God, which is Jesus Christ, came down to earth. He put on mortality, which he also nailed to the cross. Your holinesses know that when that proud and stiff-necked people grumbled against God in the desert, they began to be bitten by serpents and to die of the bites. In his mercy God provided a remedy, a remedy that restored health at the time but also foretold the wisdom that was to come in the future. SERMON 6.7.[1]

THE CONQUERING CROSS. CAESARIUS OF ARLES: That staff, dearly beloved, prefigured the mystery of the cross. Just as through the staff Egypt was struck by ten plagues, so also the whole world was humiliated and conquered by the cross. Just as Pharaoh and his people were afflicted by the power of the staff, with the result that he released the Jewish people to serve God, so the devil and his angels are wearied and oppressed by the mystery of the cross to such an extent that they cannot recall the Christian people from God's service. SERMON 95.5.[2]

SYMBOLS OF DEATH, RESURRECTION AND JUDGMENT. TERTULLIAN: But we know that prophecy expressed itself by things no less than by words. By words and also by deeds is the resurrection foretold. When Moses puts his hand into his bosom and then draws it out again dead, and again puts his hand into his bosom and plucks it out living, does not this apply as an anticipation of the resurrection to all humankind?—inasmuch as those three signs denoted the threefold power of God: when it shall, first, in the appointed order, subdue to man the old serpent, the devil, however formidable; then, second, draw forth the flesh from the bosom of death; and then, at last, shall pursue all blood [shed] in judgment. ON THE RESURRECTION OF THE FLESH 28.1-2.[3]

4:4 Take It by the Tail

See AUGUSTINE ON Exodus 7:10.

4:6-7 Disease and Restoration

MOSES' HAND REPRESENTS HUMAN DEEDS. ORIGEN: It is difficult to see what this sign can symbolize for us. But since we must not stop seeking and must deliver to the reader what occurs to us as an interpretation, we will say that in many passages the hand is a symbol of deeds. Now the bosom of Moses has two meanings. The first, in accordance with the sense of the letter, makes the deed of the doer like snow, as it says in the Hebrew, and leprous. The second, however, in accordance with the spiritual law, shows that the conduct is pure and that it is restored to the will of the nature of the Word. COMMENTARY ON THE GOSPEL OF JOHN 32.268.[4]

CHRIST'S GLORY AND FLESH. AMBROSE: Again, another sign which Moses gave points to our Lord Jesus Christ. He put his hand into his

---

[1]*WSA* 3 1:229-30. [2]FC 47:67-68. [3]ANF 3:565. [4]FC 89:392.

bosom and drew it out again, and his hand had become as snow. A second time he put it in and drew it out, and it was again like the appearance of human flesh. This signified first the original glory of the Godhead of the Lord Jesus and then the assumption of our flesh, in which truth all nations and peoples must believe. So he put in his hand, for Christ is the right hand of God; and whosoever does not believe in his Godhead and incarnation is punished as a sinner; like that king[5] who, while not believing open and plain signs, yet afterwards, when punished, prayed that he might find mercy. DUTIES OF THE CLERGY 3.15.95.[6]

MOSES' HAND POINTS TO ISRAEL. CASSIODORUS: Just as Moses was allowed to perform miracles with a rod, so he was ordered to thrust his hand into his bosom, and when it was brought out again it was found to be leprous; then he was ordered to insert it again, and it was at once healed. This indicates that the Jewish people was to become impure by abandoning the Lord Christ but that it would recover its former health by returning to him. EXPOSITION OF THE PSALMS 73.11.[7]

---

[5]That is, Pharaoh. [6]NPNF 2 10:83*. [7]ACW 52:217.

4:10-17 AARON'S OFFICE AS ASSISTANT

[10]*But Moses said to the LORD, "Oh, my LORD, I am not eloquent*[*]*, either heretofore or since thou hast spoken to thy servant; but I am slow of speech and of tongue." *[11]*Then the LORD said to him, "Who has made man's mouth? Who makes him dumb, or deaf, or seeing, or blind? Is it not I, the LORD? *[12]*Now therefore go, and I will be with your mouth and teach you what you shall speak." *[13]*But he said, "Oh, my Lord, send, I pray, some other person." *[14]*Then the anger of the LORD was kindled against Moses and he said, "Is there not Aaron, your brother, the Levite? I know that he can speak well; and behold, he is coming out to meet you, and when he sees you he will be glad in his heart. *[15]*And you shall speak to him and put the words in his mouth; and I will be with your mouth and with his mouth, and will teach you what you shall do. *[16]*He shall speak for you to the people; and he shall be a mouth for you, and you shall be to him as God."*

[*]*Lit.* not a man of words

OVERVIEW: Moses received both word and reason from God (ORIGEN). Moses became eloquent when God began to speak to him (AUGUSTINE). The phrase "uncircumcised lips" is to be interpreted figuratively (ORIGEN). God can inspire anyone to speak courageously (CYPRIAN). Whatever we suffer, we suffer justly (AUGUSTINE). Through the Holy Spirit God gives us wisdom in speech (AMBROSE). God is the cause of all that happens. God reproached Moses for not putting all his hope in him. Moses was a true prophet who spoke to people what he heard from God (AUGUSTINE). Scripture uses the title *gods* of people who are distinguished by their love for God (PSEUDO-DIONYSIUS).

4:10 I Am Not Eloquent

Israel Received the Word in Moses. Origen: Moses himself once said: "I am *alogos* ("wordless"). The Latin version uses a different expression, but we can translate the word *alogos* exactly as "without words and reason." After he said this, he received reason and speech, which he admitted that he did not have before. When the people of Israel were in Egypt, before they had received the law, they too were without words and reason and thus in a sense mute. Then they received the Word; Moses was the image of it. So these people do not admit now what Moses had once admitted—that they are mute and wordless—but show by signs and silence that they have neither words nor reason. Do you not realize that the Jews are confessing their folly when none of them can give a reasonable explanation of the precepts of their law and of the predictions of their prophets? Homilies on the Gospel of Luke 5.3.[1]

Moses Could Become Eloquent. Augustine: [Moses] believes that by God's will he can suddenly become eloquent when he says, "or since the time you began to speak to your servant." He shows that it could happen that one who was not eloquent the day before, or the day before that, could suddenly become eloquent, from the time when the Lord began to speak to him. Questions on Exodus 7.[2]

"Uncircumcised in Lips" Calls for Spiritual Interpretation. Origen: But I shall also bring forth still another passage for you which you cannot contradict. In Exodus where we have written in the codices of the church Moses responding to the Lord and saying, "Provide, Lord, another whom you will send. For I am feeble in voice and slow in tongue," you have in the Hebrew copies, "But I am uncircumcised in lips." Behold, you have a circumcision of lips according to your copies, which you say to be more accurate. If therefore according to you Moses still says that he is unworthy because he has not been circumcised in his lips, he certainly indicates this, that he would be worthier and holier who is circumcised in his lips. Therefore apply the pruning hook also to your lips and cut off the covering of your mouth since indeed such an understanding pleases you in the divine letters. But if you refer circumcision of lips to allegory and say no less that circumcision of ears is allegorical and figurative, why do you not also inquire after allegory in circumcision of the foreskin? Homilies on Genesis 3.5.[3]

4:11 Who Has Made Man's Mouth?

God Can Give Us the Courage to Speak. Cyprian: Just as in Exodus God speaks to Moses, when he delays and fears to go to the people, saying, "Who gave a mouth to man and who made the dumb and the deaf, the seeing and the blind? Did not I the Lord God? Go now, and I shall open your mouth, and I will teach you what you shall speak." It is not difficult for God to open the mouth of a man devoted to him and to inspire constancy and confidence in speaking in one who confesses him, who in the book of Numbers made even a female ass speak against Balaam the prophet.[4] Therefore let no one consider in persecutions what danger the devil brings, but rather let him bear in mind what assistance God affords. Let not the disturbances of men weaken the mind, but let divine protection strengthen the faith, since each one according to the Lord's promises and the merits of his faith receives so much of God's help as he thinks he receives, and since there is nothing which the Almighty cannot grant, except if the frail faith of the recipient be deficient. Exhortation to Martyrdom 10.[5]

God Wills All Things Justly. Augustine: There are some who bring false charges against God, or rather against the Scriptures of the Old Testament,[6] because God said that he himself

---

[1]FC 94:21. [2]CCL 33:71. [3]FC 71:96. [4]Num 22:28-30. [5]FC 36:330-31. [6]Augustine means Marcion and his followers.

makes a man blind or mute. So what do they say about Christ the Lord, who says openly in the Gospel, "I have come so that those who are blind may see and those who see might be made blind"?[7] Who besides a fool would believe that something can happen to a man in regard to corporeal defects that God did not will? No one doubts that God wills all things justly. QUESTIONS ON EXODUS 8.[8]

4:12 I Will Teach You

THE HOLY SPIRIT TEACHES THE SAINTS TO SPEAK. AMBROSE: The Lord himself also opened his mouth and said to the apostles, "Receive the Holy Spirit."[9] By these words he declared that he was the one who said to Moses, "I will open your mouth and will teach you what you are to say." Therefore this wisdom, divine, "indescribable,"[10] "unmixed and uncorrupted," pours its grace into the souls of the saints and reveals knowledge, so that they may look upon his glory. LETTER 2(65).4.[11]

GOD'S GRACE AND THE HUMAN WILL. AUGUSTINE: It is clear that not only the instruction that comes from his mouth but also its being opened pertains to the will and grace of God. For God does not say, "You open your mouth, and I will instruct you," but promised both: "I shall open, and I shall instruct." Elsewhere he says in a psalm, "Open your mouth, and I shall fill it."[12] There it signifies the will in man to receive what God gives to one who is willing, so that "open your mouth" pertains to the initiative of the will and "I shall fill it" to the grace of God. But here the sense is "I shall both open your mouth and instruct you." QUESTIONS ON EXODUS 9.[13]

4:14 The Lord's Anger Was Kindled

WHAT THE ANGER OF GOD MEANS. AUGUSTINE: How can the anger of God be understood, since God is not gripped by any irrational disturbance, as man is? Where Scripture says something like this, we should have a consistent explanation to avoid repeating the same account too often. But one can rightly ask why God says here that he is angry with Moses about his brother Aaron, because he would speak to the people for Moses. For it means that God had not given Moses the fullest ability that he was going to give, because he was diffident. God wished the deed to be carried out by two men. He could also have done it through one, if that man had believed. But all these words, when they are considered more diligently, do not mean that the Lord in his anger had handed over Aaron for punishment. For he says this: "Behold, is your brother Aaron not a Levite? I know that when he speaks, he will speak eloquently." These words show that God rather reproached Moses, who feared to go because he was less suitable, since he had a brother through whom he could say to the people what he wanted, because Moses himself had a weak voice and a slow tongue. Still, he should have put all his hope in God. Then he says the same things that he had promised shortly before and afterward grown angry. For he had said, "I shall open your mouth and instruct you." But now he says, "I shall open your mouth and his mouth, and I shall teach you what to do." But since he added, "And he will speak for you to the people," the opening of the mouth seems to be provided, because Moses says he is slow of tongue. But the Lord did not will to supply [vocal strength] for the weakness of his voice but added the help of his brother Aaron. Moses could use Aaron's voice, which was sufficient to teach the people. So when he says, "and you will put my words in his mouth," he shows that he was going to provide him with words. For if he were only given things to hear for the people, God would have said, "into his ears." Then it says a little later, "and he will speak for you to the people," he shows clearly

---

[7]Jn 9:39. [8]CCL 33:72. [9]Jn 20:22. [10]Wis 17:1. [11]CSEL 82 1:16. [12]Ps 81:10. [13]CCL 33:72.

enough that the leading role was for Moses, the subordinate role for Aaron. What he says thereafter, "You will be to him as God," perhaps this great mystery is to be examined closely. The figure suggests that Moses was the mediator between God and Aaron, and Aaron the mediator between Moses and the people. QUESTIONS ON EXODUS 10.[14]

4:16 Aaron Shall Speak for You

THE TRUE FUNCTION OF A PROPHET. AUGUSTINE: One should notice that when Moses is sent to the people, God does not say to him, "Behold, I gave you as a god to the people, and your brother will be your prophet," but he says, "[Your brother] will speak to the people for you." For Scripture had said, "He will be your mouth, and you will be to him as God." It did not say, "You are god to him." But to Pharaoh Moses is said to be given as god, and according to analogy, Aaron is a prophet of Moses, but to Pharaoh. Here it is suggested to us that prophets of God say what they hear from him. A prophet of God is nothing but one who speaks the words of God to men—those who either cannot hear God or do not deserve to. QUESTIONS ON EXODUS 17.[15]

THE TITLE GODS. PSEUDO-DIONYSIUS: You will also notice how God's Word gives the title of "gods" not only to those heavenly beings who are our superiors[16] but also to those sacred men among us who are distinguished for their love of God. CELESTIAL HIERARCHY 12.3.[17]

---

[14]CCL 33:72-73. [15]CCL 33:75-76. [16]Ps 82:1; 95:3. [17]PDCW 176.

4:18-31 MOSES' RETURN TO EGYPT

[20]*So Moses took his wife and his sons and set them on an ass, and went back to the land of Egypt; and in his hand Moses took the rod of God.*
[21]*And the LORD said to Moses, . . . "Do before Pharaoh all the miracles which I have put in your power; but I will harden his heart.*
[22]*"And you shall say to Pharaoh, 'Thus says the LORD, Israel is my first-born son,* [23]*and I say to you, "Let my son go that he may serve me"; if you refuse to let him go, behold, I will slay your first-born son.'"*
[24]*At a lodging place on the way the LORD* met him and sought to kill him.* [25]*Then Zipporah took a flint and cut off her son's foreskin, and touched Moses' feet with it, and said, "Surely you are a bridegroom of blood to me!"* [26]*So he let him alone. Then it was that she said, "You are a bridegroom of blood," because of the circumcision.*

*LXX angel of the LORD

OVERVIEW: Two passages in Exodus are not contradictory (AUGUSTINE). The passage in which Scripture says that God hardened Pharaoh's heart troubled many early Christians because it appeared to deny free will and teach fatalism or determinism (ORIGEN). Both God and Pharaoh caused the hardening of his heart (AUGUSTINE). Indeed, Pharaoh's sins caused his heart to be hardened (CAESARIUS OF ARLES). Interpreters of Scripture must take care to defend God's justice. Israel, even in dispersion, was God's firstborn, and Jesus died to gather them into one (ORIGEN). Christ is God's firstborn, not because God had other sons but because he was begotten from the beginning (CYRIL OF JERUSALEM). The statement in Scripture that the Lord wishes to kill Moses is troubling (ORIGEN). The grammar of the statement is unclear (AUGUSTINE). Moses' wife carried out the commandment to circumcise the child (EPHREM). Circumcision is a symbol of celibacy (JEROME). Circumcision was a sacrament of the Old Law, and as such it once had great power. The sign of circumcision is fulfilled in baptism. The stone that Zipporah used was Christ, who cuts away the body of sin (AUGUSTINE).

4:20 Moses Took His Wife and His Sons

CONCORDANCE OF TWO PASSAGES. AUGUSTINE: What was said above, that Moses placed his wife and his children on carts so that he might go with them into Egypt, but afterwards his father-in-law Jethro met him with them [in his company], after Moses had led the people out of Egypt, one can ask how both assertions can be true. One should realize that after the killing of Moses or of the child that the angel was going to carry out, his wife returned with the children. For some interpreters thought that the angel threatened them to keep a woman from accompanying Moses and thus forming an obstacle to the ministry that God had imposed on him. QUESTIONS ON EXODUS 12.[1]

4:21 I Will Harden Pharaoh's Heart

THE PROBLEM OF FREE CHOICE. ORIGEN: Now many have been troubled by the story of Pharaoh, in dealing with whom God says several times, "I will harden Pharaoh's heart." For if he is hardened by God and through being hardened sins, he is not himself responsible for the sin; and

if this is so, Pharaoh has no free will. And someone will say that in the same way those who are lost have no free will and will not be lost on their own account. Also the saying in Ezekiel, "I will take away their stony hearts and will put in them hearts of flesh, that they may walk in my statutes and keep my judgments,"[2] might lead one to suppose that it was God who gave the power to walk in the commandments and to keep the judgments, by his removing the hindrance, the stony heart, and implanting something better, the heart of flesh. ON FIRST PRINCIPLES 3.1.7.[3]

PHARAOH STILL HAD FREE CHOICE. AUGUSTINE: And you must not deny free will to Pharaoh just because God says in a number of places, "I have hardened Pharaoh" or "I will harden the heart of Pharaoh," for it does not thereby follow that it was not Pharaoh himself that hardened his own heart. Furthermore, we read that this happened to Pharaoh after the plague of flies had been removed from the Egyptians, as the Scripture testifies: "And Pharaoh's heart was hardened so that neither this time would he let the people go." Thus it was that both God and Pharaoh caused this hardening of the heart: God, by his just judgments, Pharaoh, by his free will. ON GRACE AND FREE WILL 23.[4]

PHARAOH'S WICKEDNESS AND PRIDE HARDENED HIS HEART. CAESARIUS OF ARLES: Now let no one along with pagans or Manichaeans dare to censure or blame the justice of God. It is to be believed as most certain that not the violence of God but his own repeated wickedness and indomitable pride in opposition to God's commands caused Pharaoh to become hardened. What does that mean which God said, "I will make him obstinate," except that when my grace is withdrawn from him his own iniquity will harden him? In order that this may be known more clearly, we propose to your charity a com-

---

[1]CCL 33:74-75; the passages are Ex 4:20 and 18:1-5. [2]Ezek 11:19-20. [3]OFP 167. [4]FC 59:307.

parison with visible things. As often as water is contracted by excessive cold, if the heat of the sun comes upon it, it becomes melted; when the same sun departs the water again becomes hard. Similarly the charity of many men freezes because of the excessive coldness of their sins, and they become as hard as ice; however, when the warmth of divine mercy comes upon them again, they are melted. SERMON 101.4.[5]

4:22 Israel Is My Firstborn Son

OUR UNDERSTANDING OF GOD'S JUSTICE. ORIGEN: Why too does he blame Pharaoh, saying, "You will not let my people go; behold, I will smite all the firstborn in Egypt, even your firstborn," and all the rest that is recorded as being said by God through Moses to Pharaoh? It is incumbent on him who believes that the Scriptures are true and that God is just, if he is a thoughtful man, to take pains to show how God, in using such expressions as these, can be clearly conceived to be just. ON FIRST PRINCIPLES 3.1.9.[6]

THE BEAUTY OF CALLING ISRAEL GOD'S FIRSTBORN SON. ORIGEN: And is there anything more profound to say of Israel, not of nature but of grace, of whom it was written, "Israel is my firstborn son," when Israel was in dispersion? You yourself will also understand that these are the scattered children of God for whom Jesus was to die in order to gather them together into one. COMMENTARY ON THE GOSPEL OF JOHN 28.185.[7]

GOD'S TRUE FIRSTBORN SON IS CHRIST. CYRIL OF JERUSALEM: When you hear "firstborn," do not think of this in human fashion; for among humans the firstborn have other brothers; and it is somewhere written, "Israel is my son, my firstborn." But like Reuben, Israel was a rejected firstborn; for Reuben went up to his father's bed,[8] and Israel cast the Son of the Father out of the vineyard[9] and crucified him.

To others also Scripture says, "You are children of the Lord your God"[10] and elsewhere, "I said, you are gods; all of you sons of the Most High."[11] Note "I said," not "I begot." They, from the fact that God said it, received adoption which they did not have, but he was not begotten to be other than he was before. Rather he was begotten Son from the beginning, Son of the Father, like in all things to his Genitor, begotten Life of Life, Light of Light, Truth of Truth, Wisdom of Wisdom, King of King, God of God, Power of Power. CATECHETICAL LECTURE 11.4.[12]

4:24 The Lord Sought to Kill Him

WHO SOUGHT TO KILL MOSES? ORIGEN: We must also inquire who that being was of whom it is said in Exodus that he wished to kill Moses because he was setting out for Egypt. And afterwards, who is it that is called the "destroying angel,"[13] and who also is he who in Leviticus is described as Apopompeus, that is, the Averter, of whom the Scripture speaks thus: "One lot for the Lord, and one lot for Apopompeus"?[14] ON FIRST PRINCIPLES 3.2.1.[15]

A SCRIPTURAL PROBLEM. AUGUSTINE: We ask first, whom did the angel wish to kill? Was it Moses, because Scripture says, "The angel approached him and sought to kill him"? For whom will he be thought to have approached except him who was in charge of his entire people and by whom the others were led? Or did the angel seek to kill the boy, whom his mother aided by circumcising him? Then one would understand that the reason why God wished to kill the child was that he was not circumcised and thus sanctioned the precept of circumcision by the severity of the punishment. If this is the case, it is unclear of whom it was said previously, "he sought to kill him," because we do not know

---

[5]FC 47:100-101. [6]OFP 171-72. [7]FC 89:330. [8]Gen 49:4. [9]Mt 21:39. [10]Deut 14:1. [11]Ps 82:6. [12]FC 61:212-13. [13]Ex 12:23. [14]Lev 16:8; in Hebrew, Azazel. [15]OFP 211.

who it was until we discover it from what follows. It is a remarkable and unusual expression to say "he approached him and sought to kill him" about someone who had not been mentioned before. But there is such a usage in a psalm: "Its foundations are on the holy mountains; the Lord loves the gates of Zion."[16] For the psalm begins at that point and had not said anything about the Lord or about that city whose foundations were meant to be understood when the psalm said, "Its foundations are on the holy mountains." But because of what follows, "the Lord loves the gates of Zion," the foundations, either those of the Lord or of Zion—"of Zion" yields the better sense—are understood as the foundation of a city. But the gender of this pronoun, "its," is ambiguous, for it can be masculine, feminine or neuter.[17] In Greek, however, the feminine is *autēs,* whereas the masculine and neuter are *autou,* and the Greek text has *autou,* so we must understand that the foundations are those not of Zion but of the Lord. That is, [they are] the foundations that the Lord constitutes, of which Scripture has said, "the Lord building Jerusalem."[18] But when the psalm said, "Its foundations are on the holy mountains," it had not previously mentioned either Zion or the Lord. Here too it is said, "He met him and sought to kill him," although the child had not yet been named, so that we do not know of whom he was speaking in the words that follow. But still, if someone wants to hold that Moses is meant, he should not be strongly opposed. We should rather understand what follows, if we can, what it means when the text says that the angel refrained from killing any of them because the woman said, "The blood of the infant's circumcision has stopped flowing." She does not say that "he drew back from him" because she circumcised the infant but that "the blood of circumcision stopped." Not that it flowed but that it stopped—in a great mystery, if I am not wrong. Questions on Exodus 11.[19]

4:25 Zipporah Took a Flint

Moses and His Wife Were at Odds.

Ephrem the Syrian: At the place where they were spending the night, the Lord came upon Moses and wanted to kill him, because he had discontinued circumcision in Midian for one of his sons who had not been circumcised. From the day [the Lord] spoke with him on Horeb, he had not been united to his wife, who was distressed; and she was under judgment because she had not put full faith in his word. [Moses] blamed her for keeping his son from being circumcised. They spent the night [preoccupied] with these thoughts. Suddenly an angel appeared for both of these reasons, while seeming to appear only because of circumcision.

[The angel] appeared to Moses in anger so that his departure [from Midian] would not be ridiculed because he had discontinued circumcision without necessity, while the Hebrews had not interrupted it in spite of the death of their children. Now whom should he have feared, God, who prescribed circumcision, or his wife, who had stood in the way of circumcision?

When Moses' wife saw that he was about to die because she had stood in the way of circumcision, about which and on account of which he had argued with her that evening, "she took a piece of flint" and, still trembling from the vision of the angel, "circumcised her son," letting him be spattered with his [own] blood. Then she held the angel's feet and said, "I have a husband of blood. Do not cause suffering on the day of the celebration of circumcision." Because there was great joy on the day Abraham circumcised Isaac, she said, "I too have a husband of blood. If you do not [refrain from harm] on account of me, who circumcised my son with my own hands, or on account of Moses, refrain on account of the commandment of circumcision itself which has been observed." Commentary on Exodus 4.4.1-3.[20]

Circumcision a Symbol of Celibacy. Je-

---

[16]Ps 87:1-2. [17]The Latin pronoun *eius* represents all three genders. [18]Ps 147:2. [19]CCL 33:73-74. [20]FC 91:234-36.

ROME: As regards Moses, it is clear that he would have been in peril at the inn, if Zipporah, which is by interpretation "a bird," had not circumcised her son and cut off the foreskin of marriage with the knife which prefigured the gospel. AGAINST JOVINIAN 1.20.[21]

CIRCUMCISION A SACRAMENT OF THE OLD LAW. AUGUSTINE: If I had been a Jew in the times of the ancient people, when there was nothing better to be, I would surely have accepted circumcision. That "seal of the justice of the faith"[22] had so much power at that time, before it was rendered void by the coming of the Lord, that the angel would have strangled the infant son of Moses if his mother had not taken up a stone and circumcised the child and thus by this sacrament warded off his imminent destruction. This sacrament even tamed the river Jordan and reduced it to a brook. The Lord himself received this sacrament after birth, although on the cross he made it void. LETTER 23.[23]

JUSTIFICATION AND THE SEAL OF BAPTISM.

AUGUSTINE: And this was made manifest by the message of an angel in the case of Moses' son, for when he was carried by his mother, being yet uncircumcised, it was required, by manifest present peril, that he should be circumcised. And when this was done, the danger of death was removed. As therefore in Abraham the justification of faith came first and circumcision was added afterwards as the seal of faith, so in Cornelius the spiritual sanctification came first in the gift of the Holy Spirit. And the sacrament of regeneration was added afterward in the laver of baptism. ON BAPTISM 4.24.32.[24]

THE FLINT WAS CHRIST. AUGUSTINE: Christ was the rock whence was formed the stony blade for the circumcision, and the flesh of the foreskin was the body of sin. ON THE GRACE OF CHRIST AND ORIGINAL SIN 2.31.36.[25]

---

[21]NPNF 2 6:361. [22]Rom 4:11. [23]FC 12:61-62. [24]NPNF 1 4:461. [25]NPNF 1 5:250.

5:1-14 PHARAOH'S OBDURACY

[1]*Afterward Moses and Aaron went to Pharaoh and said, "Thus says the LORD, the God of Israel, 'Let my people go, that they may hold a feast to me in the wilderness.'"* [2]*But Pharaoh said, "Who is the LORD, that I should heed his voice and let Israel go? I do not know the LORD, and moreover I will not let Israel go. . . .* [9]*Let heavier work be laid upon the men that they may labor at it and pay no regard to lying words."*

OVERVIEW: God said he wanted to lead the people out of Egypt, but Pharaoh was told that they only wanted to make a three days' journey. But God was not lying. He foreknew Pharaoh would not agree. He intended to obtain a just judgment (AUGUSTINE). Arrogance abased Pharaoh and made him lower than flies and frogs (CHRYSOSTOM). Both Pharaoh and Moses afflicted the people, but with wholly different motives: pride in the one case, love in the other (AUGUSTINE).

5:1 A Feast in the Wilderness

GOD DID NOT LIE. AUGUSTINE: Some ask how the people can be told that God gave the order that he would lead them from Egypt into the land of Canaan, while Pharaoh was told that they wanted to make three days' journey into the desert to offer sacrifice to their god by his command. But the passage should be understood thus: although God knew what he was going to do and knew that Pharaoh would not agree to dismiss the people, that fact was to be stated first that would also happen first, if Pharaoh let the people go. The contumacy of Pharaoh and his courtiers merited everything that happened, to which the Scripture afterward attests. God is not lying when he commands what he knows is not going to be done by the one he commands; his purpose is to obtain a just judgment. QUESTIONS ON EXODUS 13.[1]

5:2 I Do Not Know the Lord

PHARAOH MADE INFERIOR TO FLIES AND FROGS. CHRYSOSTOM: Let us then become lowly, that we may be high. For most utterly does arrogance abase. This abased Pharaoh. For, "I know not," he says, "the Lord," and he became inferior to flies and frogs and the locusts, and after that with his very arms and horses was he drowned in the sea. In direct opposition to him, Abraham says, "I am dust and ashes" and prevailed over countless barbarians, and having fallen into the midst of Egyptians, returned, bearing a trophy more glorious than the former, and, cleaving to this virtue, grew ever more high. HOMILIES ON THE GOSPEL OF MATTHEW 65.6[2]

5:9 Heavier Work Alloted

AFFLICTION WITH DIFFERENT INTENTIONS. AUGUSTINE: When both the good and the bad do the same things and suffer the same things, they are to be distinguished by their intentions, not by their acts and penalties. Pharaoh oppressed the people of God with hard labors; Moses afflicted the same people, who had fallen into idolatry, with severe punishments.[3] They did the same things, but they did not aim at the same result. The former was puffed up with pride of power, the latter was animated by love. LETTER 93.[4]

---

[1]CCL 33:75. [2]NPNF 1 10:403. [3]Ex 32:27. [4]FC 18:62.

5:15-21 COMPLAINT OF THE FOREMEN

[15]*Then the foremen of the people of Israel came and cried to Pharaoh, "Why do you deal thus with your servants?" . . . [17]But he said, "You are idle, you are idle; therefore you say, 'Let us go and sacrifice to the LORD.' [18]Go now, and work; for no straw shall be given you, yet you shall deliver the same number of bricks." [19]The foremen of the people of Israel saw that they were in evil plight, when they said, "You shall by no means lessen your daily number of bricks." [20]They met Moses and Aaron, who were waiting for them, as they came forth from Pharaoh; [21]and they said to them, "The LORD look upon you and judge, because you have made us offensive in the sight of Pharaoh and his servants, and have put a sword in their hand to kill us."*

OVERVIEW: It is proper to seek God when one is at leisure (BASIL). The shepherd of souls should listen to the complaints of his charges and guide them through their temptations (PATERIUS).

5:17 You Are Idle

LEISURE CAN BE GOOD OR EVIL. BASIL THE GREAT: Even Pharaoh knew that it was proper for one to seek God when he was unoccupied, and for this reason he reproached Israel: "You are unoccupied, you are idle, and you say, 'We shall offer prayers to the Lord, our God.'" Now leisure itself is good and useful to him who is unoccupied, since it produces quiet for the acquisition of salutary doctrines. But the leisure of the Athenians was evil, "who used to spend all their leisure telling or listening to something new."[1] Even at the present time some imitate this, misusing the leisure of life for the discovery of some newer teaching. EXEGETIC HOMILIES 18.8.[2]

5:20 They Met Moses and Aaron

THE PEOPLE COMPLAIN. PATERIUS: In Moses and Aaron the law and the prophets are prefigured. A sick soul often murmurs to itself against the sacred words. After it has begun to hear and follow the heavenly words, the opposition of the Egyptian king—that is, the temptation of an evil spirit—rises up. So the physician should carefully make known to the soul that is making progress which temptations will attack it, so that it can carefully prepare itself for the snares of an evil spirit. EXPOSITION OF THE OLD AND NEW TESTAMENT, EXODUS 11.[3]

---

[1]Acts 17:21. [2]FC 46:307. [3]PL 79:726, citing Gregory the Great *Homilies on Ezekiel* 12.24-25.

5:22—6:13 RENEWAL OF GOD'S PROMISE

[22]*Then Moses turned again to the* LORD *and said, "O* LORD, *why hast thou done evil to this people? Why didst thou ever send me?"* . . .
[2]*And God said to Moses, "I am the* LORD. [3]*I appeared to Abraham, to Isaac, and to Jacob, as God Almighty,[h]* but by my name the* LORD *I did not make myself known to them.* . . .
[10]*And the* LORD *said to Moses,* [11]*"Go in, tell Pharaoh king of Egypt to let the people of Israel go out of his land."*

h *Heb* El Shaddai **LXX being their God*

OVERVIEW: Moses' words may seem like a complaint, but they were a prayerful inquiry (AUGUSTINE). God does not appear to people; God reveals himself through his Son (EUSEBIUS). No human speech can describe and name God's greatness (CASSIODORUS).

5:22 Moses Turned to the Lord

MOSES COMPLAINS TO GOD. AUGUSTINE: The words that Moses speaks to the Lord are not words of contumacy or indignation but of inquiry and prayer. This fact is clear from the way the Lord answered him. For he did not accuse him of infidelity but revealed what he was about to do. QUESTIONS ON EXODUS 14.[1]

6:3 I Appeared to Abraham

HOW IT IS POSSIBLE FOR THE TRANSCEN-

---

[1]CCL 33:75.

35

DENT GOD TO APPEAR. EUSEBIUS: It will naturally be asked how he that is beyond the universe, himself the only almighty God, appeared to the fathers. And the answer will be found if we realize the accuracy of Holy Scripture. For the Septuagint rendering, "I was seen of Abraham, Isaac and Jacob, being their God," Aquila[2] says, "And I was seen by Abraham, Isaac and Jacob as a sufficient God," clearly showing that the almighty God himself, who is one, was not seen in his own person and that he did not give answers to the fathers, as he did to Moses by an angel, or a fire or a bush, but "as a sufficient God." Thus the Father was seen by the fathers through the Son, according to his saying in the Gospels, "He that has seen me has seen the Father."[3] For the knowledge of the Father was revealed in him and by him. But in cases when he appeared to save men, he was seen in the human form of the Son, giving an earnest before the time[4] to the godly of that salvation which should come through him to all men. But when he was going to be the avenger and chastiser of the wicked Egyptians, he appeared no longer as a sufficient God but as an angel ministering punishment, and in form of fire and flame, ready at once to devour them like wild and thorny undergrowth. So they say that the bush darkly refers to the wild, savage and cruel character of the Egyptians and the fire to the avenging power of the chastisement that overtook them. PROOF OF THE GOSPEL 5.13.240.[5]

GOD'S NAME IS SECRET. CASSIODORUS: The God of gods is the Lord Christ; with the Father and Holy Spirit he is truly called God of gods, though the title is not wholly appropriate to the Godhead because the human tongue cannot, as we have already said, indicate the height of the Godhead beyond this. *Deus* ("God")[6] in the Greek language means "fear," and since he alone is to be feared the word attained the role of a title. We read in Exodus: "My name Adonai I did not show them." From this we are to realize that the name is secret and is known to have been revealed not even to chosen ministers. So he spoke through prophets, through apostles and more powerfully through his own mouth. EXPOSITION OF THE PSALMS 49.1.[7]

6:11 Go, Tell Pharaoh

See CLEMENT OF ALEXANDRIA ON EXODUS 3:19.

---

[2]A Jewish translator of the Hebrew Scriptures into Greek. [3]Jn 14:9. [4]2 Cor 1:22; 5:5; Eph 1:14. [5]POG 1:258-59. [6]*Deus* means "God" in Latin; the Greek word is *Theos*. [7]ACW 51:480.

6:14-27 GENEALOGY OF MOSES AND AARON

[14]*These are the heads of their fathers' houses. . . .* [24]*The sons of Korah: Assir, Elkanah, and Abiasaph; these are the families of the Korahites.* [25]*Eleazar, Aaron's son, took to wife one of the daughters of Puti-el; and she bore him Phinehas. These are the heads of the fathers' houses of the Levites by their families.*

[26]*These are the Aaron and Moses to whom the* LORD *said: "Bring out the people of Israel from the land of Egypt by their hosts."* [27]*It was they who spoke to Pharaoh king of Egypt about bringing out the people of Israel from Egypt, this Moses and this Aaron.*

OVERVIEW: Moses' descent from Levi was a descent from the priestly tribe (AUGUSTINE). The three sons of Korah speak as one voice and one soul (ORIGEN).

6:14 The Heads of Houses

THE DESCENT OF MOSES AND AARON FROM LEVI. AUGUSTINE: There is no doubt that this is a mysterious passage. The Scripture wishes to demonstrate the origin of Moses, because his action now required it. His descent began from the firstborn of Jacob, that is, Reuben, and then to Simeon, and then to Levi. It went no further, because Moses was descended from Levi. These men who are mentioned here had already been mentioned among the seventy-five men in whom Israel entered Egypt. For God did not want the first or the second tribe, but the third—that is, the tribe of Levi—to be the priestly tribe. QUESTIONS ON EXODUS 15.[1]

6:24 The Sons of Korah

SPEAKING AS WITH ONE VOICE. ORIGEN: For though there were three sons of Korah whose names we find in the book of Exodus—Aser, which is, by interpretation, "instruction," and the second Elkana, which is translated "possession of God," and the third Abiasaph, which in the Greek tongue might be rendered "congregation of the father"—yet the prophecies were not divided but were both spoken and written by one spirit and one voice and one soul, which worked in true harmony. And the three speak as one, "As the hart pants after the springs of the water, so pants my soul after you, O God."[2] COMMENTARY ON THE GOSPEL OF MATTHEW 14.1.[3]

---

[1]CCL 33:75. [2]Ps 42:1. [3]ANF 9:495.

6:28—7:7 MOSES AND AARON BEFORE PHARAOH

[28]On the day when the LORD spoke to Moses in the land of Egypt, [29]the LORD said to Moses, "I am the LORD; tell Pharaoh king of Egypt all that I say to you." [30]But Moses said to the LORD, "Behold, I am of uncircumcised lips.". . . [1]And the LORD said to Moses, "See, I make you as God to Pharaoh. . . . [3]But I will harden Pharaoh's heart, and though I multiply my signs and wonders in the land of Egypt, [4]Pharaoh will not listen to you; then I will lay my hand upon Egypt and bring forth my hosts, my people the sons of Israel, out of the land of Egypt by great acts of judgment." . . . [6]And Moses and Aaron did so; they did as the LORD commanded them." [7]Now Moses was eighty years old, and Aaron eighty-three years old, when they spoke to Pharaoh.

OVERVIEW: Was Moses' voice so weak that not even one man could hear him? (AUGUSTINE). The Scripture says that God made Moses as god to Pharaoh; what does this mean? If Moses is god to Pharaoh, Christ is God to all (NOVATIAN). Moses' being called god designates a power he received,

---

not a divine nature (Basil). Moses may have been god to Pharaoh, but he was a servant of the true God (Gregory of Nazianzus). Moses' great virtue earned him the title *god*. When Christ is called God, he is God in a way different from all others who are given this title (Ambrose). If we are called gods, it is by grace, not nature; only Christ is son of God by nature (Jerome). The miracles Moses performs are the occasion of his being called a god (Peter Chrysologus). Human beings are made in the image of God; hence they may be called gods (John of Damascus). When God hardened Pharaoh's heart, the evil in Pharaoh's heart was the result of his own evildoing (Augustine). Moses' father abstained from relations with his wife until the child was weaned (Clement of Alexandria).

6:30 *Uncircumcised Lips*

Moses Had a Weak Voice. Augustine: Moses says, "Behold, I have a weak voice, how will Pharaoh listen to me?" He appears to excuse himself for the weakness of his voice, not only due to the great number of the people but also due to the condition of one man. It would be remarkable if his voice were so weak that he could not be heard even by one man. Or perhaps the royal dignity did not allow them to speak at close range? For God says to Moses, "Behold, I gave you as a god to Pharaoh, and Aaron your brother will be your prophet." Questions on Exodus 16.[1]

7:1 *I Make You as God to Pharaoh*

Christ Is Lord of Creation. Novatian: Why in the world, after reading that this name was also given to Moses, when it is stated, "I have made you as god to Pharaoh," should they deny this title to Christ who we find has been constituted not a god to Pharaoh but rather the Lord and God of all creation? The Trinity 20.7.[2]

Power, Not Nature. Basil the Great: Moses was appointed god of the Egyptians when

he who was giving the revelation spoke to him in this manner: "I have appointed you the god of Pharaoh." Therefore the title conveys an indication of some power, either protective or active. But the divine nature in all the names which may be contrived remains, just as it is, inexplicable, as is our teaching. Letter 189.[3]

Moses the True God's Servant. Gregory of Nazianzus: So Moses was a god to Pharaoh, but a servant of God, as it is written. The stars which illumine the night are hidden by the sun, so much that you could not even know of their existence by daylight. A little torch brought near a great blaze is neither destroyed nor seen nor extinguished; but it is all one blaze, the bigger one prevailing over the other. Letter 101.[4]

Moses' Virtue Earned Him the Title God. Ambrose: He so far exceeded the dignity of his human state that he was given the title of "god" as we read in the Scriptures, where the Lord speaks: "I have appointed you the god of Pharaoh." He was in fact victorious over all his passions and was not allured by the enticements of the world. He enveloped this our habitation here in the body with a purity that savored of a "citizenship that is in heaven."[5] By directing his mind and by subduing and castigating his flesh with an authority that was almost regal, he was given the name of "god," by whom he had modeled his life through numerous acts of perfect virtue. Cain and Abel 1.2.7.[6]

Christ Is Not Called God in the Way Others Are. Ambrose: But if they think [Christ] is called God because he had an indwelling of the Godhead within him, as many holy men were (for the Scripture calls them gods to whom the word of God came)[7]—they do not place him before other men but think he is to be compared with them. They consider him

---

[1]CCL 33:75. [2]FC 67:77. [3]FC 28:33. [4]LCC 3:220. [5]Phil 3:20. [6]FC 42:364. [7]Jn 10:35.

to be the same as he granted other men to be, even as he says to Moses: "I have made you a god unto Pharaoh." Similarly it is also said in the psalms: "I have said, you are gods."[8] ON THE CHRISTIAN FAITH 5.1.23.[9]

HUMAN BEINGS ARE "GODS" BY GRACE. JEROME: "I said: You are gods, all of you sons of the Most High." Let Eunomius hear this, let Arius, who says that the Son of God is son in the same way that we are. That we are gods is not so by nature but by grace. "But to as many as received him he gave the power of becoming sons of God."[10] I made man for that purpose, that from men they may become gods. "I said: You are gods, all of you sons of the Most High."[11] Imagine the grandeur of our dignity; we are called gods and sons! I have made you gods just as I made Moses a god to Pharaoh, so that after you are gods, you may be made worthy to be sons of God. Reflect upon the divine words: "With God there is no respect of persons."[12] God did not say, "I said, you are gods, you kings and princes"; but "all" to whom I have given equally a body, a soul and a spirit, I have given equally divinity and adoption. We are all born equal, emperors and paupers; and we die as equals. Our humanity is of one quality. HOMILIES ON THE PSALMS 14.[13]

WHY MOSES IS CALLED A GOD. PETER CHRYSOLOGOS: Hence it is that through the influence of these three things Moses is made a god: for the sake of his military triumphs he brings all the elements under his control. He bids the sea to withdraw, its waves to solidify, its bottom to become dry[14] and the sky to drop its rain. He supplies food, compels the winds to scatter meats,[15] illumines the night with the splendor of the sun, tempers the sun by the veil of the cloud.[16] He strikes the rock to make it yield from its fresh wound cool streams of water for those who thirst.[17] He first gives to the earth heaven's law, writes down the norms of living, sets the terms of disciplinary control.[18] SERMON 43.[19]

IMAGES OF GOD. JOHN OF DAMASCUS: I say that they are gods, lords and kings not by nature but because they have ruled over and dominated sufferings and because they have kept undebased the likeness of the divine image to which they were made—for the image of the king is also called a king. Finally . . . they have freely been united to God and [by] receiving him as a dweller within themselves have through association with him become by grace what he is by nature. ORTHODOX FAITH 4.15.[20]

7:3 I Will Harden Pharaoh's Heart

GOD DID NOT SUPPRESS PHARAOH'S FREE CHOICE. AUGUSTINE: God constantly says, "I will harden Pharaoh's heart," and gives the reason why he does this. He says, "I will harden Pharaoh's heart and fulfill my signs and my portents in Egypt," as if the hardening of Pharaoh's heart were necessary so that God's signs might be multiplied and fulfilled in Egypt. God makes good use of bad hearts for what he wishes to show to those who are good or those he is going to make good. And the quality of evil in each heart (that is, what sort of heart is disposed to evil) came about through its own evildoing, which grew from the choice of the will. Still, those evils in quality, so that the heart is moved this way or that, when it is moved to evil this way or that way, comes to be by causes by which the soul is driven. And whether these causes either exist or do not exist is not within the power of man. They come from the providence of God that is hidden, most just and clearly most wise, who disposes and administers the universe that he created. So that Pharaoh had such a heart, which was not moved by God's patience to piety but rather to impiety, was the result of his own vice. But that those things happened by which his heart, so evil by its own vice,

---

[8]Ps 82:6. [9]NPNF 2 10:287. [10]Jn 1:12. [11]Ps 82:6. [12]Rom 2:11. [13]FC 48:106. [14]Ex 14:21. [15]Ex 16:12-13; Num 11:31. [16]Ex 13:21-22. [17]Num 20:11. [18]Ex 20:1-17. [19]FC 17:91-92. [20]FC 37:367.

resisted God's command—it is called "hardened" because it did not bend and agree but resisted unbendingly—was of divine dispensation. It was not unjust to such a heart. It was clearly a just punishment [that] was being prepared, by which those who feared God would be corrected. For example: when money is offered for the commission of homicide, a greedy man is moved in one way, but one who disdains money is moved in another way. The former is moved to commit the crime, the latter to being cautious. Yet the offer of the money itself was not under the control of either of them. Thus motives come to evil men that indeed are not under their control, but they act from these motives as they find them already established from their own past willing. We should consider whether the phrase can be understood in this way: "I shall harden," as if he were saying, "I

shall show how hard his heart is." QUESTIONS ON EXODUS 18.[21]

7:7 Moses Was Eighty Years Old

RESPECT FOR A NURSING MOTHER. CLEMENT OF ALEXANDRIA: On the same basis, you would not be able to point to anyone of the past generations approaching a pregnant woman in the pages of Scripture. Only later, after the birth and weaning of the child, would you again find the wives in physical relations with their husbands. You will find that Moses' father observed this point. He left a three-year gap after Aaron's birth before fathering Moses. STROMATEIS 3.11.72.[22]

---

[21]CCL 33:76-77. [22]FC 85:300-301.

7:8-13 THE STAFF TURNED INTO A SNAKE

[8]And the LORD said to Moses and Aaron, [9]"When Pharaoh says to you, 'Prove yourselves by working a miracle,' then you shall say to Aaron, 'Take your rod and cast it down before Pharaoh, that it may become a serpent.'" [10]So Moses and Aaron went to Pharaoh and did as the LORD commanded; Aaron cast down his rod before Pharaoh and his servants, and it became a serpent. [11]Then Pharaoh summoned the wise men and the sorcerers; and they also, the magicians of Egypt, did the same by their secret arts.

OVERVIEW: Moses and Aaron were both great men. Moses was the lawgiver and gave the letter and spirit of the law; Aaron was a priest and the minister of the tabernacle (GREGORY OF NAZIANZUS). Why did Aaron cast down Moses' rod? (AUGUSTINE). Moses' rod or staff was a figure of the cross (EPHREM). As the rod became a serpent and devoured the other serpents, so the Word became flesh and destroyed the power of sin

(AMBROSE). When the serpent became a rod again, it was a sign that Christ would take up the whole of his body, which is the church, into the resurrection. God is more powerful than the Egyptian magicians. Moses' power came from holiness. In the name of God and helped by angels, he triumphed over the Egyptian wonderworkers. Yet sometimes the wicked seem able to work wonders when the good cannot. But the

Lord predicted that false prophets would work signs. Acts that appear the same are often done from different motives (AUGUSTINE).

7:8-9 Instructions for Moses and Aaron

MOSES THE LAWGIVER AND AARON THE PRIEST. GREGORY OF NAZIANZUS: Great indeed was Moses, who afflicted Egypt grievously and saved his people by many signs and prodigies, who went within the cloud and instituted the twofold law: the law of the letter without and the law of the spirit within. Aaron also, the brother of Moses according to the flesh and the spirit, sacrificed and prayed on behalf of the people,[1] as consecrated minister of the great and holy tabernacle, "which the Lord has erected and not man."[2] ORATION 43, ON ST. BASIL 72.[3]

WHY AARON CAST DOWN MOSES' ROD. AUGUSTINE: Here indeed there was no need to use the service of the voice, for which Aaron was provided out of necessity, on account of the weakness of Moses' voice. But the staff was to be cast down so that it would become a serpent. Why did Moses himself not do this, except because that mediation of Aaron himself between Moses and Pharaoh was the symbol of some great matter? QUESTIONS ON EXODUS 19.[4]

7:10 Aaron's Rod Becomes a Serpent

THE STAFF PREFIGURED THE CROSS. EPHREM THE SYRIAN: The staff is a sign of the cross. It caused all the plagues when it swallowed the snakes, just as [the cross] would destroy all idols. With [the staff], [Moses] divided the sea and drowned the Egyptians. That prefigured the destruction of the Canaanites. COMMENTARY ON EXODUS 7.4.[5]

MOSES' ROD FORESHADOWED THE INCARNATION. AMBROSE: He cast down his rod, and it became a serpent which devoured the serpents of Egypt. This signified that the Word should become flesh to destroy the poison of the dread serpent by the forgiveness and pardon of sins. For the rod stands for the Word that is true, royal, filled with power and glorious in ruling. As the rod became a serpent, so he who was the Son of God begotten of the Father became the Son of man born of a woman. Like the serpent, he was lifted up on the cross, poured his healing medicine on the wounds of humanity. Wherefore the Lord himself says, "As Moses lifted up the serpent in the wilderness, so must the Son of Man be lifted up."[6] DUTIES OF THE CLERGY 3.15.94.[7]

DEATH AND RESURRECTION ARE SIGNIFIED. AUGUSTINE: For by the serpent is to be understood death, which was brought about by the serpent in paradise, according to the manner of speech which attributes the effect to the cause. Therefore the rod was turned into a serpent, and the whole Christ, together with his body which is the church,[8] into the resurrection, that will take place at the end of time. This is signified by the tail of the serpent which Moses held, in order that it might be turned again into a rod.[9] But the serpents of the magicians are like those who are dead in the world, for, unless by believing in Christ they have been as it were swallowed up and entered into his body, they will not be able to rise in him. THE TRINITY 3.20.[10]

7:11 The Magicians Did the Same

THE EGYPTIAN MAGICIANS INFERIOR TO MOSES. AUGUSTINE: We read that the magicians of the Egyptians were very skilled in those arts, but they were outdone by Moses, the servant of God. Yet when they performed certain wonders by their forbidden arts, he overturned

---

[1]Ex 29:1. [2]Heb 8:2. [3]FC 22:90-91. [4]CCL 33:77. [5]FC 91:240. [6]Jn 3:14. [7]NPNF 2 10:82-83*. [8]Col 1:24. [9]Ex 4:4. [10]FC 45:117.

all their trickery by simply calling on God. LET-
TER 137.[11]

THE MAGICIANS' FEATS PROVED MOSES'
FEATS GREATER. AUGUSTINE: The magicians of
Pharaoh, the king of Egypt who was tyrannizing
over this people, were permitted to accomplish
certain wonders merely that they might be outdone by more genuine miracles. These magicians worked by the kind of sorceries and
incantations to which evil spirits or demons are
addicted, while Moses was powerful by his holiness and helped by the angels, and so, in the
name of God, creator of heaven and earth, he
easily triumphed over them. CITY OF GOD
10.8.[12]

WHY SINNERS SEEM TO WORK MIRACLES
AND SAINTS DO NOT. AUGUSTINE: Conse-
quently it happens that the holy servants of
God, when it is useful for them to have this gift,
in accord, the power of the most high God, have
command over the lowest powers in order to
perform certain visible miracles. This power
thus becomes publicly known, as if it were imperial law. For it is God himself who rules in them,
whose temple they are, and whom they, having
despised their own private power, love most fer-
vently. However, in magical imprecation, in order to make the deception attractive so as to
subjugate to themselves those [magicians] to
whom they grant such things, [the lowest pow-
ers] give effect to their prayers and rituals, and
they dispense through that private law what
they are allowed to dispense to those who honor
them and serve them and keep certain covenants
with them in their mystery rites. And when the
magicians appear to have command, they
frighten their inferiors with the names of more
elevated [powers] and exhibit to those looking
on with wonder some visible effects. Due to the
weakness of the flesh, these seem momentous to
those unable to behold eternal things, which the
true God offers through himself to those who
love him. However, God permits these things

through his righteous government of all things,
in order that he may distribute to them the
kinds of bondage or the kinds of freedom that
are proportioned to their own desires and
choices. And if they gain something for their
own evil desires when they call upon the most
high God, that is a punishment and not a kindness. Indeed not without reason does the apostle
say, "God has given them over to the desires of
their hearts."[13] For the opportunity to commit
certain sins is a punishment for other preceding
sins. . . .

But as for the Lord's claim that false prophets
will perform many signs and wonders so as to
deceive, if possible, even the elect,[14] clearly he is
urging us to understand that even wicked men
do certain miracles of a kind which the saints
cannot do. Still, they must not be thought to be
in a better position with God on that account,
for the magicians of the Egyptians were not
more acceptable to God than were the Israelite
people because the latter could not do what the
magicians were doing, although Moses had been
able to do greater things by the power of God.
However, the reason for not granting these miracles to all the saints is this: to prevent the weak
from being deceived by a most pernicious error
of supposing that there are greater gifts in such
feats than in the works of righteousness
whereby one obtains eternal life. Accordingly
the Lord prohibits his disciples from rejoicing
on this account when he says, "Do not rejoice in
this, that the spirits are subject to you; rather,
rejoice in this, that your names are written in
heaven."[15]

When therefore magicians do things of a kind
which the saints sometimes do, remember that
their deeds appear to the eye to be alike, but
they are done both for a different purpose and
under a different law. For the former act seeking
their own glory; the latter, the glory of God.
Again, the former act through certain things
granted to the powers in their own sphere, as if

---

[11]FC 20:29. [12]FC 14:129-30. [13]Rom 1:26. [14]Mt 24:24. [15]Lk 10:20.

through business arrangements and magic arts of a private nature; but the latter, by a public administration at the command of him to whom the entire creation is subject. For it is one thing for an owner to be compelled to give his horse to a soldier; it is another thing for him to hand it over to a buyer or to give or lend it to someone. And just as a great many evil soldiers, whom imperial discipline condemns, terrify some owners with the ensigns of their commander and extort from them something which is not in accord with public law, so evil Christians or schismatics or heretics sometimes exact through the name of Christ or Christian words or sacraments something from the powers who have been enjoined to defer to the honor of Christ. However, when the powers submit to the bidding of evil men, they do so willingly in order to seduce others, in whose error they rejoice. Consequently it is one thing for magicians to perform miracles, another for good Christians, and another for evil Christians. Magicians do so through private contracts, good Christians through a public righteousness, and evil Christians through the "ensigns" or symbols of this public righteousness. On Eighty-three Varied Questions 79.1, 3-4.[16]

---

[16]FC 70:201-3.

7:14-24 FIRST PLAGUE: WATER TURNED INTO BLOOD

[14]Then the Lord said to Moses, "Pharaoh's heart is hardened, he refuses to let the people go." . . . [19]And the Lord said to Moses, "Say to Aaron, 'Take your rod and stretch out your hand over the waters of Egypt, over their rivers, their canals, and their ponds, and all their pools of water, that they may become blood; and there shall be blood throughout all the land of Egypt, both in vessels of wood and in vessels of stone.'"

[20]Moses and Aaron did as the Lord commanded; in the sight of Pharaoh and in the sight of his servants, he lifted up the rod and struck the water that was in the Nile, and all the water that was in the Nile turned to blood. [21]And the fish in the Nile died; and the Nile became foul, so that the Egyptians could not drink water from the Nile; and there was blood throughout all the land of Egypt. . . . [24]And all the Egyptians dug round about the Nile for water to drink, for they could not drink the water of the Nile.

OVERVIEW: The sign of blood means that the people were preoccupied with thoughts of the flesh (Cassiodorus). The blood is the speculation of philosophers, who think of the world only carnally (Isidore of Seville). If Moses changed all the water of Egypt into blood, how did Pharaoh's magicians find any water that they could transform? (Augustine).

7:20 All the Water Turned to Blood

CHANGE FOR THE WORSE. CASSIODORUS: Just

as we read in the Gospel that water was turned into wine,[1] which denoted that people were changed for the better, so here its transformation into blood announces that sinners interpret the causes of spiritual things in a bodily sense. Blood is introduced here to denote the flesh, and undoubtedly the Jewish people took this materialistic view. He further says that both their rivers and their rain showers were turned into blood, so that in their preoccupation with the thoughts of the flesh they did not understand the heavenly preaching in a spiritual sense. The literal sense of this and of what follows is clear, for the words of the divine history show that these events occurred in Egypt. EXPOSITION OF THE PSALMS 77.44.[2]

THE PLAGUE AS A FIGURE. ISIDORE OF SEVILLE: Then the plagues are visited upon Egypt. They were carried out corporally among the Egyptians; they are now carried out spiritually in us, for Egypt is the figure of this world. The first plague is the one in which the waters are turned into blood. The waters of Egypt are erratic, just as the dogmas of the philosophers are inconstant. These waters are deservedly turned into blood, because when the philoso-phers ponder the causes of things they think carnally. But when the cross of Christ shows the light of truth to this world, it will reproach the world with censures of this sort, so that from the kind of punishment it suffers, the world might recognize its errors. QUESTIONS ON THE OLD TESTAMENT, EXODUS 14.1-2.[3]

7:24 Searching for Water

HOW THE EGYPTIANS FOUND WATER. AUGUSTINE: You asked . . . how, when all the water of Egypt was turned into blood, the magicians of Pharaoh found any [water] with which they could transform in like manner. This difficulty is usually solved in two ways. They did it either because some sea water could be brought or, what is more likely, because in that part of the country where the children of Israel were those plagues did not take place. In certain passages of that Scripture this is very clearly expressed,[4] and it warns us what is to be understood even when it is not expressed. LETTER 143.[5]

---

[1]Jn 2:9. [2]ACW 52:266. [3]PL 83:292. [4]Ex 8:22; 9:4; 10:23; 11:7. [5]FC 20:150.

7:25—8:15 SECOND PLAGUE: THE FROGS

[1i]*Then the LORD said to Moses, "Go in to Pharaoh and say to him, 'Thus says the LORD, "Let my people go, that they may serve me. [2]But if you refuse to let them go, behold, I will plague all your country with frogs."'" . . . [6]So Aaron stretched out his hand over the waters of Egypt; and the frogs came up and covered the land of Egypt. . . .*

[8]Then Pharaoh called Moses and Aaron, and said, "Entreat the LORD to take away the frogs from me and from my people; and I will let the people go to sacrifice to the LORD." [9]Moses said to Pharaoh, "Be pleased to command me when I am to entreat, for you and for your servants and for your people, that the frogs be destroyed from you and your houses and be left only in the

Nile." [10]And he said, "Tomorrow." Moses said, "Be it as you say, that you may know that there is no one like the Lord our God."

i Ch 7.26 in Heb

Overview: The plague of frogs humiliated the Egyptians (Augustine). The croaking of frogs is like the loquacity of the poets (Isidore of Seville). In these passages Pharaoh is often said to pray (Origen). Pharaoh procastinated and was indifferent to the punishments that the Egyptians suffered (Ambrose).

8:2 Plaguing Egypt with Frogs

God Humiliated the Egyptians with Frogs. Augustine: For what reason do you puff yourself up with human pride? A man insulted you, and you swelled up and were angered. Rid yourself of the fleas that you may sleep. Find out who you are! For that you may know, brothers, that these things which would bother us were created to enable us to control our pride, [remember], God could have tamed the proud people of Pharaoh with bears, with lions or with snakes; he sent flies and frogs upon them that their pride might be tamed by the most ignoble of things. Tractate on the Gospel of John 1.15.[1]

Songs of the Poets. Isidore of Seville: In the second plague frogs are brought forth. They are thought to stand figuratively for the songs of the poets. The poets have brought deceptive fables into this world, with their empty and conceited songs that are like the croaking of frogs. For the frog stands for empty loquacity. That animal is good for nothing else but to give out the sounds of its voice in offensive and annoying noises. Questions on the Old Testament, Exodus 14.3.[2]

8:8 Entreat the Lord

The Meaning of the Term Prayer. Origen: One should also observe that the term *prayer*, which often differs in meaning from "invocation," is here employed in the case of one who promises in a vow to do certain things if God grants him certain other things. But the term is also used in the ordinary way. For example, we found this to be so in Exodus after the description of the plague of the frogs, which was the second of the ten plagues: . . . "But Pharaoh called Moses and Aaron and said to them: 'Pray to the Lord on my account to take away the frogs from me and my people; and I will let the people go to sacrifice to the Lord.'" When Pharaoh employs the word *prayer* the habitual meaning of "prayer" is conveyed in addition to the above meaning. If anyone finds this difficult to see, it becomes clear in what follows, namely: "And Moses said to Pharaoh: 'Set me a time when I shall pray for you, and for your servants, and for your people, that the frogs may be driven away from you and from your house and from your people, and may remain only in the river.'"

We noted, however, that in the case of the sciniphs,[3] the third plague, Pharaoh does not ask that prayer be made, nor does Moses pray. And in the case of the flies, the fourth plague, he says, "Pray therefore for me to the Lord." And then Moses said, "I will go out from you and will pray to the Lord. And the flies shall depart from Pharaoh, and from his servants, and from his people tomorrow."[4] And a little further on we read: "So Moses went out from Pharaoh and prayed to God."[5] Again in the case of the fifth and also of the sixth plague Pharaoh did not ask that prayer be made, nor did Moses pray. In the seventh plague "Pharaoh sent and called Moses and Aaron, saying to them, 'I have sinned this

---

[1]FC 78:54-55. [2]PL 83:292. [3]Greek *sknips*, a gnat found under the bark of trees. [4]Ex 8:28-29. [5]Ex 8:30.

time. The Lord is just, but I and my people are wicked. Pray to the Lord, that the thunderings of God and the hail and the fire may cease.' "[6] And a little further on we read: "And Moses went from Pharaoh out of the city and stretched forth his hands to the Lord; and the thunders . . . ceased."[7] We shall discuss more suitably at another time why it is not said as on the previous occasions that "he prayed" but rather that "he stretched forth his hands to the Lord." And in the case of the eighth plague Pharaoh says, "And pray to the Lord your God, that he take away from me this death. And Moses going forth from the presence of Pharaoh, prayed to the Lord."[8] On Prayer 3.2-3.[9]

8:10 Pharaoh Said, "Tomorrow"

Pharaoh Was Not Eager for Deliver-

ance. Ambrose: Take the example of Pharaoh, a man given to vain, empty thoughts. His land of Egypt was afflicted with a plague of frogs. They gave forth a surfeit of sound, meaningless and senseless. Moses said to Pharaoh, "Set me a time when I shall pray for you and for your servants and for your people that the Lord may exterminate the frogs."[10] Pharaoh, who because of his plight should have besought him to offer prayer, replied, "Tomorrow," thus showing himself indifferent to the punishment that the delay would bring, although he was still intent on saving Egypt from the plague. And so, when his prayer was finally granted, he was unmindful of gratitude. Being puffed up in heart, he forgot God. Cain and Abel 1.9.33.[11]

---

[6]Ex 9:29. [7]Ex 9:33. [8]Ex 10:17. [9]ACW 19:22-23. [10]Ex 8:9. [11]FC 42:390.

8:16-19 THIRD PLAGUE: THE GNATS

[16]Then the LORD said to Moses, "Say to Aaron, 'Stretch out your rod and strike the dust of the earth, that it may become gnats throughout all the land of Egypt.' " . . . [18]The magicians tried by their secret arts to bring forth gnats, but they could not. So there were gnats on man and beast. [19]And the magicians said to Pharaoh, "This is the finger of God." But Pharaoh's heart was hardened, and he would not listen to them; as the LORD had said.

Overview: The plague of gnats suggest the hidden subtle stings of heretics. At the third plague, the Egyptian magicians discerned the finger of God, which is a figure of the Holy Spirit (Isidore of Seville). All power, even the power to inflict suffering, comes from God (Augustine).

8:18 The Magicians Try to Bring Forth Gnats

Gnats Are Heretics. Isidore of Seville: After these plagues, gnats are brought forth. This animal flies through the air suspended on wings. But it is so subtle and minute that it escapes being seen by the eye unless one looks closely. But when it lands on the body it drills in with a sharp sting. If anyone cannot see it flying, he still feels its sting immediately.

This sort of animal can be compared with the subtlety of heretics, who drill into souls with the subtle stings of their words. They attack with such cunning that one who is deceived neither sees nor understands the source of his deception. At the third sign the magicians yielded and said, "The finger of God is here."[1] Those magicians stand for heretics and their animosity.

The apostle states this when he says, "Just as Jannes and Jambres resisted Moses, so too these men resisted the truth. They are corrupt in mind and reprobate in matters of faith. But they will not advance any further. Their madness will be manifested to everyone, just as Jannes' and Jambres' was."[2] The minds of the Egyptian magicians were disquieted by their own corruption, and their power failed at the third sign. They confessed that the Holy Spirit was against them, for the Spirit was in Moses.

The Holy Spirit is put in the third place, and he is the finger of God. Thus the magicians failed at the third sign and said, "The finger of God is here." The Holy Spirit, well disposed and favorable, gives rest to the meek and humble of heart but, when he is opposed, stirs up disquiet against the merciless and the proud. Those tiny gnats signified this disquiet, at which Pharaoh's magicians failed and said, "The finger of God is here." QUESTIONS ON THE OLD TESTAMENT, EXODUS 14.4-7.[3]

8:19 The Finger of God

THE MAGICIANS CONFESS GOD'S POWER.
AUGUSTINE: Here I see a difficulty occurring to one of limited knowledge [of Scripture], that is, why miracles are also done by magical arts, for

the magicians of Pharaoh also made serpents and other similar things. But what is a much greater cause of wonder is how the power of the magicians, who could make serpents, utterly failed when it came to very small gnats. For the sciniphs,[4] by which the proud people of Egypt were afflicted, are very small flies. And there certainly the magicians who failed, exclaimed, "This is the finger of God." We are thereby given to understand that not even the angels and the spirits of the air, who transgressed and were cast from that home of sublime and ethereal beauty into this most profound darkness, as into a prison peculiar to them, could do anything that they could by means of their magical arts, if the power had not been given to them from above. THE TRINITY 3.7.12.[5]

THE FINGER OF GOD IS THE HOLY SPIRIT.
AUGUSTINE: Isn't the finger of God to be understood as being the Holy Spirit? Read the Gospel, and see that where one Evangelist has the Lord saying, "If I with the Spirit of God cast out demons,"[6] another says, "If I with the finger of God cast out demons."[7] So if that law too was written by the finger of God, that is, by the Spirit of God, the Spirit by which Pharaoh's magicians were defeated, so they said, "This is the finger of God, . . . why can it not be said of it, "For the law of the Spirit of life in Christ Jesus has delivered you from the law of sin and death"?[8] SERMON 155.3.[9]

---

[1]Ex 8:19. [2]2 Tim 3:8-9. [3]PL 83:292-93. [4]See note on Ex 8:8. [5]FC 45:107. [6]Mt 12:28. [7]Lk 11:20. [8]Rom 8:2. [9]WSA 3 5:86.

8:20-32 FOURTH PLAGUE: THE FLIES

[20]Then the LORD said to Moses, "Rise up early in the morning and wait for Pharaoh, as he goes out to the water, and say to him, 'Thus says the LORD, "Let my people go, that they may

serve me. [21]*Else, if you will not let my people go, behold, I will send swarms of flies on you and your servants and your people, and into your houses."' "* . . .

[25]*Then Pharaoh called Moses and Aaron, and said, "Go, sacrifice to your God within the land."* [26]*But Moses said, "It would not be right to do so; for we shall sacrifice to the LORD our God offerings abominable to the Egyptians. . . .* [27]*We must go three days' journey into the wilderness and sacrifice to the LORD our God as he will command us."* [28]*So Pharaoh said, "I will let you go, to sacrifice to the LORD your God in the wilderness; only you shall not go very far away. Make entreaty for me."* . . . [32]*But Pharaoh hardened his heart this time also, and did not let the people go.*

OVERVIEW: The proper understanding of the term for flies is "every genus of flies" (JEROME). But others see it especially in references to the restlessness of the dog fly (ISIDORE OF SEVILLE). The Egyptians despised sheep and thus hated pure sacrifices (AMBROSE). The righteous are marked by purity and gentleness (PATERIUS).

8:21 Swarms of Flies

THE NATURE OF THE PLAGUE. JEROME: *Kynomyia*[1] does not represent "dog fly," as the Latins translated it, with the Greek letter upsilon; according to the sense of the Hebrew the diphthong *oi* should be written so that the word is *koinomyia*, that is, "every genus of flies." LETTER 106.86.[2]

FLIES ARE CARNAL LUST. ISIDORE OF SEVILLE: In the fourth place, Egypt is struck with flies. The fly is an insolent and restless animal. What does it stand for except the arrogant concerns of carnal desires? Egypt is struck with flies because the hearts of those who love this world are battered by the disquiet of their desires.[3]

The translators of the Septuagint put *cynomyia* here, which means "dog fly." This word meant the habits of a dog, in which the pleasures of the mind and the indulgence of the flesh are constantly expressed. By dog fly this passage can also mean the eloquence of lawyers, which they use to tear at one another like dogs. QUESTIONS ON THE OLD TESTAMENT, EXODUS 14.8-9.[4]

8:26 Offerings Abominable to the Egyptians

THE EGYPTIANS DESPISED THE SHEPHERD AND THE FLOCK. AMBROSE: You[5] wrote to me that you were disturbed by what you read: "Let us sacrifice the abominations of the Egyptians to God." But you had the means to explain it: that in Genesis it is written, "The Egyptians abominated the shepherd of flocks."[6] This was certainly not because of the man, but because of the sheep. For the Egyptians cultivated the earth with the plow; Abraham and Jacob, however, and later Moses and David, were shepherds and bestowed a certain royal discipline upon this occupation.

Thus the Egyptians hated pure sacrifices, that is, zeal complete and perfect for virtue and discipline. For what wicked men hate is pure and pious among good men. The indulgent man hates the labor of virtue; the glutton shrinks back from it. And so the Egyptian body, because it loves allurements, turns away from the virtues of the soul. It hates authority, and shrinks from the discipline of the virtues and all labors of this sort.

The Egyptian, then flees these things; he is an Egyptian and not a man. You have knowledge of human nature; you will understand this. But reject what they follow and choose, since these

---

[1]The Greek word for fly in Ex 8:21. [2]CSEL 55:289. [3]Isidore quotes this passage from Gregory the Great *Moral Interpretation of Job* 18.43.68. [4]PL 83:293. [5]Irenaeus, a resident of Milan, expressed this concern in a previous letter to Ambrose. [6]Gen 46:34.

two—prudence and folly—cannot be in accord with one another. And so, just as the virtues of prudence and continence exclude whatever belongs in any way to imprudence and intemperance, so every foolish man and every incontinent man has no part in what good men have or in the inheritance of the wise and continent man. LETTER 4(27).1-3.[7]

A CLEAN CONSCIENCE. PATERIUS: The Egyptians disdained the eating of sheep. But what the Egyptians abhor, the Israelites offer to God. The unjust despise a clean conscience as weak and abject, but the just turn it into a sacrifice to God of virtue. The righteous, as they worship God, offer their purity and gentleness to him. The reprobate despise these virtues and consider them foolishness. EXPOSITION OF THE OLD AND NEW TESTAMENT, EXODUS 13.[8]

8:27 Three Days' Journey

See CAESARIUS OF ARLES ON EXODUS 19:16.

8:28 Entreat for Me

See ORIGEN ON EXODUS 8:8.

8:32 Pharaoh Hardened His Heart

See AUGUSTINE ON EXODUS 4:21.

---

[7]CSEL 82 1:26-27. [8]PL 79:727, citing Gregory the Great *Moral Interpretation of Job* 10.29.48.

9:1-7 FIFTH PLAGUE: THE PESTILENCE

[1]Then the LORD said to Moses, "Go in to Pharaoh, and say to him, 'Thus says the LORD, the God of the Hebrews, "Let my people go, that they may serve me. [2]For if you refuse to let them go and still hold them, [3]behold, the hand of the LORD will fall with a very severe plague upon your cattle which are in the field, the horses, the asses, the camels, the herds, and the flocks."'" . . . [7]And Pharaoh sent, and behold, not one of the cattle of the Israelites was dead. But the heart of Pharaoh was hardened, and he did not let the people go.

OVERVIEW: The Egyptians worshiped their gods in the form of animals and showed thereby their irrationality (ISIDORE OF SEVILLE).

9:3 A Plague on Cattle

GODS IN THE FORM OF ANIMALS. ISIDORE OF SEVILLE: In the fifth place, Egypt is struck with the slaughter of animals or cattle. Frenzy is demonstrated here, and the stupidity of men who, like irrational animals, gave worship and the name of god to figures carved in wood or stone—figures not only of men but of animals, too. They worshiped Jupiter Ammon in a ram,[1] Anubis in a dog,[2] and Apis in a bull,[3] and others, too, which Egypt admired as symbols of its gods. They believed that the divine splendor was present in these forms and offered pathetic acts of worship to them. QUESTIONS ON THE OLD TESTAMENT, EXODUS 14.10.[4]

---

[1]A cult of Jupiter practiced in Africa. [2]An Egyptian deity, tutelary of the chaste. [3]The ox, worshiped in Egypt as a god. [4]PL 83:293.

9:8-12 SIXTH PLAGUE: THE BOILS

[8]And the LORD said to Moses and Aaron, "Take handfuls of ashes from the kiln, and let Moses throw them toward heaven in the sight of Pharaoh. [9]And it shall become fine dust over all the land of Egypt, and become boils breaking out in sores on man and beast throughout all the land of Egypt." . . . [12]But the LORD hardened the heart of Pharaoh, and he did not listen to them; as the LORD had spoken to Moses.

OVERVIEW: Ulcers and cysts are signs of pride, anger and rage (ISIDORE OF SEVILLE).

9:9 Boils Breaking Out in Sores

SIGNS OF PRIDE AND RAGE. ISIDORE OF SEVILLE: After these plagues came rotten and swollen cysts, along with fever, as the sixth plague. In the ulcers the troubled and purulent evil of this age is signified; in the cysts swollen and inflated pride; in the fevers anger and the madness of rage. Up to this point such punishments as were inflicted on the world were tempered, insofar as its errors were represented by signs. QUESTIONS ON THE OLD TESTAMENT, EXODUS 14.11.[1]

[1]PL 83:293-94.

9:13-35 SEVENTH PLAGUE: THE HAIL

[13]Then the LORD said to Moses, "Rise up early in the morning and stand before Pharaoh, and say to him, 'Thus says the LORD, the God of the Hebrews, . . . [15]"For by now I could have put forth my hand and struck you and your people with pestilence, and you would have been cut off from the earth; [16]but for this purpose have I let you live, to show you my power. . . . [18]Behold, tomorrow about this time I will cause very heavy hail to fall, such as never has been in Egypt from the day it was founded until now."'"

[23]Then Moses stretched forth his rod toward heaven; and the LORD sent thunder and hail, and fire ran down to the earth. And the LORD rained hail upon the land of Egypt; [24]there was hail, and fire flashing continually in the midst of the hail, very heavy hail, such as had never been in all the land of Egypt since it became a nation. [25]The hail struck down everything that was in the field throughout all the land of Egypt, both man and beast; and the hail struck down every plant of the field, and shattered every tree of the field. [26]Only in the land of Goshen, where the people of Israel were, there was no hail.

[27]Then Pharaoh sent, and called Moses and Aaron, and said to them, "I have sinned this

time; the Lord *is in the right, and I and my people are in the wrong.* [28]*Entreat the* Lord. . . . [34]*But when Pharaoh saw that the rain and the hail and the thunder had ceased, he sinned yet again, and hardened his heart, he and his servants.*

Overview: God used Pharaoh to show forth the power of his grace, which separated the redeemed from the lost (Augustine). Thunder, hail and fire come together on Egypt, offered to correct the vices of this world (Isidore of Seville). The hail and fire together were terrifying. Pharaoh's sin grows more serious (Ephrem). Pharaoh confesses that he has sinned, after God has hardened his heart (Origen). Even Pharaoh affirmed God's justice; Christians should do the same (Caesarius of Arles).

9:16 *To Show My Power*

Grace Is Deliverance from Perdition. Augustine: With God there is no injustice. Thus [Paul] immediately added, "For the Scripture says to Pharaoh, 'For this very purpose I raised you up, that I may show through you my power and that my name may be proclaimed in all the earth.'"[1] Then, having said this, he draws a conclusion that looks both ways, that is, toward mercy and toward judgment: "Therefore," he says, "he has mercy on whom he wills, and whom he wills he hardens." He shows mercy out of his great goodness; he hardens out of no unfairness at all. In this way neither does he who is saved have a basis for glorying in any merit of his own; nor does the man who is damned have a basis for complaining of anything except what he has fully merited. For grace alone separates the redeemed from the lost, all having been mingled together in the one mass of perdition, arising from a common cause which leads back to their common origin. Enchiridion 25.99.[2]

9:18 *Heavy Hail Fell*

Reproaches and Divine Rebukes. Isidore of Seville: After these plagues come blows

from on high: voices, thunder and hail, and flashing fire. Thunder means reproaches and divine rebukes, because it does not strike in silence. It makes sounds and sends its teaching down from heaven. By its teaching the world is castigated and can acknowledge its guilt.

And he sends hail, which destroys the young vices that are still tender. He sends fire, too, knowing that there are thorns and spiny plants which that fire might feed on. The Lord says of them, "I came to cast fire on the earth."[3] This fire consumes the incentives to pleasure and lust. Questions on the Old Testament, Exodus 14.12-13.[4]

9:24 *Hail and Fire*

How Hail and Fire Fell Together. Ephrem the Syrian: "Hail and fire fell" together; neither did the hail extinguish the fire, nor did the fire melt the hail. Rather, it burst into flames in the hail as in a thicket and turned [the hail] as red as iron in the fire, blazing in the hail, and careful of the trees. The force [of the hail] "splintered the ancient trees,"[5] but the fire in [the hail] protected the hedges, seed beds and vineyards. Commentary on Exodus 9.3.[6]

9:27 *I Have Sinned*

Pharaoh Confesses His Sin. Ephrem the Syrian: Pharaoh said to Moses, "This time I have sinned." And the previous times he hardened his heart, did he not sin? And even if he sinned the previous times, he did not sin the way he did this time. [The Lord] warned him to bring in the cattle, but he was not persuaded.

---

[1]Rom 9:17. [2]LCC 7:398. [3]Lk 12:49. [4]PL 83:294. [5]Ex 9:25. [6]FC 91:243.

This is why his offense was more serious in this plague than in all the [other] plagues. COMMENTARY ON EXODUS 9.4.[7]

GOD WORKS TO EDUCATE PHARAOH. ORIGEN: See whether it is for this reason that God hardens the heart of Pharaoh, so that at a moment when he was not hardened he could say, "The Lord is just: I and my people are wicked."[8] His heart has to be hardened further, and he has to suffer more, that he may not, because he has been freed of his hardheartedness too quickly, think too lightly of that hardheartedness and so may have to have his heart hardened over and over again. ON PRAYER 29.16.[9]

PHARAOH CONFESSED THAT GOD IS JUST. CAESARIUS OF ARLES: Moreover, as we are wont

to sing in the hymn, "God is faithful, without deceit." For this reason, as I mentioned above, we should believe without any doubt concerning Pharaoh that he became hardened because of God's patience rather than his power. This fact we know clearly from his own admission, for when he was being punished he confessed in this way as justice compelled him: "The Lord is just; it is I and my subjects who are at fault." With what feelings then does a Christian complain that God is unjust, when even a wicked king admits that he is just?" SERMON 101.5.[10]

9:28 Ask the Lord

See ORIGEN ON EXODUS 8:8.

---

[7]FC 91:243. [8]Cf. Deut 32:4. [9]ACW 19:124. [10]FC 47:101-2.

10:1-20 EIGHTH PLAGUE: THE LOCUSTS

[3]*So Moses and Aaron went in to Pharaoh, and said to him, "Thus says the LORD, the God of the Hebrews, 'How long will you refuse to humble yourself before me? Let my people go, that they may serve me.* [4]*For if you refuse to let my people go, behold, tomorrow I will bring locusts into your country.'"* . . .

[7]*And Pharaoh's servants said to him, "How long shall this man be a snare to us? Let the men go, that they may serve the LORD their God; do you not yet understand that Egypt is ruined?"* . . .

[12]*Then the LORD said to Moses, "Stretch out your hand over the land of Egypt for the locusts, that they may come upon the land of Egypt, and eat every plant in the land, all that the hail has left."* . . . [16]*Then Pharaoh called Moses and Aaron in haste, and said, "I have sinned against the LORD your God, and against you.* [17]*Now therefore, forgive my sin, I pray you, only this once, and entreat the LORD your God only to remove this death from me."* . . . [20]*But the LORD hardened Pharaoh's heart, and he did not let the children of Israel go.*

OVERVIEW: The locusts signify dissent and discord or the restless quest of pleasure (ISIDORE OF SEVILLE). God's signs had an effect on Pharaoh, and he yielded before God's marvelous works

(ORIGEN). The locusts are the ministers of divine punishment (AMBROSE).

10:4 I Will Bring Locusts

INCONSTANCY AND DISCORD. ISIDORE OF SEVILLE: In the eighth place locusts are mentioned. Some interpreters think that this sort of plague confutes the inconstancy of the human race, filled with dissent and discord. In another sense, the locusts can be interpreted as representing flittering mobility, like the pleasures of this world in a restless and skittish soul. QUESTIONS ON THE OLD TESTAMENT, EXODUS 14.14.[1]

10:7 Let the Men Go

PHARAOH'S HEART COULD BE SOFTENED. ORIGEN: And the briefly recorded fact that the heart of Pharaoh experienced a kind of softening when he said, "But you shall not proceed far; you shall go a three days' journey and leave your wives behind," and whatever else he spoke when yielding before the marvelous works makes it clear that these signs had some effect even on him, though they did not entirely accomplish their object. Yet not even this would have happened if the idea held by most people about the words, "I will harden Pharaoh's heart," rightly represented what was wrought by him, that is, by God. ON FIRST PRINCIPLES 3.1.11.[2]

10:12 Stretch Out Your Hand for the Locusts

ON THE NATURE OF LOCUSTS. AMBROSE: Divine grace has penetrated even into the life of a locust. When a locust swarms over and takes possession of some extent of land, no harm at first is done to the land. Nothing is devoured by these unfriendly invaders except when a sign from heaven has been received. A passage in Exodus provides an example of this. There the locust as minister of divine vengeance inflicts punishment for an offense against heaven. SIX DAYS OF CREATION 5.23.82.[3]

10:17 Entreat the Lord Your God

See ORIGEN ON EXODUS 8:8.

---

[1]PL 83:294. [2]OFP 175-76. [3]FC 42:221.

10:21-29 NINTH PLAGUE: THE DARKNESS

[21]Then the LORD said to Moses, "Stretch out your hand toward heaven that there may be darkness over the land of Egypt, a darkness to be felt." [22]So Moses stretched out his hand toward heaven, and there was thick darkness in all the land of Egypt three days. . . . [28]Then Pharaoh said to him, "Get away from me; take heed to yourself; never see my face again; for in the day you see my face you shall die." [29]Moses said, "As you say! I will not see your face again."

OVERVIEW: Darkness is the blindness of minds or the obscurity of the working of providence. The Egyptians were too bold and fell into the darkness of ignorance (ISIDORE OF SEVILLE).

10:22 Thick Darkness Throughout Egypt

THE DIVINE MYSTERY. ISIDORE OF SEVILLE: In the ninth plague, darkness fell. Either it means the blindness of their minds or that they should realize that the workings of the divine economy and of providence are most obscure. For God made darkness his hiding place.[1] But they desired boldly and rashly to investigate it and, drawing one conclusion after another, fell into the dense and palpable darkness of ignorance. QUESTIONS ON THE OLD TESTAMENT, EXODUS 14.15.[2]

---

[1]Ps 18:11. [2]PL 83:294.

11:1-10 TENTH PLAGUE: THE DEATH OF THE FIRSTBORN

[1]The LORD said to Moses, "Yet one plague more I will bring upon Pharaoh and upon Egypt; afterwards he will let you go hence; when he lets you go, he will drive you away completely. [2]Speak now in the hearing of the people, that they ask, every man of his neighbor and every woman of her neighbor, jewelry of silver and of gold." [3]And the LORD gave the people favor in the sight of the Egyptians. Moreover, the man Moses was very great in the land of Egypt, in the sight of Pharaoh's servants and in the sight of the people.

[4]And Moses said, "Thus says the LORD: About midnight I will go forth in the midst of Egypt; [5]and all the first-born in the land of Egypt shall die, from the first-born of Pharaoh who sits upon his throne, even to the first-born of the maidservant who is behind the mill; and all the first-born of the cattle." . . .

[10]Moses and Aaron did all these wonders before Pharaoh; and the LORD hardened Pharaoh's heart, and he did not let the people of Israel go out of his land.

OVERVIEW: Christians should make good use of the spoils of Egypt (GREGORY OF NAZIANZUS). Moses was not as great as Abraham and Isaac; he still had some of the bonds of mortality about him. Jesus is the last one whom Scripture calls great (ORIGEN). Midnight is the time of the antichrist (METHODIUS). Great events take place at midnight (CASSIODORUS). The firstborn of the Egyptians are the source of idolatry, and the truth of Christ puts an end to them (ISIDORE OF SEVILLE).

11:2 Silver and Gold Jewelry

BE AN HONEST ROBBER. GREGORY OF NAZI-ANZUS: What say you? Thus it has pleased him that you should come forth out of Egypt, the iron furnace; that you should leave behind the idolatry of that country and be led by Moses and his lawgiving and martial rule. I give you a piece of advice which is not my own, or rather which is very much my own, if you consider the matter spiritually. Borrow from the Egyptians vessels of gold and silver. With these take your journey. Supply yourself for the road with the goods of strangers, or rather with your own. There is money owing to you, the wages of your bondage and of your brick making. Be clever on your side too in asking retribution. Be an honest robber. You did suffer wrong there while you were fighting with the clay (that is, this troublesome and filthy body) and were building cities foreign and unsafe, whose memorial perishes with a cry. What then? Do you come out for nothing and without wages? But why will you leave to the Egyptians and to the powers of your adversaries that which they have gained by wickedness and will spend with yet greater wickedness? It does not belong to them. They have ravished it and have sacrilegiously taken it as plunder from him who says, "The silver is mine and the gold is mine, and I give it to whom I will."[1] Yesterday it was theirs, for it was permitted to be so. Today the master takes it and gives it to you that you may make a good and saving use of it. Let us make to ourselves friends of the mammon of unrighteousness, that when we fail, they may receive us in the time of judgment. ORATION 45.20.[2]

11:3 Moses Was Very Great

MOSES NOT AS GREAT AS ABRAHAM AND ISAAC. ORIGEN: When Moses had come to the place which God shows him, he is not permitted to ascend, but first God says to him, "Loose the tie of the shoes from your feet."[3] None of these things are said to Abraham and Isaac, but they ascend and do not put aside their shoes. The reason for this is perhaps that although Moses was "great," he was nevertheless coming from Egypt, and some fetters of mortality were bound to his feet. Abraham and Isaac, however, have none of these, but "they come to the place."[4] HOMILIES ON GENESIS 8.7.[5]

WHO IS CALLED GREAT. ORIGEN: About Isaac it is said that "he grew strong until he became great, exceedingly great."[6] Moses was called "great," and John the Baptist was called "great,"[7]

and now Jesus is called "great,"[8] and after this no one is any longer called "great." For before he who is truly "great" had come, in comparison with the rest of men, the saints whom we mentioned earlier were called "great." HOMILIES ON LEVITICUS 12.2.5.[9]

11:4 About Midnight I Will Go Forth

THE TIME OF THE ANTICHRIST. METHODIUS: Midnight stands for the reign of the antichrist, when the destroying angel will pass over the houses. BANQUET OF THE TEN VIRGINS 6.4.[10]

WHAT HAPPENED AT MIDNIGHT. CASSIODORUS: The words "I rose at midnight"[11] are not without value. They knew that at that hour the firstborn of the Egyptians were smitten, that at that time the bonds of Peter, Paul and Silas who lay in prison were loosed,[12] that the bridegroom would also come at midnight.[13] EXPOSITION OF THE PSALMS 118.62.[14]

11:5 All the Firstborn in Egypt Shall Die

TYRANNY AND ERROR ARE DESTROYED. ISIDORE OF SEVILLE: Finally the firstborn of the Egyptians are destroyed. They are the principalities and powers and the rulers of this world of darkness. Or they are the originators and inventors of the false religions that existed in this world. The truth of Christ put an end to these religions and wiped them out, along with their inventors. QUESTIONS ON THE OLD TESTAMENT, EXODUS 14.16.[15]

---

[1]Hag 2:8. [2]NPNF 2 7:430. [3]Ex 3:5. [4]Gen 22:9. [5]FC 71:142. [6]Gen 26:13. [7]Lk 1:15. [8]Lk 1:32. [9]FC 83:221. [10]ACW 27:94. [11]Ps 119:62. [12]Acts 12:6. [13]Mt 25:6. [14]ACW 53:201*. [15]PL 83:294.

12:1-20 THE PASSOVER RITUAL PRESCRIBED

¹*The* Lord *said to Moses and Aaron in the land of Egypt,* ²*"This month shall be for you the beginning of months; it shall be the first month of the year for you.* ³*Tell all the congregation of Israel that on the tenth day of this month they shall take every man a lamb according to their fathers' houses, a lamb for a household;* ⁴*and if the household is too small for a lamb, then a man and his neighbor next to his house shall take according to the number of persons; according to what each can eat you shall make your count for the lamb.* ⁵*Your lamb shall be without blemish, a male a year old; you shall take it from the sheep or from the goats;* ⁶*and you shall keep it until the fourteenth day of this month, when the whole assembly of the congregation of Israel shall kill their lambs in the evening.*ᵒ ⁷*Then they shall take some of the blood, and put it on the two door-posts and the lintel of the houses in which they eat them.* ⁸*They shall eat the flesh that night, roasted; with unleavened bread and bitter herbs they shall eat it.* ⁹*Do not eat any of it raw or boiled with water, but roasted, its head with its legs and its inner parts.* ¹⁰*And you shall let none of it remain until the morning, anything that remains until the morning you shall burn.* ¹¹*In this manner you shall eat it: your loins girded, your sandals on your feet, and your staff in your hand; and you shall eat it in haste. It is the* Lord's *passover.* ¹²*For I will pass through the land of Egypt that night, and I will smite all the first-born in the land of Egypt, both man and beast; and on all the gods of Egypt I will execute judgments: I am the* Lord. ¹³*The blood shall be a sign for you, upon the houses where you are; and when I see the blood, I will pass over you, and no plague shall fall upon you to destroy you, when I smite the land of Egypt.*

¹⁴*"This day shall be for you a memorial day, and you shall keep it as a feast to the* Lord; *throughout your generations you shall observe it as an ordinance for ever."*

o *Heb* between the two evenings

OVERVIEW: Christians pondered virtually every detail of the Passover ritual. Exodus 12 was one of the chapters of the Old Testament upon which the Fathers meditated most profoundly. By ancient tradition, Exodus 12 was read at the paschal service, the primitive Easter, on the night that led into Easter Sunday. The result was a rich interpretation of this whole chapter.

Spring, the time of Passover, was also the time of creation and of the Lord's passion (AMBROSE). Spring is the time when winter ends and flowers bloom. Spring is a season of joy and of resurrection (PSEUDO-MACARIUS). Christians celebrate Easter between March 22 and April 21,[1] but al-

ways on Sunday in the first month of the year by Hebrew reckoning (MARTIN OF BRAGA).

The lamb was chosen on the fifth day before it was slaughtered (as the Romans counted),[2] and on the fifth day before Passover Jesus was teaching in the temple (BEDE).[3] The lamb was for the just; the goat was for penitent sinners (JEROME, AUGUSTINE).

Christ died on the cross in the evening, the time when the lambs were being slaughtered

---

[1]In current practice, between March 22 and April 25. [2]Romans counted both the beginning and ending day; thus Christ's resurrection "on the third day." [3]Jn 12:1, 12.

(Cyprian). The evening represents the end of the ages (Jerome). The Jewish rites are clear types of the Christian mystery (Augustine). The fourteenth day of the month is the day of the full moon; Christ is offered in perfect light (Jerome).

Moses and Ezekiel gave signs, but the sign for Christians is the blood of the lamb (Basil). If animal blood had great power, how much more power does Christ's blood have? (Chrysostom). The lamb is a type of the sheep led to slaughter that Isaiah prophesied (Augustine). Christ the lamb, by his blood, frees us from the slavery of death (Martin of Braga). The lamb was eaten in the evening, so Christ suffered in the evening of the world.

Christ is the bread of life, the living bread, prefigured in the unleavened bread of the Passover.

Bitter herbs are the medicine that brings us healing and health. Bitter herbs signify repentance (Origen). The words of Christ's precepts can be harsh and bitter (Maximus of Turin). Raw food is savage; boiled food is watery and limp; hence the lamb is eaten roasted (Origen). The head of the lamb prefigures Christ's divinity, the feet his humanity (Cyril of Jerusalem). Or, the head, the shanks and the inner organs are three ways to understand Scripture (Jerome). Ezekiel, as well as Moses, commanded the people to eat only fresh food (Origen).

One whose loins are girt is ready to act, ready to carry out God's command (Cyril of Alexandria). Sandals provide protection against injury from animals and serpents. To eat in haste is to give proof of one's determination (Ambrose).

The word *pascha* ("Passover") is Hebrew, although some interpreters associate it with the Greek word *paschein* ("to suffer"); the error is useful (Augustine). Passover has a double sense: the Lord passed over the houses of the Hebrews, and the Hebrews passed over the Red Sea from slavery into freedom (Bede). The temples of Egypt were destroyed, and error took flight (Isidore of Seville). The offering

of Christ, prefigured in the lamb, effected the forgiveness of original sin (Caesarius of Arles). Jesus Christ, the true Light, has revealed the meaning of these signs to us (Athanasius).

12:2 *The Beginning of Months*

Creation Took Place in Spring. Ambrose: In like manner also we can understand this statement: "This month shall be to you the beginning of months." This statement is to be interpreted in reference to time. There is reference to the pasch of the Lord, which is celebrated at the beginning of spring. Therefore he created heaven and earth at the time when the months began, from which time it is fitting that the world took its rise. Then there was the mild temperature of spring, a season suitable for all things. Six Days of Creation 1.4.13.[4]

The Month of Flowers. Pseudo-Macarius: After having inflicted the Egyptians with many plagues, he led them out of Egypt in the month of flowers, when the most pleasant spring appears and the sadness of winter passes away. Homily 47.3.[5]

The Time of the Resurrection. Pseudo-Macarius: This, I say, is the first month of the year. This brings joy to every creature. It clothes the naked trees. It opens the earth. This produces joy in all animals. It brings mirth to all. This is for Christians *Xanthicus*,[6] the first month, the time of the resurrection in which their bodies will be glorified by means of the light which even now is in them hidden. This is the power of the Spirit who will then be their clothing, food, drink, exultation, gladness, peace, adornment and eternal life. Homily 5.9.[7]

---

[4]FC 42:12. [5]*PMFSH* 233. [6]The Greek name for the month of April. [7]*PMFSH* 73.

THE CREATION OF THE WORLD AND THE DATE OF EASTER. MARTIN OF BRAGA: Consequently our elders decided that one full month must be observed for the birthday of the world and that Easter should be observed in whatever part of it both the day and the moon coincided. This is not without scriptural authority, for Moses said, "This month shall stand at the head of your calendar, the first month of the year." With these words he consecrated a whole month for the day of the world's birth. Thus our elders, who had found that March 22 was the birthday of the world, defined April 21 as a limit in determining the first month. So it will be permitted to celebrate Easter neither before March 22 nor after April 21. But when during this month both the moon and the day coincide, that is, the fourteenth day of the moon and Sunday, then Easter is to be celebrated. Now again, since the fourteenth day of the moon frequently does not fall on Sunday, they preferred to have the moon extended for seven days, provided they observed Sunday in the joy of the resurrection. So when the day falls thus, we always postpone Easter as far as the twenty-first day of the moon for the sake of Sunday, so that Easter is celebrated neither before March 22 nor after April 21. In this way it is found that the month and the day and the moon are retained in the observance of Easter. ON THE PASCHA 7.[8]

12:3, 5 A Lamb from the Sheep or Goats

FIVE DAYS BEFORE THE PASSOVER. BEDE: It was commanded that the paschal lamb, by whose immolation the people of Israel were freed from slavery in Egypt, should be selected five days before the [feast of] Passover, that is, on the tenth [day of the lunar] month, and immolated on the fourteenth [day of the lunar] month at sundown. This signified the one who was going to redeem us by his blood, since five days before the [feast of] Passover (that is, today), accompanied by the great joy and praise of people going ahead and following, he came

into God's temple, and he was there teaching daily. At last, after five days, having observed up to that point the sacraments of the old Passover, he brought them to perfect fulfillment, and he handed over the new sacraments to his disciples to be observed henceforth.[9] [Then], having gone out to the Mt. of Olives, he was seized by the Jews[10] and crucified [the next] morning.[11] He redeemed us from the sway of the devil on that very day when the ancient people of the Hebrews cast aside the yoke of slavery under the Egyptians by the immolation of the lamb. HOMILIES ON THE GOSPELS 2.3.[12]

THE GOAT IS FOR PENITENT SINNERS. JEROME: "The lamb," the Lord says, "must be without blemish. You may take it from either the sheep or the goats." In another place of Holy Writ, it is prescribed that if anyone is unable to keep the Passover in the first month, he is to do so in the second.[13] According to the regulation above, anyone who is unable to sacrifice a lamb may substitute a kid. In the house of the church, moreover, Christ is offered in a twofold manner: if we are just, we eat of the flesh of the lamb; if we are sinners and do penance, for us a goat is slain. This does not mean that Christ is from the goats that stand, as he has taught, on his left hand, but that Christ becomes a lamb or a goat in conformity with individual and personal merit. HOMILY 91.[14]

THE RIGHTEOUS AND THE WICKED. AUGUSTINE: The bridegroom, who was to call good and bad to his marriage,[15] was pleased to assimilate himself to his guests, in being born of good and bad. He thus confirms as typical of himself the symbol of the Passover, in which it was commanded that the lamb to be eaten should be taken from the sheep or from the goats—that is, from the righteous or the wicked. Preserving

---

[8]FC 62:107-8*. See Overview on the dating of Easter. [9]Lk 22:14-20. [10]Lk 22:39-54. [11]Mk 15:25. [12]HOG 2:23-24. [13]Num 9:10-11. [14]FC 57:237. [15]Mt 22:10.

throughout the indication of both divinity and humanity, as man he consented to have both bad and good as his parents, while as God he chose the miraculous birth from a virgin. AGAINST FAUSTUS, A MANICHAEAN 22.64.[16]

12:6 The Sacrifice of the Lambs

THE FULL MOON IS PERFECT LIGHT. JEROME: We read in Exodus that on the fourteenth day a lamb is sacrificed; on the fourteenth day when the moon is a full moon, when its light is at its brightest. You see Christ is not immolated except in perfect and full light. HOMILIES ON THE PSALMS 5.[17]

EVENING AND MORNING. CYPRIAN: It was fitting for Christ to offer the sacrifice in evening of the day in order that the very hour might show the setting and evening of the world as it is written in Exodus: "And the whole multitude of the children of Israel shall slaughter it in the evening." And again in the Psalms: "The lifting up of my hands as evening sacrifice."[18] But we celebrate the resurrection of the Lord in the morning. LETTER 63.16.[19]

THE MEANING OF THE EVENING. JEROME: Why is this lamb offered up in the evening and not during the day? The reason is plain enough, for our Lord and Savior suffered his passion at the close of the ages. So John says in his letter: "Dear children, it is the last hour."[20] Since, moreover, it is the last hour, it is the beginning of night, for day has come to an end. It must be understood, however, that as long as we are in this world, as long as we abide in Egypt, we are not in a clear light but in a dark mist. Although the church shines as the moon in the nighttime, nevertheless we cannot yet dwell in the full splendor of the true sun. HOMILY 91.[21]

JEWISH RITES MANIFEST CHRIST. AUGUSTINE: But now then, can there be anybody who is not curious to know what the meaning can be of the fact that the Jews answered from Scripture the inquiry of the magi about where the Christ would be born and yet did not go with them to worship him themselves? Don't we see the same thing even now, when by the very rites and sacraments to which they are subjected for their hardness of heart, nothing else is indicated but the very Christ in whom they refuse to believe? Even when they kill the sheep and eat the Passover, aren't they demonstrating to the Gentiles the very Christ whom they themselves don't worship along with them?

And isn't it the same sort of thing, when people have their doubts about the prophetic testimonies in which Christ was foretold and wonder if they haven't perhaps been compiled by Christians after the event, not before? We appeal to the codices in the possession of the Jews to set the minds of doubters at rest. Don't the Jews on such occasions too show the Gentiles the Christ whom they decline to worship with the Gentiles? SERMON 202.3.[22]

12:7 Blood on the Two Doorposts

THE MEANING OF THE SIGN. BASIL THE GREAT: Moses caused the doorposts of the Israelites to be signed with the blood of a lamb; but you have given us a sign, the blood itself of a Lamb without blemish, slain for the sin of the world. Ezekiel says that a sign was given on the foreheads of the persons.[23] EXEGETIC HOMILIES 20.3.[24]

BLOOD: TYPE AND REALITY. CHRYSOSTOM: Now if its type had so much power, both in the temple of the Hebrews and in the midst of the Egyptians, when sprinkled on the doorposts, how much more power does the reality have. In its types this blood sanctified the golden altar. Without it, the High Priest did not dare to enter

---

[16]NPNF 1 4:296. [17]FC 48:38. [18]Ps 141:2. [19]FC 51:213. [20]1 Jn 2:18. [21]FC 57:237. [22]WSA 3 6:92-93. [23]Ezek 9:4. [24]FC 46:337-38.

the sanctuary. This blood has ordained priests. In its types it has washed away sins. And if it had such great power in its types, if death shuddered so much at the figure, how would it not even more so be in terror of the reality itself, pray tell? Homilies on the Gospel of John 46.[25]

Marked with the Blood of the Lamb. Augustine: For why would the Lord instruct them to kill a sheep on this very feast day except that it was he about whom it was prophesied: "As a sheep is led to the slaughter."[26] The doorposts of the Jews were marked with the blood of a slaughtered animal. Our foreheads are marked with the blood of Christ. And that sign, because it was a sign, was said to keep the destroyer away from the houses marked with the sign. The sign of Christ drives the destroyer away from us insofar as our heart receives the Savior. Tractate on the Gospel of John 50.3.[27]

Marked with the Blood of Christ. Martin of Braga: The sacrifice of this lamb was so great that even the shadow of its truth was sufficient for salvation in freeing the Jews from the slavery of Pharaoh, as though already the liberation of the creature from the slavery of corruption was prefigured, the image of Christ's coming passion worked for the advent of salvation. Therefore it was declared by God that in the first month of the year on the fourteenth day of the moon, a year-old lamb without blemish should be sacrificed. With its blood they were to make signs upon the doorposts of their houses, lest they be frightened by the angel of destruction. And on that very night when the lamb was eaten in their homes, which was the celebration of the Passover, they should receive liberation through the figure of slavery. It is not difficult to interpret the spotless lamb of Christ[28] and his sacrifice made to free the slavery of our death. For, marked by the sign of his cross as by the sprinkling of blood, we shall

be saved from the angels of destruction even to the consummation of the world. On the Pascha 2.[29]

12:8 Roasted Meat, Unleavened Bread, Bitter Herbs

Evening and Morning, Weeping and Gladness. Origen: Christians eat the flesh of the lamb every day, that is, they consume daily the flesh of the Word. "For Christ our pasch is sacrificed."[30] And because the law of the pasch is such that it is eaten in the evening, for this reason the Lord suffered in the evening of the world, that you may always eat of the flesh of the Word, because you are always in the evening until the morning comes. And if in this evening you shall be anxious and "in weeping and fasting"[31] and shall lead your life in every labor of justice, you shall be able to say, "In the evening weeping shall have place and in the morning gladness."[32] For you shall rejoice in the morning, that is, in the world to come, if in this world you have gathered "the fruit of justice"[33] in weeping and labor. Homilies on Genesis 10.3.[34]

The Meaning of Bread. Origen: And we must eat the meat roasted with fire with unleavened bread. For the Word of God is not only flesh. He says, indeed, "I am the bread of life,"[35] and "This is the bread which comes down from heaven that one may eat of it and not die. I am the living bread which came down from heaven. If anyone eat of this bread he shall live forever."[36]

We must not, however, fail to remark that all food is loosely said to be bread, as it is written in the case of Moses in Deuteronomy: "He did not eat bread for forty days, and he did not drink water,"[37] instead of saying he partook of neither dry nor wet nourishment.

Now I have noted this because it is also said

---

[25]FC 33:469-70. [26]Is 53:7. [27]FC 88:261. [28]1 Cor 5:7. [29]FC 62:104. [30]1 Cor 5:7. [31]Job 2:12. [32]Ps 30:5. [33]Phil 1:11; Jas 3:18. [34]FC 71:163. [35]Jn 6:48. [36]Jn 6:50-51. [37]Ex 34:28; Deut 9:9.

in the Gospel according to John, "And also the bread which I shall give for the life of the world is my flesh."[38] COMMENTARY ON THE GOSPEL OF JOHN 10.99-101.[39]

BITTER MEDICINE CURES US. ORIGEN: Then too the unleavened bread is commanded to be eaten with bitter herbs; nor is it possible to attain the promised land unless we pass through bitterness. For just as physicians put bitter substances in medicines with a view to the health and healing of the infirm, so also the Physician of our souls with a view to our salvation has wished us to suffer the bitterness of this life in various temptations. [He knows] that the end of this bitterness gains the sweetness of salvation for our soul, just as, on the contrary, the end of the sweetness found in corporeal pleasure, as the example of that rich man teaches,[40] brings a bitter end: torments in hell. HOMILIES ON NUMBERS 27.10.[41]

BITTER HERBS ARE GRIEF OR TRIALS. ORIGEN: But we eat the flesh of the lamb and the unleavened bread with bitter herbs either by being grieved with a godly grief because of repentance for our sins, a grief which produces in us a repentance unto salvation which brings no regret,[42] or by seeking and being nurtured from the visions of the truth which we discover because of our trials. COMMENTARY ON THE GOSPEL OF JOHN 10.102.[43]

THE BITTER WORDS OF CHRIST. MAXIMUS OF TURIN: Yet they were also completely ignorant of the commands of Moses himself, who ordered them specially to eat this bitterness when he established the paschal sacraments for them to observe and said, "You will eat it with bitterness, for it is the pasch of the Lord." For he did not order, as they think, the consuming of the very bitter juices of insignificant herbs with the roasted flesh of a lamb. Rather, he commanded the fruitful devouring of the bitter words of Christ's precepts with the sacrament of the

Lord's passion. For do not the words of the Lord seem to be bitter when he says: "If you wish to be perfect, leave all that you have and come, follow me?"[44] And when he says that one is not to possess two tunics or a wallet or sandals,[45] that bitterness of such words is a medicine for souls. SERMON 25.2.[46]

12:9 Lamb Not Raw or Boiled

RAW SCRIPTURE IS THE LITERAL SENSE. ORIGEN: One must not therefore eat the flesh of the lamb raw, as the slaves of the letter do in the manner of animals which are irrational and quite savage. In relation to men who are truly rational through their desire to understand the spiritual aspects of the world, the former [slaves of the letter] share the company of wild beasts.

We must strive, however, in transforming the rawness of Scripture into boiled food, not to transform what has been written into what is flaccid, watery and limp. This is what they do who "have itching ears and" turn them away "from the truth"[47] and transform the anagogical meanings so far as they are concerned to the carelessness and wateriness of their manner of life. COMMENTARY ON THE GOSPEL OF JOHN 10.103-4.[48]

THE LAMB IS CHRIST. CYRIL OF JERUSALEM: Children of purity and disciples of chastity, let us celebrate the praises of the virgin-born God with lips all pure. Being counted worthy to partake of the flesh of the spiritual Lamb, let us take the head with the feet, understanding the head as the divinity and the feet as the humanity. CATECHETICAL LECTURE 12.1.[49]

THE LAMB IS THE SCRIPTURES. JEROME: "You shall eat it with its head and shanks and inner organs." To me, the head seems to be that of the Lamb, written of in St. John's Gospel: "In the

---

[38]Jn 6:51. [39]FC 80:276-77. [40]Lk 16:19-31. [41]OEM 259-60. [42]2 Cor 7:9-10. [43]FC 80:277. [44]Mt 19:21. [45]Mt 10:10. [46]ACW 50:62. [47]2 Tim 4:3-4. [48]FC 80:277. [49]FC 61:227.

beginning was the Word, and the Word was with God; and the Word was God; he was in the beginning with God."[50] The shanks represent the human nature that he deigned to assume for our salvation. Another interpretation, however, is also possible. The head may be taken to signify spiritual understanding; the shanks, historical narrative; the inner organs are whatever lies hidden within the letter, whatever is not perceived on the surface but is brought to light by exegetes only after they have well considered it in painstaking investigation. HOMILY 91.[51]

12:10 Let None Remain Until Morning

WE ARE TO EAT FRESH FOOD. ORIGEN: Consequently let us compare the divine Scripture with itself and follow the path of the solution that it would open to us. For we find in the sacrifice of the Passover that it is ordered to be offered "in the evening." In like manner, the command is given that "nothing will remain of the flesh until morning." It is not insignificant that the divine word wants us to eat not yesterday's meat, but always fresh and new, particularly those who offer to God the Passover sacrifice or "the sacrifice of praise."[52] It commands them to eat this new and fresh meat of the same day. It prohibits yesterday's meat. I remembered the prophet Ezekiel said something similar when the Lord had commanded him to bake cakes for them in "human dung."[53] For he answered the Lord and said, "O Lord, never was my soul contaminated, and dead or unclean things did not enter my mouth. Even yesterday's meat never entered my mouth."[54] In this case I was often asking myself what this exultation of the prophet was that as something great he brought mean before the Lord and said, "I never ate yesterday's meat." But as I see from this place, taught and instructed by these mysteries, this prophet spoke to the Lord saying, I am not a priest so cast down and ignoble that "I eat yesterday's meat," that is, old meat. HOMILIES ON LEVITICUS 5.8.2.[55]

12:11 Preparing to Leave Egypt

CHRISTIANS MUST BE READY TO ACT. CYRIL OF ALEXANDRIA: And let us know that the law also of the most wise Moses is found to have commanded something of this kind to the Israelites. For a lamb was sacrificed on the fourteenth day of the first month, as a type of Christ. For our Passover, Christ is sacrificed, according to the testimony of most sacred Paul. The hierophant Moses, then, or rather God by his means, commanded them, when eating its flesh, saying, "Let your loins be girt, and your shoes on your feet, and your staves in your hands." For I affirm that it is the duty of those who are partakers of Christ to beware of a barren indolence. Yet it is a further duty not to have as it were their loins ungirt and loose but to be ready cheerfully to undertake whatever labors become the saints; and to hasten besides with alacrity wherever the law of God leads them. And for this reason he very appropriately made them wear the garb of travelers [at the Passover]. HOMILIES ON THE GOSPEL OF LUKE 92.[56]

SANDALS PROVIDE PROTECTION. AMBROSE: [The father of the prodigal son] orders the shoes to be brought out, for he who is about to celebrate the Lord's Passover, about to feast on the Lamb, ought to have his feet protected against all attacks of spiritual wild beasts and the bite of the serpent. CONCERNING REPENTANCE 2.3.18.[57]

THE JUST PERSON ACTS QUICKLY. AMBROSE: The just man gives an added force to his vow by acting quickly. Accordingly our fathers ate the paschal lamb in haste, girding up their reins, and with shoes on their feet, and standing ready, equipped for departure. The pasch is the passage of the Lord from passion to the exercise of virtue. It is called the pasch of the Lord because

---

[50]Jn 1:1-2. [51]FC 57:239. [52]Ps 50:23. [53]Ezek 4:12. [54]Ezek 4:14. [55]FC 83:104-5*. [56]CGSL 371. [57]NPNF 2 10:347.

the truth of the passion of the Lord was then indicated in the type of the lamb, and its benefits are now being observed. CAIN AND ABEL 1.8.31.[58]

PASCHA IS HEBREW, NOT GREEK. AUGUSTINE: [The word] *pascha* is not, as some think, a Greek word, but a Hebrew one;[59] yet most conveniently there occurs in this name a certain congruity between the two languages. Because in Greek [the word for] "to suffer" is *paschein*. For this reason "pascha" has been thought of as a passion, as though this name has been derived from [a Greek word for] "suffering." But in its own language, that is, in Hebrew, "pascha" means "a passing over." For this reason the people of God celebrated the pascha for the first time when, fleeing from Egypt, they "passed over" the Red Sea. So now that prophetic figure has been fulfilled in truth when Christ is led as a sheep to the slaughter.[60] By his blood, after our doorposts have been smeared [with it], that is, by the sign of his cross, after our foreheads have been marked [with it], we are freed from the ruin of this world as though from the captivity or destruction in Egypt. And we effect a most salutary passing over when we pass over from the devil to Christ and from this tottering world to his most solidly established kingdom. And therefore we pass over to God who endures so that we may not pass over with the passing world. TRACTATE ON THE GOSPEL OF JOHN 55.1.[61]

THE MEANING OF PASSOVER. BEDE: Passover means "passing over." It derives its ancient name from the Lord's passing over on this [day] through Egypt, striking the firstborn of the Egyptians and freeing the children of Israel, and from the children of Israel's passing over on that night from their slavery in Egypt in order that they might come to the land which had once been promised to their heirs as a land of peace. Mystically it signifies that on this [day] our Lord would pass over from this world to his

Father. Following his example, the faithful, having cast off temporal desires and having cast off their slavery to vices by their continual practice of the virtues, should pass over to their promised heavenly fatherland. HOMILIES ON THE GOSPELS 2.5.[62]

12:12 Judgment on the Gods of Egypt

TEMPLES ARE DESTROYED. ISIDORE OF SEVILLE: In what follows, "on their gods I shall pass judgment," the Hebrews affirm that on the night on which the people departed, all the temples in Egypt were destroyed, either by an earthquake or by a bolt of lightning. But we say, spiritually, that when we depart from Egypt, the idols of error take flight and the whole culture of perverse dogmas is crushed. QUESTIONS ON THE OLD TESTAMENT, EXODUS 14.17.[63]

12:13 I Will Pass Over You

THE DEVIL LOST WHAT HE HELD. CAESARIUS OF ARLES: Original sin could not have easily been forgiven, if a victim had not been offered for it, if that sacred blood of propitiation had not been shed. Even then the words in Exodus were not vainly said of our Lord: "I shall see the blood and shall protect you." That figure of the lamb represented this passion of Christ our Lord. Blood is given for blood, death for death, a victim for sin, and thus the devil lost what he held. SERMON 11.5.[64]

12:14 A Feast to the Lord

HOW THE PEOPLE LOOKED. ATHANASIUS: As also the Word of God, when desirous [to establish the paschal feast] said to his disciples,

---

[58]FC 42:388-89. [59]Augustine is right. The Hebrew *pesach*, Aramaic *pascha*, means "Passover." Jewish exegetes applied it both to God's passing over the Israelites' houses and to the Israelites' passing over the Red Sea. Greek-speaking Christians readily connected the Passover with Christ's suffering. [60]Is 53:7. [61]FC 90:3-4. [62]HOG 2:43-44. [63]PL 83:294. [64]FC 31:66.

"With desire I have desired to eat this Passover with you."[65] Now that is a wonderful account, for a man might have seen them at that time girded as for a procession or a dance and going out with staves and sandals and unleavened bread. These things, which took place before in shadows, were typical anticipatory symbols. But now the truth has drawn near to us, "the image of the invisible God,"[66] our Lord Jesus Christ, the true Light. Instead of a staff, he is our scepter; instead of unleavened bread, he is the bread which came down from heaven; who instead of sandals has furnished us with the preparation of the gospel.[67] It is he who, to speak briefly, by all these means has guided us to his Father. And if enemies afflict us and persecute us, he again, instead of Moses, will encourage us with better words, saying, "Be of good cheer; I have overcome the wicked one."[68] And if after we have passed over the Red Sea, heat should again vex us or some bitterness of the waters befall us, even then again the Lord will appear to us, imparting to us of his sweetness and his life-giving fountain, saying, "If any man thirst, let him come to me and drink."[69] FESTAL LETTERS 14.3.[70]

---

[65]Lk 22:15. [66]Col 1:15. [67]Eph 6:15. [68]Jn 16:33. [69]Jn 7:37. [70]NPNF 2 4:542-43.

12:21-28 PROMULGATION OF THE PASSOVER

[21]*Then Moses called all the elders of Israel, and said to them, "Select lambs for yourselves according to your families, and kill the passover lamb.* [22]*Take a bunch of hyssop and dip it in the blood which is in the basin, and touch the lintel and the two doorposts with the blood which is in the basin; and none of you shall go out of the door of his house until the morning.* [23]*For the LORD will pass through to slay the Egyptians; and when he sees the blood on the lintel and on the two doorposts, the LORD will pass over the door, and will not allow the destroyer to enter your houses to slay you.* [24]*You shall observe this rite as an ordinance for you and for your sons for ever.* [25]*And when you come to the land which the LORD will give you, as he has promised, you shall keep this service."*

OVERVIEW: The blood of the lamb saved the people because it was the type of the Lord's blood (CHRYSOSTOM). The baptized are purified both according to the law and according to the gospel (AMBROSE). Hyssop is a mild and humble plant, but its roots are strong and penetrating (AUGUSTINE). The doorposts were anointed, even though they were not conscious (GREGORY OF NAZIANZUS). The cross protects us from the fate of the Egyptians (JEROME). The sign on the doorpost inspires fear in all Christ's enemies (MAXIMUS OF TURIN). The destroying angel of Exodus is Azazel, mentioned in Leviticus. The devil destroys those who obey him (ORIGEN). The cross is a shield and a trophy against the enemy (JOHN OF DAMASCUS).

12:21 Kill the Passover Lamb

THE BLOOD SAVES US. CHRYSOSTOM: What

then did Moses do? "Sacrifice an unblemished lamb," he said, "and smear your doors with its blood." What do you mean? Can the blood of an irrational animal save one who expresses reason? "Yes," he says. "Not because it is blood but because it prefigures the Master's blood." Although statues of the emperor have neither life nor perception, they can save the men endowed with perception and life who flee to them for refuge, not because they are bronze but because they are images of the emperor. So too that blood which lacked life and perception saved the men who had life, not because it was blood but because it was an anticipatory type of the Master's blood. BAPTISMAL INSTRUCTIONS 3.14.[1]

12:22 Hyssop and Blood

THE BAPTIZED ARE PURIFIED. AMBROSE: For he who is baptized is seen to be purified both according to the law and according to the gospel. According to the law, because Moses sprinkled the blood of the lamb with a bunch of hyssop. According to the gospel, because Christ's garments were white as snow, when in the gospel he showed forth the glory of his resurrection. ON THE MYSTERIES 7.34.[2]

HYSSOP IS MILD BUT PENETRATING. AUGUSTINE: They are to bear in mind that those who celebrated the Passover at the time through figures and shadows, when they were commanded to mark their doorpost with the blood of the lamb, marked them with hyssop. This is a mild and humble plant, but it has very strong and penetrating roots. So, "being rooted and grounded in love," we may be able "to comprehend with all the saints what is the breadth and length and height and depth,"[3] that is, the cross of the Lord. ON CHRISTIAN TEACHING 2.41.62.[4]

ANOINTING DOORPOSTS AND BAPTIZING CHILDREN. GREGORY OF NAZIANZUS: Be it so,

some will say, in the case of those who ask for baptism; what have you to say about those who are still children and conscious neither of the loss nor of the grace? Are we to baptize them too? Certainly, if any danger presses. For it is better that they should be unconsciously sanctified than that they should depart unsealed and uninitiated.

A proof of this is found in the circumcision on the eighth day, which was a sort of typical seal. It was conferred on children before they had use of reason. And so is the anointing of the doorposts, which preserved the firstborn, though applied to things which had no consciousness. ORATION 40. 28.[5]

12:23 The Lord Will Pass

THE CROSS PROTECTS US. JEROME: I cull these few flowers in passing from the fair field of the Holy Scriptures. They will suffice to warn you that you must shut the door of your breast and fortify your brow by often making the sign of the cross. Thus alone will the destroyer of Egypt find no place to attack you. Thus alone will the firstborn of your soul escape the fate of the firstborn of the Egyptians. Thus alone will you be able with the prophet to say, "My heart is fixed, O God, my heart is fixed; I will sing and give praise."[6] LETTER 130.9.[7]

THE SIGN MAKES THE DEVIL TREMBLE. MAXIMUS OF TURIN: [The Son of God's] cross is our victory, and his gibbet is our triumph. With joy let us take this sign on our shoulders, let us bear the banners of victory. Let us bear such an imperial banner, indeed, on our foreheads! When the devil sees this sign on our doorposts, he trembles. Those who are not afraid of gilded temples are afraid of the cross, and those who disdain regal scepters and the purple and the banquets of the Caesars stand in fear of the

---

[1]ACW 31:60-61. [2]NPNF 2 10:321. [3]Eph 3:17-18. [4]FC 2:115. [5]NPNF 2 7:370. [6]Ps 57:7-8. [7]NPNF 2 6:266.

loneliness and the fasts of the Christian. Sermon 45.2.[8]

Who Is the Destroyer? Origen: We must also inquire who that being was of whom it is said in Exodus that he wished to kill Moses because he was setting out for Egypt.[9] And afterwards, who is it that is called the "destroying angel"? And who also is he who in Leviticus is described as Apopompeus, that is, the Averter, of whom the Scripture speaks thus: "One lot for the Lord, and one lot for Apopompeus"?[10] On First Principles 3.2.1.[11]

The Identity of the Destroyer. Origen: And who else could be the destroyer in Exodus, which Moses wrote, except the one who is the cause of destruction to those who obey him and who do not resist and struggle against his wickedness? Against Celsus 6.43.[12]

The Cross Is Our Shield. John of Damascus: This [cross] we have been given as a sign on our forehead, just as Israel was given the circumcision. For by it we faithful are set apart from the infidels and recognized. It is a shield and armor and a trophy against the devil. It is a seal that the destroyer may not strike us, as Scripture says. Orthodox Faith 4.11.[13]

---

[8]ACW 50:249-50*. [9]Ex 4:24. [10]Lev 16:8; in Hebrew, Azazel. [11]OFP 211. [12]OCC 360. [13]FC 37:350.

12:29-30 DEATH OF THE FIRSTBORN

[29]At midnight the Lord smote all the first-born in the land of Egypt, from the first-born of Pharaoh who sat on his throne to the first-born of the captive who was in the dungeon, and all the first-born of the cattle. [30]And Pharaoh rose up in the night, he, and all his servants, and all the Egyptians; and there was a great cry in Egypt, for there was not a house where one was not dead.

Overview: Even the lowliest criminal in a dungeon was slain, if he was the firstborn. (Basil).

12:29 To the Firstborn of the Captive

Pit and Well Distinguished. Basil the Great: "He that has opened a pit and dug it."[1] We do not find the name of "pit" (lakkos) ever assigned in the divine Scriptures in the case of something good, nor a "well" of water (phrear) in the case of something bad. That into which Joseph was thrown by his brothers is a pit (lakkos).[2] And there is a slaughter "from the firstborn of Pharaoh unto the firstborn of the captive woman that was in the prison (lakkos)." Exegetic Homilies 11.8.[3]

---

[1]Ps 7:15; the Greek word for dungeon in Ex 12:29 is lakkos. [2]Gen 37:24. [3]FC 46:179.

12:31-36 PERMISSION TO DEPART

[35]*The people of Israel had also done as Moses told them, for they had asked of the Egyptians jewelry of silver and gold, and clothing;* [36]*and the LORD had given the people favor in the sight of the Egyptians, so that they let them have what they asked. Thus they despoiled the Egyptians.*

OVERVIEW: Just as the people of Israel despoiled the Egyptians, so Christians can make good use of pagan learning (AUGUSTINE).

12:36 They Despoiled the Egyptians

THE TEACHINGS OF THE PAGANS. AUGUSTINE: The Egyptians not only had idols and crushing burdens which the people of Israel detested and from which they fled. They also had vessels and ornaments of gold and silver, and clothing, which the Israelites leaving Egypt secretly claimed for themselves as if for a better use. Not on their own authority did they make this appropriation, but by the command of God. Meanwhile, the Egyptians themselves, without realizing it, were supplying the things which they were not using properly. In the same way, all the teachings of the pagans have counterfeit and superstitious notions and oppressive burdens of useless labor. Any one of us, leaving the association of pagans with Christ as our leader, ought to abominate and shun them. ON CHRISTIAN TEACHING 2.40.60.[1]

[1]FC 2:112-13.

12:37-42 DEPARTURE FROM EGYPT

[37]*And the people of Israel journeyed from Rameses to Succoth, about six hundred thousand men on foot, besides women and children.*

OVERVIEW: The growth of the people of Israel in Egypt is a sign of God's generosity (GREGORY OF NAZIANZUS). The people were in fact even more numerous than six hundred thousand (AUGUSTINE).

12:37 About Six Hundred Thousand Men

A SIGN OF GOD'S GENEROSITY. GREGORY OF NAZIANZUS: Joseph came into Egypt alone, and soon thereafter six hundred thousand depart from Egypt. What is more marvelous than this? What greater proof of the generosity of God, when from persons without means he wills to supply the means for public affairs? ORATION 42.5.[1]

WHO THE PEOPLE WERE. AUGUSTINE: From their single ancestor, in not much more than four hundred years, the Hebrew people became

[1]NPNF 2 7:387*.

so numerous that at the time of the exodus from Egypt there were, we are told, six hundred thousand men of military age. This number does not include the Idumeans, who were not reckoned with the people of Israel, although they were descended from Israel's brother Esau, who was a grandson of Abraham. Nor does it include those other descendants of Abraham who were not of the line of his wife Sarah. City of God 15.8.[2]

---

[2]FC 14:432.

12:43-51 PASSOVER REGULATIONS

[43]*And the* Lord *said to Moses and Aaron, "This is the ordinance of the passover: no foreigner shall eat of it;* [44]*but every slave that is bought for money may eat of it after you have circumcised him.* [45]*No sojourner or hired servant may eat of it.* [46]*In one house shall it be eaten; you shall not carry forth any of the flesh outside the house; and you shall not break a bone of it.* [47]*All the congregation of Israel shall keep it. . . ."*

OVERVIEW: The deceitful are strangers and may not eat the Passover (ATHANASIUS). The one house is the one church, and the Eucharist may be received only there. The church is indivisible and invisible (CYPRIAN). The Passover is eaten in one house, just as Noah had one ark. Only in the church is salvation possible (JEROME). The command in Exodus not to break a bone of the lamb was a prophecy, fulfilled in Christ (CHRYSOSTOM). The legs of the thieves were broken, but Christ's were not (AUGUSTINE).

12:43 No Foreigner Shall Eat It

SINNERS MAY NOT EAT THE PASSOVER. ATHANASIUS: But the deceitful, and he that is not pure of heart and possesses nothing that is pure (as Proverbs says, "To a deceitful man there is nothing good")[1] shall assuredly, being a stranger and of a different race from the saints, be accounted unworthy to eat the Passover, for "a foreigner shall not eat of it."[2] Thus Judas, when he thought he kept the Passover, because he plotted deceit against the Savior, was estranged from the city which is above and from the apostolic company. For the law commanded the Passover to be eaten with due observance. But he, while eating it, was sifted of the devil,[3] who had entered his soul. FESTAL LETTERS 6.11.[4]

12:46 Eaten in One House

THE ONE HOUSE IS THE CHURCH. CYPRIAN: God says, "In one house shall it be eaten; you shall not cast the flesh abroad out of the house." The flesh of Christ and the holy thing of the Lord cannot be cast out. The faithful have no home but the one church. This home, this house of unanimity, the Holy Spirit announces unmistakably in the Psalms: "God who makes men to dwell together of one mind as in a house."[5] THE UNITY OF THE CATHOLIC CHURCH 8.[6]

---

[1]Prov 13:13. [2]Ex 12:43. [3]Lk 22:31. [4]NPNF 2 4:522-23. [5]Ps 68:6. [6]LCC 5:129.

The Unity of the Church. Cyprian: The faith of the divine Scripture manifests that the church is not outside and that it cannot be rent in two or divided against itself, but that it holds the unity of an inseparable and invisible house. It is written concerning the rite of the Passover and of the lamb, which lamb signifies Christ: "It shall be eaten in one house; you shall not take any of its flesh outside the house." Letter 69.4.[7]

The One House and Ark. Jerome: All such efforts are only of use when they are made within the church's pale. We must celebrate the Passover in the one house. We must enter the ark with Noah.[8] We must take refuge from the fall of Jericho with the justified harlot, Rahab.[9] Letter 22.38.[10]

Prophecy and Fulfillment. Chrysostom: That well-known prophecy likewise was fulfilled: "Not a bone of him shall you break." For even if this was spoken with reference to the lamb among the Jews, the type preceded for the sake of truth and was, rather, fulfilled in this event. Moreover, that is why the Evangelist cited the prophet. Since he might not seem to be worthy of credence because he was repeatedly making reference to his own testimony, he summoned Moses to testify that this not only did not take place by accident but that it had been foretold in writing from of old. This is the meaning of that famous prophecy: "Not a bone of him shall be broken."[11] Homilies on the Gospel of John 85.[12]

A Prophecy of Christ. Augustine: Now next, that the legs of those two were broken, while his [Christ's] were not. He was already dead. Why this happened was stated in the Gospel itself.[13] It was fitting, you see, to demonstrate by this sign as well that the true point and purpose of the Jewish Passover, which contained this instruction, not to break the lamb's bones, was to be a prophetic preenactment of his death. Sermon 218.13.[14]

---

[7]FC 51:246. [8]1 Pet 3:20-21. [9]Jas 2:25. [10]NPNF 2 6:39. [11]Ex 12:46; Num 9:12. [12]FC 41:436. [13]Jn 19:33. [14]WSA 3 6:186.

13:1-16 CONSECRATION OF FIRSTBORN

[1]The Lord said to Moses, [2]"Consecrate to me all the first-born; whatever is the first to open the womb among the people of Israel, both of man and of beast, is mine."

[3]And Moses said to the people, "Remember this day, in which you came out from Egypt, out of the house of bondage, for by strength of hand the Lord brought you out from this place; no leavened bread shall be eaten. [4]This day you are to go forth, in the month of Abib. [5]And when the Lord brings you into the land of the Canaanites, the Hittites, the Amorites, the Hivites, and the Jebusites, which he swore to your fathers to give you, a land flowing with milk and honey, you shall keep this service in this month. . . .

[13]"Every firstling of an ass you shall redeem with a lamb, or if you will not redeem it you shall break its neck. Every first-born of man among your sons you shall redeem. [14]And when in time

to come your son asks you, 'What does this mean?' you shall say to him, 'By strength of hand the Lord *brought us out of Egypt, from the house of bondage. . . .'"*

Overview: Scripture speaks not only of persons but also of animals and things as consecrated or holy (Origen). Only the Son of God truly opened a closed womb (Tertullian). The birth of Jesus opened Mary's womb (Origen). When people cry out to God, God sends a new Moses to deliver them. Deliverance takes place in springtime (Pseudo-Macarius). The unclean ass is not sacrificed to God, but the clean sheep is (Ambrose).

13:2 Consecrate All the Firstborn

What Scripture Calls Holy. Origen: Therefore let us draw together from the divine Scriptures instances in which we find "holy"[1] used, and discover not only persons but also mute animals that are called "holy," and also find both "the vessels" of the ministry that are called "holy,"[2] and the garments which are said to be "holy,"[3] and even the places which were located in cities and suburbs and counted as priestly.[4] Indeed, among the brute animals it is commanded through the law that "the firstborn" of calves or cattle be sacrificed to the Lord, and it says, You will not do any work with them because they have been consecrated to the Lord. Homilies on Leviticus 11.1.2.[5]

The Text Applies Preeminently to Christ. Tertullian: For who is really holy but the Son of God? Who properly opened the womb but he who opened a closed one? But it is marriage which opens the womb in all cases. The Virgin's womb, therefore, was especially opened, because it was especially closed. On the Flesh of Christ 23.4-5.[6]

Christ Truly Opened Mary's Womb. Origen: Males were sacred because they opened their mothers' wombs. They were offered before the altar of the Lord. Scripture says, "Every male that opens the womb. . . ." This phrase has a spiritual meaning. For you might say that "every male is brought forth from the womb" but does not open the womb of his mother in the way that the Lord Jesus did. In the case of every other woman, it is not the birth of an infant but intercourse with a man that opens the womb. But the womb of the Lord's mother was opened at the time when her offspring was brought forth, because before the birth of Christ a male did not even touch her womb, holy as it was and deserving of all respect. Homilies on the Gospel of Luke 14.7-8.[7]

See also Jerome on Exodus 34:19.

13:4 In the Month of Abib

The Meaning of Abib. Pseudo-Macarius: But if man groans and cries out to God, he sends him the spiritual Moses, who redeems him from the slavery of the Egyptians. But man first cries out and groans and then he receives the beginning of deliverance. And he is delivered in the month of new flowers, in the springtime when the ground of the soul is able to shoot forth the beautiful and flowering branches of justification. The bitter winter storms of the ignorance of darkness have passed, as well as the great blindness that was born of sordid deeds and sins. Homily 47.7.[8]

13:5 Land Promised to the Ancestors

See Maximus of Turin on Exodus 3:8.

13:13 Redeeming a Firstborn Animal

---

[1]In Greek it is clear that the word for "consecrate" or "make holy" is derived from the adjective *holy*. [2]Ex 40:9. [3]Ex 28:2. [4]Num 35:1-8. [5]FC 83:208. [6]ANF 3:541. [7]FC 94:60. [8]PMFSH 234.

LABOR AND PRODUCE. AMBROSE: The law has established that an unclean animal shall not be a part of a sacrifice but in its place a clean animal be offered. The law orders that the offspring of an ass, which is unclean, should be changed for a sheep, which is a clean animal and suitable for sacrifice. This is the literal meaning. If one were to pursue this matter further and seek for the spiritual sense of this passage, he will discover that the ass is a laborious animal, whereas the sheep is productive. This may be interpreted to mean that labor should be exchanged for produce, since the final results of work is the produce thereof. Or we may interpret the passage in this manner: Every action or labor of yours you can make commendable by the pure and simple manner in which you perform it. CAIN AND ABEL 2.2.8.[9]

[9]FC 42:408-9.

13:17—14:9 TOWARD THE RED SEA

[17]*When Pharaoh let the people go, God did not lead them by way of the land of the Philistines, although that was near; for God said, "Lest the people repent when they see war, and return to Egypt."* [18]*But God led the people round by the way of the wilderness toward the Red Sea. And the people of Israel went up out of the land of Egypt equipped for battle. . . .* [21]*And the Lord went before them. . . .*

14 [8]*And the Lord hardened the heart of Pharaoh king of Egypt and he pursued the people of Israel as they went forth defiantly.* [9]*The Egyptians pursued them, all Pharaoh's horses and chariots and his horsemen and his army, and overtook them encamped at the sea, by Pi-ha-hiroth, in front of Baal-zephon.*

OVERVIEW: As the Jews were saved through the waters of the Red Sea, so Christians are saved through the waters of baptism. Even the waters of baptism are red, since they are tinged with Christ's blood (CASSIODORUS). God makes himself known through creaturely means (AUGUSTINE). God has appeared in a burning bush, in a pillar of fire and in a pillar of cloud (PETER CHRYSOLOGUS). Fire evokes dread, but clouds are soothing (GREGORY THE GREAT). The columns of fire and cloud prefigure the light of grace (BEDE). Christ, the pillar of fire, now leads the Christian people through the waters of baptism (MAXIMUS OF TURIN).

13:18 The Red Sea

THE WATERS OF BAPTISM RED. CASSIODORUS: Just as the Jews were saved and extricated through the waters of the Red Sea, so we are delivered from the land of Egypt, that is, from the sins of the flesh, and reborn through regeneration by the sacred water. The very name of the Red Sea is not superfluous. Just as it is known as Red, so the baptismal water can be labeled red, for it came forth mixed with blood from the Lord Savior's side. EXPOSITION OF THE PSALMS 80.6.[1]

[1]ACW 52:296.

13:21 A Pillar of Cloud, a Pillar of Fire

God Appears Through Creaturely Means. Augustine: Who can doubt that here too God appeared to the eyes of mortal men by a corporeal creature made subject to him and not by his own substance? But it is also not apparent whether it was the Father, or the Son, or the Holy Spirit, or the Trinity itself, the one God. Nor, as far as I can judge, has this distinction been made in that place where it is written: "And the glory of the Lord appeared in the cloud, and the Lord spoke to Moses saying, 'I have heard the grumbling of the children of Israel.'"[2] The Trinity 2.14.24.[3]

God Appears in Different Forms. Peter Chrysologus: At one time he appears all aglow in a bush.[4] For you are cold with the perfidy of infidelity, and he wants to enkindle you with the heat of faith. At another time he glows like fire in a pillar extending toward heaven, that the darkness of your ignorance may be removed and that you can follow the way of saving knowledge through the wilderness of this world. At yet another time he is changed for you into a pillar of cloud, in order to restrain the burning ebullience of your passions. Sermon 170.[5]

Fire Evokes Fear, but Clouds Console. Gregory the Great: It was also fitting that a pillar of fire preceded the Israelites as they progressed through the desert during the night and a pillar of a cloud during the day. There is dread in fire but a gentle soothing quality in the sight of a cloud. "Day" is understood to point toward the life of the righteous and "night" that of the sinner. Hence Paul said to sinners who had been converted, "You were once darkness but are now light in the Lord."[6] The pillar was revealed as a cloud during the day and as a fire during the night since almighty God will appear soothing to the righteous and dreadful to the unrighteous. When he comes at the judgment, he will reassure the former by his gentleness and mildness and cause dread in the latter by the strictness of his justice. Homily 21.[7]

The Pillar of Fire and the Light of Grace. Bede: The freeing of the children of Israel and their being brought out into the fatherland once promised them is also linked with the mystery of our redemption. By means of it we make our way to the light of the dwelling place on high with the grace of Christ lighting our way and guiding us. That cloud and column of fire that both protected them throughout the whole of their journey from the darkness of the nights and led them by a sure path to the promised homes of the fatherland also prefigured the light of this grace. Commentary on 1 Peter at 2:9.[8]

14:8 Pharaoh Pursued Israel

Faith Drives Out Fear. Maximus of Turin: But the same Christ the Lord who did all these things now goes through baptism before the Christian people in the pillar of his body—he who at that time went through the sea before the children of Israel in the pillar of fire. This, I say, is the column which at that time offered light to the eyes of those who followed and now ministers light to the hearts of those who believe, which then made firm a watery path in the waves and now strengthens the traces of faith in the washing. Through this faith—as was the case with the children of Israel—the one who walks calmly will not fear Egypt in pursuit. Sermon 100.3.[9]

---

[2]Ex 16:10-12. [3]FC 45:80. [4]Ex 3:2. [5]FC 17:277. [6]Eph 5:8. [7]CS 123:159. [8]CS 82:88. [9]ACW 50:227.

14:10-20 CROSSING OF THE RED SEA

^{15}The LORD said to Moses, "Why do you cry to me? Tell the people of Israel to go forward. ^{16}Lift up your rod, and stretch out your hand over the sea and divide it, that the people of Israel may go on dry ground through the sea. ^{17}And I will harden the hearts of the Egyptians so that they shall go in after them, and I will get glory over Pharaoh and all his host, his chariots, and his horsemen. ^{18}And the Egyptians shall know that I am the LORD, when I have gotten glory over Pharaoh, his chariots, and his horsemen."

^{19}Then the angel of God who went before the host of Israel moved and went behind them; and the pillar of cloud moved from before them and stood behind them, ^{20}coming between the host of Egypt and the host of Israel. And there was the cloud and the darkness; and the night passed^p without one coming near the other all night.

p Gk: *Heb* and it lit up the night

OVERVIEW: Through prayer, we cry out to God in a way that he alone hears (ORIGEN). God hears the blood of just persons and their good works as if they were voices (BASIL). The word *cry* in Scripture means the cry of the heart, not of the voice (JEROME). The silent longings of the heart are a cry to God (CASSIODORUS). Moses worked all his signs with the mysterious wood of his staff, which was a sign of the future cross (CAESARIUS OF ARLES). The body is an obstacle between us and God, as the pillar of cloud was between the Egyptians and the Hebrews (GREGORY OF NAZIANZUS). The angel protected the Jews and prayed for them (CYRIL OF ALEXANDRIA).

14:15 Why Do You Cry to Me?

GOD HEARS THE VOICE OF PRAYER. ORIGEN: But if the mental voice of those who pray should not be extremely loud, though it is not weak, and should they not raise a cry and shout, God still hears those who pray thus. For it is he who says to Moses, "Why do you cry out to me?" when he had not cried out audibly (for this is not recorded in Exodus), but through prayer he had cried out loudly in that voice which is heard by God alone. COMMENTARY ON THE GOSPEL OF JOHN 6.101.[1]

GOOD WORKS CRY TO GOD. BASIL THE GREAT: Or do you not hear how Moses, although he said nothing but met the Lord with his inexpressible groanings, was heard by the Lord, who said, "Why do you cry to me?" God knows how to hear even the blood of a just man, to which no tongue is attached and of which no voice pierces the air. The presence of good works is a loud voice before God. EXEGETIC HOMILIES 22.[2]

THE CRY OF THE HEART. JEROME: The word *cry* in Scripture does not refer to the cry of the voice but to the cry of the heart. In fact, the Lord says to Moses, "Why are you crying out to me?" when Moses had not muttered any cry at all. HOMILIES ON THE PSALMS 2.[3]

THE SILENT LONGINGS OF THE HEART. CASSIODORUS: The heart reveals its silent longing, to which the Godhead listens more than to the most thundering voices of nations. He said to

[1]FC 80:197. [2]FC 46:353. [3]FC 48:16.

Moses, "Why do you cry to me?" although we do not read that Moses had said anything. So the faithful man said that his heart was speaking to the Lord, since he seemed to offer his thoughts by this means. Exposition of the Psalms 26.8.[4]

14:16 Lift Your Rod

THE MEANING OF MOSES' STAFF. CAESARIUS OF ARLES: Moses performed no sign without the mysterious wood, for he received from the Lord a rod to work wonders and prodigies in Egypt. Moreover, as a sign that he had heard things divinely, it was said to him, "Lift up your staff." God, of course, did not need the assistance of a staff. But it was raised so that we might know how great was the mystery of that future wood which was prefigured by the shadow of this staff. SERMON 112.4.[5]

14:20 The Cloud and the Darkness

THE BODY STANDS BETWEEN US AND GOD. GREGORY OF NAZIANZUS: Therefore this dark-ness of the body has been placed between us and God, like the cloud of old between the Egyptians and the Hebrews. This is perhaps what is meant by "He made darkness his separate place,"[6] namely, our dullness, through which few can see even a little. THEOLOGICAL ORATION 2.12.[7]

THE ANGEL OF GOD PROTECTED THE ISRAELITES. CYRIL OF ALEXANDRIA: And it is written also in Exodus that when the ruler of the land of the Egyptians with his warriors was pursuing after the Israelites and was already upon the point of engaging with them in battle, the angel of God stood between the camp of the Israelites and of the Egyptians, and the one came not near the other all the night. There is therefore nothing unbefitting in supposing here also that the holy angel who was the guardian of the synagogue offered supplications in its behalf and prayed for a respite, if perchance yielding to better influence it might yet bring forth fruit. HOMILIES ON THE GOSPEL OF LUKE 96.[8]

---

[4]ACW 51:267. [5]FC 47:154. [6]Ps 18:11. [7]LCC 3:144. [8]CGSL 389.

14:21-31 DESTRUCTION OF THE EGYPTIANS

[21]Then Moses stretched out his hand over the sea; and the LORD drove the sea back by a strong east wind all night, and made the sea dry land, and the waters were divided. [22]And the people of Israel went into the midst of the sea on dry ground, the waters being a wall to them on their right hand and on their left. [23]The Egyptians pursued, and went in after them into the midst of the sea, all Pharaoh's horses, his chariots, and his horsemen. [24]And in the morning watch the LORD in the pillar of fire and of cloud looked down upon the host of the Egyptians, and discomfited the host of the Egyptians, [25]clogging[q] their chariot wheels so that they drove heavily; and the Egyptians said, "Let us flee from before Israel; for the LORD fights for them against the Egyptians."

[26]Then the LORD said to Moses, "Stretch out your hand over the sea, that the water may come back upon the Egyptians, upon their chariots, and upon their horsemen." [27]So Moses stretched

forth his hand over the sea, and the sea returned to its wonted flow when the morning appeared; and the Egyptians fled into it, and the LORD routed[r] the Egyptians in the midst of the sea. [28]The waters returned and covered the chariots and the horsemen and all the host[s] of Pharaoh that had followed them into the sea; not so much as one of them remained. [29]But the people of Israel walked on dry ground through the sea, the waters being a wall to them on their right hand and on their left.

[30]Thus the LORD saved Israel that day from the hand of the Egyptians; and Israel saw the Egyptians dead upon the seashore. [31]And Israel saw the great work which the LORD did against the Egyptians, and the people feared the LORD; and they believed in the LORD and in his servant Moses.

q *Or binding. Sam Gk Syr: Heb* removing   r *Heb* shook off   s *Gk Syr: Heb* to all the host

OVERVIEW: Weapons need faith, but faith needs no weapons (PAULINUS). Moses accomplished his works by prayer, whereas Christ exercised his own power (CHRYSOSTOM). One who follows the law of the Lord finds a dry path to the heavenly reward (ORIGEN). The chosen people are saved by water, but the spirits of evil perish in water (GREGORY OF NYSSA). Moses and Peter both mastered the power of water (PAULINUS). Baptism, which was consecrated by the blood of Christ, washes away sins (AUGUSTINE). The Egyptians did not fear the Lord; they drove their chariots at full speed until the wheels were clogged (EPHREM). The sea closed in on the Egyptians. This event is still credible (GREGORY OF NYSSA). The tracks and ruts of the Egyptians' chariots are still visible on the shores of the Red Sea (PAULUS OROSIUS). The same water saved one people and destroyed another (AMBROSE). The Egyptians perished because their hearts were hardened, despite the signs and wonders they witnessed (CLEMENT OF ROME). Moses was a type of Christ, not of the Holy Spirit (BASIL).

14:21 Moses Stretched Out His Hand

THE EGYPTIANS LACKED FAITH. PAULINUS: We find that arms have always needed faith, but faith has never needed arms. The rod of faith parted the sea which submerged the army bereft of faith together with its wicked leader. POEM 26.150.[1]

MOSES AND PETER COMPARED. PAULINUS: Note how the teachers of the Old and New Testaments differ in their deeds but are paired in glory, for the one Wisdom issued twin laws in the two Testaments, so equal distinction gives the same weight to differing powers. Peter did not divide the sea with a rod, but then Moses did not walk on the waters. However, both have the same bright glory, for the one Creator inspired both the cleavage of the waters with a rod and the treading of the waves underfoot. POEM 26.366.[2]

THE JEWS CROSS THE SEA, CHRIST WALKS ON THE WATER. CHRYSOSTOM: Now the Jews also had crossed the Red Sea, under the leadership of Moses, but there is a great difference here. Moses accomplished everything by praying and in the manner of a servant, whereas Christ acted altogether by his own power. And in the episode of the Red Sea the water gave way by means of the wind which then was blowing, so as to make a passage on dry land, while in this episode[3] a greater wonder took place. Though the sea kept its own nature, even so it carried the Lord on its

---

[1]ACW 40:259. [2]ACW 40:267. [3]Jn 6:18-19.

surface, to bear out that scriptural testimony to one "who walks upon the seas as on a pavement."[4] HOMILIES ON THE GOSPEL OF JOHN 43.[5]

14:22 The People Went on Dry Ground

THE LAW OF GOD DELIVERS US. ORIGEN: How hard a temptation it is to pass through the midst of the sea, to see the waves rise piled up, to hear the noise and rumbling of the raging waters! But if you follow Moses, that is, the law of God, the waters will become for you walls on the right and left, and you will find a path on dry ground in the midst of the sea. Moreover, it can happen that the heavenly journey that we say the soul takes may hold peril of waters. Great waves may be found there. HOMILIES ON NUMBERS 27.10.[6]

THOSE FLEEING FROM SIN ARE SAVED BY WATER. GREGORY OF NYSSA: Again, according to the view of the inspired Paul,[7] the people itself, by passing through the Red Sea, proclaimed the good tidings of salvation by water. The people passed over, and the Egyptian king with his host was engulfed, and by these actions this sacrament was foretold. For even now, whensoever the people is in the water of regeneration, fleeing from Egypt, from the burden of sin, it is set free and saved. But the devil with his own servants (I mean, of course, the spirits of evil) is choked with grief and perishes, deeming the salvation of men to be his own misfortune. ON THE BAPTISM OF CHRIST.[8]

THE SEA WASHES AWAY THE EGYPTIANS. AUGUSTINE: This people of God, freed from a great and broad Egypt, is led, as through the Red Sea, that in baptism it may make an end of its enemies. For by the sacrament as it were of the Red Sea, that is by baptism consecrated with the blood of Christ, the pursuing Egyptians, the sins, are washed away. EXPLANATION OF THE PSALMS 107.3.[9]

14:25 Clogging the Chariot Wheels

THE EGYPTIANS WERE MIRED IN CONFUSION. EPHREM THE SYRIAN: The Egyptians pursued the Hebrews with no fear of the darkness that separated them from the Hebrews and without being disturbed by the sea that was divided. During the night, through a sea that was divided, they went rushing forward to do battle with the people who were led by the column of fire. During the morning watch, the Lord appeared to the Egyptians and threw them into confusion. He clogged the wheels of their chariots so that they could neither pursue the people nor escape from the sea. But they did not fear the Lord who appeared to them, and they were not deterred by their wheels that were clogged. They boldly drove their chariots with full force. COMMENTARY ON EXODUS 14.5.[10]

14:27 The Sea Returned to Its Flow

EVIDENCE IS STILL VISIBLE. GREGORY OF NYSSA: But after that the surface of the sea became one again, and the temporary gap was flooded over. So this remains a unique event which occurred in such a way that the marvel did not lose credibility because of the passage of time, since it continues to be testified to by visible traces. That is the way the affair of the marshy lake is both described and shown. THE LIFE OF GREGORY THE WONDERWORKER 7.55.[11]

EVIDENCE OF THE EGYPTIANS' PURSUIT. PAULUS OROSIUS: The Hebrews proceeded safely over the dry passage, and the masses of stationary water collapsed behind them. The entire Egyptian multitude with their king was overwhelmed and killed, and the entire province, which had previously been tortured by plagues, became empty by this last slaughter. Even today there exists most reliable evidence of these

---

[4]Job 9:8. [5]FC 33:439-40. [6]OEM 59. [7]1 Cor 10:1-2. [8]NPNF 2 5:522. [9]NPNF 1 8:533. [10]FC 91:250-51. [11]FC 98:65.

events. For the tracks of chariots and the ruts made by the wheels are visible not only on the shore but also in the deep, as far as sight can reach. And if perchance for the moment they are disturbed either accidentally or purposely, they are immediately restored through divine providence by winds and waves to their original appearances, so that whoever is not taught to fear God by the study of revealed religion may be terrified by his anger through this example of his accomplished vengeance. SEVEN BOOKS OF HISTORY AGAINST THE PAGANS 1.10.[12]

14:28 The Waters Returned

WATER SAVES AND DESTROYS. AMBROSE: The waters of the sea were held back yet at the same time surrounding the Hebrews. They then poured back and brought death upon the Egyptians, so that they destroyed one people and saved the other. What too do we find in the Gospel itself? Did not our Lord show there that the sea grew calm at his word, that the storm clouds of heaven were scattered, that the blasts of the winds subsided and that the dumb elements obeyed him and the shores were quieted?[13] ON

HIS BROTHER, SATYRUS 2.74.[14]

FOR THE HARDNESS OF THEIR HEARTS. CLEMENT OF ROME: Pharaoh and his army and all the leaders of Egypt, "the chariots and their riders," were drowned in the Red Sea and perished for no other reason than that their foolish hearts were hardened, after the working of signs and wonders in the land of Egypt by God's servant Moses. LETTER TO THE CORINTHIANS 51.[15]

14:31 Belief in the Lord and Moses

FAITH IN MOSES AS A TYPE OF CHRIST. BASIL THE GREAT: But belief in Moses not only does not show our belief in the Spirit to be worthless, but, if we adopt our opponents' line of argument, it rather weakens our confession in the God of the universe. "The people," it is written, "believed the Lord and his servant Moses." Moses then is joined with God, not with the Spirit; and he was a type not of the Spirit but of Christ. ON THE SPIRIT 14.33.[16]

---

[12]FC 50:31. [13]Mt 8:26-27. [14]FC 22:229-30. [15]FC 1:49. [16]NPNF 2 8:20.

15:1-21 SONG OF MOSES

[1]Then Moses and the people of Israel sang this song to the LORD, saying,
"I will sing to the LORD, for he has triumphed gloriously;
    the horse and his rider[t] he has thrown into the sea.
[2]The LORD is my strength and my song,
    and he has become my salvation;
this is my God, and I will praise him,
    my father's God, and I will exalt him.
[3]The LORD is a man of war;
    the LORD is his name.

⁴"Pharaoh's chariots and his host he cast into the sea;
   and his picked officers are sunk in the Red Sea.
⁵The floods cover them;
   they went down into the depths like a stone.
⁶Thy right hand, O Lord, glorious in power,
   thy right hand, O Lord, shatters the enemy.
⁷In the greatness of thy majesty thou overthrowest thy adversaries;
   thou sendest forth thy fury, it consumes them like stubble.
⁸At the blast of thy nostrils the waters piled up,
   the floods stood up in a heap;
   the deeps congealed in the heart of the sea.
⁹The enemy said, 'I will pursue, I will overtake,
   I will divide the spoil, my desire shall have its fill of them.
   I will draw my sword, my hand shall destroy them.'
¹⁰Thou didst blow with thy wind, the sea covered them;
   they sank as lead in the mighty waters.

¹¹"Who is like thee, O Lord, among the gods?
   Who is like thee, majestic in holiness,
   terrible in glorious deeds, doing wonders?
¹²Thou didst stretch out thy right hand,
   the earth swallowed them.

¹³"Thou hast led in thy steadfast love the people whom thou hast redeemed,
   thou hast guided them by thy strength to thy holy abode.
¹⁴The peoples have heard, they tremble;
   pangs have seized on the inhabitants of Philistia.
¹⁵Now are the chiefs of Edom dismayed;
   the leaders of Moab, trembling seizes them;
   all the inhabitants of Canaan have melted away.
¹⁶Terror and dread fall upon them;
   because of the greatness of thy arm, they are as still as a stone,
till thy people, O Lord, pass by,
   till the people pass by whom thou hast purchased.
¹⁷Thou wilt bring them in, and plant them on thy own mountain,
   the place, O Lord, which thou hast made for thy abode,
   the sanctuary, O Lord, which thy hands have established.
¹⁸The Lord will reign for ever and ever."
¹⁹For when the horses of Pharaoh with his chariots and his horsemen went into the sea, the

Lord *brought back the waters of the sea upon them; but the people of Israel walked on dry ground in the midst of the sea.* [20]*Then Miriam, the prophetess, the sister of Aaron, took a timbrel in her hand; and all the women went out after her with timbrels and dancing.* [21]*And Miriam sang to them:*

"Sing to the Lord, *for he has triumphed gloriously;*
the horse and his rider he has thrown into the sea."

t *Or its chariot*

Overview: The Song of Moses is the first great song in Scripture. The song prefigures the song that the bride sings to Christ her husband (Origen). Christians must leave behind Egypt and all that it stands for (Jerome). Baptism cleanses Christians of all that is dark and unclean. The armies of pride and arrogance are obliterated in baptism. Like the Egyptians, our sins have been put to death. The three-horse team is a triple fear: of pain, humiliation and death (Augustine). The elite officers of the Egyptians are luxury, wickedness and pride (Caesarius of Arles). Horses represent the irrational, passionate part of the soul, as Plato taught (Clement of Alexandria). Despair can drive us into the depths (Augustine). God's left hand tolerates the prosperity of the wicked, but his right hand destroys them (Gregory the Great). God is not like other gods; there is no comparison between him and demons (Chrysostom). The enemy fails to understand the power of baptism and continues in pursuit (Augustine). The sea swallows up guilt and error but leaves virtue and innocence unharmed (Ambrose). The earth figuratively devours the godless when they imagine themselves victorious (Augustine). When they are converted, the Gentiles will cease to be stone and will receive new human and rational natures in Christ (Origen).

The Bible attests that both men and women were prophets (Constitutions). Miriam was a prophetess (Ephrem) and a type of the church (Ambrose). The song of Miriam should be our song too (Augustine). The same name suits the sister of Moses and the mother of Jesus (Peter Chrysologus). The tambourine is a sign of virginity (Gregory of Nyssa).

15:1 *Moses and the People of Israel Sang*

Who May Sing the Perfect Song. Origen: As the perfect Bride of the perfect husband, then, she has received the words of perfect doctrine. Moses and the children of Israel sang the first song to God when "they saw the Egyptians dead on the seashore"[1] and when they saw "the strong hand" and the mighty strong arm "of the Lord and [when they] believed in God and Moses his servant."[2] Then they sang, therefore, saying, "Let us sing to the Lord, for he is gloriously magnified."[3] And I think that nobody can attain to that perfect and mystical song and to the perfection of the Bride which this Scripture contains unless he first marches "through the midst of the sea upon dry land" and, with "the water becoming to him as a wall on the right hand and on the left,"[4] so makes his escape "from the hands of the Egyptians." [Then] he "beholds them dead on the seashore"[5] and, seeing the strong hand with which the Lord has acted against the Egyptians, believes in the Lord and in his servant Moses. In Moses, I say—in the law, and in the Gospels and in all the divine Scriptures. For them he will have good cause to sing and say, "Let us sing unto the Lord, for he is gloriously magnified." Commentary on the Song of Songs, prologue 4.[6]

What the Horse and Rider Are. Clement

---

[1]Ex 14:30. [2]Ex 14:31. [3]Ex 15:1. [4]Ex 14:22. [5]Ex 14:30. [6]ACW 26:47.

of Alexandria: It is said in the ode, "For he has triumphed gloriously: the horse and his rider has he cast into the sea." The many-limbed and brutal affection, lust, with the rider mounted, who gives reigns to pleasures, "he has cast into the sea," throwing them away into the disorders of the world. Thus also Plato, in his book *On the Soul*, says that the charioteer and the horse that ran off—the irrational part, which is divided in two, into anger and concupiscence—fall down. So the myth intimates that it was through the licentiousness of the steeds that Phathon was thrown out. Stromateis 5.8.[7]

Christians Delivered from the Adversary. Jerome: Our motive in going over all this, dearly beloved brethren, is that we may be on our guard, for fear that, after coming out from Egypt and hastening through the desert for forty days[8]—for forty years, as it were—to reach the land of promise, we should long for the fleshpots of Egypt[9] and be bitten to death by the serpents.[10] We have left Egypt; what have we to do with the food of Egypt? We who have bread from heaven; why do we go in search of earthly foods? We who have left Pharaoh, let us call upon the help of the Lord so that the Egyptian king may be drowned in the baptism of those who believe. Let his horses and their riders perish there; let the raging army of the adversary be destroyed. Let us not murmur against the Lord lest we be struck down by him. Homily 90.[11]

What God Has Cast into the Sea. Augustine: "For he has been gloriously extolled" who has already granted us in the bath of regeneration what we have been singing about: "horse and rider he has cast into the sea." All our past sins, you see, which have been pressing on us, as it were, from behind, he has drowned and obliterated in baptism. These dark things of ours were being ridden by unclean spirits as their mounts, and like horsemen they were riding them wherever they liked. That's why the apos-

tle calls them "rulers of this darkness."[12] We have been rid of all this through baptism, as through the Red Sea, so called because sanctified by the blood of the crucified Lord. Let us not turn back to Egypt in our hearts, but with him as our protector and guide let us wend our way through the other trials and temptations of the desert toward the kingdom. Sermon 223e.2.[13]

Sin Cast into the Sea. Augustine: As far as we are concerned, you see, they are dead, because they cannot lord it over us anymore; because our very misdeeds, which made us into their subjects, have been, so to say, sunk and obliterated in the sea, when we were set free by the bath of holy grace. Sermon 363.2.[14]

15:3 The Lord Is His Name

See Gregory Nazianzus on Exodus 3:14.

15:4 Pharaoh's Chariots and Host

Sins Obliterated in Baptism. Augustine: And the worldly pride and arrogance and the troops of innumerable sins which were fighting for the devil in us, he obliterated in baptism. Sermon 363.2.[15]

The Three Fears That Terrorize Us. Augustine: The devil had placed "teams of three"[16] in each chariot, who were to terrorize us by haunting us with the fear of pain, the fear of humiliation, the fear of death. All these things were sunk in the Red Sea, because "together with him," together with the One who for our sakes was scourged, dishonored and slain, "we were buried through baptism into death."[17] Thus he overwhelmed all our enemies in the Red Sea, having consecrated the waters of baptism with the bloody death which was utterly to consume

---

[7]ANF 2:457. [8]Jerome means the forty days of Lent. [9]Ex 16:3. [10]Num 21:6. [11]FC 57:234. [12]Eph 6:12. [13]*WSA* 3 6:227. [14]*WSA* 3 10:270-71. [15]*WSA* 3 10:271. [16]So the LXX at Ex 15:4. [17]Rom 6:4.

our sins. SERMON 363.2.[18]

THE PICKED OFFICERS. CAESARIUS OF ARLES: "The elite of his officers, who were standing three deep, he submerged in the Red Sea." Who are the elite of his officers? Surely those chosen by the devil for luxury, wickedness and pride, the source of all evil. Moreover, these, standing three deep, occupy those three ways in order to subvert man to evil deeds, to tempt him to evil speech or to win him to evil thoughts. SERMON 97.4.[19]

15:5 Into the Depths

THE DEVIL KEEPS THOSE WHO DESPAIR. AUGUSTINE: But if our enemies "went down into the depths like a stone," the only ones the devil remains in possession of and the only ones who have the hardness of the devil are those about whom it is written, "When the sinner has come into the depths of evil, he behaves disdainfully."[20] They don't believe, you see, that they can be forgiven for what they have done; and in that mood of despair they plummet to greater depths than ever. SERMON 363.2.[21]

15:6 The Lord Shatters the Enemy

GOD'S RIGHT AND LEFT HANDS. GREGORY THE GREAT: For this reason it is written again: "Your right hand, O Lord, has destroyed the enemy." For the enemies of God, though prosperous in his left hand, are destroyed by his right hand, because very often the present life raises up the wicked, but the coming of eternal bliss condemns them. PASTORAL CARE 3.26.[22]

15:9 The Enemy Said, "I Will Pursue"

THE ENEMY MISUNDERSTANDS BAPTISM. AUGUSTINE: The enemy does not understand the power of the Lord's sacrament, which is available in saving baptism for those who believe and hope in him. He still thinks that sins can prevail even over the baptized, because they are

being tempted by the frailty of the flesh. He doesn't know where and when and how the complete renewal of the whole person is to be perfected, which is begun and prefigured in baptism and is already grasped by the most assured hope. SERMON 363.2.[23]

15:10 The Sea Covered the Egyptians

THE WIND IS THE SPIRIT. AMBROSE: Moses himself says in his song, "You sent your Spirit, and the sea covered them." You observe that even then holy baptism was prefigured in that passage of the Hebrews, wherein the Egyptian perished, the Hebrew escaped. For what else are we daily taught in this sacrament but that guilt is swallowed up and error done away, but that virtue and innocence remain unharmed? ON THE MYSTERIES 3.12.[24]

15:11 Who Is Like the Lord?

GOD IS INCOMPARABLE. CHRYSOSTOM: The Old Testament . . . says, "Who is like to you among the gods, O Lord?" What do you mean, Moses? Is there any comparison at all between the true God and false gods? Moses would reply, "I did not say this to make a comparison; but since I was talking to the Jews, who had a lofty opinion of demons, I condescended to their weakness and brought in the lesson I was teaching in this way." Let me also say that since my discussion is with the Jews, who consider that Christ is mere man and one who violated their law, I compared him with those whom the pagan Greeks admire. DISCOURSES AGAINST JUDAIZING CHRISTIANS 5.3.3.[25]

15:12 The Earth Swallowed Them

DID THE EARTH DEVOUR THE EGYPTIANS?

---

[18]WSA 3 10:271. [19]FC 47:77. [20]Prov 18:3. [21]WSA 3 10:271. [22]ACW 11:184. [23]WSA 3 10:272. [24]NPNF 2 10:318. [25]FC 68:105-6.

AUGUSTINE: Certainly at that time no yawning chasm of the earth swallowed up any of the Egyptians; they were covered by water, they perished in the sea. So what's the meaning of "You stretched out your right hand, the earth devoured them"? Or are we correct in understanding God's right hand to be the one of whom Isaiah says, "And the arm of the Lord, to whom has it been revealed"?[26] That, you see, is the only Son, whom the Father did not spare "but handed him over for us all."[27] And thus he stretched out his right hand on the cross, and the earth devoured the godless, when they thought of themselves as victorious and of him as despicable in defeat. SERMON 363.2.[28]

15:16 Still as a Stone

THE GENTILES BECAME STONES. ORIGEN: God is asked that for a short while the Gentiles might be changed into stones—that is what the Greek word apolithōthētōsan really means—"until the Jewish people passes through." There is no doubt but that after they have passed through, the Gentiles will cease to be stone and will receive in place of their hard hearts a human and rational nature in Christ, to whom is glory and power for ages of ages. Amen. HOMILIES ON THE GOSPEL OF LUKE 22.10.[29]

15:19 Israel Walked on Dry Ground

See ORIGEN ON EXODUS 15:1.

15:20 Miriam the Prophetess

WOMEN WHO PROPHESIED. ANONYMOUS: Now women prophesied also. Of old, Miriam the sister of Moses and Aaron, and after her Deborah,[30] and after these Huldah[31] and Judith[32]—the former under Josiah, the latter under Darius. The mother of the Lord also prophesied, and her kinswoman Elisabeth, and Anna;[33] and in our time the daughters of Philip.[34] Yet were not these elated against their husbands but preserved their

own measures. CONSTITUTIONS OF THE HOLY APOSTLES 8.1.2.[35]

HOW MIRIAM BECAME A PROPHETESS. EPHREM THE SYRIAN: "The prophetess Miriam took. . . ." How did she become a prophetess? Either, like Isaiah's wife, she had the honorary title of prophecy, although she was not a prophetess, or because she was just a woman. COMMENTARY ON EXODUS 15.4.2.[36]

MIRIAM WAS A TYPE OF THE CHURCH. AMBROSE: And Miriam taking the timbrel led the dances with maidenly modesty. But consider whom she was then prefiguring. Was she not a type of the church, who as a virgin with unstained spirit joins together the religious gatherings of the people to sing divine songs? CONCERNING VIRGINS 1.3.12.[37]

WE TOO SING MIRIAM'S SONG. AUGUSTINE: This is what Moses sang and the sons of Israel with him, what Miriam the prophetess sang and the daughters of Israel with her. It is what we too now should sing, whether it means men and women or means our spirit and our flesh. "Those who belong to Christ Jesus," you see, as the apostle says, "have crucified their flesh with its passions and desires."[38] This can be suitably understood in the drum which Miriam took to accompany this song: flesh, you see, is stretched over wood to make a drum. So they learn from the cross how to accompany in confession the sweet strains of grace. SERMON 363.4.[39]

MIRIAM AND MARY. PETER CHRYSOLOGUS: This name is related to prophecy and salutary to those reborn. It is the badge of virginity, the glory of purity, the indication of chastity, the sacrificial gift of God, the height of hospitality,

---

[26]Is 53:1. [27]Rom 8:32. [28]WSA 3 10:272-73. [29]FC 94:96. [30]Judg 4:4. [31]2 Kings 22:14. [32]Jdt 8:11. [33]Lk 1:46; 2:38. [34]Acts 21:9. [35]ANF 7:481. [36]FC 91:253. [37]NPNF 2 10:365. [38]Gal 5:24. [39]WSA 3 10:274.

the sum total of sanctity. Rightly therefore is this motherly name that of the mother of Christ. SERMON 146.[40]

GREGORY OF NYSSA: This reminds us that the prophetess, Miriam, immediately after the crossing of the sea, took a dry, tuneful "tambourine in her hand" and led a chorus of women. Perhaps by the tambourine Scripture means to suggest the virginity of the first Mary, who was, I think, the prototype of Mary the mother of God. For as the tambourine produces a loud sound, having no moisture in it and being quite dry, so also virginity is clear and noised abroad and has nothing in itself of the life-preserving moisture of this life. ON VIRGINITY 19.[41]

---

[40]FC 17:241-42. [41]FC 58:60-61.

15:22-27 AT MARAH AND ELIM

[24]*And the people murmured against Moses, saying, "What shall we drink?"* [25]*And he cried to the LORD; and the LORD showed him a tree, and he threw it into the water, and the water became sweet.*

There the LORD[v] *made for them a statute and an ordinance and there he proved them,* [26]*saying, "If you will diligently hearken to the voice of the LORD your God, and do that which is right in his eyes, and give heed to his commandments and keep all his statutes, I will put none of the diseases upon you which I put upon the Egyptians; for I am the LORD, your healer."*

[27]*Then they came to Elim, where there were twelve springs of water and seventy palm trees; and they encamped there by the water.*

v Heb he

OVERVIEW: The wood that restores the sweetness to water is Christ (TERTULLIAN). The waters of baptism are of no avail unless the cross of Christ is preached (AMBROSE). The seventy palm trees remind us of Christ's seventy disciples (JEROME). The bitter water was the law of the Old Testament, which needed to be tempered by the cross of Christ (MAXIMUS OF TURIN). Marah and Elim stand in sharp contrast. Marah had one bitter spring; Elim had twelve sweet ones. This is a contrast between the law and the gospel (MAXIMUS OF TURIN). Elim means "of rams" and refers to the apostles (BEDE).

15:25 The Water Became Sweet

CHRIST HEALS NATURE. TERTULLIAN: Again, water is restored from its defect to its native grace of "sweetness" by the tree of Moses. That tree was Christ, restoring of himself the veins of what had been envenomed and bitter nature into the allsalutary waters of baptism. ON BAPTISM 9.2.[1]

BAPTISM COMPRISES WATER AND THE WORD. AMBROSE: Marah was a fountain of most bitter water. Moses cast wood into it and it became sweet. For water without the preaching of the cross of the Lord is of no avail for future salvation. But after it has been consecrated by the

---

[1]ANF 3:673.

mystery of the saving cross, it is made suitable for the use of the spiritual laver and of the cup of salvation. As then Moses, that is, the prophet, cast wood into that fountain, so too the priest utters over this font the proclamation of the Lord's cross, and the water is made sweet for the purpose of grace. ON THE MYSTERIES 3.14.[2]

PALM TREES AND DISCIPLES OF CHRIST. JEROME: As wood sweetens Marah so that seventy palm trees are watered by its streams, so the cross makes the waters of the law lifegiving to the seventy who are Christ's apostles.[3] LETTER 69.6.[4]

THE LAW AND THE CROSS. MAXIMUS OF TURIN: In this mystical number, I say, the children of Israel, arriving at Marah and being unable to draw the water because of its bitterness (for the well had water but no sweetness, and it was pleasing to the eye but polluted to the taste), drank water that became sweet and mild as soon as wood was thrown into it by Moses. The sacrament of the wood removed the harshness that the noxious water bore. I believe that this happened as a sign, for I think that the bitter water of Marah is the Old Testament law, which was harsh before it was tempered by the Lord's cross. SERMON 67.4.[5]

15:27 Elim: Springs and Palm Trees

THE CONTRAST BETWEEN MARAH AND ELIM. MAXIMUS OF TURIN: They arrived at a place called Elim, where there were twelve very pure springs of water and a multitude of seventy flourishing palm trees. See the mystery of God—how, after the bitterness of the law, the richness of gospel piety abounds. There the one spring is harsh to drink, but here the many are all sweet to imbibe. Once there was no refreshment after weariness, but now there is refreshment after labor. For springs are at the disposal of the thirsty, and palms are offered to victors. Palms are offered to victors, I say, because after the hardness of the law it is a victory to have arrived at the grace of the gospel. For part of the victor's reward is to moisten his mouth from a flowing spring and to take the triumphal palm in his hand. With the spring the confessor's tongue is purified, and with the palm the martyr's hand is honored—the former because it has praised the glory of Christ, the latter because it has refused the altar of sacrilege. SERMON 68.2.[6]

THE MEANING OF ELIM. BEDE: When the people of God went out from Egypt, their sixth resting place, in which "there were twelve fountains of water and seventy palm trees," was called Elim (that is, "of rams"), so that both by its name and by its appearance it might contain the figure of the apostles and the apostolic men. ON THE TABERNACLE 2.4.[7]

---

[2]NPNF 2 10:319. [3]Lk 10:1. [4]NPNF 2 6:145. [5]ACW 50:165. [6]ACW 50:166-67. [7]TTH 18:63-64.

16:1-3 THE DESERT OF SIN

[3]"*Would that we had died by the hand of the* LORD *in the land of Egypt, when we sat by the fleshpots and ate bread to the full; for you have brought us out into this wilderness to kill this whole assembly with hunger.*"

OVERVIEW: The people of Israel were freed from Egypt and then desired to return; only a few of them were allowed to enter the Promised Land (JOHN CASSIAN). The people preferred the food of Egypt to heavenly manna (NOVATIAN).

16:3 Would That We Had Died in Egypt

THE TRUE RENUNCIATION OF EGYPT. JOHN CASSIAN: Although this manner of speaking first referred to that people, nonetheless we see it now daily fulfilled in our life and profession. For everyone who has first renounced this world and then returns to his former pursuits and his erstwhile desires proclaims that in deed and in intention he is the same as they were, and he says, "It was well with me in Egypt."

I fear that there will be found as many such people as we read there were multitudes of sinners in the time of Moses. For although six hundred and three thousand armed men were said to have left Egypt,[1] no more than two of these entered the Promised Land.[2] Hence we must strive to take our models of virtue from the few and far between, since, according to that figure of speech in the Gospel, many are said to be called but few are said to be chosen.[3] Bodily renunciation and removal from Egypt, as it were, will be of no value to us, therefore, if we have been unable to obtain at the same time the renunciation of heart which is more sublime and more beneficial. CONFERENCE 3.7.6-7.[4]

THEY PREFERRED BITTER FOOD. NOVATIAN: Since they dared to prefer the bitterest of Egyptian foods to the heavenly food of manna and preferred the succulent meats of their hostile masters to their own freedom, did they deserve anything else than to have their joy in foods curtailed? They truly deserved to bear the brand of the slavery they had longed for, since a better food—the food of the free—displeased them so. JEWISH FOODS 4.5.[5]

---

[1]Ex 38:26. [2]Num 14:38; Joshua and Caleb. [3]Mt 22:14. [4]ACW 57:126. [5]FC 67:151.

16:4-21 THE QUAIL AND MANNA

[4]Then the LORD said to Moses, "Behold, I will rain bread from heaven for you; and the people shall go out and gather a day's portion every day, that I may prove them, whether they will walk in my law or not. [5]On the sixth day, when they prepare what they bring in, it will be twice as much as they gather daily." [6]So Moses and Aaron said to all the people of Israel, "At evening you shall know that it was the LORD who brought you out of the land of Egypt, [7]and in the morning you shall see the glory of the LORD, because he has heard your murmurings against the LORD. For what are we, that you murmur against us?" . . .

[13]In the evening quails came up and covered the camp; and in the morning dew lay round about the camp. [14]And when the dew had gone up, there was on the face of the wilderness a fine, flake-like thing, fine as hoarfrost on the ground. [15]When the people of Israel saw it, they said to one another, "What is it?"ᵂ For they did not know what it was. And Moses said to them, "It is the bread which the LORD has given you to eat. [16]This is what the LORD has commanded: 'Gather

of it, every man of you, as much as he can eat; you shall take an omer apiece, according to the number of the persons whom each of you has in his tent.'" [17] *And the people of Israel did so; they gathered, some more, some less.* [18] *But when they measured it with an omer, he that gathered much had nothing over, and he that gathered little had no lack; each gathered according to what he could eat.* [19] *And Moses said to them, "Let no man leave any of it till the morning."* [20] *But they did not listen to Moses; some left part of it till the morning, and it bred worms and became foul; and Moses was angry with them.* [21] *Morning by morning they gathered it, each as much as he could eat; but when the sun grew hot, it melted.*

w *Or "It is manna." Heb* man hu

OVERVIEW: The manna was a gift from heaven and required no human labor (PETER CHRYSOLOGUS). The Lord spoke not of manna but of bread from heaven; he is that bread (CASSIODORUS). The small, thin food was angelic in nature (ORIGEN). Manna means "What is this?" (CASSIODORUS), a question we should always ask about the Scriptures (CAESARIUS OF ARLES). The food that God gives nourishes the souls of the wise. The Word of God delights and illuminates those who receive it (AMBROSE). Just as one measure of manna sufficed for each person, so the Holy Spirit is given equally to all (CYPRIAN). Those who took too much manna found that it bred worms; so are gluttons and drunkards punished (CHRYSOSTOM). "The glory of the Lord" is one of the many titles that Scripture would later give to the first-begotten Son (JUSTIN MARTYR).

16:4 *Bread from Heaven*

BREAD WITHOUT LABOR. PETER CHRYSOLOGUS: The rain of manna fed the Jewish people for forty years in the desert. It did not by its customary service cause an increase of sprouts from the earth but streamed on the earth like harvested grains. It took away all the toil of human labor and by its pleasant dew[1] offered and spread out heavenly produce for the hungry. SERMON 166.[2]

THE NATURE OF TRUE MANNA. CASSIODORUS: These incidents are quite well known from our reading of Exodus, for quails rained down like the heaviest shower, and the Jews received manna to get their fill. But to demonstrate that this was a prefiguration, he spoke not of manna but of the bread of heaven, so that the Lord Savior's coming could be visualized in this blessing, for he is "the living bread which came down from heaven."[3] The meaning of manna, as was stated at Psalm 77, is "What is this?"[4] He disposed of the problem surrounding the name, and with the statement "He filled them with the bread of heaven,"[5] he explained the answer to the question about manna, for the Lord of heaven is indicated by the phrase, and the nature of manna is clearly acknowledged. EXPOSITION OF THE PSALMS 104.40.[6]

16:7 *The Glory of the Lord*

THE GLORY OF THE LORD IS THE SON. JUSTIN MARTYR: "So, my friends," I said, "I shall now show from the Scriptures that God has begotten of himself a certain rational power as a beginning before all other creatures. The Holy Spirit indicates this power by various titles, sometimes the glory of the Lord, at other times Son, or Wisdom, or angel, or God, or Lord or Word. He even called himself Commander-in-chief when he appeared in human guise to Joshua, the son of Nun. Indeed, he can justly

[1]Ex 16:13. [2]FC 17:273. [3]Jn 6:51. [4]Ex 16:15; Ps 78:24. [5]Ps 105:40. [6]ACW 53:62-63.

lay claim to all these titles from the fact that he performs the Father's will and that he was begotten by an act of the Father's will. DIALOGUE WITH TRYPHO 61.[7]

16:14 Fine as Hoarfrost

A SMALL, THIN FOOD. ORIGEN: But if there are some who have come out of Egypt and, following the pillar of fire and cloud, are entering the wilderness, then he comes down from heaven to them and offers them a small, thin food, like to the food of angels; so that "man eats the bread of angels."[8] COMMENTARY ON THE SONG OF SONGS 1.4.[9]

16:15 Bread the Lord Has Given

THE MEANING OF MANNA. CAESARIUS OF ARLES: Manna is interpreted as "What is this?" See whether the very power of the name does not provoke you to learn it, so that when you hear the law of God read in church you may always ask and say to the teachers: What is this? This it is that the manna indicates. Therefore if you want to eat the manna, that is, if you desire to receive the word of God, know that it is small and very fine like the seed of the coriander. SERMON 102.3.[10]

THE BREAD IS GOD'S COMMANDMENT. AMBROSE: "This is the bread that God gave" to you "to eat." Hear who this bread is: "The word," Scripture says, "which God has ordained." This then is the ordination of God; this food nourishes the soul of the wise. It illuminates and it sweetens, resplendent with the gleam of truth and soothing, as if with a honeycomb, by the sweetness of different virtues and the word of wisdom. For "good words are sweeter than a honeycomb," as it is written in Proverbs.[11] LETTER 54(64).2.[12]

THE BREAD IS THE WORD OF GOD. AMBROSE: That this is heavenly food is demonstrated by the person speaking: "I shall rain upon you bread from heaven." Manna is a cause (aition), because God, who waters minds with the dew of wisdom, uses it as an instrument. And manna is a kind of matter (hyle), because souls that see it and taste it are delighted and ask whence it comes, manna which is more splendid that light and sweeter than honey. They can be answered with a chain of quotations from Scripture: "This is the bread that the Lord gave to you to eat," and "This is the Word of God which God has established" or ordained. By this bread the souls of the prudent are fed and delighted, since it is fair and sweet, illuminating the souls of the hearers with the splendor of truth and drawing them on with the sweetness of the virtues. LETTER 55(8).7.[13]

16:16 Gather the Manna

THE MANNA COLLECTED. CYPRIAN: Nay, rather, the Holy Spirit is not given from a measure but is poured out completely upon the believer. For if the day is born to all equally, and if the sun shines upon all with equal and similar light, how much more does Christ, the Sun and the true Day, bestow equally in his church the light of eternal life with equal measure! We see that the pledge of this equality is celebrated in Exodus, when the manna from heaven fell and, with a prefiguring of the future, showed the nourishment of heavenly bread and the food of the coming Christ. For there, without distinction either of sex or of age, a measure was collected for each equally. LETTER 69.14.[14]

16:20 The Manna Became Foul

COVETOUSNESS MADE THE MANNA ROT. CHRYSOSTOM: If anyone cannot endure what I have said but still clings to the poverty of worldly things, snatching at the things which

---

[7]FC 6:244. [8]Ps 78:25. [9]ACW 26:78. [10]FC 47:105. [11]Prov 16:24. [12]CSEL 82 2:73. [13]CSEL 82 2:79. [14]FC 51:255.

undergo diminution, let him call to mind the food of manna. Let him tremble at the example of that punishment. For what happened in that instance, this same result one may now also see in the case of covetous people. But what then happened to them? Worms were bred from their covetousness. This also now happens in their case. For the measure of the food is the same for all. You have but one stomach to fill. Only you who feed luxuriously have more to get rid of.

Those who gathered in their houses more than the lawful quantity gathered not manna but more worms and rottenness. Just so both in luxury and in covetousness, the gluttonous and drunken gather not more delicacies but more corruption. Homilies on 1 Corinthians 40.5.[15]

---

[15]NPNF 1 12:248*.

16:22-36 REGULATIONS REGARDING THE MANNA

[29]"See! The Lord has given you the sabbath, therefore on the sixth day he gives you bread for two days; remain every man of you in his place, let no man go out of his place on the seventh day." [30]So the people rested on the seventh day.

[31]Now the house of Israel called its name manna; it was like coriander seed, white, and the taste of it was like wafers made with honey. [32]And Moses said, "This is what the Lord has commanded: 'Let an omer of it be kept throughout your generations, that they may see the bread with which I fed you in the wilderness, when I brought you out of the land of Egypt.'" [33]And Moses said to Aaron, "Take a jar, and put an omer of manna in it, and place it before the Lord, to be kept throughout your generations." [34]As the Lord commanded Moses, so Aaron placed it before the testimony, to be kept. [35]And the people of Israel ate the manna forty years, till they came to a habitable land; they ate the manna, till they came to the border of the land of Canaan. [36](An omer is the tenth part of an ephah.)

Overview: Some passages of Scripture do not readily admit of a literal sense. The manna, though one food, tasted like each one's favorite food (Origen). The number forty is a sacred number in Scripture (Maximus of Turin). The three measures are sense perception, reason and intellect (Clement of Alexandria).

16:29 Manna for Two Days

A Spiritual Sense. Origen: Moreover in regard to the celebrated sabbath, a careful reader

will see that the command, "You shall sit each one in your dwellings; let none of you go out from his place on the sabbath day," is an impossible one to observe literally, for no living creature could sit for a whole day and not move from his seat. On First Principles 4.3.2.[1]

16:31 Israel Called It Manna

To Each One's Taste. Origen: The Word of

---

[1]OFP 291.

God becomes all these things to each and every one according as the capacity or the desire of the participant requires. In just the same way the manna also, although it was one food, yielded its flavor to each person after his desire.[2] So he does not offer himself only as bread to those who hunger and as wine to those who thirst, but he presents himself also as fragrant apples to those who crave delights. COMMENTARY ON THE SONG OF SONGS 3.8.[3]

16:35 The People Ate Manna for Forty Years

THE SIGNIFICANCE OF THE NUMBER FORTY. MAXIMUS OF TURIN: Let us also see if we are able to find Quadragesima's[4] mystical number somewhere else in the Scriptures. We read that holy Moses fed the children of Israel with heavenly manna in the desert for the space of forty years. Good is the number, then, which always opens heaven. Good is the number, I say, by which Noah's righteousness is preserved and the children of Israel are fed. For this reason let us also observe this number so that the heavens

might be opened to us in order that the rain of spiritual grace might fall upon us and the manna of the spiritual sacraments refresh us. For, after the fashion of our fathers, by this observance of Quadragesima we are both made righteous and nourished: we are made righteous by the washing [of baptism] and nourished by the sacraments [of bread and wine]. SERMON 50.3.[5]

16:36 Omers and Ephahs

THE MEANING OF THE MEASURES. CLEMENT OF ALEXANDRIA: Anyway, when the instruction is given to consecrate in a golden vessel the memorial of the food sent down by God from heaven, "the gomor," it is written, "is a tenth part of three measures." For our purposes, "three measures" means three sources of judgment: perception of sensible objects; reason, for evaluating sentences, nouns and verbs; and the intellect, for intelligible objects. STROMATEIS 2.50.1.[6]

---

[2]Wis 16:20-21. [3]ACW 26:198. [4]That is, the forty days of Lent. [5]ACW 50:120. [6]FC 85:192.

17:1-7 WATER FROM THE ROCK

[3]*The people thirsted there for water, and the people murmured against Moses, and said, "Why did you bring us up out of Egypt, to kill us and our children and our cattle with thirst?"* [4]*So Moses cried to the LORD, "What shall I do with this people? They are almost ready to stone me."* [5]*And the LORD said to Moses, "Pass on before the people, taking with you some of the elders of Israel; and take in your hand the rod with which you struck the Nile, and go.* [6]*Behold, I will stand before you there on the rock at Horeb; and you shall strike the rock, and water shall come out of it, that the people may drink." And Moses did so, in the sight of the elders of Israel.*

OVERVIEW: It is better to thirst for justice than for water (CAESARIUS OF ARLES). Even though the people threatened to stone Moses, he prayed for them (JEROME). Christ, who was the rock,

was pierced on the cross, and blood and water flowed from his side (CAESARIUS OF ARLES). Grace can work contrary to nature, as when water flows from a rock. As a rock poured forth

---

water, a virgin gave birth (AMBROSE).

17:3 The People Thirsted for Water

FOR WHAT DID THE PEOPLE THIRST? CAESARIUS OF ARLES: What then does Scripture mention in what follows? "In their thirst for water, the people grumbled against Moses." Perhaps this word that he said may seem superfluous, that the people thirsted for water. For since he said, "In their thirst," what need was there to add "for water"? Thus indeed the ancient translation has it. Why did he add this, except because they thirsted for water when they should have thirsted for justice? "Blessed are they who hunger and thirst for justice";[1] and again, "thirst is my soul for the living God."[2] Many people are thirsty, both the just and sinners; the former thirst after justice, the latter after dissipation. The just are thirsty for God; sinners for gold. For this reason the people thirsted after water when they should have thirsted after justice. SERMON 103.2.[3]

17:4 What Shall I Do?

MOSES SOUGHT TO IMITATE CHRIST. JEROME: When [Moses] was being stoned by the people, he made intercession for them. Even more so he wished to be blotted out of God's book sooner than that the flock committed to him should perish.[4] He sought to imitate the Shepherd who would, he knew, carry on his shoulders even the wandering sheep. LETTER 82.3.[5]

17:6 Strike the Rock

CHRIST THE ROCK HAD TO SUFFER. CAESARIUS OF ARLES: Then the Lord said to Moses, "Take the staff and strike the rock, that it may produce water for the people." Behold, there is a rock, and it contains water. However, unless this rock is struck, it does not have any water at all. But when it has been struck, it produces fountains and rivers, as we read in the Gospel: "He who believes in me, from within him there shall flow rivers of living water."[6] When Christ was struck on the cross, he brought forth the fountains of the New Testament. Therefore it was necessary for him to be pierced. If he had not been struck, so that water and blood flowed from his side, the whole world would have perished through suffering thirst for the word of God. SERMON 103.3.[7]

GRACE WORKS CONTRARY TO NATURE. AMBROSE: The people of the fathers thirsted, Moses touched the rock, and water flowed out of the rock. Did not grace work a result contrary to nature, so that the rock poured forth water, which by nature it did not contain? ON THE MYSTERIES 9.51.[8]

THE ROCK AND THE VIRGIN MARY. AMBROSE: It does not surpass faith that a virgin gave birth, when we read that even a rock poured out water and that the waves of the sea were made solid in the form of a wall. LETTER 15 EXTRA COLL. (42).7.[9]

---

[1]Mt 5:6. [2]Ps 42:2. [3]FC 47:109. [4]Ex 32:31-32. [5]NPNF 2 6:171-72. [6]Jn 7:38. [7]FC 47:109-10. [8]NPNF 2 10:324. [9]CSEL 82 3:306.

17:8-16 BATTLE WITH AMALEK

[8]*Then came Amalek and fought with Israel at Rephidim.* [9]*And Moses said to Joshua, "Choose for us men, and go out, fight with Amalek; tomorrow I will stand on the top of the hill with the rod of God in my hand."* [10]*So Joshua did as Moses told him, and fought with Amalek; and Moses, Aaron, and Hur went up to the top of the hill.* [11]*Whenever Moses held up his hand, Israel prevailed; and whenever he lowered his hand, Amalek prevailed.* [12]*But Moses' hands grew weary; so they took a stone and put it under him, and he sat upon it, and Aaron and Hur held up his hands, one on one side, and the other on the other side; so his hands were steady until the going down of the sun.* [13]*And Joshua mowed down Amalek and his people with the edge of the sword.*

OVERVIEW: The name Amalek means "a sinful people." Amalek denied passage to the Israelites and had to be conquered by the cross of Christ (AUGUSTINE). When eyes are raised in thought and hands are lifted in deeds, our enemies are conquered (ORIGEN). How are we to arm ourselves against the wicked one? We do as Moses did (GREGORY OF NAZIANZUS). Moses performed his work with deliberation and virtuously (AMBROSE). The stone that supported Moses was Christ (JUSTIN MARTYR). Why did Moses sit as he prayed, when prayer should be offered kneeling or prostrate? (TERTULLIAN). Moses is the type; Christ is the truth (CHRYSOSTOM). The sign of the cross is to be seen everywhere (MAXIMUS OF TURIN). This passage prefigures the mediatorship of Christ (GREGORY THE GREAT). The battle lasted until evening, and Christ died in the evening (JUSTIN MARTYR).

17:8 Then Came Amalek

AMALEK MEANS "A SINFUL PEOPLE." AUGUSTINE: There is no vice which the divine law resists more [than pride]. That most proud spirit becomes an obstacle to things above and a mediator to things below. It thereby receives a greater power of domination, unless one avoids the secret snares he is laying by going along a different way. If he is openly raging through a sinful people, he is like Amalek.[1] By his opposition he denies the passage to the land of promise. He then must be overcome by the cross of Christ, which was prefigured by the extended hands of Moses. THE TRINITY 4.15.20.[2]

17:11 Moses Held Up His Hand

LIFTING HANDS IN SACRIFICE. ORIGEN: For in this way, when the eyes are lifted up through thought and contemplation and the hands are lifted up in deeds which lift up and exalt the soul, as Moses lifted up his hands, one may consequently say, "The lifting up of my hands is as the evening sacrifice."[3] In this way the Amalekites and all the unseen enemies will be worsted, and the Israelite reasonings in us will prevail. COMMENTARY ON THE GOSPEL OF JOHN 28.37.[4]

HOW TO CONQUER THE WICKED ONE? GREGORY OF NAZIANZUS: For my own warfare, however, I am at a loss what course to pursue, what alliance, what word of wisdom, what grace to devise, with what panoply to arm myself against the wiles of the wicked one.[5] What Moses did is

---

[1]Ex 17:16. [2]FC 45:156. [3]Ps 141:2. [4]FC 89:299. [5]Eph 6:11.

to conquer him by stretching out his hands upon the mount, in order that the cross, thus typified and prefigured, may prevail. ORATION 2.88.[6]

17:12 Moses' Hands Grew Weary

VICTORY THROUGH COURAGE. AMBROSE: Moses showed this when his hands became so heavy that Joshua the son of Nun could hardly hold them up. For that reason the people conquered when they performed works not carelessly but with full consideration and virtue—not with faltering souls nor with a wavering disposition but with the stability of a firm mind. LETTER 7 (37).33.[7]

MOSES REPRESENTED THE CROSS. JUSTIN MARTYR: In truth it was not because Moses prayed that his people were victorious, but because, while the name of Jesus[8] was at the battle front, Moses formed the sign of the cross. Who among you does not know that that prayer is the most pleasing to God which is uttered with lamentation and tears? But on this occasion Moses (or any after him) did not pray in such a manner; he was seated on a stone. And I have shown that even the stone is symbolical of Christ. DIALOGUE WITH TRYPHO 90.[9]

WHY MOSES SAT TO PRAY. TERTULLIAN: But, to come now to Moses, why, I wonder, did he merely at the time when Joshua was battling against Amalek, pray sitting with hands expanded, when, in circumstances so critical, he ought rather, surely, to have commended his prayer by knees bent, and hands beating his breast, and a face prostrate on the ground; except it was that there, where the name of the Lord Jesus was the theme of speech—destined as he was to enter the lists one day singly against the devil—the figure of the cross was also necessary, [that figure] through which Jesus was to win the victory?[10] ANSWER TO THE JEWS 10.10.[11]

MOSES COMPARED WITH CHRIST. CHRYSOSTOM: See how the type was given through Moses but the truth came through Jesus Christ. And again, on Mt. Sinai, when the Amalekites were waging war on the Hebrews, the hands of Moses were propped up, held by Aaron and Hur standing on either side. But Christ, when he came, himself held his hands extended on the cross by his own power. Do you see how the type "was given" and "the truth came"?[12] HOMILIES ON THE GOSPEL OF JOHN 14.[13]

HOW OFTEN WE SEE THE CROSS. MAXIMUS OF TURIN: When Moses' hands were lifted up Amalek was conquered; when they came down a little he grew strong. The sailyards of ships and the ends of the sailyards move about in the form of our cross. The very birds, too, when they are borne to the heights and fly through the air, imitate the cross with their wings outstretched. Trophies themselves are crosses, and so are adorned victories of triumphs. These we ought to have not only on our foreheads but also on our souls so that, thus armed, we may trample upon the adder and the serpent,[14] in Christ Jesus, to whom be glory forever. SERMON 45.3.[15]

MOSES AND THE STONE ARE THE LAW AND CHRIST. GREGORY THE GREAT: When Moses sat on the stone, it prefigured the law resting on the church. But this law had heavy hands, because it did not deal mercifully with those who were sinners but treated them with extreme harshness. "Aaron" means "mountain of strength," and "Hur" means "fire." Who is meant by "mountain of strength"? Our Redeemer, of whom the prophet said, "It shall come to pass in the latter days that the mountain of the house of the Lord shall be established as the highest of the mountains."[16] And who is prefigured by "fire" but the

---

[6]NPNF 2 7:222. [7]CSEL 82 1:59. [8]Joshua in Greek is "Jesus." [9]FC 6:292. [10]Col 2:14-15. [11]ANF 3:165-66. [12]Jn 1:17. [13]FC 33:138. [14]Ps 91:13. [15]ACW 50:250*. [16]Is 2:2.

Holy Spirit, of whom our Redeemer said, "I have come to cast fire upon the earth"?[17] Aaron and Hur support the heavy hands of Moses and make them lighter by their support. Similarly the "Mediator between God and men,"[18] coming with the fire of the Holy Spirit, revealed that the heavy commandments of the law, which cannot be borne when taken literally, become more tolerable for us when they are understood spiritually. It is as if he made the hands of Moses light when he changed the weight of the law's commandments into the strength that comes from confession. HOMILY 33.[19]

ON THE CROSS UNTIL EVENING. JUSTIN MARTYR: Besides, the fact that the prophet Moses remained until evening in the form of the cross, when his hands were held up by Aaron and Hur, happened in the likeness of this sign. For the Lord also remained upon the cross until evening, when he was buried. Then he rose from the dead on the third day. DIALOGUE WITH TRYPHO 97.[20]

---

[17]Lk 12:49. [18]1 Tim 2:5. [19]CS 123:276-77. [20]FC 6:300.

[18:1-12 MEETING WITH JETHRO]

18:13-27 APPOINTMENT OF MINOR JUDGES

[5]*And Jethro, Moses' father-in-law, came with his sons and his wife to Moses in the wilderness where he was encamped at the mountain of God. . . .*

[14]*When Moses' father-in-law saw all that he was doing for the people, he said, "What is this that you are doing for the people? Why do you sit alone, and all the people stand about you from morning till evening?" . . .*

[17]*Moses' father-in-law said to him, "What you are doing is not good.* [18]*You and the people with you will wear yourselves out, for the thing is too heavy for you; you are not able to perform it alone.* [19]*Listen now to my voice; I will give you counsel, and God be with you! You shall represent the people before God, and bring their cases to God;* [20]*and you shall teach them the statutes and the decisions, and make them know the way in which they must walk and what they must do.* [21]*Moreover choose able men from all the people, such as fear God, men who are trustworthy and who hate a bribe; and place such men over the people as rulers of thousands, of hundreds, of fifties, and of tens.* [22]*And let them judge the people at all times; every great matter they shall bring to you, but any small matter they shall decide themselves; so it will be easier for you, and they will bear the burden with you." . . .*

[24]*So Moses gave heed to the voice of his father-in-law and did all that he had said.*

OVERVIEW: Moses could take the good advice even of a pagan, his father-in-law, since all truth comes from God (AUGUSTINE). Moses needed to devote himself to spiritual matters (GREGORY

THE GREAT). The Septuagint attests that Moses appointed teachers of reading and writing for God's people (Augustine). Moses was a deeply humble man (Chrysostom).

18:19 Listen to My Counsel

Moses Listened to Jethro. Augustine: God spoke to Moses, did he not? Yet Moses very prudently and humbly yielded to the advice of his father-in-law, foreigner though he was, with regard to governing and directing such a mighty nation. For he realized that from whatever intellect right counsel proceeded, it should be attributed not to him who conceived it but to the One who is the Truth, the immutable God. On Christian Teaching, Prologue 7.[1]

18:21 Choose Able Men

Moses Freed to Learn Spiritual Matters. Gregory the Great: Moses, who speaks with God, is judged by the reproof of Jethro, a man of alien race, on the ground that he devotes himself by his ill-advised labor to the earthly affairs of the people. At the same time counsel is given him to appoint others in his place for the reconciling of quarrels, so that he himself may be more free to learn the secrets of spiritual matters for teaching the people. Pastoral Care 2.7.[2]

Moses Appointed Teachers. Augustine: Moses in fact took care to appoint teachers of reading and writing for God's people before they had any written record of God's law. The Septuagint Scripture calls these instructors *grammatoeisagogoi*,[3] which is Greek for "bringers-in of letters," because they brought them, in a sense, into their students' minds or perhaps introduced their students to them. City of God 18.39.[4]

18:24 Moses Heeds Jethro

The Humility of Moses. Chrysostom: For nothing was ever more humble than he, who, being leader of so great a people, and having overwhelmed in the sea the king and the host of all the Egyptians, as if they had been flies, and having wrought so many wonders both in Egypt and by the Red Sea and in the wilderness, and received such high testimony, yet felt exactly as if he had been an ordinary person. As a son-in-law he was humbler than his father-in-law; Moses took advice from him and was not indignant. Nor did he say, "What is this? After such and so great achievements, have you come to us with your counsel?" Homilies on 1 Corinthians 1.4.[5]

---

[1]FC 2:23. [2]ACW 11:70. [3]Many mss. of the LXX add this office to the ones listed in the MT, here and at Ex 18:25. [4]FC 24:147. [5]NPNF 1 12:4-5.

19:1-15 ARRIVAL AT SINAI

[1]On the third new moon after the people of Israel had gone forth out of the land of Egypt, on that day they came into the wilderness of Sinai. [2]And when they set out from Rephidim and came into the wilderness of Sinai, they encamped in the wilderness; and there Israel encamped before the mountain. [3]And Moses went up to* God, and the LORD called to him out of the moun-

---

tain, saying, "Thus you shall say to the house of Jacob, and tell the people of Israel: ⁴You have seen what I did to the Egyptians, and how I bore you on eagles' wings and brought you to myself. ⁵Now therefore, if you will obey my voice and keep my covenant, you shall be my own possession among all peoples; for all the earth is mine, ⁶and you shall be to me a kingdom of priests and a holy nation. These are the words which you shall speak to the children of Israel."

⁷So Moses came and called the elders of the people, and set before them all these words which the Lord had commanded him. ⁸And all the people answered together and said, "All that the Lord has spoken we will do." And Moses reported the words of the people to the Lord. ⁹And the Lord said to Moses. "Lo, I am coming to you in a thick cloud, that the people may hear when I speak with you, and may also believe you for ever."

Then Moses told the words of the people to the Lord. ¹⁰And the Lord said to Moses, "Go to the people and consecrate them today and tomorrow, and let them wash their garments, ¹¹and be ready by the third day; for on the third day the Lord will come down upon Mount Sinai in the sight of all the people. ¹²And you shall set bounds for the people round about, saying, 'Take heed that you do not go up into the mountain or touch the border of it; whoever touches the mountain shall be put to death; ¹³no hand shall touch him, but he shall be stoned or shot; whether beast or man, he shall not live.' When the trumpet sounds a long blast, they shall come up to the mountain."

* LXX *adds* the mountain of

OVERVIEW: On the fiftieth day after Passover, Moses received the law, written by the finger of God, which is the Holy Spirit (AUGUSTINE). The people were to purify themselves to receive the law (AMBROSE, AUGUSTINE). An interval of fifty days is found in both Testaments (AUGUSTINE). Not everyone is worthy to ascend the mountain. Those who are not yet prepared to ascend the mountain should stand afar (GREGORY OF NAZIANZUS). Titles once given to the Israelites are later applied to the Christian people (AMBROSE, BEDE). It was God the Son who spoke eschatologically to the people from the pillar of cloud (EUSEBIUS). In the Old Testament, fear holds the people back; in the New, the people eagerly await the coming of the Holy Spirit (AUGUSTINE).

19:1 On the Third New Moon

FROM SLAYING THE LAMB TO GIVING THE LAW. AUGUSTINE: The Pentecost too we observe, that is, the fiftieth day from the passion

and resurrection of the Lord, for on that day he sent to us the Holy Paraclete whom he had promised. This was prefigured in the Jewish Passover, for on the fiftieth day after the slaying of the lamb, Moses on the mount received the law written with the finger of God. AGAINST FAUSTUS, A MANICHAEAN 32.12.[1]

FIFTY-DAY INTERVALS IN SCRIPTURE. AUGUSTINE: But the fifty-day period is also praised in Scripture, not only in the Gospel, because the Holy Spirit came on the fiftieth day, but even in the Old Testament. Therein fifty days are numbered from the celebration of the pasch by the killing of a lamb to the day on which the law was given on Mt. Sinai to the servant of God, Moses. LETTER 55.[2]

FIFTY DAYS AND THREE DAYS. AUGUSTINE: We come now to the desert, where the law was

¹NPNF 1 4:336. ²FC 12:285.

given, and this is what Scripture says: "But in the third month from when the people were brought out of Egypt." The Lord spoke to Moses that those who were going to receive the law should purify themselves in readiness for the third day, on which the law was to be given. So at the beginning of the third month a purification is commanded in readiness for the third day. SERMON 272B.6.[3]

19:3 Moses Went Up to God

WHO MAY ASCEND THE MOUNTAIN? GREGORY OF NAZIANZUS: Now when I go up eagerly into the mount—or, to use a truer expression, when I both eagerly long and at the same time am afraid (the one through my hope and the other through my weakness), to enter within the cloud and hold converse with God, for so God commands: If any be an Aaron,[4] let him go up with me, and let him stand near, being ready, if it must be so, to remain outside the cloud. THEOLOGICAL ORATION 2.2.[5]

19:6 A Kingdom of Priests and a Holy Nation

ISRAEL CALLED. AMBROSE: How indeed but in his body did Christ expiate the sins of the people? In what did he suffer, save in his body— even as we said: "Christ having suffered in the flesh"? In what is he a priest, save in that which he took unto himself the vocation of a priestly nation? ON THE CHRISTIAN FAITH 3.11.86.[6]

ISRAEL'S TITLES APPLIED TO CHRISTIANS. BEDE: The apostle Peter now rightly gives to the Gentiles this attestation of praise which formerly was given by Moses to the ancient people of God, because they believed in Christ, who like a cornerstone brought the Gentiles into that salvation which Israel had had for itself. He calls them "a chosen race"[7] on account of their faith, that he may distinguish them from those who by rejecting the living stone have themselves

become rejected. They are "a royal priesthood,"[8] however, because they have been joined to his body who is their real king and true priest, who as king grants to his own a kingdom and as their high priest cleanses them of their sins by the sacrificial victim of his own blood. He names them "a royal priesthood" that they may remember both to hope for an eternal kingdom and always to offer to God the sacrifices of a stainless way of life. COMMENTARY ON 1 PETER AT 2:9.[9]

19:9 Appearing in a Thick Cloud

THE PILLAR OF CLOUD WAS THE WORD. EUSEBIUS: The people then beheld the pillar of cloud, and it spoke to Moses. But who was the speaker? Obviously the pillar of cloud, which before appeared to the fathers in a corporeal form. And I have already shown that this was not directly and visibly the almighty God as such but the One whom we name as the Word of God, the Christ who was seen for the sake of the multitude of Moses and the people in a pillar of cloud, because it was not possible for them to see him like their fathers in human shape. For surely it was reserved for the perfect to be able to see beforehand his future incarnate appearance among men. And since it was impossible then for the whole people to bear it, he was seen now in fire in order to inspire fear and wonder, and now in a cloud, as it were in a shadowy and veiled form ruling them, as he was also seen by Moses for their sake. PROOF OF THE GOSPEL 5.14.241.[10]

19:10 Let The People Wash Their Garments

WHAT IT MEANS TO WASH YOUR CLOTHES. AMBROSE: However, even the people had to be purified two or three days beforehand, so as to come clean to the sacrifice, as we read in the Old

---

[3]WSA 3 7:308. [4]Ex 19:24. [5]LCC 3:136. [6]NPNF 2 10:255*. [7]1 Pet 2:9. [8]1 Pet 2:9. [9]CS 82:87. [10]POG 1:258.

Testament. They even used to wash their clothes. If such regard was paid in what was only the figure, how much ought it to be shown in the reality! Learn then, priest and Levite, what it means to wash your clothes. You must have a pure body wherewith to offer up the sacraments. If the people were forbidden to approach their victim unless they washed their clothes, do you, while foul in heart and body, dare to make supplication for others? Do you dare to make an offering for them? DUTIES OF THE CLERGY 1.50.258.[11]

19:12 Setting Bounds for the People

A FEARFUL THING. AUGUSTINE: In this wonderful agreement there is the very great difference, that in the Old Testament the people is held back by a fearful dread from approaching the place where the law was given; whereas in the New the Holy Spirit comes upon those who were assembled together waiting for his promised coming. ON THE SPIRIT AND THE LETTER 17.29.[12]

19:13 Whether Beast or Human

EVIL PEOPLE MAY NOT SPECULATE ON CHRISTIAN TEACHING. GREGORY OF NAZIANZUS: But if any is an evil and savage beast and altogether incapable of taking in the subject matter of contemplation and theology, let him not hurtfully and malignantly lurk in his den among the woods, to catch hold of some dogma or saying by a sudden spring and to tear sound doctrine to pieces by his misrepresentations. But let him stand yet afar off and withdraw from the mount, or he shall be stoned and crushed and shall perish miserably in his wickedness. THEOLOGICAL ORATION 2.2.[13]

---

[11]NPNF 2 10:41. [12]LCC 8:217. [13]LCC 3:137.

19:16-25 THE GREAT THEOPHANY

[16]*On the morning of the third day there were thunders and lightnings, and a thick cloud upon the mountain, and a very loud trumpet blast, so that all the people who were in the camp trembled.* [17]*Then Moses brought the people out of the camp to meet God; and they took their stand at the foot of the mountain.* [18]*And Mount Sinai was wrapped in smoke, because the LORD descended upon it in fire; and the smoke of it went up like the smoke of a kiln, and the whole mountain quaked greatly.* [19]*And as the sound of the trumpet grew louder and louder, Moses spoke, and God answered him in thunder.* [20]*And the LORD came down upon Mount Sinai, to the top of the mountain; and the LORD called Moses to the top of the mountain, and Moses went up.*

OVERVIEW: Many great mysteries have happened on the third day (ORIGEN). The fiftieth day from Passover is reckoned as the day when the law was given (AUGUSTINE). The number three represents the Trinity in Scripture (CAESARIUS OF ARLES). Lightning and thunder had a unique meaning at Sinai. God's manifestations in material form do not mean that he is mutable. Smoke and fire are not God's substance; not even the Arians would say that (AUGUSTINE).

Fire enlightens the humble; smoke blinds the proud (BEDE). As the trumpet grew louder, the living Word was spread abroad everywhere (CYRIL OF ALEXANDRIA). Right speech is sweet speech (ORIGEN). Carnal-minded people, content with the letter, cannot ascend the mountain (BEDE).

19:16 On the Morning of the Third Day

THE THIRD DAY IS APPLIED TO MYSTERIES. ORIGEN: The third day, however, is always applied to mysteries. For when the people had departed from Egypt, they offer sacrifice to God on the third day and are purified on the third day. And the third day is the day of the Lord's resurrection.[1] Many other mysteries also are anticipated in this day. HOMILIES ON GENESIS 8.4.[2]

THE INTERVAL OF FIFTY DAYS. AUGUSTINE: The law then was obviously given on the third day of the third month. Now count the days from the fourteenth of the first month, when the pasch was kept, to the third day of the third month. You will have seventeen of the first month, thirty of the second, three of the third, which makes fifty. LETTER 55.[3]

THE MYSTERY OF THE TRINITY. CAESARIUS OF ARLES: When Abraham offered his son Isaac, he was a type of God the Father, while Isaac prefigured our Lord and Savior. The fact that he arrived at the place of sacrifice on the third day is shown to represent the mystery of the Trinity. That the third day should be accepted in the sense of a promise or mystery of the Trinity is found frequently in the sacred books. In Exodus we read, "We will go a three days' journey into the wilderness."[4] Again, upon arriving at Mt. Sinai it is said to the people, "Be sanctified, and be ready for the third day." When Joshua was about to cross the Jordan, he admonished the people to be ready on the third day. Moreover, our Lord rose on the third day. We have men-

tioned all this because blessed Abraham on the third day came to the place which the Lord had shown him. SERMON 84.2.[5]

THE MIRACLE WAS IN THE MEANING. AUGUSTINE: Again God produces the ordinary lightnings and thunders. But because they were done in an unusual manner on Mt. Sinai, and those voices were spoken there without a confused noise but in such a manner that it was evident from the most unmistakable proofs, . . . certain significant meanings were attached to them. Then they were miracles. THE TRINITY 3.5.11.[6]

See also AUGUSTINE ON EXODUS 13:21.

19:18 Sinai Wrapped in Smoke

GOD'S NATURE IS NOT MUTABLE. AUGUSTINE: But the sound of that voice and the corporeal appearance of the dove and the "parted tongues as it were of fire that sat upon every one of them,"[7] like those terrible manifestations that happened on Mt. Sinai and that pillar of cloud by day and of fire by night,[8] were performed and carried out as figurative acts. Now in these matters special care must be taken lest anyone believe that the nature of God, either the Father, the Son or the Holy Spirit, is subject to change or transformation. And let no one be troubled because sometimes the sign receives the name of the thing signified. Thus the Holy Spirit is said to have descended on Christ in the corporeal appearance, as it were, of a dove and to have remained upon him. Thus also the rock is called Christ because it signifies Christ.[9] LETTER 169.[10]

SMOKE, FIRE AND CLOUD ARE NOT GOD'S SUBSTANCE. AUGUSTINE: What shall I say about this except that no one is so insane as to

---

[1]Mt 27:63; Mk 8:31. [2]FC 71:140. [3]FC 12:286-87. [4]Ex 8:27. [5]FC 47:16-17. [6]FC 45:105-6. [7]Acts 2:3. [8]Ex 13:21. [9]1 Cor 10:4. [10]FC 30:57-58.

believe that the smoke, the fire, the cloud and the darkness and everything else of a similar nature are the substance of either the Word and the Wisdom of God which Christ is or of the Holy Spirit. For not even the Arians have dared to say this about God the Father. Therefore all those things were produced by a creature serving its Creator and were manifested by a suitable dispensation to the human senses. . . . Perhaps carnal thoughts will suggest that the cloud was certainly seen by the people but that within the cloud Moses saw the Son of God with his bodily eyes, whom the raving heretics will have to be seen in his own substance, because it was said, "Moses entered the cloud where God was."[11] THE TRINITY 2.15.25.[12]

SMOKE AND FIRE, PRIDE AND HUMILITY. BEDE: When about to give the law, the Lord descended in fire and smoke. Through the brilliance of his manifestation he enlightened the humble, and through the murky smoke of error he dimmed the eyes of the proud. COMMENTARY ON THE ACTS OF THE APOSTLES 2.[13]

19:19 *The Sound of the Trumpet*

THE GOSPEL PROCLAIMED BY MANY. CYRIL OF ALEXANDRIA: And this is pictured for you in the writings of Moses. For the God of all came down in the likeness of fire on Mt. Sinai, and there was a cloud, and darkness, and gloom and the voice of the trumpet with a loud ringing sound, according to the Scripture. The notes of the trumpet were, it says, few at first, but afterwards they waxed longer and became louder and louder continually. What then was it which the

shadow of the law signified to us by these things? Was it not this: that at first there were but few to publish the gospel tidings; but afterwards they became many? HOMILIES ON THE GOSPEL OF LUKE 60.[14]

THE SWEETNESS OF SPEECH. ORIGEN: But when she [the bride] has become worthy to have it said of her, as also it was said of Moses, that "Moses spoke, and God answered him," then there is fulfilled in her that which he says: "Make me to hear your voice."[15] It is indeed high praise of her that is disclosed in that saying, "Sweet is your voice."[16] For thus also said the most wise prophet David: "Let my speech be sweet to him."[17] And the voice of the soul is sweet when it utters the word of God, when it expounds the faith and the doctrines of the truth, when it unfolds God's dealings and his judgments. COMMENTARY ON THE SONG OF SONGS 3.15.[18]

19:20 *Moses Went Up*

ONLY THE PERFECT MAY ASCEND. BEDE: Moses alone ascended to its very top, where the divine majesty shone forth in fire and a dark cloud. Only the more perfect know how to grasp and observe the deeper and most secret mysteries of the law; the carnal-minded people, content with the external aspects of the letter, and gathered apart, as it were, and below, stood to hear the words from heaven. HOMILIES ON THE GOSPELS 11.17.[19]

---

[11]Ex 20:21. [12]FC 45:81. [13]CAA 32-33. [14]CGSL 259. [15]Song 2:14. [16]Song 2:14. [17]Ps 104:34. [18]ACW 26:250-51. [19]HOG 2:172.

20:1-17 THE TEN COMMANDMENTS

¹*And God spoke all these words, saying,*

²*"I am the* Lord *your God, who brought you out of the land of Egypt, out of the house of bondage.*

³*"You shall have no other gods before^f me.*

⁴*"You shall not make for yourself a graven image, or any likeness of anything that is in heaven above, or that is in the earth beneath, or that is in the water under the earth;* ⁵*you shall not bow down to them or serve them; for I the* Lord *your God am a jealous God, visiting the iniquity of the fathers upon the children to the third and the fourth generation of those who hate me,* ⁶*but showing steadfast love to thousands of those who love me and keep my commandments.*

⁷*"You shall not take the name of the* Lord *your God in vain; for the* Lord *will not hold him guiltless who takes his name in vain.*

⁸*"Remember the sabbath day, to keep it holy.* ⁹*Six days you shall labor, and do all your work;* ¹⁰*but the seventh day is a sabbath to the* Lord *your God; in it you shall not do any work, you, or your son, or your daughter, your manservant, or your maidservant, or your cattle, or the sojourner who is within your gates;* ¹¹*for in six days the* Lord *made heaven and earth, the sea, and all that is in them, and rested the seventh day; therefore the* Lord *blessed the sabbath day and hallowed it.*

¹²*"Honor your father and your mother, that your days may be long in the land which the* Lord *your God gives you.*

¹³*"You shall not kill.*

¹⁴*"You shall not commit adultery.*

¹⁵*"You shall not steal.*

¹⁶*"You shall not bear false witness against your neighbor.*

¹⁷*"You shall not covet your neighbor's house; you shall not covet your neighbor's wife, or his manservant, or his maidservant, or his ox, or his ass, or anything that is your neighbor's."*

f *Or* besides

Overview: The two tablets of the law correspond to the two great commandments of the gospel (Caesarius of Arles). Catechumens should be instructed on the whole of the Decalogue (Augustine). The first commandment is spoken by the Father and the Son; both are the Lord God (Fulgentius). The only-begotten Son is true God and not of another nature, as the Arians say (Gregory of Nyssa). Christians should not bow down before idols, even to save themselves from martyrdom. The Jews worship only the one true God. Both Jews and Christians prefer death to any form of idolatry. The jealousy of God means that he does not want anything alien to come into the souls of those who believe in him. God's jealousy is like that of a husband who wants his wife to remain chaste.

The name of God points to his most personal characteristic, which is holiness (Origen). The commandments refer in a veiled way to both the

Father and the Son (Eusebius). The second commandment calls us to revere the divinity of Christ.

The commandment to observe the sabbath bids us observe a true holiday, with a humble and quiet mind. The true sabbath observance is that of love that rests in God. The servile work from which we are to abstain is sin; and sin is a form of slavery (Augustine). The observance of a spiritual sabbath comprises prayer and spiritual reading (Caesarius of Arles). To rest on the seventh day is to imitate the Lord (Bede). The command to observe the sabbath includes a reason, because this commandment is not part of the natural law (Chrysostom).

To honor one's parents means first of all to provide what they need to live. Paul reinforced this commandment by quoting it verbatim (Origen). We should honor our parents even if they are poor, because their greatest gift to us is their final blessing (Ambrose). The commandment bids us support poor parents (Jerome). How close we are to our parents! Fathers are warned not to buy their sons' love with promises of an inheritance (Augustine).

Conscience itself teaches us not to kill (Chrysostom). Yet there are instances of justified homicide. The commandment also prohibits suicide. Both commandments and counsels are measured by the standard of love (Augustine). The full observance of the prohibition of adultery includes rejecting every form of superstition (John Cassian). The law forbade immoral acts; Christ goes further and condemns even immoral thoughts (Gregory the Great). The commandment that prohibits bearing false witness forbids every kind of lie.

Greed can darken our minds to the truth (Augustine). Love of money is an old vice (Ambrose). The commandment "You shall not covet" moves us to seek the medicine of grace. It makes us admit our pride. Fear of punishment is not a sufficient reason for observing the commandments. Do not look with longing on some-

one else's fine house (Augustine). David is an example of a man who gave in to lust (Gregory the Great). To cease lusting is to accomplish the good (Augustine).

20:1 God Spoke All These Words

The Two Tablets of the Law. Caesarius of Arles: We should also know that the ten commandments of the law are also fulfilled by the two gospel precepts, love of God and love of neighbor. For the three commandments which were written on the first tablet pertain to the love of God, while on the second tablet seven commandments were inscribed, one of which is "Honor your father and your mother." Doubtless all of the latter are recognized as pertaining to love of neighbor. The Lord said in the Gospel: "On these two commandments depend the whole Law and the Prophets."[1] Likewise we read what the apostle James said: "But whoever offends in one point has become guilty in all."[2] What does it mean to offend in one point and lose all, except to have fallen from the precept of charity and so to have offended in all the other commands? According to the apostle, without charity nothing in our virtues can be shown to avail at all. Sermon 100A.12.[3]

20:2 I Am the Lord Your God

Love of God and Love of Neighbor. Augustine: Let [my opponents] insist, if they like, in contradiction to their own assertion, that worship of the one true God and the prohibition against idolatry is not to be preached to the unbaptized but to the already baptized. Do not, however, let them any longer say to those who are going to receive baptism that they need be instructed only on belief in God and after the reception of the sacrament they will be taught the manner of living required by the second pre-

---

[1]Mt 22:40. [2]Jas 2:10. [3]FC 47:96.

cept on the love of neighbor. For both are contained in the law which the people received after the Red Sea, that is, after baptism. The commandments were not so distributed that before crossing the Red Sea the Jews were warned against idolatry and not until after their escape taught to honor father and mother, not to commit adultery, not to kill, and the remaining prescriptions for a rational and godly way of living. ON FAITH AND WORKS 11.17.[4]

BOTH FATHER AND SON SPOKE THE FIRST COMMANDMENT. FULGENTIUS: In the first commandment of the Decalogue, just as the worship and service of the one Lord God is most clearly commanded, so for adoration and service to be shown by the faithful to any creature is most vehemently forbidden. For it is said there: "I am the Lord your God, who brought you out of the land of Egypt, out of the house of slavery; you shall have no other gods before me." If this is taken as spoken simultaneously by the Father and the Son, the Father and the Son are believed to be one Lord God. But if either the Father is believed to have said this without the Son or the Son without the Father, it is necessary that the Father or the Son be denied to be the Lord God. Concerning this he said, "I am the Lord your God who brought you out of the land of Egypt, out of the house of slavery; you shall have no other gods before me." LETTER 8.4.9.[5]

20:3 No Other Gods Before Me

THE NATURE OF THE FATHER AND THE SON. GREGORY OF NYSSA: Again, he who says "you shall never worship a strange god" forbids us to worship another god, and the strange god is so called in contradistinction to our own God. Who then is our own God? Clearly, the true God. And who is the strange god? Surely, he who is alien from the nature of the true God. If therefore our own God is the true God, and if, as the heretics say, the only-begotten God is not

of the nature of the true God, he is a strange God and not our God. ON THE FAITH.[6]

20:5 You Shall Not Bow Down to Images

TO WORSHIP AND TO BOW DOWN ARE DISTINCT. ORIGEN: [God] warns a man inclined to idolatry not to practice it. But when a man who is not so inclined but yet through cowardice, which he calls "accommodation," pretends to worship idols as the masses do, he does not, it is true, worship idols, but he does bow before them. And I would say that they who abjure Christianity in the courtroom or even before they are brought there do not worship idols, but they do bow down before them; for they apply to inanimate and unheeding matter the name of the Lord God, namely "God". EXHORTATION TO MARTYRDOM 6.[7]

THE JEWS WORSHIP THE ONE GOD. ORIGEN: It is obvious that the Jews follow the law where God is represented as saying, "You shall have none other gods but me; you shall not make for yourself an idol nor any likeness of anything in the heaven above and in the earth beneath and in the waters under the earth; you shall not bow down to them nor worship them." And they worship none other than the supreme God who made heaven and everything else. It is clear then that since those who live according to the law reverence him who made the heavens, they do not reverence the heavens together with God. Furthermore, none of those who serve the Mosaic law worship the angels in heaven. And in the same way that they do not worship the sun, moon and stars, "the world of heaven," they avoid worshiping heaven and the angels in it. AGAINST CELSUS 5.6.[8]

CHRISTIANS ABHOR IDOLATRY. ORIGEN: Christians and Jews are led to avoid temples

---

[4]FC 27:242. [5]FC 95:371. [6]NPNF 2 5:337. [7]ACW 19:146. [8]OCC 267-68.

and altars and images by the command "You shall fear the Lord your God and him only shall you serve." . . . And not only do they avoid them, but when necessary they readily come to the point of death to avoid defiling their conception of the God of the universe by any act of this kind contrary to his law. AGAINST CELSUS 7.64.[9]

GOD IS JEALOUS. ORIGEN: When men try to seduce us to apostasy, it is useful to reflect upon what God wishes to teach us when he says, "I am the Lord your God, jealous." In my view, just as the bridegroom who wishes to make his bride live chastely so as to give herself entirely to him and beware of any relationship whatever with any man other than her husband, pretends, though he be wise, to be jealous—he uses this pretense as a kind of antidote for his bride—so the Lawgiver, especially when he reveals himself as "the firstborn of every creature,"[10] says to his bride, the soul, that he is a jealous God. In this way he keeps his followers from any fornication with demons and pretended gods. EXHORTATION TO MARTYRDOM 9.[11]

THE HOUSE OF GOD IS EACH OF US. ORIGEN: Now Christ is especially jealous for the house of God in each of us, not wishing it to be a house of merchandise[12] or that the house of prayer become a den of thieves,[13] since he is Son of a jealous God. This is the case if we understand such words from the Scriptures in a reasonable manner, which were spoken metaphorically from the human viewpoint to set forth the fact that God wishes nothing alien to his will to be mingled with the soul of any, but especially with the soul of those who wish to receive [the teachings of the] most divine faith. COMMENTARY ON THE GOSPEL OF JOHN 10.221.[14]

20:7 Not Taking the Lord's Name in Vain

HOW WE COME TO UNDERSTAND GOD. ORI-

GEN: Although making a variety of suppositions about him, we all know something of God but do not all know what he is, for few indeed and fewer (if I may say so) than few are they who grasp his holiness in all things. Thus we are rightly taught to pray that our concept of God may be hallowed among us. Thus we shall see his holiness in creating, in providing, in judging, in choosing and abandoning, in accepting and rejecting, in rewarding and punishing each one according to his merits.

In these activities and others like them is found, so I may say, the stamp of the personal character of God, that which in my opinion is called in Scripture the "name of God." So in Exodus: "You shall not take the name of your God in vain." ON PRAYER 24.2-3.[15]

THE LORD AND THE LORD. EUSEBIUS: Here too the Lord himself teaches in the passage before us about another Lord. For he says, "I am the Lord thy God," and adds, "You shall not take the name of the Lord your God in vain." The second Lord is here mystically instructing his servant about the Father, that is to say, the God of the universe. And you could find many other similar instances occurring in Holy Scripture, in which God speaks as if in a second voice about another. The Lord himself speaks as if about another. PROOF OF THE GOSPEL 5.16.243.[16]

THE NAME OF THE LORD IS TRUTH. AUGUSTINE: The second commandment: "You shall not take the name of the Lord your God in vain; for whoever takes the name of the Lord his God in vain will not be purified." The name of the Lord our God Jesus Christ is Truth: he himself said, "I am the truth."[17] So truth purifies; futility defiles. And because whoever speaks the truth speaks from what is God's—for "whoever speaks falsehood speaks from what is his

[9]OCC 448. [10]Col 1:15. [11]ACW 19:149. [12]Jn 2:16. [13]Mt 21:13. [14]FC 80:303-4. [15]ACW 19:81-82. [16]POG 1:260. [17]Jn 14:6.

own"[18]—to speak the truth is to speak reasonably, whereas to speak futility is to make a noise rather than to speak. Rightly, because the second commandment means love of the truth, the opposite of that is love of futility. Sermon 8.5.[19]

Christ Is Not a Creature. Augustine: You are told "Do not take the name of the Lord your God in vain"; do not regard Christ as a creature because for your sake he put on the creature. And you, you despise him who is equal to the Father and one with the Father. Sermon 9.3.[20]

20:8 Remember the Sabbath

The Sabbath Means a Peaceful Mind. Augustine: The third commandment: "Remember the sabbath day to sanctify it." This third commandment imposes a regular periodical holiday—quietness of heart, tranquility of mind, the product of a good conscience. Here is sanctification, because here is the Spirit of God. Well, here is what a true holiday, that is to say, quietness and rest, means "Upon whom," he says, "shall my spirit rest? Upon one who is humble and quiet and trembles at my words."[21] So unquiet people are those who recoil from the Holy Spirit, loving quarrels, spreading slanders, keener on argument than on truth, and so in their restlessness they do not allow the quietness of the spiritual sabbath to enter into themselves. Sermon 8.6.[22]

Pure Rest Is Found in God Alone. Augustine: We are not ordered to keep the sabbath day by a literal corporal abstinence from work, as the Jews observe it—and, indeed, that observance of theirs, because it is so commanded, is considered ludicrous unless it signifies some other spiritual rest. From this we understand that all the truths which are expressed figuratively in the Scriptures are appropriately designed to arouse love. By love we attain to rest. The only commandment that is given figuratively is the one by which rest is enjoined.

Rest is universally loved but found pure and entire in God alone.

However, the Lord's day was not made known to Jews but to Christians by the resurrection of the Lord, and from that event it began to acquire its solemnity. Doubtless the souls of all the saints prior to the resurrection of the body enjoy repose, but they do not possess that activity which gives power to risen bodies. Letter 55.[23]

No Perfect Rest in This Life. Augustine: But the rite of the sabbath was taught to our ancient fathers which we Christians observe spiritually so that we abstain from all servile work, that is, from all sin (for the Lord says, "Everyone who commits a sin is a slave of sin"),[24] and we have rest in our hearts, that is, spiritual tranquility. And, however we try in this world, we shall nevertheless not arrive at that perfect rest except when we have departed this life. Tractate on the Gospel of John 20.2.[25]

Servile Work Is Sin. Augustine: To teach a Christian anything about the observance of the sabbath would seem to be rather superfluous. On the contrary, not only is it not superfluous, but it is in fact basic, bedrock doctrine, because it is a shadow of things to come.[26] The people, you see, are forbidden to perform servile works on the sabbath. Now are we, I ask you, not forbidden to perform servile works? Listen to the Lord: "Everyone who commits sin is the slave of sin."[27] And yet to celebrate the sabbath is to hope to receive from God this very thing, of not committing sin. That's why it is written, "God rested on the seventh day from all his works."[28] God rested; God enables you to rest. For God himself to rest, well when did he tire himself out working, seeing that he created all things with a word? Sermon 179A.3.[29]

---

[18]Jn 8:44. [19]WSA 3 1:242-43. [20]WSA 3 1:261. [21]Is 66:2. [22]WSA 3 1:244. [23]FC 12:278. [24]Jn 8:34. [25]FC 79:164. [26]Col 2:17. [27]Jn 8:34. [28]Gen 2:2. [29]WSA 3 5:308.

OBSERVE A SPIRITUAL SABBATH. CAESARIUS OF ARLES: The third precept is "Remember to keep holy the sabbath day." In this third commandment is suggested a certain idea of freedom, a repose of the heart or tranquility of the mind which a good conscience effects. Indeed, sanctification is there because the Spirit of God dwells there. Now look at the freedom or repose; our Lord says, "Upon whom shall I rest but upon the man who is humble and peaceable, and who trembles at my words?"[30] Therefore restless souls turn away from the Holy Ghost. Lovers of strife, authors of calumnies, devotees of quarrels rather than of charity, by their uneasiness they do not admit to themselves the repose of a spiritual sabbath. Men do not observe a spiritual sabbath unless they devote themselves to earthly occupations so moderately that they still engage in reading and prayer, at least frequently, if not always. As that apostle says, "Be diligent in reading and in teaching";[31] and again, "Pray without ceasing."[32] Men of this kind honor the sabbath in a spiritual manner. SERMON 100.4.[33]

SIX DAYS OF GOD'S WORKS. BEDE: Under the law the people were ordered to work for six days and to rest on the seventh, [and] to plow and reap for six years and desist during the seventh,[34] because the Lord completed the creation of the world in six days and desisted from his work on the seventh.[35] Mystically speaking, we are counseled by all this that those who in this age (which is comprised of six periods), devote themselves to good works for the Lord's sake, are in future led by the Lord to a sabbath, that is, to eternal rest. HOMILIES ON THE GOSPELS 2.17.[36]

20:10 A Sabbath to the Lord

THE COMMANDMENTS AND THE NATURAL LAW. CHRYSOSTOM: When he speaks to us of another commandment, not known to us by the dictate of conscience, he not only prohibits but

also adds the reason. When, for instance, he gave the commandment respecting the sabbath, "On the seventh day you shall do no work," he subjoined also the reason for this cessation. What was this? "Because on the seventh day God rested from all his works which he had begun to make." And again, "Because you were a servant in the land of Egypt."[37] For what purpose then, I ask, did he add a reason respecting the sabbath but did no such thing in regard to murder? Because this commandment was not one of the leading ones. It was not one of those which were accurately defined in our conscience but a kind of partial and temporary one. And for this reason it was later experienced. HOMILIES CONCERNING THE STATUES 12.9.[38]

20:12 Honor Your Parents

WHAT HONORING PARENTS MEANS. ORIGEN: And God said, "Honor your father and your mother," teaching that the child should pay the honor which is due to his parents. Of this honor to parents one part was to share with them the necessaries of life, such as food and clothing, and if there was any other thing in which it was possible for them to show favor toward their own parents. COMMENTARY ON THE GOSPEL OF MATTHEW 11.9.[39]

THE COMMANDMENT IS BINDING. ORIGEN: And again, who would deny that the command which says, "Honor your father and your mother, that it may be well with you," is useful quite apart from any spiritual interpretation and that it ought certainly to be observed, especially when we remember that the apostle Paul has quoted it in the same words?[40] ON FIRST PRINCIPLES 4.3.4.[41]

THE HONOR DUE TO PARENTS. AMBROSE: The

---

[30]Is 66:2. [31]1 Tim 4:13. [32]1 Thess 5:17. [33]FC 47:87. [34]Ex 23:10-11. [35]Gen 2:2. [36]HOG 2:174-75. [37]Deut 5:15; 15:15; 16:12; 24:18. [38]NPNF 1 9:421-22. [39]ANF 9:438. [40]Eph 6:2-3. [41]OFP 295.

formation of the children is then the prerogative of the parents. Therefore honor your father, that he may bless you. Let the godly man honor his father out of gratitude and the ingrate do so on account of fear. Even if the father is poor and does not have plenty of resources to leave to his sons, still he has the heritage of his final blessing with which he may bestow the wealth of sanctification on his descendants. And it is a far greater thing to be blessed than it is to be rich. THE PATRIARCHS 1.1.[42]

DUTY TO POOR PARENTS. JEROME: [The Lord] declares that [this commandment] is to be interpreted not of mere words, which while offering an empty show of regard may still leave a parent's wants unrelieved, but by the actual provision of the necessaries of life. The Lord commanded that poor parents should be supported by their children and that these should pay them back when old for those benefits which they had themselves received in their childhood. LETTER 123.6.[43]

PARENTS ARE TO BE CHERISHED. AUGUSTINE: It's your parents you see when you first open your eyes, and it is their friendship that lays down the first strands of this life. If anyone fails to honor his parents, is there anyone he will spare? SERMON 9.7.[44]

A WARNING TO PARENTS. AUGUSTINE: So if you are afraid your son won't take care of you once he has his hands on the money, you are in fact making filial piety a commodity for sale, not a quality to be loved. How much better a poor man's son, the son, for instance, of an old man in the direst poverty, who expects nothing from his father because he hasn't got anything he can leave him but who all the same supports his father with his labor and the sweat of his brow. Sometimes, of course, the children of rich people too take the fear of God seriously, and that's why they show consideration to their parents, not because they expect something from them but because they are

their parents who brought them into the world and brought them up, and God gave a commandment which says "Honor your father and your mother." But where the reward is there for all to see, the genuineness of their sentiments is not so obvious. SERMON 45.2.[45]

20:13 *You Shall Not Kill*

THE NATURAL LAW PROHIBITS MURDER. CHRYSOSTOM: How was it then when he said, "You shall not kill," that he did not add, "because murder is a wicked thing?" The reason was that conscience had already taught this beforehand. He speaks thus, as if to those who know and understand the point. HOMILIES CONCERNING THE STATUES 12.9.[46]

JUSTIFIED HOMICIDE. AUGUSTINE: "What about the prohibition, 'You shall not kill,' which is also there? If killing is evil in every respect, how will the just who, in obedience to a law, have killed many, be excused from this charge?" The answer to this question is that he does not kill who is the executor of a just command. ON LYING 13.23.[47]

THE QUESTION OF SUICIDE. AUGUSTINE: It is significant that in Holy Scripture no passage can be found enjoining or permitting suicide either in order to hasten our entry into immortality or to void or avoid temporal evils. God's command, "You shall not kill," is to be taken as forbidding self-destruction, especially as it does not add "your neighbor," as it does when it forbids false witness, "You shall not bear false witness against your neighbor." CITY OF GOD 1.20.[48]

20:14 *You Shall Not Commit Adultery*

THE STANDARD OF MORALS. AUGUSTINE: Therefore whatsoever things God commands

---

[42]FC 65:243. [43]NPNF 2 6:231-32. [44]WSA 3 1:265. [45]WSA 3 2:252. [46]NPNF 1 9:421. [47]FC 16:85. [48]FC 8:52.

(and one of these is "You shall not commit adultery") and whatsoever things are not positively ordered but are strongly advised as good spiritual counsel (and one of these is, "It is a good thing for a man to not touch a woman")[49]—all of these imperatives are rightly obeyed only when they are measured by the standard of our love of God and our love of our neighbor in God. A Handbook on Faith, Hope and Love 32.121.[50]

The Higher Sense of the Commandment. John Cassian: It is written in the law, "You shall not commit fornication." This is required in a beneficial way according to the simple sound of the letter by the person who is still entangled in the passions of fleshly impurity. It is necessarily observed in spiritual fashion, however, by one who has already left behind this filthy behavior and impure disposition, so that he also rejects not only all idolatrous ceremonies but also every superstition of the Gentiles and the observance of auguries and omens and of all signs and days and times. And he is certainly not engaged in the divination of particular words or names, which befouls the wholesomeness of our faith. Conference 14.11.2.[51]

Acts and Thoughts. Gregory the Great: The law suppressed physical sins, but our Redeemer condemned even unlawful thoughts.[52] And so "if they do not hear Moses and the prophets, neither will they believe one who rises from the dead."[53] When will those who neglect to fulfill the less important commandments of the law be strong enough to obey our Savior's more demanding precepts? This much is clear: anyone whose sayings they decline to fulfill, they have refused to believe. Homily 40.[54]

20:16 You Shall Not Bear False Witness

All Lies Are Forbidden. Augustine: In the Decalogue itself it is written, "You shall not bear false witness," in which classification every lie is embraced, for whoever pronounces any statement gives testimony to his own mind. If anyone should argue that not every lie should be called false witness, what will he answer to this statement which is also in the sacred Scriptures: "The mouth that belies, kills the soul"?[55] If anyone should think that this passage can be interpreted to except certain lies, he may read in another passage: "You will destroy all that speak a lie."[56] In this connection, our divine Lord said with his own lips, "Let your speech be 'yes, yes'; 'no, no'; and whatever is more comes from the evil one."[57] Hence the apostle too, when he directs that the old man should be put off, under which term all sins are understood, goes on to explain his remark and specifically says, "Therefore put away lying and speak the truth."[58] On Lying 5.6.[59]

Greed and Avarice. Augustine: The law says to you, for example, "You shall not bear false witness."[60] If you know what the truth of the evidence is, you have light in your mind. But if you are overcome by greed for sordid gain and decide in your heart of hearts to bear false witness for the sake of it, then you are already beginning to be tossed about by the storm in the absence of Christ. You are being heaved up and down by the waves of your avarice, you are being endangered by the tempest of your desires, and with Christ apparently absent, you are on the verge of sinking. Sermon 75.5.[61]

20:17 You Shall Not Covet

An Ancient Vice. Ambrose: Love of money then is an old, an ancient vice, which showed itself even at the declaration of the divine law; for a law was given to check it. Duties of the Clergy 2.26.130.[62]

The Commandment Leads Us to Grace.

---

[49]1 Cor 7:1. [50]LCC 7:411. [51]ACW 57:515. [52]Mt 5:28. [53]Lk 16:31. [54]CS 123:382. [55]Wis 1:11. [56]Ps 5:6. [57]Mt 5:37. [58]Eph 4:25. [59]FC 16:61. [60]Ex 20:16; Deut 5:20. [61]WSA 3 3:306. [62]NPNF 2 10:63.

AUGUSTINE: The law said, "You shall not covet," in order that, when we find ourselves lying in this diseased state, we might seek the medicine of grace. By that commandment [we might] know both in what direction our endeavors should aim as we advance in our present mortal condition and to what a height it is possible to reach in the future immortality. For unless perfection could somewhere be attained, this commandment would never have been given to us. ON MARRIAGE AND CONCUPISCENCE 1.32.[63]

COVETOUSNESS CONVICTS US OF SIN. AUGUSTINE: There you are then, the law tells you "you shall not covet." You know the law which says, "You shall not covet." Covetousness surges up in you, which you didn't know. It was there inside, you see, but it wasn't known. You started to make an effort to overcome what was inside, and what was hidden came to light. Proud fellow, through the law you have been made into a transgressor. Acknowledge grace, and become a singer of praise. SERMON 26.9.[64]

FEAR OF PUNISHMENT IS NOT ENOUGH. AUGUSTINE: Even a lion can be shooed off its prey by the terrifying threat of arms and weapons and the crowd of people perhaps surrounding it or coming to attack it; and yet the lion comes, the lion returns. It hasn't seized its prey; it hasn't either laid aside its evil intention. If that's what you're like, your justice is still the sort by which you take care not to get tortured. What's so great about being afraid of punishment? Who isn't afraid of it? SERMON 169.8.[65]

WHAT IT MEANS TO CEASE LUSTING. AUGUSTINE: What is the accomplishing of good except the cessation and end of evil? But what is the cessation of evil except what the law says, "You shall not lust"?[66] To lust not at all is the accomplishing of good because it is the cessation of evil. He said this: "To accomplish good is not there for me," because he was unable to bring it about that he did not lust. He only brought it about that he reined in lust, that he did not consent to lust and that he did not offer his members to lust for its service. TRACTATE ON THE GOSPEL OF JOHN 41.12.[67]

AVOID COVETING PROPERTY. AUGUSTINE: To save me from saying a lot, among other commandments it contains "You shall not covet your neighbor's property." Don't covet; don't go up and down in front of that country house belonging to someone else and sigh because it's such a fine one. Do not covet your neighbor's property. "The Lord's is the earth and its fullness."[68] What haven't you acquired, if you have got hold of God? So don't covet your neighbor's property. SERMON 252A.6.[69]

DAVID LUSTED. GREGORY THE GREAT: Old Testament law forbids anyone to lust after another man's wife, but it does not decree punishment for the king who commands his soldiers to perform dangerous feats or who desires a drink of water. We all know that David was pricked by lust and desired another man's wife and took her.[70] The blows his sin deserved followed, and he made amends for the evil he had done by tears of repentance. HOMILY 34.[71]

---

[63]NPNF 1 5:276. [64]WSA 3 2:98. [65]WSA 3 5:227. [66]Rom 7:7 quoting Ex 20:17. [67]FC 88:148. [68]Ps 24:1. [69]WSA 3 7:145-46. [70]2 Sam 11:2-4. [71]CS 123:295.

20:18-26 THE FEAR OF GOD

[18]Now when all the people perceived the thunderings and the lightnings and the sound of the trumpet and the mountain smoking, the people were afraid and trembled; and they stood afar off, [19]and said to Moses, "You speak to us, and we will hear; but let not God speak to us, lest we die." . . .

[24]"An altar of earth you shall make for me and sacrifice on it your burnt offerings and your peace offerings, your sheep and your oxen; in every place where I cause my name to be remembered I will come to you and bless you. [25]And if you make me an altar of stone, you shall not build it of hewn stones; for if you wield your tool upon it you profane it. [26]And you shall not go up by steps to my altar, that your nakedness be not exposed on it."

OVERVIEW: There is a great contrast between the giving of the law on Sinai and the coming of the Holy Spirit on Pentecost (AUGUSTINE). God has no need of sacrifices (CONSTITUTIONS). To sacrifice on an altar of earth is to acknowledge the Lord's incarnation (PATERIUS). God is one and is not approached in steps or stages of divinity (CASSIODORUS).

20:18 The Mountain Smoking

See AUGUSTINE ON EXODUS 19:18.

20:19 Let Not God Speak to Us

SINAI AND PENTECOST. AUGUSTINE: But notice how it happened there and how it happened here. There, the people stood a long way off; there was an atmosphere of dread, not of love. I mean, they were so terrified that they said to Moses, "Speak to us yourself, and do not let the Lord speak to us, lest we die." So God came down, as it is written, on Sinai in fire; but he was terrifying the people who stood a long way off, and "writing with his finger on stone,"[1] not on the heart.

Here, however, when the Holy Spirit came, the faithful were gathered together as one; and he didn't terrify them on a mountain but came

in to them in a house. There came a sudden sound, indeed, from heaven, as of a fierce squall rushing upon them; it made a noise, but nobody panicked. You have heard the sound, now see the fire too, because each was there on the mountain also, both fire and sound; but there, there was smoke as well, here, though, the fire was clear. "There appeared to them," Scripture says, you see, "divided tongues, as of fire." Terrifying them from a long way off? Far from it. Because "it settled upon each one of them, and they began to talk in languages, as the Spirit gave them utterance."[2] Hear a person speaking a language, and understand the Spirit writing not on stone but on the heart. SERMON 155.6.[3]

20:24 An Altar of Earth

GOD NEEDS NO SACRIFICES. ANONYMOUS: For he says, "If you will make an altar, you shall make it of earth." It does not say "make one" but "if you will make." It does not impose a necessity but gives leave to their own free liberty. For God does not stand in need of sacrifices, being by nature above all want. CONSTITUTIONS OF THE HOLY APOSTLES 6.4.20.[4]

---

[1]Ex 31:18. [2]Acts 2:1-4. [3]WSA 3 5:87. [4]ANF 7:459.

THE LORD'S INCARNATION. PATERIUS: To make an altar of earth for the Lord is to place our hope in the incarnation of the Mediator. Our gift is accepted by God when, on this altar, our humility rests whatever it does upon faith in the Lord's incarnation. We place the gift we offer on an altar made of earth if we base all our actions on faith in the Lord's incarnation. EXPOSITION OF THE OLD AND NEW TESTAMENT, EXODUS 30.[5]

20:26 Not Going Up by Steps to God's Altar

GOD IS ONE. CASSIODORUS: Unity knows no number, equality allows no scale. As Scripture says, "You shall not go up by steps to my altar." EXPOSITION OF THE PSALMS 116.2.[6]

---

[5]PL 79:735, citing Gregory the Great *Moral Interpretation of Job* 3.26.51. [6]ACW 53:162.

21:1-11 LAWS REGARDING SLAVES

[2]*"When you buy a Hebrew slave, he shall serve six years, and in the seventh he shall go out free, for nothing. [3]If he comes in single, he shall go out single; if he comes in married, then his wife shall go out with him. [4]If his master gives him a wife and she bears him sons or daughters, the wife and her children shall be her master's and he shall go out alone. [5]But if the slave plainly says, 'I love my master, my wife, and my children; I will not go out free,' [6]then his master shall bring him to God, and he shall bring him to the door or the doorpost; and his master shall bore his ear through with an awl; and he shall serve him for life."*

OVERVIEW: The true sabbath rest is eternal life (JEROME). To belong only to God is to enjoy true freedom (AMBROSE).

21:2 Hebrew Slaves Serve Six Years

THE TRUE AND ETERNAL SABBATH. JEROME: We read that every Hebrew keeps the same Passover, and that in the seventh year every prisoner is set free, and that at Jubilee, that is, the fiftieth year,[1] every possession returns to its owner. All this refers not to the present but to the future. For being in bondage during the six days of this world, on the seventh day, the true and eternal sabbath, we shall be free. If we wish to be free, we will be free even while still in bondage in the world. If, however, we do not desire it, our ear will be bored in token of our disobedience. We shall, with our wives and children, remain in perpetual slavery if we prefer the flesh and its works to liberty. AGAINST JOVINIAN 2.25.[2]

21:5 I Will Not Go Out Free

SLAVERY TO THE WORLD. AMBROSE: That man is truly free, a true Hebrew, who is entirely God's. Everything that he possesses shares in freedom. He has nothing in common with the man who rejects freedom and says, "I have loved my master. . . . I will not go out free." The man who subjects himself to the world is returned not only to his master but also to his infirmity, because he loves the world or his mind, that is,

---

[1]Lev 25:10-12. [2]NPNF 2 6:408.

his *nous*, the author of this desire. He is returned not only to his wife but even to those pleasures which make him so bound to household matters that he does not care for what is eternal. Thus "at his threshold and door his master shall

pierce his ear," in order that he might remember the decision by which he chose slavery. LETTER 1(7).14.[3]

[3] CSEL 82 1:9-10.

21:12-32 PERSONAL INJURY

[12] "Whoever strikes a man so that he dies shall be put to death. [13] But if he did not lie in wait for him, but God let him fall into his hand, then I will appoint for you a place to which he may flee. . . .

[15] "Whoever strikes his father or his mother shall be put to death.

[16] "Whoever steals a man, whether he sells him or is found in possession of him, shall be put to death.

[17] "Whoever curses his father or his mother shall be put to death. . . .

[22] "When men strive together, and hurt a woman with child, so that there is a miscarriage, and yet no harm follows, the one who hurt her shall[b] be fined, according as the woman's husband shall lay upon him; and he shall pay as the judges determine. [23] If any harm follows, then you shall give life for life, [24] eye for eye, tooth for tooth, hand for hand, foot for foot, [25] burn for burn, wound for wound, stripe for stripe."

b *Heb* he shall

OVERVIEW: How does a Christian deal with the law of retaliation, which Christ abrogated? The law did not permit personal revenge but restrained violence (TERTULLIAN). The law and the gospel are not contradictory but can ultimately be reconciled (ORIGEN). Even murderers are subject to God's providence (AMBROSE). Both Testaments provide for a refuge from persecution (ATHANASIUS). The lowest sort of justice demands a penalty greater than the injury. The justice of the Pharisees seeks punishment proportionate to the offense. Perfect peace seeks no retaliation (AUGUSTINE). The law of retaliation was a temporary dispensation and part of a process of education (CYRIL OF ALEXANDRIA). The

gospel asks us to go beyond the law and to endure suffering patiently (JOHN CASSIAN). To speak well of our parents merits a great reward (CHRYSOSTOM).

21:13 A Place to Flee

THE MURDERER IN GOD'S PLAN. AMBROSE: Even the person who unwittingly committed a murder was still within the ministry of God, since the law makes this statement regarding him: "God delivered him into his hands." His hands therefore served as an instrument of divine punishment. The Levite is then the minister who remits, whereas the man who (in the example just cited) unwittingly and unwillingly struck another in a homicidal act became in fact an administrator of divine punishment. See to it that Christ is infused into the act of slaying an impious man and that sanctification accompany and be part of your attempt to abolish what is abominable. Cain and Abel 2.4.15.[1]

CITIES OF REFUGE. ATHANASIUS: For there was a command under the law that cities of refuge should be appointed, in order that they who were sought after to be put to death might at least have some means of saving themselves. And when he who spoke to Moses, the Word of the Father, appeared in the end of the world, he also gave this commandment, saying, "But when they persecute you in this city, flee into another."[2] DEFENSE OF HIS FLIGHT 11.[3]

21:17 One Who Curses Parents

TO SPEAK WELL OF PARENTS. CHRYSOSTOM: One who speaks ill of his mother or father will die the death. One who speaks well of them will have full enjoyment of the rewards of life. If our parents in the flesh should enjoy such good will from us, so much the more would this hold true for our parents in the spirit. HOMILY 6.1.[4]

21:24 Eye for Eye, Tooth for Tooth

THE LAW RESTRAINS VIOLENCE. TERTULLIAN: But what parts of the law can I defend as good with a greater confidence than those which heresy has shown such a longing for—as the statute of retaliation, requiring eye for eye, tooth for tooth and stripe for stripe? Now there is not here any smack of permission to mutual injury. There is rather, on the whole, a provision for restraining violence. To a people which was very obdurate and wanting in faith toward God, it might seem tedious and even incredible to expect from God that vengeance which was subsequently to be declared by the prophet: "Vengeance is mine; I will repay, says the Lord."[5] Therefore, in the meanwhile, the commission of wrong was to be checked by the fear of retribution immediately to happen. So the permission of this retribution was to be the prohibition of provocation. In this way a stop might thus be put to all hot-blooded injury. By the permission of the second the first is prevented by fear. By this deterring of the first the second act of wrong fails to be committed. AGAINST MARCION 2.18.1.[6]

CONCORDANCE OF OLD AND NEW TESTAMENTS. ORIGEN: Celsus[7] does not quote any passages from the law which are apparently in contradiction to what stands in the gospel, so that we might compare them. He says, "And to a man who has struck one once one should offer oneself to be struck again."[8] But we will say that we are aware that "it was said to them of old time, 'An eye for an eye and a tooth for a tooth,' "[9] and that we have read also the words "But I say unto you, to him that strikes you on one cheek offer the other one also."[10] However, I imagine that Celsus derived some of his vague notions from those who say that the God of the gospel is different from the God of the law and so made remarks like this. I would reply to his objection that the Old Testament also knows the doctrine that to him that strikes you on the right cheek you should offer the other one also. At any rate, it is written in the Lamentations of Jeremiah: "It is good for a man when he bears a yoke in his youth, he will sit alone and in silence when he has taken it on himself. He will give a cheek to the man who smites him and shall be filled with reproaches."[11] The gospel then does not lay down laws in contradiction to the God of the law, not even if we interpret literally the saying about a blow on the jaw.

---

[1]FC 42:416. [2]Mt 10:23. [3]NPNF 2 4:259. [4]FC 72:164-65. [5]Deut 32:35; Rom 12:19; Heb 10:30. [6]ANF 3:311*. [7]Celsus was a pagan who attacked Christianity in the late second century in a book entitled *The True Word*. [8]Mt 5:39. [9]Ex 21:24; Lev 24:20; Mt 5:38. [10]Mt 5:38-39. [11]Lam 3:27-29.

And neither Moses nor Jesus "is wrong." Nor did the "Father forget when he sent Jesus the commands which he had given to Moses." Nor did he "condemn his own laws, and change his mind and send his messenger for the opposite purpose."[12] AGAINST CELSUS 7.25.[13]

THREE LEVELS OF JUSTICE. AUGUSTINE: Not to exceed due measure in inflicting punishment, lest the requital be greater than the injury— that is the lesser justice of the Pharisees. And it is a high degree of justice, for it would not be easy to find a man who, on receiving a fisticuff, would be content to give only one in return and who, on hearing one word from a reviler, would be content to return one word exactly equivalent. On the contrary, either he exceeds moderation because he is angry, or he thinks that, with regard to one who has inflicted an injury on another, justice demands a penalty greater than the injury suffered by the innocent person. To a great extent, such a spirit is restrained by the law, in which is written the directive, "An eye for an eye" and "A tooth for a tooth." Moderation is signified by these words, so that the penalty may not be greater than the injury. And this is the beginning of peace. But to have absolutely no wish for any such retribution—that is perfect peace. ON THE LORD'S SERMON ON THE MOUNT 1.19.56.[14]

GOD LEADS HIS PEOPLE GENTLY. CYRIL OF ALEXANDRIA: Such an enactment required a man not to injure others. Supposing him to have sustained an injury, his anger at the wrongdoer must not go beyond an equal retribution. But the general bearing of the legal mode of life was by no means pleasing to God. It was even given to those of old time as a schoolmaster, accustoming them little by little to a fitting righteousness and leading them on gently toward the possession of the perfect good. For it is written, "To do what is just is the beginning of the good way";[15] but finally all perfection is in Christ and his precepts. "For to him that strikes you on the cheek," he says, "offer also the other."[16] HOMILIES ON THE GOSPEL OF LUKE 29.[17]

THE LAW AND GRACE. JOHN CASSIAN: The law does not forbid the retaliation of wrongs and revenge for injustices when it says, "An eye for an eye, a tooth for a tooth." Grace wants our patience to be proven by a redoubling of the mistreatment and the blows that come upon us, and it commands us to be ready to endure double hurt when it says, "Whoever strikes you on your right cheek, offer him the other. And to him who wants to contend with you at law and to take away your coat, give him your cloak as well."[18] The former says that enemies must be hated, but the latter decrees that they are to be loved to such an extent that we must even pray to God continually on their behalf.[19] CONFERENCE 21.32.4.[20]

---

[12]Origen is quoting Celsus. [13]OCC 414-15. [14]FC 11:80. [15]Prov 16:5. [16]Lk 6:29. [17]CGSL 136-37. [18]Mt 5:39-40. [19]Mt 5:44. [20]ACW 57:744.

21:33—22:6 PROPERTY DAMAGE

[33]"When a man leaves a pit open, or when a man digs a pit and does not cover it, and an ox or an ass falls into it, [34]the owner of the pit shall make it good; he shall give money to its owner, and the dead beast shall be his.

[35]"When one man's ox hurts another's, so that it dies, then they shall sell the live ox and divide the price of it; and the dead beast also they shall divide. [36]Or if it is known that the ox has been accustomed to gore in the past, and its owner has not kept it in, he shall pay ox for ox, and the dead beast shall be his.

22 [1i]"*If a man steals an ox or a sheep, and kills it or sells it, he shall pay five oxen for an ox, and four sheep for a sheep. [j]He shall make restitution; if he has nothing, then he shall be sold for his theft. [4]If the stolen beast is found alive in his possession, whether it is an ox or an ass or a sheep, he shall pay double.*"

i Ch 21.37 in Heb   j Restoring the second half of verse 3 and the whole of verse 4 to their place immediately following verse 1

OVERVIEW: The commands of the Old Testament are no stricter than those of the New. The Old forbids us to steal; the New commands us to be generous (GREGORY THE GREAT). Zaccheus, in the Gospel, followed the law and restored what he had stolen fourfold (CHRYSOSTOM).

21:33 An Open Pit

See GREGORY THE GREAT ON EXODUS 34:34.

22:1 Stealing an Ox

THE OLD TESTAMENT IS NOT STRICTER THAN THE NEW. GREGORY THE GREAT: Some people consider the commandments of the Old Testament stricter than those of the New, but they are deceived by a shortsighted interpretation. In the Old Testament, theft, not miserliness, is punished: wrongful taking of property is punished by fourfold restitution.[1] In the New Testament[2] the rich man is not censured for having taken away someone else's property but for not having given away his own. He is not said to have forcibly wronged anyone but to have prided himself on what he received. HOMILY 40.[3]

22:1 Four Sheep for a Sheep

VIOLENCE IS WORSE THAN THEFT. CHRYSOSTOM: Therefore the thief being taken pays fourfold, but he that spoils by violence is worse than if he steals. And if this last ought to give fourfold what he stole, the extortioner should give tenfold and much more. Even so he can make atonement for his justice. For of almsgiving not even then will he receive the reward. Therefore says Zaccheus, "I will restore what I have taken by false accusation fourfold, and the half of my goods I will give to the poor."[4] And if under the law one ought to give fourfold, much more under grace. And if this is so for one who steals, much more it is so for one who spoils by violence. HOMILIES ON THE GOSPEL OF MATTHEW 52.6.[5]

[1]Cf. Lev 6:5; 2 Sam 12:6.   [2]See Lk 16:19-31.   [3]CS 123:374-75.   [4]Lk 19:8.   [5]NPNF 1 10:326.

[22:7-15 TRUSTS AND LOANS]

22:16—23:9 SOCIAL LAWS

²⁰*"Whoever sacrifices to any god, save to the L*ORD *only, shall be utterly destroyed. . . .*

²⁵*"If you lend money to any of my people with you who is poor, you shall not be to him as a creditor, and you shall not exact interest from him.* ²⁶*If ever you take your neighbor's garment in pledge, you shall restore it to him before the sun goes down;* ²⁷*for that is his only covering, it is his mantle for his body; in what else shall he sleep? And if he cries to me, I will hear, for I am compassionate.*

²⁸*"You shall not revile God, nor curse a ruler of your people.*

²⁹*"You shall not delay to offer from the fulness of your harvest and from the outflow of your presses.*

"The first-born of your sons you shall give to me. ³⁰*You shall do likewise with your oxen and with your sheep: seven days it shall be with its dam; on the eighth day you shall give it to me.*

³¹*"You shall be men consecrated to me; therefore you shall not eat any flesh that is torn by beasts in the field; you shall cast it to the dogs.*

23 ¹*"You shall not utter a false report. You shall not join hands with a wicked man, to be a malicious witness.* ²*You shall not follow a multitude to do evil; nor shall you bear witness in a suit, turning aside after a multitude, so as to pervert justice;* ³*nor shall you be partial to a poor man in his suit.*

⁴*"If you meet your enemy's ox or his ass going astray, . . .* ⁵*you shall help him."*

OVERVIEW: Pagan sacrifices feed and nourish the demons (ORIGEN). The Old Testament imposed a dreadful penalty on idolatry (AUGUSTINE). To take interest on a loan is to put a restraint on charity (CLEMENT OF ALEXANDRIA). The law showed admirable compassion for the poor and the destitute (PSEUDO-BASIL). How much reverence should we show to the one true High Priest (AUGUSTINE). What we owe to God should be given promptly (AMBROSE). Grace bids us to go beyond the law (JOHN CASSIAN). The gentleness of the law is shown well in its tender care even for newborn animals (CLEMENT OF ALEXANDRIA). Justice should play no favorites, neither to the poor nor to the rich (CHRYSOSTOM). Nobility of spirit requires us to hold no grudges. We should not overburden beasts, nor should we take pleasure in others' misfortunes (CLEMENT OF ALEXANDRIA). If it is good to relieve a beast's burden, how much better is it to help one's fellow Christians (CAESARIUS OF ARLES).

22:20 Sacrifices to Other Gods Punished by Death

SACRIFICES NOURISH DEMONS. ORIGEN: Some people give no thought to the question of demons, that is to say, to the fact that these demons, in order to be able to exist in the heavy atmosphere that encircles the earth, must have the nourishment of exhalations and consequently are always on the lookout for the savor of burnt sacrifices, blood and incense.[1] Since they attach no importance to the matter of sacri-

---

[1]Origen believed that demons, as spirits of the lower air, had to feed on the smoke of sacrifices, blood that evaporated, and other such nourishment.

fice, we would express ourselves also on this subject. If men who give sustenance to robbers, murderers and barbarian enemies of the great king are punished as criminals against the state, how much more will they be punished justly who through offering sacrifice proffer sustenance to the minions of evil and thus hold them in the atmosphere of the earth! And this holds true especially if knowing the text, "He that sacrifices to gods other than the Lord alone will be destroyed utterly," they nevertheless sacrifice to these authors of evil on earth. In my opinion, when there is question of crimes committed by these demons operating against men, they who sustain them by sacrificing to them will be held no less responsible than the demons themselves that do the crimes. For the demons and they that have kept them on earth, where they could not exist without the exhalations and nourishment considered vital to their bodies, work as one in doing evil to mankind. EXHORTATION TO MARTYRDOM 45.[2]

THE SEVERITY OF THE LAW. AUGUSTINE: In the law of the true God it is written, "He that sacrifices to gods shall be put to death, save only to the Lord." The dreadful sanction of this command makes it clear that God wanted no sacrifices offered to such gods, good or bad. CITY OF GOD 19.21.[3]

22:25 You Shall Not Exact Interest

WHAT TRUE INTEREST IS. CLEMENT OF ALEXANDRIA: There is a great deal about sharing and exchanging, but it is enough to say that the law forbids lending at interest to a brother.[4] By brother it means not merely one born of the same parents but a member of the same tribe or one of the same faith, who shares in the same Logos. The law does not deem it right to collect interest on the capital. It seeks to enable free giving to those in need, with hands and minds wide open. God is the creator of this free gift. It is he who shares his goods, exacting as the only reasonable

interest the most precious things human beings possess: gentleness, goodness, high-mindedness, repute, glory. STROMATEIS 2.84.[5]

22:27 God Is Compassionate

COMPASSION FOR THE POOR. PSEUDO-BASIL: It appears also that one who does not give back his pledge to a poor man stands condemned with God, for the following threat is directed against such a one: "He who does not receive back his pledge will cry to me," says the Lord, "and I will hear him because I am compassionate."[6] [Of old] it was wicked and unlawful to gather the sheaves left after the harvest, or to glean the vines after the vintage or to gather up the olives that remain after the trees were picked, because these things were to be left for the poor.[7] Now if this was commanded of those who were under the law, what shall we say of those who are in Christ? To them the Lord says, "Unless your justice abound more than that of the scribes and Pharisees, you shall not enter the kingdom of heaven."[8] ON MERCY AND JUSTICE.[9]

22:28 You Shall Not Curse a Ruler

AN APPLICATION OF THE LAW. AUGUSTINE: "Brethren, I did not know that he was the high priest; for it is written, 'You shall not speak ill of a ruler of your people.'"[10] The mildness of this prompt reply shows how calmly he had spoken what he seemed to have uttered in anger, for such a reply could not be given by those who are angered or perturbed. And in the reply, "I did not know that he was the high priest," he spoke the truth to those who understand him. It is as though he were saying, "I have come to know another High Priest for whose name's sake I am suffering these injuries—a High Priest whom it is not lawful to revile but whom you are reviling,

---

[2]ACW 19:188. [3]FC 24:235. [4]Lev 25:36-37. [5]FC 85:214. [6]Ex 22:27. [7]Deut 24:19-21. [8]Mt 5:20. [9]FC 9:510-11. [10]Acts 23:5; Ex 22:28.

116

because in me you hate nothing else than his name." On the Lord's Sermon on the Mount 1.19.58.[11]

22:29 You Shall Not Delay

The First Fruits of the Senses. Ambrose: Those emotions therefore which are morally good are the first fruits of our senses, whereas the others are of common and indifferent stock. This classification was used by Moses, following in that respect the language of the Jews, in his reference to the threshing floor of the law: "The tithes of your threshing floor and of your wine vat you shall not delay to pay: you shall give the firstborn of your sons to me." All the morally good emotions of your senses are the first fruits of the threshing floor of the soul in such a manner as grain is separated in an actual barn floor.[12] Cain and Abel 2.1.5.[13]

Grace Goes Beyond the Law. John Cassian: The law says, "You shall not delay in offering your tithes and first fruits." But grace says, "If you wish to be perfect, go, sell all that you have and give to the poor."[14] Conference 21.32.3.[15]

22:30 Compassion for Animals

The Law Is Kind Even to Animals. Clement of Alexandria: Scripture says, "At least grant the offspring to its mother for its first seven days."[16] For if nothing comes to be without reason and milk flows in the mothers for the nourishment of the offspring, then in taking the offspring away from the providential endowment of milk, a person is doing violence to nature. So Greeks and anyone else who runs the law down ought to blush for shame if the law is generous over irrational beasts, whereas they actually expose human offspring to die. Yet for a long time with prophetic authority the law has cut short their ferocity through the commandment of which we have been speaking. For if the law refuses to allow the offspring of irrational creatures to be separated from their mother before taking milk, it is far more forceful in preparing human beings against that cruel, uncivilized view. If they ignore nature, at least they may not ignore the lessons of the law. Stromateis 2.18.92.[17]

23:3 No Partiality to a Poor Person

Justice May Not Be Corrupted. Chrysostom: "You shall not favor a poor man in his lawsuit," Scripture says. What therefore is the meaning of these words? "Do not be overcome by pity or unduly influenced if the wrongdoer happens to be a poor man," it means. And if we must not show favor to the poor man, much more must we not do so for the rich. Moreover, I address these words not only to judges but also to all men, so that justice may nowhere be corrupted but everywhere kept inviolate. Homilies on the Gospel of John 49.[18]

23:4 Returning a Neighbor's Stray Animals

Do Not Hold a Grudge. Clement of Alexandria: A reputation for nobility follows the refusal to remember ills and leads to the cessation of hostility. From this we become disposed to concord, and concord leads to happiness. If you catch anyone you regard as a traditional enemy acting stupidly and irrationally out of desire or temper, turn him toward good behavior. Stromateis 2.18.90.[19]

23:5 Helping an Enemy

Take No Joy in Others' Misfortunes. Clement of Alexandria: The Lord tells us to relieve and lighten the burden of beasts of burden, even when they belong to our enemies.[20] He is teaching us at a distance not to take pleasure in

---

[11]FC 11:84-85. [12]Num 15:20. [13]FC 42:404. [14]Mt 19:21. [15]ACW 57:744. [16]Lev 22:27. [17]FC 85:219. [18]FC 41:22. [19]FC 85:217-18. [20]Lk 6:27-28.

the misfortunes of others and not to laugh at our enemies. He wants to teach those who have exercised themselves in these disciplines to pray for their enemies. STROMATEIS 2.18.90.[21]

DUTIES TO FELLOW CHRISTIANS. CAESARIUS OF ARLES: You are commanded to pull out the ass or the ox which is lying in the mud. Do you then see a Christian like yourself, who was redeemed by the blood of Christ, lying in the sewer of drunkenness and wallowing in the mud of dissipation and remain silent? Do you pass by and not stretch forth the hand of mercy by shouting to him or rebuking him or instilling fright in him? If he neglects to listen to you,

mention it to the priest somewhat secretly, in order that he may accomplish by his authority what you were unable to obtain by your humble admonition. Know for a most certain fact that unless you first in secret and with great love admonish sinners and later publicly do so if you have been rejected, that sentence must be directed at you: "If you do not warn the wicked man about his wicked conduct," it exclaims to careless bishops, "I will hold you responsible for his death."[22] SERMON 225.4.[23]

---

[21]FC 85:217. [22]Ezek 3:18. [23]FC 66:154.

23:10-19 RELIGIOUS LAWS

[15]*"You shall keep the feast of unleavened bread; as I commanded you, you shall eat unleavened bread for seven days at the appointed time in the month of Abib, for in it you came out of Egypt. None shall appear before me empty-handed. . . .*
[19]*"You shall not boil a kid in its mother's milk."*

OVERVIEW: Sacrifice is good, but it is better to lead others into the church (CHRYSOSTOM). To mix life and death is repulsive (CLEMENT OF ALEXANDRIA).

23:15 None Shall Appear Empty-Handed

BRING OTHERS INTO THE CHURCH. CHRYSOSTOM: "You shall not appear before the Lord empty," that is, enter not into the temple without sacrifices. Now if it is not right to go into the house of God without sacrifices, much more ought we to enter the assembly accompanied by our brethren. For this sacrifice and offering is better than that, when you bring a soul with you

into the church. HOMILY TO THOSE WHO HAD NOT ATTENDED THE ASSEMBLY 4.[1]

23:19 Not Boiling a Kid in Its Mother's Milk

DO NOT MIX LIFE AND DEATH. CLEMENT OF ALEXANDRIA: Our physical nature rebels against the thought of making the nourishment of the living a garnish for the dead or the cause of life an accessory to the death of the body. STROMATEIS 2.18.94.[2]

---

[1]NPNF 1 9:227*. [2]FC 85:220.

23:20-33 REWARD OF FIDELITY

²⁰"Behold, I send an angel before you, to guard you on the way and to bring you to the place which I have prepared. ²¹Give heed to him and hearken to his voice, do not rebel against him, for he will not pardon your transgression; for my name is in him. . . .

²⁶"None shall cast her young or be barren in your land; I will fulfil the number of your days."

OVERVIEW: Both Joshua and John the Baptist are called angels in Scripture. Joshua had great powers and exercised the prophetic office (TERTULLIAN). Joshua, whose name is also Jesus, is the leader who brings the people into eternal life (AUGUSTINE). Spiritual love makes one fruitful in the spirit (ORIGEN).

23:20 I Send an Angel Before You

JOSHUA AND JOHN THE BAPTIST. TERTULLIAN: For Joshua was to introduce the people into the land of promise, not Moses. Now he called him an angel on account of the magnitude of the mighty deeds which he was to achieve (which mighty deeds Joshua the son of Nun did, as you can yourselves read) and on account of his office of prophet announcing the divine will. Similarly the Spirit, speaking in the person of the Father, calls the forerunner of Christ, John, a future angel, through the prophet: "Behold, I send my angel before your"—that is, Christ's—"face, who shall prepare your way before you."[1] ANSWER TO THE JEWS 9.23.[2]

JOSHUA CALLED AN ANGEL. TERTULLIAN: He called him an angel indeed, because of the greatness of the powers which he was to exercise and because of his prophetic office, while announcing the will of God. He is called Joshua (also Jesus), because it was a type of his own future name. AGAINST MARCION 3.16.5.[3]

THE ANGEL WAS JOSHUA (JESUS). AUGUSTINE: Consider these words. Let the Jew, not to

speak of the Manichaean, say what other angel he can find in Scripture to whom these words apply, but this leader who was to bring the people into the land of promise. Then let him inquire who it was that succeeded Moses and brought in the people. He will find that it was Jesus and that this was not his name at first but after his name was changed. It follows that he who said, "My name is in him"[4] is the true Jesus, the leader who brings his people into the inheritance of eternal life, according to the New Testament, of which the Old was a figure. No event or action could have a more distinctly prophetical character than this, where the very name is itself a prediction. AGAINST FAUSTUS, A MANICHAEAN 16.19.[5]

23:26 None Shall Be Barren

CARNAL LOVE AND SPIRITUAL LOVE. ORIGEN: And we notice that the saying, "The barren has borne seven, and she that has many children is weakened,"[6] is in accord with this;[7] as also is that which is said in the blessings: "There shall not be one among you that is childless or barren."[8] This being so, it follows that just as there is one love, known as carnal and also known as Cupid by the poets, according to which the lover sows in the flesh. So also is there another, a spiritual love, by which the inner man who loves sows in the

---

[1]Mal 3:1. [2]ANF 3:163. [3]ANF 3:335. [4]Ex 23:21. [5]NPNF 1 4:226. [6]1 Sam 2:5. [7]The preceding statement to which "this" refers is "Now then . . . one person is childless and barren according to the inner man, while another has plenty of offspring." [8]Ex 23:26.

spirit.[9] And, to speak more plainly, if anyone still bears the image of the earthly according to the outer man, then he is moved by earthly desire and love; but the desire and love of him who bears the image of the heavenly according to the inner man are heavenly.[10] COMMENTARY ON THE SONG OF SONGS, PROLOGUE 2.[11]

---

[9]Gal 6:8. [10]1 Cor 15:49. [11]ACW 26:29.

24:1-11 RATIFICATION OF THE COVENANT

[1]And he said to Moses, "Come up to the LORD, you and Aaron, Nadab, and Abihu, and seventy of the elders of Israel, and worship afar off. [2]Moses alone shall come near to the LORD; but the others shall not come near, and the people shall not come up with him." . . .

[9]Then Moses and Aaron, Nadab, and Abihu, and seventy of the elders of Israel went up, [10]and they saw the God of Israel; and there was under his feet as it were a pavement of sapphire stone, like the very heaven for clearness. [11]And he did not lay his hand on the chief men of the people of Israel; they beheld God, and ate and drank.

Overview: Not everyone may draw near God; Moses was able to behold God's glory (GREGORY OF NAZIANZUS). The manifestations of God are only visible and tangible signs; God, one and three, cannot be seen with human eyes (AUGUSTINE).

24:2 Moses Alone Came Near to God

WHO MAY DRAW NEAR TO GOD? GREGORY OF NAZIANZUS: For it is not everyone who may draw near to God but only one who, like Moses, can bear the glory of God. Moreover, before this, when the law was first given, the trumpet blasts, and lightnings, and thunders, and darkness, and the smoke of the whole mountain,[1] and the terrible threats that if even a beast touched the mountain it should be stoned,[2] and other like alarms kept back the rest of the people, for whom it was a great privilege, after careful purification, merely to hear the voice of God. But Moses actually went up, and entered into the cloud,[3] and was charged with the law and received the tables. For the multitude, the tables of law are viewed according to the letter. But for those who are above the multitude, these are viewed according to the spirit.[4] ORATION 2.92.[5]

24:10 They Saw the God of Israel

WHAT MOSES SAW SIGNIFIED THE TRINITY. AUGUSTINE: Moses, of course, might be thought to have seen God with bodily eyes, if not only the Wisdom of God which is Christ but even the wisdom itself . . . [which] can be seen with the eyes of the flesh, or because it is written of the elders of Israel that "they beheld the place where the God of Israel had stood"[6] and that there was "under his feet as it were a work of sapphire stone and a likeness of the firmament of heaven."[7] We might therefore be led to imagine that the Word and the Wisdom of God, who extends from end to end mightily and orders all

---

[1]Ex 19:16. [2]Ex 19:12-13; Heb 12:20. [3]Ex 24:15, 18. [4]2 Cor 3:6-7. [5]NPNF 2 7:223. [6]Ex 24:10. [7]Ex 24:10.

things sweetly,[8] stood in his own substance within the space of an earthly place. And thus the Word of God, through whom all things were made,[9] is thought changeable so that now he draws himself together and now he expands. May God cleanse the hearts of his faithful from such thoughts! But, as we have often declared, all these visible and tangible signs were displayed through a creature that has been made subject, in order to signify the invisible and intelligible God, not only the Father but also the Son and the Holy Spirit, from whom are all things, through whom are all things, and in whom are all things.[10] Since the creation of the world, the invisible attributes of God, his everlasting power also and divinity, are seen, being understood through the things that are made.[11] THE TRINITY 2.15.25.[12]

---

[8]Wis 8:1. [9]Jn 1:3. [10]Rom 11:36. [11]Rom 1:20. [12]FC 45:81-82.

24:12-18 MOSES ON THE MOUNTAIN

[12]*The LORD said to Moses, "Come up to me on the mountain, and wait there; and I will give you the tables of stone, with the law and the commandment, which I have written for their instruction."* . . .

[18]*And Moses entered the cloud, and went up on the mountain. And Moses was on the mountain forty days and forty nights.*

OVERVIEW: Only those who are friends of God may enter the cloud (AMBROSE). When Moses spent forty days on the mountain, he was transformed (PETER CHRYSOLOGUS). Moses' fast on the mountain stands in sharp contrast to the people's indulgence (CHRYSOSTOM). The stone of the law must be rolled away so that Christ's resurrection may be revealed (BEDE).

24:12 *Tables of Stone*

THE STONE OF THE LAW. BEDE: Mystically the rolling away of the stone[1] implies the disclosure of the sacraments, which were formerly hidden and closed up by the letter of the law. The law was written on stone. Indeed in the case of each of us, when we acknowledge our faith in the Lord's passion and resurrection, his tomb, which had been closed, is opened up. HOMILIES ON THE GOSPELS 2.10.[2]

24:18 *Moses Entered the Cloud*

TO HAVE GOD AS A FRIEND. AMBROSE: If anyone therefore desires to behold this image of God, he must love God so as to be loved by him, no longer as a servant but as a friend who observes his commandments, that he may enter the cloud where God is. ON HIS BROTHER, SATYRUS 2.110.[3]

MOSES WAS TRANSFIGURED. PETER CHRYSOLOGUS: Moses himself was so purified and freed from his body by a fast of forty days that his whole self took on a glorious appearance of divinity. Still in the darkness of our body, he gleamed with the full radiance of divinity. The eyes of mortals could not gaze upon him who, long nourished by the substance of God, had

---

[1]Lk 24:2. [2]HOG 2: 90. [3]FC 22:248.

forgotten all about the aids provided by mortals' food. From this he learned that the sustenance of life does not fail those who live in God's sight and with him. SERMON 166.[4]

THE REWARDS OF FASTING. CHRYSOSTOM: Do you now recognize the harm caused by intemperance? Look in turn at the instances of good behavior due to fasting. The great Moses, after keeping his fast for forty days, was able to get the tables of the law. When he came down from the mountain and saw the people's sin, the tablets which he had been successful in obtaining through such intercession he threw down and smashed,[5] thinking it was preposterous that an indulgent and sinful people should receive laws of the Lord's own making. HOMILIES ON GENESIS 1.7.[6]

---

[4]FC 17:274. [5]Ex 32:19. [6]FC 74:24.

25:1-9 COLLECTING MATERIALS FOR THE TABERNACLE

[1]*The LORD said to Moses, . . .* [3]*"This is the offering which you shall receive from them: gold, silver, and bronze,* [4]*blue and purple and scarlet stuff and fine twined linen, goats' hair,* [5]*tanned rams' skins, goatskins, acacia wood,* [6]*oil for the lamps, spices for the anointing oil and for the fragrant incense,* [7]*onyx stones, and stones for setting, for the ephod and for the breastpiece.* [8]*And let them make me a sanctuary, that I may dwell in their midst.* [9]*According to all that I show you concerning the pattern of the tabernacle, and of all its furniture, so you shall make it."*

OVERVIEW: Twice-dyed scarlet suggests the twofold love of God and neighbor (GREGORY THE GREAT). The tabernacle was only a model, and transitory, which was yet to be fulfilled in the church (EPHREM).

25:4 Scarlet Stuff

THE TWO GREAT COMMANDMENTS. GREGORY THE GREAT: Scarlet cloth, twice dyed,[1] was to be offered to adorn the tabernacle so that our love of God and neighbor might have the color of love in God's sight. That person truly loves himself who loves his Creator completely. Scarlet cloth is twice dyed when a soul is set on fire toward itself and its neighbor as a result of its love of truth. HOMILY 17.[2]

25:9 The Pattern of the Tabernacle

ONLY A PATTERN OR MODEL. EPHREM THE SYRIAN: By saying [to him], "You shall make everything according to the model of the tabernacle that I will show you," he first called it a model and a temporal tabernacle to indicate that it was transitory and that it would be replaced by the church, the perfect prototype which lasts forever. And so . . . they would esteem it because of its likeness to the heavenly tabernacle. COMMENTARY ON EXODUS 25.1.[3]

---

[1]The LXX and the Vulgate add "twice-dyed" to "scarlet" to suggest its high quality. [2]CS 123:142. [3]FC 91:261.

25:10-22 PLAN OF THE ARK

[10]"*They shall make an ark of acacia wood; two cubits and a half shall be its length, a cubit and a half its breadth, and a cubit and a half its height.* [11]*And you shall overlay it with pure gold, within and without shall you overlay it, and you shall make upon it a molding of gold round about.* [12]*And you shall cast four rings of gold for it and put them on its four feet, two rings on the one side of it, and two rings on the other side of it. . . .*

[18]"*And you shall make two cherubim of gold; of hammered work shall you make them, on the two ends of the mercy seat.* [19]*Make one cherub on the one end, and one cherub on the other end; of one piece with the mercy seat shall you make the cherubim on its two ends.* [20]*The cherubim shall spread out their wings above, overshadowing the mercy seat with their wings, their faces one to another; toward the mercy seat shall the faces of the cherubim be.* [21]*And you shall put the mercy seat on the top of the ark; and in the ark you shall put the testimony that I shall give you.*"

OVERVIEW: It is risky to seek a deeper meaning in every detail of the tabernacle (ORIGEN). The ark prefigures the church, and the rings of gold at the four corners that support it are the four Gospels (GREGORY THE GREAT). Intellect and mind are golden, whereas language and speech are silver (ORIGEN). The two cherubim represent the two Testaments, which are the fullness of knowledge (GREGORY THE GREAT). The plate or mercy seat over the ark was the place from which God spoke to the high priest as he prayed (ISAAC OF NINEVEH).

25:10 Making an Ark

THE ARK AND ITS DETAILS ARE TYPES. ORIGEN: But when the passage about the equipment of the tabernacle is read, believing that the things described therein are types, some seek for ideas which they can attach to each detail that is mentioned in connection with the tabernacle. Now so far as concerns their belief that the tabernacle is a type of something they are not wrong. But in rightly attaching the word of Scripture to the particular idea of which the tabernacle is a type, here they sometimes fall into error. ON FIRST PRINCIPLES 4.2.2.[1]

25:12 Four Rings of Gold

THE RINGS AND THE STAVES. GREGORY THE GREAT: What is symbolized by the ark but holy church? The orders are that it is to be provided with four rings of gold in the four corners—obviously because, being extended to the four parts of the world, it is declared to be equipped with the four books of the holy Gospels. And staves of setim wood are made and inserted into these rings for carrying, because strong and persevering teachers, like incorruptible timbers, are to be sought out, who, always adhering to the instructions of the sacred volumes, proclaim the unity of holy church, and, as it were, carry the ark, by their being let into the rings. Indeed, to carry the ark with staves is to bring holy church through preaching to the untutored minds of unbelievers. Furthermore, they are ordered to be overlaid with gold, that when the sound of their preaching goes forth to others, they may themselves shine in the splendor of their way of life. PASTORAL CARE 2.11.[2]

---

[1]*OFP* 273. [2]*ACW* 11:87-88.

25:18 Two Cherubim of Gold

**CHERUBIM ARE THE FULLNESS OF KNOWL-
EDGE.** ORIGEN: We are told too that "the words
of the Lord are pure words, as silver tried in the
fire";[3] again, in another place "the tongue of the
just" is said to be "as silver tried by fire."[4] And
the cherubim are described as golden, because
they are by interpretation the plentitude of
knowledge. And it is commanded also that a
candlestick of solid gold should be put in the
tabernacle of the testimony; and that, it seems
to us, is a type of the natural law in which the
light of knowledge is contained. But what need
is there to multiply proof texts when those who
will can easily see for themselves from many
Scripture passages that gold is applied to the
intellect and mind, whereas silver is referred
only to language and the power of speech? COM-
MENTARY ON THE SONG OF SONGS 2.8.[5]

THE TWO TESTAMENTS. GREGORY THE GREAT:
The two cherubim which covered the mercy seat
beheld one another with their countenances
turned toward it. The word *cherubim* means
"fullness of knowledge." What do the two cherubim signify but the two Testaments? And what

does the mercy seat prefigure but the Lord
become a man? John says of him, "For he is the
expiation"[6] for our sins. HOMILY 25.[7]

25:21 The Mercy Seat

REVELATIONS ARE GIVEN IN PRAYER. ISAAC
OF NINEVEH: The same applied to the plate
placed on top of the ark, from which the priest
learned from God whatever was necessary by
revelation once a year, when the high priest
entered, at the solemn moment of prayer, while
all the tribes of Israel were gathered and standing in awe and trembling in the outer tent in
prayer. The high priest entered the inner sanctuary, and while he lay prostrate on his face, the
utterances of God were audible from within that
plate which was over the ark, by means of an
awesome and ineffable revelation. How fearful
was that mystery which was carried out on that
occasion. It is the same with all the revelations
and visions which have come to the saints: they
have all occurred at the time of prayer. DIS-
COURSE 22.[8]

---

[3]Ps 12:6. [4]Prov 10:20. [5]ACW 26:151-52. [6]1 Jn 2:2. [7]CS 123:191.
[8]CS 101:261-62.

25:23-30 THE TABLE

[23]"*And you shall make a table of acacia wood; two cubits shall be its length, a cubit its
breadth, and a cubit and a half its height.*"

OVERVIEW: The temple was so constructed that
the smoke of the incense filled the inner sanctuary (BEDE).

25:23 A Table of Acacia Wood

THE LAYOUT OF THE SANCTUARY. BEDE: A
dividing wall of cedar planks, twenty cubits
high, was built in the temple to separate the
inner sanctuary, that is, the Holy of Holies,
from the forepart of the temple. The inner sanc-

tuary was twenty cubits deep, twenty cubits wide and twenty cubits high.[1] The [part of the temple] in front of the inner sanctuary was forty cubits long,[2] and in it were tables and the golden candelabrum, as well as the golden altar near the door of the inner sanctuary. This was done so that when incense was offered upon it, the cloud of smoke might rise up and cover the inner sanc-

tuary, where the ark of the covenant was,[3] "and above it the cherubim of glory overshadowing the mercy seat."[4] HOMILIES ON THE GOSPELS 25.[5]

---

[1]1 Kings 6:20. [2]1 Kings 6:17. [3]Lev 16:13. [4]Heb 9:5. [5]HOG 2:264-65.

25:31-40 THE LAMPSTAND

[31]*"And you shall make a lampstand of pure gold. . . . [40]And see that you make them after the pattern for them, which is being shown you on the mountain."*

OVERVIEW: There are three steps in the history of salvation: the law as schoolmaster, the perfect precepts of Christ and finally the eternal gospel of heaven (ORIGEN). The tabernacle was at the second remove from the heavenly reality (METHODIUS). The tabernacle was matter, and yet its Creator was present there (JOHN OF DAMASCUS).

25:40 After the Pattern

THE LAW WAS A SCHOOLMASTER. ORIGEN: Moreover it was said to Moses himself, "See that you make all things according to the form and likeness which was shown to you in the mount." It seems to me, therefore, that . . . in this earth the law was a kind of schoolmaster to those who by it were appointed to be led to Christ[1] and to be instructed and trained in order that after their training in the law they might be able with greater facility to receive the more perfect precepts of Christ. So also that other earth, when it receives all the saints, first imbues and educates them in the precepts of the true and eternal law in order that they may with greater facility

accept the precepts of heaven which are perfect and to which nothing can ever be added. And in heaven will truly exist what is called the "eternal gospel"[2] and the Testament that is always new, which can never grow old.[3] ON FIRST PRINCIPLES 3.6.8.[4]

THE TABERNACLE WAS A SHADOW OF AN IMAGE. METHODIUS: If, according to the apostle, "the law is spiritual"[5] and contains within itself the images "of the good things to come,"[6] then let us remove "the veil"[7] of the letter which is spread over it and contemplate its true meaning stripped bare. The Jews were commanded to adorn their tabernacle as a proleptic imitation of the church, that through the things of sense they might be able to prefigure the image of things divine. For the exemplar which was shown forth on the mountain and on which Moses gazed when he constructed the tabernacle was in a way an accurate picture of the dwelling in heaven, to which indeed we pay homage

---

[1]Gal 3:24. [2]Rev 14:6. [3]Heb 8:13; 9:15. [4]OFP 254. [5]Rom 7:14. [6]Heb 10:1. [7]2 Cor 3:6, 16.

insofar as it far surpasses the types in clarity and yet is far fainter than the reality. The fact is that the unmingled truth has not yet come to humanity as it is in itself, for here we would be unable to contemplate its pure incorruptibility, just as we cannot endure the rays of the sun with unshielded eyes. The Jews announced what was a shadow of an image, at a third remove from reality, whereas we ourselves clearly behold the image of the heavenly dispensation. But the reality itself will be accurately revealed after the resurrection when we shall see the holy tabernacle, the heavenly city, "whose builder and maker is God,"[8] face to face, and not "in a dark manner" and only "in part."[9] BANQUET OF THE TEN VIRGINS 5.7.[10]

THE SACRAMENTALITY OF MATTER. JOHN OF DAMASCUS: Behold, the glorification of matter,

which you despise! What is more insignificant than colored goatskins? Are not blue and purple and scarlet merely colors? Behold the handiwork of men becoming the likeness of the cherubim! Was not the meeting tent an image in every way? "And see that you make them after the pattern for them, which is being shown you on the mountain." Yet all the people stood around it and worshiped! Were not the cherubim kept where all the people could see them? Did not the people gaze upon the ark, and the lampstand, and the table, the golden urn and Aaron's rod, and fall down in worship? I do not worship matter. I worship the Creator of matter, who became matter for me, taking up his abode in matter and accomplishing my salvation through matter. ON DIVINE IMAGES 14.[11]

---

[8]Heb 11:10. [9]1 Cor 13:12. [10]ACW 27:88-89. [11]ODI 61.

26:1-14 THE TENT CLOTH

[1]*"Moreover you shall make the tabernacle with ten curtains of fine twined linen and blue and purple and scarlet stuff; with cherubim skilfully worked shall you make them."*

OVERVIEW: The curtain of twice-dyed scarlet is the double love of God and neighbor, by which we enter the tabernacle of God (GREGORY THE GREAT).

26:1 Scarlet Curtains

SCARLET SIGNIFIES LOVE. GREGORY THE GREAT: Surely no access to the heavenly city is given us if we do not keep the love of God and neighbor in this church, which because it is outside is called a porch. This is why it was ordered

that the curtains of the tabernacle be woven from scarlet cloth twice dyed.[1] You, my friends, you are the curtains of the tabernacle, since by your faith you veil the heavenly secrets in your hearts. Scarlet twice dyed must be used for the curtains of the tabernacle. Scarlet has the look of fire, and what is love but fire? This love must be twice dyed, dyed by love of God and dyed by love of our neighbor. HOMILY 38.[2]

---

[1]See note on Ex 25:4. [2]CS 123:348.

26:15-30 THE WOODEN WALLS

[15]*"And you shall make upright frames for the tabernacle of acacia wood . . .* [19]*and forty bases of silver you shall make under the twenty frames, two bases under one frame for its two tenons, and two bases under another frame for its two tenons."*

OVERVIEW: The silver bases prefigure the prophets who were the first to speak of the Lord's incarnation, and the frames prefigure the apostles who spread the gospel into the whole world (PATERIUS).

26:19 Forty Bases of Silver

APOSTLES AND PROPHETS. PATERIUS: What can the silver bases of the frames signify, except the order of prophets? They were the first to speak openly of the Lord's incarnation. They were like bases, and we see them rising from the foundations and sustaining the weight of the structure built on them. So when the Lord bade Moses build the frames of the tabernacle, Moses had the builders set them on their silver bases. What do the frames mean, except the apostles, who were spread out into the world by their preaching? What do the silver bases mean, except the prophets? They are firm, cast metal, and sustain the frames placed on them. The apostles' lives are guided by their proclamation and strengthened by their authority. So two bases are joined and placed under each frame.[1]

For when the holy prophets agree in what they say about the incarnation of the Mediator, they undoubtedly build up the preachers in the church who follow them. They do not disagree among themselves, and they make the preachers stronger. God rightly commands that the bases, which signify the prophets, should be cast in silver. The gleam of silver is maintained by use; when it is not used, it turns black. The prophets spoke before the Mediator came. Since their words were not joined into one spiritual understanding and could not be seen clearly because of the darkness, they remained, as it were, black. But afterwards, the Mediator came and cleansed our eyes with the hand of his incarnation. Whatever light was concealed in our eyes[2] he made clear. He made the intentions of the ancient fathers useful, because he confirmed their words with his deeds. EXPOSITION OF THE OLD AND NEW TESTAMENT, EXODUS 43.[3]

---

[1]Ex 26:18-25; the ratio of bases to frames is 2 to 1. [2]In antiquity, sight was believed to result from the meeting of light from the eyes and light from the object seen. [3]PL 79:742, citing Gregory the Great *Moral Interpretation of Job* 28.7.18.

26:31-37 THE VEILS

[31]*"And you shall make a veil of blue and purple and scarlet stuff and fine twined linen; in skilled work shall it be made, with cherubim;* [32]*and you shall hang it upon four pillars of acacia overlaid with gold, with hooks of gold, upon four bases of silver.* [33]*And you shall hang the veil*

from the clasps, and bring the ark of the testimony in thither within the veil; and the veil shall separate for you the holy place from the most holy."

OVERVIEW: The veil that divides the tabernacle prefigures the distinction in the coming *ecclesia* between those who are pilgrims on earth and those who reign with the Lord in heaven (BEDE). The divine word is as clear as silver and supports the church and its preaching (PATERIUS). The outer sanctuary is the church as it now is, where all Christians, because they are priests, minister and offer sacrifice (ORIGEN).

26:31 *Making a Veil*

THE LORD ALONE HAS PASSED INTO HEAVEN. BEDE: The temple was divided by a veil [hung across] the wall in the center [of the building], and the outer [section of this part of the] building was called the sanctuary; the inner [section], where the ark of the covenant was placed, was called the Holy of Holies. The church is in part on pilgrimage on earth, [away from] the Lord, and in part it reigns with the Lord in heaven. The wall [across the] center is understood [as indicating] heaven, and the ark of the covenant [as indicating] the Lord, who alone is conscious of the Father's hidden mysteries and has passed into the inner reaches of heaven. HOMILIES ON THE GOSPELS 2.1.[1]

26:32 *Four Bases of Silver*

THE WORD OF GOD IS REFINED SILVER. PATERIUS: The tabernacle is a type of the church. So God says to Moses that the bases of the four pillars placed within it should be silver. What does silver mean except the clarity of the divine Word? Scripture says, "The words of the Lord are chaste words, silver tried by fire, cleansed from earth."[2] The bases are overlaid with silver and hold up the four pillars of the tabernacle, just as the preachers of the church are adorned with divine eloquence. They provide an example in every way; they have the words of the four Evangelists on their lips and in their deeds. EXPOSITION OF THE OLD AND NEW TESTAMENT, EXODUS 44.[3]

26:33 *The Veil Separates the Holy Place from the Most Holy*

THE FIRST SANCTUARY IS THE CHURCH. ORIGEN: If the ancient custom of sacrifices is clear to you, let us see what these things also contain according to the mystical understanding. You heard that there were two sanctuaries, one, as it were, visible and open to the priests; the other, as it were, invisible and inaccessible. With the exception of the high priest alone, the others were outside. I think this first sanctuary can be understood as this church in which we are now placed in the flesh, in which the priests minister "at the altar of the whole burnt offerings,"[4] with that fire kindled about which Jesus said, "I came to send fire unto the earth, and how I wish it to be ignited."[5] And I do not want you to marvel that this sanctuary is open only to the priests. For all who have been anointed with the chrism of the sacred anointing have become priests, just as Peter also says to all the church, "But you are an elect race, a royal priesthood, a holy people."[6] Therefore you are "a priestly race," and because of this you approach the sanctuary. HOMILIES ON LEVITICUS 9.9.3.[7]

---

[1]HOG 2:10. [2]Ps 12:6. [3]PL 79:742, citing Gregory the Great *Moral Interpretation of Job* 18.7.17. [4]Ex 29:25. [5]Lk 12:49. [6]1 Pet 2:9. [7]FC 83:196.

27:1-8 THE ALTAR OF HOLOCAUSTS

¹"You shall make the altar of acacia wood."

OVERVIEW: The altar of sacrifice signified the fleshly-minded worship of the Old Covenant; the altar of incense signified the order of grace in the New Covenant (BEDE).

27:1 The Altar of Acacia Wood

THE ALTARS AND TWO COVENANTS. BEDE: There were two altars in the temple, which expressed the two covenants in the church. The first, the altar of burnt offerings, which was plated with bronze and was situated in front of the doors of the temple, was for the offering up of victims and sacrifices. It signified the fleshly minded worshipers of the Old Covenant. And then there was the altar of incense, which was covered with gold[1] and set near the entrance of the Holy of Holies and was to burn fragrant gums on. This prefigured the interior and more perfect grace of the New Covenant and its worshipers. HOMILIES ON THE GOSPELS 2.19.[2]

---

[1]Ex 30:3. [2]HOG 2:195-96.

[27:9-19 COURT OF THE DWELLING]

[27:20-21 OIL FOR THE LAMPS]

28:1-30 THE PRIESTLY VESTMENTS

⁶"And they shall make the ephod of gold, of blue and purple and scarlet stuff, and of fine twined linen, skilfully worked. ⁷It shall have two shoulder-pieces attached to its two edges, that it may be joined together. ⁸And the skilfully woven band upon it, to gird it on, shall be of the same workmanship and materials, of gold, blue and purple and scarlet stuff, and fine twined linen. ⁹And you shall take two onyx stones, and engrave on them the names of the sons of Israel, ¹⁰six of their names on the one stone, and the names of the remaining six on the other stone, in the order of their birth. . . .

²¹"There shall be twelve stones with their names according to the names of the sons of Israel; they shall be like signets, each engraved with its name, for the twelve tribes. . . . ³⁰And in the breastpiece of judgment you shall put the Urim and the Thummim, and they shall be upon

Aaron's heart, when he goes in before the LORD; thus Aaron shall bear the judgment of the people of Israel upon his heart before the LORD continually."

OVERVIEW: The priest must possess wisdom, the understanding of heavenly things, true virtue and charity, as well as a spirit of abstinence (GREGORY THE GREAT). The number twelve recurs often in Scripture (TERTULLIAN). All twelve stones are needed to preserve the faith intact (AMBROSE). The twelve stones encircle the Urim and Thummim, which point toward Christ as manifestation and truth (CYRIL OF ALEXANDRIA).

28:8 Gold, Blue, Purple and Scarlet

THE QUALIFICATIONS OF A PRIEST. GREGORY THE GREAT: Further, it is rightly enjoined that the humeral[1] veil be made of gold, hyacinth, purple, scarlet twice dyed,[2] and fine twisted linen, so that it may be evident with what variety of virtues the priest should be conspicuous. Thus in the vesture of the priest the gold is resplendent beyond all else; so should he especially shine beyond all others in the understanding of wisdom. Hyacinth is added, brilliant with the color of the skies, that by every matter which he penetrates with his understanding, he may not stoop to the base favors of earth but rise up to the love of heavenly things. He must beware of being incautiously snared by praise, thus despoiling himself of even the appreciation of truth.

With the gold and blue of the vesture there is also a mingling of purple. That is to say, the heart of the priest, while hoping for those high matters about which he preaches, should repress in itself the remotest suggestions of vice. He should, as it were, with kingly power reject them, ever setting his gaze on the nobility of his interior regeneration and safeguarding by his way of living his right to the heavenly kingdom. . . .

Now to gold, blue and purple is added twice-dyed scarlet, to signify that in the eyes of the Judge of the heart all that is good in virtues must be adorned with charity and that everything that is resplendent in human eyes must in the sight of the Judge within be lit up with the flame of love coming from the heart. Moreover, because this charity embraces both God and neighbor, its radiance is, as it were, of a double hue. He therefore that sighs for the beauty of his Maker but neglects the care of his neighbor, or who so compasses the care of the neighbor as to grow listless in divine love, in neglecting either of these does not know what it means to have twice-dyed scarlet in the adornment of the humeral.

But while the mind is intent on the precepts of charity, it remains, beyond doubt, that the flesh must be mortified by abstinence. Consequently fine-twisted linen is joined with the twice-dyed scarlet. Now fine linen comes from the earth with radiant hue. And what else is designated by linen but chastity, radiant in the comeliness of bodily cleanness? The twisted linen is also woven into the beauty of the humeral, for then chastity issues into the perfect radiance of purity, when the flesh is spent with abstinence. While thus, in company with the other virtues, the merit of mortified flesh is revealed, as it were, the twisted linen is resplendent in the variegated beauty of the humeral. PASTORAL CARE 2.3.[3]

28:21 Twelve Stones

THE NUMBER TWELVE. TERTULLIAN: But why was it that [Christ] chose twelve apostles, and not some other number? In truth, I might from this very point conclude of my Christ that he was foretold not only by the words of prophets

---

[1]Shoulder vestment. [2]See note on Ex 25:4. [3]ACW 11:49-51.

but by the embodied language of facts. For of this number I find figurative hints up and down the Creator's dispensation in the twelve springs of Elim;[4] in the twelve gems of Aaron's priestly vestment;[5] and in the twelve stones appointed by Joshua to be taken out of the Jordan and set up for the ark of the covenant. AGAINST MARCION 4.13.3-4.[6]

TWELVE STONES AND TWELVE APOSTLES. AMBROSE: Of these twelve, as of twelve precious stones, is the pillar of our faith built up. For these are the precious stones—sardius, jasper, smaragd, chrysolite, and the rest—woven into the robe of holy Aaron, even of him who bears the likeness of Christ, that is, of the true Priest. [These] stones [are] set in gold and inscribed with the names of the sons of Israel, twelve stones close joined and fitting one into another, for if any should sunder or separate them, the whole fabric of the faith falls in ruins. ON THE CHRISTIAN FAITH 2, INTRODUCTION 4.[7]

THE MANIFESTATION AND TRUTH OF EMMANUEL. CYRIL OF ALEXANDRIA: And on the breast of the high priest were certain stones hanging, twelve in number, in the midst of which were placed two other stones, manifestation and

truth.[8] By means of a riddle through these the chorus of the holy apostles is clearly signified being, as it were, in a circle around Emmanuel, who is manifestation and truth. For he manifested the truth by having taken away the worship of God in shadows and in types. LETTER 55.28.[9]

28:30 Aaron Bears the Judgment of the People

TRUE AND JUST JUDGMENT. GREGORY THE GREAT: The priest bearing the judgment of the children of Israel on his breast in the sight of the Lord means that he examines the causes of his subjects in accordance only with the mind of the Judge within. So . . . he allows no admixture of human reason in what he dispenses in the place of God, lest personal displeasure embitter him in his zeal for correction. While showing himself zealous against the transgressions of others, he should punish his own, lest his latent ill will stain the calmness of his judgment or hasty anger distort it. PASTORAL CARE 2.2.[10]

---

[4]Num 33:9. [5]Ex 28:21. [6]ANF 3:364. [7]NPNF 2 10:223-24. [8]The LXX translated the "Urim and the Thummim" of Ex 28:30 as "Manifestation and Truth." [9]FC 77:26. [10]ACW 11:47.

28:31-43 OTHER VESTMENTS

[31]"And you shall make the robe of the ephod all of blue. [32]It shall have in it an opening for the head, with a woven binding around the opening, like the opening in a garment,[p] that it may not be torn. [33]On its skirts you shall make pomegranates of blue and purple and scarlet stuff, around its skirts, with bells of gold between them, [34]a golden bell and a pomegranate, a golden bell and a pomegranate, round about on the skirts of the robe."

p *The Hebrew word is of uncertain meaning*

OVERVIEW: The pomegranate has many seeds protected by one rind; so the church embraces countless people (GREGORY THE GREAT).

28:34 A Golden Bell and a Pomegranate

THE UNITY OF FAITH. GREGORY THE GREAT: Hence in the vesture of the priest, in accordance with the divine Word, pomegranates are added to the little bells. What else is symbolized by pomegranates but the unity of faith? For as in the pomegranate many seeds within are protected by one outer rind, so unity in faith comprehends numberless people of holy church, who, though varying in merits, are retained within it. PASTORAL CARE 2.4.[1]

---

[1]ACW 11:54.

29:1-9 CONSECRATION OF THE PRIESTS

[1]*"Now this is what you shall do to them to consecrate them, that they may serve me as priests. Take one young bull and two rams without blemish,* [2]*and unleavened bread, unleavened cakes mixed with oil, and unleavened wafers spread with oil. You shall make them of fine wheat flour.* [3]*And you shall put them in one basket and bring them in the basket, and bring the bull and the two rams.* [4]*You shall bring Aaron and his sons to the door of the tent of meeting, and wash them with water."*

OVERVIEW: Priests are consecrated by faith and good works and by the grace of divine illumination (BEDE). The one who prays for others must first be baptized (CYRIL OF JERUSALEM).

29:1 Consecrate Priests

CONSECRATION BY FAITH AND GOOD WORKS. BEDE: What follows next explains ... the proper manner of consecration which is to be used in dedicating [Aaron and his sons] as well as the tabernacle with all its furnishings. [That manner] is to offer the Lord a calf and two rams and wheat bread that is not only unleavened but also sprinkled with oil or even covered with an application of the oil of unction. Figuratively all of these things doubtless indicate either devotion to good works and purity of faith or the grace of divine illumination, which is the only proper means of consecrating priests. For who does not know that the sacrifice of those animals and [the sprinkling of] their blood designate the death of our Lord and the sprinkling of his blood, through which we are set free from sins and strengthened for good works? ON THE TABERNACLE 3.10.[1]

29:4 Washing with Water

CLEANSING WATER COMES FIRST. CYRIL OF JERUSALEM: The high priest washes himself, then offers incense; for Aaron was first washed, then became high priest. For how could one who had not yet been cleansed by water pray for others? Further, the laver had been set within the tabernacle, as a symbol of baptism. CATECHETICAL LECTURE 3.5.[2]

---

[1]TTH 18:144. [2]FC 61:111.

29:10-46 ORDINATION SACRIFICES

[10]*"Then you shall bring the bull before the tent of meeting. Aaron and his sons shall lay their hands upon the head of the bull,* [11]*and you shall kill the bull before the* Lord, *at the door of the tent of meeting,* [12]*and shall take part of the blood of the bull and put it upon the horns of the altar with your finger, and the rest of* [r] *the blood you shall pour out at the base of the altar.* [13]*And you shall take all the fat that covers the entrails, and the appendage of the liver, and the two kidneys with the fat that is on them, and burn them upon the altar.* [14]*But the flesh of the bull, and its skin, and its dung, you shall burn with fire outside the camp; it is a sin offering. . . .*

[22]*"You shall also take the fat of the ram, and the fat tail, and the fat that covers the entrails, and the appendage of the liver, and the two kidneys with the fat that is on them, and the right thigh (for it is a ram of ordination),* [23]*and one loaf of bread, and one cake of bread with oil, and one wafer, out of the basket of unleavened bread that is before the* Lord; [24]*and you shall put all these in the hands of Aaron and in the hands of his sons, and wave them for a wave offering before the* Lord. [25]*Then you shall take them from their hands, and burn them on the altar in addition to the burnt offering, as a pleasing odor before the* Lord; *it is an offering by fire to the* Lord.

[26]*"And you shall take the breast of the ram of Aaron's ordination and wave it for a wave offering before the* Lord; *and it shall be your portion.* [27]*And you shall consecrate the breast of the wave offering, and the thigh of the priests' portion, which is waved, and which is offered from the ram of ordination, since it is for Aaron and for his sons.* [28]*It shall be for Aaron and his sons as a perpetual due from the people of Israel, for it is the priests' portion to be offered by the people of Israel from their peace offerings; it is their offering to the* Lord. . . .

[41]*"And the other lamb you shall offer . . . for a pleasing odor. . . .* [42]*It shall be a continual burnt offering throughout your generations at the door of the tent of meeting before the* Lord, *where I will meet with you, to speak there to you.* [43]*There I will meet with the people of Israel, and it shall be sanctified by my glory;* [44]*I will consecrate the tent of meeting and the altar; Aaron also and his sons I will consecrate, to serve me as priest.* [45]*And I will dwell among the people of Israel, and will be their God.* [46]*And they shall know that I am the* Lord *their God, who brought them forth out of the land of Egypt that I might dwell among them; I am the* Lord *their God."*

r *Heb* all

Overview: Christ was crucified not in the temple or in the city but outside the city because he initiated a new order of worship (Leo the Great). The priest should surpass the people in virtue and right conduct. The priest must have right thoughts and no concern for the things of this world (Gregory the Great). The incense God wants comes from a pure heart and a good conscience (Origen).

29:14 Outside the Camp

Christ Died Outside the Camp. Leo the Great: Indeed consequently, "Christ our Passover has been sacrificed,"[1] as the apostle says. Offering himself to the Father as a new and real sacrifice of reconciliation, he was crucified—not in the temple whose due worship is now completed, nor within the enclosure of the city which was to be destroyed because of its crime, but "outside and beyond the camp." That way, as the mystery of the ancient sacrifices was ceasing, a new victim would be put on a new altar, and the cross of Christ would be the altar not of the temple but of the world. SERMON 59.5.[2]

See also AMBROSE ON EXODUS 33:7.

29:22 The Right Thigh

ALWAYS TO DO WHAT IS UPRIGHT. GREGORY THE GREAT: Therefore by divine ordinance the priest receives a shoulder for sacrifice, and that too the right one and separate. His conduct should be not only profitable but also outstanding. He should not only do what is upright in the midst of the wicked but also surpass the well-doers among his subjects. And as he surpasses them in the dignity of his rank, so should he in the virtue of his conduct. PASTORAL CARE 2.3.[3]

29:25 The Burnt Offering

See ORIGEN ON EXODUS 26:33.

29:28 The Priests' Portion

THE VIRTUES OF A PRIEST. GREGORY THE GREAT: Again, the breast of the victim together with the shoulder are assigned to him for eating, so that he may learn to immolate to the Giver of all things those parts of himself which correspond to the parts of the sacrifice which he is ordered to take. Not only in his heart must he have right thoughts, but also he must invite those who behold him, by the shoulder[4] of his deeds to sublime heights. He may not covet the good things of this present life nor fear any adversity. He must despise the blandishments of the world by heeding the fear they inspire in his conscience yet despise all fears in view of the sweet delights which his conscience holds out to him. PASTORAL CARE 2.3.[5]

29:41 For a Pleasing Odor

A PURE HEART AND A GOOD CONSCIENCE. ORIGEN: For do not think that the omnipotent God commanded this and consecrated this in the law that incense be brought to him from Arabia. But this is the incense that God seeks to be offered by human beings to him, from which he receives "a pleasing odor," prayers from a pure heart and good conscience in which God truly receives a pleasing warmth. HOMILIES ON LEVITICUS 13.5.2.[6]

---

[1] 1 Cor 5:7. [2] FC 93:257. [3] ACW 11:48-49. [4] Represented by his humeral vestment. [5] ACW 11:49. [6] FC 83:242.

30:1-10 ALTAR OF INCENSE

[1] "You shall make an altar to burn incense upon; of acacia wood shall you make it. . . . [6] And you shall put it before the veil that is by the ark of the testimony, before the mercy seat that is over the testimony, where I will meet with you. [7] And Aaron shall burn fragrant incense on it; every morning when he dresses the lamps he shall burn it, [8] and when Aaron sets up the lamps in

the evening, he shall burn it, a perpetual incense before the LORD throughout your generations. [9]*You shall offer no unholy incense thereon, nor burnt offering, nor cereal offering; and you shall pour no libation thereon.* [10]*Aaron shall make atonement upon its horns once a year; with the blood of the sin offering of atonement he shall make atonement for it once in the year throughout your generations; it is most holy to the LORD."*

OVERVIEW: The ark of the covenant and its contents foreshadow the new dispensation (BEDE). The high priest could both have relations with his wife and be permitted to offer incense (AUGUSTINE). The Day of Atonement in the new covenant lasts until the end of the world (ORIGEN).

30:6 Before the Veil

THE ARK IS CHRIST. BEDE: The ark of the covenant, which was inside the veil, . . . very suitably symbolizes the nature of [Christ's] humanity. The urn [containing] manna symbolizes the fullness of his divinity. The staff of Aaron symbolizes the indestructible power of his priesthood, [and] the tablets of the covenant symbolize that it is he who gave the law and will also give his blessing to those who fulfill the law. HOMILIES ON THE GOSPELS 2.25.[1]

30:7 Burning Fragrant Incense

AUGUSTINE CORRECTS HIS EARLIER MISINTERPRETATION. AUGUSTINE: In the third book[2] there is also a discussion of how the high priest begot sons, since he had the obligation to enter the Holy of Holies twice a day where the altar of incense was, to offer incense morning and evening. Into [this], as the law states, he could not enter while unclean, and the law says that a man is even made unclean as a result of conjugal coition,[3] and indeed it orders him to be washed with water, but it states also that he, although washed, "is unclean until evening."[4] Hence I said, "It follows logically that he either be continent or that, on some days, the offering of incense be interrupted." I did not realize that

this is not a logical consequence. For what is written, "he will be unclean until evening," can be understood to mean that he was no longer unclean during the evening itself but up to the evening, so that, cleansed, he could offer incense during the evening even though, after morning offering of incense, he had had conjugal relations with his wife for the procreation of children. RECONSIDERATIONS 81.2.[5]

30:10 Once a Year

THE DAY OF ATONEMENT LASTS UNTIL THE END. ORIGEN: Therefore, if I should consider how the true "high priest," my Lord Jesus Christ,[6] having indeed been placed in the flesh, was with the people all year, that year about which he himself says, "He sent me to proclaim good news to the poor and to announce the acceptable year of the Lord and the day of forgiveness,"[7] I perceive how "once" in this "year" on the Day of Atonement he enters into "the Holy of Holies." That is, when with his dispensation fulfilled "he penetrates the heavens"[8] and goes to the Father to make atonement for the human race and prays for all those who believe in him. Knowing this atonement by which he propitiates the Father for humans, the apostle John says, "I say this, little children, that we may not sin. But if we should sin, we have an advocate before the Father, Jesus Christ the just; and he himself is the propitiation for our sins."[9] But Paul also in a similar way mentions this atonement when he says

---

[1]HOG 2:265. [2]*Questions on the Heptateuch* 3.82; 3.85. [3]Lev 15:18. [4]Lev 15:16. [5]FC 60:241. [6]Heb 4:14. [7]Is 61:1-2. [8]Heb 4:14. [9]1 Jn 2:1-2.

concerning Christ, "Whom God appointed as a propitiator by his blood through faith."[10] Therefore the Day of Atonement remains for us until the sun sets;[11] that is, until the world comes to an end. HOMILIES ON LEVITICUS 9.8-9.[12]

---

[10]Rom 3:25. [11]Lev 23:32. [12]FC 83:186-87

30:11-21 CENSUS TAX AND THE LAVER

[17]The LORD said to Moses, [18]"You shall also make a laver of bronze, with its base of bronze, for washing. And you shall put it between the tent of meeting and the altar, and you shall put water in it, [19]with which Aaron and his sons shall wash their hands and their feet."

OVERVIEW: The laver of bronze represents the tears of compunction, with which we should approach the heavenly mysteries (BEDE).

30:18 A Laver of Bronze

WATER OF BAPTISM AND TEARS OF COMPUNCTION. BEDE: In the first instance, we can understand this basin (or flanged bowl, as it is called further on) to be the water of baptism, in which all those who enter the doors of the church must bathe in order to be cleansed. It was put between the tabernacle of the testimony and the altar of the holocaust, and the priests were commanded to wash themselves in it twice a day (that is, morning and evening) when they were going to the altar of incense to offer to the Lord. We, however, are not supposed to be washed in the water of baptism more than once; consequently the basin commends to us that washing of compunction and of tears which is required of us at all times, and especially when we draw near to minister at the heavenly mysteries. ON THE TABERNACLE 3.14, AT EXODUS 3:18-20.[1]

---

[1]TTH 18:159.

30:22-38 THE ANOINTING OIL AND THE INCENSE

[34]And the LORD said to Moses, "Take sweet spices, stacte, and onycha, and galbanum, sweet spices with pure frankincense (of each shall there be an equal part), [35]and make an incense blended as by the perfumer, seasoned with salt, pure and holy; [36]and you shall beat some of it very small, and put part of it before the testimony in the tent of meeting where I shall meet with you; it shall be for you most holy."

Overview: As in all things, we should follow God's command (Bede).

30:34 Take Sweet Spices

The Composition of Incense. Bede: "You shall not offer upon it incense of another composition." Later in this book the spices from which this incense was to be composed are specified by name: stacte,[1] and onycha,[2] galbanum[3] of pleasing fragrance, and the purest frankincense. It is obvious that all of these signify the eternal goods which we ought to seek from the Lord before anything else. Consequently upon the altar of gold they were not supposed to offer incense of any composition other than that which the Lord had decreed, because when we pray we ought to seek from the Lord nothing other than that which he himself has commanded and has promised to give us. And we ought to believe nothing concerning him other than that which he himself has taught. On the Tabernacle 3.12, at Exodus 30:9.[4]

---

[1]A sweet spice used in making incense. [2]An ingredient of incense from mollusks. [3]A bitter aromatic gum extracted from an Asian plant. [4]TTH 153.

[31:1-11 CHOICE OF ARTISANS]

31:12-18 SABBATH LAWS

[15]"*'Six days shall work be done, but the seventh day is a sabbath of solemn rest, holy to the Lord; whoever does any work on the sabbath day shall be put to death.* [16]*Therefore the people of Israel shall keep the sabbath, observing the sabbath throughout their generations, as a perpetual covenant.* [17]*It is a sign for ever between me and the people of Israel that in six days the Lord made heaven and earth, and on the seventh day he rested, and was refreshed.'*"

[18]*And he gave to Moses, when he had made an end of speaking with him upon Mount Sinai, the two tables of the testimony, tables of stone, written with the finger of God.*

Overview: The sabbath is a rest from labor and freedom from the burden of sin (Ambrose). The sevenfold grace of the Holy Spirit means that Christians should be free of the burden of sin every day of the week (Bede). It was the Holy Spirit, the finger of God, who wrote the law on the tablets. The law of the two tablets binds all Christians; it was not a part of the law that Christ abrogated (Augustine).

31:15 The Seventh Day Is a Sabbath

Sabbath Is Relief from Burdens. Ambrose: They were also commanded to celebrate the sabbath as a feast on one day of the week, so that they would not be subjected to any burdens. Would that they, who were freed from worldly labors, have departed in such a way. That they would not carry with themselves any burdens of serious sin into that perpetual sabbath of ages to come. But since God knew that the people were fickle, he prescribed for the more feeble a part [of that sabbath] by the observation of one day; he reserved its fullness for the stronger. The synagogue observes a single day; the church observes a day without end. In the law then is the part; in the gospel there is completion. LETTER 64(74).5.[1]

FREEDOM FROM THE BURDEN OF SIN. BEDE: Indeed by the fleshly sabbath, which was kept according to the letter, the people were ordered to keep free from all servile work on the seventh day. [The meaning of] the spiritual sabbath, in the light of the sevenfold spiritual grace which we have received, is that we should remain on holiday from the unrest of vices not only on one day but every day. For if, according to the Lord's voice, "Everyone who commits sin is a servant of sin,"[2] it is clear that sins are properly understood as servile works, and we are ordered to walk free of them, as it were on the seventh day, in the partaking of spiritual grace. [We are ordered] not only to keep from wrong deeds but also to devote ourselves to good deeds. HOMILIES ON THE GOSPELS 1.23.[3]

31:18 Written with the Finger of God

THE FINGER OF GOD AND THE HOLY SPIRIT. AUGUSTINE: This law was "written with the finger of God," and this finger of God the New Testament explicitly identifies with the Holy Spirit. For when one Evangelist has "By the finger of God, I cast out devils,"[4] another says this same thing thus: "By the spirit of God, I cast out dev-

ils."[5] Who would not have this joy in the divine mysteries, when the redemptive doctrine shines with so clear a light, rather than all the powers of this world though they be infused with unwonted peace and happiness? LETTER 55.[6]

THE COMMANDMENTS ARE BINDING ON CHRISTIANS. AUGUSTINE: Let us look at the Decalogue itself. Undoubtedly Moses received on the mount a law to be ministered to the people, written on tables of stone by the finger of God. It is comprised in ten commandments, among which there is no charge of circumcision or of the animal sacrifices which by Christians are no longer offered. In these ten commandments, apart from the observance of the sabbath, I would ask what the Christian is not bound to observe. Of the commands, not to make or worship idols or any other gods but the one true God, not to take God's name in vain, to honor parents, to avoid fornication, murder, theft, false witness, adultery, and the coveting of that which is another's—which among these commands can be said not to bind the Christian? What the apostle calls "the letter that kills"[7] is not this law, written on the two tables, but that of circumcision and the other ancient ordinances now done away. For in the law of the tables comes "You shall not covet," the command by which (says Paul), "though it is holy and righteous and good, sin deceived me and thereby slew me"[8]—which can only be "the letter killing." ON THE SPIRIT AND THE LETTER 14.23.[9]

---

[1]CSEL 82 2:152. [2]Jn 8:34. [3]HOG 1:226. [4]Lk 11:20. [5]Mt 12:28. [6]FC 12:285. [7]2 Cor 3:6. [8]Rom 7:11-12. [9]LCC 8:213.

32:1-29 THE GOLDEN CALF

[1]When the people saw that Moses delayed to come down from the mountain, the people gathered themselves together to Aaron, and said to him, "Up, make us gods, who shall go before us; as for this Moses, the man who brought us up out of the land of Egypt, we do not know what has become of him." . . . [6]And they rose up early on the morrow, and offered burnt offerings and brought peace offerings; and the people sat down to eat and drink, and rose up to play.

[7]And the Lord said to Moses, "Go down; for your people, whom you brought up out of the land of Egypt, have corrupted themselves; [8]they have turned aside quickly out of the way which I commanded them; they have made for themselves a molten calf, and have worshiped it and sacrificed to it, and said, 'These are your gods, O Israel, who brought you up out of the land of Egypt!'" [[9]And the Lord said to Moses, "I have seen this people, and behold, it is a stiff-necked people;]* [10]now therefore let me alone, that my wrath may burn hot against them and I may consume them; but of you I will make a great nation."

[11]But Moses besought the Lord his God, and said, "O Lord, why does thy wrath burn hot against thy people, whom thou hast brought forth out of the land of Egypt with great power and with a mighty hand? [12]Why should the Egyptians say, 'With evil intent did he bring them forth, to slay them in the mountains, and to consume them from the face of the earth'? Turn from thy fierce wrath, and repent of this evil against thy people. [13]Remember Abraham, Isaac, and Israel, thy servants, to whom thou didst swear by thine own self, and didst say to them, 'I will multiply your descendants as the stars of heaven, and all this land that I have promised I will give to your descendants, and they shall inherit it for ever.'" [14]And the Lord repented of the evil which he thought to do to his people.

[15]And Moses turned, and went down from the mountain with the two tables of the testimony in his hands, tables that were written on both sides; on the one side and on the other were they written. [16]And the tables were the work of God, and the writing was the writing of God, graven upon the tables. [17]When Joshua heard the noise of the people as they shouted, he said to Moses, "There is a noise of war in the camp." [18]But he said, "It is not the sound of shouting for victory, or the sound of the cry of defeat, but the sound of singing that I hear." [19]And as soon as he came near the camp and saw the calf and the dancing, Moses' anger burned hot, and he threw the tables out of his hands and broke them at the foot of the mountain. [20]And he took the calf which they had made, and burnt it with fire, and ground it to powder, and scattered it upon the water, and made the people of Israel drink it. . . .

[27]And he said to them, "Thus says the Lord God of Israel, 'Put every man his sword on his side, and go to and fro from gate to gate throughout the camp, and slay every man his brother, and every man his companion, and every man his neighbor.'" [28]And the sons of Levi did accord-

ing to the word of Moses; and there fell of the people that day about three thousand men. [29]*And Moses said, "Today you have ordained yourselves."*

* Heb., Vulgate; absent in LXX

OVERVIEW: When Moses was absent, the people worshiped the calf and openly committed the sin that was hidden in their hearts (EPHREM). The people acted irrationally, and the law had to educate them with the power of reason (CLEMENT OF ALEXANDRIA). Self-indulgence leads to idolatry (AMBROSE). When the people are virtuous, they are God's people, but when they sin, they are not (ORIGEN). The stiff-necked people are subjected to the yoke of humility (CASSIODORUS). God allows us the chance to intercede with him (EPHREM) and to pray to him. We ought to be persistent in prayer, just as Moses was (JEROME). Moses, in his love for the people, acted like a mother toward them (AUGUSTINE). In answer to Moses' prayer, God tempers his justice with gentleness (CASSIODORUS). When God is said to change his mind, it happens in our perception of him, not in his decree. The spirit must be added to the letter of the law (AUGUSTINE). God acted toward the people as a schoolmaster does (CHRYSOSTOM). The trial by ordeal forced the people to swallow their own idol. But in a different sense idolaters are converted and become part of Christ's body—swallowed up, as it were (AUGUSTINE). God justly designated those who were to be punished for idolatry (EPHREM). The death of a few delivered many from death (CAESARIUS OF ARLES). The sons of Levi can serve as models for the Christian pastor. The tribe of Levi hallowed itself by carrying out God's command (GREGORY THE GREAT).

32:1 What Has Become of Moses?

THE PEOPLE REJECT MOSES. EPHREM THE SYRIAN: Bitter signs had accompanied [Israel] as far as the [Red] Sea so that they would fear [God]. And blessed wonders surrounded [Israel] in the desert waste so that they would be recon-

ciled [to him]. But for want of faith [Israel] rejected [the signs] with the feeble excuse: "As for the man Moses who brought us out, we do not know what has become of him." They no longer considered the triumphs that had accompanied them. They only saw that Moses was not near. And so, with this as a convenient excuse, they could draw near to the paganism of Egypt. Therefore Moses was not seen by them for a while, so that the calf could be seen with them [and] so that they could worship openly what they had been worshiping in their hearts.

When their paganism came out of hiding and into the open, Moses also came out of hiding and into the open to deliver openly the penalty to those whose paganism had become unrestrained beneath the holy cloud that overshadowed them. God deprived the flock of its shepherd for forty days, so that it would show that it trusted securely in the calf as the god that had pastured it with every delight. It made as its shepherd a calf which could not even graze! Moses, who inspired fear in them, was taken away from them, so that idolatry, which fear of Moses had quieted in their hearts, would cry out from their own mouths. And they did cry out: "Make gods for us to lead us."[1] HOMILY ON OUR LORD 17.3—18.1.[2]

32:6 The People Rose to Play

THE LAW WAS AN EDUCATOR. CLEMENT OF ALEXANDRIA: Of old, the Word educated through Moses and after that through the prophets; even Moses was in fact a prophet. For the law was the education of children difficult to control. "Having eaten their fill," Scripture says, "they got up to play," using a Greek word which means not food but cattle fodder, because of

---

[1]Ex 32:1. [2]FC 91:292-93.

their irrational gorging.

And since they were continually filling themselves without obeying reason and playing without listening to reason, the law and fear followed them to restrain them from sin and to encourage them to reform themselves. CHRIST THE EDUCATOR 1.11.96-97.[3]

THE EFFECTS OF VICE. AMBROSE: He who wallows and sinks in mud pits falls into the snares of treachery. For "the people sat down to eat and drink," and they demanded that gods be made for them. Whence the Lord teaches that he who gives his soul over to these two types of shameful deeds is divested of a garment not of wool but of living virtue, for the cloak of virtue is not temporal but eternal. LETTER 27(58).16.[4]

32:7 Your People

MOSES' PEOPLE AND GOD'S PEOPLE. ORIGEN: Therefore just as the people are God's when they do not sin but are no longer said to be his when they sin, so also the feats are the feats of sinners when they are hated by the Lord's soul, but when they are ordained by the Lord, they are called the Lord's. COMMENTARY ON THE GOSPEL OF JOHN 10.80.[5]

32:9 A Stiff-Necked People

ACCEPT GOD'S YOKE. CASSIODORUS: So these sinners undergo a contrary experience: their necks which they fatally raised against the Lord are subjected to his sweet yoke with the humility which brings salvation. We recall that this often befell persecutors, so that having earlier maintained their idols by the most sacrilegious compulsion, they became proclaimers of our most holy religion. EXPOSITION OF THE PSALMS 128.4.[6]

32:10 Now Let Me Alone

THE POWER OF INTERCESSION. EPHREM THE

SYRIAN: When he wished that [the fig tree] be uprooted, the event was similar to that earlier one, when the Father said to Moses, "Permit me to destroy the people." He [thus] gave him a reason to intercede with him. Here too he showed the vinedresser that he wished to uproot it. The vinedresser made known his plea, and the merciful one showed his pity, that if, in a further year, [the fig tree] did not yield fruit, it would be uprooted.[7] COMMENTARY ON TATIAN'S DIATESSARON 14.27.[8]

GOD INVITES US TO PRAYER. JEROME: On another occasion God said to Moses, "Let me alone . . . that I may consume this people," showing by the words "let me alone" that he can be withheld from doing what he threatens. The prayers of his servant hindered his power. Who, think you, is there now under heaven able to stay God's wrath, to face the flame of his judgment and to say with the apostle, "I could wish that I myself were accursed for my brethren"?[9] LETTER 128.4.[10]

PERSISTENCE IN PRAYER. JEROME: Moses resisted God and prevented him from destroying his people when God said to him: "Let me alone, that I may strike this people." Just see the power of Moses! What does God say to him? Let me alone; you are compelling me, your prayers, as it were, restrain me; your prayers hold back my hand. I shoot an arrow; I hurl a javelin; and your prayers are the shield of the people. Let me alone that I might strike down this people. Along with this, consider the compassionate kindness of God. When he says, "Let me alone," he shows that if Moses will continue to importune him, he will not strike. If you, too, will not let me alone, I shall not strike; let me alone, and I shall strike. In other words, what does he say? Do not cease your persistent entreaty, and I

---

[3]FC 23:85. [4]CSEL 82 1:186. [5]FC 80:272. [6]ACW 53:309. Cassiodorus is commenting on the Vulgate. [7]Lk 13:7-9. [8]JSSS 2:227. [9]Rom 9:3. [10]NPNF 2 6:260.

shall not strike. HOMILIES ON THE PSALMS 26.[11]

MOSES PRAYS AS A MOTHER DOES. AUGUSTINE: And in case you should suppose that he acted like this more from necessity than from charity, God actually offered him another people: "And I will make you," he said, "into a great nation," so leaving himself free to eliminate those others. But Moses wouldn't accept this: he sticks to the sinners; he prays for the sinners. And how does he pray? This is a wonderful proof of his love, brothers and sisters. How does he pray? Notice something I've often spoken of, how his love is almost that of a mother. When God threatened that sacrilegious people, Moses' maternal instincts were roused, and on their behalf he stood up to the anger of God. "Lord," he said, "if you will forgive them this sin, forgive; but if not, blot me out from the book you have written."[12] What sure maternal and paternal instincts, how sure his reliance, as he said this, on the justice and mercy of God! He knew that because he is just he wouldn't destroy a just man, and because he is merciful he would pardon sinners. SERMON 88.24.[13]

32:12 Turn from Thy Fierce Wrath

JUSTICE AND GENTLENESS. CASSIODORUS: By his very love and charm he begs the Lord to temper his justice with a little gentleness, so that he can be prevailed upon by those sinners with whom he was known to be justly angry. But we must notice that he did not say, "Change your ways wholly" but "Change your ways a little," for this is more profitable to us when some lash of tribulation afflicts us. Often when admonished we can gain pardon for our sins by a most wholesome conversion. EXPOSITION OF THE PSALMS 89.13.[14]

32:14 The Lord Repented

DOES GOD CHANGE HIS MIND? AUGUSTINE: Though we sometimes hear the expression "God

changed his mind" or even read in the figurative language of Scripture that "God repented,"[15] we interpret these sayings not in reference to the decisions determined on by almighty God but in reference to the expectations of man or to the order of natural causes. CITY OF GOD 14.11.[16]

32:15 The Two Tables of the Testimony

THE LAW WITHOUT GRACE. AUGUSTINE: For if we should designate a number which signifies the law, what will it be except ten? For indeed we hold it as most certain that the Decalogue of the law, that is, those very well known ten commandments, were first written by the finger of God on two stone tablets.[17] But the law, when grace gives no aid, makes transgressors and exists only in the letter. For because of this especially the apostle says, "The letter kills, but the spirit gives life."[18] Therefore let the spirit be added to the letter so that the letter may not kill him to whom the spirit does not give life, but that we may practice the commandments, not by our own strength but by the gift of the Savior. TRACTATE ON THE GOSPEL OF JOHN 122.8.[19]

32:19 Moses Broke the Tablets

GOD IS A SCHOOLMASTER. CHRYSOSTOM: And Moses broke their tablet, having written for them, as it were, certain words; just as a schoolmaster would do, who having taken up the writing tablet and found it badly written, throws away the tablet itself, desiring to show great anger; and if he has broken it, the father is not angry. For he indeed was busy writing, but they were not attending to him. Turning themselves other ways, [they] were committing disorder. And as in school they strike each other, so also on that occasion he bade them strike and slay each other. HOMILIES ON COLOSSIANS 4.[20]

[11]FC 48:211-12. [12]Ex 32:32. [13]WSA 3 3:435. [14]ACW 52:377. [15]Gen 6:6; 1 Sam 15:11. [16]FC 14:375. [17]Ex 31:18, 32:15-16; Deut 9:10. [18]2 Cor 3:6. [19]FC 92:69. [20]NPNF 1 13:278.

32:20 *Moses Made the People Drink It*

IDOLATERS DIED. EPHREM THE SYRIAN: Moses pulverized the calf and made them drink it in the waters of testing, so that all who had lived to worship the calf would die by drinking it. HOM-ILY ON OUR LORD 6.2.[21]

FAITH SOFTENS THE PEOPLE'S HEARTS. AMBROSE: Moses ground the head of the golden calf into powder and cast it into water and gave it to the people to drink—for "their hearts were fat" with gross faithlessness—so that their hearts might be softened and they might embrace the keenness of faith. Finally, the woman who grinds well will be accepted, but she who grinds poorly will be rejected.[22] LETTER 54(64).3.[23]

ISRAEL OVERCOMES IDOLATRY. AUGUSTINE: Therefore perhaps that calf, being ground to powder, was cast into the water and given to the children of Israel to drink, that so the body of ungodliness might be swallowed up by Israel. EXPLANATION OF THE PSALMS 35.26.[24]

UNBELIEVERS ARE CONVERTED. AUGUSTINE: For Moses ground down the calf's head, and sprinkled it upon the water, and made the children of Israel drink it. All the unbelieving are ground: they believe by degrees; and they are drunk by the people of God and pass into Christ's body. EXPLANATION OF THE PSALMS 89.23.[25]

32:27 *Every Man Puts On His Sword*

THE GUILTY WERE SLAIN. EPHREM THE SYR-IAN: The sons of Levi, who rallied to Moses with drawn swords, attacked them. But the sons of Levi did not know whom they should kill, because those who had worshiped mixed with those who had not worshiped. But the One for whom distinctions are easy to make separated those who committed idolatry from those who had not, so that the innocent would be grateful that their innocence had not

escaped the notice of the just one, and the guilty would be brought to justice because their crime had not escaped the judge. HOM-ILY ON OUR LORD 6.2.[26]

See also AUGUSTINE ON EXODUS 5:9.

A FEW DIE. CAESARIUS OF ARLES: Behold true and perfect charity: he ordered the death of a few people in order to save six hundred thousand, with the women and children excepted. If he had not been aroused with zeal for God to punish a few men, God's justice would have destroyed them all. SERMON 40.1.[27]

PUTTING ALL VICE TO DEATH. GREGORY THE GREAT: To put the sword on the thigh is to prefer the zeal for preaching to the pleasures of the flesh, so that when one is zealous for speaking of holy matters, he must be careful to overcome forbidden temptations. To go from gate to gate is to hasten with rebuke from vice to vice, whereby death enters the soul. To pass through the midst of the host is to live with such perfect impartiality within the church as to rebuke the faults of sinners and not to turn aside to favor anyone. Therefore it is properly added: "Let every man kill his brother and friend and neighbor"; that is, a man kills brother and friend and neighbor when, discovering what should be punished, he does not refrain from using the sword of reproof, even in the case of those whom he loves for his kinship with them. PASTORAL CARE 3.25.[28]

32:29 *Ordained for the Lord's Service*

LEVI APPEASES GOD'S WRATH. GREGORY THE GREAT: Therefore we must consider well when we desist from chiding the wicked, how sinful it is to maintain peace with the very wicked, if so great a prophet offered to God, as it were, in sacrifice, the fact that he had aroused the enmities

---

[21]FC 91:282. [22]Mt 24:41. [23]CSEL 82 2:73-74. [24]NPNF 1 8:86. [25]NPNF 1 8:434. [26]FC 91:282. [27]FC 31:201. [28]ACW 11:179.

of the wicked against himself in behalf of the
Lord. This is the reason that the tribe of Levi,
when it took up the sword and passed through
the midst of the host and did not spare the sinners who were to be smitten, is said to have consecrated its hand to God. Hence Phinehas,

spurning the favor of his fellow countrymen,
smote those associated with the Midianites and
by his own wrath appeased the wrath of God.
PASTORAL CARE 3.22.[29]

---

[29]ACW 11:166.

32:30—33:6 THE ATONEMENT

[30]*On the morrow Moses said to the people, "You have sinned a great sin. And now I will go up
to the LORD; perhaps I can make atonement for your sin."* [31]*So Moses returned to the LORD and
said, "Alas, this people have sinned a great sin; they have made for themselves gods of gold.* [32]*But
now, if thou wilt forgive their sin—and if not, blot me, I pray thee, out of thy book which thou
hast written."* [33]*But the LORD said to Moses, "Whoever has sinned against me, him will I blot out
of my book.* [34]*But now go, lead the people to the place of which I have spoken to you; behold, my
angel shall go before you. Nevertheless, in the day when I visit, I will visit their sin upon them."*

[35]*And the LORD sent a plague upon the people, because they made the calf which Aaron made.*

OVERVIEW: Moses was a gentle man and offered
himself for the people to spare them God's
wrath (AMBROSE). Moses was at one time angry
with the people and at another prayed that he
would be destroyed rather than they (CAS-
SIODORUS). Moses, David and Peter all made
amends for their sins (JEROME). Moses, the
leader of the people, prayed for them (AM-
BROSE). Passover—and therefore Easter—is a
special season of forgiveness (CHRYSOSTOM).
Both Moses and Paul were willing to be cut off
for the sake of the people (JEROME). Moses was
the educator of the people (CLEMENT OF ALEXAN-
DRIA). The death of some people was a salutary
example for others (SALVIAN).

32:30 Perhaps I Can Atone

ATONEMENT IS POSSIBLE. JEROME: By a threefold confession Peter blotted out his threefold

denial.[1] If Aaron committed sacrilege by fash-
ioning molten gold into the head of a calf, his
brother's prayers made amends for his transgressions. If holy David, meekest of men, committed the double sin of murder and adultery, he
atoned for it by a fast of seven days. LETTER
77.4.[2]

32:32 If Not, Blot Me Out of Thy Book

IN PRAISE OF MOSES' GENTLENESS. AMBROSE:
What reproaches Moses had to bear from his
people! But when the Lord would have avenged
him on those who reviled him, he often used to
offer himself for the people that he might save
them from the divine anger. What gentle words
he used to address the people, even after he was
wronged! He comforted them in their labors,

---

[1]Jn 18:17, 25, 27; 21:15-17. [2]NPNF 2 6:159.

consoled them by his prophetic declarations of the future and encouraged them by his works. And though he often spoke with God, yet he was inclined to address men gently and pleasantly. Worthily was he considered to stand above all men. For they could not even look on his face[3] and refused to believe that his sepulcher was found.[4] He had captivated the minds of all the people to such an extent that they loved him even more for his gentleness than they admired him for his deeds. DUTIES OF THE CLERGY 2.7.31.[5]

MOSES' CONCERN FOR ALL THE PEOPLE. AMBROSE: The greater the sin, the more worthy must be the prayers that are sought. For it was not any one of the common people who prayed for the Jewish people, but Moses, when forgetful of their covenant they worshiped the head of a calf. Was Moses wrong? Certainly he was not wrong in praying, who both merited and obtained that for which he asked. For what should such love not obtain as that of his when he offered himself for the people and said, "And now, if you will forgive their sin, forgive; but if not, blot me out of the book of life." We see that he does not think of himself, like a man full of fancies and scruples, whether he may incur the risk of some offense, as Novatian says he dreads that he might. But rather, thinking of all and forgetful of himself, he was not afraid lest he should offend, so that he might rescue and free the people from danger and offense. CONCERNING REPENTANCE 1.9.42.[6]

THE TIME OF FORGIVENESS. CHRYSOSTOM: For such is the compassion of the saint that he thinks death with his children sweeter than life without them. He will also make the special season his advocate and shelter himself behind the sacred festival of the Passover and will remind the emperor of the season when Christ remitted the sins of the whole world. HOMILIES CONCERNING THE STATUES 3.2.[7]

MOSES COMPARED WITH PAUL. JEROME: He sought to imitate the shepherd who would, he knew, carry on his shoulders even the wandering sheep. "The good shepherd"—these are the Lord's own words—"lays down his life for the sheep."[8] One of his disciples can wish to be anathema from Christ for his brothers' sake, his kinsmen according to the flesh who were Israelites. If then Paul can desire to perish that the lost may not be lost, how much should good parents not provoke their children to wrath[9] or by too great severity embitter those who are naturally mild. LETTER 82.3.[10]

See also AUGUSTINE ON EXODUS 32:10.

MOSES PUT THE NATION AHEAD OF HIMSELF. CASSIODORUS: What a holy man, most worthy of all praise! When he came down from Mt. Sinai to the camp and saw the people exultantly and sacrilegiously posturing before the idol, he was roused to anger, broke the tablets in front of them and ordered one or other of them to be slain by the sword. But when comprehensive disaster loomed, he prayed that he himself should be destroyed rather than that the entire nation should perish. Both attitudes were devoted and splendid. Moses was right to converse with the divine clemency, for he loved to carry out its decrees. At the same time that power is revealed by which we often escape the punishment of deserved death through the prayers of the saints. Not that anyone can change the Lord's dispositions, but [we] must realize that the outcome is foreknown by him. EXPOSITION OF THE PSALMS 105.23.[11]

32:34 Lead the People

MOSES AN EDUCATOR. CLEMENT OF ALEXANDRIA: In this passage, he teaches him the art of

---

[3]Ex 34:30. [4]Deut 34:6. [5]NPNF 2 10:48. [6]NPNF 2 10:336. [7]NPNF 1 9:355. [8]Jn 10:11. [9]Eph 6:4. [10]NPNF 2 6:172. [11]ACW 53:75.

educating. And well he might, for it was through Moses, in fact, that the Lord of the ancient people was the educator of his children. It is in his own person, however, face to face, that he is the guide of the new people. Christ the Educator 1.7.58.[12]

32:35 The Lord Sent a Plague

Love Exceeds Judgment. Salvian the Presbyter: Thus is it written: "The Lord therefore struck the people for their guilt on the occasion of the calf which Aaron had made." What greater and more manifest judgment could God have made regarding sinners than that punishment immediately follow their sins? Yet, since all were guilty, why was not condemnation visited on all? Because the good Lord struck some with the swords of his sentence in order to correct others by example and to prove to all at the same time, his judgment by correcting, his love by pardoning. When he punished, he judged; when he pardoned, he loved. His judgment and love were unequal: his love was more evident than was his severity. The Governance of God 1.11.48.[13]

[12]FC 23:53. [13]FC 3:49.

33:7-23 MOSES' INTIMACY WITH GOD

[7]Now Moses used to take the tent and pitch it outside the camp, far off from the camp; and he called it the tent of meeting. And every one who sought the Lord would go out to the tent of meeting, which was outside the camp. [8]Whenever Moses went out to the tent, all the people rose up, and every man stood at his tent door, and looked after Moses, until he had gone into the tent. [9]When Moses entered the tent, the pillar of cloud would descend and stand at the door of the tent, and the Lord would speak with Moses. [10]And when all the people saw the pillar of cloud standing at the door of the tent, all the people would rise up and worship, every man at his tent door. [11]Thus the Lord used to speak to Moses face to face, as a man speaks to his friend. When Moses turned again into the camp, his servant Joshua the son of Nun, a young man, did not depart from the tent.

[12]Moses said to the Lord, "See, thou sayest to me, 'Bring up this people'; but thou hast not let me know whom thou wilt send with me. Yet thou hast said, 'I know you by name, and you have also found favor in my sight.' [13]Now therefore, I pray thee, if I have found favor in thy sight, show me now thy ways,* that I may know thee and find favor in thy sight. Consider too that this nation is thy people." [14]And he said, "My presence will go with you, and I will give you rest." [15]And he said to him, "If thy presence will not go with me, do not carry us up from here. [16]For how shall it be known that I have found favor in thy sight, I and thy people? Is it not in thy going with us, so that we are distinct, I and thy people, from all other people that are upon the face of the earth?"

[17]And the Lord said to Moses, "This very thing that you have spoken I will do; for you have found favor in my sight, and I know you by name." [18]Moses said, "I pray thee, show me thy

glory." [19]And he said, "I will make all my goodness pass before you, and will proclaim before you my name 'The LORD'; and I will be gracious to whom I will be gracious, and will show mercy on whom I will show mercy. [20]But," he said, "you cannot see my face; for man shall not see me and live." [21]And the LORD said, "Behold, there is a place by me where you shall stand upon the rock; [22]and while my glory passes by I will put you in a cleft of the rock, and I will cover you with my hand until I have passed by; [23]then I will take away my hand, and you shall see my back; but my face shall not be seen."

* LXX show yourself to me, that I may see you clearly

OVERVIEW: The meaning of being outside the camp is to be above the world and thus with Jesus (AMBROSE). Through their lives, the saints became friends of God (BASIL). Through fasting Moses was made more ready to behold God (MAXIMUS OF TURIN). Moses beheld God's glory, but not in the way we shall behold it in the life to come (AUGUSTINE). To say that God is in darkness is to say that he is invisible and unimaginable (CLEMENT OF ALEXANDRIA). No one can see God, but God is visible in Christ's human nature (CYRIL OF JERUSALEM). God did not and could not appear to Moses in his own nature (AUGUSTINE). Love that longs to see God manifests a spirit of true devotion (PETER CHRYSOLOGUS). The theophany to Moses anticipated in a veiled manner the revelation of the Father and the Son (CYRIL OF JERUSALEM). To think that God's nature is knowable is to be deceived (GREGORY OF NYSSA). It is impossible to see God in this life. To see God's back is a sign of the future incarnation of the Son (AUGUSTINE). We cannot behold God's power, which is life and knowledge in repose (MARIUS VICTORINUS). Even the sun can blind us; in this sinful life we cannot see God (AMBROSE). When we behold God's face, sin is impossible. To see God's substance is to be raised to a state beyond that we are now in (AUGUSTINE). By hope ancient Israel stood on Christ after his resurrection and believed in him (PATERIUS). When one contemplates God, he beholds the incarnate nature of Christ (GREGORY OF NAZIANZUS). The cleft in the rock is the way God is revealed to us. To see the back of God is not an

impious or scandalous expression, as some say; we know God rather than seeing him (ORIGEN). The world was captive to sin; hence punishment is just. Salvation is due to God's mercy and not to human merits (AUGUSTINE).

33:7 Moses Pitched the Tent Outside the Camp

MOSES SAW GOD OUTSIDE THE CAMP.
AMBROSE: For that reason Jesus departed from the city, so that when you depart from this world, you may be above the world. Moses, who alone saw God, kept the tabernacle outside the camp when he spoke with God. And while the blood of the sacrificial victims, which was shed for sin, was carried to the altars, the carcasses, however, were burnt beyond the camp, because no one located within the vices of this world puts off sin nor is his blood accepted by God, unless he departs from the filth of this body. LETTER 14 EXTRA COLL. (63).104.[1]

33:11 As a Man Speaks to His Friend

MOSES' FRIENDSHIP WITH GOD. BASIL THE GREAT: The whole life of the saints and of the blessed, the example of the Lord himself while he was with us in the flesh, are aids to us in this matter. Moses, through long perseverance in fasting and prayer,[2] received the law and heard

---

[1]CSEL 82 3:291-92. [2]Deut 9:9.

the words of God, "as a man is inclined to speak to his friend." THE LONG RULES 16.[3]

THE VALUE OF FASTING. MAXIMUS OF TURIN: Fasting these forty days and nights holy Moses too merited to speak with God, to stand and stay with him and to receive the precepts of the law from his hand. For although this human condition prevented him from seeing God, yet the grace of his fasting drew him into close contact with the Divinity. For to fast frequently is a portion of God's virtues in ourselves, since God himself always fasts. He is more familiar, intimate and friendly with the person in whom he sees more of his works, as Scripture says: "And Moses spoke with God face to face like one speaking with his friend." SERMON 35.3.[4]

33:13 Show Me Thy Ways

AN ANSWER FOR THIS LIFE. AUGUSTINE: Again, in ancient times, in the case of the faithful servant of God, Moses, who was destined to labor on this earth and to rule the chosen people, it would not be surprising that what he asked was granted: that he might see the glory of the Lord, to whom he said, "If I have found favor before you, show me yourself openly." He received an answer adapted to present conditions: that he could not see the face of God, because no man could see him and live. Thus God made clear that the vision belongs to another and better life. In addition to that, the mystery of the future church of Christ was foreshadowed by the words of God. LETTER 147.32.[5]

GOD IS FOUND IN THE DARKNESS. CLEMENT OF ALEXANDRIA: As a result Moses, convinced that God will never be known to human wisdom, says, "Reveal yourself to me," and finds himself forced to enter "into the darkness" where the voice of God was present; in other words, into the unapproachable, imageless, intellectual concepts relating to ultimate reality. For God does not exist in darkness. He is not in

space at all. He is beyond space and time and anything belonging to created beings. Similarly he is not found in any section. He contains nothing. He is contained by nothing. He is not subject to limit or division. STROMATEIS 2.2.6.[6]

WE SEE GOD IN THE FACE OF CHRIST. CYRIL OF JERUSALEM: Moses says to him, "Show me yourself."[7] You see that then also the prophets saw Christ, that is, in the measure each was able. "Show me yourself, that I may see you clearly." But he said, "No one sees me and still lives." Therefore, because no one could see the face of the Godhead and live, he assumed the face of human nature, that seeing this we might live. Yet when he wished to show even this with a little majesty, at the time when "his face shone as the sun,"[8] the disciples fell to the earth terrified. His bodily countenance shined, not according to the full power of him who wrought it but in the measure the disciples could bear. Now if this terrified them and even thus they could not bear it, how could anyone gaze upon the majesty of the Godhead? It is a great thing which you desire, O Moses, the Lord says; and I approve your insatiable longing and "this word will I do"[9] for you, but according to your capacity. "Behold, I will set you in the hollow of the rock";[10] for as you are small, you will lodge in a small place. CATECHETICAL LECTURE 10.7.[11]

33:18 Show Me Thy Glory

MOSES SAW A MANIFESTATION OF GOD. AUGUSTINE: The saintly Moses, his faithful servant, showed the flame of this desire of his when he said to God, with whom he spoke face to face as to a friend: "If I have found favor before you, show me yourself." What, then? Was it not himself? If it were not himself, he would not have said "Show me yourself" but "Show me God"; yet, if he really beheld his very nature and sub-

---

[3]FC 9:269. [4]ACW 50:86. [5]FC 20:200. [6]FC 85:160-61. [7]Ex 33:13 LXX. [8]Mt 17:2. [9]Ex 33:17. [10]Ex 33:22. [11]FC 61:199-200.

stance, he would have been far from saying "Show me yourself." It was himself, therefore, under that aspect in which he willed to appear (but he did not appear in his own very nature) which Moses longed to see, inasmuch as that is promised to the saints in another life. Hence the answer made to Moses is true that no one can see the face of God and live; that is, no one living in this life can see him as fully as he is. Many have seen, but they saw what his will chose, not what his nature formed . . . when he willed . . . not in his nature under which he lies hidden within himself even when he is seen. LETTER 147.20.[12]

PEOPLE LONG TO SEE GOD'S FACE. PETER CHRYSOLOGUS: This is why love which longs to see God, even if it lacks judgment, does have the spirit of devotion. This is why Moses dares to say, "If I have found favor in your sight, show me your face." This is why another man says, "Show us your face."[13] Finally, this is why the Gentiles fashioned idols. In their errors they wanted to see with their eyes what they were worshiping. SERMON 147.[14]

33:19 Graciousness and Mercy

"LORD" AND "LORD" ARE FATHER AND SON. CYRIL OF JERUSALEM: Now here please note carefully what I am to say, because of the Jews. For it is our purpose to demonstrate that the Lord, Jesus Christ, was with the Father. The Lord then said to Moses, "I will make all my beauty pass before you, and in your presence I will pronounce my name, 'Lord.'" Being himself the Lord, what Lord does he proclaim? You see how in a veiled manner he was teaching the holy doctrine of Father and Son. Again, in what follows, it is written in express terms: "Having come down in a cloud, the Lord stood with him there and proclaimed his name, 'Lord.' Thus the Lord passed before him and cried out, 'The Lord, the Lord, merciful and gracious, slow to anger and rich in kindness and fidelity, and guarding justice and continuing his kindness for a thousand generations, and forgiving wickedness and crime and sin.'"[15] And thereafter: "Moses at once bowed down to the ground in worship" before the Lord proclaiming the Father, and said, "O Lord, do come along in our company."[16] CATECHETICAL LECTURE 10.8.[17]

THE WORLD WAS CONDEMNED BY ITS SIN. AUGUSTINE: So if the whole world was being detained in captivity, it was quite in order to say, "I will be merciful to whom I will be merciful and show mercy to whom I will show mercy."[18] If the whole world is in captivity, the whole world in sin, the whole world very justly sentenced to punishment, but part of it set free through mercy, who can say to God, "Why do you condemn the world?" How can God, the just judge, be indicted when the guilty world is convicted? You're guilty. If you consider what you owe, it is called punishment, and you cannot in fairness blame the one who inflicts it for exacting from you what you owe. You may blame the debt collector if he seizes what you don't owe, but who can blame a creditor for demanding payment of a debt, even though you are hoping he will let you off? SERMON 27.3.[19]

MERCY, NOT MERIT. AUGUSTINE: What did he here teach us but that as death is the just due of the clay of the first man, it belongs to the mercy of God and not to the merits of man that anyone is saved. And . . . therein there is no injustice with God, because he is not unjust either in forgiving or in exacting the penalty. Mercy is free where just vengeance could be taken. From this it is more clearly shown what a great benefit is conferred on the one who is delivered from a just penalty and freely justified, while another, equally guilty, is punished without injustice on the part of the avenger. LETTER 186.[20]

---

[12]FC 20:188-89*. [13]Ps 80:3. [14]FC 17:246. [15]Ex 34:5-7. [16]Ex 34:8-9. [17]FC 61:200. [18]Rom 9:15. [19]WSA 3 2:105. [20]FC 30:203.

33:20 *You Cannot See My Face*

DESIRE FOR THE VISION OF GOD NEVER CEASES. GREGORY OF NYSSA: He would not have shown himself to his servant if the sight were such as to bring the desire of the beholder to an end, since the true sight of God consists in this, that the one who looks up to God never ceases in that desire. For he says, "You cannot see my face, for man cannot see me and live."

Scripture does not indicate that this causes the death of those who look, for how would the face of life ever be the cause of death to those who approach it? On the contrary, the divine is by its nature life-giving. Yet it is the characteristic of the divine nature to transcend all characteristics. Therefore he who thinks God is something to be known does not have life, because he has turned from true being to what he considers by sense perception to have being. LIFE OF MOSES 2.233-34.[21]

GOD IS INCOMPREHENSIBLE BY EYES AND BY MIND. AUGUSTINE: Hence the answer made to Moses is true that no one can see the face of God and live, that is, no one living in this life can see him as he is. Many have seen, but they saw what his will chose, not what his nature formed, and this is what John said, if he is rightly understood: "Dearly beloved, we are the sons of God, and it has not yet appeared what we shall be. We know that when he shall appear, we shall be like to him, because we shall see him as he is";[22] not as men saw him when he willed under the appearance that he willed; not in his nature under which he lies hidden within himself even when he is seen, but as he is. This is what was asked of him by the one who spoke to him face to face, when he said to him, "Show me yourself," but no one can at any time experience the fullness of God through the eyes of the body any more than by the mind itself. LETTER 147.8-9.[23]

THE INCARNATION OF CHRIST PREFIGURED. AUGUSTINE: And as a matter of fact the words which the Lord later says to Moses ... are commonly and not without reason understood to prefigure the person of our Lord Jesus Christ. Thus the back parts are taken to be his flesh, in which he was born of the Virgin and rose again, whether they are called the back parts [*posteriora*] because of the posteriority of his mortal nature or because he deigned to take it near the end of the world, that is, at a later period [*posterius*]. But his face is that form of God in which he thought it not robbery to be equal to God the Father,[24] which no one surely can see and live. ... After this life, in which we are absent from the Lord,[25] where the corruptible body is a load upon the soul,[26] we shall see "face to face," as the apostle says.[27] (For it is said of this life in the Psalms, "Indeed all things are vanity: every man living,"[28] and again, "For in your sight no man living shall be justified."[29] In [this] life too, according to John, "it has not yet appeared what we shall be. For we know," he said, "that when he shall appear we shall be like to him, because we shall see him as he is."[30] And he certainly meant this to be understood as after this life, when we shall have paid the debt of death and shall have received the promise of the resurrection.) Or [is it] that even now, to whatever extent we spiritually grasp the Wisdom of God, through which all things were made, to that same extent we die to carnal affections. ... Since we regard this world as dead to us, we also die to this world, and may say as did the apostle: "The world is crucified to me and I to the world."[31] THE TRINITY 2.17.28.[32]

KNOWLEDGE OF GOD AND SELF-FORGETFULNESS. MARIUS VICTORINUS: No one sees the power itself alone, for "no one has ever seen God."[33] And since power is life in repose and knowledge in repose but life and knowledge are actions, if someone were to see God he must die,

---

[21]GNLM 115. [22]1 Jn 3:2. [23]FC 20:188-89. [24]Phil 2:6. [25]2 Cor 5:6. [26]Wis 9:15. [27]1 Cor 13:12. [28]Ps. 39:5. [29]Ps 143:2. [30]1 Jn 3:2. [31]Gal 6:14. [32]FC 45:84-85. [33]Jn 1:18.

because the life and knowledge of God remain in themselves and are not in act. But every act is exterior. Indeed, for us to live is to live externally [in a body]; to see God is therefore a death. "No one," says the Scripture, "has ever seen God and lived." Indeed, like is seen by like. External life therefore must be forgotten, knowledge must be forgotten, if we wish to see God, and this for us is death. AGAINST ARIUS 3.3.1.[34]

THE FACE OF THE CREATOR. AMBROSE: "Who shall see my face and live?" Scripture said, and rightly so. For our eyes cannot bear the sun's rays, and whoever turns too long in its direction is generally blinded, so they say. Now if one creature cannot look upon another creature without loss and harm to himself, how can he see the dazzling face of his eternal Creator while covered with the clothing that is this body? For who is justified in the sight of God,[35] when the infant of but one day cannot be clean from sin[36] and no one can glory in his uprightness and purity of heart?[37] DEATH AS A GOOD 11.49.[38]

PRECLUDING ALL SIN. AUGUSTINE: As regards this life, Moses is told, "Nobody has seen the face of God and lived." You see, we are not meant to live in this life in order to see that face; we are meant to die to the world in order to live forever in God. Then we won't sin, not only by deed but not even by desire, when we see that face which beats and surpasses all desires. Because it is so lovely, my brothers and sisters, so beautiful, that once you have seen it, nothing else can give you pleasure. It will give insatiable satisfaction of which we will never tire. We shall always be hungry and always have our fill. SERMON 170.9.[39]

CAN WE BEHOLD GOD'S SUBSTANCE? AUGUSTINE: Another point that can trouble us is how it was possible for the very substance of God to be seen by some while still in this life, in view of what was said to Moses: "No man can see my face and live," unless it is possible for the human

mind to be divinely rapt from this life to the angelic life, before it is freed from the flesh by our common death. LETTER 147.31.[40]

33:21 Standing on the Rock

ISRAEL'S CONVERSION AFTER EASTER. PATERIUS: The place is the church, the rock is the Lord, Moses is the multitude of the people of Israel, who did not believe in the Lord when he preached on the earth. So that multitude stood on the rock and beheld the back parts of the Lord as he passed by. After the Lord's passion and ascension they were led into the church and merited to receive faith in Christ. They did not recognize him face to face on earth but later acknowledged him "from behind." EXPOSITION OF THE OLD AND NEW TESTAMENT, EXODUS 58.[41]

33:22 In a Cleft of the Rock

GREGORY'S ASCENT TO GOD. GREGORY OF NAZIANZUS: What is this that has happened to me, O friends and initiates and fellow lovers of the truth? I was running to lay hold on God, and thus I went up into the mount and drew aside the curtain of the cloud and entered away from matter and material things. And as far as I could I withdrew within myself. And then when I looked up, I scarce saw the back parts of God, although I was sheltered by the rock, the Word that was made flesh for us. And when I looked a little closer, I saw not the first and unmingled nature known to itself—to the Trinity, I mean; not that which abides within the first veil and is hidden by the cherubim; but only that nature which at last even reaches to us. And that is, as far as I can learn, the majesty or, as holy David calls it, the glory which is manifested among the creatures, which it produced and governs. For

---

[34]FC 69:221. [35]Ps 143:2. [36]Job 14:5 LXX. [37]Prov 20:9. [38]FC 65:106. [39]WSA 3 5:243. [40]FC 20:199. [41]PL 79:751, citing Gregory the Great Moral Interpretation of Job 25.10.25.

these are the back parts of God, which he leaves behind him as tokens of himself, like the shadows and reflection of the sun in the water, which show the sun to our weak eyes, because he is too strong for our power of perception. THEOLOGICAL ORATION 2.3.[42]

33:23 You Shall See My Back

AND THE ROCK WAS CHRIST. ORIGEN: Like to these is the saying of God to Moses: "Lo, I have set you in a cleft of the rock, and you shall see my back parts." That rock which is Christ is therefore not completely closed but has clefts. But the cleft of the rock is he who reveals God to men and makes him known to them; for "no one knows the Father, save the Son."[43] So no one sees the back parts of God—that is to say, the things that are come to pass in the latter times—unless he be placed in the cleft of the rock, that is to say, when he is taught them by Christ's own revealing. COMMENTARY ON THE SONG OF SONGS 3.15.[44]

THESE TERMS ARE NOT IMPIOUS. ORIGEN: For it is well known that he, that is, the one who gave the oracles to Moses, says, "You shall not see my face but my back." Certainly these statements must be understood by the aid of that symbolism which is appropriate to the understanding of divine sayings, and those old wives' fables, which ignorant people invent on the subject of the front and back parts of God, must be utterly rejected and despised. Nor indeed must anyone suppose that we have entertained some impious thought in saying that the Father is not visible even to the Savior, but he must consider the exact meaning of the terms we use in controverting the heretics. For we have said that it is one thing to see and be seen, another to perceive and be perceived or to know and be known. To see and be seen is a property of bodies, which it would certainly not be right to apply either to the Father or to the Son or to the Holy Spirit in their relations one with another. For the Trinity by its nature transcends the limits of vision, although it grants to those who are in bodies, that is, to all other creatures, the property of being seen one by another. But incorporeal and above all intellectual nature is capable of nothing else but to know and be known, as the Savior himself declares when he says, "No one knows the Son save the Father, neither does any know the Father save the Son, and he to whom the Son wills to reveal him."[45] It is clear then that he did not say, "No one sees the Father save the Son" but "No one knows the Father save the Son." ON FIRST PRINCIPLES 2.3.[46]

---

[42]LCC 3:137-38. [43]Mt 11:27. [44]ACW 26:250. [45]Mt 11:27. [46]OFP 99.

34:1-9 RENEWAL OF THE TABLETS

[6]The LORD passed before him, and proclaimed, "The LORD, the LORD, a God merciful and gracious, slow to anger, and abounding in steadfast love and faithfulness, [7]keeping steadfast love for thousands, forgiving iniquity and transgression and sin, but who will by no means clear the guilty, visiting the iniquity of the fathers upon the children and the children's children, to the third and the fourth generation."

Overview: Sin can be visited upon children through their parents' bad example; but the guilt of original sin is remitted in baptism (Paterius).

34:7 Visiting Iniquity on the Children

How Iniquity Is Passed Down. Paterius: What does it mean that the Lord now says through Moses, "You visit the iniquity of fathers on their sons and grandsons"? In these two passages[1] a different sense is found, but the mind of the hearer is taught to inquire subtly along the path of discernment. We inherit original sin from our parents, and unless we are washed by the grace of baptism, we bear even our parents' sins, because up to that point we are one with them. So God will visit the iniquity of the fathers upon their sons, for, through original sin, the soul of the offspring is stained by the guilt of the parent. But then God does not visit the iniquity of fathers on their sons, because, when we are freed from original guilt through baptism, we no longer have our parents' guilt but only the guilt for sins we ourselves committed. This passage can also be understood in another way, because when each one imitates the iniquity of his sinful parent, he is rendered guilty through his parent's fault. But whoever does not imitate the iniquity of his parent is not burdened with his sin. Thus it happens that the sinful son of a sinful father pays the penalty not only for his own sins, which he committed, but also for his father's sins. For he does not fear to add his own malice to his father's vices, even though he knows that the Lord is angered by them. It is just that a man who does not fear to imitate the ways of his wicked father before a busy judge is forced in this present life to pay the penalty for the faults of his wicked father. So Scripture says, "The soul of my father is mine; . . . the soul that sins, that one will die."[2] For in the flesh sons sometimes perish for their father's sin. But when the original sin that comes from the parents' iniquity is forgiven, it is no longer kept in the soul. What does it mean that small children are often snatched away by demons, unless the son's flesh suffers to punish the father? For the wicked father is struck at in his very self and refuses to sense the force of the blow. Generally he is struck in his sons, so that he burns painfully, and the father's sorrow is visited on the son's flesh, insofar as the father's evil heart is punished by the son's suffering. But when the sons who are punished for their fathers' guilt are not little children but already grown, what else should we understand except that they are suffering the punishments of those people whose deeds they imitated? Thus Scripture says rightly, "To the third and fourth generation."[3] For the sons can see the lives of the parents they imitate up to the third and fourth generation. Punishment extends up to them, for they saw what they would imitate sinfully. Exposition of the Old and New Testament, Exodus 60.[4]

---

[1]Gregory has just quoted Jer 31:29-30 and Ezek 18:2-3, which say that God does not punish children for their parents' sins. [2]Ezek 18:4. [3]Ex 34:7. [4]PL 79:751-52, citing Gregory the Great *Moral Interpretation of Job* 15.51.57.

34:10-26 RELIGIOUS LAWS

[12]*"Take heed to yourself, lest you make a covenant with the inhabitants of the land whither you go, lest it become a snare in the midst of you. . . .*

[17]"You shall make for yourself no molten gods.

[18]"The feast of unleavened bread you shall keep. Seven days you shall eat unleavened bread, as I commanded you, at the time appointed in the month Abib; for in the month Abib you came out from Egypt. [19]All that opens the womb is mine. . . .

[23]"Three times in the year shall all your males appear before the LORD God, the God of Israel. [24]For I will cast out nations before you, and enlarge your borders; neither shall any man desire your land, when you go up to appear before the LORD your God three times in the year.

[25]"You shall not offer the blood of my sacrifice with leaven; neither shall the sacrifice of the feast of the passover be left until the morning. [26]The first of the first fruits of your ground you shall bring to the house of the LORD your God. You shall not boil a kid in its mother's milk."

OVERVIEW: Through baptism all sins are forgiven. To sin after baptism is to make a covenant with sin once more (CAESARIUS OF ARLES). Idolatry is wrong because it is impossible to make an image of the incorporeal and invisible God (JOHN OF DAMASCUS). The phrase "all that opens the womb is mine" is especially understandable in the light of Christ, who truly opened the womb of the Virgin Mary (JEROME).

34:12 Lest It Become a Snare

SIN AFTER BAPTISM. CAESARIUS OF ARLES: When the Lord handed over to you the land of the Canaanites, he said, "Take care, therefore, not to make a covenant with these inhabitants of the land that you are to enter; else they will immediately become a snare among you." Now we believe that by the grace of baptism all sins and offenses have been banished from us. If we afterward make a covenant with those same sins and vices, doubtless this covenant will become a snare for us because of our consent to avarice or dissipation. SERMON 81.4.[1]

34:17 No Molten Gods

TO MAKE AN IMAGE. JOHN OF DAMASCUS: "You shall make for yourself no molten gods." You see that he forbids the making of images because of idolatry and that it is impossible to make an image of the bodiless, invisible and uncircumscribed God. "You saw no form on the day that the Lord spoke. . . ."[2] And St. Paul, standing in the midst of the Areopagus, says, "Being therefore God's offspring, we ought not to think that the Deity is like gold, or silver or stone, a representation by the art and imagination of man."[3] ON DIVINE IMAGES 8.[4]

34:19 All That Opens the Womb Is Mine

THE TEXT IS TRUE ESPECIALLY OF CHRIST. JEROME: All the heretics have gone astray by not understanding the mystery of his nativity. The statement "He who opens the womb shall be called holy to the Lord" is more applicable to the special nativity of the Savior than to that of all humanity. For Christ alone opened the closed doors of the womb of virginity, which nevertheless remained permanently closed. This is the closed east door, through which only the high priest enters and leaves, and nevertheless it is always closed. AGAINST THE PELAGIANS 2.4.[5]

34:23 All Males Shall Appear Before the Lord

See ORIGEN ON EXODUS 13:2.

---

[1]FC 47:6. [2]Deut 4:15. [3]Acts 17:29. [4]*ODI* 56. [5]FC 53:299.

34:26 *You Shall Not Boil a Kid in Its Mother's Milk*

See COMMENT ON EXODUS 23:19.

34:27-35 RADIANCE OF MOSES' FACE

²⁷*And the* LORD *said to Moses, "Write these words; in accordance with these words I have made a covenant with you and with Israel."* ²⁸*And he was there with the* LORD *forty days and forty nights; he neither ate bread nor drank water. And he wrote upon the tables the words of the covenant, the ten commandments.*^t

²⁹*When Moses came down from Mount Sinai, with the two tables of the testimony in his hand as he came down from the mountain, Moses did not know that the skin of his face shone because he had been talking with God. . . .* ³³*He put a veil on his face;* ³⁴*but whenever Moses went in before the* LORD *to speak with him, he took the veil off, until he came out; and when he came out, and told the people of Israel what he was commanded,* ³⁵*the people of Israel saw the face of Moses, that the skin of Moses' face shone; and Moses would put the veil upon his face again, until he went in to speak with him.*

t *Heb* words

OVERVIEW: The gospel is in accord with the Law and the Prophets; Moses, Elijah and Christ all fasted for forty days (AUGUSTINE). Seeing God restored Moses' youth (EPHREM THE SYRIAN). One who contemplates God, who is true beauty, receives a share in that beauty (BASIL). The veil on Moses' face concealed his appearance but called attention to his words (CYRIL OF ALEXANDRIA). One who turns to the Lord and is enlightened by the Holy Spirit can read the Scripture with unveiled eyes (ORIGEN). Knowledge of profound things must not be revealed indiscriminately (GREGORY THE GREAT).

34:28 Moses Fasted

FASTING FOR FORTY DAYS. AUGUSTINE: The forty-day fast of Lent draws its authority from the Old Testament, from the fasts of Moses and Elijah,[1] and from the gospel, because the Lord fasted that many days,[2] showing that the gospel is not at variance with the Law and the Prophets. The Law is personified by Moses, the Prophets by Elijah, between whom the Lord appeared transfigured on the mountain.[3] LETTER 55.[4]

34:29 Moses' Face Shone

MOSES IS A PARABLE. EPHREM THE SYRIAN:
In Moses he depicted for you a parable:
his cheeks, ashen with age,
became shining and fair,
a symbol of old age
that in Eden again becomes young.
HYMNS ON PARADISE 7.10.[5]

---

[1]1 Kings 19:8. [2]Mt 4:2. [3]Mt 17:2-5. [4]FC 12:283. [5]HOP 122.

THE NATURE OF BEAUTY. BASIL THE GREAT: Every soul is beautiful which is considered by the standard of its own virtues. But most beautiful, true and lovely, which can be contemplated by him alone who has purified his mind, is that of the divine and blessed nature. He who gazes steadfastly at the splendor and graces of it receives some share from it, as if from an immersion, tinging his own face with a sort of brilliant radiance. Whence Moses also was made resplendent in face by receiving some share of beauty when he held converse with God. Therefore he who is conscious of his own beauty utters this act of thanksgiving: "O Lord, in your favor, you gave strength to my beauty."[6] EXEGETIC HOMILIES 14.5.[7]

34:33 Moses Veiled His Face

THE BEAUTY WITHIN. CYRIL OF ALEXANDRIA: The shadows bring forth the truth, even if they are not at all the truth themselves. Because of this, the divinely inspired Moses placed a veil upon his face and spoke thus to the children of Israel, all but shouting by this act that a person might behold the beauty of the utterances made through him, not in outwardly appearing figures but in meditations hidden within us.[8] LETTER 41.7.[9]

THE SCRIPTURE TOO IS VEILED. ORIGEN: For so long as a man does not attend to the spiritual meaning "a veil lies upon his heart," in consequence of which veil, in other words his duller understanding, the Scripture itself is said or thought to be veiled. This is the explanation of the veil which is said to have covered the face of Moses when he was speaking to the people, that is, when the law is read in public. But if we turn to the Lord, where also the Word of God is and where the Holy Spirit reveals spiritual knowledge, the veil will be taken away, and we shall then with unveiled face behold in the holy Scriptures the glory of the Lord. ON FIRST PRINCIPLES 1.1.2.[10]

34:34 Moses Told the People What He Was Commanded

KNOWLEDGE MUST NOT BE USED TO MISLEAD. GREGORY THE GREAT: When Moses comes forth from the sanctuary of God, he veils his shining countenance when in the presence of the people, because he is not going to reveal to the multitude the secrets received in profound enlightenment. Hence God speaking through him enjoined that if anyone dug a pit and neglected to cover it over, then if an ox or an ass fell into it, he should pay the price of the animal.[11] So when a man who has arrived at the deep streams of knowledge does not cover them up before the unlearned hearts of his hearers, he is judged liable to punishment if by his words a soul, whether clean or unclean, takes scandal. Hence it is said to blessed Job: "Who gave the cock understanding?"[12] PASTORAL CARE 3.39.[13]

---

[6]Ps 30:7 LXX. [7]FC 46:221. [8]Cf. 2 Cor 3:13-18. [9]FC 76:172. [10]OFP 8. [11]Ex 21:33-34. [12]Job 38:36 Vulgate. [13]ACW 11:231-32.

[35:1-3 SABBATH REGULATIONS]

[35:4-29 COLLECTION OF MATERIALS AND CALL FOR ARTISANS]

35:30 — 36:7 THE ARTISANS

[30]*And Moses said to the people of Israel, "See, the Lord has called by name Bezalel the son of Uri, son of Hur, of the tribe of Judah;* [31]*and he has filled him with the Spirit of God, with ability, with intelligence, with knowledge, and with all craftsmanship,* [32]*to devise artistic designs, to work in gold and silver and bronze,* [33]*in cutting stones for setting, and in carving wood, for work in every skilled craft."*

OVERVIEW: Bezalel was first inspired and then constructed the tabernacle (GREGORY OF NYSSA).

35:30 The Lord Called Bezalel

THE CALLING OF BEZALEL. GREGORY OF NYSSA: For we are not wrong in saying just the same of Bezalel, that being entrusted by Moses with the building of the tabernacle, he became the constructor of those things there mentioned. He would not have taken the work in hand had he not previously acquired his knowledge by divine inspiration. He ventured upon the undertaking on Moses' entrusting him with its execution. Accordingly the term *entrusted* suggests that his office and power in creation came to him as something adventitious, in the sense that before he was entrusted with that commission he had neither the will nor the power to act. But when he received authority to execute the works and power sufficient for the works, then he became the artificer of things that are, the power allotted to him on high being, as Eunomius[1] says, sufficient for the purpose. AGAINST EUNOMIUS II.5.[2]

---

[1]A Neo-Arian, opposed by Basil the Great and Gregory of Nyssa.
[2]NPNF 2 5:237.

36:8-19 THE TENT CLOTH AND COVERINGS

[13]*And he made fifty clasps of gold, and coupled the curtains one to the other with clasps; so the tabernacle was one whole.*

OVERVIEW: The fifty rings designate true rest in the Holy Spirit, prefiguring the One who came fifty days after Easter. From this the church unites two peoples into one (BEDE).

36:13 Fifty Clasps of Gold

TRUE REST IN THE HOLY SPIRIT. BEDE: Since the number fifty designates true rest in the Holy Spirit, and a ring seems to have neither beginning nor end, and gold is the most precious of metals, excelling all others in its brightness, what is expressed in the fifty golden rings except the perpetual brightness and bright perpetuity of the highest repose? And the rings grip the loops of the curtains in such a way that one tabernacle might be made out of them all when the glory of the heavenly kingdom graciously pours itself into the pure minds of the faithful, so that with the glue of such healing inspiration the church is made perfect out of the two peoples, or

perhaps we should say out of all Christ's elect. On the Tabernacle 2.2, at Exodus 26:6.[1]

---

[1]TTH 18:55.

36:20-34 THE BOARDS

[27]And for the rear of the tabernacle westward he made six frames. [28]And he made two frames for corners of the tabernacle in the rear. [29]And they were separate beneath, but joined at the top, at the first ring; he made two of them thus, for the two corners. [30]There were eight frames with their bases of silver: sixteen bases, under every frame two bases.

[31]And he made bars of acacia wood, five for the frames of the one side of the tabernacle, [32]and five bars for the frames of the other side of the tabernacle, and five bars for the frames of the tabernacle at the rear westward. [33]And he made the middle bar to pass through from end to end halfway up the frames.

Overview: The rear of the tabernacle westward represents the old life before exodus and baptism (Bede). Sometimes a figure in Scripture can signify two things (Augustine). Christ reached out both to Jews and to Gentiles, as one bar unifying held both sides of the tabernacle (Bede).

36:27 The Rear of the Tabernacle Westward

The West Signifies Destruction in the Sea. Bede: And since the reprobate perish in eternity while the righteous are reigning with the Lord, rightly is it said further on that this side of the tabernacle looks to the sea.[1] Now this signifies the Red Sea, in which Pharaoh with his host was drowned and from which Israel, having been saved by the Lord, went up to Mt. Sinai where they made the tabernacle. Therefore the western side of the tabernacle looks back to the sea when after the perfection of good works the holy church is crowned in Christ and gazes

freely upon the failings or the punishments of the impious, which [Christ] has decreed by his own command. On the Tabernacle 2.6.[2]

36:30 Eight Frames

Eight Faithful Souls Were Saved. Augustine: Sometimes, however, under one figure of either an act or an utterance, two terms may have one meaning. Thus the boards which were fitted together into the construction of the ark signify both the faithful and the eight souls who were saved in the same ark. Similarly, in the Gospel, in the parable of the sheepfold, Christ himself is both the shepherd and the door.[3] Letter 164.[4]

36:33 The Middle Bar

Christ Reaches Out to Jews and Gen-

---

[1]Ex 36:27 Vulgate. [2]TTH 1873. [3]Jn 10:7, 11. [4]FC 20:393-94.

TILES. BEDE: Here, therefore, we must assume that a bar was stretched across the ten cubits of the width of the tabernacle, from the top of the boards in front to the top on the other side. [It was] firmly positioned with a head on the boards on each side in such a way that by means of it that side of the tabernacle which rested not on boards but on pillars might also remain immovable, no less firmly fixed than the other [side], even when the wind was blowing against it.

If you should also wish to understand the sacrament of this bar, in a figurative manner it unambiguously signifies our Redeemer himself, who passed through from corner to corner, as it were. He reached out from the Jewish people, which he had previously chosen for himself, to make atonement also for the sake of the salvation of the multitude of the Gentiles. Hence, just as in the prophets he can for good reason be called the "cornerstone,"[5] so also in the law can he be called the "corner bar." He is "cornerstone," evidently, in relation to the temple which is constructed for God out of living stones.[6] He is "corner bar" in relation to the tabernacle which is built for him out of imperishable wood, that is, out of the souls of the elect, which are free from the stain of corruption. ON THE TABERNACLE 2.10.[7]

---

[5]Is 28:16. [6]1 Pet 2:4-8. [7]TTH 18:85.

36:35—37:16 THE VEIL, THE ARK AND THE TABLE

[35]And he made the veil of blue and purple and scarlet stuff and fine twined linen; with cherubim skilfully worked he made it. . . .

37 [1]Bezalel made the ark of acacia wood. . . .
[16]And he made the vessels of pure gold which were to be upon the table, its plates and dishes for incense, and its bowls and flagons with which to pour libations.

OVERVIEW: The true pastor should teach God's Word to the people as each person is able to receive it (GREGORY THE GREAT).

37:16 Bowls and Flagons

PREACH AS YOU ARE ABLE. GREGORY THE GREAT: We know that in God's tabernacle not only bowls but ladles too were made at the Lord's bidding. The bowls signify a more than sufficient teaching, the ladles a small and limited knowledge. One full of true teaching fills the minds of his hearers and in this way provides a bowl by what he says. Another cannot expound what he perceives, but because he proclaims it as best he can he truly offers a ladle to taste. You who are in God's tabernacle, in his holy church, if you cannot fill bowls with the wisdom of your teaching, give to your neighbors ladles filled with a good word, as much as you have from the divine bounty. Draw others as far as you consider you have advanced. Desire to have comrades on your way toward God. HOMILY 5.[1]

---

[1]CS 123:32.

37:17—38:20 THE LAMPSTAND, THE ALTARS OF INCENSE AND HOLOCAUSTS, AND THE COURT

[17]He also made the lampstand of pure gold. . . . [25]He made the altar of incense of acacia wood. . . .

38 [1]He made the altar of burnt offering also of acacia wood. . . . [8]And he made the laver of bronze and its base of bronze, from the mirrors of the ministering women who ministered at the door of the tent of meeting. [9]And he made the court. . . .

OVERVIEW: We must first be cleansed of sin by compunction and then enter into the secrets of God (GREGORY THE GREAT).

38:8 The Laver of Bronze

THE LAVER OF COMPUNCTION. GREGORY THE GREAT: Moses put there a bronze basin in which the priests had to wash themselves and enter the Holy of Holies, because God's law prescribes that we first wash ourselves by compunction, that in our uncleanness we may not be unworthy to enter the cleanness of the secrets of God. HOMILY 19.[1]

See also BEDE ON EXODUS 30:18.

[1]CS 123:141.

[38:21-31 AMOUNT OF METAL USED]

39:1-21 THE VESTMENTS

[1]And of the blue and purple and scarlet stuff they made finely wrought garments, for ministering in the holy place; they made the holy garments for Aaron; as the LORD had commanded Moses. [2]And he made the ephod of gold, blue and purple and scarlet stuff, and fine twined linen. [3]And gold leaf was hammered out and cut into threads to work into the blue and purple and the scarlet stuff, and into the fine twined linen, in skilled design. [4]They made for the ephod shoulder-pieces, joined to it at its two edges.

OVERVIEW: The vestment was double-sided; so our good works should be seen by our neighbor but kept unblemished in God's sight (BEDE).

39:4 Joined at Its Two Edges

GOOD WORKS: THE OUTSIDE AND THE

INSIDE. BEDE: From this it appears to have been the case that the borders of two pieces were joined together from top to bottom on both sides into a doubled garment. In [this] way . . . half of the garment would be visible to the eyes of those looking at it from the outside while the other half would be concealed on the inside, but the joined borders of the two would come all the way down to the lowest point below. What else are we to understand by means of this type, except that while we are displaying good works on the outside before our neighbors, we must keep them unblemished on the inside before the Lord? ON THE TABERNACLE 3.4, AT EXODUS 28:7.[1]

---

[1]TTH 18:115.

[39:22-31 THE OTHER VESTMENTS]

[39:32-43 PRESENTATION OF THE WORK TO MOSES]

40:1-38 ERECTION OF THE DWELLING

[42]*According to all that the LORD had commanded Moses, so the people of Israel had done all the work.* [43]*And Moses saw all the work, and behold, they had done it; as the LORD had commanded, so had they done it. And Moses blessed them.*

40 [1]*The LORD said to Moses,* [2]*"On the first day of the first month you shall erect the tabernacle of the tent of meeting."*

OVERVIEW: The tabernacle was erected on the first day of the first month, because this is the time when God created the world and Christ underwent his saving passion (THEODORET OF CYR).

40:2 On the First Day of the First Month

WHEN THE WORLD WAS CREATED. THEODORET OF CYR: Why did God command Moses to erect the tabernacle on the first day of the first month? Because at that time he created the world. The sprouting of the trees attests to this fact. For Scripture says, "Let the earth sprout forth grass for fodder, and sow seed according to its kind and its likeness, and fruit-bearing trees that produce fruit, with its seed within it in its likeness, according to its kind upon the earth."[1] When spring begins, the meadows bloom, the fields grow like waves, and the trees germinate their fruit. So too in this very season God set

---

[1]Gen 1:11.

Israel free from slavery under the Egyptians and the archangel Gabriel brought the holy virgin the good news of her mysterious childbearing. In this same season the Lord Christ underwent his saving passion. Most fittingly, the Lord God of all ordered the tabernacle to be erected on the first day of the first month because it was the image of the entire world, and also so that the people would prepare for the feast of Passover, which the law commanded the Jews to celebrate as the first feast. At that time, they were going to celebrate this feast for the first time in the desert, for this was the second year after their deliverance from slavery. QUESTIONS ON EXODUS 72.[2]

---

[2]PG 80:297.

LEVITICUS

1:1-17 HOLOCAUSTS

¹*The Lord called Moses, and spoke to him from the tent of meeting, saying,* ²*"Speak to the people of Israel, and say to them, When any man of you brings an offering to the Lord, you shall bring your offering of cattle from the herd or from the flock. . . .*

⁶*"And he shall flay the burnt offering and cut it into pieces. . . .* ⁹*And the priest shall burn the whole on the altar, as a burnt offering, an offering by fire, a pleasing odor to the Lord.*

¹⁰*"If his gift for a burnt offering is from the flock, from the sheep or goats, he shall offer a male without blemish;* ¹¹*and he shall kill it on the north side of the altar before the Lord, and Aaron's sons the priests shall throw its blood against the altar round about. . . .*

¹⁴*"If his offering to the Lord is a burnt offering of birds, then he shall bring his offering of turtledoves or of young pigeons."*

OVERVIEW: The detailed ritual instructions for the holocaust sacrifices of the old law have an analogy in ourselves, in our quest to be cleansed of sin, to deal with temptation and to grow in holiness (PATERIUS). The birds to be offered in sacrifice are symbols of virtue (BEDE).

1:6 Flay and Cut the Burnt Offering

DEALING WITH TEMPTATION. PATERIUS: We strip off the skin of a victim when we remove the illusion of virtue from the eyes of our mind. We cut its limbs into pieces when we carefully distinguish the content of a virtue and ponder it step by step. We should take care, so that when we conquer evil we do not replace it with frivolous goods. Otherwise those goods might produce inconstancy; they might lay hold of frivolity; they might wander off on the path of error; they might be broken by laziness and lose the value of work already done. In all things the mind should look around carefully and persevere in its provident concern. We should also note that we are sometimes afflicted by an impulse to illicit thoughts, because we are engaged in some earthly business, even if it is legitimate. When an earthly act is tinged with desire, even in a small way, the power of the ancient enemy grows against us and our minds are corrupted by no small oppression of temptation. Hence the priest of the law is bidden to burn in fire part of the victim that has been cut into pieces, namely, the head and the parts around the liver; but the feet and the intestines of the victim he must first wash in water. We burn the head and what is near the liver when, in the senses that rule the whole body and in our hidden desires, we burn with the flame of divine love. And the priest is commanded to wash the victim's feet and intestines. Feet touch the earth, and intestines carry excrement. We are often set on fire with longing for eternity and in our sense of devotion long for our mortification. But since we still do something earthly because of our weakness, we tolerate in our hearts some illicit thoughts that we have suppressed. And when unclean temptation fouls our thoughts, what do they contain except excrement from the victim's intestines? To burn them, they should be washed, for it is necessary that weeping in fear should wash away unclean thoughts. The heavenly fire can burn them in an acceptable sacrifice. Whatever the mind suffers in unfamiliar struggle or in the memory of its first conversion is to be washed, so that it can burn more sweetly in the sight of the one who beholds it. EXPOSITION OF THE OLD AND NEW TESTAMENT, LEVITICUS 1.[1]

1:14 Offering Turtledoves or Young Pigeons

SIMPLICITY AND CHASTITY. BEDE: In very many ceremonies of the law one who needed to be cleansed was ordered to be cleansed by [offering] these [birds]. A pigeon indicates simplicity and a turtledove indicates chastity, for a pigeon is a lover of simplicity and a turtledove is a lover of chastity—so that if by chance one loses its mate it will not subsequently seek another. HOMILIES ON THE GOSPELS 1.18.[2]

---

[1]PL 79:753-54, citing Gregory the Great *Moral Interpretation of Job* 1.36.55; 9.55.84. [2]HOG 1:181.

2:1-16 CEREAL OFFERINGS

[11]"No cereal offering which you bring to the LORD shall be made with leaven; for you shall burn no leaven nor any honey as an offering by fire to the LORD. [12]As an offering of first fruits you may bring them to the LORD, but they shall not be offered on the altar for a pleasing odor. [13]You shall season all your cereal offerings with salt; you shall not let the salt of the covenant with your God be lacking from your cereal offering; with all your offerings you shall offer salt.

[14]"If you offer a cereal offering of first fruits to the LORD, you shall offer for the cereal offering of your first fruits crushed new grain from fresh ears, parched with fire."

OVERVIEW: Honey and beeswax are ambiguous to the taste; hence they are not offered in sacrifice. Honey is a sign of sensual pleasure (JEROME). Salt, which is meditation on the Scriptures, stings and disinfects (METHODIUS). Salt is the seasoning that makes speech graceful (JEROME). Salt destroys corruption and restores health (MACARIUS). The salt of temptation may strengthen the soul (ORIGEN). The first fruits of the church are the newly baptized (AMBROSE).

2:11 Do Not Burn Leaven or Honey

HONEY AND WAX NOT OFFERED TO GOD. JEROME: They quote the passage which says that "the lips of a strange woman drop as honeycomb,"[1] which is sweet indeed in the eater's mouth but is afterward found more bitter than gall.[2] This, they argue, is the reason that neither

---

[1]Prov 5:3. [2]Rev 10:9-10.

honey nor wax is offered in the sacrifices of the Lord, and that oil, the product of the bitter olive, is burned in his temple.[3] LETTER 128.2.[4]

HONEY IS A SIGN OF PLEASURE. JEROME: Under no circumstances is there an offering of honey. "Whatever happens," it says, "will be impure." Honey is a sign of pleasure and sweetness, and believe me, sensual pleasure always brings death; sensuality as such is never pleasing to God. HOMILY 75.[5]

2:13 Salt Given with All Offerings

THE SALT OF TEMPTATION STRENGTHENS THE SOUL. ORIGEN: Just as meat, if it is not sprinkled with salt, no matter how great and special it is, becomes rotten, so also the soul, unless it is somehow salted with constant temptations, immediately becomes feeble and soft. For this reason the saying is established that every sacrifice shall be salted with salt. HOMILIES ON NUMBERS 27.12.[6]

THE SALT OF SCRIPTURE STINGS. METHODIUS: Hence in Leviticus every gift, unless it is seasoned with salt, is forbidden to be offered as an oblation to the Lord God. Now the whole spiritual meditation of the Scriptures is given to us as salt which stings in order to benefit and which disinfects. Without [this] it is impossible for a soul, by means of reason, to be brought to the Almighty; for "you are the salt of the earth,"[7] said the Lord to the apostles. BANQUET OF THE TEN VIRGINS 1.1.[8]

THE GOODNESS OF SALT. JEROME: Salt is good,

and every offering must be sprinkled with it. Therefore also the apostle has given the commandment: "Let your speech be always with grace, seasoned with salt."[9] But "if the salt have lost his savor," it is cast out.[10] LETTER 125.1.[11]

SALT CLEANSES THE SOUL. MACARIUS: If indeed the soul takes refuge in God, believes and seeks the salt of life which is the good and person-loving Spirit, then the heavenly salt comes and kills those ugly worms. The Spirit takes away the awful stench and cleanses the soul by the strength of his salt. Thus the soul is brought back to health and freed from its wounds by the true salt in order to be again useful and ordered to serve the heavenly Lord. That is why even in the law God uses this example when he ordered that all sacrifices be salted with salt. HOMILY 1.5.[12]

2:14 A Cereal Offering of First Fruits

THE FIRST FRUITS ARE THE NEWLY BAPTIZED. AMBROSE: The sacrifice should consist of a gift, the newest of the new, or it should be dried or broken into pieces, or it should be unbroken. The "newest of the new" belongs to the early season of the year and is consistent with the nature of first fruits. Now it has been made clear to us that this refers to those who are renewed by the sacrament of baptism. CAIN AND ABEL 2.6.19.[13]

---

[3]Ex 27:20. [4]NPNF 2 6:258. [5]FC 57:127. [6]OEM 263. [7]Mt 5:13. [8]ANF 6:311. [9]Col 4:6. [10]Mt 5:13. [11]NPNF 2 6:244. [12]IWG 29. [13]FC 42:420.

3:1-17 PEACE OFFERINGS

[1]"If a man's offering is a sacrifice of peace offering, if he offers an animal from the herd, male or female, he shall offer it without blemish before the LORD. . . .

[9]"Then from the sacrifice of the peace offering as an offering by fire to the LORD he shall offer its fat, the fat tail entire, taking it away close by the backbone, and the fat that covers the entrails, and all the fat that is on the entrails, [10]and the two kidneys with the fat that is on them at the loins, and the appendage of the liver which he shall take away with the kidneys. [11]And the priest shall burn it on the altar as food offered by fire to the LORD."

OVERVIEW: The tail of the victim, offered in sacrifice, makes the offering of good works complete (GREGORY THE GREAT).

3:9 The Fat Tail

THE TAIL SIGNIFIES COMPLETENESS. GREGORY THE GREAT: The law commands that the tail of the victim is to be offered in sacrifice. Now the tail is the end of a body, and that person makes a perfect offering who carries out the sacrifice of a good work to its due completion. HOMILY 25.[1]

_____

[1]CS 123:188.

4:1-12 SIN OFFERINGS: FOR PRIESTS

[3]"If it is the anointed priest who sins, thus bringing guilt on the people, then let him offer for the sin which he has committed a young bull without blemish to the LORD for a sin offering. [4]He shall bring the bull to the door of the tent of meeting before the LORD, and lay his hand on the head of the bull, and kill the bull before the LORD. [5]And the anointed priest shall take some of the blood of the bull and bring it to the tent of meeting; [6]and the priest shall dip his finger in the blood and sprinkle part of the blood seven times before the LORD in front of the veil of the sanctuary."

OVERVIEW: The dignity of the priesthood makes the priest's sins more serious (CHRYSOSTOM). The two names, Jesus and Christ, show that he is both Savior and priest (CYRIL OF JERUSALEM).

4:3 If the Priest Sins

THE SINS OF PRIESTS ARE MORE SERIOUS. CHRYSOSTOM: And before the time of the prophets, when he wanted to show that sins received a much heavier penalty when they were committed by the priests than when they were committed by ordinary people, he commanded as great a sacrifice to be offered for the priests as for all the people. This explicitly proves that the priest's wounds require greater help, indeed as much as those of all the people together. They would not have required greater help if they had not been more serious, and their seriousness is not increased by their own nature but by the extra weight of dignity belonging to the priest who dares to commit them. ON THE PRIEST-HOOD 6.16.[1]

4:5 The Anointed Priest

JOSHUA AND AARON PREFIGURE CHRIST.
CYRIL OF JERUSALEM: He is called by two names, Jesus Christ; Jesus because he is a savior, Christ because he is a priest. With this in mind the divinely inspired prophet Moses gave these two titles to two men eminent above all, changing the name of his own successor in the sovereignty, Auses, to Jesus,[2] and giving his own brother, Aaron, the surname Christ,[3] that through these two chosen men he might represent at once the high priesthood and the kingship of the one Jesus Christ who was to come. CATECHETICAL LECTURE 10.11.[4]

---

[1]COP 151. [2]According to Num 13:16, Moses changed Hoshea's name to Joshua; Auses and Iesous are the Greek forms of these names. [3]Aaron, as priest, was anointed, which in Greek is *christos*. [4]FC 61:202.

[4:13-21 FOR THE COMMUNITY]

4:22—5:13 FOR PRINCES, PRIVATE PERSONS AND SPECIAL CASES

[22]*"When a ruler sins, doing unwittingly any one of all the things which the LORD his God has commanded not to be done, and is guilty,* [23]*if the sin which he has committed is made known to him, he shall bring as his offering a goat, a male without blemish. . . .*

[27]*"If any one of the common people sins unwittingly in doing any one of the things which the LORD has commanded not to be done, and is guilty,* [28]*when the sin which he has committed is made known to him he shall bring for his offering a goat, a female without blemish, for his sin which he has committed. . . .*

5 [1]*"If any one sins in that he hears a public adjuration to testify and though he is a witness, whether he has seen or come to know the matter, yet does not speak, he shall bear his inquity. . . .*

[7]*"If he cannot afford a lamb, then he shall bring, as his guilt offering to the LORD for the sin which he has committed, two turtledoves or two young pigeons, one for a sin offering and the other for a burnt offering."*

OVERVIEW: To whom is one obliged to reveal an act of perjury (AUGUSTINE)? In reparation for sin, we should offer signs of gentleness and lack of guile (CLEMENT OF ALEXANDRIA). The Holy

Spirit is represented under two signs, depending on whether he reveals mysteries or the simple truths of the faith (ORIGEN).

5:1 If Anyone Is to Testify

THE OBLIGATION TO SPEAK THE TRUTH. AUGUSTINE: "But if a soul should sin or hear the utterance of an oath, and he himself is a witness or sees or knows about it: if he does not make it known, he too will incur sin." That is, "If he does not make it known, he will incur sin." The addition of "and" is a common expression in the Scriptures. But this particular meaning, since it is obscure, seems to need an explanation. For it seems to say that a man sins when someone swears falsely in his hearing and he knows that that man is swearing falsely and remains silent. He knows this, if he was a witness to this matter about which an oath was taken, either having seen it or having known about it. That is, in some way he knows it. Either he saw it with his own eyes or the one who swears told him. For thus he could be aware of it. But between fear of this sin and fear of the treachery of men, there often arises no small temptation. For we can call someone back who is prepared to perjure himself by admonishing him or by preventing him from committing so grave a sin. If, however, he does not listen, and he swears in front of us about something that we know is false, a different question arises: should he be exposed—even if, once he is exposed, he comes into danger of death? But Scripture does not say here to whom this wrong should be made known—whether to the one to whom he swears, or to a priest or to someone who not only is unable to proceed against him by imposing a punishment but can even pray for him. It seems to me that one would free oneself even from the bond of sin if he reveals the fact to those who are able to help the perjurer rather than harm him, either by correcting him or by praying to God for him, if he himself uses the remedy of confession. QUESTIONS ON LEVITICUS 1.[1]

5:7 Two Turtledoves or Two Young Pigeons

THE INNOCENCE OF THE BIRDS. CLEMENT OF ALEXANDRIA: Through Moses God orders that two young birds, a pair of pigeons or of turtledoves, be offered for any sin. This means that the sinlessness of such gentle birds and their guilelessness and forgetfulness of injury is very acceptable to God. So he is instructing us to offer a sacrifice bearing the character of that against which we have offended. The plight of the poor doves, moreover, will instill into us a beginning of abhorrence for sin. CHRIST THE EDUCATOR 1.5.14.[2]

THE HOLY SPIRIT UNDER TWO FIGURES. ORIGEN: Not without reason are "a pair of turtledoves and two young doves" accepted in the sacrifices. For they are worth the same, and you never find separate mention of just a pair of doves but "a pair of turtledoves and two young doves." The dove denotes the Holy Spirit. But when the great and more hidden mysteries are in question and the things that many people cannot grasp, then the Holy Spirit is represented under the appellation of a turtledove—of the bird, that is to say, that always dwells on mountain ridges and in the tops of trees. But in the valleys, in the things that all men understand, he figures as a dove. HOMILIES ON THE SONG OF SONGS 2.12.[3]

See also BEDE ON LEVITICUS 1:14.

---

[1]CCL 33:175. [2]FC 23:15. [3]ACW 26:303.

5:14—6:7 GUILT OFFERINGS

[14]The Lord said to Moses, [15]"If any one commits a breach of faith and sins unwittingly in any of the holy things of the Lord, he shall bring, as his guilt offering to the Lord, a ram without blemish out of the flock. . . .

[2]"If any one sins and commits a breach of faith against the Lord . . . [3]or has found what was lost and lied . . . in any of all the things which men do and sin therein, . . . [5]he shall restore it in full, and shall add a fifth to it, and give it to him to whom it belongs, on the day of his guilt offering."

OVERVIEW: The moral law of the Old Testament obliges Christians too (AUGUSTINE). Indeed, the New Testament places higher moral demands on us than the Old Testament does (GREGORY THE GREAT).

6:3 Finding What Was Lost

THE LAW TEACHES AND BINDS US. AUGUSTINE: Shall we therefore say that when it is written that whoever finds another man's property of any kind that has been lost, should return it to him who has lost it, doesn't pertain to us? Do not many other like things pertain whereby people learn to live piously and uprightly? Isn't especially the Decalogue itself, which is contained in those two tables of stone, apart from the carnal observance of the sabbath, which signifies spiritual sanctification and rest? AGAINST TWO LETTERS OF THE PELAGIANS 3.10.[1]

6:5 Making Restoration in Full

THE NEW TESTAMENT MORE DEMANDING THAN THE OLD. GREGORY THE GREAT: Some people consider the commandments of the Old Testament stricter than those of the New, but they are deceived by such a shortsighted interpretation. In the former theft, not miserliness, is punished; wrongful taking of property is punished in the latter by fourfold restitution. In this place the rich man is not censured for having taken away someone else's property but for not having sufficiently given away his own.[2] HOMILY 40.[3]

---

[1]NPNF 1 5:406. [2]Mk 10:1-23. [3]CS 123:374-75.

6:8-13 THE DAILY HOLOCAUST

[9]"Command Aaron and his sons, saying, This is the law of the burnt offering. The burnt offering shall be on the hearth upon the altar all night until the morning, and the fire of the altar shall be kept burning on it. [10]And the priest shall put on his linen garment, and put his

linen breeches upon his body, and he shall take up the ashes to which the fire has consumed the burnt offering on the altar, and put them beside the altar."

Overview: Analogous to the all-night burning of the sacrificial holocaust, the life of a Christian should be marked by the burning fire of charity, so that he or she performs good works all through life (Bede). The flame of charity should always burn in the Christian's heart (Paterius). The priest who offers the holocaust represents the Lord, who offers us the example of his own passion, death and resurrection (Bede).

6:9 The Law of the Burnt Offering

Holocausts and the Fire of Charity.
Bede: A holocaust is burned on the altar when a good work is performed with the burning fire of charity in the heart of any elect person who is devoted to God completely (that is, with both body and soul). This is done all night until the morning when one does not cease to persevere in good works throughout all the time of his life, until one is taken from the body and merits seeing the morning of the world to come. The fire will be on the same altar, because we ought to be burning with that charity alone which the Lord gives to his church through the Holy Spirit. On the Tabernacle 2.11.[1]

Fueled by the Daily Recollection of Scripture and the Fathers. Paterius: That fire is perpetual that is never extinguished on the altar. The altar of God is our heart. Fire must always burn in it, for the flame of charity must always burn on it for God. Day by day, the priest puts wood on the fire, lest it go out. Everyone who has faith in Christ has been made a member of the high priest. The apostle Peter says to all the faithful, "You are an elect people, a royal priesthood."[2] The apostle John says, "You have made us a kingdom and a priesthood for our God."[3] The priest who feeds the fire on the altar and puts wood on it each day is each one of the

faithful. To keep the flame of charity from going out in himself, he does not cease to gather both the examples of the elders and the testimonies of Holy Scripture. To call to mind the examples of the fathers or the precepts of the Lord in the practice of charity is to put fuel on the fire. Since this inner newness of ours grows old in the daily living of life, wood must be used to feed that fire. While the fire grows dim as we age, it grows bright again through the testimonies and examples of the fathers. And the command is good, to gather wood each day in the morning. This cannot be done except when the night of darkness is banished. Since morning is the first part of the day and comes when we have put off thoughts of this present life, each of the faithful should think of this task first so that the practice of charity can inflame whatever is just about to die out in him, by the efforts he can make. For that fire on the altar of God—that is, in our hearts—is soon extinguished unless it is carefully maintained by the examples of the fathers and the testimonies of the Lord. Exposition of the Old and New Testament, Leviticus 5.[4]

6:10 The Priest's Linen Garment

The Priest Who Offers Is the Lord.
Bede: The priest who offers the holocaust is the Lord who is himself accustomed to kindle in us the fire of his charity and through it to make the sacrifices of our good actions acceptable to himself. And he is clothed in linen garments when he does these things because, in order that he may excite us to works of virtue, he sets before us the examples of his own incarnation, passion and death, which can be signified by linen, as we have frequently said. On the Tabernacle 2.11.[5]

---

[1]TTH 18:88. [2]1 Pet 2:9. [3]Rev 1:6. [4]PL 79:756, citing Gregory the Great *Moral Interpretation of Job* 25.7.15. [5]TTH 18:88.

6:14—7:10 DAILY CEREAL OFFERING, SIN OFFERINGS, GUILT OFFERINGS

[23]"*Every cereal offering of a priest shall be wholly burned; it shall not be eaten.*"

[24]*The LORD said to Moses,* [25]"*Say to Aaron and his sons, This is the law of the sin offering. In the place where the burnt offering is killed shall the sin offering be killed before the LORD; it is most holy. . . .*

7 [2]"*In the place where they kill the burnt offering they shall kill the guilt offering, and its blood shall be thrown on the altar round about.* [3]*And all its fat shall be offered, the fat tail, the fat that covers the entrails,* [4]*the two kidneys with the fat that is on them at the loins, and the appendage of the liver.*"

OVERVIEW: Every good work we begin should be brought to completion (PATERIUS).

7:3 The Fat Tail

CARRY GOOD WORKS THROUGH TO THE END. PATERIUS: What is the tail, except the end of the body? And that man sacrifices well who contin- ues his offering of good works right to the end of the required action. So the tail of a beast must be offered on the altar so that we will carry out to the end every good work that we begin. EXPOSITION OF THE OLD AND NEW TESTA- MENT, LEVITICUS 7.[1]

---

[1]PL 79:757, citing Gregory the Great *Homilies on the Gospels* 25.

[7:11-21 PEACE OFFERINGS]

[7:22-27 PROHIBITION AGAINST FAT AND BLOOD]

7:28-38 THE PORTIONS FOR PRIESTS

[19]"*Flesh that touches any unclean thing shall not be eaten; it shall be burned with fire. All who are clean may eat flesh,* [20]*but the person who eats of the flesh of the sacrifice of the LORD's peace offerings while an uncleanness is on him, that person shall be cut off from his people. . . .*
[33]*He among the sons of Aaron who offers the blood of the peace offerings and the fat shall*

*have the right thigh for a portion. . . . *[35]*This is the portion of Aaron and of his sons from the offerings made by fire to the LORD, consecrated to them on the day they were presented to serve as priests of the LORD."*

OVERVIEW: The true priest is superior in virtue (PATERIUS).

7:33 The Right Thigh

DUTIES OF A PRIEST. PATERIUS: What does it mean that the priest, by a precept of the law, receives not only the right shoulder, but receives it "separated"?[1] Not only is his work useful; it is also unique. Not only does he do what is right among wicked men, but he surpasses those who live well and are subject to him by the honor of his orders and thus surpasses them in his virtuous life. When the breast and the shoulder are given to him as food—since he is bidden to consume part of the sacrifice—he learns to sacrifice something of himself to God. Not only should he think right thoughts in his breast, but also by the work of his shoulder draw his hearers to things above. Nothing in this present life should he desire, nothing should he fear. He should despise the pleasures of this world and reject the fear within, and he should scorn fear as he meditates on the pleasures of inner sweetness. EXPOSITION OF THE OLD AND NEW TESTAMENT, LEVITICUS 8.[2]

---

[1]Thus the Latin text. [2]PL 79:757, citing Gregory the Great *Pastoral Care* 2.3.

8:1-13 ORDINATION OF AARON AND HIS SONS

[3]*"Assemble all the congregation at the door of the tent of meeting." *[4]*And Moses did as the LORD commanded him; and the congregation was assembled at the door of the tent of meeting. . . .*

[10]*Then Moses took the anointing oil, and anointed the tabernacle and all that was in it, and consecrated them. *[11]*And he sprinkled some of it on the altar seven times, and anointed the altar and all its utensils, and the laver and its base, to consecrate them. *[12]*And he poured some of the anointing oil on Aaron's head, and anointed him, to consecrate him.*

OVERVIEW: The word that later meant "church" occurs here for the first time in Scripture, where the Lord establishes Aaron as a priest. Moses, when he appointed Aaron a priest, had him wash and then anointed him. These actions prefigured baptism and confirmation (CYRIL OF JERUSALEM).

8:3 Assemble the Congregation

THE WORD CHURCH IN SCRIPTURE. CYRIL OF JERUSALEM: Well is the church named *ecclesia* ["assembly"], because it calls forth and assembles all men, as the Lord says in Leviticus: "Then assemble the whole community at the entrance of the meeting tent." It is worthy of note that this word *assemble* is used in the Scriptures for the first time[1] in the passage when the Lord established Aaron in the high priesthood. In Deuteronomy God says to Moses, "Assemble the people for me; I will have them hear my words, that they may learn to fear me."[2] He mentions the name of the church again when he says of the tablets: "And on them were inscribed all the words that the Lord spoke to you on the mountain from the midst of the fire on the day of the assembly";[3] as if he would say more plainly, "on the day on which you were called and gathered together." And the psalmist says, "I will give you thanks in a great church [*ecclesia*], in the mighty throng I will praise you."[4] CATECHETICAL LECTURE 18.24.[5]

8:12 Moses Anointed Aaron

CHRIST CONFERS THE ANOINTING. CYRIL OF JERUSALEM: You must know that this chrism [*chrismation*] is prefigured in the Old Testament. When Moses, conferring on his brother the divine appointment, was ordering him high priest, he anointed him after he had bathed in water, and thenceforward he was called "christ" ["anointed"], clearly after the figurative Chrism. CATECHETICAL LECTURE 3.6.[6]

---

[1]The Greek word *ekklēsia*, which later meant "church," is found in the LXX for the first time here. [2]Deut 4:10. [3]Deut 9:10. [4]Ps 35:18. [5]FC 64:132-33. [6]FC 64:172-73.

[8:14-36 ORDINATION SACRIFICES]

9:1-21 OCTAVE OF THE ORDINATION

[7]*Then Moses said to Aaron, "Draw near to the altar, and offer your sin offering and your burnt offering, and make atonement for yourself and for the people; and bring the offering of the people, and make atonement for them; as the* LORD *has commanded."*

OVERVIEW: All were guilty of sin and all needed to ask for forgiveness (AUGUSTINE).

9:7 Make Atonement

PRIESTS MUST PRAY FOR FORGIVENESS. AUGUSTINE: It seems that they have not paid sufficient attention to the fact that Zachary was a priest and that all priests at that time were obliged by the law of God to offer sacrifice first for their own sins and then for those of the people. Therefore, as it is now proved by the sacrifice of prayer that we are not sinless, since we are [daily] commanded to say, "Forgive us our debts,"[1] so it was proved then by the sacrifice of animal victims that the priests were not sinless, since they were commanded to offer the victim for their own sins. LETTER 177.[2]

---

[1]Mt 6:12; Lk 11:4. [2]FC 30:106.

9:22-24 REVELATION OF THE LORD'S GLORY

²²*Then Aaron lifted up his hands toward the people and blessed them; and he came down from offering the sin offering and the burnt offering and the peace offerings.* ²³*And Moses and Aaron went into the tent of meeting; and when they came out they blessed the people, and the glory of the LORD appeared to all the people.* ²⁴*And fire came forth from before the LORD and consumed the burnt offering and the fat upon the altar; and when all the people saw it, they shouted, and fell on their faces.*

OVERVIEW: The one who bestows a blessing needs to be raised above the many by his works (ORIGEN).

9:22 Aaron Blessed the People

ADORNED WITH GOOD WORKS. ORIGEN: Something of this sort has also been written about Aaron in the book of Leviticus, namely, that "he raised up his hands over the people and blessed them." I gather from this that the saying expresses a mystery, namely, that the one who blesses someone must be adorned with works that distinguish him from the many and raise him above them. For when he is going to bless the people, the hands of Aaron are raised on high. So if someone has his hands down toward earthly things, he does not intend to bless anyone. FRAGMENT ON THE GOSPEL OF LUKE 257.[1]

---

[1]FC 94:227.

10:1-3 NADAB AND ABIHU

¹*Now Nadab and Abihu, the sons of Aaron, each took his censer, and put fire in it, and laid incense on it, and offered unholy fire before the LORD, such as he had not commanded them.* ²*And fire came forth from the presence of the LORD and devoured them, and they died before the LORD.*

OVERVIEW: No one may turn away from the tradition that comes from God and follow mere human authority. In particular, heretics may not administer baptism (CYPRIAN). Unfortunately some Christian priests are overcome with cupidity (BEDE).

10:1 Aaron's Sons Offered Unholy Fire

GOD REJECTS HUMAN AUTHORITY. CYPRIAN: The sons of Aaron also, who set upon the altar a strange fire not commanded by the Lord, were at once blotted out in the sight of the avenging

Lord. These examples, you will see, are being followed wherever the tradition which comes from God is despised by lovers of strange doctrine and replaced by teaching of merely human authority. THE UNITY OF THE CATHOLIC CHURCH 18-19.[1]

HERETICS MAY NOT BAPTIZE. CYPRIAN: The same penalty awaits those who bring strange water to a false baptism. The censure and vengeance of God overtakes heretics who do, against the church, what only the church is allowed to do. THE BAPTISMAL CONTROVERSY 8.[2]

THE CUPIDITY OF PRIESTS. BEDE: This is not far from being a sign of our unhappy time, in which some who have attained positions as priests and teachers—merely to mention it is both distressing and sad enough—are consumed by the fire of heavenly vengeance because they prefer the fire of cupidity to the fire of heavenly love. Their eternal damnation was prefigured by the temporal death of Aaron's sons. ON THE TABERNACLE 3.2.[3]

---

[1]LCC 5:137. [2]LCC 5:162. [3]TTH 18:110.

10:4-11 CONDUCT OF THE PRIESTS

[9]*"Drink no wine nor strong drink, you nor your sons with you, when you go into the tent of meeting, lest you die; it shall be a statute for ever throughout your generations.* [10]*You are to distinguish between the holy and the common, and between the unclean and the clean;* [11]*and you are to teach the people of Israel all the statutes which the* LORD *has spoken to them by Moses."*

OVERVIEW: The law forbade the priests of the Old Testament to drink any intoxicating drink (JEROME).

10:9 No Wine or Strong Drink

PRIESTS MAY NOT DRINK INTOXICANTS. JEROME: Priests given to wine are both condemned by the apostle[1] and forbidden by the old law. Those who serve the altar, we are told, must drink neither wine nor *shechar.*[2] Now every

intoxicating drink is in Hebrew called *shechar,* whether it is made of corn or of the juice of apples, whether you distil from the honeycomb a rude kind of mead or make a liquor by squeezing dates or strain a thick syrup from a decoction of corn. Whatever intoxicates and disturbs the balance of the mind avoid as you would wine. LETTER 52.11.[3]

---

[1]1 Tim 3:3. [2]The Greek word *sikera*, borrowed from Hebrew, occurs six times in the Pentateuch; it means "strong drink." [3]NPNF 2 6:94.

[10:12-20 EATING THE PRIESTLY PORTIONS]

11:1-47 CLEAN AND UNCLEAN FOOD

¹And the LORD said to Moses and Aaron, ²"Say to the people of Israel, These are the living things which you may eat among all the beasts that are on the earth. ³Whatever parts the hoof and is cloven-footed and chews the cud, among the animals, you may eat. . . .

⁹"These you may eat, of all that are in the waters. Everything in the waters that has fins and scales, whether in the seas or in the rivers, you may eat. ¹⁰But anything in the seas or the rivers that has not fins and scales, of the swarming creatures in the waters and of the living creatures that are in the waters, is an abomination to you. . . .

¹³"And these you shall have in abomination among the birds, they shall not be eaten, they are an abomination: the eagle, the vulture, the osprey, ¹⁴the kite, the falcon according to its kind, ¹⁵every raven according to its kind, ¹⁶the ostrich, the nighthawk, the sea gull, the hawk according to its kind, ¹⁷the owl, the cormorant, the ibis, ¹⁸the water hen, the pelican, the carrion vulture, ¹⁹the stork, the heron according to its kind, the hoopoe, and the bat.

²⁰"All winged insects that go upon all fours are an abomination to you. . . .

³⁹"And if any animal of which you may eat dies, he who touches its carcass shall be unclean until the evening, ⁴⁰and he who eats of its carcass shall wash his clothes and be unclean until the evening; he also who carries the carcass shall wash his clothes and be unclean until the evening.

⁴¹"Every swarming thing that swarms upon the earth is an abomination; it shall not be eaten. . . . ⁴⁴For I am the LORD your God; consecrate yourselves therefore, and be holy, for I am holy."

OVERVIEW: Just persons seek spiritual nourishment. They sanctify this life and prepare themselves for the life to come (CLEMENT OF ALEXANDRIA). The bride enjoys the fruit of the Word's teaching (ORIGEN). The horns of clean animals symbolize strength in faith and being unconquered in the battle with vices (BEDE). The unclean animals represent various vices (NOVATIAN). The sow is the symbol of all that is filthy-minded and disgusting (CLEMENT OF ALEXANDRIA). Fish with scales can leap upward (GREGORY THE GREAT). As birds that are scavengers may not be eaten, so should we avoid those who plunder (CLEMENT OF ALEXANDRIA). Holiness consists in total self-offering (JEROME). To be holy is to be totally dependent on God (LEO THE GREAT). To be holy is the duty of all Christians. Those who are holy are solicitous for the things of heaven (CAESARIUS OF ARLES).

11:3 Whatever Parts the Hoof and Chews the Cud

THE SIGNS OF JUSTICE. CLEMENT OF ALEXANDRIA: With whom then should we live? With the just, he replies, again under a metaphor. Everything "of split hoof and chewing the cud" is clean, because the split hoof obviously is a sign of evenly balanced justice, which chews the cud of its own food of justice, the word, which enters from without through instruction. And, once within, [it] is recalled as if from the stomach of the mind for the musings of reason. The just man chews the cud of spiritual nourishment, because he holds the Word in his mouth. Justice undoubtedly divides the hoof, in that it both sanctifies in this life and

prepares us as well for the life to come. CHRIST THE EDUCATOR 3.11.76.[1]

CHEWING THE CUD. ORIGEN: [In Songs], the bride desires to sit down in the shadow of this apple tree. This prefigures either the church, as we said, under the protection of the Son of God, or else the soul fleeing all other teachings and cleaving to the Word of God alone. She chews the Word, whose fruit, moreover, she finds sweet in her throat by continual meditation on the law of God, chewing as if it were like the cud of a clean animal. COMMENTARY ON THE SONG OF SONGS 3.5.[2]

THE STRENGTH OF FAITH. BEDE: Hence it is properly decreed in the law that the only animals which are clean and suitable to be eaten by the people of God are those that have horns. For it is well known that those animals that chew the cud and divide the hoof are also those that have horns. So . . . it is mystically disclosed that the only people who can be incorporated into a spiritual union with the church of God are those who by the strength of their faith prove that they are unconquered in their battles with the vices. ON THE TABERNACLE 3.11.[3]

11:4-13 Forbidden Foods

THE MEANING OF FORBIDDEN FOODS. NOVATIAN: Fish with rough scales are considered clean, just as persons with austere, rough, unpolished, steadfast and grave traits are commended. Fish without scales are considered unclean, just as loose, fickle, insincere and effeminate traits are censured. What does the law mean when it states, "You shall not eat the camel"?[4] From the example of an animal, it censures an unruly life and one distorted by unpleasantness. What does the law mean when it forbids one to partake of the flesh of swine?[5] It condemns, you can be sure, a foul and filthy life—one that delights in sordid vices by placing its supreme good not in nobility of spirit but in the flesh alone. What does the law

want to indicate when it forbids the hare?[6] It denounces nervous, effeminate men. Who would use as food the flesh of the weasel?[7] In it the law condemns theft.

Who would dare partake of the skink?[8] The law abhors a capricious and fickle life. Who would eat the newt?[9] The law detests aberrations of the mind. Who would dare partake of the hawk, the kite[10] or the eagle? The law hates marauders and those who live by violence. Who does not loathe the vulture? The law execrates those who look for booty in someone else's death. Who would eat the crow? The law detests immoral and shady intentions. When the law prohibits ostrich, it disapproves of intemperance. When it condemns the nightjar,[11] it hates those who shun the light of truth. When it bans the swan, it loathes stiff-necked pride. When it excludes the heron, it dislikes a garrulous and undisciplined tongue. When it detests the bat, it condemns those who seek out the darkness of error that is like night. The law execrates these and similar characteristics in animals. Since the animals, however, are born with such characteristics, they are without reproach. Conversely such qualities are reprehensible in humanity, which was not created with them but learns from them by comparison with contrary nature, through the exercise of their own error. JEWISH FOODS 3.13-23.[12]

SWINE STAND FOR UNCLEAN PEOPLE. CLEMENT OF ALEXANDRIA: The all-wise Educator, by the lips of Moses, compared association with corrupt men to living with swine when he forbade the ancient people to partake of swine. He made it plain in those words that they who invoke God should not seek the company of the unclean who, like swine, revel in bodily pleasures and filthy habits of life and impure delights, itching for evil-minded pleasures of

---

[1]FC 23:257. [2]ACW 26:181. [3]TTH 18:148. [4]Lev 11:4. [5]Lev 11:7. [6]Lev 11:6. [7]Lev 11:5. [8]A species of lizard. [9]A salamander. [10]A predatory bird. [11]A bird, also called goatsucker. [12]FC 67:149-50*.

sex. CHRIST THE EDUCATOR 3.11.75.[13]

FISH WITH FINS CAN LEAP TOWARD HEAVEN.
GREGORY THE GREAT: Believing people are forbidden to use fish without its fins for food. Fish
with fins and scales even leap up above the
water. What do the fish with fins represent if
not chosen souls? They alone pass over into the
body of the heavenly church. HOMILY 31.[14]

FORBIDDEN BIRDS. CLEMENT OF ALEXANDRIA:
He adds too that they are not to eat "kite or
mastophage[15] or eagle," meaning "You shall not
go near those who make their livelihood by
plundering others." He says other similar things
under some sort of allegory. CHRIST THE EDU-
CATOR 3.11.75.[16]

THE FILTHY HABITS OF THE SOW. CLEMENT
OF ALEXANDRIA: It is then proper that the
barbarian[17] philosophy, on which it is our business to speak, should prophesy also obscurely
and by symbols, as was evinced. Such are the
injunctions of Moses: "These common things,
the sow, the hawk, the eagle and the raven, are
not to be eaten."[18] For the sow is the emblem of
voluptuous and unclean lust of food and lecher-
ous and filthy licentiousness in venery, always
prurient, and material, and lying in the mire and
fattening for slaughter and destruction. STRO-
MATEIS 5.8.[19]

11:44 Be Holy, for I Am Holy

THE HOLINESS OF THE APOSTLES. JEROME:
"Be holy, says the Lord, for I am holy." The
apostles boasted that they had left all things and
had followed the Savior.[20] We do not read that
they left anything except their ship and their
nets; yet they were crowned with the approval of
him who was to be their judge. Why? Because in
offering up themselves they had indeed left all

that they had. LETTER 118.5.[21]

**HOLINESS MEANS TOTAL DEDICATION TO
GOD.** LEO THE GREAT: He himself says, "Be
holy, for I am holy," that is to say, choose me and
keep away from what displeases me. Do what I
love; love what I do. If what I order seems difficult, come back to me who ordered it, so that
from where the command was given help might
be offered. I who furnished the desire will not
refuse support. Fast from contradiction, abstain
from opposition. Let me be your food and drink.
None desire in vain what is mine, for those who
stretch out toward me seek me because I first
sought them. SERMON 94.2.[22]

THE MEANING OF HOLINESS. CAESARIUS OF
ARLES: Pious souls of the Lord, what the Lord
admonishes us is not to be considered merely in
passing, for he says, "Be holy because I am holy."
Although this term properly belongs to all the
Christian people, according to what blessed Peter
says, "You, however, are a chosen race, a royal
priesthood, a holy nation,"[23] this term seems particularly to apply to all priests in a special way. In
all the letters which are addressed to the Lord's
priests by any men whatsoever, it is specially indicated that they are holy. Since then this term is
applied to us, we ought to inquire what precisely
is its meaning. It is only through Greek that the
interpretation of this word *holy* can be discovered.
For *agios* is the Greek for "holy," and *agios* has the
meaning "not of the earth."[24] Therefore if we are
more solicitous for heavenly things than for those
of earth, this term is not unfittingly applied to us.
SERMON 1.19.[25]

---

[13] FC 23:256-57. [14] CS 123:255. [15] A bird of prey. [16] FC 23:257.
[17] Clement means the Hebrews, who did not speak Greek. [18] Lev
11:7, 13-16. [19] ANF 2:456. [20] Lk 18:28. [21] NPNF 2 6:223. [22] FC
93:392. [23] 1 Pet 2:9. [24] Caesarius indulges in a false etymology, deriv-
ing *hagios* from *a* ("not") and *gē* ("earth"). [25] FC 31:20-21.

12:1-8 CLEANSING AFTER CHILDBIRTH

¹The Lord said to Moses, ²"Say to the people of Israel, If a woman conceives, and bears a male child, then she shall be unclean seven days; as at the time of her menstruation, she shall be unclean. ³And on the eighth day the flesh of his foreskin shall be circumcised. . . .

⁶"And when the days of her purifying are completed, whether for a son or for a daughter, she shall bring to the priest at the door of the tent of meeting a lamb a year old for a burnt offering, and a young pigeon or a turtledove for a sin offering, ⁷and he shall offer it before the Lord, and make atonement for her; then she shall be clean from the flow of her blood. This is the law for her who bears a child, either male or female. ⁸And if she cannot afford a lamb, then she shall take two turtledoves or two young pigeons, one for a burnt offering and the other for a sin offering; and the priest shall make atonement for her, and she shall be clean."

OVERVIEW: The eighth day for circumcision prefigures the Lord's day. The stone or rock of circumcision prefigures Christ (AUGUSTINE). The Son not only became man but also became poor so that he might make us partakers in his divinity and his riches (BEDE).

12:3 Circumcised on the Eighth Day

BY WHAT KNIFE ON WHAT DAY. AUGUSTINE: It was certainly not for nothing that the commandment was given for the child "to be circumcised on the eighth day"; it can only have been because the rock, the stone with which we are circumcised, was Christ. It was "with knives of rock" or stone that the people were circumcised;[1] "now the rock was Christ."[2] So why on the eighth day? Because in seven-day weeks the first is the same as the eighth; once you've completed the seven days, you are back at the first. The seventh is finished, the Lord is buried; we are back at the first, the Lord is raised up. The Lord's resurrection, you see, promised us an eternal day and consecrated for us the Lord's day. It's called the Lord's because it properly belongs to the Lord, because on it the Lord rose again. The rock has been restored to us; let those be circumcised who wish to say, "For we are the circumcision."[3] SERMON 169.3.[4]

12:8 If She Cannot Afford a Lamb

THE LORD BECAME POOR FOR US. BEDE: The Lord commanded in the law that those who could were to offer a lamb for a son or a daughter, along with a turtledove or a pigeon. But one who did not have sufficient wealth to offer a lamb should offer two turtledoves or two young pigeons. Therefore the Lord, mindful in everything of our salvation, not only deigned for our sake to become a human being, though he was God, but also he deigned to become poor for us, though he was rich, so that by his poverty along with his humanity he might grant us to become sharers in his riches and his divinity. HOMILY 18.[5]

---

[1]Josh 5:2. [2]1 Cor 10:4. [3]Phil 3:3. [4]NCP 3 5:223. [5]CS 110 1:181.

13:1-46 LEPROSY

[1]*The Lord said to Moses and Aaron,* [2]*"When a man has on the skin of his body a swelling or an eruption or a spot, and it turns into a leprous disease on the skin of his body, then he shall be brought to Aaron the priest or to one of his sons the priests. . . .*

[13]*"Then the priest shall make an examination, and if the leprosy has covered all his body, he shall pronounce him clean of the disease; it has all turned white, and he is clean.* [14]*But when raw flesh appears on him, he shall be unclean."*

Overview: True conversion leads to the fullness of truth (Tertullian).

13:13 A Person Is Clean

The Cleansing of Faith. Tertullian: Thus he wished us to understand that the man who is changed from his former carnal state to the whiteness of faith (which the world considers a blemish and a stain) and who is completely renewed is clean. He is no longer spotted, no longer mottled with both the old and the new. On Purity 20.7.[1]

[1]ACW 28:116.

13:47-59 LEPROSY OF CLOTHES

[47]*"When there is a leprous disease in a garment, whether a woolen or a linen garment,* [48]*in warp or woof of linen or wool, or in a skin or in anything made of skin,* [49]*if the disease shows greenish or reddish in the garment, whether in warp or woof or in skin or in anything made of skin, it is a leprous disease and shall be shown to the priest.* [50]*And the priest shall examine the disease, and shut up that which has the disease for seven days. . . .*

[56]*"But if the priest examines, and the disease is dim after it is washed, he shall tear the spot out of the garment or the skin or the warp or woof;* [57]*then if it appears again in the garment, in warp or woof, or in anything of skin, it* is spreading; you shall burn with fire that in which is the disease."*

* LXX leprosy

Overview: Leprosy that reappears is like those who repent of their sins and then are tainted with pride (Paterius).

13:57 If Leprosy Appears Again in a Garment

Sin That Might Follow Repentance. Paterius: Sometimes we know we have done something poorly and avoid including it in our work. But the guilt of it insinuates itself into other acts of ours. For there are some who are subject to carnal uncleanness but reflect on it and return to themselves; they acknowledge the guilt of their depravity. But when they have recovered from their unclean act, they immediately boast of the good of their chastity and swell up with foolish pride. First an unclean act held sway over their bodies; then unclean pride reigns in their minds. What takes hold of them spiritually is like roaming leprosy.[1] It does not wholly leave the garment but changes its place on it. The garment is each of the faithful in the holy church. A roaming and wandering leprosy lays hold of a garment when, by an unreformed fault, guilt takes hold of that soul that seems to be faithful. Let's suppose someone boasts when he possesses riches in this world but then hears from the mouth of a preacher that all these material things are going to perish; he then distributes what he has to the poor. But when he does so, pride swells up in his heart. First he took pride in his possessions; then he took pride in his generosity! This is analogous to the leprosy changing its place on the garment. Another man is given to immoderate and undisciplined expressions of pleasure. Perhaps he is admonished by a preacher. He practices gravity and self-control and tries to restrain himself so that he does not indulge in dissolute pleasure. Often, though, he restrains himself from pleasure, immoderately—more than he should. His soul turns to anger. His sadness gives rise to motives for wrath and disturbs his mind, constricted as it is with the barb of rage. And so the vice of immoderate pleasure passed through immoderate restraint into the vice of anger. It is like a roaming and wandering leprosy which left the place it had and occupied a place it had not had. EXPOSITION OF THE OLD AND NEW TESTAMENT, LEVITICUS 11.[2]

---

[1]The Vulgate has "roaming and wandering leprosy" at Lev 13:57.
[2]PL 79:758. Not found in Gregory the Great.

14:1-9 PURIFICATION AFTER LEPROSY

[6]"*Take the living bird with the cedarwood and the scarlet stuff and the hyssop, and dip them and the living bird in the blood of the bird that was killed over the running water;* [7]*and . . . sprinkle it seven times upon him who is to be cleansed of leprosy; then . . . pronounce him clean, and . . . let the living bird go into the open field.* [8]*And he who is to be cleansed shall wash his clothes, and shave off all his hair, and bathe himself in water, and he shall be clean; and after that he shall come into the camp, but shall dwell outside his tent seven days.* [9]*And on the seventh day he shall shave all his hair off his head; he shall shave off his beard and his eyebrows, all his hair. Then he shall wash his clothes, and bathe his body in water, and he shall be clean.*"

OVERVIEW: Hyssop is a small plant, but it can break up rocks; so the blood of Christ can forgive sin (CASSIODORUS). Four different baptisms are prefigured in the Scriptures before Christ's baptism (JOHN OF DAMASCUS).

14:7 Sprinkled Seven Times

THE MEANING OF HYSSOP. CASSIODORUS: Though hyssop is a tiny plant, its roots are said to penetrate the heart of rocks. It is also known to be good for a person's internal wounds. In Leviticus it was dipped in sacrificial blood and sprinkled seven times on the body of a leper, revealing by way of anticipation that inward stains of sins could be effectively removed by the precious blood of the Lord Savior. EXPOSITION OF THE PSALMS 50.9.[1]

14:8 The Cleansed Person Shall Bathe

THE THIRD BAPTISM PREFIGURED BEFORE CHRIST. JOHN OF DAMASCUS: A first baptism was that of the flood [of Noah] that cut away of sin. A second was that by the [Red] Sea and the cloud,[2] for the cloud is a symbol of the Spirit, while the sea is a symbol of the water. A third is that of the [Levitical] law, for every unclean person washed himself with water and also washed his garments and thus entered into the camp. A fourth is that of John, which was an introductory baptism leading those thus baptized to penance, so that they might believe in Christ. ORTHODOX FAITH 4.9.[3]

---

[1]ACW 51:501. [2]1 Cor 10:2. [3]FC 37:346.

14:10-20 PURIFICATION SACRIFICES

[10]*"And on the eighth day he shall take two male lambs without blemish, and one ewe lamb a year old without blemish, and a cereal offering of three tenths of an ephah of fine flour mixed with oil, and one log of oil.* [11]*And the priest who cleanses him shall set the man who is to be cleansed and these things before the LORD, at the door of the tent of meeting."*

OVERVIEW: The offering of flour foreshadows the Eucharist (JUSTIN MARTYR).

14:10 Fine Flour Mixed with Oil

FLOUR AND THE EUCHARIST. JUSTIN MARTYR: "Likewise," I continued, "the offering of flour, my friends, which was ordered to be presented for those cleansed from leprosy, was a prototype of the eucharistic bread, which our Lord Jesus Christ commanded us to offer in remembrance[1] of the passion he endured for all those souls who are cleansed from sin. And . . . at the same time we should thank God for having created the world and everything in it, for the sake of humankind, and for having saved us from the sin in which we were born, and for the total destruction of the powers and principalities of evil through him who suffered in accordance with his will. DIALOGUE WITH TRYPHO 41.[2]

---

[1]Lk 22:19. [2]FC 6:209-10.

[14:21-32 A POOR LEPER'S SACRIFICE]

14:33-57 LEPROSY OF HOUSES

21"But if he is poor and cannot afford so much, then he shall take one male lamb for a guilt offering to be waved, to make atonement for him, and a tenth of an ephah of fine flour mixed with oil for a cereal offering, and a log of oil; 22also two turtledoves or two young pigeons, such as he can afford; the one shall be a sin offering and the other a burnt offering. 23And on the eighth day he shall bring them for his cleansing to the priest, to the door of the tent of meeting, before the LORD. . . .

35"He who owns the house shall come and tell the priest, 'There seems to me to be some sort of disease in my house.' 36Then the priest shall command that they empty the house before the priest goes to examine the disease, lest all that is in the house be declared unclean. . . .

44"Then the priest shall go and look; and if the disease has spread in the house, it is a malignant leprosy in the house; it is unclean. 45And he shall break down the house, its stones and timber and all the plaster of the house; and he shall carry them forth out of the city to an unclean place. 46Moreover he who enters the house while it is shut up shall be unclean until the evening; 47and he who lies down in the house shall wash his clothes; and he who eats in the house shall wash his clothes."

OVERVIEW: The recurrence of leprosy in a house raises the question of sins committed after baptism (TERTULLIAN).

14:44 If Disease Has Spread in a House

SINS AFTER BAPTISM. TERTULLIAN: But if [in a case of leprosy] after its rehabilitation and transformation, the priest again observes in that same house any of the old pocks or stains, may he pronounce it unclean and order its timbers and its stones and its whole structure to be torn down and cast forth into an unclean place. This is a type of the man, body and soul, who is transformed after baptism, that is to say, after the entrance of the priest, and then takes up once more the scabrous contaminations of the flesh. He is cast forth outside the city into an unclean place. That is to say, he is "given over to Satan for the destruction of the flesh."[1] On Purity 20.11.12.[2]

---

[1]1 Cor 5:5. [2]ACW 28:117-18.

15:1-33 PERSONAL UNCLEANNESS

[1]"The Lord said to Moses and Aaron, [2]"Say to the people of Israel, When any man has a discharge from his body, his discharge is unclean. . . . [5]And any one who touches his bed shall wash his clothes, and bathe himself in water, and be unclean until the evening. . . . [10]And whoever touches anything that was under him shall be unclean until the evening; and he who carries such a thing shall wash his clothes, and bathe himself in water, and be unclean until the evening. . . .

[18]"If a man lies with a woman and has an emission of semen, both of them shall bathe themselves in water, and be unclean until the evening."

Overview: There are three kinds of washing: the ordinary bath, the Jews' practice of purification and Christian baptism (Chrysostom). The Spirit of God moved over the waters and gave them the power to cleanse (John of Damascus). Purification after intercourse is no longer required, since one baptism has replaced the many ablutions (Clement of Alexandria).

15:5 Bathing in Water

Three Sorts of Washing. Chrysostom: The washing which is common to all persons is that of the baths, which usually cleanses away the filth of the body. There is also the washing of the Jews, which is more solemn than that of the baths but much inferior to the bath of grace. While this [baptismal] bath cleanses bodily filth, it does not merely remove the uncleanness of the body but also that which clings to a weak conscience. Baptismal Instructions 9.13.[1]

The Power of Water. John of Damascus: For from the beginning "the spirit of God moved over the waters,"[2] and over and again Scripture testifies to the fact that water is purifying. It was with water that God washed away the sin of the world in the time of Noah. It was with water that every one who was unclean was purified in accordance with the law, and even their garments were washed with water. Orthodox Faith 4.9.[3]

15:18 Bathing After Intercourse

Many Washings and One Baptism. Clement of Alexandria: In the past, a man coming from marital intercourse was required to wash. It cannot be too strongly said that the providence of God revealed through the Lord no longer makes this demand. The Lord eliminates washing after intercourse as unnecessary since he has cleansed believers by one single baptism for every such encounter, just as he takes in the many washings prescribed by Moses by one single baptism. Stromateis 3.82.6.[4]

---

[1]ACW 31:136. [2]Gen 1:2. [3]FC 37:345. [4]FC 85:307-8.

16:1-19 THE DAY OF ATONEMENT

⁶"And Aaron shall offer the bull as a sin offering for himself, and shall make atonement for himself and for his house. ⁷Then he shall take the two goats, and set them before the LORD at the door of the tent of meeting; ⁸and Aaron shall cast lots upon the two goats, one lot for the LORD and the other lot for Azazel. ⁹And Aaron shall present the goat on which the lot fell for the LORD, and offer it as a sin offering; ¹⁰but the goat on which the lot fell for Azazel shall be presented alive before the LORD to make atonement over it, that it may be sent away into the wilderness to Azazel.

¹⁶"Thus he shall make atonement for the holy place, because of the uncleannesses of the people of Israel, and because of their transgressions, all their sins; and so he shall do for the tent of meeting, which abides with them in the midst of their uncleannesses."

OVERVIEW: The two goats represent Christ's two natures: one is rejected, as Christ was in his passion; the other is taken up into the order of grace (TERTULLIAN). Christ is impassible in his divine nature and passible in his human nature (THEODORET OF CYR).

16:8 The Two Goats

THE TWO GOATS AND CHRIST'S TWO NATURES. TERTULLIAN: May I offer, moreover, an interpretation of the two goats which were presented on "the great day of atonement"? Do they not also prefigure the two natures of Christ? They were of like size and very similar in appearance, owing to the Lord's identity of aspect. He is not to come in any other form. He had to be recognized by those by whom he was also wounded and pierced. One of these goats was bound with scarlet and driven by the people out of the camp into the wilderness, amid cursing, and spitting, and pulling and piercing, being thus marked with all the signs of the Lord's own passion. The other, by being offered up for sins and given to the priests of the temple for meat, afforded proofs of his second appearance, when (after all sins have been expiated) the priests of the spiritual temple, that is, the church, are to enjoy the flesh, as it were, of the Lord's own grace. The rest will deport from salvation without tasting it. AGAINST MARCION 3.7.7.[1]

CHRIST'S GODHEAD AND MANHOOD. THEODORET OF CYR: I will however mention the sacrifice in which two goats were offered, the one being slain and the other let go. In these two goats there is an anticipative image of the two natures of the Savior; in the one let go, of the impassible Godhead, in the one slain, of the passible manhood. DIALOGUE 3.[2]

---

[1]ANF 3:327*. [2]NPNF 2 3:226.

16:20-34 THE SCAPEGOAT AND THE FAST

²²*"The goat shall bear all their iniquities upon him to a solitary land; and he shall let the goat go in the wilderness. . . .*

²⁹*"And it shall be a statute to you for ever that in the seventh month, on the tenth day of the month, you shall afflict yourselves, and shall do no work, either the native or the stranger who sojourns among you;* ³⁰*for on this day shall atonement be made for you, to cleanse you; from all your sins you shall be clean before the Lord."*

OVERVIEW: The spiritual effects of fasting and watching purify sinful hearts (CAESARIUS OF ARLES).

16:29 *Afflict Yourselves*

THE POWER OF PENANCE. CAESARIUS OF ARLES: "On the days of your solemn feasts you shall mortify yourselves." Why did he say this? Because fasts and vigils and holy mortifications afflict bodies that are humbled, but they purify hearts that have been defiled. They may take strength away from limbs, but they add a bright sheen to conscience. Sins of pleasure are redeemed by bodily weariness while the physical delights of dissipation are punished by the distresses of a hard cross. Thus by present mortification the sentence of future death is suspended. SERMON 197.1.[1]

---

[1]FC 66:45.

17:1-16 SACREDNESS OF BLOOD

¹¹*"For the life of the flesh is in the blood; and I have given it for you upon the altar to make atonement for your souls; for it is the blood that makes atonement, by reason of the life.* ¹²*Therefore I have said to the people of Israel, No person among you shall eat blood, neither shall any stranger who sojourns among you eat blood."*

OVERVIEW: Beasts are distinguished from human beings insofar as in beasts, the soul is in the blood; in human beings, the soul is incorporeal and immortal (CHRYSOSTOM).

17:11 *The Life Is in the Blood*

THE HUMAN SOUL. CHRYSOSTOM: In the case of the human person: first its body is created from the dust, and afterward the power of life is given to it, and this is the being of the soul. Accordingly Moses said about the beasts, "Its blood is its life." But in the case of the human person its being is incorporeal and immortal and has a great superiority over the body, to the same extent as incorporeal form surpasses the corporeal. HOMILIES ON GENESIS 13.10.[1]

---

[1]FC 74:173-74.

18:1-30 THE SANCTITY OF SEX

[5]"*You shall therefore keep my statutes and my ordinances, by doing which a man shall live: I am the LORD. . . .*

[30]"*So keep my charge never to practice any of these abominable customs which were practiced before you, and never to defile yourselves by them: I am the LORD your God.*"

OVERVIEW: The law did not promise eternal life but rewards in this world (JEROME). The righteousness of the law consists in the fact that it forces us to recognize our own infirmity (AUGUSTINE). The earthly promises of the law are contrasted with the heavenly promises of the Beatitudes (JOHN CASSIAN).

18:5 Keeping the Lord's Law

THE LAW PROMISES MERIT. JEROME: "The man who carries out the law will find life through it."[1] Scripture did not say he will find life through it, in the sense that through the law he will live in heaven, but he will find life through it to the extent that what he merits, he reaps in the present world. HOMILY 76.[2]

THE LAW IS RIGHTEOUS. AUGUSTINE: The righteousness of the law, of which it is said that if a man does it he shall live in it, is set forth to this end: that every man may recognize his own infirmity. It is not in his own strength or through the letter of the law (which cannot be) but only by receiving through faith the favor of the Justifier that he may attain and do and live in righteousness. ON THE SPIRIT AND THE LETTER 29.50.[3]

CONSOLATION IN THIS LIFE. JOHN CASSIAN: For the law promises those who practice it not the rewards of the heavenly kingdom but the consolations of this life when it says, "The one who does these things shall live in them." But the Lord says to his disciples, "Blessed are the poor in spirit, for theirs is the kingdom of heaven."[4] CONFERENCE 21.5.2.[5]

---

[1]Rom 10:5. [2]FC 57:137. [3]LCC 8:235. [4]Mt 5:3. [5]ACW 57:721-22.

19:1-37 VARIOUS RULES OF CONDUCT

[2]"*Say to all the congregation of the people of Israel, You shall be holy; for I the LORD your God am holy. . . .*

[9]"*When you reap the harvest of your land, you shall not reap your field to its very border, neither shall you gather the gleanings after your harvest.* [10]*And you shall not strip your vineyard bare, neither shall you gather the fallen grapes of your vineyard; you shall leave them for the poor and for the sojourner: I am the LORD your God.*

¹¹*"You shall not steal, nor deal falsely, nor lie to one another.* ¹²*And you shall not swear by my name falsely, and so profane the name of your God: I am the* LORD.

¹³*"You shall not oppress your neighbor or rob him. The wages of a hired servant shall not remain with you all night until the morning.* ¹⁴*You shall not curse the deaf or put a stumbling block before the blind, but you shall fear your God: I am the* LORD.

¹⁵*"You shall do no injustice in judgment; you shall not be partial to the poor or defer to the great, but in righteousness shall you judge your neighbor.* ¹⁶*You shall not go up and down as a slanderer among your people, and you shall not stand forth against the life^g of your neighbor: I am the* LORD.

¹⁷*"You shall not hate your brother in your heart, but you shall reason with your neighbor, lest you bear sin because of him.* ¹⁸*You shall not take vengeance or bear any grudge against the sons of your own people, but you shall love your neighbor as yourself: I am the* LORD.

¹⁹*"You shall keep my statutes. You shall not let your cattle breed with a different kind; you shall not sow your field with two kinds of seed; nor shall there come upon you a garment of cloth made of two kinds of stuff.*

²⁰*"If a man lies carnally with a woman who is a slave, betrothed to another man and not yet ransomed or given her freedom, an inquiry shall be held. They shall not be put to death, because she was not free;* ²¹*but he shall bring a guilt offering for himself to the* LORD, *to the door of the tent of meeting, a ram for a guilt offering.* ²²*And the priest shall make atonement for him with the ram of the guilt offering before the* LORD *for his sin which he has committed; and the sin which he has committed shall be forgiven him.*

²³*"When you come into the land and plant all kinds of trees for food, then you shall count their fruit as forbidden;^h three years it shall be forbidden to you, it must not be eaten."*

g *Heb* blood   h *Heb* their uncircumcision

OVERVIEW: The law offers beautiful examples of generosity toward the poor and the needy. The law proclaims God's justice and goodness (CLEMENT OF ALEXANDRIA). To deny a laborer his or her wages is deeply sinful in God's eyes (AMBROSE). The blind and the deaf should not be taken advantage of (GREGORY THE GREAT), nor, however, should a judge be partial to a poor person. Each case must be judged on its own merits (JEROME). The second great commandment, love of neighbor, presupposes the first, the love of God (AUGUSTINE). Love of neighbor must be carried out by deeds (GREGORY THE GREAT). We should not expect praise for our good works in this life but in the life to come (PATERIUS).

19:2 You Shall Be Holy

See COMMENTS ON LEVITICUS 11:44.

19:9-10 Laws About Harvesting

AN EXAMPLE OF GENEROSITY. CLEMENT OF ALEXANDRIA: During the harvest, [the law] forbids owners to gather up the bits which fall from the sheaves and similarly advises that in harvesting something should be left behind unreaped.[1] By this it gives excellent teaching to owners in the practice of generous sharing by leaving some of their property for those in need

---

[1] Deut 24:20-21.

and providing the poor with a chance for food. STROMATEIS 2.85.3.[2]

TO TITHE HONORS GOD. CLEMENT OF ALEXANDRIA: Do you see how the law proclaims simultaneously the justice and goodness of God, who provides food unstintingly for all? Again, in the grape harvest the harvesters are forbidden to go back and cut anything that has been left over or to collect fallen grapes. The same rules are applied to olive gatherers.[3] In fact the principle of tithing crops and flocks was an education in honoring the divine. We are not to be totally absorbed by profit but to share humanely with the neighbor as well. STROMATEIS 2.86.1.[4]

19:13 The Wages of a Hired Servant

WE MUST NOT DEFRAUD LABORERS. AMBROSE: Let no one deny the hireling the wage he is owed, since we too are hirelings of our God, and from him we look forward to the reward of our labor. And if you indeed, whatever type of businessman you are, deny your hireling a monetary payment that is a perishable trifle, you shall be denied the reward of heaven that has been promised. You shall not defraud, as the law says, the hireling of his pay. LETTER 62 (19).3.[5]

19:14 Do Not Curse the Deaf

SINS AGAINST JUSTICE. GREGORY THE GREAT: To speak evil of the deaf is to disparage one who is absent and does not hear. To put a block before the blind is to do a thing that is proper of itself but which affords an occasion of scandal to one who fails to understand the propriety of it. PASTORAL CARE 3.35.[6]

19:15 Do Not Be Partial to the Poor

PITY MUST YIELD TO JUSTICE. JEROME: "You shall not be partial to the poor," a precept given lest under pretext of showing pity we should

judge an unjust judgment. For each individual is to be judged not by his personal importance but by the merits of his case. His wealth need not stand in the way of the rich man, if he makes a good use of it; and poverty of itself can be no recommendation to the poor if in the midst of squalor and want he fails to stay away from wrongdoing. LETTER 79.1.[7]

19:18 Love Your Neighbor as Yourself

THE TWO GREAT COMMANDMENTS. AUGUSTINE: Long before Christ it had been said, "You shall not covet";[8] long before it had been said, "You shall love your neighbor as yourself," a phrase which, as the apostle says, expresses the fulfillment of the whole law.[9] And as no one loves himself unless he loves God, the Lord says that the whole Law and the Prophets depend on these two commandments.[10] LETTER 177.[11]

LOVE IN PRACTICE. GREGORY THE GREAT: A person who does not divide with his needy neighbor what is necessary to him proves that he loves him less than himself. The command is to share two tunics with one's neighbor:[12] he could not have spoken of a single tunic, since if one is shared no one is clothed. Half a tunic leaves the person who receives it naked, as well as the person who gives it. HOMILY 6.[13]

19:23 Planting Trees for Food

DO NOT EAT FRUIT OUT OF SEASON. PATERIUS: Fruitbearing trees are works that bring forth virtues. We circumcise trees[14] when we are suspicious of how weak our first efforts are and do not approve of the first fruits of our work. We call the fruit that grows unclean and do not

---

[2]FC 85:215*. [3]Deut 24:20-21. [4]FC 85:215. [5]CSEL 82 2:122. [6]ACW 11:226. [7]NPNF 2 6:163. [8]Ex 20:17. [9]Rom 13:8. [10]Mt 22:37-40. [11]FC 30:101. [12]Lk 3:11. [13]CS 123:43. [14]The Hebrew text speaks of trees in their first three years as uncircumcised; the RSV calls their fruit forbidden. The Vulgate follows the Hebrew here.

take it as our food. When the first fruits of good works are praised, it is proper that this fruit should not feed the soul of the worker. Otherwise the praise we receive is plucked, and the fruit of our work is eaten out of season. So one who receives praise from a human mouth for a virtue just undertaken eats the fruit of a tree he has planted before its time. Truth said this through the psalmist: "It is vain for you to rise before dawn; rise up after you have sat down."[15]

To rise before dawn is to rejoice in the night of this present life, before the clear light of eternal rewards appears. We should first sit down and then rise up rightly, because whoever does not willingly humble himself now will not be exalted in the glory to come. EXPOSITION OF THE OLD AND NEW TESTAMENT, LEVITICUS 14.[16]

---

[15]Ps 127:2. [16]PL 79:759, citing Gregory the Great *Moral Interpretation of Job* 8.47.79-80

20:1-27 PENALTIES FOR VARIOUS SINS

[7]*"Consecrate yourselves therefore, and be holy; for I am the LORD your God. [8]Keep my statutes, and do them; I am the LORD who sanctify you. [9]For every one who curses his father or his mother shall be put to death; he has cursed his father or his mother, his blood is upon him.*

[10]*"If a man commits adultery with the wife of[i] his neighbor, both the adulterer and the adulteress shall be put to death. . . .*

[26]*"You shall be holy to me; for I the LORD am holy, and have separated you from the peoples, that you should be mine."*

i *Heb repeats* if a man commits adultery with the wife of

OVERVIEW: Matthew quotes the Old Testament but in an adapted form (ORIGEN). An example of pharisaic interpretation of the law about adultery is found in the Gospels (AMBROSE).

20:7 Be Holy

See COMMENTS ON LEVITICUS 11:44.

20:9 One Who Curses Parents

HOW MATTHEW QUOTES THE LAW. ORIGEN: But when we wish to examine the very letter of the words as given by Matthew, "He that speaks evil of father or mother, let him die the death,"[1] consider whether it was taken from the place where it was written, "Whoso strikes his father

or mother, let him die the death; and he that speaks evil of father or mother, let him die the death."[2] For such are the exact words taken from the law with regard to the two commandments; but Matthew has quoted them in part and in an abridged form, and not in the very words. COMMENTARY ON THE GOSPEL OF MATTHEW 11.9.[3]

20:10 Adulterous Persons Put to Death

JESUS AND THE LAW. AMBROSE: A woman accused of adultery was brought by the scribes and Pharisees to the Lord Jesus. But the woman was presented with guile, so that if Jesus should absolve her, he would appear to break the law.

---

[1]Mt 15:4. [2]Ex 21:15. [3]ANF 9:437-38.

But if Jesus should condemn her, he would deviate from the purpose for which he came, since he came to forgive the sins of all. Earlier he said, "I do not judge anyone." But presenting her, they said, "We found this woman openly committing adultery. Now it is written in the law of Moses

that every adulteress is to be stoned. But what do you have to say about her?" LETTER 68 (26).11.[4]

[4]CSEL 82 2:174.

21:1-15 SANCTITY OF THE PRIESTHOOD

[7]*"For the priest is holy to his God.* [8]*You shall consecrate him, for he offers the bread of your God; he shall be holy to you; for I the LORD, who sanctify you, am holy.* [9]*And the daughter of any priest, if she profanes herself by playing the harlot, profanes her father; she shall be burned with fire."*

OVERVIEW: High demands are made on priests and even on their families (CHRYSOSTOM).

21:9 Burned with Fire

EVEN DAUGHTERS OF PRIESTS ARE PUNISHED SEVERELY. CHRYSOSTOM: But why speak of the men engaged in the ministry? Even the daughters of priests, who are of no significance for the priestly office, incur a far more severe penalty than do others for the same sins, because of their fathers' dignity. The offense is the same (it is prostitution in both cases) when committed by them and the daughters of ordinary people, but their punishment is far greater. You see how thoroughly God proves to you that he demands much more punishment of the ruler than of the subjects. ON THE PRIESTHOOD 6.16.[1]

[1]COP 151.

21:16-24 IRREGULARITIES

[17]*"Say to Aaron, None of your descendants throughout their generations who has a blemish may approach to offer the bread of his God.* [18]*For no one who has a blemish shall draw near."*

OVERVIEW: The priest without blame is the one who is ready to offer his life in witness to the faith (ORIGEN). The perfect sacrifice presupposes integrity of soul (GREGORY OF NAZIANZUS).

21:17 Unblemished Priests

One Ready for Martyrdom. Origen: Moreover, blameless priests served the Godhead by offering blameless sacrifices, while those who were blemished and offered blemished sacrifices and whom Moses described in Leviticus were separated from the altar. And who else is the blameless priest offering a blameless sacrifice than the person who holds fast to his confession and fulfills every requirement the account of martyrdom demands? He is the one we have spoken of before. Exhortation to Martyrdom 30.[1]

Unblemished Body and Integrity of Soul. Gregory of Nazianzus: I know also that not even bodily blemishes in either priests or victims passed without notice, but that it was required by the law that perfect sacrifices must be offered by perfect men—a symbol, I take it, of integrity of soul. Oration 2 (In Defense of His Flight to Pontus) 94.[2]

---

[1]OEM 62. [2]NPNF 2 7:223.

22:1-16 SACRIFICIAL BANQUETS

[10]"An outsider shall not eat of a holy thing. . . . [14]And if a man eats of a holy thing unwittingly, he shall add the fifth of its value to it, and give the holy thing to the priest. [15]The priests shall not profane the holy things of the people of Israel, which they offer to the Lord, [16]and so cause them to bear iniquity and guilt, by eating their holy things: for I am the Lord who sanctify them."

Overview: The law punished wrongdoing done in ignorance. Full knowledge is punished more severely under the gospel (Jerome).

22:14 Eating Unknowingly of a Holy Thing

Reverence for the Eucharist. Jerome: At the end, it is stated, "If a man eats of the sanctified things through ignorance, iniquity and wickedness are laid at his feet, and he shall be bound by a vow." Thus also the apostle teaches us that we are to eat the Eucharist of the Lord with caution, lest we eat to our condemnation and judgment.[1] If ignorance is condemned under the law, how much more will full knowledge be condemned according to the gospel? Against the Pelagians 1.34.[2]

---

[1]1 Cor 11:28-29. [2]FC 53:284.

22:17-33 UNACCEPTABLE VICTIMS

²⁰*"You shall not offer anything that has a blemish, for it will not be acceptable for you. . . .*
²⁷*"When a bull or sheep or goat is born, it shall remain seven days with its mother; and from the eighth day on it shall be acceptable as an offering by fire to the* LORD. ²⁸*And whether the mother is a cow or a ewe, you shall not kill both her and her young in one day.* ²⁹*And when you sacrifice a sacrifice of thanksgiving to the* LORD, *you shall sacrifice it so that you may be accepted.* ³⁰*It shall be eaten on the same day, you shall leave none of it until morning: I am the* LORD."

OVERVIEW: The law expresses beautiful generosity even toward helpless beasts (CLEMENT OF ALEXANDRIA).

22:27 Seven Days with Its Mother

KINDNESS EVEN TO BEASTS. CLEMENT OF ALEXANDRIA: Scripture says, "At least grant the offspring to its mother for its first seven days." For if nothing comes to be without reason and milk flows in the mothers for the nourishment of the offspring, then in taking the offspring away from the providential endowment of the milk, a person is doing violence to nature. So Greeks and anyone else who runs the law down ought to blush for shame if the law is generous over irrational beasts. Yet some people actually expose human offspring to abortive death. By prophetic authority the law has for a long time cut short their ferocity through this commandment of which we have been speaking. For if the law refuses to allow the offspring of irrational creatures to be separated from their mother before taking milk, it is far more forceful in preparing human beings against that cruel, uncivilized view [exposure to death of infants]. If they ignore nature, at least they may not ignore the lessons of the law. STROMATEIS 2.92.2-4.[1]

---

[1]FC 85:219.

23:1-14 HOLY DAYS—PASSOVER

¹*The* LORD *said to Moses,* ²*"Say to the people of Israel, The appointed feasts of the* LORD *which you shall proclaim as holy convocations, my appointed feasts, are these. . . .*
⁷*"Do no laborious work."*

OVERVIEW: The true sabbath consists in tranquility of heart and the serenity of a good conscience (AUGUSTINE).

23:7 No Laborious Work

TRANQUILITY AND A GOOD CONSCIENCE.

AUGUSTINE: The sabbath was given to the Jews to be observed literally, like other things, as rites symbolically signifying something deeper. A particular kind of vacation, you see, was enjoined on them. Take care to carry out what that vacation signifies. A spiritual vacation, I mean, is tranquility of heart; but tranquility of heart issues from the serenity of a good conscience. So the person who really observes the sabbath is the one who doesn't sin. This, after all, is the way the command was given to those who were commanded to observe the sabbath: "You shall perform no servile work."[1] "Everyone who commits sin is the slave of sin."[2] SERMON 270.[3]

[1]Lev 23:3. [2]Jn 8:34. [3]WSA 3 7:293.

23:15-22 PENTECOST

[15]"And you shall count from the morrow after the sabbath, from the day that you brought the sheaf of the wave offering; seven full weeks shall they be, [16]counting fifty days to the morrow after the seventh sabbath; then you shall present a cereal offering of new grain to the LORD. [17]You shall bring from your dwellings two loaves of bread to be waved, made of two tenths of an ephah; they shall be of fine flour, they shall be baked with leaven, as first fruits to the LORD.

[22]"And when you reap the harvest, . . . you shall not . . . gather the leanings."

OVERVIEW: The two loaves stand for the two peoples whom the church embraces, Jews and Gentiles (BEDE).

23:17 Two Loaves of Bread

THE CHURCH SANCTIFIES JEWS AND GENTILES. BEDE: Two loaves of bread made from the first fruits of the new harvest were rightly ordered to be offered, for the church gathers those it can consecrate to its Redeemer as a new family from both peoples, the Jews and the Gentiles. HOMILIES ON THE GOSPELS 2.17.[1]

23:22 When You Reap the Harvest

See COMMENTS ON LEVITICUS 19:9.

[1]HOG 2:173.

[23:23-25 NEW YEAR'S DAY]

23:26—24:23 THE DAY OF ATONEMENT, THE FEAST OF BOOTHS, THE SANCTUARY LIGHT AND THE SHOWBREAD; PUNISHMENT OF BLASPHEMY

^{27}"On the tenth day of this seventh month is the day of atonement; it shall be for you a time of holy convocation. . . .

^{34}"On the fifteenth day of this seventh month and for seven days is the feast of booths^k to the LORD." . . .

24 ^{1}The LORD said to Moses, ^{2}"Command the people of Israel to bring you pure oil from beaten olives for the lamp, that a light may be kept burning continually. ^{3}Outside the veil of the testimony, in the tent of meeting, Aaron shall keep it in order from evening to morning before the LORD continually; it shall be a statute for ever throughout your generations. ^{4}He shall keep the lamps in order upon the lampstand of pure gold before the LORD continually.

^{5}"And you shall take fine flour, and bake twelve cakes of it; two tenths of an ephah shall be in each cake. ^{6}And you shall set them in two rows. . . . ^{7}And you shall put pure frankincense with each row. . . . ^{8}Every sabbath day Aaron shall set it in order. . . . ^{9}And it shall be for Aaron and his sons. . . .

^{19}"When a man causes a disfigurement, . . . ^{20}as he has disfigured a man, he shall be disfigured."

k Or tabernacles

OVERVIEW: The twelve loaves prefigure the apostles and all the teachers of the New Covenant, who must be virtuous and must live in concord (BEDE). The New Covenant offers heavenly bread and the cup of salvation (CYRIL OF JERUSALEM). The twelve apostles helped in the feeding of the five thousand. Frankincense stands for the prayers of the saints. The succession of loaves prefigures the succession of ministers. To eat the holy loaves is to enter into heaven or to be nourished unto eternal life by the example of the fathers (BEDE).

24:5 Fine Flour for Making Cakes

LOAVES SET OUT IN PAIRS. BEDE: The twelve loaves on the table of the tabernacle then are the twelve apostles and all those in the church who follow their teaching. Since until the end of time they do not cease to renew the people of God with the nourishment of the word, they are the twelve loaves of proposition which never depart from the table of the Lord. And those same loaves are properly ordered to be made not from just any flour but from the finest wheat, doubtless because all those who minister the word of life to others must first devote themselves to the fruits of virtue. [Thus] they may commend by their actions those things that they counsel in their preaching, being conformed to the example of him who says concerning himself, "Unless a grain of wheat falls into the ground and dies, it remains alone."[1] Those

---

[1]Jn 12:24.

same loaves are also properly commanded to be set on the table in two rows of six for the sake of concord (that is to say, charity and fellowship), for the Lord is also said to have sent his disciples out to preach two by two.[2] This suggests figuratively that the holy teachers never disagree with one another in either their defense of truth or their ardor for love. ON THE TABERNACLE 1.7.[3]

THE TWO COVENANTS. CYRIL OF JERUSALEM: The Old Covenant had its loaves of proposition, but they, as belonging to that covenant, have come to an end. The New Covenant has its heavenly bread and cup of salvation to sanctify both body and soul. For as the bread is for the body, the Word suits the soul. CATECHETICAL LECTURE 4.5.[4]

TWELVE APOSTLES GIVE FOOD TO ALL NATIONS. BEDE: In the first place, the figure of the twelve apostles is clearly foretold here in the very number of the loaves, for when the Lord appeared in flesh he chose them to be the first of those by whose ministry he gave the food of life to all nations. And then to these same disciples of his (that is, to our apostles), he says in reference to the multitudes hungering in the wilderness, "You give them something to eat."[5] And when five thousand men had been satisfied from the five loaves, they "gathered twelve baskets of fragments,"[6] doubtless because those sacraments of the Scriptures which the multitudes are not able to receive belong to the apostles and the apostolic men. ON THE TABERNACLE 1.7.[7]

24:7 Pure Frankincense

FRANKINCENSE AND THE POWER OF PRAYER. BEDE: Now that clearest frankincense which is put upon the loaves designates the power of prayer, because the same teachers commit both their ministry of preaching and their labor of devotion unto the Lord. Prayer is symbolized by frankincense, as the psalmist testifies when he says, "Let my prayer be set forth in your sight as

incense."[8] The clearest frankincense is put upon the loaves as a memorial of the oblation of the Lord when the pure prayer of the saints is added to their pious action and teaching, so that when each is duly joined to the other, the remembrance of the sacred oblation will always appear in the sight of the supreme Judge. ON THE TABERNACLE 1.7.[9]

24:8 Every Sabbath Day

THE LOAVES AND THE SUCCESSION OF PREACHERS. BEDE: The loaves are properly commanded to be changed before the Lord every sabbath day. For surely the loaves that were set out on the table of the Lord through the six days of work are exchanged for new loaves on the sabbath when all the teachers in the holy church, once the time of their holy labor is completed, are rewarded in heaven with eternal peace and leave others behind them in the same work, laboring in the word with the hope of the same reward. And in this way it is brought to pass that the table of the Lord is never left destitute of bread, but as soon as one loaf is taken away another is put in its place, as long as the churches never lack ministers of the word who follow one another in succession. In their words and in their deeds, they always manifest the faith of apostolic piety and the purity of apostolic action, continuing as in that most beautiful verse in which it is said in praise of that same holy church: "Instead of your fathers, sons are born to you; you will make them princes over all the earth."[10] In other words, that is as if it were being said to the tabernacle of the Lord: "Instead of your old loaves, new ones are prepared for you; you will designate them for the refreshment of the spiritual hearts of the faithful in all the world." ON THE TABERNACLE 1.7.[11]

24:9 For Aaron and His Sons

---

[2]Mk 6:7. [3]TTH 18:28-29. [4]FC 64:182. [5]Mt 14:16. [6]Mt 14:20. [7]TTH 18:28. [8]Ps 141:2. [9]TTH 18:29. [10]Ps 45:16. [11]TTH 18:29.

THE HIGH PRIEST INCREASES HIS HEAVENLY BODY. BEDE: And that which is added in conclusion, "And they shall be for Aaron and his sons," contains a mystery which can be understood in two ways. For surely Aaron in company with his sons eats the holy loaves that are taken from the table of the tabernacle when our High Priest takes his elect out of this life and leads them into the increase of his body which is in heaven (that is, the whole multitude of his elect). Or perhaps the holy loaves belong to Aaron and his sons when all the leaders and the peoples who are subjected to them in the Lord are nourished unto life eternal by the examples of the fathers who have gone before. ON THE TABERNACLE 1.7.[12]

24:20 *Like for Like*

See COMMENTS ON Exodus 21:24.

---

[12]TTH 18:31.

25:1-7 THE SABBATICAL YEAR

[4]*"In the seventh year there shall be a sabbath of solemn rest for the land, a sabbath to the* LORD; *you shall not sow your field or prune your vineyard.* [5]*What grows of itself in your harvest you shall not reap, and the grapes of your undressed vine you shall not gather; it shall be a year of solemn rest for the land."*

OVERVIEW: The land rests in the seventh year (CLEMENT OF ALEXANDRIA).

25:4 *A Sabbath for the Land*

FOOD FOR THE POOR. CLEMENT OF ALEXANDRIA: So do we now understand how the law educates us in piety, sharing, justice and humanity? Well? Does it not enjoin that the land lie fallow through the seventh year and invites the poor not to be afraid to use any crops that grow by God's grace, nature acting as farmer for any who will?[1] STROMATEIS 2.86.4-5.[2]

---

[1]Ex 23:10. [2]FC 85:215.

25:8-24 THE JUBILEE YEAR

[10]*"And you shall hallow the fiftieth year, and proclaim liberty throughout the land to all its inhabitants; it shall be a jubilee for you, when each of you shall return to his property and each of you shall return to his family."*

OVERVIEW: The year of jubilee is a great mystery (ORIGEN). The jubilee meant the restoration of the old order (BASIL). Psalm 50 (51), when prayed rightly, has the effect of the jubilee (CASSIODORUS). The jubilee is the anticipation of eternal tranquillity. The number fifty, the number of the year of jubilee, is also the number associated with the coming of the Holy Spirit on Pentecost (BEDE).

25:10 Hallowing the Fiftieth Year

THE MYSTERY OF THE JUBILEE. ORIGEN: Who is there who has grasped the mind of Christ so well that he knows the meaning of the seventh year of freedom of Hebrew slaves[1] and the remission of debts and the intermission of the cultivation of the holy land? Over and above the feast of every seventh year is the feast called the jubilee. No one can ever come near divining its precise meaning or the true import of the prescriptions enjoined by it, except him who knows the Father's will and his disposition for every age according to "his incomprehensible judgments and unsearchable ways."[2] ON PRAYER 27.14.[3]

THE YEAR OF JUBILEE. BASIL THE GREAT: Seven weeks of years in ancient times produced the celebrated jubilee, in which the earth kept the sabbath, debts were canceled, slaves were set free and, as it were, a new life was established again, the old one in a certain way attaining its fulfillment in the number seven. These things are figures of this present age which revolves through the seven days and passes us by; an age in which the penalties for the lesser sins are paid according to the loving care of the good Lord, so that we may not be handed over for punishment in the age without end. LETTER 260.[4]

PSALM 50 AND THE JUBILEE. CASSIODORUS: The number of this psalm[5] is not without reason. It has reference to the year of the jubilee, which among the Jews dissolved old contracts and obligations and which in Leviticus the Lord ordered

all dwellers on earth to call the year of remission. The number also refers to Pentecost, when after the Lord's ascension the Holy Spirit came on the apostles, working miracles and imparting the gift of charisms. So too this psalm, which is given the number 50, if recited with a pure heart, looses sins, cancels the bond of our debt and, like the year of remission, frees us through the Lord's kindness of the debts of our sins. EXPOSITION OF THE PSALMS 50, CONCLUSION.[6]

THE JUBILEE AND ETERNAL PEACE. BEDE: In the law the fiftieth year was ordered to be called [the year] of jubilee, that is, "forgiving" or "changed." During it the people were to remain at rest from all work, the debts of all were to be canceled, slaves were to go free [and] the year itself was to be more notable than other years because of its greater solemnities and divine praises. Therefore by this number is rightly indicated that tranquility of greatest peace when, as the apostle says, at the sound of the last trumpet "the dead will rise and we shall be changed"[7] into glory. Then, when the labors and hardships of this age come to an end and our debts, [that is] all our faults, have been forgiven, the entire people of the elect will rejoice eternally in the sole contemplation of the divine vision. And that most longed-for command of our Lord and Savior will be fulfilled: "Be still, and see that I am God."[8] HOMILIES ON THE GOSPELS 2.17.[9]

THE JUBILEE AND PENTECOST. BEDE: We read in the law that the fiftieth year was ordered to be designated as a jubilee (that is, a [year for] releasing or exchanging), in which the whole people should rest from all cultivation of the land and everyone's debts should be canceled. And we know that in the New Testament the grace of the Holy Spirit came upon the apostles on the day of Pentecost (that is, the fiftieth day

---

[1]Ex 21:2. [2]Rom 11:33. [3]ACW 19:103-4. [4]FC 28:224. [5]That is, 50 (51 in the Hebrew numbering). [6]ACW 51:512. [7]1 Cor 15:52. [8]Ps 46:10. [9]HOG 2:174.

of the Lord's resurrection) and hallowed the beginnings of the church that was being brought into existence by its coming.[10] It is agreed then that by this number can rightly be figured either the grace of the Holy Spirit or the joy of future blessedness, to which one is brought through

the gift of the same Spirit and in the perception of which alone is true rest and joy. ON THE TABERNACLE 2.2.[11]

---

[10]Acts 2:1-2. [11]TTH 18:54.

25:25—26:46 THE REDEMPTION OF PROPERTY, THE REWARD OF OBEDIENCE AND THE PUNISHMENT OF DISOBEDIENCE

[25]*"If your brother becomes poor, and sells part of his property, then his next of kin shall come and redeem what his brother has sold. . . .*

26 [1]*"You shall make for yourselves no idols. . . . [3]If you walk in my statutes and observe my commandments and do them, [4]then I will give you your rains in their season, and the land shall yield its increase, and the trees of the field shall yield their fruit. [5]And your threshing shall last to the time of vintage, and the vintage shall last to the time for sowing; and you shall eat your bread to the full, and dwell in your land securely. [6]And I will give peace in the land, and you shall lie down, and none shall make you afraid; and I will remove evil beasts from the land, and the sword shall not go through your land. [7]And you shall chase your enemies, and they shall fall before you by the sword. [8]Five of you shall chase a hundred, and a hundred of you shall chase ten thousand; and your enemies shall fall before you by the sword. [9]And I will have regard for you and make you fruitful and multiply you, and will confirm my covenant with you. [10]And you shall eat old store long kept, and you shall clear out the old to make way for the new. [11]And I will make my abode among you, and my soul shall not abhor you. [12]And I will walk among you, and will be your God, and you shall be my people. [13]I am the LORD your God, who brought you forth out of the land of Egypt, that you should not be their slaves; and I have broken the bars of your yoke and made you walk erect.*

[14]*"But if you will not hearken to me, and will not do all these commandments, [15]if you spurn my statutes, and if your soul abhors my ordinances, so that you will not do all my commandments, but break my covenant, [16]I will do this to you. . . ."*

OVERVIEW: Idolatry has been brought about by demons and rebellious angels (TERTULLIAN). What was promised to the Jews corporeally is fulfilled spiritually in Christians (CAESARIUS OF ARLES). Hence we need to study both Old and New Testaments intently (AMBROSE). The old store is the words of the prophets, and the new words are the gospel (ORIGEN). In the New Testament, hunger and bread have deep meanings (CAESARIUS OF ARLES). The old grain is the commandments of the Mosaic law (BEDE). Just persons enjoy security when they are founded in faith and build their houses on solid ground. Christ gives his followers not worldly peace but the peace that surpasses all understanding (CAESARIUS OF ARLES). God is the ultimate object of all our desires (AUGUSTINE). Fear God and you will fear nothing else. The beasts from which the land is to be freed cannot be corporeal beasts. One who brings the body into subjection suffers less the consequences of spiritual warfare. The numbers five and one hundred are complex symbols. The sword that destroys our enemies is the word of God. Peter, who fell through sin, was raised up to the place from which he had fallen (CAESARIUS OF ARLES).

26:1 Make No Idols

IDOLATRY MAKES GODS AGAINST GOD. TERTULLIAN: For this reason, in order to root out the materials of idolatry, God's law proclaims, "You shall not make an idol"; and by adding, "Nor the likeness of any thing that is in heaven or in the earth or in the sea," it utterly forbade such crafts to the servants of God.[1] Enoch had anticipated this law when he prophesied that the demons and the spirits of the rebellious angels would turn to idolatry every element and property of the universe, everything which heaven and sea and earth contain, to be consecrated as a god against God.[2] So it is that human error worships everything but the very Creator of everything. Their images are idols; the consecration of images is idolatry. Whatever sin idolatry commits must be put down to all the makers of all the idols. ON IDOLATRY 4.1-2.[3]

26:4 Rains in Season

THE CORPOREAL AND THE SPIRITUAL. CAESARIUS OF ARLES: If we faithfully and diligently pay attention to it, brethren, everything which

was promised corporally to the Jews is fulfilled spiritually in us; for all the blessings of God which they received on earth we have obtained in our souls through the grace of baptism. Therefore, with his help, let us labor with all our strength so that we may be able to receive God's blessings and avoid his curses. SERMON 105.1.[4]

26:5 Eating Bread to the Full

THE HEAVENLY BREAD IS THE WORD OF GOD. CAESARIUS OF ARLES: I do not consider this as a material blessing, as though the man who observes God's law will obtain that common bread in abundance. Why not? Do not wicked sinners also eat bread, not only in abundance but even in luxury? Therefore let us look rather to him who says, "I am the living bread that has come down from heaven."[5] And "he who eats this bread shall live forever."[6] As we notice that he who said this is the word with which our soul is fed, we realize of what bread it was said by God in blessing that: "You will have food to eat in abundance." Solomon proclaims something similar concerning the just man, when he says in the book of Proverbs, "When the just man eats, his hunger is appeased, but the souls of the wicked suffer want."[7] If this is understood only according to the letter, it seems utterly false, for the souls of the wicked eat more greedily and strive for satiety, while the just sometimes even suffer hunger. Finally, Paul was a just man, and he said, "To this very hour we hunger and thirst, and we are naked and buffeted";[8] and again he says, "In hunger and thirst, in fastings often."[9] How then does Solomon say that the just man eats and satisfies his soul? What we understood before concerning the rain we ought to consider at this point also with regard to the bread. That heavenly bread, that is, the Word of God who said, "I am the living bread,"[10] none but the just eat, to whom it is

---

[1]Ex 20:3-4; Deut 5:7-8. [2]Cf. *Enoch* 19:1. [3]LCC 5: 85-86. [4]FC 47:119. [5]Jn 6:51. [6]Jn 6:51. [7]Prov 13:25. [8]1 Cor 4:11. [9]2 Cor 11:27. [10]Jn 6:51.

said, "Taste, and see how good the Lord is."[11] With what kind of a conscience then do sinners who are defiled by many sins dare to eat? SERMON 105.3.[12]

TRUE SECURITY. CAESARIUS OF ARLES: The wicked man is never secure but is always disturbed and wavering. He is tossed about by every wind of doctrine to deceitful error, by the craft of men. However, the just man who observes God's law dwells in security on his land, because he governs his body in fear of God and brings it into subjection. His understanding is firm when he says to God, "Strengthen me according to your words, O Lord."[13] Strengthened, secure and well rooted, he dwells on the earth, founded in faith. His house is not built upon sand but is established on solid ground. SERMON 105.4.[14]

26:6 Peace in the Land

THE PEACE THAT GOD GIVES. CAESARIUS OF ARLES: Then follow the words "and I will establish peace in your lands." What peace does God give? The peace which the world possesses? Christ says he does not give that kind of peace, for he declares, "Peace I leave with you, my peace I give to you; not as this world gives peace do I give to you."[15] Therefore he denies that he will give the peace of the world to his disciples. Do you want to see then what peace God gives in our land? If the land is good so that it produces fruit a hundredfold, sixtyfold or thirtyfold, it will receive from God that peace which the apostle describes: "May the peace of God which surpasses all understanding guard your hearts."[16] SERMON 105.5.[17]

FEAR GOD, AND YOU WILL FEAR NOTHING ELSE. CAESARIUS OF ARLES: "You may lie down to rest without anxiety." Moreover, Solomon says in the book of Proverbs, "When you sit down, you need not be afraid. When you lie down, your sleep will be sweet and you will not be afraid of sudden terror or of the attack of the wicked when it comes."[18] These words he spoke concerning the just and wise man. Furthermore it is said in blessing, "You may lie down to rest without anxiety." If you are just, no one can frighten you. If you fear God, you will fear nothing else. "The just man, like a lion, feels sure of himself";[19] and in the words of David, "I shall not fear the terror of the night,"[20] and so forth. He adds still further: "The Lord is my light and my salvation; whom should I fear? The Lord is my life's refuge; of whom should I be afraid?"[21] and again, "Though an army encamp against me, my heart will not fear."[22] Do you see the courage and constancy of the soul that observes the commandments of God? SERMON 105.6.[23]

WHAT EVIL BEASTS ARE. CAESARIUS OF ARLES: After this we read, "I will rid your country of ravenous beasts." These material beasts are not entirely evil or wholly good but rather in between, for they are mute animals. However, those other beasts are spiritual evils, and the apostle calls them "spiritual forces of wickedness on high."[24] That is the evil beast of which Scripture says, "The serpent was more cunning than all the beasts on earth."[25] This is the evil beast which God promises to drive out of our land if we keep his commandments. Do you also wish to see another evil beast? Listen to the apostle Peter: "Your adversary the devil, as a roaring lion, goes about seeking someone to devour. Resist him, steadfast in the faith."[26] Under a vision in the desert which he entitled that of the quadrupeds, the prophet Isaiah spoke in a prophetic spirit concerning beasts: "The lion and the young of the lion are in tribulation. Here spring up the flying basilisks which carry their riches upon asses and camels to a people whose help is futile and vain."[27] Can these words in any way seem to have been said with regard to corporeal beasts, in the minds of those who are very fond of the letter? How can

---

[11]Ps 34:8. [12]FC 47:120-21. [13]Ps 119:28. [14]FC 47:121. [15]Jn 14:27. [16]Phil 4:7. [17]FC 47:121. [18]Prov 3:24-25. [19]Prov 28:1. [20]Ps 91:5. [21]Ps 27:1. [22]Ps 27:3. [23]FC 47:121-22. [24]Eph 6:12. [25]Gen 3:1. [26]1 Pet 5:8. [27]Is 30:6.

the lion, the young of the lion or the flying basilisk carry the riches upon asses and camels? However, the prophet enumerates the opposing powers of the most wicked demons, by the Holy Ghost seeing them put the riches of their deceits upon asses and camels, that is, upon souls that are stupid and mindful of nothing else except bodily pleasure. Thus he designates them figuratively, comparing them with camels and asses. Lest he be delivered to these beasts, the God-fearing soul prays to the Lord: "Give not to the vulture the life of your dove."[28] SERMON 105.7.[29]

SPIRITUAL WARFARE IN OUR BODIES. CAESARIUS OF ARLES: "I will rid your country of ravenous beasts and keep war from sweeping across your land." There are many fights which pass over our land, if we do not observe the law of God and keep his commands. Let each one return to his own soul or conscience and examine himself with interior recollection. Let him see how our land, that is, our body, is oppressed at one time by the spirit of fornication, at another by anger or fury. Again it is disturbed by the darts of avarice or struck by the javelins of envy; then it is darkened by the vice of pride. In whatever way the flesh lusts against the spirit or the spirit against the flesh, our land is agitated by exceedingly dangerous battles. Therefore, if a man observes the divine commands, by the Holy Ghost brings his body into subjection, keeps God's precepts and fulfills them, he suffers this fight and war less or endures them in such a way that he is victorious. Indeed, God takes them away from his land and does not allow them to pass over the land, that is, the soul of the just. SERMON 105.8.[30]

26:7 Chasing Your Enemies

OUR ENEMY IS THE DEVIL. CAESARIUS OF ARLES: "You will rout your enemies." Of what enemies do we speak, except the devil himself and his angels? We rout them not only by driving them from our own hearts, but we repel them far away from others whom they disturb or attack or overcome. We do this by our advice or reproof or prayer, if we preserve the divine precepts. Thus through death the enemy falls in our sight. Whose death? I think it is ours when we mortify our members which are on earth, namely, fornication and impurity. If we bring this death to our members, that is, to our concupiscences and sins, our enemies, the devil and his angels, will fall in our sight. How will they fall in your sight? If you are just, injustice falls at sight of you; if chaste, lust falls; if devout, you kill the spirit of impiety. SERMON 105.9.[31]

26:8 Five Shall Chase a Hundred

THE FIVE STAND FOR WISDOM. CAESARIUS OF ARLES: "Five of you will put a hundred to flight." Who are those five who can pursue a hundred? The number five is applied to both the praiseworthy and the culpable, for there were five wise virgins and five foolish; so also the number one hundred can be accepted in either way. Therefore if we belong to the five laudable ones, that is, the five wise virgins, we pursue one hundred of the foolish. If we fight wisely in matters of God's Word, if we discuss the law of the Lord prudently, we convince and put to flight a multitude of unbelievers. Similarly the number one hundred indicates both the faithful and the unfaithful. Under that number of years Abraham is recorded to have believed in God and been justified, while "the sinner of a hundred years shall be thought accursed."[32] Now here a hundred unfaithful souls are put to flight by five wise men. Again, a hundred just men, who are so designated because of their perfection rather than their number, pursue many thousands of unbelievers. Indeed, devout teachers drive away countless demons, so they will not deceive the souls of believers with their old deceits. SERMON 105.10.[33]

---

[28]Ps 74:19. [29]FC 47:122-23. [30]FC 47:123. [31]FC 47:123-24*. [32]Is 65:20. [33]FC 47:124.

SHARPER THAN ANY SWORD. CAESARIUS OF ARLES: "Your foes will be cut down by your sword." Who they are we mentioned above, but let us find out by what sword they are said to fall. The apostle Paul teaches us what this sword is when he says, "For the Word of God is living and efficient and keener than every two-edged sword and extending even to the joints of soul and spirit, of the members also and the marrow, and a discerner of the thoughts and intentions of the heart."[34] This is the sword at whose edge our enemies will fall. For it is the Word of God which casts down all enemies and puts them under its feet, so that the whole world becomes subject to God. Do you wish to learn from still another epistle of Paul that the sword with which spiritual enemies are overcome is the Word of God? Listen to him as he provides arms for the soldiers of Christ: "Take unto you the helmet of salvation and the sword of the spirit, that is, the Word of God. With all prayer and supplication pray."[35] By these words he declares very clearly that by the Word of God which is a two-edged sword our enemies will fall in our sight. SERMON 105.11.[36]

26:9 I Will Make You Fruitful

THE POWER OF CHRIST'S REGARD. CAESARIUS OF ARLES: "I will look with favor upon you and make you fruitful." Full of blessedness is the man upon whom God looks with favor. Do you want to understand how great is the salvation of a man upon whom the Lord looks [with favor]? Peter had once perished and at the prompting of the devil through the lips of a servant of the high priest had destroyed the consecration of his apostolic rank. But when the Lord looked at him, he was lifted up at once. SERMON 105.12.[37]

26:10 The Old Store and the New

THE LAW AND THE GOSPEL. ORIGEN: For we eat with blessing the old things, the prophetic words and the old things of the old things, the

words of the law. And, when the new and evangelical words came, living according to the gospel, we bring forth the old things of the letter from before the new. He sets his tabernacle in us, fulfilling the promise which he spoke, "I will dwell among them and walk in them."[38] COMMENTARY ON THE GOSPEL OF MATTHEW 10.15.[39]

READ THE WHOLE OF THE SCRIPTURE. AMBROSE: There ought to be a concurrence of the old and the new, as in the case of the Old and New Testament. It is written, "Eat the oldest of the old store and, new coming on, cast away the old." Let our food be knowledge of the patriarchs. Let our minds banquet in the prophetic books of the prophets. Such nourishment should our minds partake of, the truth of the body of Christ, and not just the external appearance of a lamb. Our eyes should not be affected by the shadow cast by the law. Rather, the clear grace of the Lord's passion and the splendor of his resurrection should illuminate our vision. CAIN AND ABEL 2.6.19.[40]

TO EAT OLD GRAIN. BEDE: And we eat the oldest of the old [grain] when we retain in our hearts the sweet memory of the old commandment which was given to the human race from the beginning, by loving the Lord our God with all our heart, all our soul and all our strength, and by loving our neighbor as ourselves.[41] And we cast away the old [to make room] for the new that is coming on when we cease to keep the typic statutes of the Mosaic law according to the letter but keep these same statutes quite gladly as they are understood through the Spirit. Our hearts [are] being renewed in the hope of the heavenly kingdom in accordance with that [saying] of the apostle: "If then anyone is in Christ a new creature, the old things have passed away; behold, things have been made new,"[42] and [with

---

[34]Heb 4:12. [35]Eph 6:17-18. [36]FC 47:124-25. [37]FC 47:125. [38]Lev 26:12; 2 Cor 6:16. [39]ANF 9:423. [40]FC 42:420. [41]Deut 6:5; Mk 12:30-31. [42]2 Cor 5:17.

that saying] in the Apocalypse: "And he that sat upon the throne said, 'Behold, I make all things new.'"[43] ON THE TABERNACLE 1.9.[44]

26:12 I Will Be Your God

THE CONSUMMATION OF OUR DESIRES. AUGUSTINE: God will be the source of every satisfaction, more than any heart can rightly crave, more than life and health, food and wealth, glory and honor, peace and every good—so that God, as St. Paul said, "may be all in all."[45] He will be the consummation of all our desiring—the object of our unending vision, of our unlessening love, of our unwearying praise. And in this gift of vision, this response of love, this paean of praise, all alike will share, as all will share in everlasting life. CITY OF GOD 22.30.[46]

---

[43]Rev 21:5. [44]TTH 18:41. [45]1 Cor 15:28. [46]FC 24:506.

[27:1-25 REDEMPTION OF VOTIVE OFFERINGS]

27:26-34 OFFERINGS NOT TO BE REDEEMED

[9]"All of such that any man gives to the LORD is holy. . . . [13]But if he wishes to redeem it, he shall add a fifth to the valuation. . . .

[28]"But no devoted thing that a man devotes to the LORD, of anything that he has, whether of a man or beast, or of his inherited field, shall be sold or redeemed; every devoted thing is most holy to the LORD. [29]No one devoted, who is to be utterly destroyed from among men, shall be ransomed; he shall be put to death.

[30]"All the tithe of the land, whether of the seed of the land or of the fruit of the trees, is the LORD's; it is holy to the LORD."

OVERVIEW: The precepts of the Redeemer are more demanding than the prescriptions of the law (GREGORY THE GREAT).

27:30 The Tithe of the Land

THE OLD LAW AND THE NEW. GREGORY THE GREAT: What is said by the law is less exacting than what is commanded by the Lord. The law prescribed the giving of a tithe, but our Redeemer ordered those who would follow the way of perfection to give up everything.[1] HOMILY 40.[2]

---

[1]Cf. Mk 10:21. [2]CS 123:381-82.

NUMBERS

1:1-19 MOSES' ASSISTANTS

[4]"And there shall be with you a man from each tribe, each man being the head of the house of his fathers. [5]And these are the names of the men who shall attend you. From Reuben, Elizur the son of Shedeur; [6]from Simeon, Shelumi-el the son of Zurishaddai; [7]from Judah, Nahshon the son of Amminadab; [8]from Issachar, Nethanel the son of Zuar; [9]from Zebulun, Eliab the son of Helon; [10]from the sons of Joseph, from Ephraim, Elishama the son of Ammihud, and from Manasseh, Gamaliel the son of Pedahzur; [11]from Benjamin, Abidan the son of Gideoni; [12]from Dan, Ahi-ezer the son of Ammishaddai; [13]from Asher, Pagiel the son of Ochran; [14]from Gad, Eliasaph the son of Deuel; [15]from Naphtali, Ahira the son of Enan."*

OVERVIEW: Even the proper names of the Old Testament can be a prophecy of Christ (AMBROSE).

1:7 Nahshon the Son of Amminadab

AMMINADAB MEANS "FATHER OF A PEOPLE."
AMBROSE: "It made me like the chariots of Aminadab," which name means "the father of a peo-ple." Now he that is a father of a people is likewise the father of Nahashon, which is "of the serpent." Now recall who hung like a serpent upon the cross for the salvation of all men, and you will understand that the soul is at peace that has God as its protector and Christ as its captain. ISAAC, OR THE SOUL 8.65.[1]

[1]FC 65:54.

1:20 — 2:34 COUNT AND ARRANGEMENT OF THE TWELVE TRIBES

[45]So the whole number of the people of Israel, by their fathers' houses, from twenty years old and upward, every man able to go forth to war in Israel—[46]their whole number was six hundred and three thousand five hundred and fifty. . . .
2 [33]But the Levites were not numbered among the people of Israel, as the LORD commanded Moses.

Overview: The tribe of Levi was set apart from the rest of Israel for holy service (Origen).

2:33 The Levites Were Not Numbered

The Levites Were More Excellent. Origen: We gather from the book of Numbers that there may be something greater than Israel too. For there the whole of Israel is numbered and reckoned in twelve tribes, as under a fixed number. But the tribe of Levi, being of greater eminence than the others, is accounted extra to this number and never thought of as being one of Israel's number [of twelve]. Commentary on the Song of Songs, prologue.[1]

---

[1]ACW 26:53-54.

3:1-13 THE SONS OF AARON

⁵And the Lord said to Moses, ⁶"Bring the tribe of Levi near, and set them before Aaron the priest, that they may minister to him. ⁷They shall perform duties for him and for the whole congregation before the tent of meeting, as they minister at the tabernacle.

Overview: In Israel's hierarchy, priests stood above Levites as Levites stood above the people (Origen).

3:5 Bring the Tribe of Levi Near

Priests Are More Eminent Than Levites. Origen: Further, the priests are described as being more eminent than the Levites; for this same Scripture tells us that "the Lord spoke to Moses, saying, 'Bring the tribe of Levi and make them stand in the sight of Aaron the priest, to minister to him.'" Do you see how here too he both speaks of the priests as superior to the Levites and once more makes the Levites appear as more eminent than the children of Israel? Commentary on the Song of Songs, Prologue.[1]

---

[1]ACW 26:54.

[3:14-20 CENSUS OF THE LEVITES]

[3:21-39 DUTIES OF THE LEVITICAL CLANS]

[3:40-51 CENSUS AND RANSOM OF FIRSTBORN]

4:1-33 DUTIES FURTHER DEFINED

¹The LORD said to Moses and Aaron, ²"Take a census of the sons of Kohath from among the sons of Levi, by their families and their fathers' houses, ³from thirty years old up to fifty years old, all who can enter the service, to do the work in the tent of meeting. ⁴This is the service of the sons of Kohath in the tent of meeting: the most holy things. ⁵When the camp is to set out, Aaron and his sons shall go in and take down the veil of the screen, and cover the ark of the testimony with it; ⁶then they shall put on it a covering of goatskin, and spread over that a cloth all of blue, and shall put in its poles. ⁷And over the table of the bread of the Presence they shall spread a cloth of blue, and put upon it the plates, the dishes for incense, the bowls, and the flagons for the drink offering; the continual bread also shall be on it; ⁸then they shall spread over them a cloth of scarlet, and cover the same with a covering of goatskin, and shall put in its poles."

OVERVIEW: There is a distinction between blue veils and purple veils. Blue suggests the sky and heaven, whereas purple signifies a kingdom (THEODORET OF CYR).

4:6, 8 A Cloth of Blue, a Cloth of Scarlet

THE MEANING OF BLUE AND PURPLE. THE-ODORET OF CYR: Why did God command that some of the sacred vessels should be covered with blue veils and others with purple[1] veils?

Only the veils of the more precious vessels were blue. The color suggests the sky. For this reason God commanded the objects behind the veil to be covered with blue tapestry but the objects outside it with purple and colors like it. For the sky is not subject to punishment, but the earth is punished for transgressions of the law. The color purple signifies a kingdom. The kingdom of God is divine, without beginning and indestructible. Hence the objects outside the tent were covered with veils both purple and blue. When the household of Kohath[2] exercised their office, the law commanded that the priests should first enter the sanctuary and cover the ark and the other vessels with the veils already mentioned. Only then would the household of Kohath transport these objects, lest they lay eyes on things that are sacred and secret and that would destroy those who see them accidentally. QUESTIONS ON NUMBERS 6.[3]

---

[1] The word used in the LXX is "purple," not "scarlet." [2] Num 4:2. [3] PG 80:356.

[4:34-49 NUMBER OF ADULT LEVITES]

5:1-4 THE UNCLEAN EXPELLED

[46]*All those who were numbered of the Levites . . . were eight thousand five hundred and eighty.* [49]*According to the commandment of the LORD through Moses they were appointed, each to his task of serving or carrying; thus they were numbered by him, as the LORD commanded Moses.*

[1]*The LORD said to Moses,* [2]*"Command the people of Israel that they put out of the camp every leper, and every one having a discharge, and every one that is unclean through contact with the dead."*

OVERVIEW: Sexually transmitted diseases, being related to voluntary acts, are more subject to censure than are involuntary conditions. The phrase "unclean in soul" refers to one who has touched a corpse (THEODORET OF CYR).

5:2 Lepers and Persons with a Discharge

LEARN FROM SMALL THINGS. THEODORET OF CYR: Why did he command these men,[1] and lepers, and those with gonorrhea, to dwell outside the camp?

He teaches us great things from small things. For if one who touches a dead body is unclean, so much the more is one who kills a man, because he incurs blood guilt. And if a leper is unclean, so much the more is one who perpetrates various forms of iniquity. And through the condemnation of one with gonorrhea, adultery is condemned. For if an involuntary act is abominable, so much the more is an act committed deliberately. QUESTIONS ON NUMBERS 8.[2]

TO BE UNCLEAN IN SOUL. THEODORET OF CYR: What does "unclean in soul"[3] mean?

The man who has touched a corpse or approached the bones of a dead man. QUESTIONS ON NUMBERS 7.[4]

---

[1]Those unclean by contact with a corpse, as in the following question. [2]PG 80:356. [3]Where the RSV has "unclean through contact with the dead," the LXX has "unclean in soul." [4]PG 80:356.

5:5-10 UNJUST POSSESSION

[5]*And the LORD said to Moses,* [6]*"Say to the people of Israel, When a man or woman commits any of the sins that men commit by breaking faith with the LORD, and that person is guilty,* [7]*he shall confess his sin which he has committed; and he shall make full restitution for his wrong, adding a fifth to it, and giving it to him to whom he did the wrong."*

OVERVIEW: Everyone is guilty of some sin. The law establishes the order of sanguinity or closeness of blood relation in which reparations are to be made (THEODORET OF CYR).

5:6 Breaking Faith

FORGIVENESS OF LESS SERIOUS SINS. THE-
ODORET OF CYR: What does this mean: "if any
man or woman commits one of all the human
sins"?[1] Scripture call the smaller sins human. It
is not possible for human nature, subject to
change as it is, to be delivered from every sin.
For "no one is clean from filth, even if his life is
one day long."[2] This is why holy David says, "Do
not enter into judgment with your servant, for
in your sight no living man will be justified."[3]
Only Christ the Lord, both as God and as man,
is blameless. The prophet Isaiah foresaw this
and said, "He committed no transgression, nor
was deceit found in his mouth."[4] For this reason
he took upon himself the sins of others, for he
had none of his own. For Isaiah also says, "He
bears our sins, and he is afflicted for us."[5] And
the great John says, "Behold the lamb of God,
who bears the sins of the world."[6] For this reason he is also called "free among the dead,"[7] since
he suffered death unjustly. The divine law
teaches how those who have sinned moderately
are to be healed. For the law commands that he
who has done wrong in a matter of contracts
should first confess the sin and then give back
what was taken to the one he wronged, adding
one fifth to the principal.[8] If it happens that the
one wronged dies before the sinner repents of
his sin, he should pay the amount to the man's
nearest relative. The law names as his nearest
relative the one related to him by generation.
The order of generation is this: first his son,
then his daughter, then the brother of his father,
then the brother of his grandfather. If there is
none of these, then it should be another close
kinsman. If no kinsman can be found, the law
declares that he should offer the stated sum to
God. For the law says this: "If the man has no
near relative, so that the sinner can give him
what he owes, then the debt is paid to the Lord
in the person of the priest, except for the ram of
expiation, through which expiation is made for
him."[9] The law mandates that the priests should
eat the first fruits that are offered. For the Levites were the first fruits of the people, and the
priests were the first fruits of the Levites. As
first fruits, then, they acquire the first fruits.
QUESTIONS ON NUMBERS 9.[10]

---

[1]Thus the LXX for "the sins that men commit" (RSV). [2]Ps 143:2. [3]Ps
143:2. [4]Is 53:9. [5]Is 53:4. [6]Jn 1:29. [7]Ps 88:5 LXX. [8]Num 5:7.
[9]Num 5:8. [10]PG 80:356-57.

[5:11-31 ORDEAL FOR A SUSPECTED ADULTERESS]

6:1-21 LAWS CONCERNING NAZIRITES

[29]*"This is the law in cases of jealousy, when a wife, though under her husband's authority,
goes astray and defiles herself, [30]or when the spirit of jealousy comes upon a man and he is jealous of his wife; then he shall set the woman before the LORD, and the priest shall execute upon
her all this law. . . .*

6 [13]*"And this is the law for the Nazirite, when the time of his separation has been completed:
he shall be brought to the door of the tent of meeting. . . . [18]And the Nazirite shall shave his*

consecrated head at the door of the tent of meeting, and shall take the hair from his consecrated head and put it on the fire which is under the sacrifice of the peace offering."

Overview: The significance of the Nazirite vow lies in continence, the restraint of superfluous thoughts and the pure love of God (Paterius).

6:18 Hair from a Nazirite's Head

Nazirites and Christian Perfection.
Paterius: What does it mean that Nazirites cultivate their hair, except that they cultivate pleasing thoughts through their lives of continence? What does it mean that, when the time of his vow is fulfilled, the Nazirite is bidden to shave his head and to put his hair in the sacrifi-cial fire? It means that we reach the height of perfection when we have so conquered external vices that we restrain even superfluous thoughts in our minds. And to burn these thoughts in sacrificial fire means to burn them in the flame of divine love, so that one's whole heart burns with the love of God. We burn up our superfluous thoughts and consume the hair of the Nazirite, as it were, in perfect devotion. Exposition of the Old and New Testament, Numbers 1.[1]

---

[1]PL 79:761, citing Gregory the Great *Moral Interpretation of Job* 2.52.84.

[6:22-27 THE PRIESTLY BLESSING]

[7:1-88 OFFERINGS OF PRINCES]

7:89 THE VOICE

[22]*The Lord said to Moses,* [23]*"Say to Aaron and his sons, Thus you shall bless the people of Israel: you shall say to them,*
[24]*The Lord bless you and keep you:*
[25]*The Lord make his face to shine upon you, and be gracious to you:*
[26]*The Lord lift up his countenance upon you, and give you peace.*
[27]*"So shall they put my name upon the people of Israel, and I will bless them." . . .*
7[2]*The leaders of Israel, heads of their fathers' houses, the leaders of the tribes, who were over those who were numbered,* [3]*offered and brought their offerings before the Lord. . . .*
[89]*And when Moses went into the tent of meeting to speak with the Lord, he heard the voice speaking to him from above the mercy seat that was upon the ark of the testimony, from between the two cherubim; and it spoke to him.*

OVERVIEW: As Moses consulted the Lord in the ark, so should officeholders consul Scripture and give themselves to contemplation while not ceasing show compassion for the weak (PATERIUS).

7:89 Into the Tent of Meeting

ACTION AND CONTEMPLATION. PATERIUS: What does it mean that Moses often enters the tabernacle and comes out, except that he, whose mind is raised up in contemplation, must go out to deal with the affairs of the weak? Inside he contemplates the mysteries of God. Outside he bears the burdens of carnal persons. And Moses, who always has recourse to the tabernacle in matters of doubt and consults the Lord in the ark of the covenant, undoubtedly offers an example to officeholders. When in their public lives they are unsure of what to decide, they should always pon-der in their minds, as in the tabernacle. They would seek advice, as it were, at the ark of the covenant, if they study the pages of sacred Scripture in their hearts when they deal with a doubt. Truth himself, manifested to us by taking on our humanity, devoted himself to prayer on the mountain and performed miracles in the cities. Thus he showed good pastors a model to imitate. They should desire what is highest in contemplation but care for the needs of the weak by their compassion. Charity rises up to the heights in a marvelous way when it mercifully turns to the depths of the neighbor's needs. When it descends in kindness to the lowest, it returns in vigor to the highest. EXPOSITION OF THE OLD AND NEW TESTAMENT, NUMBERS 2.[1]

---

[1]PL 79:761, citing Gregory the Great *Pastoral Care* 2.5.

[8:1-4 THE LAMPS SET UP]

8:5-22 PURIFICATION OF THE LEVITES

[4]*And this was the workmanship of the lampstand, hammered work of gold; from its base to its flowers, it was hammered work; according to the pattern which the LORD had shown Moses, so he made the lampstand.*

[5]*And the LORD said to Moses,* [6]*"Take the Levites from among the people of Israel, and cleanse them.* [7]*And thus you shall do to them, to cleanse them: sprinkle the water of expiation upon them, and let them go with a razor over all their body, and wash their clothes and cleanse themselves."*

OVERVIEW: The shaving of body hair among the Levites symbolizes the casting away of all carnal thoughts (PATERIUS).

8:7 Let the Levites Shave Their Bodies

PURITY OF THE MINISTER'S MIND. PATERIUS: Hairs of the flesh mean whatever human corruption is left. Hairs of the flesh are the thoughts of the old life, which we so expel from our minds that no grief at their loss fatigues us. *Levite* means "one taken up." So all Levites should shave the hairs of the flesh. For he who is taken up into divine service should appear before the eyes of God cleansed of all carnal thoughts. His mind should not bring forth illicit thoughts and deform the beautiful shape of his soul with unruly hair. But as much as the virtue of holy conversation draws a man up, as we said, he was still born into the old life, and he bears it with him. Thus the hairs of the Levites are to be shaved off, not pulled out. For when hairs have been shaved off the flesh the roots remain, and the hairs grow and are shaved off again. Vain thoughts should be cut off with great effort, but they can never be entirely rooted out. For the flesh always begets what is vain, and the spirit cuts it back with the knife of watchful concern. We see this happening in us more subtly when we reach the heights of contemplation. EXPOSITION OF THE OLD AND NEW TESTAMENT, NUMBERS 3.[1]

---

[1]PL 79:762-63, citing Gregory the Great *Moral Interpretation of Job* 5.33.59.

8:23-26 AGE LIMITS FOR LEVITICAL SERVICE

[24]*"This is what pertains to the Levites: from twenty-five years old and upward they shall go in to perform the work in the service of the tent of meeting;* [25]*and from the age of fifty years they shall withdraw from the work of the service and serve no more,* [26]*but minister to their brethren in the tent of meeting, to keep the charge, and they shall do no service. Thus shall you do to the Levites in assigning their duties."*

OVERVIEW: Young men need to battle against vice. From the age of fifty on, one enjoys internal peace and tranquility of mind. Those still struggling with vices should not presume to undertake the care of others (PATERIUS).

8:24-25 The Work of Service

OLD AGE AND THE CARE OF SOULS. PATERIUS: What is indicated by the twenty-fifth year, in which the flower of young manhood blooms, except those battles against every vice? And what is meant by fifty, which contains the repose of the jubilee, except the internal peace that comes when the war of the mind is won? What do the vessels of the tabernacle mean, except the souls of the faithful? Hence the Levites serve the tabernacle from their twenty-fifth year, and from their fiftieth year they become the keepers of the vessels.[1] This means that those who are still struggling with vices and risk consenting to them should not presume to undertake the care of others. For when the elect are still subject to temptation, they must be subjected and engage in service and grow tired through their duties and labors. But when they have won the war against temptations and are secure in their inner tranquillity, they are given the care of souls. For in the tranquil age of the mind, when the heat of temptation abates, they are guardians of the vessels and become healers of souls. EXPOSITION OF THE OLD AND NEW TESTAMENT, NUMBERS 4.[2]

---

[1]The Vulgate reads Num 8:25 as "but from their fiftieth year they should become guardians of the vessels." [2]PL 79:763, citing Gregory the Great *Moral Interpretation of Job* 23.11.21.

9:1-14 SECOND PASSOVER

⁶*And there were certain men who were unclean through touching the dead body of a man, so that they could not keep the passover on that day; and they came before Moses and Aaron on that day;* ⁷*and those men said to him, "We are unclean through touching the dead body of a man; why are we kept from offering the LORD's offering at its appointed time among the people of Israel?"* ⁸*And Moses said to them, "Wait, that I may hear what the LORD will command concerning you."*

⁹*The LORD said to Moses,* ¹⁰*"Say to the people of Israel, If any man of you or of your descendants is unclean through touching a dead body, or is afar off on a journey, he shall still keep the passover to the LORD.* ¹¹*In the second month on the fourteenth day in the evening they shall keep it; they shall eat it with unleavened bread and bitter herbs.* ¹²*They shall leave none of it until the morning, nor break a bone of it; according to all the statute for the passover they shall keep it."*

OVERVIEW: A good pastor withdraws from the concerns of the world and seeks the voice of God in hidden inspiration (PATERIUS). The second celebration of the pasch prefigures new birth in the church (PSEUDO-CYRIL).

9:8 What the Lord Will Command

MOSES WENT OFTEN TO THE TENT. PATERIUS: To leave the crowds and return to the tabernacle means to leave the tumult of external things behind and enter the hidden places of the mind. For the Lord is consulted there, and one hears, silently and within, what should be done outside and publicly. Good pastors do this every day. When they do not know how to decide about doubtful matters, they return to the hidden place of the mind as if to some tabernacle. They ponder the divine law, as if they were seeking advice from the Lord at the ark of the covenant. What they first hear silently within, they later make known when they act publicly. To fulfill their external offices without blame, they have recourse unceasingly to the secret places of the heart, and thus they hear the voice of God through his hidden inspiration, as they with-

draw from carnal sensations in spiritual meditation. EXPOSITION OF THE OLD AND NEW TESTAMENT, NUMBERS 5.[1]

9:11 In the Second Month

A SECOND BIRTH. PSEUDO-CYRIL: Those who also lived farther off or had been unclean in soul were commanded to celebrate the pasch in the second month. This is understood as a type of the holy church, which, since it has been defiled by all demons, was seen to be unclean in soul, but cleansed by a saving confession, is commanded to pass over unto a second birth, as if to a second month. However, before the month of new fruits is the last old month, in which it is completely forbidden that the true pasch be held. LETTER 87.11.[2]

9:12 Not Breaking a Bone of the Lamb

See CHRYSOSTOM ON EXODUS 12:46.

---

[1]PL 79:763, citing Gregory the Great *Moral Interpretation of Job* 23.20.38. [2]FC 77:125.

[9:15-23 THE FIERY CLOUD]

10:1-10 THE SILVER TRUMPETS

[15]*On the day that the tabernacle was set up, the cloud covered the tabernacle, the tent of the testimony; and at evening it was over the tabernacle like the appearance of fire until morning.* [16]*So it was continually. . . .*

10[2]*"Make two silver trumpets; of hammered work you shall make them; and you shall use them for summoning the congregation, and for breaking camp."*

OVERVIEW: The preacher must be like the silver trumpets: trained through suffering, and subtle and concise in speech (PATERIUS).

10:2 Make Two Silver Trumpets

THE TWO COMMANDS OF CHARITY. PATERIUS: "Make for yourself two trumpets of hammered silver." The army is led by two trumpets because the people are called to readiness in faith by the two commandments of charity. Scripture bids them to be made of silver, so that the words of the preachers may shine with gleaming light and not confuse the minds of the hearers with any darkness of their own. They are to be hammered, because those who preach the life to come grow through the blows of the present tribulations. Scripture says well, "When the short signal sounds, the camps will move."[1] When the preacher's word is subtle and concise, the hearers are aroused more ardently for the struggle against temptation. EXPOSITION OF THE OLD AND NEW TESTAMENT, NUMBERS 6.[2]

---

[1]Num 10:5. [2]PL 79:763-64, citing Gregory the Great *Moral Interpretation of Job* 30.3.14.

10:11-32 DEPARTURE FROM SINAI WITH HOBAB AS GUIDE

[11]*In the second year, in the second month, on the twentieth day of the month, the cloud was taken up from over the tabernacle of the testimony,* [12]*and the people of Israel set out by stages from the wilderness of Sinai. . . .*
[29]*And Moses said to Hobab the son of Reuel the Midianite, Moses' father-in-law, "We are setting out for the place of which the LORD said, 'I will give it to you'; come with us, and we will do you good; for the LORD has promised good to Israel." * [30]*But he said to him, "I will not go; I will depart to my own land and to my kindred." * [31]*And he said, "Do not leave us, I pray you, for you*

214

know how we are to encamp in the wilderness, and you will serve as eyes for us. [32] *And if you go with us, whatever good the LORD will do to us, the same will we do to you."*

OVERVIEW: The pride of others can easily be turned to good by complimenting them (PATE-RIUS).

10:29 We Will Do You Good

MOSES DEALT WISELY WITH THE PROUD.
PATERIUS: We can better persuade proud men to do what is useful if we say that their setting out will profit us rather than them, or if we say that improvement will profit us rather than them and ask that the cost be on our account, not theirs. For pride is easily turned to good if it can be adapted to the profit of others. Thus Moses, with God guiding him, advanced through the desert with a column of cloud going before him. When he wished to draw his relative Hobab away from his life with the Gentiles and subject him to the lordship of almighty God, he said, "We are going to the place that the Lord will give us. Come with us, so that we can do you good, for the Lord has promised good to Israel." When Hobab answered, "I will not go with you but will return to my land, where I was born,"[1] Moses added, "Do not leave us. You know where we should make camp in the desert, and you will be our guide."[2] Moses' mind was not limited by ignorance of the route. For knowledge of the Deity had made him familiar with prophecy. The column had gone before him. Familiar speech had taught him about all things interiorly, through careful conversation with God. But this prudent man, speaking to a proud listener, asked Hobab to give him help. Moses needed Hobab as a guide along the way, so that he could be Hobab's guide in life. So Moses acted so that the proud listener, as he urged the better way on him, would become more devoted to him if he were thought to be indispensable. He thought he outranked Moses, who asked him for help, and thus yielded to Moses' words as Moses entreated him. EXPOSITION OF THE OLD AND NEW TESTAMENT, NUMBERS 7.[3]

---

[1]Num 10:30. [2]Num 10:31. [3]PL 79:764, citing Gregory the Great *Pastoral Care* 3.17.

[10:33-36 INTO THE DESERT]

11:1-15 DISCONTENT OF THE PEOPLE

[4] *Now the rabble that was among them had a strong craving; and the people of Israel also wept again, and said, "O that we had meat to eat!* [5] *We remember the fish we ate in Egypt for nothing, the cucumbers, the melons, the leeks, the onions, and the garlic;* [6] *but now our strength is dried up, and there is nothing at all but this manna to look at."*

OVERVIEW: The people's murmuring against the Lord was a reprehensible act. The Israelites rejected the food they had. They should have asked to be freed from their loathing of it (AUGUSTINE). How ironic it was that the Israelites longed for onions! (CHRYSOSTOM). The faithful should not yearn for the Egypt of this world (JOHN CASSIAN).

11:4 O That We Had Meat to Eat!

MURMUR AGAINST THE LORD. AUGUSTINE: The people in the desert deserved to be reprimanded, not because they desired meat but because they murmured against the Lord as a result of this desire for meat. CONFESSIONS 10.31.46.[1]

WE SHOULD ASK THAT GOOD THINGS WILL DELIGHT US. AUGUSTINE: Do we not see that the Israelites got to their own hurt what their guilty lusting craved? For while manna was raining down on them from heaven, they desired to have meat to eat.[2] They disdained what they had, and they shamelessly sought what they had not, as if it were not better for them to have asked not that their unbecoming desires be gratified with food that was wanting, but that their own dislike be removed, and that they be made to receive rightly the food that was provided. For when evil becomes our delight and good the opposite, we ought to entreat God to win us back to the love of the good rather than to grant us the evil. TRAC-

TATE ON THE GOSPEL OF JOHN 73.2.[3]

11:5 The Onions and the Garlic

THEY PREFERRED ONIONS TO MANNA. CHRYSOSTOM: Prosperity has a way of bringing about the downfall and complete dissolution of the unwary. Thus the Jews, who from the beginning enjoyed the favor of God, repeatedly turned to the law of the kingdom of the Gentiles. When they were in the desert, after receiving manna, they kept recalling onions! HOMILIES ON THE GOSPEL OF JOHN 85.[4]

THE EGYPT OF THIS WORLD. JOHN CASSIAN: We would be censured along with those who dwelled in the desert and who desired the disgusting food of vice and filthiness after having eaten the heavenly manna, and we would seem to complain like them: "It was well with us in Egypt, when we sat over pots of flesh and ate onions and garlic and cucumbers and melons." Although this manner of speaking first referred to that people, nonetheless we see it now daily fulfilled in our life and profession. For everyone who has first renounced this world and then returns to his former pursuits and his erstwhile desires proclaims that in deed and in intention he is the same as they were, and he says, "It was well with me in Egypt." CONFERENCE 3.7.5-6.[5]

---

[1]FC 21:305. [2]Num 11:32. [3]NPNF 1 7:331. [4]FC 41:427. [5]ACW 57:126.

11:16-23 THE SEVENTY ELDERS

---

[16]And the LORD said to Moses, "Gather for me seventy men of the elders of Israel, whom you know to be the elders of the people and officers over them; and bring them to the tent of meeting, and let them take their stand there with you. [17]And I will come down and talk with you there;

---

and I will take some of the spirit which is upon you and put it upon them; and they shall bear the burden of the people with you, that you may not bear it yourself alone. [18]And say to the people, 'Consecrate yourselves for tomorrow, and you shall eat meat; for you have wept in the hearing of the LORD, saying, "Who will give us meat to eat? For it was well with us in Egypt."

OVERVIEW: The words of Scripture need to be examined carefully. In this case, a man may be an elder in body but not in mind. It was given to Moses to discern the difference (ORIGEN). The Holy Spirit proceeds from the Father and the Son as from one principle (AUGUSTINE).

11:16 Gather Seventy Men

ELDERS IN BODY AND IN SPIRIT. ORIGEN: But the Lord also says to Moses, "Choose for yourself presbyters whom you yourself know to be presbyters."[1] Let us examine very carefully the word of the Lord. What does that addition appear to mean, which says, "Whom you yourself know to be presbyters"? Was it not obvious to the eyes of all that he was a presbyter, that is, old, who was bearing old age in his body? Why then is that special inspection commanded to Moses alone, such a great prophet, that those be chosen, not whom others knew, not whom the ignorant multitude recognized, but whom the prophet full of God should choose? For in respect to them it is not a judgment about their body or their age but about

their mind. HOMILIES ON GENESIS 3.3.[2]

11:17 Some of the Spirit

THE HOLY SPIRIT GIVEN TO MOSES IS GIVEN TO THE ELDERS. AUGUSTINE: The same meaning is to be understood in the case of Moses when the Lord said to him, "I will take of your spirit and give to them," that is, I will give to them of the Holy Spirit which I have already given to you. If that which is also given has the giver for its principle, because it did not receive from any other source than that which proceeds from him, then we have to confess that the Father and the Son are the principle of the Holy Spirit, not two principles. But as the Father and the Son are one God, and in relation to the creature are one Creator and one Lord, so they are one principle in relation to the Holy Spirit. But in relation to the creature, the Father, the Son and the Holy Spirit are one principle, as they are one Creator and one Lord. THE TRINITY 5.14.15.[3]

---

[1]Num 11:16 LXX. [2]FC 71:92-93. [3]FC 45:194.

11:24-30 THE SPIRIT ON THE ELDERS

[24]*So Moses . . . gathered seventy men of the elders of the people, and placed them round about the tent. [25]Then the LORD . . . took some of the spirit that was upon him and put it upon the seventy elders; and when the spirit rested upon them, they prophesied. But they did so no more. . . .*

[27]*And a young man ran and told Moses, "Eldad and Medad are prophesying in the camp." [28]And Joshua the son of Nun, the minister of Moses, one of his chosen men, said, "My lord*

Moses, forbid them." ²⁹But Moses said to him, "Are you jealous for my sake? Would that all the Lord's people were prophets, that the Lord would put his spirit upon them!" ³⁰And Moses and the elders of Israel returned to the camp.

OVERVIEW: It was not the Spirit that was divided, but God's gifts were distributed according to the capacity of the recipient. Even those outside the assembly may receive the gift of prophecy (CYRIL OF JERUSALEM).

11:25 The Spirit That Was on Moses

THE SPIRIT BESTOWS THE GIFT. CYRIL OF JERUSALEM: This Spirit descended upon the seventy elders in Moses' day. My object is to prove that he knew all things and worked according to his will. The seventy elders were chosen: "The Lord then came down in the cloud, and taking some of the spirit that was on Moses, he bestowed it on the seventy elders." It was not that the Spirit was divided, but his gifts were distributed according to the vessels and the capacity of the recipients. Now there were sixty-eight present, and they prophesied. Eldad and Medad were not present. To make it clear that it was not Moses who bestowed the gift but the Spirit who wrought, Eldad and Medad, who had been called but had not yet presented them-

selves, also prophesied. CATECHETICAL LECTURE 16.25.[1]

11:28 My Lord Moses, Forbid Them

GRACE IS A GIFT FROM HEAVEN. CYRIL OF JERUSALEM: Joshua, the son of Nun and successor of Moses, was amazed, and coming to Moses said to him, Have you heard that Eldad and Medad are prophesying? They were called and did not come forward; "Moses, my lord, stop them." I cannot forbid them, he said, for the grace is from heaven. So far am I from forbidding them that I consider it a favor. But I think you have not spoken thus in envy. Do not be overzealous on my account, because they have prophesied, and you do not yet prophesy. Await the proper time. "Would that all the people of the Lord might prophesy, whenever the Lord shall give them his spirit."[2] CATECHETICAL LECTURE 16.26.[3]

---

[1]FC 64:91. [2]Num 11:29. [3]FC 64:91-92.

11:31-35 THE QUAIL

³²*And the people rose all that day, and all night, and all the next day, and gathered the quails; he who gathered least gathered ten homers; and they spread them out for themselves all around the camp. ³³While the meat was yet between their teeth, before it was consumed, the anger of the Lord was kindled against the people, and the Lord smote the people with a very great plague. ³⁴Therefore the name of that place was called Kibroth-hattaavah,ᶠ because there they buried the people who had the craving.*

f *That is Graves of craving*

OVERVIEW: The Israelites received what they asked for but were punished for their lust (AUGUSTINE). The graves of the Israelites are to be seen even to this day in the wilderness (JEROME).

11:33 The Anger of the Lord

THE LORD PUNISHED THE PEOPLE. AUGUSTINE: To some, indeed, who lack patience, the Lord God in his wrath grants them what they ask, just as in his mercy, on the other hand, he refused it to his apostle. We read what and how the Israelites asked and received, but when their lust had been satisfied, their lack of patience was severely punished. LETTER 130.[1]

11:34 Kibroth-hattaavah

GOD'S WRATH ON THE GLUTTONS. JEROME: How is it that the graves of lust where the people fell in their devotion to flesh remain even to this day in the wilderness? Do we not read that the stupid people gorged themselves with quails until the wrath of God came upon them? AGAINST JOVINIAN 2.17.[2]

---

[1]FC 18:396. [2]NPNF 2 6:402.

12:1-8 JEALOUSY OF AARON AND MIRIAM

[1]*Miriam and Aaron spoke against Moses because of the Cushite* woman whom he had married, for he had married a Cushite* woman;* [2]*and they said, "Has the LORD indeed spoken only through Moses? Has he not spoken through us also?" And the LORD heard it.* [3]*Now the man Moses was very meek, more than all men that were on the face of the earth. . . .* [5]*And the LORD came down in a pillar of cloud, and stood at the door of the tent, and called Aaron and Miriam; and they both came forward.* [6]*And he said, "Hear my words: If there is a prophet among you, I the LORD make myself known to him in a vision, I speak with him in a dream.* [7]*Not so with my servant Moses; he is entrusted with all my house.* [8]*With him I speak mouth to mouth, clearly, and not in dark speech; and he beholds the form of the LORD. Why then were you not afraid to speak against my servant Moses?"*

* LXX Ethiopian

OVERVIEW: Miriam represents the synagogue and the Ethiopian woman the church of the Gentiles. The faith of the Gentiles freed Miriam from leprosy (AMBROSE). Miriam and Aaron complained and claimed that God had not spoken only to Moses. The highest praise of Moses in all of Scripture is here (ORIGEN). Moses remained true to his essential nature by transcending anger and desire (GREGORY OF NYSSA). In many of his deeds, Moses foreshadowed Christ (CHRYSOSTOM). Despite all of God's gifts to him, Moses never boasted (CLEMENT OF ROME). Others saw God in visions and dreams; Moses saw God's very glory (AUGUSTINE).

12:1 Moses' Cushite Wife

THE CHURCH OF THE GENTILES. AMBROSE: The prophetess Mary [Miriam] herself, who crossed the straits of the sea on foot with her brothers, did not yet know the mystery of the Ethiopian [Cushite] woman and murmured against her brother Moses. She shuddered at the white spots of leprosy, which she would hardly have been freed from if Moses had not prayed for her. That murmuring stands very much as a type of the synagogue, which daily murmurs and does not grasp the mystery of the Ethiopian woman, that is, the church of the Gentiles. She envies that people by whose faith even she herself is freed from the leprosy of faithlessness, according to the verse of Scripture: "Blindness has stretched through part of Israel until the full number of Gentiles shall enter and thus shall all of Israel be saved."[1] LETTER 14 EXTRA COLL. (63).57.[2]

12:2 Has the Lord Spoken Only Through Moses?

THE FORSAKEN SYNAGOGUES AND THE PRIESTHOOD. ORIGEN: So then in the book of Numbers we find Moses taking an Ethiopian wife—that is to say, one who is dark or black. Because of her Mary and Aaron speak ill of him and say with indignation, "Has the Lord spoken to Moses only? Has he not also spoken to us?" Now on careful consideration the narrative here seems to lack coherence. What has their saying "Has the Lord spoken to Moses only? Has he not also spoken to us?" to do with their indignation about the Ethiopian woman? If that was the trouble, they ought to have said, "Moses, you should not have taken an Ethiopian wife and one of the seed of Ham. You should have married one of your own race and of the house of Levi." They say not a word about this. They say instead, "Has the Lord spoken to Moses only? Has he not also spoken to us?" Rather, it seems to me that in so saying they understood the thing Moses had done more in terms of the mystery. They saw Moses— that is, the spiritual law—entering now into wedlock and union with the church that is gathered together from among the Gentiles. This is the reason, apparently, why Mary [Miriam], who typified the forsaken synagogue, and Aaron, who stood for the priesthood according to the flesh, seeing their kingdom taken away from them and given to a nation bringing forth the fruits thereof, say, "Has the Lord spoken to Moses only? Has he not also spoken to us?" COMMENTARY ON THE SONG OF SONGS 2.1.[3]

12:3 Moses Was Very Meek

MOSES IS PRAISED BY GOD. ORIGEN: Moreover, Moses himself, in spite of all the great and splendid achievements of faith and patience that are recorded of him, was never so highly praised by God as on this occasion when he took the Ethiopian wife. It is said of him, in reference to this: "Moses was a man exceeding meek above all men that are upon earth." COMMENTARY ON THE SONG OF SONGS 2.1.[4]

MOSES WAS ABOVE ANGER AND DESIRE. GREGORY OF NYSSA: [Macrina replied,] It is said of Moses that he was superior to anger and desire. History testifies that he was the "meekest" of men. An incapacity for anger is shown through mildness and an aversion to wrath. He desired none of the things toward which the desiring element in many people is directed. This would not have been so if these qualities had been natural to him and logically in keeping with his essence, for it is not possible for that which is unnatural to remain in the essence. Moses, you see, was true to his essence and not involved in desire and anger, which are in addition to our nature and not our nature itself, for nature is truly that in which being has its essence. ON THE SOUL AND THE RESURRECTION.[5]

MOSES COMPARED WITH CHRIST. CHRYSOSTOM: What was the characteristic of Moses of

---

[1]Rom 11:25-26. [2]CSEL 82 3:264. [3]ACW 26:96-97. [4]ACW 26:97. [5]FC 58:218*.

old?"Moses was the meekest of all men on earth." One would not be wrong in describing this other Moses [i.e., Christ] in these same terms, for certainly the meekest of spirits is with him, being related to him by consubstantiality. In those days Moses stretched forth his hands to heaven and brought down the bread of angels, manna. This second Moses stretches forth his hands to heaven and brings down the food of eternal life. Moses struck the rock and made streams of water flow. This second Moses touches the table, strikes the spiritual board and makes the fountains of the Spirit gush forth. Consequently the table, like the fountain, lies in the middle, in order that the flocks may surround the fountain on every side and enjoy the benefit of the saving waters. BAPTISMAL INSTRUCTIONS 3.26.[6]

HIGH PRAISE OF MOSES. CHRYSOSTOM: To learn the power of gentleness and restraint, and how virtue alone suffices to render the person who practices it devoutly worthy of those ineffable encomiums, listen to the eulogy bestowed to blessed Moses. The crown was awarded him for this reason: "Moses was the mildest of all people on the earth," Scripture says. Do you see the greatness of the encomium, which conferred on him equality of esteem with the whole human race—or, rather, gave him precedence over all humankind? HOMILIES ON GENESIS 34.3.[7]

12:7 Moses Entrusted with All God's House

MOSES NEVER BOASTED. CLEMENT OF ROME: Moses was called "faithful in all God's house." God used him to bring his judgment on Egypt with scourges and torments. Yet even he, despite the great glory he was given, did not boast. But when he was granted an oracle from the bush, he said, "Who am I that you send me? I have a feeble voice and a slow tongue."[8] And again he says, "I am but steam from a pot."[9] LETTER TO THE CORINTHIANS 17.[10]

12:8 Moses Sees the Form of the Lord

MOSES BEHELD GOD AS HE IS. AUGUSTINE: As I started to say, it is shown later in the book of Numbers that even what he asked was granted to his desire, for thereby the Lord rebuked the sister of Moses for her obstinacy. The Lord appeared to the other prophets in visions and dreams but to Moses plainly and not by riddles. He added the words "And he saw the glory of the Lord." Why then did God make such an exception of him, if not perhaps that he considered him such a ruler of his people, so faithful a minister of his whole house, that he was worthy, even then, of that contemplation, so that, as he desired, he saw God as he is—a contemplation promised to all his sons at the end of life?[11] LETTER 147.32.[12]

---

[6]ACW 31:64-65. [7]FC 82:290. [8]Ex 3:11; 4:10. [9]The source is unknown. [10]LCC 1:52. [11]1 Jn 3:2. [12]FC 20:200.

12:9-16 MIRIAM'S LEPROSY

---

[9]And the anger of the LORD was kindled against them, and he departed; [10]and when the cloud removed from over the tent, behold, Miriam was leprous, as white as snow. And Aaron turned towards Miriam, and behold, she was leprous. [11]And Aaron said to Moses, "Oh, my lord, do

not[g] punish us because we have done foolishly and have sinned. [12]Let her not be as one dead, of whom the flesh is half consumed when he comes out of his mother's womb." [13]And Moses cried to the Lord, "Heal her, O God, I beseech thee." [14]But the Lord said to Moses, "If her father had but spit in her face, should she not be shamed seven days? Let her be shut up outside the camp seven days, and after that she may be brought in again."

g *Heb* lay not sin upon us

Overview: Even though Miriam offended him, Moses prayed that she should be spared punishment (Chrysostom).

12:13 Moses Pleads for Miriam's Healing

How People Desire Vengeance. Chrysostom: Miriam and her company spoke evil of Moses, and he immediately begged them off from their punishment. No, he would not so much as let it be known that his cause was avenged. But not so we. On the contrary, this is what we most desire; to have everyone know that they have not passed unpunished. Homilies on Acts 14.[1]

[1]NPNF 1 11:93.

13:1-24 THE TWELVE SCOUTS

[16]*These were the . . . men whom Moses sent to spy out the land. And Moses called Hoshea the son of Nun Joshua. . . .*

[23]*And they . . . cut down from there a branch with a single cluster of grapes. . . . [24]That place was called the Valley of Eshcol.*

Overview: When Moses changed Hoshea's name to Joshua, he introduced the name Jesus (Eusebius). The bunch of grapes (which is the meaning of Eshcol) foreshadowed the passion of Christ (Clement of Alexandria).

13:16 Moses Called the Son of Nun Joshua

How Joshua Was Like Jesus. Eusebius: And the same [Moses] by divine inspiration foresaw the name Jesus very clearly and again also endowed this with special privilege. The name of Jesus, which had never been uttered among men before it was made known to Moses, Moses applied first to this one alone. He knew that Joshua, again as a type and a symbol, would receive the rule over all after Moses' death. His successor, at any rate, had never before used the title Jesus. He had been called by another name, Auses,[1] which his parents had bestowed upon him. Moses himself proclaims Jesus, as a privilege of honor far greater than a royal crown, giving him the name because Jesus, the son of Nave,[2] himself bore a resemblance to our Savior, who alone, after Moses and the completion of the symbolic worship transmitted by him,

[1]The Greek form of Hoshea. [2]The Greek form of Nun.

received the rule of true and pure religion. ECCLESIASTICAL HISTORY 1.3.[3]

See CYRIL OF JERUSALEM ON LEVITICUS 4:5.

13:24 The Valley of Eshcol

ESHCOL MEANS "BUNCH OF GRAPES." CLEMENT OF ALEXANDRIA: Later on, a sacred vine put forth a cluster of grapes that was prophetic. To those who had been led by the Educator to a place of rest after their wanderings it was a sign, for the great cluster of grapes is the Word crushed on our account.[4] The Word desired that the "blood of the grape"[5] be mixed with water as a symbol that his own blood is an integral element in salvation. CHRIST THE EDUCATOR 2.2.19.[6]

---

[3]FC 19:46-47. [4]Is 53:5, 10. [5]Gen 49:11; Sir 50:15. [6]FC 23:111.

13:25 — 14:38 THE SPIES' RETURN, THREATS OF REVOLT, THE LORD'S SENTENCE

[25]*At the end of forty days they returned from spying out the land. . . .*

14 [1]*Then all the congregation raised a loud cry; and the people wept that night.* [2]*And all the people of Israel murmured against Moses and Aaron. . . .*

[11]*And the* LORD *said to Moses, "How long will this people despise me? And how long will they not believe in me, in spite of all the signs which I have wrought among them?* [12]*I will strike them with the pestilence and disinherit them, and I will make of you a nation greater and mightier than they."*

[13]*But Moses said to the* LORD, *"Then the Egyptians will hear of it. . . .* [18]'*The* LORD *is slow to anger, and abounding in steadfast love, forgiving iniquity and transgression, but he will by no means clear the guilty, visiting the iniquity of fathers upon children, upon the third and upon the fourth generation.'* [19]*Pardon the iniquity of this people, I pray thee, according to the greatness of thy steadfast love, and according as thou hast forgiven this people, from Egypt even until now." . . .*

[26]*And the* LORD *said to Moses and to Aaron,* [27]"*How long shall this wicked congregation murmur against me? I have heard the murmurings of the people of Israel, which they murmur against me.* [28]*Say to them, 'As I live, says the* LORD, *what you have said in my hearing I will do to you:* [29]*your dead bodies shall fall in this wilderness; and of all your number, numbered from twenty years old and upward, who have murmured against me,* [30]*not one shall come into the land where I swore that I would make you dwell, except Caleb the son of Jephunneh and Joshua the son of Nun."*

OVERVIEW: The new nation was to be raised up from among the Gentiles (CAESARIUS OF ARLES). Moses did not wish to be saved alone (SYMEON THE NEW THEOLOGIAN). Moses prayed for the people, even though they were ungrateful and faithless (CYPRIAN). God does not punish us at

---

once but delays retribution until later (JEROME).
Only God is most fully alive, because only God
has life unchangeably (ORIGEN). The number
twenty represents the fullness of both Testaments (AUGUSTINE). The penalty exacted for sin
is a great one (CAESARIUS OF ARLES).

14:12 A Nation Great and Mighty

THE NEW NATION IS THE CHURCH. CAESARIUS OF ARLES: Now the Lord said to Moses,
"I will strike them with death and wipe them
out. Then I will make the house of your father a
nation, greater and mightier than they." This
threat is not a sign of wrath but a prophecy.
Another nation was to be taken over, that is, the
people of the Gentiles, but not through Moses.
Moses excused himself, for he knew that the
great nation which was promised was not to be
called through him but through Jesus Christ.
Those people would not be called Mosaic but
Christian. SERMON 108.1.[1]

MOSES DID NOT WISH TO BE SAVED ALONE.
SYMEON THE NEW THEOLOGIAN: The attitude
[of one brother] was like that of Moses and
indeed of God himself in that he did not in any
way wish to be saved alone. Because he was spiritually bound to them by holy love in the Holy
Spirit he did not want to enter into the kingdom
of heaven itself if it meant that he would be separated from them. O sacred bond! O unutterable
power! O soul of heavenly thoughts, or, rather,
soul borne by God and greatly perfected in love
of God and of neighbor! DISCOURSE 8.2.[2]

14:13 Moses Entreats the Lord

MOSES PRAYED FOR THE PEOPLE. CYPRIAN:
Moses was often scorned by an ungrateful and
faithless people and almost stoned, and yet with
mildness and patience he prayed to the Lord in
their behalf. THE GOOD OF PATIENCE 10.[3]

14:18 Iniquity of Parents Falls on the Children

WHO OUR OFFSPRING ARE. JEROME: That is
to say, God will not punish us at once for our
thoughts and resolves but will send retribution
upon their offspring, that is, upon the evil deeds
and habits of sin which arise out of them. LETTER 130.8.[4]

14:28 "As I Live," Says the Lord

ONLY GOD MOST TRULY LIVES. ORIGEN: We
must also consider the words "as I live, says the
Lord." Perhaps living in the proper sense, especially on the basis of what has been said about
living, occurs with God alone. And see if the
apostle . . . considered the superiority of the life
of God to be beyond comparison and understood the words "as I live says the Lord" in a
manner worthy of God. Can [he] for this reason
have said of God, "Who alone has immortality,"[5]
because none of the living beings with God has
the life which is absolutely unchangeable and
immutable? And why are we uncertain about the
remaining beings, when not even the Christ had
the Father's immortality? For he tasted death for
all.[6] COMMENTARY ON THE GOSPEL OF JOHN
2.123.[7]

14:29 From Twenty Years Old

**A PEOPLE INSTRUCTED IN THE KINGDOM OF
HEAVEN.** AUGUSTINE: Of such inflexibility
were those youths of twenty years, who foretokened in figure God's new people; they entered
the land of promise; they, it is said, turned neither to the right hand nor to the left.[8] Now this
age of twenty is not to be compared with the age
of children's innocence, but if I mistake not, this
number is the shadow and echo of a mystery. For
the Old Testament has its excellence in the five
books of Moses, while the New Testament is
most refulgent in the authority of the four Gospels. These numbers, when multiplied together,

---

[1]FC 47:136. [2]SNTD 144-45. [3]FC 36:273. [4]NPNF 2 6:266.
[5]1 Tim 6:16. [6]Heb 2:9. [7]FC 80:127. [8]Josh 23:6.

reach to the number twenty: four times five, or five times four, are twenty. Such a people (as I have already said), instructed in the kingdom of heaven by the two Testaments—the Old and the New—turning neither to the right hand, in a proud assumption of righteousness, nor to the left hand, in a reckless delight in sin, shall enter into the land of promise. [There] we shall have no longer either to pray that sins may be forgiven to us or to fear that they may be punished in us. [We have] been freed from them all by that Redeemer, who, not being "sold under sin,"[9] "has redeemed Israel out of all his iniquities,"[10] whether committed in the actual life or derived from the original transgression. ON THE MERITS AND FORGIVENESS OF SINS AND ON INFANT BAPTISM 2.35.57.[11]

14:34 For Every Day a Year

THE SEVERITY OF GOD'S JUDGMENT. CAESARIUS OF ARLES: For my part I am afraid to examine the secrets of this mystery, for I see comprehended in it the calculation of sins and punishment. If each sinner is assigned punishment for the sin of one day and according to the number of days he sins must spend so many years in punishment, I fear that perhaps for us who sin daily and spend no day of our life without offense, even ages and ages will not suffice to pay our penalties. In the fact that for forty days of sin those people were afflicted in the desert for forty years and not permitted to enter the holy land, a kind of similarity to the future judgment seems to be evident. At that time the number of sins will have to be calculated, unless perchance there is the balance of good works or of evils which a man has suffered in his life, as Abraham taught concerning Lazarus. However, it is within the power of no one to know these things perfectly, except him to whom "the Father has given all judgment."[12] SERMON 108.2.[13]

---

[9]Rom 7:14. [10]Ps 25:22. [11]NPNF 1 5:67. [12]Jn 5:22. [13]FC 47:136.

[14:39-45 UNSUCCESSFUL INVASION]

15:1-21 SECONDARY OFFERINGS

[44]*But they presumed to go up to the heights of the hill country, although neither the ark of the covenant of the* LORD, *nor Moses, departed out of the camp.* [45]*Then the Amalekites and the Canaanites who dwelt in that hill country came down, and defeated them and pursued them, even to Hormah. . . .*

15 [17]*The* LORD *said to Moses,* [18]*"Say to the people of Israel, When you come into the land to which I bring you* [19]*and when you eat of the food of the land, you shall present an offering to the* LORD. [20]*Of the first of your coarse meal you shall present a cake as an offering; as an offering from the threshing floor, so shall you present it.* [21]*Of the first of your coarse meal you shall give to the* LORD *an offering throughout your generations."*

Overview: The thoughts of our minds must be sifted, to separate what is nourishing from what is useless (Ambrose).

15:20 An Offering from the Threshing Floor

Sifting Our Thoughts. Ambrose: All the morally good emotions of your senses are the first fruits of the threshing floor of the soul in the same manner as grain is separated in an actual barn floor. On this barn floor the wheat and the barley are separated by a winnowing process from the chaff and from other impurities, while the solid parts, now rid of their lighter coating, settle on the floor. In a similar fashion our thoughts, when sifted, provide a solid food and pure nourishment for the exercise of virtue. Cain and Abel 2.1.5.[1]

---

[1]FC 42:404-5.

[15:22-31 SIN OFFERING]

15:32-36 THE SABBATH BREAKER

[32]*While the people of Israel were in the wilderness, they found a man gathering sticks on the sabbath day.* [33]*And those who found him gathering sticks brought him to Moses and Aaron, and to all the congregation.* [34]*They put him in custody, because it had not been made plain what should be done to him.* [35]*And the* Lord *said to Moses, "The man shall be put to death; all the congregation shall stone him with stones outside the camp."*

Overview: The terrible punishment of the man who gathered sticks on the sabbath day was the occasion of much speculation. Even a single act of disobedience can be viewed eschatologically in relation to final judgment and thus can be punished with death (Basil, John Cassian). The people needed to be taught to respect the sabbath (Chrysostom). The law punishes; the gospel enlightens (Chrysostom). People are punished even for less serious faults as an example to others of final judgment (John Cassian). God's mercy is shown in that by the death of one, all are admonished to be cautious (Salvian).

15:32 A Man Gathering Sticks

The Dreadful Consequences of Obsti- **nancy. Basil the Great:** I find, in taking up the Holy Scripture, that in the Old and New Testament stubbornness toward God is clearly condemned not in consideration of the number or heinousness of transgressions but in terms of a single violation of any precept whatsoever, and, further, that the judgment of God covers all forms of disobedience. In the Old Testament, I read of the frightful end of Achar[1] and the account of the man who gathered wood on the sabbath day. Neither of these men was guilty of any other offense against God, nor had they wronged others in any way, small or great. But the one, merely for his first gathering of wood, paid the inescapable penalty and did not have an

---

[1]Josh 7:19-26.

opportunity to make amends. By the command of God, he was forthwith stoned by all his people. Preface on the Judgment of God15.32-36.[2]

The Law Had to Be Respected. Chrysostom: Why was he punished just for gathering sticks? Because if the laws were obstinately despised even at the beginning, of course they would scarcely be observed afterwards. For indeed the sabbath did at the first confer many and great benefits. It made them gentle toward those of their household and humane. It taught them God's providence and the creation, as Ezekiel says;[3] it trained them by degrees to abstain from wickedness and disposed them to regard the things of the Spirit. Homilies on the Gospel of Matthew 39.3.[4]

Law and Gospel Contrasted. Chrysostom: The law, if it arrests a murderer, puts him to death. The gospel, if it arrests a murderer, enlightens and gives him life. And why do I cite a murderer? The law laid hold on one that gathered sticks on a sabbath day and stoned him. This is the stark import of "the letter kills." Homilies on 2 Corinthians 6.2.[5]

Even Less Serious Faults Are Punished Seriously. John Cassian: We have in fact noticed that even for less serious faults some people have suffered the very sentence of death by which those who we said were the authors of sacrilegious prevarication were also punished. This happened in the case of the man who had been collecting wood on the sabbath, as well as in that of Ananias and Sapphira, who by their misguided faithlessness kept back a little bit of their property.[6] It is not that these sins were equally grave but that when these persons had been found committing a new offense, they had to furnish a kind of example to others of the penalty and terror of sinfulness. Thus, from then on, whoever was tempted to do the same thing would know that at the future judgment he would receive the same condemnation as the others, even if in this life his punishment was deferred. Conference 6.11.11.[7]

Severity Overcame Mercy. Salvian the Presbyter: When a man of the Israelite community gathered wood on the sabbath, he was killed, and this by the judgment and order of God, a judge most loving and merciful and who doubtless preferred to spare rather than kill him if the reason for severity had not overcome the reason for mercy. One man who was more unmindful perished, lest many be undone afterwards through lack of caution. The Governance of God 6.10.55.[8]

---

[2]FC 9:43. [3]Ezek 20:12. [4]NPNF 1 10:257. [5]NPNF 1 12:307. [6]Acts 5:2. [7]ACW 57:231. [8]FC 3:169.

[15:37-41 TASSELS ON THE CLOAK]

16:1-11 REBELLION OF KORAH

[1]*Now Korah the son of Izhar, son of Kohath, son of Levi, and Dathan and Abiram the sons of Eliab, and On the son of Peleth, sons of Reuben,* [2]*took men; and they rose up before Moses, with a number of the people of Israel, two hundred and fifty leaders of the congregation, chosen from*

the assembly, well-known men; [3]*and they assembled themselves together against Moses and against Aaron, and said to them, "You have gone too far! For all the congregation are holy, every one of them, and the Lord is among them; why then do you exalt yourselves above the assembly of the Lord?"* [4]*When Moses heard it, he fell on his face;* [5]*and he said to Korah and all his company, "In the morning the Lord will show who is his, and who is holy, and will cause him to come near to him; him whom he will choose he will cause to come near to him."*

Overview: Dathan and Abiram gave in to envy and were jealous of the favor God had bestowed on Aaron and Moses (Cassiodorus). The earth swallowed up those who rebelled against God's plan and will (Cyrian). The rebels claimed the priesthood for themselves and exercised it unworthily (Ambrose). The rebels did not differ from Moses and Aaron in faith but in community order (Cyprian). God does not deign to know those who have turned away from him (Origen).

16:2 Rising Before Moses

Dathan and Abiram Yielded to Envy. Cassiodorus: Their bellies' fullness was followed by rebellion, which often rouses occasions of destructive danger. We say that a person is provoked when roused to anger by wicked deeds or very harsh words of others. The verse[1] points to the incident when Dathan and Abiram roused strife and sought distinction for themselves.[2] So their punishment ensued; for they provoked the holy men, which led to their own destruction, for they spoke through jealousy, and this is acknowledged to have displeased the Lord. This is aptly mentioned among the Lord's praises because he is seen to have avenged his servants.

As Numbers attests, it is clear that this befell the men who with the poisonous teeth of envy sought the heavenly favor bestowed on Aaron and Moses. Thus Dathan and Abiram wantonly seized for themselves the distinction which had been bestowed by the Lord's kindness on Aaron and Moses. A similar end came on both of them because their motive in causing division was the same. They were swallowed up by the earth because they were steeped in earthly things, so that the nature of their punishment itself witnesses to their criminal deeds. Exposition of the Psalms 105.16-17.[3]

16:3 Assembling Against Moses and Aaron

People May Not Oppose God's Plan. Cyprian: Thus Korah, Dathan and Abiram, who tried to assume for themselves in opposition to Moses and Aaron the freedom to sacrifice, immediately paid the penalty for their efforts. The earth, breaking its bonds, opened up into a deep chasm, and the opening of the receding ground swallowed up the standing and the living.[4] And not only did the anger of the indignant God strike those who had been the authors [of the revolt], but also fire that went out from the Lord in speedy revenge consumed 250 others, participants and sharers in the same madness, who had been joined together with them in the daring plan. Clearly [this] warned and showed that whatever the wicked attempt by human will to destroy God's plan is done against God. The Unity of the Catholic Church 18.[5]

The Unworthy Exercise of Priesthood. Ambrose: Let the dissidents learn to fear the agitation of the Lord and to obey the priests. What does this mean? Did the cleft in the earth not swallow Dathan and Abiram and Korah because of their dissention? For when Korah and Dathan and Abiram incited 250 men to

---

[1]Ps 105:16. [2]See Num 16:1-3. [3]ACW 53:72-73*. [4]Num 16:32. [5]FC 36:113-14.

rebel against Moses and Aaron and separate themselves from them, they rose up and said, "Let it be sufficient for you that the whole assembly is holy, every one of them, and that the Lord is in them." Whence the Lord was angered and spoke to the entire assembly. He examined them. Since "the Lord knows who are his," he led the holy ones to himself. Those whom he did not choose he did not lead to himself. And the Lord commanded that Korah and all those who had risen up with him against Moses and Aaron, the priests of the Lord, select for themselves altars and put incense upon them, in order that the one elected by the Lord might himself be confirmed as holy among the Levites of the Lord.

And Moses said to Korah, "Listen to me, sons of Levi: is this insignificant to you that God has separated you from the assembly of Israel?" And further down: "Do you thus seek to exercise the priesthood, you and your entire assembly who have congregated against the Lord? What is Aaron that you murmur against him?"

You are considering then what the causes of their offense were. They were willing to exercise the priesthood unworthily, and for that reason they dissented. Moreover, they murmured and disapproved of the judgment of God in their election of their priests. Therefore a great dread seized all the people. The terror of punishment enveloped them all. Nevertheless, because all the people prayed that not all of them perish because of the insolence of a few, those guilty of the crime were singled out, and 250 men with their leaders were set apart from the body of the people. The earth bellows and is rent apart in the midst of the people. A gulf is opened into the depths. The guilty are snatched up and removed from every element of this world, so that they will not contaminate the air by their breath, or the sky by their sight, or the sea by their touch or the earth by their tombs. LETTER 14 EXTRA COLL. (63).52-55.[6]

ONE IN DOCTRINE AND IN WORSHIP. CYPRIAN: The argument that they acknowledge the same God the Father, the same son Christ and the same Holy Spirit is no use to them either. Korah, Dathan and Abiram acknowledged the same God as Aaron the priest and Moses. They lived by the same law and the same religious practices, invoking the one true God who should properly be worshiped and invoked. All the same, when they went beyond the limits of their own ministry and claimed for themselves authority to perform sacrifices in opposition to Aaron the priest, who had received the lawful priesthood by the favor of God and the ordination of the Lord, they were struck from on high and at once paid the penalty for their unlawful attempt. The sacrifices which they offered impiously and unlawfully against God's will and ordinance could be neither valid nor efficacious. LETTER 69.8.[7]

16:5 The Lord Will Show Who Is His

THOSE WHOM GOD KNOWS. ORIGEN: We say therefore with confidence that according to the Scriptures God does not know [in the sense of acknowledge] all people. God does not know sin, and God does not know sinners. He is ignorant, so to speak, of those alienated from himself. Hear the Scripture saying "The Lord knows those who are his"[8] and "Let everyone depart from iniquity who calls on the name of the Lord." The Lord knows his own, but he does not know the wicked and the impious. . . .

We say these things, however, not thinking anything blasphemous about God or ascribing ignorance to him, but thus we understand that these whose activity is considered unworthy of God are also considered to be unworthy of God's knowing them. For God does not deign to know one who has turned away from him and does not know that one. HOMILIES ON GENESIS 4.6.[9]

---

[6]CSEL 82 3:262-63. [7]LCC 5:155. [8]2 Tim 2:19. [9]FC 71:109-10*.

[16:12-14 REBELLION OF DATHAN AND ABIRAM]

[16:15-24 KORAH]

16:25-35 PUNISHMENT OF DATHAN AND ABIRAM

[12]And Moses sent to call Dathan and Abiram the sons of Eliab; and they said, "We will not come up." . . .

[23]And the LORD said to Moses, [24]"Say to the congregation, Get away from about the dwelling of Korah, Dathan, and Abiram."

[25]Then Moses rose and went to Dathan and Abiram; and the elders of Israel followed him. [26]And he said to the congregation, "Depart, I pray you, from the tents of these wicked men, and touch nothing of theirs, lest you be swept away with all their sins." . . .

[31]And as he finished speaking all these words, the ground under them split asunder; [32]and the earth opened its mouth and swallowed them up, with their households and all the men that belonged to Korah and all their goods. [33]So they and all that belonged to them went down alive into Sheol; and the earth closed over them, and they perished from the midst of the assembly.

OVERVIEW: The faithful people should separate themselves from sinful leaders (CYPRIAN). The dreadful punishment of Korah and the others is a sign to us (BASIL). Those who separated themselves from the community were destroyed (AUGUSTINE). To go down alive into hell is a terrible thing (GREGORY THE GREAT).

16:26 Depart from These Wicked Men

THE FAITHFUL SHOULD SEPARATE FROM SINNERS. CYPRIAN: We find that also made clear in Numbers when Korah and Dathan and Abiram claimed for themselves the liberty of sacrificing in opposition to Aaron the priest. There also the Lord teaches through Moses that the people should be separated from them lest they be bound by the same guilt with the criminals and contaminate themselves by the same crime.

"Keep away," he says, "from the tents of most shameless wicked men, and do not touch anything that is theirs, lest you perish at the same time in their sin." Because of this, a people who obey the precepts of the Lord and fear God ought to separate themselves from a sinful leader and should not take part in the sacrifices of a sacrilegious bishop, especially since they themselves have the power either of electing worthy bishops or of refusing the unworthy. LETTER 67.3.[1]

16:32 The Earth Swallowed Them

PRIESTS MUST BE CALLED. BASIL THE GREAT: In the Old Testament, as, for instance, in the case of Korah and the men who dared to enter

---

[1]FC 51:233-34.

the priesthood without being called to it and by the severity of the wrath which came upon them to their utter destruction, we see how grave a thing it is to do that which is unsuitable as regards the person. CONCERNING BAPTISM, QUESTION 8.[2]

See also AMBROSE ON NUMBERS 16:3B.

THE WICKED SEPARATED THEMSELVES.
AUGUSTINE: Then there were the miracles of the seditious among the people of God. They separated themselves from the divinely ordered community. They were swallowed alive by the earth, as a visible token of an invisible punishment. CITY OF GOD 10.8.[3]

16:33 *Going Alive into Sheol*

SINNING FROM IGNORANCE. GREGORY THE GREAT: It is evident that those who are alive know and feel what is done to them, but the dead feel nothing. People would be dead in going down to hell if they did evil out of ignorance; but if they have knowledge of evil and yet commit it, they go down alive—wretched and conscious—to the hell of iniquity. PASTORAL CARE 3.31.[4]

---

[2]FC 9:412. [3]FC 14:131. [4]ACW 11:210

16:36-50 PUNISHMENT OF KORAH

[39]*So Eleazar the priest took the bronze censers, which those who were burned had offered; and they were hammered out as a covering for the altar,* [40]*to be a reminder to the people of Israel, so that no one who is not a priest, who is not of the decendants of Aaron, should draw near to burn incense before the LORD, lest he become as Korah and as his company—as the LORD said to Eleazar through Moses.*

[41]*But on the morrow all the congregation of the people of Israel murmured against Moses and against Aaron, saying, "You have killed the people of the LORD." . . .* [46]*And Moses said to Aaron, "Take your censer, and put fire therein from off the altar, and lay incense on it, and carry it quickly to the congregation, and make atonement for them; for wrath has gone forth from the LORD, the plague has begun."* [47]*So Aaron took it as Moses said, and ran into the midst of the assembly; and behold, the plague had already begun among the people; and he put on the incense, and made atonement for the people.*

OVERVIEW: The censers represented the Scriptures, which heretics misinterpret (CAESARIUS OF ARLES). Severe as the punishment of the rebels was, God spared most of the people (SALVIAN).

Aaron was a true priest and offered himself for the good of the people (AMBROSE). The true priest, Jesus Christ, offered his own flesh to reverse the course of death (CAESARIUS OF ARLES).

16:39 Bronze Censers as a Covering for the Altar

HERETICS MISINTERPRET SCRIPTURE. CAESARIUS OF ARLES: When the divine lesson was read just now, dearly beloved, we heard that our Lord told Moses to forge the censers in which those haughty, rebellious men had offered incense, beat them flat and fasten them to the altar as a sign of the rebellious and proud. "Because the sinners have consecrated the censers at the cost of their lives," said the Lord, "have them hammered into plates to cover the altar, because in being presented before the Lord they have become sacred." By this figure it seems to have been shown that those censers which Scripture calls brazen represent the sacred writings. Heretics put strange fire in these writings, that is, they introduce a perverse meaning and a sense that is foreign to God and contrary to the truth, thus offering to the Lord an incense that is not sweet but abominable. If we bring these brazen censers, that is, words of the heretics, to the altar of God where there is divine fire, the true preaching of the faith, the same truth will shine all the better in comparison with what is false. SERMON 110.1.[1]

16:41 The People Murmured Against Moses

GOD'S JUSTICE AND MERCY. SALVIAN THE PRESBYTER: When their crimes were so great, heavenly solicitude was of no avail. As often as they were corrected, so often amendment did not follow. As we are not corrected, even though soundly scourged, so they, though constantly struck down, did not mend their ways. What is written? "The following day all the multitude of the children of Israel murmured against Moses and Aaron, saying 'You have killed the people of the Lord.'" What followed? Fourteen thousand and seven hundred men were struck down and consumed by divine fire.

Since the multitude all had sinned, why were not all punished, especially since, as I have said, none escaped from Korah's mutiny? Why did God wish the whole assembly of sinners to be killed on the former occasion but only a portion at the latter time? It is because the Lord is filled with both justice and mercy and in his indulgence he gives way to his love, and in his will to teach a lesson he gives way to his severity. THE GOVERNANCE OF GOD 1.12.57-58.[2]

16:47 The Plague Among the People

AARON OFFERED HIMSELF. AMBROSE: Clearly the man [Aaron], who is proposed as a leader to all, is worthy. For when fateful death crept into the midst of the people because of the insolent, he threw himself between the "living and the dead" to restrain death, lest many should perish. Truly the man is priestly in mind and heart who throws himself with pious love before the flock of the Lord like a good shepherd. In this way he broke the sting of death.[3] He held off the attack; he put an end to the dying. Piety assisted merit, since he offered himself for those who resisted. LETTER 14 EXTRA COLL. (63).51.[4]

CHRIST THE TRUE PRIEST. CAESARIUS OF ARLES: Then Moses encouraged the high priest to offer incense in the camp and to pray for the people: "For the people have already begun to be destroyed." Moses saw in spirit what was happening, and therefore Aaron departed to offer incense for the people. He stood between the living and the dead, and the Lord's fury was alleviated. If you know the course of history and have been able to perceive with your eyes, so to speak, the priest standing in the middle between the living and the dead, rise now to the loftier heights of these words. See how the true priest, Jesus Christ, took the censer of human flesh, put fire on the altar which doubtless is that splendid soul with which he was born in the flesh, further

---

[1]FC 47:144. [2]FC 3:53. [3]1 Cor 15:55. [4]CSEL 82 3:261-62.

added incense which is his pure spirit, stood between the living and the dead and did not allow death to proceed any farther.

[5]FC 47:145-46.

17:1-11 AARON'S STAFF

[2]*"Speak to the people of Israel, and get from them rods, one for each fathers' house, from all their leaders according to their fathers' houses, twelve rods. Write each man's name upon his rod, [3]and write Aaron's name upon the rod of Levi. For there shall be one rod for the head of each fathers' house. [4]Then you shall deposit them in the tent of meeting before the testimony, where I meet with you. [5]And the rod of the man whom I choose shall sprout."* . . .

[8]*And on the morrow Moses went into the tent of the testimony; and behold, the rod of Aaron for the house of Levi had sprouted and put forth buds, and produced blossoms, and it bore ripe almonds.*

OVERVIEW: Some in the community revolted against Aaron. God allowed Aaron's staff to blossom and bear fruit as a way to teach the people (CHRYSOSTOM). The priest or prophet promotes what is truly beneficial rather than what is merely enjoyable. Election to the priesthood is a work of grace, even in the case of Christ. The preaching of the patriarchs and apostles flourished in the hearts of all (AMBROSE). Almonds comprise three parts: the bitter outer covering, the hard shell and the nourishment within. Such too is the knowledge of the Scriptures (CAESARIUS OF ARLES).

17:2 Rods from Each House

AARON'S STAFF WAS A SIGN OF ELECTION. CHRYSOSTOM: We can also learn from other sources how awesome was the dignity of the priesthood. Indeed, there was a day when some wicked and evil men revolted against Aaron, quarreled with him over his position in the community and tried to drive him from his leadership. Moses, the mildest of men,[1] wanted to persuade them by the facts themselves that he had not brought Aaron to the leadership because he was a brother, relative or member of his family but that it was in obedience to God's decree that he had entrusted the priesthood to him. So he ordered each tribe to bring a staff, and Aaron was instructed to do the same.

When each tribe had brought a staff, Moses took all of them and put them inside the meeting tent. Once he had put them there, he gave orders that they await the decision of God which would come to them through those staves. Then all the other staves kept their same appearance, but a single one—Aaron's—blossomed and put forth leaves and fruit. So the Lord of nature used leaves instead of letters to teach them that he had again elected Aaron. DISCOURSES AGAINST JUDAIZING CHRISTIANS 6.1-2.[2]

17:8 Aaron's Rod Sprouted

[1]Num 12:3. [2]FC 68:167-68.

THE ROD STANDS FOR AUTHORITY. AMBROSE: In the book of the prophet Scripture says, "Take up for yourself a rod from a nut tree."[3] Consider the reason why the Lord said this to the prophet. For indeed, what was written is not inconsequential, since also in the Pentateuch we read that the priest Aaron's staff, cut from a nut tree, blossomed when it had been put away for some time. Now it seems to mean that prophetic or priestly authority ought to be direct, so that it urges not so much what is enjoyable as what is beneficial. LETTER 1 EXTRA COLL. (41).2.[4]

THE PRIEST MUST BE CALLED. AMBROSE: For that reason, too, [God] himself chose Aaron as priest, in order that not human cupidity but the grace of God would be the preponderant force in choosing the priest. It would not be a voluntary offering or one's own assumption but a heavenly vocation. The one who can suffer on behalf of sinners may offer gifts on behalf of sins, because "even he himself," Scripture says, "bears infirmity."[5] No one should assume the honor for himself but be called by God, just as Aaron was. In this way even Christ did not claim the priesthood but received it. LETTER 14 EXTRA COLL. (63).48.[6]

THE PATRIARCHS AND PAUL. AMBROSE: Paul came to preach the cross of the Lord, an oak that is always verdant. And almonds appear, which are rather hard in shell but more tender in meat—it was right that Aaron's priestly rod was of the almond tree, and Jeremiah's staff as well[7]—and double money too.[8] Who would doubt that these gifts were useful? For the life of the patriarch and the preaching of the apostle are always verdant in the heart of each man, and the speech of the saints shines brightly with the splendor of the precepts of salvation, like silver tried by the fire.[9] And it is with reason that they carry double money, for in them there is prefigured the coming of Paul, who presented presbyters who labor in the word and in the teaching with a double honor.[10] JOSEPH 9.46.[11]

THE ALMOND INTERPRETED. CAESARIUS OF ARLES: There is only one true high priest, as Scripture says, of whom the high priest Aaron presented a figure. For this reason his rod blossomed. Just as Aaron's rod sprouted among the Jewish people, so the cross of Christ flowered among the Gentiles. However, since Christ is the true high priest, as we have often said, he is the only one whose rod of the cross not only sprouted but also blossomed and produced the fruit of all believers.

What is the fruit which it bore? "Ripe almonds." Almonds are nuts, brethren. This fruit is bitter indeed in its first covering, is protected and defended by the second, but in the third part [it] feeds and nourishes whoever eats it. Such then is knowledge of the law and the prophets in Christ's church. The first appearance of the letter is quite bitter, because it commands circumcision of the flesh, enjoins sacrifices and ordains other things which are designated as the killing letter. Throw away all these things as the bitter shell of the nut. In the second place, you will come to the protective covering, in which is indicated moral doctrine or the idea of self-restraint. This is necessary for the protection of what is kept inside but doubtless must sometimes be broken and destroyed. For example, fasting and chastisement of the body are no doubt necessary as long as we are in this corruptible body which is subject to suffering. However, when it has been destroyed and dissolved at the approach of death, it will become incorruptible at the time of the resurrection when it has been restored from corruption, spiritual after being natural, and without any flattery to the body will dominate, with no difficult suffering or propitiatory fasting but by its own nature. Thus then that rather hard covering of the nut seems to be a means of self-control at present that will not be sought later. Third, you will find hidden as in the nut the

---

[3]Jer 1:11. [4]CSEL 82 3:145-46. [5]Heb 5:2. [6]CSEL 82 3:260. [7]Jer 1:11. [8]Gen 43:12, 15. [9]Ps 12:6. [10]1 Tim 5:17. [11]FC 65:220.

secret meaning of the mysteries of God's wisdom and knowledge. With these, holy souls are nourished and fed not only in the present life but also in the future one. This is that priestly fruit concerning which it is promised to those

"who hunger and thirst for justice, for they shall be satisfied."[12] SERMON III.1-2.[13]

[12]Mt 5:6. [13]FC 47:147-48.

[17:12—18:7 CHARGE OF THE SACRED THINGS]

18:8-20 THE PRIESTS' SHARE OF THE SACRIFICES

[1]*So the LORD said to Aaron, . . .* [15]*"Everything that opens the womb of all flesh, whether man or beast, which they offer to the LORD, shall be yours." . . .* [20]*And the LORD said to Aaron, "You shall have no inheritance in their land, neither shall you have any portion among them; I am your portion and your inheritance among the people of Israel."*

OVERVIEW: There is a distinction between "firstborn child" and "only child" (JEROME). The number of tribes, twelve, was maintained after Levi was excepted by naming two tribes for Joseph's sons (AUGUSTINE). The priests of God have no land, for God is their portion (ORIGEN).

18:15 Redeeming the Firstborn

THE DEFINITION OF FIRSTBORN. JEROME: Every only child is a firstborn child; but not every firstborn is an only child. A firstborn child is not only one after whom other children are also born but also one before whom no other child is born. "All that opens the womb," says the Lord to Aaron, "of all flesh that are offered to the Lord, of men and beasts, shall belong to you; only the firstborn of men shall be redeemed with a price and the firstborn of beasts that are unclean."[1] The Word of God defined what was meant by a "firstborn." "All," it says, "that opens

the womb." Otherwise, if no child is a firstborn child but only one who subsequently has brothers, the firstborn are not due the priests until others are also born, lest perchance a child be an only child and not the firstborn child, in the event that no other child shall be born subsequently. AGAINST HELVIDIUS 10.[2]

18:20 Inheritance in the Land

WHETHER THE LEVITES WERE NUMBERED. AUGUSTINE: For all this people had twelve tribes after the number of the twelve sons of Jacob. What we call tribes are as it were distinct houses and congregations of people. This people, I say, had twelve tribes, out of which twelve tribes one tribe was Judah, out of which came the kings. There was another tribe, Levi, out of which came the priests. To the priests serving

[1]Ex 34:19-20. [2]FC 53:23-24.

the temple no land was allotted. So it was necessary that among twelve tribes all the land of promise should be shared. Having separated one tribe of higher dignity, the tribe of Levi, which was of the priests, there would have remained eleven, unless by the adoption of the two sons of Joseph the number twelve were completed. EXPLANATION OF THE PSALMS 76.1.[3]

THE ALLOTMENT OF PRIESTS IS GOD. ORIGEN: Indeed, do you wish to know what the difference is between the priests of God and the priests of Pharaoh? Pharaoh grants lands to his priests. The Lord, on the other hand, does not grant his priests a portion in the land but says to them, "I am your portion." You therefore who read these words, observe all the priests of the Lord and notice what difference there is between the priests, lest perhaps they who have a portion in the land and have time for earthly cares and pursuits may appear not so much to be priests of the Lord as priests of Pharaoh. For it is Pharaoh who wishes his priests to have possessions of lands and to work at the cultivation of the soil not of the soul, to give attention to the fields and not to the law. But let us hear what Christ our Lord admonishes his priests: "He who has not renounced all he possesses," he says, "cannot be my disciple."[4] HOMILIES ON GENESIS 16.5.[5]

---

[3]NPNF 1 8:355. [4]Lk 14:33. [5]FC 71:221-22.

[18:21-24 TITHES DUE THE LEVITES]

[18:25-32 TITHES PAID BY THE LEVITES]

19:1-10 ASHES OF THE RED HEIFER

[24]"For the tithe of the people of Israel, which they present as an offering to the LORD, I have given to the Levites for an inheritance; therefore I have said of them that they shall have no inheritance among the people of Israel."

[25]And the LORD said to Moses, [26]"Moreover you shall say to the Levites, 'When you take from the people of Israel the tithe which I have given you from them for your inheritance, then you shall present an offering from it to the LORD, a tithe of the tithe.'"...

19 [1]Now the LORD said to Moses and to Aaron, [2]"This is the statute of the law which the LORD has commanded: Tell the people of Israel to bring you a red heifer without defect. . . . [8]He who burns the heifer shall wash his clothes in water and bathe his body in water, and shall be unclean until evening. [9]And a man who is clean shall gather up the ashes of the heifer, and deposit them outside the camp in a clean place; and they shall be kept for the congregation of the *people of Israel for the water for impurity, for the removal of sin.* [10]*And he who gathers the ashes of the heifer shall wash his clothes, and be unclean until evening."*

OVERVIEW: The whole burnt offering of the red heifer prefigures the Lord's passion (BEDE). In baptism the water is sprinkled, and the faith of the minister and the recipient must be unblemished (CYPRIAN).

19:2 A Red Heifer Without Defect

THE ASHES OF THE HEIFER PREFIGURE THE LORD'S PASSION. BEDE: Now [Moses] declares that the ashes of the victims (which ought to be taken as a great mystery) are "the sprinkled ashes of a red heifer," which (as the apostle also bears witness) sanctified "those who have been defiled, so that [their] flesh is made clean."[1] He also understands that the sacrament of the Lord's passion, which saves us by purifying us forever, is prefigured in these ashes. Thus the burning of a red heifer designates the actual time and event of Christ's passion, and the burnt ashes which were kept for the cleansing of those who were unclean suggest the mystery of that same passion which has already been completed, by which we are daily purged from our sins. ON THE TABERNACLE 2.11.[2]

19:9 The Water for Impurity

IF FAITH IS PURE IN BAPTISM. CYPRIAN: And again: "The water of sprinkling is a purification." From this it appears that the sprinkling with water is also equal to the life-giving bath. And when these things are done in the church, when the faith of both the recipient and of the minister is unblemished, everything is present and can be accomplished and consummated through the majesty of the Lord and the truth of faith. LETTER 69.12.[3]

---

[1]Heb 9:13. [2]TTH 18:87. [3]FC 51:254.

19:11-22 USE OF THE ASHES

[14]*"This is the law when a man dies in a tent: every one who comes into the tent, and every one who is in the tent, shall be unclean seven days.* [15]*And every open vessel, which has no cover fastened upon it, is unclean."*

OVERVIEW: The sealed cover of a vessel is analogous to self-discipline in a person (PATERIUS).

19:15 An Open Vessel Is Unclean

THE DISCIPLINE OF SILENCE. PATERIUS: The cover of a vessel, or a seal, is the control of discipline. Discipline keeps a man from being overwhelmed, as if he were an unclean or polluted vessel that is rejected. For a vessel without a cover or a seal is spoiled, like as in the case of one who devotes himself to ostentation and is not covered by any veil of silence. EXPOSITION OF THE OLD AND NEW TESTAMENT, NUMBERS 15.[1]

---

[1]PL 79:770, citing Gregory the Great *Moral Interpretation of Job* 23.10.17.

20:1 DEATH OF MIRIAM

¹And the people of Israel, the whole congregation, came into the wilderness of Zin in the first month, and the people stayed in Kadesh; and Miriam died there, and was buried there.

OVERVIEW: Wisdom can bring healing waters even to the hearts of obdurate sinners (CASSIODORUS).

20:1 The People Stayed in Kadesh

THE UNFAITHFUL GATHER IN THE DESERT.
CASSIODORUS: Next comes "And the Lord shall shake the desert of Kadesh." This still refers to the spirit of piety. The account in Numbers carefully explains this reference when it tells how the people of Israel came to Kadesh and were suffering from excessive thirst because of the aridity of that place. Moses struck a rock at the Lord's command and suddenly provided an abundance of water for them. In a remarkable way the earth, which lay foul with unwatered dustiness, was irrigated. By this comparison the prophet says that the most obdurate hearts of sinners can be liquefied into waters of wisdom. The example of Kadesh must be reenacted in human hearts. The term *desert* is often used of places where unfaithful people are known to gather, as the Gospel says: "The voice of one crying in the desert."[1] John could not have preached in the desert where none could hear. Rather, "desert" is used to describe those who had not as yet apprehended the gifts of faith. EXPOSITION OF THE PSALMS 28.8.[2]

---

[1]Mk 1:3; Is 40:3. [2]ACW 51:281.

20:2-13 WATER FAMINE AT KADESH, SIN OF MOSES AND AARON

²Now there was no water for the congregation; and they assembled themselves together against Moses and against Aaron. . . .
¹⁰And Moses and Aaron gathered the assembly together before the rock, and he said to them, "Hear now, you rebels; shall we bring forth water for you out of this rock?" ¹¹And Moses lifted up his hand and struck the rock with his rod twice; and water came forth abundantly, and the congregation drank, and their cattle. ¹²And the LORD said to Moses and Aaron, "Because you did not believe in me, to sanctify me in the eyes of the people of Israel, therefore you shall not bring this assembly into the land which I have given them."

OVERVIEW: Moses sinned in a small way and was not pardoned (BASIL). The punishment of Moses and Aaron remains a lesson to us (JEROME). The rock was Christ, and the sign of the cross brought forth water from it (AUGUSTINE). When the rock was struck twice, the cross was signified (CAESARIUS OF ARLES). In the journey of this life, we thirst for Christ (AUGUSTINE).

20:10 Water Out of This Rock?

AN EXAMPLE OF GOD'S SEVERITY. BASIL THE GREAT: The people were murmuring because there was no water. Moses merely had said to his people, "Can we bring you forth water out of this rock?" Thus he wavered only slightly, yet for this alone he immediately received the threat that he should not enter into the land of promise, which was at that time the chief of all the promises made to the Jews. When I behold this man asking and not obtaining pardon, when I see him not deemed worthy of forgiveness because of those few words, even in consideration of so many righteous deeds, truly I discern, in the words of the apostle, "the severity of God."[1] I am fully persuaded that these words are true: "If the just man shall scarcely be saved, where shall the ungodly and the sinner appear?"[2] PREFACE ON THE JUDGMENT OF GOD.[3]

20:11 Moses Struck the Rock

AARON AND MOSES WERE PUNISHED. JEROME: Priests also must take care lest they be insincere, lest they doubt the power of God. If Aaron and Moses (who seemed to waver at the waters of contradiction) did not deserve to enter the Promised Land, does it not stand to reason that we, bent under the burden of sin, shall be far less able to cross the river Jordan and reach Gilgal, the place of circumcision,[4] if we shall cause one of these little ones to sin?[5] HOMILY 90.[6]

THE ROCK WAS CHRIST. AUGUSTINE: The rock is Christ in a sign, the true Christ in the Word and in the flesh. And how did they drink? The rock was struck twice with a rod. The double striking prefigures the two pieces of wood on the cross. TRACTATE ON THE GOSPEL OF JOHN 26.12.2.[7]

THE TWO PLANKS OF THE CROSS. CAESARIUS OF ARLES: "Therefore Moses struck the rock twice with his staff." What does this mean, brethren? I do not think it is without mystery. What does it mean that the rock was not struck once but twice with the staff? The rock was struck a second time because two trees were lifted up for the gibbet of the cross: the one stretched out Christ's sacred hands, the other spread out his sinless body from head to foot. SERMON 103.3.[8]

OUR THIRST QUENCHED BY CHRIST. AUGUSTINE: We recognize that we are taking a trip in a wasteland. If we recognize ourselves in a wasteland, we are in a wasteland. What does it mean, in a wasteland? In a desert. Why in a desert? Because in this world, one thirsts on a waterless road. But let us thirst that we may be filled. For "blessed are they who hunger and thirst for justice; for they shall have their fill."[9] And our thirst is filled from a rock in the wasteland. For "the rock was Christ."[10] And it was struck with a rod that water might flow. But that it might flow, it was struck twice; for there are the two pieces of wood on the cross. TRACTATE ON THE GOSPEL OF JOHN 28.9.4.[11]

---

[1]Rom 11:22. [2]1 Pet 4:18. [3]FC 9:44-45*. [4]Deut 11:30. [5]Lk 17:2. [6]FC 57:235. [7]FC 79:270. [8]FC 47:110. [9]Mt 5:6. [10]1 Cor 10:4. [11]FC 88:11-12.

20:14-21 EDOM'S REFUSAL

[14]Moses sent messengers from Kadesh to the king of Edom, . . . [17]"Now let us pass through your land." . . . [20]But he said, "You shall not pass through."

OVERVIEW: Both vice and ignorance can make us turn aside from the king's highway (GREGORY OF NAZIANZUS).

20:17 Going Along the King's Highway

THE SHEPHERD MUST WALK THE STRAIGHT PATH. GREGORY OF NAZIANZUS: So in the case of one of us, if he leans to either side, whether from vice or ignorance, no slight danger of a fall into sin from vice or ignorance, no slight danger of a fall into sin is incurred, both for himself and those who are led by him. But we must really walk in the king's highway and take care not to turn aside from it either to the right hand or to the left, as the Proverbs say.[1] For such is the case with our passions, and such in this matter is the straight path of the good shepherd, if he is to know properly the souls of his flock, and to guide them according to the methods of a pastoral care which is right and just and be worthy of our true Shepherd. ORATION 2 (IN DEFENSE OF HIS FLIGHT TO PONTUS) 34.[2]

---

[1]Prov 4:27. [2]NPNF 2 7:212.

20:22-29 DEATH OF AARON

[25]"Take Aaron and Eleazar his son, and bring them up to Mount Hor; [26]and strip Aaron of his garments, and put them upon Eleazar his son; and Aaron shall be gathered to his people, and shall die there."

OVERVIEW: Moses alone consecrated Eleazar, son of Aaron (AMBROSE).

20:26 Strip Aaron of His Garments

ELEAZAR IS CONSECRATED PRIEST. AMBROSE: What else does it mean that after the death of Aaron God did not command the entire people but only Moses, who is among the priests of the Lord, to clothe with the vestments of Aaron the priest his son, Eleazar, unless we understand that a priest should consecrate a priest? He himself should vest him, that is, with priestly virtues. And then, if he sees that he lacks none of the priestly vestments and that everything is appropriately in order, he admits him to the holy altars. LETTER 14 EXTRA COLL. (63).58.[1]

---

[1]CSEL 82 3:265.

21:1-9 VICTORY OVER ARAD; THE BRONZE SERPENT

⁵And the people spoke against God and against Moses, "Why have you brought us up out of Egypt to die in the wilderness? For there is no food and no water, and we loathe this worthless food." ⁶Then the LORD sent fiery serpents among the people, and they bit the people, so that many people of Israel died. . . . So Moses prayed for the people. ⁸And the LORD said to Moses, "Make a fiery serpent, and set it on a pole; and every one who is bitten, when he sees it, shall live." ⁹So Moses made a bronze serpent, and set it on a pole; and if a serpent bit any man, he would look at the bronze serpent and live.

OVERVIEW: The bronze serpent looked like the fiery serpents, but it did not wound, analogous to the human flesh that Christ took on in overcoming sin (BEDE). The power of the serpent of Egypt was broken on the cross (JUSTIN MARTYR). Serpents can both kill and heal (EPHREM). When one rightly beholds Christ, who died, one is delivered from death (AUGUSTINE). There is a great contrast between the bronze serpent and the crucified Christ (GREGORY OF NAZIANZUS).

21:6 The Lord Sent Fiery Serpents

SERPENTS IN THE SCRIPTURES. BEDE: The wounds caused by the fiery serpent are the poisonous enticements of the vices, which afflict the soul and bring about its spiritual death. The people were murmuring against the Lord. They were stricken by the serpents' bites. This provides an excellent instance of how one may recognize from the results of an external scourge what a great calamity a person might suffer inwardly by murmuring. In the raising up of the bronze serpent (when those who were stricken beheld it, they were cured) is prefigured our Redeemer's suffering on the cross, for only by faith in him is the kingdom of death and sin overcome. The sins which drag down soul and body to destruction at the same time are appro-

priately represented by the serpents, not only because they were fiery and poisonous [and] artful at bringing about death but also because our first parents were led into sin by a serpent,[1] and from being immortal they became mortal by sinning. The Lord is aptly made known by the bronze serpent, since he came in the likeness of sinful flesh.[2] Just as the bronze serpent had the likeness of a fiery serpent but had absolutely none of the strength of harmful poison in its members—rather by being lifted up it cured those who had been stricken by the [live] serpents—so the Redeemer of the human race did not merely clothe himself in sinful flesh but entered bodily into the likeness of sinful flesh, in order that by suffering death on the cross in [this likeness] he might free those who believed in him from all sin and even from death itself. **HOMILIES ON THE GOSPELS 2.18.**[3]

21:9 Moses Made a Bronze Serpent

CONTRAST BETWEEN TWO SERPENTS. JUSTIN MARTYR: Tell me, did not God, through Moses, forbid the making of an image or likeness of anything in the heavens or on earth? Yet didn't he himself have Moses construct the brazen serpent in the desert? Moses set it up as a sign by

[1]Gen 3:1-7. [2]Rom 8:3. [3]HOG 2:184-85.

which those who had been bitten by the serpents were healed. In doing so, was Moses not free of any sin? By this, as I stated above, God through Moses announced a mystery by which he proclaimed that he would break the power of the serpent, who prompted the sin of Adam. He promises that he would deliver from the bites of the serpent (that is, evil actions, idolatries and other sins) all those who believe in him who was to be put to death by this sign, namely, the cross. DIALOGUE WITH TRYPHO 94.[4]

CHRIST IS THE SPIRITUAL SERPENT. EPHREM THE SYRIAN: The serpent struck Adam in paradise and killed him. [It also struck] Israel in the camp and annihilated them. "Just as Moses lifted up the serpent in the desert, the Son of Man will be lifted up."[5] Just as those who looked with bodily eyes at the sign which Moses fastened on the cross lived bodily, so too those who look with spiritual eyes at the body of the Messiah nailed and suspended on the cross and believe in him will live [spiritually]. Thus it was revealed through this brazen [serpent], which by nature cannot suffer, that he who was to suffer on the cross is one who by nature cannot die. COMMENTARY ON TATIAN'S DIATESSARON 16.15.[6]

DELIVERANCE FROM DEATH. AUGUSTINE: To be made whole of a serpent is a great sacrament.

What is it to be made whole of a serpent by looking upon a serpent? It is to be made whole of death by believing in one dead. And nevertheless Moses feared and fled.[7] What is it that Moses fled from that serpent? What, brethren, save that which we know to have been done in the gospel? Christ died, and the disciples feared and withdrew from that hope wherein they had been.[8] EXPLANATION OF THE PSALMS 74.4.[9]

CONTRAST BETWEEN THE SERPENT AND CHRIST. GREGORY OF NAZIANZUS: That brazen serpent was hung up as a remedy for the biting serpents, not as a type of him that suffered for us but as a contrast. It saved those that looked upon it, not because they believed it to live but because it was killed, and killed with it were the powers that were subject to it, being destroyed as it deserved. And what is the fitting epitaph for it from us? "O death, where is your sting? O grave, where is your victory?"[10] You are overthrown by the cross. You are slain by him who is the giver of life. You are without breath, dead, without motion, even though you keep the form of a serpent lifted up high on a pole. ORATION 45.22.[11]

---

[4]FC 6:297*. [5]Jn 3:14. [6]JSSS 2:250. [7]Ex 4:3. [8]Lk 24:21. [9]NPNF 1 8:344. [10]Hos 13:14; 1 Cor 15:55. [11]NPNF 2 7:431.

[21:10-20 JOURNEY AROUND MOAB]

[21:21-31 VICTORY OVER SIHON]

[21:32-35 VICTORY OVER OG]

22:1-14 BALAAM SUMMONED

⁴*So Balak the son of Zippor, who was king of Moab at that time,* ⁵*sent messengers to Balaam the son of Beor at Pethor, which is near the River, in the land of Amaw to call him, saying, "Behold, a people has come out of Egypt; they cover the face of the earth, and they are dwelling opposite me.* ⁶*Come now, curse this people for me, since they are too mighty for me."* . . .

OVERVIEW: Balaam was a famous and powerful man (CAESARIUS OF ARLES).

22:5 A People Out of Egypt

BALAAM WAS TO CURSE ISRAEL. CAESARIUS OF ARLES: This Balaam was exceedingly famous for his magical art and very powerful with his harmful verses. He did not possess the power or skill of words in blessing but only in cursing, for the demons are invited to curse but not to bless. As he was experienced in such matters, for this reason he was esteemed by all men in the Orient.

Indeed, abundant proofs of it had happened before when he had frequently turned back an armed enemy with his curses. Otherwise the king surely would not have presumed that what could not be accomplished by iron and the sword could be done by words. Therefore Balak was sure of it and had frequently tried it, for he put aside all instruments and aids of war and sent ambassadors to him saying, "A people has come here from Egypt, who now cover the face of the earth and are settling down opposite us." SERMON 113.2.[1]

---

[1] FC 47:156.

22:15-20 SECOND APPEAL TO BALAAM

¹⁵*Once again Balak sent princes, more in number and more honorable than they.* ¹⁶*And they came to Balaam and said to him, "Thus says Balak the son of Zippor: 'Let nothing hinder you from coming to me;* ¹⁷*for I will surely do you great honor, and whatever you say to me I will do; come, curse this people for me.'"*

OVERVIEW: Balaam was tempted by love of money (AMBROSE).

22:17 Great Honor

BALAAM'S AVARICE. AMBROSE: Love of money then is an old and ancient vice, which showed itself even at the declaration of the divine law;

for a law was given to check it.[1] On account of love of money Balak thought Balaam could be tempted by rewards to curse the people of our fathers. Love of money would have won the day too, had not God bidden him hold back from cursing. DUTIES OF THE CLERGY 2.26.130.[2]

---

[1] Ex 20:17. [2] NPNF 2 10:63.

22:21-40 THE TALKING ASS

²¹*So Balaam rose in the morning, and saddled his ass, and went with the princes of Moab.* ²²*But God's anger was kindled because he went; and the angel of the* Lord *took his stand in the way as his adversary. Now he was riding on the ass, and his two servants were with him.* ²³*And the ass saw the angel of the* Lord *standing in the road, with a drawn sword in his hand; and the ass turned aside out of the road, and went into the field; and Balaam struck the ass, to turn her into the road.* ²⁴*Then the angel of the* Lord *stood in a narrow path between the vineyards, with a wall on either side.* ²⁵*And when the ass saw the angel of the* Lord, *she pushed against the wall, and pressed Balaam's foot against the wall; so he struck her again.* ²⁶*Then the angel of the* Lord *went ahead, and stood in a narrow place, where there was no way to turn either to the right or to the left.* ²⁷*When the ass saw the angel of the* Lord, *she lay down under Balaam; and Balaam's anger was kindled, and he struck the ass with his staff.* ²⁸*Then the* Lord *opened the mouth of the ass, and she said to Balaam, "What have I done to you, that you have struck me these three times?"*

Overview: The angel appeared to the ass and not to Balaam. In this way Balaam was humiliated for his greed (Ambrose). When a soul is swollen with pride, the flesh suffers and humiliates it (Gregory the Great). The ass saw the angel of God and even received human speech (Origen).

22:25 The Donkey Saw the Angel

An Angel Is Revealed, but Not to Balaam. Ambrose: What offense does Balaam commit, except that he said one thing and plotted another? For God seeks out a pure vessel, one not corrupted by impurity and squalor. Balaam was tested, therefore, but he was not found acceptable: "For he was full of lies and guile." In short, when he first inquired whether he ought to go to that vain people and was stopped, he made excuses. Later, when more important legates were sent and more copious things were promised, he was enticed by the richer gifts—although he should have renounced them—and decided that there should be another consultation, as though God could be affected either by a

bribe or by gifts. The response was given as though to a greedy man and not as to one seeking the truth, so that he might be mocked rather than informed. He set out, and an angel met him in a narrow place. He revealed himself to the ass. He did not reveal himself to the seer. He revealed himself to the one; he disgraced the other. Nevertheless, in order that he himself might at some point come to recognition, "he opened his eyes." He saw and still did not believe the clear oracle. He who should have believed his own eyes responded obscurely and ambiguously. Letter 28 (50).6-7.[1]

The Flesh Holds Back the Mind. Gregory the Great: The spirit which is carried out of itself to pride is made to remember the condition to which it is subject, owing to the ills of the flesh which it bears. This was rightly indicated though Balaam (if only he had been willing to follow obediently the voice of God!) in that his journey was retarded. For we see Balaam on the way to attain his purpose, but

---

[1]CSEL 82 1:189-90.

the beast under him thwarts his intention. The ass, stopped by a command, perceives an angel not seen by the mind of the man. For commonly the flesh, retarded by affliction, manifests to the mind the God whom the mind itself did not see, though it dominates the flesh, owing to the scourgings it receives. PASTORAL CARE 3.12.[2]

22:28 The Donkey's Mouth Opened

BALAAM'S ASS IS BLESSED. ORIGEN: I marvel at Balaam's ass and heap blessings on it, because it was worthy not only to see the angel of God but even to have its mouth opened and break into human speech. HOMILIES ON THE GOSPEL OF LUKE 14.9.[3]

---

[2]ACW 11:123-24*. [3]FC 94:61.

22:41—23:12 THE FIRST ORACLE

[5]*And the* LORD *put a word in Balaam's mouth, and said, "Return to Balak, and thus you shall speak." . . .*
    [10]*"Who can count the dust of Jacob,*
        or number the fourth part[s] of Israel?
    Let me die the death of the righteous,
        and let my end* be like his!"
[11]*And Balak said to Balaam, "What have you done to me? I took you to curse my enemies, and behold, you have done nothing but bless them."*

s Or dust clouds   *LXX *understands this to be* generations *or* seed

OVERVIEW: Instead of a curse, Balaam uttered a blessing and began to proclaim Christ (TERTULLIAN). Balaam foresaw the mystery of Christ's passion and resurrection (AMBROSE).

23:5 The Lord Gives Words to Balaam

THE SPIRIT MOVED BALAAM. TERTULLIAN: The prophet Balaam, in Numbers, was sent forth by king Balak to curse Israel, with whom he was commencing war. But at the same moment he was filled with the spirit. Instead of the curse which he came to pronounce, he uttered the blessing which the spirit at that very hour inspired him with. This is he who had previously declared to the king's messengers, and then to the king himself, that he could only speak forth that which God should put into his mouth. The novel [heretical] doctrines of the new Christ are such as the Creator's servants initiated long before! AGAINST MARCION 4.28.8.[1]

23:10 Let Me Die the Death of the Righteous

BALAAM FORESAW CHRIST'S RISING. AMBROSE: You have caused me, my brother, not to fear death, and I only would that my life might die with yours! This Balaam wished for as the greatest good for himself, when, inspired by the spirit of prophecy, he said, "Let my soul

---

[1]ANF 3:396.

die in the souls of the righteous, and let my seed be like the seed of them." And in truth he wished this according to the spirit of prophecy, for as he saw the rising of Christ, so also he saw his triumph; he saw his death but saw also in him the everlasting resurrection of humanity and therefore feared not to die as he was to rise again. Let not then my soul die in sin or admit sin into itself, but let it die in the soul of the righteous, that it may receive his righteousness. Then too, he who dies in Christ is made a partaker of his grace in the font. On His Brother Satyrus 2.43.[2]

---

[2]NPNF 2 10:180.

23:13—24:9 THE SECOND AND THIRD ORACLES

[22]"God brings them out of Egypt;
   they have as it were the horns of the wild ox.
[23]For there is no enchantment against Jacob,
   no divination against Israel." . . .
24 [8]"God brings him out of Egypt;
      he has as it were the horns of the wild ox,
   he shall eat up the nations his adversaries,
   and shall break their bones in pieces,
   and pierce them through with his arrows."

Overview: Balaam foresaw the flight of Mary and Joseph with Jesus into Egypt (Eusebius).

24:8 Out of Egypt

Truth Will Shout. Eusebius: The oracle in the previously quoted prophecy,[1] in saying that the Lord would come into Egypt, foretold the journey of our Lord Jesus Christ when he went into Egypt with his parents. Here we have the prophecy of his return from Egypt in its natural order, when he came back with his parents into the land of Israel, in the words "God led him out of Egypt." For our Lord and Savior Jesus, the Christ of God, was the only one of the seed of Israel and of the Jewish race who has rule over many nations, so that it is indisputable that he is the fulfillment of the prophecy which says, literally, "that a man will come from the Jewish race and rule over many nations." If he is not, let him who will suggest some other famous man among the Hebrews who has ruled over many nations. But this he cannot do, for such a man never existed. But with regard to our Savior, truth itself will shout and cry aloud, even if we say nothing. This shows plainly that his divine power has ruled, through the human he took of the seed of Israel according to the flesh, and even now will rule many nations. Proof of the Gospel 8.3.[2]

---

[1]Num 24:3-9. [2]POG 2:156.

24:10-25 THE FOURTH ORACLE

^{15}And he took up his discourse, and said, . . .
^{17}"I see him, but not now;
I behold him, but not nigh:
a star shall come forth out of Jacob,
and a scepter shall rise out of Israel;
it shall crush the forehead^w of Moab,
and break down all the sons of Sheth.
^{18}Edom shall be dispossessed,
Seir also, his enemies, shall be dispossessed,
while Israel does valiantly.
^{19}By Jacob shall dominion be exercised,
and the survivors of cities be destroyed!"
^{20}Then he looked on Amalek, and took up his discourse, and said,
"Amalek was the first of the nations,
but in the end he shall come to destruction."
^{21}And he looked on the Kenite, and took up his discourse, and said,
"Enduring is your dwelling place,
and your nest is set in the rock;
^{22}nevertheless Kain shall be wasted.
How long shall Asshur take you away captive?"

w Heb corners (of the head)

OVERVIEW: Why was it that Balaam spoke more plainly of Christ than almost any other prophet? (JEROME). Balaam's eyes were opened to the sin he had committed (PATERIUS). The magi were Balaam's successors and had a record of his prophecy (EUSEBIUS). Christ was God in flesh and the mediator between God and man (LACTANTIUS). Both Balaam and Caiaphas were inadvertently prophets (CHRYSOSTOM). The magi recalled Balaam's prophecy and followed its lead as far as Jerusalem (LEO THE GREAT). Balaam's prophecy had been preserved in writing in Mesopotamia (CAESARIUS OF ARLES). The seed of Amalek was destined to be destroyed (AMBROSE). The holy person is nourished with Christ's exalted humility and ascends to the heights (PATERIUS).

24:15 The Oracle of Balaam

BALAAM SPOKE PLAINLY OF CHRIST. JEROME: One day we had before us the book of Numbers written by Moses, and [Fabiola] modestly questioned me as to the meaning of the great mass of names there to be found. Why was it, she inquired, that single tribes were differently associated in this passage and in that, how came it to be that the soothsayer Balaam, in prophesying of the future mysteries of Christ, spoke more plainly of him than almost any other prophet? I replied as best I could and tried to satisfy her inquiries. LETTER 77.7.[1]

THE EYES OF THE WICKED. PATERIUS: The unholy man does not know the evil he does unless he begins to be punished for the same evils. For Balaam offered counsel against the Israelites and afterwards saw in his punishment what sin he had previously committed. But the elect, who should not sin, are watchful. Their eyes are open before they fall. The eyes of the wicked man are open only after he falls, because after his sin he sees, in his punishment, that he should have avoided the evil he did. EXPOSITION OF THE OLD AND NEW TESTAMENT, NUMBERS 20.[2]

24:17 A Star from Jacob

BALAAM AND THE MAGI. EUSEBIUS: We are told that Balaam's successors moved by this[3] (for the prediction was preserved most likely among them)[4] when they noticed in the heavens a strange star besides the usual ones, fixed above the head, so to say, and vertically above Judea, hastened to arrive at Palestine, to inquire about the king announced by the star's appearance. PROOF OF THE GOSPEL 9.1.[5]

CHRIST THE MEDIATOR. LACTANTIUS: Moses himself [wrote] in the book of Numbers: "There shall come a star out of Jacob, and a man shall arise out of Israel." For this cause, therefore, being God, he took upon him flesh, that, becoming a mediator between God and man, having overcome death, he might by his guidance lead man to God. EPITOME OF THE DIVINE INSTITUTES 44.[6]

BALAAM PROPHESIED THE SAVIOR'S COMING. CHRYSOSTOM: Listen to the Evangelist's words about Caiaphas, the high priest of the Jews: "He did not give this as a personal opinion, but in his capacity of high priest that year he prophesied that Jesus was destined to die, not for the person

alone but to bring together into one also the nations that had been scattered."[7] You will find something like it occurring again in the story of Balaam also: When urged to curse the people, he not merely did not curse them but even prophesied great and wonderful things, not merely about the people but also about the coming of the Savior. HOMILIES ON GENESIS 21.16.[8]

THE THREE WISE MEN FOLLOW THE STAR. LEO THE GREAT: Although it was a gift of divine favor that the birth of the Savior should become recognizable to the nations, nevertheless, to understand the wonder of the sign, the wise men were also able to be reminded through the ancient pronouncements of Balaam, for they knew that it had at one time been spread abroad in a famous and memorable prediction: "A star will appear out of Jacob, and a man will rise up from Israel. He will rule over the nations." So the three men, stirred by God through the shining of this unusual star, follow the course of its gleaming light ahead of them, thinking that they would find the indicated child in the royal city of Jerusalem.

When this conjecture had failed them, however, they learned from scribes and teachers of the Jews what the sacred Scriptures had told about the birth of Christ. Encouraged by the double evidence, they sought him out with an even more ardent faith, the one to whom both the brightness of the star and the authority of prophets pointed. SERMON 34.2.[9]

THE MAGI HAD COPIES OF BALAAM'S PROPHECIES. CAESARIUS OF ARLES: If God's prophecies were inserted in the sacred books by Moses, how much more so were they copied by men who then lived in Mesopotamia, for they considered Balaam splendid and certainly were disci-

---

[1]NPNF 2 6:161. [2]PL 79:772, citing Gregory the Great *Moral Interpretation of Job* 15.51.58. [3]That is, the star that appeared at the birth of Jesus. [4]That is, the Gentiles. [5]POG 2:150-51. [6]ANF 7:239-40. [7]Jn 11:51-52. [8]FC 82:62. [9]FC 93:144-45.

ples of his art! After his time the profession and instruction of the seers is said to have flourished in parts of the Orient. Possessing copies of everything which Balaam prophesied, they even have it written: "A star shall advance from Jacob, and a man shall rise from Israel." The magi kept these writings more among themselves, and so when Jesus was born they recognized the star and understood that the prophecy was fulfilled more than did the people of Israel who disdained to hear the words of the holy prophets. Therefore, only from the writings which Balaam had left, they learned that the time was approaching, came and immediately sought to adore him. Moreover, in order to show their great faith, they honored the little boy as a king. SERMON 113.2.[10]

24:20 Amalek the First of the Nations

AMALEK MEANS "KING OF THE WICKED." AMBROSE: Scripture also says in the book called Numbers: "Amalek, the beginning of nations, whose seed will be destroyed." And of course Amalek is not the first of all nations. Amalek in fact is interpreted to mean the king of the wicked, and by the wicked it is intended to mean the Gentiles. There is no reason why we should not accept him as one whose seed shall perish. His seed are the wicked and the unfaithful, to whom the Lord says, "You are the voice of your father the devil."[11] SIX DAYS OF CREATION 1.4.14.[12]

24:21 He Looked on the Kenite

THE HOLY MAN HAS HIS NEST IN THE CLIFFS. PATERIUS: Kenite means "possession." And who are those who possess present things but the ones who are skilled in the study of secular wisdom? They are those who, by their study, truly build themselves a sturdy dwelling, if they make themselves into little children with humility and are nourished by Christ's grandeur. They sense that they are weak, and [they] place their trust in the exalted humility of the Redeemer they have acknowledged and foster that trust. They do not seek out the heights. They transcend, by the flight of their hearts, everything that is passing. Let us ponder the holy man, how he builds his nest on the rock. For he says, "our conversation is in heaven,"[13] and "who revived and made us be seated in heaven."[14] This holy man has his nest in the cliffs, because he took counsel on high. He does not want to cast his mind down into the depths; he does not want to dwell in the depths through dejected human conversation. Paul was imprisoned when he attested that he was seated with Christ in heaven. He was where he had fixed his mind, already afire, and not where sluggish flesh retained him by force. EXPOSITION OF THE OLD AND NEW TESTAMENT, NUMBERS 22.[15]

---

[10]FC 47:159. [11]Jn 8:44. [12]FC 42:14. [13]Phil 3:20. [14]Eph 2:6. [15]PL 79:772, citing Gregory the Great *Moral Interpretation of Job* 31.47.94-95.

25:1-5 WORSHIP OF BAAL OF PEOR

[1]*While Israel dwelt in Shittim the people began to play the harlot with the daughters of Moab.* [2]*These invited the people to the sacrifices of their gods, and the people ate, and bowed*

down to their gods. ³*So Israel yoked himself to Baal of Peor. And the anger of the LORD was kindled against Israel.*

OVERVIEW: There is a distinction between bowing down to idols and worshiping them; the Israelites did not worship the idols of Moab (ORIGEN).

25:2 Israel Bowed to Other Gods

TO BOW DOWN DIFFERS FROM WORSHIP.
ORIGEN: I might say that those who deny Christianity on oath at the tribunals or before they have been put on trial do not worship but only bow down to idols when they take "God" from the name of the Lord God and apply it to vain and lifeless wood. Thus the people who were defiled with the daughters of Moab bowed down to idols but did not worship them. Indeed, it is written in the text itself, "They invited them to the sacrifices of their idols, and the people ate of their sacrifices, and they bowed down to their idols, and performed the rites to Baal Peor." Observe that it does not say "and they worshiped their idols"; for it was not possible after such great signs and wonders in one moment of time to be persuaded by the women with whom they committed fornication to consider the idols gods. EXHORTATION TO MARTYRDOM 6.[1]

[1]OEM 45.

25:6-15 ZEAL OF PHINEHAS

⁶*And behold, one of the people of Israel came and brought a Midianite woman to his family, in the sight of Moses and in the sight of the whole congregation of the people of Israel, while they were weeping at the door of the tent of meeting.* ⁷*When Phinehas the son of Eleazar, son of Aaron the priest, saw it, he rose and left the congregation, and took a spear in his hand* ⁸*and went after the man of Israel into the inner room, and pierced both of them, the man of Israel and the woman, through her body. Thus the plague was stayed from the people of Israel.* ⁹*Nevertheless those that died by the plague were twenty-four thousand.*

¹⁰*And the LORD said to Moses,* ¹¹*"Phinehas the son of Eleazar, son of Aaron the priest, has turned back my wrath from the people of Israel, in that he was jealous with my jealousy among them, so that I did not consume the people of Israel in my jealousy.* ¹²*Therefore say, 'Behold, I give to him my covenant of peace;* ¹³*and it shall be to him, and to his descendants after him, the covenant of a perpetual priesthood, because he was jealous for his God, and made atonement for the people of Israel.'"*

OVERVIEW: Phinehas appeased God's wrath by slaying another, but Christ offered himself (CYRIL OF JERUSALEM). If we die with Christ, sin is dead within us (GREGORY OF NYSSA). Punishment may have good effects, while mercy granted in disobedience to God may merit condemnation (CHRYSOSTOM). The punishment inflicted on the fornicators was terrible (TERTULLIAN). Phinehas killed the two fornicators with one thrust of the spear, and it was imputed to him as righteousness (ORIGEN). Balaam is more rightly viewed as a diviner, not a prophet, because he was not converted to faith (AMBROSE).

25:8 Phinehas Pierced Them

PHINEHAS AND JESUS CONTRASTED. CYRIL OF JERUSALEM: If Phinehas by his zeal in slaying the evildoer appeased the wrath of God, shall not Jesus, who slew no other but "gave himself a ransom for all,"[1] take away God's wrath against humanity? CATECHETICAL LECTURE 13.2.[2]

THE DEATH OF SIN IN US. GREGORY OF NYSSA: Now if we have been conformed to his death, sin henceforth in us is surely a corpse, pierced through by the javelin of baptism, as that fornicator was thrust through by the zealous Phinehas. ON THE BAPTISM OF CHRIST.[3]

PHINEHAS AND SAMUEL CONTRASTED. CHRYSOSTOM: Slaughter has brought about righteousness, and mercy has been a cause of condemnation more than slaughter, because the latter has been according to the mind of God, but the former has been forbidden. It was reckoned to Phinehas for righteousness that he pierced to death the woman who committed fornication, together with the fornicator. But Samuel, that saint of God, although he wept and mourned and entreated for whole nights, could not rescue Saul from the condemnation which God issued against him, because he saved, contrary to the design of God, the king of the alien tribes whom he ought to have slain.[4] LETTER TO THE FALLEN THEODORE 2.3.[5]

25:9 Twenty-four Thousand Died by the Plague

PUNISHMENT FOR FORNICATION. TERTULLIAN: As far as that goes, we too have examples from this same past in favor of our own way of thinking, examples of a judgment on fornication which was not only not remiss but rather immediately executed. It is quite enough, I should think, that so great a number of the chosen people, twenty-four thousand, perished at one stroke after they had fornicated with the daughters of Midian. I prefer, however, for the glory of Christ, to derive ecclesiastical discipline from Christ. ON PURITY 6.6.12-14.[6]

25:10 Phinehas Turned Back God's Wrath

PHINEHAS'S RIGHTEOUS ANGER. ORIGEN: And lest we appear to you to bring these things forth from our own understanding rather than from the authority of the divine Scriptures, go back to the book of Numbers and recall what Phinehas the priest did when he saw a harlot of the Midianite people with an Israelite man clinging in impure embraces in the eyes of all. Filled with the wrath of divine jealousy, he drove a sword, which he had seized, through the breast of both. This work was imputed to him by God for righteousness when the Lord says, "Phinehas appeased my rage, and it shall be imputed to him for righteousness." That earthly food of anger therefore becomes our food when we use it rationally for righteousness. HOMILIES ON GENESIS 1.17.[7]

25:13 The Covenant of a Perpetual Priesthood

BALAAM WAS NOT CONVERTED. AMBROSE: God is neither unjust nor is his judgment changeable. For God laid hold of [Balaam's] mind and the secrets of his heart. For that reason he tested him as a diviner; he did not elect him as a prophet. And certainly he ought to have been converted by the grace of such great oracles

[1]1 Tim 2:6. [2]FC 64:5. [3]NPNF 2 5:524. [4]1 Sam 15:9. [5]NPNF 1 9:113. [6]ACW 28:67. [7]FC 71:70.

and the sublimity of the revelations. But his soul, full of vileness, put forth words, but it did not bring forth faith. He desired to undermine by his counsel what he announced would happen. Since he was not able to give the lie to the oracles, he proposed fraudulent counsels. By these counsels the fickle people of Israel were indeed tested, but they were not overcome. For by the justice of one man, a priest, every plan of that villainous man was undone. It is much more amazing that the multitude of our fathers could be freed through one man than be deceived through one man. LETTER 28 (50).15.[8]

---

[8]CSEL 82 1:193-94.

[25:16-18 VENGEANCE ON THE MIDIANITES]

26:1-51 THE SECOND CENSUS

[16]And the LORD said to Moses, [17]"Harass the Midianites, and smite them; [18]for they have harassed you with their wiles." . . .

26 [1]After the plague the LORD said to Moses and to Eleazar the son of Aaron, the priest, [2]"Take a census of all the congregation of the people of Israel, from twenty years old and upward, by their fathers' houses, all in Israel who are able to go forth to war."

OVERVIEW: A comparison of the first and second census reveals their differences (PROCOPIUS OF GAZA).

26:2 A Census of the Whole Congregation

THE CENSUS OF A NEW PEOPLE. PROCOPIUS OF GAZA: After Scripture has indicated that the people arrived at the border established by God, God again asks for a census of the men suitable for military service. For, since the fathers who had been counted previously had died,[1] their sons are summoned for a census. David attests that the Lord said, "If they shall enter into my rest"[2] and what follows. Their sons were the type of the faithful people who receive Christ, the end of the law.

There is a spiritual stain of blood that is also circumcision, as Paul attests: "For we," he says, "are the circumcision, as many of us as worship God in spirit."[3] And again, "You have been circumcised without the ministry of hands."[4] Joshua is the type of these men, for he circumcises those who came after him. But because that circumcision was not the true one, Scripture says elsewhere, "Cut away the hardness of your hearts."[5]

So Moses counts the sons of the dead but not in the way it had been done previously—that is, first counting the tribes that come from free women and then those born of slave women.[6] He has no reason to distinguish these two sorts. He first enumerates the five sons of Leah,[7] apart

---

[1]See Num 1:1-46; 26:64-65. [2]Ps 95:11; Heb 3:11. [3]Phil 3:3. [4]Col 2:11. [5]Joel 2:13. [6]Procopius follows the LXX, in which the order of the tribes differs between Num 1 and Num 26. In Num 1, the sons of the slaves Zilpah and Bilhah are put after the sons of Leah and Rachel. In Num 26, the slave woman Zilpah's two sons precede Rachel's. [7]Reuben, Simeon, Judah, Issachar and Zebulun; see Num 26:5-27.

---

from the beloved tribe of Levi, since that tribe is destined to have its own place, namely, that of sacred ministry. Then he counts Gad and Asher,[8] sons of the slave girl. Then he counts the three sons of the free woman Rachel, among whom he first counts the sons of Joseph, according to the order of their generation: Manasseh and Ephraim,[9] and then Rachel's last son, Benjamin.[10] To these he adds the sons of the slave girl, Dan[11] and Naphtali.[12] He has before his eyes the union of Israel, who was led by the spirit of servitude, and us, who are called through adoption into the spirit of freedom. Thus the words of Moses, "The nations rejoiced with this people."[13] And the Savior said, "There will be one flock and one shepherd."[14] The numbers of the remaining tribes decreased from the previous census, but the tribe of Levi increased.[15] For the elect people always grows, while the people opposed to them diminishes. CATENA ON THE OCTATEUCH, ON NUMBERS 26:2.[16]

[8]Num 26:15-18, 44-47. [9]Num 26:28-37. [10]Num 26:38-41. [11]Num 26:42-43. [12]Num 26:48-50. [13]Deut 32:43 LXX. [14]Jn 10:16. [15]Num 1:46 reports 603,550 men ready for service; Num 26:51 reports 601,730. [16]PG 87 1:873-74. Procopius drew part of this passage from Apollinarius of Laodicea. See Robert Devreesse, *Les anciens commentateurs Grecs de l'Octateuque et des Rois*, Studi e Testi 201 (Vatican City: Biblioteca Apostolica Vaticana, 1959), p. 146.

26:52-56 ALLOTMENT OF THE LAND

26:57-65 CENSUS OF THE LEVITES

[55]*"The land shall be divided by lot; according to the names of the tribes of their fathers they shall inherit. [56]Their inheritance shall be divided according to lot between the larger and the smaller."*

[57]*These are the Levites as numbered according to their families: . . . [62]And those numbered of them were twenty-three thousand, every male from a month old and upward; for they were not numbered among the people of Israel, because there was no inheritance given to them among the people of Israel.*

OVERVIEW: God uses lotteries as a way to express his will. The young men, who have not sinned, are given the land. The tribe of Levi is set apart (PROCOPIUS OF GAZA).

26:55 The Land Divided by Lot

LOTS AND PROVIDENCE. PROCOPIUS OF GAZA: A lottery takes place to avoid contention and to assure greater certitude and clarity. The source of this rule is the counsel of God. Devout men do not entrust their affairs to blind chance. This is what Paul means when he says, "We have been called to this destiny, predestined according to the mind of him who moves all things and according to the counsel of his will."[1] Our use of lots bespeaks grace because, by God's word, it takes place according to faith. The apostles im-

[1]Eph 1:11-12. [2]Acts 1:24.

ply the same idea when they say, "Lord, knower of hearts, designate the one we should choose from among these two."[2] Thus it is clear that the lot does not happen by chance but by the power of God's will. So what Scripture now says—whatever the lot designates—it says about God's choice by lot, not about chance. In the same way those among the Greeks who said they exercised power did not escape blame.[3]

After the people have been counted, the parts of the holy land are assigned to them at the Jordan. Those who possess their homelands in Israel, as designated by Caleb and Joshua, have been described as free, baptized young men.[4] By sons Scripture means young men and those who have passed puberty.[5] Their souls are ready for war, but their strength is untested; they have never experienced the risks of war. The sons of those who were under the law foreshadow a new people, who are judged worthy to be inscribed in the book of life. They are described one by one according to their virtues, and they inherit the earth, which belongs to the meek[6] (unless perhaps the meek enjoy it in even greater measure). This measure, Scripture says, they will pour into your lap; it will be beautiful, pressed down, shaken and rich.[7] Then, it says, you will increase his portion manyfold, so that each one receives his lot according to the count of the census. Hence it happens that the books handed over to Daniel to be explained were plural in number and their dimensions were described differently.[8] For this reason too, God ordered the peo-

ple counted by tribe and by name, although he commanded that their family relationships should be recorded too. CATENA ON THE OCTATEUCH, ON NUMBERS 26:55.[9]

26:57-65 Census of the Levites

THOSE CHOSEN FOR HOLY ORDERS. PROCOPIUS OF GAZA: These words seem to say something about the blessedness of Christ, by the fact that they decree rewards proper to each virtue, and the greatest rewards go to those who are endowed with sincere hearts. For, Scripture says, they will see God.[10] The sort of men he bids to be chosen for holy orders have an appointed description; apart from that they have no portion in the land. They could also say, "In your hands is my lot and my portion, Lord."[11] So there is no little boy among them; this signifies purity and integrity. The one who counts all of them is Christ, adumbrated in the high priest and lawgiver, who gave no lot to the unfaithful. For Scripture says, "Let them be expunged from the book of the living and not be recorded with the just."[12] CATENA ON THE OCTATEUCH, ON NUMBERS 26:55.[13]

---

[3]Mk 10:42; Mt 20:25. [4]They will be baptized because they will have crossed the Jordan. [5]Num 26:2; those twenty and older were counted. [6]Mt 5:5. [7]Lk 6:38. [8]Dan 7:10; 9:2. [9]PG 871:873-75. [10]Mt 5:8. [11]Ps 16:5. [12]Ps 69:28. [13]PG 871:875-76. Procopius uses Apollinarius of Laodicea here too; see Devreesse, *Les anciens commentateurs* (cited at Num 26:2), 147.

[27:1-4 ZELOPHEHAD'S DAUGHTERS]

[27:5-11 LAWS CONCERNING HEIRESSES]

27:12-23 JOSHUA TO SUCCEED MOSES

[7]*"The daughters of Zelophehad are right; you shall give them possession of an inheritance among their father's brethren and cause the inheritance of their father to pass to them.* [8]*And you shall say to the people of Israel, 'If a man dies, and has no son, then you shall cause his inheritance to pass to his daughter.'"*. . . [12]*The* Lord *said to Moses, "Go up into this mountain of Abarim, and see the land which I have given to the people of Israel.* [13]*And when you have seen it, you also shall be gathered to your people, as your brother Aaron was gathered,* [14]*because you rebelled against my word in the wilderness of Zin during the strife of the congregation, to sanctify me at the waters before their eyes."* (These are the waters of Meribah of Kadesh in the wilderness of Zin.) [15]*Moses said to the* Lord, [16]*"Let the* Lord, *the God of the spirits of all flesh, appoint a man over the congregation,* [17]*who shall go out before them and come in before them, who shall lead them out and bring them in; that the congregation of the* Lord *may not be as sheep which have no shepherd."* [18]*And the* Lord *said to Moses, "Take Joshua the son of Nun, a man in whom is the spirit, and lay your hand upon him."*

Overview: Our sins and the scandal we might give are far more serious than the sin of Aaron and Moses (Jerome). Moses was punished for a sin he had committed thirty-eight years earlier. How fearful is God's judgment! (Gregory the Great).

27:14 Rebellion Against God's Word

The Danger of Scandal. Jerome: If Aaron and Moses (who seemed to waver at the waters of contradiction) did not deserve to enter the Promised Land, does it not stand to reason that we, bent under the burden of sin, shall be far less able to cross the river Jordan and reach Gilgal, the place of circumcision,[1] if we shall cause one of these little ones to sin? Homily 90.[2]

Moses' Fault Recalled. Gregory the Great: But when the land of promise had at length been reached, [Moses] was called into the mountain and heard of the fault which he had committed eight and thirty years before, as I have said, in that he had doubted about drawing water from the rock. And for this reason he was told that he might not enter the land of promise. Herein it is for us to consider how formidable is the judgment of the almighty God, who did so many signs through that servant of his whose fault he still bore in remembrance for so long a time. Letter 28.[3]

---

[1]Deut 11:30-31. [2]FC 57:235. [3]NPNF 2 13:56.

[28:1-8 SACRIFICES MORNING AND EVENING]

[28:9-10 ON THE SABBATH]

[28:11-15 AT THE NEW MOON FEAST]

[28:16-25 AT THE PASSOVER]

[28:26-31 AT PENTECOST]

29:1-6 ON NEW YEAR'S DAY

[1]*The LORD said to Moses,* [2]*"Command the people of Israel, and say to them, 'My offering, my food for my offerings by fire, my pleasing odor, you shall take heed to offer to me in its due season.'* . . .

[9]*"On the sabbath day two male lambs a year old without blemish, and two tenths of an ephah of fine flour for a cereal offering, mixed with oil, and its drink offering:* [10]*this is the burnt offering of every sabbath, besides the continual burnt offering and its drink offering.* . . .

29 [1]*"On the first day of the seventh month you shall have a holy convocation; you shall do no laborious work."*

OVERVIEW: One is to make sacrifices on festal days with due solemnity (AMBROSE). Even though work is banned on the sabbath, prescribed sacrifices are to be made (CHRYSOSTOM). The Day of Atonement, celebrated on the tenth day of the seventh month, is fulfilled in Christ (ORIGEN).

28:2 In Its Due Season

AN ACT OF PERFECT VIRTUE. AMBROSE: This is indeed a full and perfect sacrifice, as the Lord tells us in speaking of gifts and contributions as his: "You will offer to me my oblation in my festal days," sparing nothing and setting nothing aside, but offering a full, complete and perfect sacrifice. By "festal day" is meant the Lord's Day, a time appropriate to acts of perfect virtue. These acts are made perfect if our souls quell the anxieties of this world and the enticements of the flesh in a victorious struggle over hedonism. Thus the soul is free from the world and dedicated to God, departing not even in the slightest way from the path of good intentions and casting aside all distractions, whether of pleasure or of toil. The wise—and no one else—celebrate with due solemnity this festal day. CAIN AND ABEL 2.2.8.[1]

28:9-10 On the Sabbath

[1]FC 42:408.

DO WHAT IS REQUIRED ON THE SABBATH.
CHRYSOSTOM: Because they could not have
borne it[2] if when giving the law for the sabbath
God had said, "Do your good works on the sabbath, but do not the works that are evil," therefore he restrained them from all alike. "You must
do nothing at all," he says, and even so they were
not kept in line. But in the very act of giving the
law of the sabbath he signified, though in
shaded language, that he restricts them from
evil works only, for he says, "You must do no
work, except what shall be done for your life."[3]
And in the temple too all went on each sabbath
with even more diligence and double toil. Thus
even by shadows he was secretly opening them
to the truth. HOMILIES ON THE GOSPEL OF
MATTHEW 39.3.[4]

29:1 The First Day of the Seventh Month

THE FEASTS OF THE SEVENTH MONTH. ORI-
GEN: After these, in the seventh month other
festivals are celebrated. "On the first day of the
month" there is the new moon of trumpets, just
as it says in the psalm, "Play the trumpet at the
beginning of the month."[5] But "on the tenth day
of the seventh month"[6] there is the festival of
atonement. Only "on this day" is the high priest
dressed with all the pontifical garments. Then

he is dressed in "the manifestation and truth."[7]
Then he goes into that inaccessible place where
he can approach only "once a year,"[8] that is, into
"the Holy of Holies." For "once a year" the high
priest, leaving the people behind, enters that
place where "the mercy seat" is, and above "the
mercy seat is the cherubim," where "the ark of
testimony" and "the altar of incense"[9] are, where
no one is permitted to enter except the high
priest alone.[10]

Therefore if I should consider how the true
"high priest," my Lord Jesus Christ,[11] having
indeed been placed in the flesh, was with the
people all year, that year about which he himself
says, "He sent me to proclaim good news to the
poor and to announce the acceptable year of the
Lord and the day of forgiveness,"[12] I perceive
how "once in" this "year" on the day of atonement he enters into "the Holy of Holies."[13] That
is, when with his dispensation fulfilled "he penetrates the heavens"[14] and goes to the Father to
make atonement for the human race and prays
for all those who believe in him. HOMILIES ON
LEVITICUS 9.5.7-8.[15]

---

[2]The judgment on their desecration of the sabbath. [3]Ex 12:16 (v. 17
LXX). [4]NPNF 1 10:257. [5]Ps 81:3. [6]Lev 16:29. [7]Ex 28:30. The
terms are the Greek translation of Urim and Thummim. [8]Ex 30:10.
[9]Ex 25:18-21; 27:1; 29:37. [10]Heb 9:7. [11]Heb 4:14. [12]Is 61:1-2.
[13]Ex 30:10. [14]Heb 4:14. [15]FC 83:186-87.

[29:7-11 ON THE DAY OF ATONEMENT]

[29:12-40 ON THE FEAST OF BOOTHS]

30:1-16 VALIDITY AND ANNULMENT OF VOWS

[7]*"On the tenth day of this seventh month you shall have a holy convocation, and afflict your-selves."* . . .

30 [1]*Moses said to the heads of the tribes of the people of Israel, "This is what the LORD has commanded. [2]When a man vows a vow to the LORD, or swears an oath to bind himself by a pledge, he shall not break his word; he shall do according to all that proceeds out of his mouth."*

OVERVIEW: To break a vow is to lie to God. Jephthah sacrificed his daughter as the result of a vow. He performed an act that was permitted only once. It is not a model because it does not follow the law. The effects of some vows are suspended (PROCOPIUS OF GAZA).

30:2 Fulfilling a Vow

THE IMPORT OF VOWS. PROCOPIUS OF GAZA: If it is a serious matter to lie to another person, how much more to lie to God. When Scripture describes his majesty, it says that God is in heaven above, and you are on the earth below. This passage was written for us to imitate God, who said, "I will not break my covenant."[1] He says this[2] about the life of each man: that is, if one has vowed abstinence from food, or shaving his head, or the offering of a sheep or a calf. Malachi commands that the best offerings should be brought forth when he says, "Cursed is he who has a male animal in his flock and makes a vow and then offers a blemished animal to the Lord."[3]

The daughter of Jephthah[4] preferred to undergo death rather than to render her father's vow unfulfilled and mendacious. She did not know that she was the type of the saving Victim, whom she prefigured in herself.[5] For this reason Jephthah's deed was immune to guilt. It is not a model, because it does not follow the law. The deed was permitted only once, as a sign, for God rejects human sacrifice.

Moreover, what is undertaken by children to the disgrace of their parents does not merit the name of vow, despite those wicked doctors and teachers who tell their parents that "whatever you would have received from me is Corban."[6] For God commands us to honor father and mother in all cases.

A man who infringes on the vow of his new bride, which she made without her father's approval, [does not sin]. The same applies to a married man who does not consent to a vow his wife made.[7] For what is vowed when the woman is subject to a greater power, if it is not carried out, does not make her guilty. But if the woman becomes a widow or is separated from her husband, her vow is binding.[8] This ancient institution of God is confirmed because the woman was made for the sake of the man, and it is just for her to obey him. There is also that verse from Paul, that the woman should revere the man.[9]

Scripture gives a similar explanation for matters concerning affliction of the soul, fasting and other practices, when it says, concerning the month of fasting, "In that month you will afflict your souls."[10] CATENA ON THE OCTATEUCH, ON NUMBERS 30:2.[11]

---

[1]Judg 2:1. [2]That is, Num 30:2. [3]Mal 1:14. [4]See Judg 11:30-39. [5]Christ, who like Jephthah's daughter died willingly. [6]Mk 7:11. [7]Num 30:5, 8. [8]Num 30:9. [9]Eph 5:33. [10]Num 29:7. [11]PG 87 1:879-82.

31:1-12 EXTERMINATION OF THE MIDIANITES

¹The Lord said to Moses, ²"Avenge the people of Israel on the Midianites; afterward you shall be gathered to your people." . . .

⁸They slew the kings of Midian with the rest of their slain, Evi, Rekem, Zur, Hur, and Reba, the five kings of Midian; and they also slew Balaam the son of Beor with the sword.

OVERVIEW: The Midianites were slaughtered because they had led the Israelites into sin (AMBROSE). Balaam attacked the people of Israel not with armed men but with seductive women (PETER CHRYSOLOGUS).

31:1 Avenging Israel on the Midianites

WHY THE MIDIANITES WERE SLAUGHTERED.
AMBROSE: But a deeper vengeance is taken on fiercer foes and on those that are false as well as on those who have done greater wrongs, as was the case with the Midianites. For they had made many of the Jewish people to sin through their women. For this reason the anger of the Lord was poured out upon the people of our fathers. Thus it came about that Moses when victorious allowed none of them to live. DUTIES OF THE CLERGY 1.29.139.[1]

31:8 Balaam Killed

BALAAM TEMPTED THE ISRAELITES. PETER CHRYSOLOGOS: The soothsayer Balaam set up a scandal for the people of Israel when he went to meet their warriors, not with men in armor but with women arrayed in all their finery. He hoped to make the men drop their arms for debauchery, change their triumph into disgrace, bring the avengers of guilt into guilt themselves and—to put it briefly—to profane all their holiness into depravity. As a result of it all, when Moses was meting out punishment, he sentenced Balaam thus: "Kill Balaam the soothsayer, because he set up a stumbling block before the children of Israel." SERMON 27.[2]

---

¹NPNF 2 10:24. ²FC 17:72.

31:13-20 TREATMENT OF CAPTIVES

¹⁵Moses said to them, "Have you let all the women live? ¹⁶Behold, these caused the people of Israel, by the counsel of Balaam, to act treacherously against the Lord in the matter of Peor, and so the plague came among the congregation of the Lord. ¹⁷Now therefore, kill every male among the little ones, and kill every woman who has known man by lying with him. ¹⁸But all the young girls who have not known man by lying with him, keep alive for yourselves."

OVERVIEW: In Hebrew usage, all females are called women, even if they are virgins (AUGUSTINE).

31:18 *Young Girls Who Have Not Known Man*

EVEN VIRGINS ARE CALLED WOMEN IN SCRIPTURE. AUGUSTINE: The same angel, however, said to the Virgin Mary, "Hail, full of grace, the Lord is with you";[1] the one who will be in you is already with you. "Blessed are you among women."[2] Holy Scripture bears witness to the fact that in the proper usage of the Hebrew language all females are habitually called women; in case some of you perhaps may be astonished and scandalized, if you are not used to hearing the Scriptures. There's a place in the Scriptures where the Lord says openly, "Set apart the women who have not known man."[3] In any case, call to mind those origins of ours; when Eve was made from the man's side, what does Scripture say? "He removed a rib from him and built it into a woman."[4] She is already called a woman, taken indeed from the man but not yet united to the man. So now, when you hear from the angel, "Blessed are you among women," take it in such a way, as if it were saying, in our usage, Blessed are you among females. SERMON 291.4.[5]

---

[1]Lk 1:28. [2]Lk 1:42. [3]Num 31:18 LXX. [4]Gen 2:21-22. [5]WSA 3 8:133.

[31:21-24 PURIFICATION AFTER COMBAT]

[31:25-31 DIVISION OF THE BOOTY]

[31:32-47 AMOUNT OF BOOTY]

[31:48-54 GIFTS OF THE OFFICERS]

32:1-5 REQUEST OF GAD AND REUBEN

[25]The LORD said to Moses, [26]"Take the count of the booty that was taken, both of man and of beast, you and Eleazar the priest and the heads of the fathers' houses of the congregation; [27]and divide the booty into two parts, between the warriors who went out to battle and all the congregation. [28]And levy for the LORD a tribute from the men of war who went out to battle." . . .

32

¹*Now the sons of Reuben and the sons of Gad had a very great multitude of cattle; and they saw the land of Jazer and the land of Gilead, and behold, the place was a place for cattle. . . . ⁴"The land which the LORD smote before the congregation of Israel, is a land for cattle; and your servants have cattle." ⁵And they said, "If we have found favor in your sight, let this land be given to your servants for a possession; do not take us across the Jordan."*

OVERVIEW: There are some in the church who defend the church but do not love it. They are like the tribes across the Jordan, who fought for the land but did not live in it (PATERIUS).

32:4 A Land for Cattle

THE DANGERS OF PRIDE. PATERIUS: There are some in the church who despise being little ones. Even where humility should prevail, they hardly cease being grand in their own eyes. You can see them being exalted with honors, enjoying pleasures, being entertained by the sheer number of things. Often they seek nothing except being in command of others. They enjoy being feared by many. They fail to live upright lives yet desire to be known as leading an upright life. They seek out flatterers; they swell up with admiration shown them. Since they are eager for things in the present life, they do not seek the joys to come. When complex business occupies them, it demonstrates that they are absent even from themselves. But if a temptation against faith arises—for in this area they are quite restrained—they defend the faith by words and labors. They defend the heavenly fatherland, but they do not love it. In the books of Moses, the sons of Reuben and Gad and the half tribe of Manasseh exemplify these men well. They possessed great flocks of sheep and herds of cattle. While they were beyond the Jordan, they wanted the pastureland that they saw. They did not wish to have their inheritance in the land of promise and said, "The land that the Lord struck in the sight of the sons of Israel is a rich region, good for pasturing animals; and we, your servants, have great herds. We ask you, if we find favor before you, to give us, your ser-

vants, this land as our possession, and do not make us cross the Jordan."[1] They own many cattle and refuse to cross the Jordan. Those who have many entanglements in this world do not seek a dwelling in the heavenly fatherland. Those entanglements hold them by their appearance. Faith threatens them, lest they grow languid in their enjoyment of leisure. By their example, they keep others from putting up with work and from dedication to patience. Thus God says to them through Moses, "Will your brethren go to battle, and you will sit here? Why do you undermine the hearts of the children of Israel?"[2] Since they blushed at not defending what they believed, they hasten to battle for the same faith that they professed and defend it, not for themselves but for their neighbor. So they say to Moses, "We will build folds for our sheep and stables for our cattle and fortified cities for our little ones; but we will go forth to battle armed and girded before the children of Israel."[3] They go forth as brave men for others; they free the land of promise from their enemies and then leave it and return to feed their flocks across the Jordan.

By analogy many people, although they are believers, are occupied with present cares, as if they were feeding flocks across the Jordan. Contrary to the faith they professed in baptism, they serve perishable things with their whole minds and all their desires. But, as we said, when a temptation against faith arises, they gird on arms to defend it. They cut down the enemies of the faith and conquer them and defend the heritage of the land of promise. That is, they do not love the fruits of faith and fight for it in such a

---

[1]Num 32:4-5. [2]Num 32:7. [3]Num 32:16-17.

way that they leave the spoils of the battle outside the faith. Because they have little ones outside the land, they do not love to dwell in it. So they return to the plains, because they will fall off the high peaks of the mountains as they do from hope for heavenly things. Outside the land of promise they pasture brute animals, because they work to pasture the irrational movements of the soul with empty desires. They do not know how clear the eternal light is, because they are blinded by transitory concerns. And while they take pride in earthly things, they shut the door to heavenly light. EXPOSITION OF THE OLD AND NEW TESTAMENT, NUMBERS 23.[4]

---

[4]PL 79:773-74, citing Gregory the Great *Moral Interpretation of Job* 27.13.24-25.

[32:6-15 MOSES' REBUKE]

[32:16-27 COUNTERPROPOSAL]

[32:28-42 AGREEMENT REACHED; OTHER CONQUESTS]

33:1-4 STAGES ON THE JOURNEY

---

[29]*And Moses said to them, "If the sons of Gad and the sons of Reuben, every man who is armed to battle before the LORD, will pass with you over the Jordan and the land shall be subdued before you, then you shall give them the land of Gilead for a possession;* [30]*but if they will not pass over with you armed, they shall have possessions among you in the land of Canaan."* . . .
33 [1]*These are the stages of the people of Israel, when they went forth out of the land of Egypt by their hosts under the leadership of Moses and Aaron.* [2]*Moses wrote down their starting places, stage by stage, by command of the LORD.*

OVERVIEW: The list of forty-two stopping places is mysterious and hard to interpret (JEROME). The list of stopping places was recorded for our benefit, and we should be able to profit from it. The stopping places help us to understand the long spiritual journey that lies ahead of us. Moses stands for knowledge of the law, Aaron

for the duties of a priest (ORIGEN).

33:1 *These Are the Stages*

THE LIST OF STOPPING PLACES. JEROME: Unrolling the book still further, [Fabiola] came to the passage in which is given the list of all the halting places by which the people after leaving Egypt made its way to the waters of Jordan. And when she asked me the meaning and reason of each of these, I spoke doubtfully about some, dealt with others in a tone of assurance and in several instances simply confessed my ignorance. Hereupon she began to press me harder still, expostulating with me as though it were a thing unallowable that I should be ignorant of what I did not know, yet at the same time affirming her own unworthiness to understand mysteries so deep. LETTER 77.7.[1]

BOTH MOSES AND AARON WERE NEEDED. ORIGEN: The one hand of Moses was not enough for going forth from Egypt, and the hand of Aaron was also needed. Moses stands for knowledge of the law; Aaron, for skill in making sacrifices and immolations to God. It is therefore necessary for us when we come forth from Egypt to have not only the knowledge of the law and of faith but also the fruits of works well pleasing to God. HOMILIES ON NUMBERS 27.6.[2]

33:2 Moses Wrote Down Their Starting Places

THE LIST MUST BENEFIT US. ORIGEN: You have heard that Moses wrote this down by the word of the Lord. Why did the Lord want him to write it down? Was it so that this passage in Scripture about the stages the children of Israel made might benefit us in some way or that it should bring us no benefit? Who would dare to say that what is written "by the Word of God" is of no use and makes no contribution to salvation but is merely a narrative of what happened and was over and done a long time ago, but pertains in no way to us when it is told? HOMILIES ON NUMBERS 27.2.[3]

OUR STARTING PLACES. ORIGEN: He wrote them down, then, "by the word of the Lord" so that when we read them and see how many starting places lie ahead of us on the journey that leads to the kingdom, we may prepare ourselves for this way of life. [Thus,] considering the journey that lies ahead of us, [we] may not allow the time of our life to be ruined by sloth and neglect. HOMILIES ON NUMBERS 27.7.[4]

---

[1]NPNF 2 6:161.　[2]OEM 253-54.　[3]OEM 248.　[4]OEM 254.

33:5-37 FROM EGYPT TO MOUNT HOR

[5]So the people of Israel set out from Rameses, and encamped at Succoth. [6]And they set out from Succoth, and encamped at Etham, which is on the edge of the wilderness. [7]And they set out from Etham, and turned back to Pi-hahiroth, which is east of Baal-zephon; and they encamped before Migdol. [8]And they set out from before Hahiroth, and passed through the midst of the sea into the wilderness, and they went a three days' journey in the wilderness of Etham, and encamped at Marah. [9]And they set out from Marah, and came to Elim; at Elim there were twelve springs of water and seventy palm trees, and they encamped there. [10]And they set out from Elim, and encamped by the Red Sea. [11]And they set out from the Red Sea, and encamped in the wilderness of Sin. [12]And they set out from the wilderness of Sin, and encamped at Dophkah. [13]And they set out from Dophkah, and encamped at Alush. [14]And they set out from Alush, and encamped at Rephidim, where there was no water for the people to drink. [15]And they set

out from Rephidim, and encamped in the wilderness of Sinai. [16]And they set out from the wilderness of Sinai, and encamped at Kibroth-hattaavah. [17]And they set out from Kibroth-hattaavah, and encamped at Hazeroth. [18]And they set out from Hazeroth, and encamped at Rithmah. [19]And they set out from Rithmah, and encamped at Rimmon-perez. [20]And they set out from Rimmon-perez, and encamped at Libnah. [21]And they set out from Libnah, and encamped at Rissah. [22]And they set out from Rissah, and encamped at Kehelathah. [23]And they set out from Kehelathah, and encamped at Mount Shepher. [24]And they set out from Mount Shepher, and encamped at Haradah. [25]And they set out from Haradah, and encamped at Makheloth. [26]And they set out from Makheloth, and encamped at Tahath. [27]And they set out from Tahath, and encamped at Terah. [28]And they set out from Terah, and encamped at Mithkah. [29]And they set out from Mithkah, and encamped at Hashmonah. [30]And they set out from Hashmonah, and encamped at Moseroth. [31]And they set out from Moseroth, and encamped at Bene-jaakan. [32]And they set out from Bene-jaakan, and encamped at Hor-haggidgad. [33]And they set out from Hor-haggidgad, and encamped at Jotbathah. [34]And they set out from Jotbathah, and encamped at Abronah. [35]And they set out from Abronah, and encamped at Ezion-geber. [36]And they set out from Ezion-geber, and encamped in the wilderness of Zin (that is, Kadesh). [37]And they set out from Kadesh, and encamped at Mount Hor, on the edge of the land of Edom.

OVERVIEW: In a spectacular tour de force, Origen interprets the forty-two stopping places of the people of Israel in the desert as stages of growth in the spiritual life. His basis for this interpretation was the Hebrew names of the places. In each case the Greek form that Origen used has been retained and the Hebrew form inserted in brackets from the Revised Standard Version. Origen was honest; in one case he writes that he does not know what a particular place name means. There is some philological interest in Origen's understanding of the Hebrew names. But far more significant is his spiritual insight into the different stages of the spiritual struggle in the Christian life.

33:5 Setting Out from Rameses

THE STARTING PLACE OF THE SPIRITUAL LIFE. ORIGEN: Now the first starting place was from Ramesse [Rameses]; and whether the soul starts out from this world and comes to the future age or is converted from the errors of life to the way of virtue and knowledge, it starts out

from Ramesse. For in our language Ramesse means "confused agitation" or "agitation of the worm." By this it is made clear that everything in this world is set in agitation and disorder and also in corruption; for this is what the worm means. The soul should not remain in such agitation but should set out and come to Sochoth [Succoth]. HOMILIES ON NUMBERS 27.9.[1]

THE SOUL IS READY FOR BATTLE. ORIGEN: Sochoth [Succoth] is interpreted "tents." Thus the first progress of the soul is to be taken away from earthly agitation and to learn that it must dwell in tents like a wanderer, so that it can be, as it were, ready for battle and meet those who lie in wait for it unhindered and free. HOMILIES ON NUMBERS 27.9.[2]

33:6 They Camped at Etham

THE SOUL MUST STRUGGLE. ORIGEN: Then when the soul thinks it is ready, it sets out from

---

[1]OEM 257-58. [2]OEM 258.

Succoth and camps at Buthan [Etham]. Buthan means "valley." Now we have said that the stages refer to progress in the virtues. And a virtue is not acquired without training and hard work, nor is it tested as much in prosperity as in adversity. So the soul comes to a valley. For in valleys and in low places the struggle against the devil and the opposing powers takes place. Homilies on Numbers 27.9.[3]

33:7 They Turned Back to Pi-hahiroth

THE SOUL MAKES SMALL CONQUESTS. Origen: Iroth [Pi-hahiroth] means "villages." For the soul has not yet come to the city, nor is what is perfect already held, but first and for the moment some small places are taken. For progress consists in coming to great things from small ones. Homilies on Numbers 27.9.[4]

THE SOUL ASCENDS TO GREAT THINGS. Origen: Iroth is situated opposite Beelsephon [Baal-zephon] and opposite Magdalum. Beelsephon means "the ascent of the watchtower or citadel." So the soul ascends from small things to great and is not yet placed in that watchtower but opposite the watchtower, that is, in sight of the watchtower. For it begins to watch and to look for the future hope and to contemplate the height of the progresses; little by little it grows, while it is more nourished by hope than worn out by toils. Homilies on Numbers 27.9.[5]

THE SOUL IS FED BY GREAT HOPES. Origen: This camp or stage is opposite Magdalum [Migdol] but not yet in Magdalum itself. For Magdalum means "grandeur." Thus, since it has in view both the ascent of watching and the grandeur of things to come, the soul, as we have said, is fed and nourished by great hopes. It is now situated in starting places and not in perfection. Homilies on Numbers 27.9.[6]

33:8 They Passed Through the Sea

THE SOUL FOLLOWS GOD'S LAW. Origen: Next they set out from Iroth and pass through the midst of the Red Sea and camp at Bitter Waters. We have said that the time of starting places is a time of dangers. How hard a temptation it is to pass through the midst of the sea, to see the waves rise piled up, to hear the noise and rumbling of the raging waters! But if you follow Moses, that is, the law of God, the waters will become for you walls on the right and left, and you will find a path on dry ground in the midst of the sea. Homilies on Numbers 27.10.[7]

THE SOUL MUST PASS THROUGH BITTERNESS. Origen: And so they camped at the Bitter Waters [Marah]. Do not be terrified or afraid when you hear of Bitter Waters. "For the moment all discipline seems bitter rather than pleasant; later it yields the sweetest and most peaceful fruit of righteousness to those who have been trained by it," as the apostle teaches.[8] Then too, the unleavened bread is commanded to be eaten with bitter herbs;[9] nor is it possible to attain the Promised Land unless we pass through bitterness. Homilies on Numbers 27.10.[10]

THE SOUL REACHES PLEASANT PLACES. Origen: Helim [Elim] is where there are twelve springs of water and seventy-two[11] palm trees. You see after bitterness, after the hardships of temptations, what pleasant places receive you! You would not have come to the palm trees unless you had endured the bitterness of temptations. Nor would you have come to the sweetness of the springs unless you had first overcome what was sad and harsh. . . . And Helim means "rams"; rams are the leaders of flocks. Thus who are the leaders of Christ's flock but the apostles, who are also the twelve springs? But since our Lord and Savior chose not only those twelve but also seventy-two others, there are not only

---

[3]OEM 258. [4]OEM 258. [5]OEM 258-59. [6]OEM 259. [7]OEM 259. [8]Heb 12:11. [9]Ex 12:8. [10]OEM 259-60. [11]The Hebrew text reads "seventy."

twelve springs but also seventy-two palm trees mentioned in Scripture. HOMILIES ON NUMBERS 27.11.[12]

33:10 They Camped by the Red Sea

THE SOUL IS DELIVERED FROM FEAR. ORIGEN: They do not enter the Red Sea, since entering it once was enough. Now they camp next to the sea, so that they look at the sea and regard its waves but in no way fear its motions and assaults. HOMILIES ON NUMBERS 27.11.[13]

33:11 They Camped in the Wilderness of Sin

THE SOUL UNDERGOES TEMPTATIONS. ORIGEN: Sin means "bramble bush" or "temptation." Thus the hope of good things now begins to smile upon you. What is the hope of good things? The Lord appeared from the bush and answered Moses; and this became the beginning of the Lord's coming to the children of Israel.[14] But it is not insignificant that Sin also means "temptation." For visions usually involve temptation. Sometimes an angel of wickedness disguises himself as an angel of light.[15] HOMILIES ON NUMBERS 27.11.[16]

33:12 They Encamped at Dophkah

THE SOUL ATTAINS HEALTH. ORIGEN: Raphaca [Dophkah] means "health." You see the order of the progresses, how when the soul is once made spiritual and begins to have the discernment of heavenly visions, it arrives at health. . . . For the soul has many infirmities. Avarice is one of the worst of its infirmities; pride, anger, boasting, fear, inconstancy, timidity, and the like. When, Lord Jesus, will you cure me of all these infirmities? When will you heal me so that I may say, "Bless the Lord, O my soul, who heals all your infirmities"[17] so that I may be able to make a stage at Raphaca [Dophkah], which is healing? HOMILIES ON NUMBERS 27.12.[18]

33:13 They Encamped at Alush

THE SOUL MUST TOIL. ORIGEN: Halus [Alush] means "toils." Nor should you be surprised if toils follow health. For the soul acquires health from the Lord in order to accept toils with delight and not unwillingly. HOMILIES ON NUMBERS 27.12.[19]

33:14 They Camped at Rephidim

THE SOUL JUDGES RIGHTLY. ORIGEN: Now Raphidin [Rephidim] means "praise of judgment." Praise most justly follows toils, but what is the praise of? Judgment, it says. Therefore the soul becomes worthy of praise when it judges rightly, discerns rightly, that is, when it judges all things spiritually and is itself judged by no one.[20] HOMILIES ON NUMBERS 27.12.[21]

33:15 In the Wilderness

THE SOUL RECEIVES GOD'S LAW. ORIGEN: Sina itself is a place in the wilderness that was earlier mentioned as Sin. But this place is, rather, the name of the mountain that is in that wilderness; it is called Sina after the name of the wilderness. Therefore, after the soul has been made praiseworthy in judgment and begins to have a right judgment, then it is given the law by God, since it has begun to be capable of receiving divine mysteries and heavenly visions. HOMILIES ON NUMBERS 27.12.[22]

33:16 They Encamped at Kibroth-hattavah

THE FLESH CEASES TO LUST. ORIGEN: From there they come to the Tombs of Lust [Kibroth-hattavah]. What are the Tombs of Lust? Doubtless it is where lusts are buried and covered over, where all desire is quenched and the flesh no

---

[12]OEM 260. [13]OEM 260-61. [14]Ex 3:2. [15]2 Cor 11:14. [16]OEM 261. [17]Ps 103:3. [18]OEM 261. [19]OEM 262. [20]1 Cor 2:15. [21]OEM 262. [22]OEM 262.

longer lusts against the spirit, since it has been put to death by the death of Christ.[23] HOMILIES ON NUMBERS 27.12.[24]

33:17 At Hazeroth

THE SOUL FREE FROM FLESHLY VICES. ORIGEN: Next they come to Aseroth [Hazeroth]. This means "perfect halls" or "blessedness." Consider quite carefully, each of you wanderers, what the order of progress is. After you have been buried and have handed over the lusts of the flesh to death, you will come to the spacious dignity of halls, you will come to blessedness. For blessed is the soul that is no longer driven by any vices of the flesh. HOMILIES ON NUMBERS 27.12.[25]

33:18 They Camped at Rithmah

THE SOUL GAINS PERFECT UNDERSTANDING. ORIGEN: From there they come to Rathma or Pharam [Rithmah]. Rathma means "completed vision," but Pharam means "visible face." Why? Unless because the soul so grows that when it has ceased being driven by the troubles of the flesh, it has completed visions and gains perfect understanding of things, since it has a fuller and higher knowledge of the reasons for the incarnation of the Word of God and the purposes of his dispensations. HOMILIES ON NUMBERS 27.12.[26]

33:19 They Encamped at Rimon-perez

THE SOUL GAINS DISCERNMENT. ORIGEN: From there they come to Remonphares [Rimon-perez], which in our language means "a high cutting through," that is, where the separation and distinction of great and heavenly things from earthly and lowly things takes place. For as the understanding of the soul grows, it is also furnished with an acquaintance with high things and is given judgment by which to cut what is eternal away from what is temporal and to distinguish what is perishable from what is ever-

lasting. HOMILIES ON NUMBERS 27.12.[27]

33:20 Encamped at Libnah

THE SOUL GROWS BRIGHT. ORIGEN: Next they came to Lebna [Libnah], which means "whitewashing." I know that in some respects whitewashing has a pejorative connotation.... But this whitewashing is that concerning which the prophet says, "You will wash me, and I shall be whiter than snow...."[28] So then, this whitewashing must be understood to come from the radiance of the true light and to descend from the brightness of heavenly visions. HOMILIES ON NUMBERS 27.12.[29]

33:21 They Camped at Rissah

TEMPTATIONS STRENGTHEN THE SOUL. ORIGEN: The next stage takes place in Ressa [Rissah], which could be put into our words as "visible or praiseworthy temptation." Why is it that however great the progress made by the soul nonetheless temptations are not taken away from it? Here it becomes clear that temptations are brought to it as a kind of protection and defense. For just as meat, if it is not sprinkled with salt, no matter how great and special it is, becomes rotten, so also the soul, unless it is somehow salted with constant temptations, immediately becomes feeble and soft. HOMILIES ON NUMBERS 27.12.[30]

33:22 Encamped at Kehelathah

THE SOUL RULES THE BODY. ORIGEN: From it they come to Macelath [Kehelathah], which is "sovereignty" or "staff." Power seems to be meant by both and that the soul has progressed so far as to rule over the body and to obtain by that the staff of power. Indeed, it is power not only over the body but also over the whole

---

[23]Gal 5:17; Rom 7:4. [24]OEM 262. [25]OEM 262. [26]OEM 262-63. [27]OEM 263. [28]Ps 51:7. [29]OEM 263. [30]OEM 263.

world that Paul means when he says, "By the cross the world has been crucified to me, and I to the world."[31] HOMILIES ON NUMBERS 27.12.[32]

33:23 They Camped at Mt. Shepher

THE SOUL GOES TO WAR. ORIGEN: From there they come to Mt. Sephar [Shepher], which has the meaning "sound of trumpets." The trumpet is a sign of war. Therefore when the soul perceives itself armed with so many and such important virtues, it necessarily goes forth to the war it has against principalities and powers and against the world rulers.[33] Or, of course, the trumpet sounds in the Word of God, that is, in preaching and teaching, to give a distinct sound by the trumpet so that the person who hears it can prepare himself for war.[34] HOMILIES ON NUMBERS 27.12.[35]

33:24 They Encamped at Haradah

THE SOUL GROWS COMPETENT. ORIGEN: Next they arrive at Charadath [Haradah], which in our language signifies "made competent." Indeed, this is just what Paul says, "He has made us competent to be ministers of a new covenant."[36] HOMILIES ON NUMBERS 27.12.[37]

33:25 At Makheloth

THE SOUL CONTEMPLATES THE BEGINNING. ORIGEN: From there a stage is made at Maceloth [Makheloth], which means "from the beginning." For the person who strives for contemplation contemplates the beginning of things, or rather he refers everything to him who was in the beginning, nor is there any time when he abandons that beginning. HOMILIES ON NUMBERS 27.12.[38]

33:26 They Encamped at Tahath

THE SOUL LEARNS ENDURANCE. ORIGEN: Next a stage is made at Cataath [Tahath], which

is "encouragement" or "endurance." For it is necessary for someone who wants to be of use to others to suffer many things and to bear them all patiently, as it is said of Paul, "For I will show him how much he must suffer for the sake of my name."[39] HOMILIES ON NUMBERS 27.12.[40]

33:27 They Camped at Terah

THE SOUL KNOWS MARVELOUS THINGS. ORIGEN: From there they come to Thara [Terah], which may be understood in our words as "contemplation of amazement. . . ." Thus the contemplation of amazement means a time when the mind is struck with amazement by the knowledge of great and marvelous things. HOMILIES ON NUMBERS 27.12.[41]

33:28 At Mithkah

WE DIE WITH CHRIST. ORIGEN: Next they come to Matheca [Mithkah], which means "new death." What is the new death? When we die with Christ so that we may live with him.[42] HOMILIES ON NUMBERS 27.12.[43]

33:29 They Encamped at Hashmonah

STRENGTH AND FIRMNESS REVEALED. ORIGEN: From there they come to Asenna [Hashmonah], which is said to mean "bone" or "bones." By this it is doubtless strength and the firmness of endurance that is revealed. HOMILIES ON NUMBERS 27.12.[44]

33:30 They Camped at Moseroth

WICKED SUGGESTIONS ARE SHUT OUT. ORIGEN: Now from here a stage is made at Mesoroth [Moseroth], which is thought to mean "shutting out." What do they shut out? Doubtless the

---

[31]Gal 6:14. [32]OEM 264. [33]Eph 6:12. [34]1 Cor 14:8. [35]OEM 264. [36]2 Cor 3:6. [37]OEM 264. [38]OEM 264. [39]Acts 9:16. [40]OEM 264. [41]OEM 264. [42]2 Tim 2:11. [43]OEM 265. [44]OEM 265.

wicked suggestions of the opposing spirit from their thoughts. HOMILIES ON NUMBERS 27.12.[45]

33:31 They Encamped at Bene-jaakan

ONE OBEYS ALL THE COMMANDMENTS. ORIGEN: Next they come to Banaim [Bene-jaakan], which means "springs" or "filterings," that is, where one draws water from the springs of divine words until one filters them by drinking. . . . Thus a person filters the word of God when he does not omit even the least commandment, indeed when he gains the understanding that not even one iota or one dot in the word of God is insignificant.[46] HOMILIES ON NUMBERS 27.12.[47]

33:32 At Hor-haggidgad

TEMPTATION STRENGTHENS THE SOUL. ORIGEN: Next they come to Galgad [Hor-haggidgad], which means "temptation" or "dense crowd." Temptation, as I think, is a kind of strength and defense for the soul. For temptation is so mingled with virtues that no virtue appears to be seemly or complete without them. HOMILIES ON NUMBERS 27.12.[48]

33:33 They Encamped at Jotbathah

THROUGH TEMPTATIONS TO GOOD THINGS. ORIGEN: When you pass through them, you will camp at Tabatha [Jotbathah]. Tabatha means "good things." Thus they do not come to good things except after the trials of temptations. HOMILIES ON NUMBERS 27.12.[49]

33:34 They Encamped at Abronah

THE SOUL'S CONTINUING PROGRESS. ORIGEN: From there, it says, they camped at Ebrona [Abronah], which is "passage." For everything must be passed through. Even if you have come to good things, you must pass through them to better things until you come to that good thing in which you should always remain. HOMILIES ON NUMBERS 27.12.[50]

33:35 Encamped at Ezion-geber

THE SOUL REACHES MATURITY. ORIGEN: Next they come to Gasiongaber [Ezion-geber], which means "the purposes of a man." If someone ceases to be a child in understanding, he arrives at the purposes of a man, just as Paul, who said, "When I became a man, I gave up childish ways."[51] HOMILIES ON NUMBERS 27.12.[52]

33:36 The Wilderness of Zin

A RETURN TO TEMPTATION. ORIGEN: From there they come again to Sin [Zin]. And again Sin is "temptation." For we said that there is no other way of furthering our embarking upon this journey. HOMILIES ON NUMBERS 27.12.[53]

THE SOUL REAPS FRUIT. ORIGEN: Next they camp at Pharancades [Kadish], which is "holy fruitfulness." You see where they come from; you see that holy fruitfulness follows the ploughed furrows of temptations. HOMILIES ON NUMBERS 27.12.[54]

33:37 They Encamped at Mt. Hor

TO DWELL ON GOD'S MOUNTAIN ALWAYS. ORIGEN: They encamped at Mt. Or [Hor], which means "mountains." For one comes to the mount of God so that he may himself become a fruitful mountain and a massive mountain[55] or because the person who always dwells on the mount of God is called a mountaineer. HOMILIES ON NUMBERS 27.12.[56]

---

[45]OEM 265. [46]Mt 5:18. [47]OEM 265. [48]OEM 265. [49]OEM 265. [50]OEM 265. [51]1 Cor 13:11. [52]OEM 265-66. [53]OEM 266. [54]OEM 266. [55]Ps 68:15. [56]OEM 266.

33:38-49 FROM MOUNT HOR TO THE
PLAINS OF MOAB

³⁸*And Aaron the priest went up Mount Hor at the command of the Lord, and died there, in the fortieth year after the people of Israel had come out of the land of Egypt, on the first day of the fifth month. ³⁹And Aaron was a hundred and twenty-three years old when he died on Mount Hor.*

⁴⁰*And the Canaanite, the king of Arad, who dwelt in the Negeb in the land of Canaan, heard of the coming of the people of Israel.*

⁴¹*And they set out from Mount Hor, and encamped at Zalmonah. ⁴²And they set out from Zalmonah, and encamped at Punon. ⁴³And they set out from Punon, and encamped at Oboth. ⁴⁴And they set out from Oboth, and encamped at Iye-abarim, in the territory of Moab. ⁴⁵And they set out from Iyim, and encamped at Dibon-gad. ⁴⁶And they set out from Dibon-gad, and encamped at Almon-diblathaim. ⁴⁷And they set out from Almon-diblathaim, and encamped in the mountains of Abarim, before Nebo. ⁴⁸And they set out from the mountains of Abarim, and encamped in the plains of Moab by the Jordan at Jericho; ⁴⁹they encamped by the Jordan from Beth-jeshimoth as far as Abelshittim in the plains of Moab.*

OVERVIEW: *See* Overview at Numbers 33:5-37.

33:41 They Encamped at Zalmonah

CHRIST AND THE HOLY SPIRIT PROTECT US. ORIGEN: The stage at Selmona [Zalmonah] follows next. Its meaning is "shadow of the portion." . . . The shadow of our portion, which gives us shade from all the heat of temptations, is Christ and the Holy Spirit. HOMILIES ON NUMBERS 27.12.[1]

33:42 Encamped at Punon

ONE MUST GUARD THE MYSTERIES. ORIGEN: Now from here they come to Phinon [Punon], which we think means "frugality of the mouth." For the person who can contemplate the mystery of Christ and of the Holy Spirit, if he sees or hears what it is not right for men to speak,[2] will necessarily have frugality of mouth, since he will know to whom, when and how he should

speak of the divine mysteries. HOMILIES ON NUMBERS 27.12.[3]

33:43 They Camped at Oboth

A NAME BAFFLES ORIGEN. ORIGEN: Next they come to Oboth. Although we have not found an interpretation of this name, nonetheless we do not doubt that in this name as in all the others the logic of the progresses is preserved. HOMILIES ON NUMBERS 27.12.[4]

33:44 At Iye-abarim

THE APPROACH TO ABRAHAM'S BOSOM. ORIGEN: There follows next the stage that is called Gai [Iye-abarim], which means "chasm." For through these progresses one approaches the bosom of Abraham, who says to those in torments, "Between you and us a great chasm has

---

[1]OEM 266. [2]2 Cor 12:4. [3]OEM 266. [4]OEM 266.

been fixed."[5] He comes so that he may also rest in his bosom, as blessed Lazarus did. HOMILIES ON NUMBERS 27.12.[6]

33:45 Encamped at Dibon-gad

THE HONEY OF THE SCRIPTURES. ORIGEN: From there they come in turn to Dibongad [Dibon-gad], which bears the meaning "beehive of temptations." How marvelous is the caution of divine providence! For look, this wanderer on his heavenly journey comes right up to the highest perfection by a succession of virtues; and nevertheless temptations do not leave him, though I hear temptations of a new kind. It means "beehive of temptations." Scripture considers the bee a praiseworthy insect, and kings and commoners use what it produces for their health. This may rightly be taken of the words of the prophets and the apostles and all who wrote the sacred books. HOMILIES ON NUMBERS 27.12.[7]

33:46 At Almon-diblathaim

THE SOUL DESPISES EARTHLY THINGS. ORIGEN: Next, then, they come to Gelmon Deblathaim [Almon-diblathaim], which means "scorn of figs," that is, where earthly things are completely scorned and despised. For unless what seems to delight us on earth is rejected and scorned, we cannot pass through to heavenly things. HOMILIES ON NUMBERS 27.12.[8]

33:47 In the Mountains of Abarim, Before Nebo

SEPARATION FROM THE WORLD. ORIGEN: There follows next the stage at Abarim opposite Nabau [Nebo], which is "passage." But Nabau means "separation." For when the soul has made its journey through all these virtues and has climbed to the height of perfection, it then "passes" from the world and "separates" from it, as it is written of Enoch, "And he was not found, because God had taken him across."[9] HOMILIES ON NUMBERS 27.12.[10]

33:48 Encamped in the Plains of Moab

THE SOUL ARRIVES AT THE RIVER OF GOD. ORIGEN: The last stage is east of Moab by the Jordan. For the whole journey takes place, the whole course is run for the purpose of arriving at the river of God, so that we may make neighbors of the flowing Wisdom and may be watered by the waves of divine knowledge, and so that purified by them all we may be made worthy to enter the promised land. HOMILIES ON NUMBERS 27.12.[11]

---

[5]Lk 16:26. [6]OEM 267. [7]OEM 267. [8]OEM 267-68. [9]Gen 5:24. [10]OEM 268. [11]OEM 268.

[33:50-56 CONQUEST AND DIVISION OF CANAAN]

[34:1-15 THE BOUNDARIES]

34:16-29 SUPERVISORS OF THE ALLOTMENT

^{16}*The Lord said to Moses, ^{17}"These are the names of the men who shall divide the land to you for inheritance: Eleazar the priest and Joshua the son of Nun. ^{18}You shall take one leader of every tribe, to divide the land for inheritance."*

Overview: The order of names and titles in Scripture is significant (Procopius of Gaza).

34:17 Eleazar the Priest and Joshua

Priest and Leader. Procopius of Gaza: He places the priest before the leader, since the priest comes closer to God. Catena on the Octateuch, on Numbers 34:17.[1]

---

[1]PG 87 1:889-90.

[35:1-8 CITIES FOR THE LEVITES]

[35:9-15 CITIES OF ASYLUM]

35:16-28 MURDER AND MANSLAUGHTER

^{8}*"And as for the cities which you shall give from the possession of the people of Israel, from the larger tribes you shall take many, and from the smaller tribes you shall take few; each, in proportion to the inheritance which it inherits, shall give of its cities to the Levites."*
^{9}*And the Lord said to Moses, ^{10}"Say to the people of Israel, When you cross the Jordan into the land of Canaan, ^{11}then you shall select cities to be cities of refuge for you, that the manslayer who kills any person without intent may flee there. . . .*
^{25}*"And the congregation shall rescue the manslayer from the hand of the avenger of blood, and the congregation shall restore him to his city of refuge, to which he had fled, and he shall live in it until the death of the high priest who was anointed with the holy oil."*

Overview: Christ is the chief high priest, who bore the sins of the world (Ambrose). We, who are sinners, are the homicide who returns for forgiveness, until Christ redeems us by his death (Paterius).

35:25 Until the Death of the High Priest

Baptism into Christ's Death. Ambrose: The man who renounces the vices and rejects the way of life of his countrymen is in flight like

Lot. Such a one does not look behind himself but enters that city which is above by the passageway of his thoughts, and he does not withdraw from it until the death of the chief priest who bore the sin of the world.[1] He indeed died once, but he dies for each person who is baptized in Christ's death, that we may be buried together with him and rise with him and walk in the newness of his life.[2] FLIGHT FROM THE WORLD 9.55.[3]

35:28 The Manslayer May Return

THE DEATH OF THE REDEEMER. PATERIUS: What does it mean that a homicide returns for absolution after the death of the high priest, except that the human race, which brought death upon itself by sinning, receives absolution for its guilt after the death of the true priest, namely, our Redeemer? EXPOSITION OF THE OLD AND NEW TESTAMENT, NUMBERS 24.[4]

---

[1]Jn 1:29. [2]Col 2:12; Rom 6:4. [3]FC 65:322. [4]PL 79:774, citing Gregory the Great *Homilies on Ezekiel* 6.15.

[35:29-34 WITNESSES; NO INDEMNITY]

36:1-13 PROPERTY OF HEIRESSES

[6]*This is what the* LORD *commands concerning the daughters of Zelophehad, "Let them marry whom they think best; only, they shall marry within the family of the tribe of their father.* [7]*The inheritance of the people of Israel shall not be transferred from one tribe to another; for every one of the people of Israel shall cleave to the inheritance of the tribe of his fathers."*

OVERVIEW: The command to marry within one's own tribe was carried out by Joseph and Mary (EUSEBIUS).

36:6 Marrying Within the Tribe

MARY AND JOSEPH BELONGED TO THE SAME TRIBE. EUSEBIUS: Now, since the genealogy of Joseph is so traced, Mary also appears virtually to have been of the same tribe as he, since,

according to the law of Moses, intermarriages between different tribes were not permitted. For it was commanded to join in marriage with one of the same family and of the same people, so that the inheritance of the race might not be changed from tribe to tribe. ECCLESIASTICAL HISTORY 1.7.[1]

---

[1]FC 19:64-65.

DEUTERONOMY

1:1 — 4:14 HISTORICAL REVIEW

[1]These are the words that Moses spoke to all Israel beyond the Jordan. . . .

[16]"I charged your judges, . . . 'Hear the cases between your brethren, and judge righteously between a man and his brother or the alien that is with him. [17]You shall not be partial in judgment; you shall hear the small and the great alike; you shall not be afraid of the face of man, for the judgment is God's; and the case that is too hard for you, you shall bring to me, and I will hear it.' [18]And I commanded you at that time all the things that you should do. . . .

[29]"Then I said to you, 'Do not be in dread or afraid of them. [30]The Lord your God who goes before you will himself fight for you, just as he did for you in Egypt before your eyes, [31]and in the wilderness, where you have seen how the Lord your God bore you, as a man bears his son, in all the way that you went until you came to this place.' [32]Yet in spite of this word you did not believe the Lord your God. . . .

4 [1]"And now, O Israel, give heed to the statutes and the ordinances which I teach you, and do them; that you may live, and go in and take possession of the land which the Lord, the God of your fathers, gives you. [2]You shall not add to the word which I command you, nor take from it; that you may keep the commandments of the Lord your God which I command you. [3]Your eyes have seen what the Lord did at Baal-peor; for the Lord your God destroyed from among you all the men who followed the Baal of Peor; [4]but you who held fast to the Lord your God are all alive this day. [5]Behold, I have taught you statutes and ordinances, as the Lord my God commanded me, that you should do them in the land which you are entering to take possession of it. [6]Keep them and do them; for that will be your wisdom and your understanding in the sight of the peoples, who, when they hear all these statutes, will say, 'Surely this great nation is a wise and understanding people.' [7]For what great nation is there that has a god so near to it as the Lord our God is to us, whenever we call upon him? [8]And what great nation is there, that has statutes and ordinances so righteous as all this law which I set before you this day?

[9]"Only take heed, and keep your soul diligently, lest you forget the things which your eyes have seen, and lest they depart from your heart all the days of your life; make them known to your children and your children's children—[10]how on the day that you stood before the Lord your God at Horeb, the Lord said to me, 'Gather the people to me, that I may let them hear my words, so that they may learn to fear me all the days that they live upon the earth, and that they may teach their children so.' "

Overview: God delivered the first law to Moses; Moses delivered the second law, Deuteronomy, to Joshua, who prefigures Jesus (Origen). Early Christian teaching shares Deuteronomy's concern with righteous judgment (Didache). Anthropomorphic analogies do not mean that God is in reality like humans (Origen).

1:1 Moses Spoke to Israel

Deuteronomy, the Second Law. Origen: And here this other fact will not appear to be without significance, that it is Moses who hears from God all that is written down in the law of Leviticus, whereas in Deuteronomy it is the people who are represented as listening to Moses and learning from him what they could not hear from God.[1] This indeed is why it is called Deuteronomy, meaning the second law. A fact which some will think points to this [is] that when the first law given through Moses[2] came to an end, a second legislation was apparently composed, and this was specially delivered by Moses to his successor Joshua.[3] And Joshua is certainly believed to be a figure of our Savior, by whose second law, that is, by the precepts of the Gospels, all things are brought to perfection. On First Principles 4.3.12.[4]

1:16 Judge Righteously

Be Judicious. Didache: Do not desire any schism, but make peace among those who fight. Judge justly, and do not show favor to anyone in correcting offenses. Do not waver whether a thing shall or shall not be. Teaching of the Twelve Apostles 4.3-4.[5]

1:31 As a Man Bears His Son

As a Father Teaches His Son. Origen: See what we are generally taught about God: "God is not as a man to be deceived nor as the son of man to be threatened,"[6] and we learn that God is not as man. But other texts say that God *is* as a man: "For the Lord your God has taught you as a man teaches his son,"[7] and again, "As a man he takes on the manners of his son." Hence, wherever the Scriptures speak theologically about God in relation to himself and do not involve his plan for human matters, they teach that he is "not as a man."[8] For "there will be no limit to his greatness,"[9] and "he is more feared than all of the gods,"[10] and "praise him, all you angels of God; praise him, all his hosts; praise him, sun and moon; praise him, all stars and light."[11] You can find many other passages in the sacred Scriptures to which you can relate the words "God is not as a man." Homily 18.3.[12]

4:10 Gather the People

See Cyril of Jerusalem on Leviticus 8:3.

---

[1]Lev 1:1; Deut 5:1. [2]Jn 1:17. [3]Deut 31:7. [4]*OFP* 309. [5]FC 1:174. [6]Num 23:19. [7]Deut 8:5. [8]Num 23:19. [9]Ps 144:3. [10]Ps 95:4. [11]Ps 148:2-3. [12]FC 97:198.

4:15-24 DANGER OF IDOLATRY

---

[15]"*Therefore take good heed to yourselves. Since you saw no form on the day that the Lord spoke to you at Horeb out of the midst of the fire,* [16]*beware lest you act corruptly by making a*

---

graven image for yourselves. . . . [19]*And beware lest you lift up your eyes to heaven, and when you see the sun and the moon and the stars, all the host of heaven, you be drawn away and worship them and serve them, things which the* LORD *your God has allotted to all the peoples under the whole heaven.* . . . [24]*For the* LORD *your God is a devouring fire, a jealous God."*

OVERVIEW: We can make within ourselves images of whatever we choose: of God or of something unworthy. The law requires that people should not make images of what is unreal. Those who have the truth worship the Creator, not the creature (ORIGEN). Only one is worthy of worship: God, who is spirit to the just and fire to sinners. When God is called a devouring fire, what he devours is sin (ORIGEN). As fire, God illuminates us (AMBROSE) or warms us (JEROME). Thus the Holy Spirit came in the form of fire (JOHN OF DAMASCUS).

4:16 Beware of Acting Corruptly

TAKING ON THE CHARACTER OF WHAT WE ADORE. ORIGEN: We create other images in ourselves instead of the Savior's image. Instead of being the image of the Word, or of wisdom, justice, and the rest of the virtues, we assume the form of the devil. Then we can be called "serpents" and "a generation of vipers."[1] When we are venomous, cruel or wily, we have taken on the character of the lion, the snake or the fox. When we are prone to pleasure, we are like the goat. I recall once explaining that place in Deuteronomy where it is written, "Do not make any image of a male or a female or an image of any beast."[2] I said that "because the law is spiritual,"[3] the passage means this. Some make themselves into the image of a male, others into the image of a female. One has the likeness of birds, another of reptiles and serpents. Still another makes himself into the image of God. Anyone who reads what I wrote will know how the passage can be understood. HOMILIES ON THE GOSPEL OF LUKE 8.3.[4]

RESPECTING THE TRUTH. ORIGEN: The intention of the law was that in everything they should look toward what is real. They should not make up things which are different from reality or misrepresent what is truly male or what is really female, or the nature of beasts or the species of birds or creeping things, or fishes. AGAINST CELSUS 4.31.[5]

4:19 Beware of Worshiping the Heavens

WE DO NOT WORSHIP HEAVEN. ORIGEN: It is clear then that since those who live according to the law reverence the One who made the heaven, they do not reverence the heaven as if God. Furthermore, none of those who serve the Mosaic law worship the angels in heaven. And in the same way that they do not worship the sun, moon, and stars and "the world of heaven." They avoid worshiping heaven as such or the angels in it. AGAINST CELSUS 5.6.[6]

WE MAY NEVER WORSHIP CREATURES. ORIGEN: It is quite likely that the enemy will want to induce us by every possible trick down to "the sun and the moon and all the host of heaven."[7] But we shall reply that the Word of God did not command us to do so. For in no way may we bow down to the creature in the presence of the Creator[8] who sustains all and anticipates their prayer. Not even the sun would wish that any friend of God or anyone else, it would seem, should bow down to it. It imitates him who says, "Why do you call me good? None is good but one, that is God"[9] the Father. EXHORTATION TO MARTYRDOM 7.[10]

---

[1]Mt 23:33. [2]Deut 4:16-17. [3]Rom 7:14. [4]FC 94:34. [5]OCC 207. [6]OCC 268*. [7]Deut 17:3. [8]Rom 1:25. [9]Mk 10:18. [10]ACW 19:148.

4:24 *The Lord Is a Devouring Fire*

God Is Spirit and Fire. Origen: "God is spirit, and those who worship him should worship in spirit and in truth."[11] Our God is also "a consuming fire." Therefore God is called by two names: "spirit" and "fire." To the just he is spirit; to sinners he is fire. Homilies on the Gospel of Luke 26.1.[12]

The God of Fire Consumes Sins. Origen: Hear what is written: "Our God is a consuming fire." What does the God of fire consume? Will we be so senseless as to think that God consumes the firewood or straw or hay?[13] But the God of fire consumes human sins. He consumes them, devours them, purges them, as he says in another place, "I will purge you with fire for purity."[14] Homilies on Leviticus 5.3.2[15]

God Appears as Fire. Ambrose: So the prophets called him a burning fire, because in those three points[16] we see more intensely the majesty of the Godhead. Since to sanctify is of the Godhead, to illuminate is the property of fire and light, and the Godhead is frequently pointed out or seen in the appearance of fire: "For our God is a consuming fire," as Moses said. On the Holy Spirit 1.14.164.[17]

God's Fire Is Warmth. Jerome: If God is fire, he is fire in order to drive out the cold of the devil. Homilies on the Psalms 57.[18]

The Holy Spirit Comes as Fire. John of Damascus: And the Holy Spirit descended upon the holy apostles in the form of fire, because he is God, and "God is a consuming fire." On the Orthodox Faith 4.9.[19]

See also Gregory of Nazianzus on Exodus 3:14.

---

[11]Jn 4:24. [12]FC 94:109. [13]1 Cor 3:12. [14]Is 1:25. [15]FC 83:94. [16]According to Ambrose, the three occasions in which John the Evangelist, Isaiah and Moses identify the Godhead to be fire or light. See Jn 1:8-9; Is 10:16-17; Ex 3:1-6. [17]NPNF 2 10:112. [18]FC 48:414. [19]FC 37:347.

[4:25-31 GOD'S FIDELITY]

[4:32-40 PROOFS OF GOD'S LOVE]

[4:41-43 CITIES OF REFUGE]

[4:44-49 INTRODUCTION TO GOD AND HIS COVENANT]

5:1-5 THE COVENANT AT HOREB

^{25}"When you beget children and children's children, and have grown old in the land, if you act corruptly by making a graven image in the form of anything, and by doing what is evil in the sight of the LORD your God, so as to provoke him to anger, ^{26}I call heaven and earth to witness against you this day, that you will soon utterly perish from the land which you are going over the Jordan to possess; you will not live long upon it, but will be utterly destroyed. . . .

^{32}"For ask now of the days that are past, which were before you, since the day that God created man upon the earth, and ask from one end of heaven to the other, whether such a great thing as this has ever happened or was ever heard of. ^{33}Did any people ever hear the voice of a god speaking out of the midst of the fire, as you have heard, and still live? ^{34}Or has any god ever attempted to go and take a nation for himself from the midst of another nation, by trials, by signs, by wonders, and by war, by a mighty hand and an outstretched arm, and by great terrors, according to all that the LORD your God did for you in Egypt before your eyes? . . . ^{37}And because he loved your fathers and chose their descendants after them, and brought you out of Egypt with his own presence, by his great power, ^{38}driving out before you nations greater and mightier than yourselves, to bring you in, to give you their land for an inheritance, as at this day; ^{39}know therefore this day, and lay it to your heart, that the LORD is God in heaven above and on the earth beneath; there is no other." . . .

5 ^{1}And Moses summoned all Israel, and said to them, "Hear, O Israel, the statutes and the ordinances which I speak in your hearing this day, and you shall learn them and be careful to do them. ^{2}The LORD our God made a covenant with us in Horeb. ^{3}Not with our fathers did the LORD make this covenant, but with us, who are all of us here alive this day."

OVERVIEW: Heaven and earth are called as witnesses to human action, for they will be present with the judged (BASIL). God has neither voice nor outward appearance (CHRYSOSTOM). The pious have an inheritance in the land created in the beginning (ORIGEN). God indeed is one (PSEUDO-CLEMENT). God had made covenants with Noah and Abraham before the covenant with Moses (EUSEBIUS).

4:26 Witnesses to Evil

HEAVEN AND EARTH TO WITNESS. BASIL THE GREAT: Not only Paul but generally all those to whom is committed any ministry of the word never cease to testify but call heaven and earth to witness, on the grounds that now every deed is done within them, and they will be present with the judged in the examination of all of life. So it is said, "He shall call to the heavens above and to earth, that he may judge his people."[1] And so Moses, when about to deliver his oracles to the people, says, "I call heaven and earth to witness this day"; and again in his song he says, "Give ear, O you heavens, and I will speak; and hear, O earth, the words of my mouth."[2] ON THE SPIRIT 13.30.[3]

---

[1]Ps 1:4. [2]Deut 32:1. [3]NPNF 2 8:18.

4:33 *The Voice of a God*

God Speaks Out of Love. Chrysostom: "You have never seen his face." Yet Isaiah, Jeremiah, Ezekiel and many others say that they have seen him. What is it, therefore, that Christ meant here? He was introducing them to a philosophical teaching, showing gradually that with regard to God there is neither voice nor outward appearance; he is superior to such forms and sounds. Just as by saying, "You have never heard his voice," he did not mean that God utters sound but is not heard, so by saying, "You have never seen his face," he did not mean that God has outward form but cannot be seen. Neither sound nor form exists with regard to God. Indeed, in order that they might not say, "You are making a display of knowledge in vain, since God spoke only to Moses" (they actually did say, "We know that God spoke to Moses; but as for this man, we do not know where he is from"),[4] he spoke in this way to show that with regard to God there is neither voice nor outward appearance. Homilies on the Gospel of John 40.[5]

4:38 *Land for an Inheritance*

Land to the Pious. Origen: If we rightly understand the matter, this is the statement of Moses at the beginning of his book: "In the beginning God created the heavens and the earth."[6] For this is the beginning of all creation; to this beginning the end and consummation of all things must be recalled, in order that this heaven and this earth may be the habitation and resting place of the pious. So all the holy ones and the meek obtain an inheritance in that land, since this is the teaching of the Law and the Prophets and the Gospels. On First Principles 3.6.8.[7]

4:39 *There Is No Other*

No Other God. Pseudo-Clement: See how by some ineffable virtue the Scripture, opposing the future errors of those who affirm that either in heaven or on earth there is any god besides the God of the Jews, decides thus: "The Lord your God is one God, in heaven above, and in the earth beneath, and besides him there is none else." How then have you dared to say that there is any god besides him who is God of the Jews? Recognitions 2.43.[8]

5:3 *The Lord Made This Covenant*

This Covenant Is New. Eusebius: See how distinctly he alludes to this [Mosaic] covenant when he says God did not give the same covenant to their fathers [Abraham and Noah]. For if he had said that absolutely no covenant was given to their fathers it would have been a false statement. For Holy Scripture testifies that a covenant of some kind was given both to Abraham and Noah. And so Moses adds that one "not the same" was given to their fathers. This points to that other greater and glorious covenant, by which all of these were shown forth as friends of God. Proof of the Gospel 1.6.[9]

---

[4]Jn 9:29. [5]FC 33:411. [6]Gen 1:1. [7]ANF 4:347-48. [8]ANF 8:109. [9]POG 1:30.

[5:6-21 THE DECALOGUE]

5:22—6:3 MOSES AS MEDIATOR

[22]"These words the LORD spoke to all your assembly at the mountain out of the midst of the fire, the cloud, and the thick darkness, with a loud voice; and he added no more. And he wrote them upon two tables of stone, and gave them to me. [23]And when you heard the voice out of the midst of the darkness, while the mountain was burning with fire, you came near to me, all the heads of your tribes, and your elders; [24]and you said, . . . [26]'For who is there of all flesh, that has heard the voice of the living God speaking out of the midst of fire, as we have, and has still lived? [27]Go near, and hear all that the LORD our God will say; and speak to us all that the LORD our God will speak to you; and we will hear and do it.'

[28]"And the LORD heard your words, when you spoke to me; and the LORD said to me, . . . [31]'You, stand here by me, and I will tell you all the commandment and the statutes and the ordinances which you shall teach them, that they may do them in the land which I give them to possess.'

OVERVIEW: On the Ten Commandments see the passages on Exodus 20:2-17. In the Old Testament the people are in fear of God, whereas in the New Covenant the people await the Holy Spirit (AUGUSTINE). God will not cause our death but comes to save us (CYRIL OF JERUSALEM). Many statements about God in Scripture, that is, those that imply human limitations, must be interpreted figuratively (ORIGEN). Moses was uniquely privileged (AMBROSE).

5:22 Tablets of Stone

TABLETS OF STONE AND HEARTS OF FLESH.
AUGUSTINE: There the finger of God worked upon tables of stone: here upon the hearts of men. So there the law was set outside men to be a terror to the unjust: here it was given within them to be their justification. "For this: you shall not commit adultery, you shall do no murder, you shall not covet, and if there be any other commandment"—written, as we know, upon those tables—"it is briefly comprehended," said the apostle, "in this saying: you shall love your neighbor as yourself. Love works not a neighbor's ill: and charity is the fullness of the law."[1] This law is not written on tables of stone but is

shed abroad in our hearts through the Holy Spirit which is given to us. Therefore the law of God is charity. To it the mind of the flesh is not subject, neither indeed can be. But when, to put fear into the mind of the flesh, the works of charity are written upon tables, we have the law of works, the letter killing the transgression. When charity itself is shed abroad in the hearts of believers, we have the law of faith, the Spirit giving life to the lover. ON THE SPIRIT AND THE LETTER 17.29.[2]

5:26 Who Is There of All Flesh?

GOD ACCOMMODATES OUR WEAKNESS. CYRIL OF JERUSALEM: If to hear the voice of God speaking is a cause of death, how will the sight of God not cause death? And why wonder? Even Moses himself says, "I am greatly terrified and trembling." What then? Would you that he who came for our salvation become a minister of destruction because men could not bear him? Or rather that he should temper his grace to our measure? CATECHETICAL LECTURE 12.13-14.[3]

---

[1]Rom 13:9-10. [2]LCC 8:217. [3]FC 61:234.

5:31 *Stand Here by Me*

Scripture Uses Anthropomorphisms.
Origen: [Celsus] continues by making further
remarks as if they were what we should agree to,
although none of those Christians who have any
intelligence would agree to them. Not one of us
says that "God participates in shape or color."
Nor does he "partake of movement"; because it
is his nature to be established and firm, he calls
the righteous man to imitate him in this respect
when he says, "But as for you, stand with me." If,
however, some texts suggest that there is movement of some sort on his part, as for example
that which says "They heard the Lord God
walking in the garden in the evening,"[4] we
should understand such sayings in the sense
that God is regarded as being moved by those
who have sinned. Or we should interpret such
texts in the same way as we do when there is a
figurative reference to God's sleep or his anger
or anything of this sort. Against Celsus 6.64.[5]

God's Blessed Words to Moses. Ambrose:
Blessed is the mind of that man who, overstep-
ping the bounds of species and race, deserves to
hear what was said to Moses when he stood
apart from his people: "Stand here with me."
Cain and Abel 1.2.7.[6]

---

[4]Gen 3:8. [5]OCC 379. [6]FC 42:363.

6:4-9 THE GREAT COMMANDMENT

[4]*"Hear, O Israel: The Lord our God is one Lord;*[e] [5]*and you shall love the Lord your God with
all your heart, and with all your soul, and with all your might."*

e Or the Lord our God, the Lord is one   Or the Lord is our God, the Lord is one   Or the Lord is our God, the Lord alone

---

Overview: The Father and the Son are one
God, not two (Hilary of Poitiers). The Father
is God, the Son is God, but there is one God
(Gregory of Nyssa). We are called to listen to
God. God is immutable and wholly one (Ambrose). The Jews were called to faith in the one
God and this faith saved them (Chrysostom).
The most blessed Trinity is one God. When the
Old Testament speaks of the one God, it speaks
of the Trinity (Augustine). The prayer "Hear,
O Israel" is addressed to the one God, yet it
does not deny the distinction of persons (Fulgentius). Love of God cannot be separated
from love of neighbor (Gregory of Nyssa). Our
first duty is to God; only then may we fulfill our
duty to our neighbor. Belief must precede love;
when it does, love can be perfect. The earth produces its fruit regularly, but we do not. To love
God with all one's heart is to love him wholly
(Ambrose). God is to be loved with the whole
heart, soul and mind. True love of God is wisdom (Augustine). Trust in God requires purity
of mind (Cassiodorus).

6:4 *The Lord Our God Is One Lord*

Christian Faith Is Monotheistic. Hilary
of Poitiers: Let us see whether the confession
of the apostle Thomas agrees with this teaching
of the Evangelist, when he says, "My Lord and

my God."[1] He is therefore his God whom he acknowledges as God. And certainly he was aware that the Lord had said, "Hear, O Israel, the Lord your God is one." And how did the faith of the apostle become unmindful of the principal commandment, so that he confessed Christ as God, since we are to live in the confession of the one God? The apostle, who perceived the faith of the entire mystery through the power of the resurrection, after he had often heard "I and the Father are one" and "All things that the Father has are mine" and "I in the Father and the Father in me,"[2] now confessed the name of the nature without endangering the faith. ON THE TRINITY 7.12.[3]

FATHER AND SON ARE ONE GOD. GREGORY OF NYSSA: Wherefore [Scripture] says, "The Lord God is one Lord." By the word *Godhead* it proclaims too the only-begotten God and does not divide the unity into a duality so as to call the Father and the Son two gods, although each is called God by holy writers. ON NOT THREE GODS.[4]

GOD BIDS US HEAR. AMBROSE: The law says, "Hear, O Israel, the Lord your God." It did not say "speak" but "hear." Eve fell because she said to the man what she had not heard from the Lord her God. The first word from God says to you, "hear." DUTIES OF THE CLERGY 1.2.7.[5]

GOD IS IMMUTABLE. AMBROSE: Such too was the teaching of the law: "Hear, O Israel, the Lord your God is one Lord," that is, unchangeable, always abiding in unity of power, always the same and not altered by any accession or diminution. Therefore Moses called him one. ON THE HOLY SPIRIT 3.15.105.[6]

FAITH IN THE ONE GOD. CHRYSOSTOM: "What then?" one may say. "Were they wronged who lived before his coming?" By no means, for men might then be saved even though they had not confessed Christ. For this was not required

of them, but not to worship idols and to know the true God. "For the Lord your God," it is said, "is one Lord." Therefore the Maccabees were admired, because for the observance of the law they suffered what they did suffer;[7] and the three children,[8] and many others too among the Jews, having shown forth a very virtuous life and having maintained the standard of this their knowledge, had nothing more required of them. For then it was sufficient for salvation, as I have said already, to know God only, but now it is so no more. There is need also of the knowledge of Christ. HOMILIES ON THE GOSPEL OF MATTHEW 36.[9]

THE TRINITY IS ONE GOD. AUGUSTINE: That Trinity is one God. Not that Father, Son and Holy Spirit are identically the same. But the Father is Father, the Son is Son, and the Holy Spirit is Holy Spirit, and this Trinity is one God, as it is written: "Hear, O Israel, the Lord your God is one God." ON FAITH AND THE CREED 9.16.[10]

"HEAR, O ISRAEL" IS SPOKEN OF THE TRINITY. AUGUSTINE: Consider now for a while the passages of Scripture which force us to confess that the Lord is one God, whether we are asked about the Father alone, or the Son alone, or the Holy Spirit alone, or about the Father and the Son and the Holy Spirit together. Certainly it is written, "Hear, O Israel, the Lord your God is one Lord." Of whom do you think that this is said? If it is said only of the Father, then our Lord Jesus Christ is not God. Why did those words come to Thomas when he touched Christ and cried out, "My Lord and my God,"[11] which Christ did not reprove but approved, saying, "Because you have seen, you have believed"?[12] LETTER 238.[13]

---

[1]Jn 20:28. [2]Jn 10:30; 16:15; 14:11. [3]FC 25:235-36. [4]LCC 3:265-66. [5]NPNF 2 10:2. [6]NPNF 2 10:150. [7]2 Macc 7:1-41. [8]Dan 3:1-30. [9]NPNF 1 10:241. [10]LCC 6:361. [11]Jn 20:28. [12]Jn 20:29. [13]FC 32:201.

ONE GOD IN THREE DISTINCT PERSONS. FUL-GENTIUS: Therefore, in whatever place you may be, because you know that you have been baptized in the one name of the Father and the Son and the Holy Spirit, according to the rule promulgated by the command of our Savior, retain this rule with your whole heart, from the start and without hesitation: the Father is God, and the Son is God, and the Holy Spirit is God. This means the holy and ineffable Trinity is by nature one God, concerning whom it is said in Deuteronomy, "Hear, O Israel, the Lord your God is one God," and "You shall adore the Lord your God and him alone shall you serve."[14] Indeed, . . . we have said that this one God who alone is true God by nature, is not the Father only, nor the Son only, nor the Holy Spirit only but is at one and the same time Father, Son and Holy Spirit. [Thus] we must be wary that while we say in truth that as the Father, Son, and Holy Spirit are one God, insofar as this is a unity of nature, we dare not say or believe something altogether blasphemous. [Such a blasphemous saying would be] that he who is the person of the Father is the same as either the Son or the Holy Spirit, or that he who is the person of the Son is the Father or the Holy Spirit. Or [it might be] that we dare to say or to believe that the person who is properly called the Holy Spirit in the confession of this Trinity is either the Father or the Son, something that is altogether wicked. TO PETER ON THE FAITH 1.3.[15]

6:5 Love the Lord Your God

LOVING OTHER CHRISTIANS. GREGORY OF NYSSA: If one does not love God with all his heart and with all his soul, how can he care wholesomely and guilelessly for the love of his brothers, since he is not fulfilling the love of the One on whose account he has a care for the love of his brothers? The person in this condition, who has not given his whole soul to God and has not participated in his love, the craftsman of evil finds disarmed and easily overpowers. ON THE

CHRISTIAN MODE OF LIFE.[16]

FIRST GIVE YOUR MIND TO GOD. AMBROSE: It is a noble thing to do one's kindnesses and duties toward the whole of the human race. But it is ever more seemly that you should give to God the most precious thing you have, that is, your mind, for you have nothing better than that. When you have paid your debt to your Creator, then you may labor for humanity, to show them kindness and to give help. Then you may assist the needy with money, or by some duty or some service that lies in the way of your ministry; by money to support him; by paying a debt, so as to free him that is bound; by undertaking a duty, so as to take charge of a trust, which he fears to lose, who has put it by in trust. DUTIES OF THE CLERGY 1.50.262.[17]

THE BEGINNING OF LOVE. AMBROSE: Now one who loves undoubtedly believes, and by believing each one begins to love. Finally, "Abraham believed,"[18] and thus he began to love. He did not believe in part but believed all things. Otherwise he could not possess full charity, since Scripture says, "Charity believes all things."[19] LETTER 66 (78).5.[20]

WE OFTEN FAIL TO LOVE. AMBROSE: To humanity it was said, "Love the Lord your God," yet the love of God is not instilled in the hearts of all. Deafer are the hearts of people than the hardest rock. The earth, in compliance with its Author, furnishes us with fruit which is not owed to us. We deny the debt when we do not give homage to the Author. SIX DAYS OF CREATION 3.17.70.[21]

TO LOVE GOD WITH ONE'S SOUL. AUGUSTINE: For while there remains any remnant of the lust of the flesh, to be kept in check by the rein of continence, God is by no means loved with all

---

[14]Deut 6:13. [15]FC 95:61. [16]FC 58:148. [17]NPNF 2 10:42. [18]Gal 3:6. [19]1 Cor 13:7. [20]CSEL 82 2:162. [21]FC 42:120.

one's soul. For the flesh does not lust without the soul, although it is the flesh which is said to lust, because the soul lusts carnally. In that perfect state the just man shall live absolutely without any sin, since there will be in his members no law warring against the law of his mind.[22] But wholly will he love God, with all his heart, with all his soul and with all his mind,[23] which is the first and chief commandment. ON THE PERFECTION OF HUMAN RIGHTEOUSNESS 8.19.[24]

THE THREEFOLD LOVE OF GOD. AUGUSTINE: The number three has an intrinsic relation to the mind. This may be understood from the text in which we are commanded to love God in a threefold manner, with the whole heart, with the whole soul, with the whole mind. EXPLANATION OF THE PSALMS 6.2.[25]

THE HOLY SPIRIT ENABLES US TO LOVE. AUGUSTINE: Therefore the supreme and true wisdom is in that first commandment: "You shall love the Lord your God with your whole heart and with your whole soul." From this it follows that wisdom is love of God, which is "poured forth in our hearts," not otherwise than "by the Holy Spirit who is given to us."[26] But "the fear of the Lord is the beginning of wisdom,"[27] and "there is no fear in love, but perfect love casts out fear."[28] LETTER 140.18.[29]

LOVE, HOPE AND PRAISE. CASSIODORUS: As the law teaches, "You shall love the Lord your God with your whole heart and your whole soul." But the person who puts his entire hope in the Lord also praises with his whole heart. He does not put his trust in the transient consolations of the world, once he has trained himself on the Lord with total purity of mind. EXPOSITION OF THE PSALMS 85.12.[30]

---

[22]Rom 7:23. [23]Mt 22:37. [24]NPNF 1 5:165. [25]NPNF 1 8:16. [26]Rom 5:5. [27]Ps 111:10. [28]1 Jn 4:18. [29]FC 20:95-96. [30]ACW 52:333.

6:10-19 FIDELITY IN PROSPERITY

[13]*"You shall fear the LORD your God; you shall serve him,* and swear by his name."*

*LXX adds and cleave to him

OVERVIEW: Justice teaches us the true rule of life. Scripture uses a distinctive word to name the worship owed to God (AUGUSTINE).

6:13 Fearing the Lord

See FULGENTIUS ON DEUTERONOMY 6:4.

TO SERVE THE ONE GOOD. AUGUSTINE: What is to be said of justice in its relation to God? As the Lord says, "No man can serve two masters,"[1] and the apostle rebukes those who serve the creature rather than the Creator,[2] so had it not been said before in the Old Testament: "You shall adore the Lord your God and him only shall you serve"? But what need is there to say more about this here since the Scriptures are full of such texts? Justice then offers this rule of life to the lover we are describing: that he serve with gladness the Lord whom he loves, that is to

---

[1]Mt 6:24. [2]Rom 1:25.

say, the supreme good, the supreme wisdom, the supreme peace; and with respect to all other things, that he govern those which are subject to him and endeavor to subject all else to the same rule. This rule of life is confirmed, as we have shown, by the authority of both Testaments. On the Catholic and the Manichaean Ways of Life 1.24.44.[3]

Worship of God Is Called Latreia. Augustine: Whoever yields assent to the supreme authority of divine Scripture should first examine these words: "The Lord your God shall you adore, and him only shall you serve." In Greek the expression used does not signify the service owed to human masters but that which is offered to God, called *latreia*. Thus idolatry is rightly condemned because the *latreia* which is due to the true God alone is offered to idols.[4] It does not say, "You shall adore only the Lord your God," but it says, "And him only shall you serve." It used the word *only* with "you shall serve," meaning, no doubt, that service which is called *latreia*. To this service belong temple, sacrifice, priest, and other like attributes. Letter 173a.[5]

---

[3]FC 56:37. [4]The word *idolatry* contains the root of *latreia*. [5]FC 30:82.

[6:20-25 INSTRUCTION TO CHILDREN]

7:1-11 DESTRUCTION OF PAGANS

[1]"*When the Lord your God brings you into the land which you are entering to take possession of it, and clears away many nations before you, . . .* [5]*thus shall you deal with them: you shall break down their altars, and dash in pieces their pillars, and hew down their Asherim, and burn their graven images with fire.*"

Overview: The seven nations that the Lord promised to Israel prefigure for Christians the virtues, which overcome innumerable vices (John Cassian). Christians should not destroy pagan idols without the consent of their owners (Augustine).

7:1 Seven Nations

More Vices Than Virtues. John Cassian: These are the seven nations whose lands the Lord promised to give to the children of Israel when they left Egypt. We must accept the fact that, according to the apostle, all the things that happened to them in a figure were written for our instruction. . . .[1] The reason that they are said to be much more numerous[2] is that there are more vices than virtues. Therefore in the list they are counted as seven nations, to be sure, but when it is a question of destroying them they are said to be innumerable. Conference 5.16.1-2.[3]

7:5 Break Down Their Altars

---

[1]1 Cor 10:11. [2]Deut 7:1 Vulgate. [3]ACW 57:196-97.

286

PRACTICAL ADVICE ON OPPOSING IDOLATRY.
AUGUSTINE: When you have received lawful
authority, do all this.[4] Where authority has not
been given to us, we don't do it; where it has
been given, we don't fail to do it. Many pagans
have these abominations on their estates. Do we
march in and smash them? The first thing we try
to do is to break the idols in their hearts. When

they too become Christians, they either invite
us in to perform this good work or else they get
in first with it before us. The thing we have to
do now is pray for them, not get angry with
them. SERMON 62.17.[5]

---

[4]That is, Deut 7:1-5. [5]WSA 3 3:165.

[7:12-26 BLESSINGS OF OBEDIENCE]

8:1-10 GOD'S CARE

[1]"All the commandment which I command you this day you shall be careful to do, that you
may live and multiply, and go in and possess the land which the LORD swore to give to your
fathers. [2]And you shall remember all the way which the LORD your God has led you these forty
years in the wilderness, that he might humble you, testing you to know what was in your heart,
whether you would keep his commandments, or not. [3]And he humbled you and let you hunger
and fed you with manna, which you did not know, nor did your fathers know; that he might
make you know that man does not live by bread alone, but that man lives by everything that
proceeds out of the mouth of the LORD. [4]Your clothing did not wear out upon you, and your foot
did not swell, these forty years. . . . [7]For the LORD your God is bringing you into a good land, . . .
[10]and you shall eat and be full, and you shall bless the LORD your God for the good land he has
given you."

OVERVIEW: The good person is never in need
and can be free of any feeling of want (CLEMENT
OF ALEXANDRIA). God cared for Israel in the
desert for forty years; surely he will care for us
(EPHREM). The preservation of the Israelites'
clothing and shoes in the desert is a figure of the
resurrection (AMBROSE). If God can preserve
clothing from decay, he can also make bodies immortal (AUGUSTINE). After bodily food we
should have a spiritual meal (CHRYSOSTOM).

8:3 Not by Bread Alone

THE GOOD PERSON IS NEVER IN WANT.
CLEMENT OF ALEXANDRIA: One who possesses
the Word, who is almighty God, needs nothing
and never lacks any of the things he desires, for
the Word is an infinite possession and the
source of all our wealth. However, someone may
object and insist that he has often seen the just
in need of food. This is rare and happens only
where no one else is just. Besides, let him read
the beautiful sentence, "It is not by bread alone
that the just man lives, but by the Word of the
Lord," who is the true bread, the bread of

heaven.[1] The good man is never really in want as long as he keeps intact his adherence to faith in God. For he can ask for and receive whatever he needs from the Father of all, and he can enjoy whatever belongs to him, if only he obey his Son. Then too, he has this advantage, that he can be free from feeling any want. The Word, who acts as our educator, gives us riches. There is no need to envy the wealth of others with those who have gained freedom from want through him. He who possesses this sort of wealth will inherit the kingdom of God. CHRIST THE EDUCATOR 3.7.39-40.[2]

8:4 Clothing That Did Not Wear Out

TRUST IN GOD. EPHREM THE SYRIAN: Nourish your soul with the fear of God, and God will nourish [your] body. Do these things, so that what you yourself are unable [to procure] may be given you by God. Take note of this, if God does not give the rain and the wind, it avails you naught, even if you are anxious. Obey God, therefore, and creation will obey your needs. If God nourished Israel for forty years in the desert, while they were murmuring and disbelieving, and effortlessly preserved their sandals and clothing, how much more so in the case of believers? COMMENTARY ON TATIAN'S DIATESSERON 6.18A.[3]

A FIGURE OF THE RESURRECTION. AMBROSE: Is he not good, who in the wilderness fed with bread from heaven such countless thousands of the people, lest any famine should assail them, without need of toil, in the enjoyment of rest? For the space of twenty years, their raiment grew not old, nor were their shoes worn, a figure, which, to the faithful, points to the resurrection that is to come. This shows that the glory of great deeds and the beauty of the power by which he has clothed us and the stream of

human life is not absurd, not for nothing. ON THE CHRISTIAN FAITH 2.2.23.[4]

THE BLESSING OF IMMORTALITY. AUGUSTINE: God granted to the garments of the Israelites their proper state without any damage for forty years. If so, how much more does he grant a very happy temperament of certain state to the bodies of those who obey his command until they may be turned into something better? This embetterment occurs not by the death of man, by which the body is deserted by the soul, but by a blessed change from mortality to immortality, from an animal to a spiritual quality. ON THE GOOD OF MARRIAGE 2.2.[5]

CHRIST'S GLORIFIED BODY. AUGUSTINE: If the garments of the Israelites could last without wearing out for so many years in the desert and the hides of dead animals could continue undestroyed for so long a time in their shoes, surely God can extend the quality of incorruption in certain bodies for as long as he wills. I think therefore that the body of the Lord is the same now in heaven as it was when he ascended into heaven. LETTER 205.[6]

8:10 You Shall Bless the Lord

PRAY AFTER EATING. CHRYSOSTOM: Do you see how it is especially appropriate after the enjoyment of food to set a spiritual meal for yourself lest the soul, after satiety of bodily food, should lose its zest and fall into some disaster and make way for the wiles of the devil, who is always looking for an opportunity and anxious to deliver us a blow at a critical moment? HOMILIES ON GENESIS 10.20.[7]

---

[1]See Jn 6:33, 41. [2]FC 23:232. [3]JSSS 2:121. [4]NPNF 2 10:226. [5]FC 27:11*. [6]FC 32:9. [7]FC 74:141.

8:11-20 DANGER OF PROSPERITY

[17]"Beware lest you say in your heart, 'My power and the might of my hand have gotten me this wealth.' [18]You shall remember the LORD your God, for it is he who gives you power to get wealth; that he may confirm his covenant which he swore to your fathers, as at this day. [19]And if you forget the LORD your God and go after other gods and serve them and worship them, I solemnly warn you this day that you shall surely perish. [20]Like the nations that the LORD makes to perish before you, so shall you perish, because you would not obey the voice of the LORD your God."

OVERVIEW: There is danger in ascribing success to our own merits (AMBROSE). We should employ the gifts God gives us to help others grow in virtue (CLEMENT OF ALEXANDRIA).

8:17 Beware of Trusting One's Own Power

FALSE TRUST IN ONE'S MERITS. AMBROSE: Such a one is he who ascribes all his success to his own merits and hence, feeling self-assured, does not recognize his own errors which drag him with their extended rope afar. For, if he believes that his acquisition of property is due either to mere chance or to shrewd cunning, there is no occasion for him to feel undue pride in matters to which there is no glory attached, or where the labor results in nothing, or where there is evidence of shameless cupidity, which prescribes no limits in its pur-suit of pleasure. SIX DAYS OF CREATION 6.8.53.[1]

8:18 God Gives Power

HOW TO USE GOD'S GIFTS WELL. CLEMENT OF ALEXANDRIA: By these words [Scripture] is showing clearly that it is God who grants us gifts of good things and that we ought as servants of the grace of God to sow God's gracious gifts and enable our neighbors to become people of honor. The aim is for the man of self-control to enable those who are continent to find their fulfillment, the man of courage to do the same for the noble, the man of practical wisdom for the understanding, and the man of justice for the just. STROMATEIS 2.18.96.4.[2]

---

[1]FC 42:267-68. [2]FC 85:221.

9:1-5 UNMERITED SUCCESS

[4]"Do not say in your heart, after the LORD your God has thrust them out before you, 'It is because of my righteousness that the LORD has brought me in to possess this land'; whereas it is because of the wickedness of these nations that the LORD is driving them out before you."

OVERVIEW: If the Lord had not helped us, our effort would have been in vain (JOHN CASSIAN).

9:4 Do Not Trust in One's Own Righteousness

THE NECESSITY OF GRACE. JOHN CASSIAN: I ask, what could be said more clearly against that pernicious opinion and presumption of ours, by which we want to attribute everything that we do to our free will and to our own effort? "Do not say in your heart, when the Lord your God has destroyed them in your sight: Because of my righteousness the Lord has led me in to possess this land." Did he not express himself clearly to those whose souls' eyes are open and whose ears hear? Namely, when you have enjoyed a notable success in warring against the carnal vices and you see that you have been freed from their filthiness and from this world's way of life, you should not be puffed up with the success of the struggle and the victory and ascribe this to your own strength and wisdom, believing that you were able to obtain victory over evil spirits and carnal vices through your own efforts and application and free will. There is no doubt that you would never have been able to prevail over these if the Lord's help had not fortified and protected you. CONFERENCE 5.15.3-4.[1]

---

[1]ACW 57:196.

9:6—10:11 THE GOLDEN CALF

[9]"When I went up the mountain to receive the tables of stone, the tables of the covenant which the LORD made with you, I remained on the mountain forty days and forty nights; I neither ate bread nor drank water. [10]And the LORD gave me the two tables of stone written with the finger of God; and on them were all the words which the LORD had spoken with you on the mountain out of the midst of the fire on the day of the assembly. . . .

[20]"And the LORD was so angry with Aaron that he was ready to destroy him; and I prayed for Aaron also at the same time. [21]Then I took the sinful thing, the calf which you had made, and burned it with fire and crushed it, grinding it very small, until it was as fine as dust; and I threw the dust of it into the brook that descended out of the mountain. . . .

10 [1]"At that time the LORD said to me, 'Hew two tables of stone like the first, and come up to me on the mountain, and make an ark of wood. [2]And I will write on the tables the words that were on the first tables which you broke, and you shall put them in the ark.'"

OVERVIEW: Moses, Elijah and Christ all fasted for forty days, and the number forty is frequent in Scripture. It indicates our need to commemorate the Lord's body (AUGUSTINE). Through fasting Moses drew closer to God (MAXIMUS OF TURIN). The word that nourishes us is manifold and varied (ORIGEN). The assembly of the Israelites anticipates the church. Aaron's sin did not prevent him from becoming high priest (CYRIL OF JERUSALEM).

9:9 Forty Days and Nights on the Mountain

THE SIGNIFICANCE OF THE NUMBER FORTY. AUGUSTINE: This is why Moses fasted for forty days, and Elijah, and the Mediator himself, our

Lord Jesus Christ: because in this time-bound state of ours restraint from bodily attractions and allurements is very necessary. The people also spent forty years wandering in the desert, and forty days of rain produced the flood.[1] The Lord spent forty days after his resurrection with his disciples, to convince them of the reality of his risen body. This suggests that in this life, in which we are in exile away from the Lord, the number forty stands, as I have just said, for our need to celebrate the memorial of the Lord's body, which we do in the church until he comes.[2] SERMON 51.32.[3]

THE GOOD EFFECTS OF FASTING. MAXIMUS OF TURIN: Fasting these forty days and nights, holy Moses too merited to speak with God, to stand and stay with him and to receive the precepts of the law from his hand. For although this human condition prevented him from seeing God, yet the grace of his fasting drew him into close contact with the Divinity. For to fast frequently is a portion of God's virtues in ourselves, since God himself always fasts. He is more familiar, intimate and friendly with the person in whom he sees more of his works, as Scripture says, "And Moses spoke with God face to face like one speaking with his friend."[4] SERMON 35.4.[5]

THE TRUE BREAD. ORIGEN: Every form of nourishment is called "bread" in the Scriptures. This is clear from what is written concerning Moses: for forty days he neither ate "bread" nor drank water. The word that nourishes is multidimensional and varied. Not everyone can receive the solid and strong nourishment of God's teachings. Therefore, wishing to give an athlete's nourishment suitable to the more perfect, [Christ] says, "The bread that I will give is

my flesh, which I will give for the life of the world."[6] ON PRAYER 27.4.[7]

9:10 *Two Tables of Stone*

See CYRIL OF JERUSALEM ON LEVITICUS 8:3 *and* AUGUSTINE ON EXODUS 32:15, 18.

THE ASSEMBLY AND THE CHURCH. CYRIL OF JERUSALEM: Moses anticipates the name of the ecclesia once again when he says of the tablets: "And on them were inscribed all the words that the Lord spoke to you on the mountain from the midst of the fire on the day of the assembly." It is as if he might have said more plainly: "you were called and gathered together." CATECHETICAL LECTURE 18.24.[8]

9:20 *Praying for Aaron Also*

AARON, ONCE FORGIVEN, BECAME HIGH PRIEST. CYRIL OF JERUSALEM: It was not the people alone that sinned but also Aaron, the high priest. For Moses says, "And the wrath of the Lord was upon Aaron"; "and I prayed for him," he says, "and God forgave him." Now Moses made supplication on behalf of the high priest who sinned and prevailed upon the Lord by his importunity. If so, will not Jesus, his only-begotten Son, imploring God in our behalf, more so prevail? If he did not prevent Aaron, because of his falling away, from acceding to the high priesthood, can it be that he will prevent you, coming from paganism, from attaining salvation? CATECHETICAL LECTURE 2.10.[9]

---

[1]Gen 7:12. [2]1 Cor 11:26. [3]*WSA* 3 3:41-42. [4]Ex 33:11. [5]ACW 50:86. [6]Jn 6:51. [7]ACW 19:94. [8]FC 64:133*. [9]FC 61:101.

10:12-22 THE LORD'S MAJESTY

[12]"And now, Israel, what does the Lord your God require of you, but to fear the Lord your God, to walk in all his ways, to love him, to serve the Lord your God with all your heart and with all your soul, [13]and to keep the commandments and statutes of the Lord, which I command you this day for your good? . . . [17]For the Lord your God is God of gods and Lord of lords, the great, the mighty, and the terrible God, who is not partial and takes no bribe. [18]He executes justice for the fatherless and the widow, and loves the sojourner, giving him food and clothing. [19]Love the sojourner therefore; for you were sojourners in the land of Egypt. [20]You shall fear the Lord your God; you shall serve him and cleave to him, and by his name you shall swear. [21]He is your praise; he is your God, who has done for you these great and terrible things which your eyes have seen. [22]Your fathers went down to Egypt seventy persons; and now the Lord your God has made you as the stars of heaven for multitude."

OVERVIEW: God needs nothing from us, yet he credits us with generosity (ORIGEN). There are no other gods but the Lord God, despite some phrases that appear in the Scriptures (JUSTIN MARTYR). When the Word took on flesh, he took on all of human nature (GREGORY OF NYSSA).

10:12 What Does the Lord Require?

GOD NEEDS NOTHING FROM US. ORIGEN: God seeks from us and entreats us, not because he needs something that we have to give him but, after we have given it to him, he will account that very thing to us for our salvation. HOMILIES ON THE GOSPEL OF LUKE 39.6.[1]

10:17 God of Gods and Lord of Lords

SCRIPTURE ATTESTS TO THE ONE GOD. JUSTIN MARTYR: [Trypho the Jew said,] "But now, return to the original topic and prove to us that the prophetic Spirit ever admits the existence of another God, besides the Creator of all things; and do be careful not the mention the sun and moon, which, Scripture tells us, God permitted the Gentiles to worship as gods.[2] Even prophets often misuse the word in this sense when they say, 'Your God is God of gods and Lord of lords,' often adding, 'the great and mighty and terrible.' Such words are used not as if they were really gods but because the word is instructing us that the true God, the Creator of all, is the sole Lord of all those who are falsely regarded as gods and lords. To convince us of this the Holy Spirit said through David: 'The gods of the Gentiles (although reputed as gods) are idols of demons, and not gods.'[3] And he places a curse upon those who make or worship such idols."

"Trypho," I answered, ". . . They who worship these idols and similar objects are justly condemned." DIALOGUE WITH TRYPHO 55.[4]

10:22 The Ancestors Numbered Seventy Persons

SOUL MEANS ALL OF HUMAN NATURE. GREGORY OF NYSSA: When we read in sacred history that Jacob went down into Egypt with seventy-five souls,[5] we understand the flesh also to be intended together with the souls. So then the

---

[1]FC 94:162. [2]Deut 4:19. [3]Ps 96:5. [4]FC 6:230. [5]So the LXX; see Acts 7:14.

Word, when he became flesh, took with the flesh the whole of human nature. And hence it was possible that hunger and thirst, fear and dread, desire and sleep, tears and trouble of spirit, and all such things, were in him. For the Godhead, in its proper nature, admits no such

affections, nor is the flesh by itself involved in them, if the soul is not affected coordinately with the body. AGAINST EUNOMIUS 2.13.[6]

---

[6]NPNF 2 5:127-28.

11:1-17 THE WONDERS OF THE LORD

[11]"But the land which you are going over to possess is a land of hills and valleys, which drinks water by the rain from heaven, [12]a land which the LORD your God cares for; the eyes of the LORD your God are always upon it, from the beginning of the year to the end of the year.

[13]"And if you will obey my commandments which I command you this day, to love the LORD your God, and to serve him with all your heart and with all your soul, [14]he[j] will give the rain for your land in its season, the early rain and the later rain, that you may gather in your grain and your wine and your oil."

j Sam Gk Vg: Heb I

OVERVIEW: The Promised Land is watered from above, by rain from heaven, and not from below, the way Egypt is (JEROME). Early rain came in the time of the law and late rain at the time of the incarnation (PATERIUS).

11:11 A Land of Hills and Valleys

SPIRITUAL ATTRACTIONS. JEROME: All this Abraham undergoes that he may dwell in a land of promise watered from above, and not like Egypt, from below, no producer of herbs for the weak and ailing but a land that looks for the early and the latter rain from heaven. It is a land of hills and valleys and stands high above the sea. The attractions of the world it entirely lacks, but its spiritual attractions are for this all the greater. LETTER 46.2.[1]

11:14 Rain in Its Season

RAIN FOR JEWS AND CHRISTIANS. PATERIUS: What do we understand here by rain, except the words of sacred preaching? We apply this passage to the holy teachers who were preachers in Judea. Of them it is written, "I will command the clouds not to pour down rain upon her."[2] We are watered by the word of their holy preaching when we acknowledge the aridity of our hearts with true humility. Thus the psalmist says rightly, "My soul is like a land without water before you."[3] The prophet urges us to be drenched with the flowing words of doctrine when he says, "You who thirst, come to the waters."[4] We, in the late ages of the world, now receive the words of holy preaching. We are watered, as it were, with late rain. This preaching of the late rain went forth from his sacrifice to us. For he says through the psalmist, "The

---

[1]NPNF 2 6:61. [2]Is 5:6. [3]Ps 143:6. [4]Is 55:1.

lifting up of my hands is an evening sacrifice."[5] Because our Redeemer suffered the attack of his persecutors in the last age of the world, he offered himself as an evening sacrifice for us. Early and late rains are promised as a gift to the people destined to enter the land of promise, and we now see this promise accomplished spiritually. He gave early rain, because he conferred understanding on his elect in the earlier time,

the time of the law. He also gave late rain, because he allowed the mystery of his incarnation to be proclaimed in the last days. EXPOSITION OF THE OLD AND NEW TESTAMENT, DEUTERONOMY 2.[6]

---

[5]Ps 141:2. [6]PL 79:775, citing Gregory the Great *Moral Interpretation of Job* 20.2.5.

[11:18-32 REWARD OF FAITHFULNESS]

[12:1-14 ONE SANCTUARY]

[12:15-28 PROFANE AND SACRED MEALS]

[12:29-31 PAGAN RITES]

12:32—13:19 PENALTIES FOR IDOLATRY

[2]*"You shall surely destroy all the places where the nations whom you shall dispossess served their gods, upon the high mountains and upon the hills and under every green tree;* [3]*you shall tear down their altars, and dash in pieces their pillars, and burn their Asherim with fire; you shall hew down the graven images of their gods, and destroy their name out of that place. . . .*

[28]*"Be careful to heed all these words which I command you, that it may go well with you and with your children after you for ever, when you do what is good and right in the sight of the* LORD *your God.*

[29]*"When the* LORD *your God cuts off before you the nations whom you go in to dispossess, and you dispossess them and dwell in their land,* [30]*take heed that you be not ensnared to follow them, after they have been destroyed before you, and that you do not inquire about their gods, saying, 'How did these nations serve their gods?—that I also may do likewise.'* [31]*You shall not do so to the* LORD *your God; for every abominable thing which the* LORD *hates they have done for their*

gods; for they even burn their sons and their daughters in the fire to their gods. . . .

13

[1]*"If a prophet arises among you, or a dreamer of dreams, and gives you a sign or a wonder,* [2]*and the sign or wonder which he tells you comes to pass, and if he says, 'Let us go after other gods,' which you have not known, 'and let us serve them,'* [3]*you shall not listen to the words of that prophet or to that dreamer of dreams; for the LORD your God is testing you, to know whether you love the LORD your God with all your heart and with all your soul. . . .*

[6]*"If your brother . . . entices you secretly, saying, 'Let us go and serve other gods,' . . .* [9]*you shall kill him."*

OVERVIEW: One is to depend on divine power to keep God's commandments (AUGUSTINE, CLEMENT OF ROME, DIDACHE). The true prophet loves the truth of God and of the church (VINCENT OF LÉRINS). When Scripture says that God "does not know," it is said for our sake, so that we can test our progress, or it means that God does not approve. God permits us to be tempted for our benefit. Some temptation leads to sin, while other temptation proves the quality of our faith (AUGUSTINE). It is not penitents that are slain but the obdurate (PACIAN OF BARCELONA).

12:3 Hew Down the Graven Images

RELY ON THE DIVINE POWER. AUGUSTINE: Give no credit to their words, neither be afraid of them. They say that we are enemies of their idols. So be it; may God give them all into our power, as he has already given us what we have broken down. For I say this, beloved, that you may not attempt to overcome those which it is not lawfully in your power to overcome. It is the way of ill-regulated men and the mad Circumcelliones[1] to be violent when they have no power and to be ever eager to die without cause. You heard what we read to you, all of you who were present in the Mappalia:[2] "When the land shall have been given into your power"—he says first "into your power" and so enjoins what is to be done—"then you shall destroy their altars and break in pieces their groves, and hew down all their images."[3] When the power has not been given us, do not do it; when it is given, do not

neglect it. SERMONS ON NEW TESTAMENT LESSONS 12.17.[4]

12:28 What Is Good and Right

LED BY GOD. CLEMENT OF ROME: For it is you, Master, the heavenly "King of eternity,"[5] who gives the sons of men glory and honor and authority over the earth's people. Direct their plans, O Lord, in accord with "what is good and pleasing to you" so that they may administer the authority you have given them with peace, consideration and reverence, and so win your mercy. LETTER TO THE CORINTHIANS 61.2.[6]

12:31 Everything I Command

THE WAY OF LIFE. DIDACHE: You must hate all hypocrisy and everything that fails to please the Lord. You must not forsake "the Lord's commandments" but "observe" the ones you have been given, "neither adding nor subtracting anything." At the church meeting you must confess your sins and not approach prayer with a bad conscience. TEACHING OF THE TWELVE APOSTLES 4.12-14.[7]

13:3 Being Put to the Test

---

[1]Radical Donatists who sometimes substituted suicide for martyrdom. [2]The burial site of Cyprian, outside the walls of Carthage. [3]Cf. Deut 7:1. [4]NPNF 1 6:303. [5]1 Tim 1:17; Tob 13:6, 10. [6]LCC 1:72. [7]LCC 1:173.

Ignore False Teachers. Vincent of Lérins: Hence [Montanus][8] richly deserved that it also ought to be said of him and his writings: "If there rises in the midst of you a prophet, you shall not hear the words of that prophet." And why not? "For," it is said, "the Lord your God tries you whether you love him or not." By virtue of these many convincing examples[9] from church history and others of the same kind, we must clearly perceive and, according to the rules of Deuteronomy, fully understand that if at any time a teacher of the church deviates from the faith, divine providence permits this to happen in order to test and to try us, "whether we love God or not with all our heart and all our soul."[10] Since this is so, we may say that a true and genuine Catholic is the person who loves the truth of God, the church and the body of Christ.[11] [Such a person] does not put anything above divine religion and the Catholic faith—neither the authority, nor the affection, nor the genius, nor the eloquence nor the philosophy of any other human being. Commonitories 18.6-20.1.[12]

In What Sense God Does Not Know. Augustine: God is said to know even when he causes someone to know, as it has been written: "The Lord your God puts you to the test that he might know if you love him." Now this manner of speaking does not mean that God does not know; rather, [it was said] in order that people might know how far they have progressed in the love of God—a thing which is not fully recognized by them except by way of the testings which come about. As for the expression "he puts to the test," it means that God permits testing. Therefore when it is also said that God does not know, this means either that he does not approve (i.e., does not recognize [as conformable to] his discipline and teaching), as it has been said: "I do not know you."[13] Or [it means] that he causes people not to know for their own good, because it serves no useful purpose for them to know. Accordingly the text "the Father alone knows"[14] is correctly grasped if under-

stood to say that he causes the Son to know, and the text "the Son does not know,"[15] if understood to say that the Son causes men not to know (i.e., does not disclose to them what would serve no useful purpose for them to know). On Eighty-three Varied Questions 60.[16]

God Allows Us to Be Tested. Augustine: He permits us to be tested not in order that he, for whom nothing lies hidden, might know but in order that he might make us know the extent of our progress in love for him. According to this same mode of speech our Lord also says that he does not know the day or the hour of the end of the world.[17] What can there be that he does not know? He was concealing it from the disciples for their benefit, and he said that he did not know it because he was causing them not to know by concealing it. On Genesis, Against the Manichaeans 1.22.34.[18]

How God Tempts Us. Augustine: Take, for instance, the text "God tempts no one":[19] it cannot be understood as meaning every kind of temptation but only of a particular kind which God doesn't tempt anyone with. Otherwise that other text, "the Lord your God is tempting you," would be false. Otherwise too we might be denying that Christ is God or that the gospel is not telling the truth when we read that he questioned one of the disciples, "tempting him, but he himself knew what he was going to do."[20] You see, there is a temptation that leads to sin, and in that way God tempts no one. Then there is a temptation or testing that proves the quality of faith, and that way even God is prepared to tempt people. In the same sort of way, when we hear "whoever blasphemes against the Holy Spirit,"[21] we shouldn't take it as meaning every kind of blaspheming, just as in the other case we don't under-

---

[8]A second-century charismatic enthusiast. [9]Vincent has just treated Origen and Tertullian. [10]Deut 6:4. [11]Eph 1:23. [12]FC 7:303-4. [13]Mt 25:12. [14]Mt 24:36. [15]Mt 24:36. [16]FC 70:114-15. [17]Mt 24:36. [18]FC 84:82. [19]Jas 1:13. [20]Jn 6:6. [21]Mk 3:29.

stand every kind of tempting. Sermon 71.15.[22]

13:9 Idolatry to Be Punished

Who Must Be Punished. Pacian of Barcelona: Do you see then that this was not said about penitents but about those who not only themselves persevere in wickedness but also do

not cease to put obstacles in our way? It is these very ones, however dear they may be, that must be relinquished. However useful they seem, they must be abandoned. Letter 3.17.[23]

[22]WSA 3 3:255. [23]FC 99:58-59.

[14:1-2 PAGAN MOURNING RITES]

14:3-21 CLEAN AND UNCLEAN ANIMALS

[3]"You shall not eat any abominable thing. [4]These are the animals you may eat: the ox, the sheep, the goat, [5]the hart, the gazelle, the roebuck, the wild goat, the ibex, the antelope, and the mountainsheep. [6]Every animal that parts the hoof and has the hoof cloven in two, and chews the cud, among the animals, you may eat. [7]Yet of those that chew the cud or have the hoof cloven you shall not eat these: The camel, the hare, and the rock badger, because they chew the cud but do not part the hoof, are unclean for you. [8]And the swine, because it parts the hoof but does not chew the cud, is unclean for you. Their flesh you shall not eat, and their carcases you shall not touch. . . .

[21]"You shall not eat anything that dies of itself; you may give it to the alien who is within your towns, that he may eat it, or you may sell it to a foreigner; for you are a people holy to the Lord your God.

"You shall not boil a kid in its mother's milk."

Overview: The wisdom of Christ the educator forbade the Jews to eat many sorts of food to train them in self-discipline (Clement of Alexandria). Clean animals have horns, so that they can repel temptation and evil (Ambrose).

14:3 No Abominable Thing

The Wisdom of the Law. Clement of Alexandria: Among the Jews, frugality was made a matter of precept by a very wise dispensation of

the law. The Educator forbade them the use of innumerable things. He explained the reasons, the spiritual ones hidden, the material ones obvious, but all of which they trusted. Some animals [were forbidden] because they were [not] cloven-footed; others, because they did not ruminate their food; a third class, because they, alone among all the fish of the seas, had no scales;[1] until finally there were only a few things left fit for

[1]Lev 11:1-47; Deut 14:3-20.

food. And even of those he permitted them to touch, he placed a prohibition on the ones found dead or offered to idols or strangled.[2] They could not even touch them. He imposed upon them a contrary course of action until the inclination engendered by habits of easy living be broken, because it is difficult for one who indulges in pleasures to keep himself from returning to them. CHRIST THE EDUCATOR 2.1.17.[3]

See also NOVATIAN ON LEVITICUS 11:4 *and* CLEMENT OF ALEXANDRIA ON LEVITICUS 11:13.

14:4 Animals You May Eat

THE MEANING OF HORNS. AMBROSE: And therefore the animals that are clean according to the law have horns, for the law is spiritual. Those who can repel the enticements of this world through the Word of God and the observance of virtue seem to be protected by horns upon their heads, so to speak, as if by weapons. And with good reason the wonderful power of

discourse that incites the good soldiers of Christ to battle, so that we may carry back the spoils from our enemy the devil, is called a horn [trumpet].[4] Therefore we are in a battle, and we perceive that many of us are captives in the camp of our enemy. Them we must deliver from a very heavy yoke of slavery. THE PATRIARCHS 11.56.[5]

14:6 Animals That Part the Hoof

See BEDE ON LEVITICUS 11:3.

14:8 The Swine Is Unclean

See CLEMENT OF ALEXANDRIA ON LEVITICUS 11:13.

14:21 Not Boiling a Kid in Its Mother's Milk

See CLEMENT OF ALEXANDRIA ON EXODUS 23:19.

---

[2]Deut 14:21; Acts 21:25. [3]FC 23:108-9. [4]Ps 98:6. [5]FC 65:273.

[14:22-29 TITHES]

[15:1-11 DEBTS AND THE POOR]

15:12-18 HEBREW SLAVES

[22]*"You shall tithe all the yield of your seed, which comes forth from the field year by year. . . .* [6]*"For the LORD your God will bless you, as he promised you, and you shall lend to many nations, but you shall not borrow; and you shall rule over many nations, but they shall not rule over you. . . .* [12]*"If your brother, a Hebrew man, or a Hebrew woman, is sold to you, he shall serve you six years, and in the seventh year you shall let him go free from you.* [13]*And when you let him go free from you, you shall not let him go empty-handed."*

Overview: The patriarch Joseph lent to the nations at interest and thereby taught them true doctrine (Ambrose).

15:6 Lending to Many Nations

The Hebrews Profited the Gentiles.
Ambrose: The Hebrew[1] lent to the nations at interest. He did not himself receive doctrine from the people but handed it down. To him the Lord opened his treasury so that the rain of his word might make the nations to grow wet and so that he might become the prince among the nations, but he himself would have no prince over himself. Letter 7 (37).14.[2]

15:12 Freed in the Seventh Year

See Basil on Leviticus 25:10.

---

[1]That is, the patriarch Joseph.   [2]CSEL 82 1:50.

15:19-23 FIRSTLINGS

[19]*"All the firstling males that are born of your herd and flock you shall consecrate to the Lord your God."*

Overview: Those who are just beginning the Christian life should not make a display of their works, lest they be deceived by praise (Paterius).

15:19 The Firstling of Herds and Flocks

The Beginnings of Christian Life. Paterius: What did Moses mean by making this prohibition, except to forbid those who have begun to live aright to engage in human occupations? To plow with the firstborn of a cow is to display the beginnings of one's conversion[1] in carrying out public activities. To shear the firstborn of sheep is to strip the cover of secrecy from our first good works and display them to human eyes. Therefore we are forbidden to work with the firstlings of cattle. When we are kept from shearing the firstlings of the sheep, we should not act openly too quickly, even if we have begun some solid work. Since our life begins as something simple and innocuous, it is proper that we should not lay aside the covering of its privacy, lest it show itself naked to human eyes once the wool has been sheared. The firstlings of cattle and sheep are suitable only for divine sacrifices. Whatever we begin with that is strong, simple and innocent, we should offer on the altar of our hearts to the honor of the secret judge. And he without a doubt receives it more gladly if it has been hidden from men and not stained with any desire for praise. But often the beginnings of a new conversion are mixed with elements of a carnal life and hence should not become known too quickly. Otherwise, when the good that is acceptable is praised, the soul is deceived by praise and cannot grasp the evils that still lie concealed in it. Exposition of the Old and New Testament, Deuteronomy 4.[2]

---

[1]Conversion, by Gregory the Great's time, often meant undertaking the monastic life, as it probably does here.   [2]PL 79:775-76, citing Gregory the Great *Moral Interpretation of Job* 8.47.78-79.

[16:1-8 FEAST OF THE PASSOVER]

16:9-12 FEAST OF WEEKS

[1]*"Observe the month of Abib, and keep the passover to the LORD your God; for in the month of Abib the LORD your God brought you out of Egypt by night. . . .*

[9]*"You shall count seven weeks; begin to count the seven weeks from the time you first put the sickle to the standing grain.* [10]*Then you shall keep the feast of weeks to the LORD your God with the tribute of a freewill offering from your hand, which you shall give as the LORD your God blesses you."*

OVERVIEW: The offering of the Old Testament was fulfilled in the preaching of the New (JOHN CASSIAN). On the day of Pentecost the sacrifice of prayers was offered up and the people received the Holy Spirit (ORIGEN).

16:9 Counting Seven Weeks

PENTECOST AND THE JUBILEE. JOHN CASSIAN: There was plainly realized the number of this festival,[1] which we read was figuratively foreshadowed in the Old Testament too, when it was ordered that at the end of seven weeks the bread of first fruits was to be offered to the Lord by the priests. This in very truth is recognized as having been offered to the Lord by the preaching of the apostles with which they are said to have exhorted the people on that day.[2] This was the true bread of the first fruits, which was proffered at the beginning of the new teaching, when five thousand men were filled with

the gift of its food and which consecrated to the Lord a Christian people newly born from the Jews. CONFERENCE 21.20.2.[3]

16:10 A Freewill Offering

FIRST FRUITS AND THE HOLY SPIRIT. ORIGEN: An offering of "first fruits," that is, from the beginning of the harvest, is commanded. If you remember well, the law commands this is to be done on the day of Pentecost. This was obviously given to them as a "shadow,"[4] but the truth was reserved for us. For on the day of Pentecost, after they offered up the sacrifice of prayers, the church of the apostles received the first fruits of the coming of the Holy Spirit.[5] HOMILIES ON LEVITICUS 2.2.5.[6]

---

[1]Pentecost, the fiftieth day of Easter. [2]Acts 2:14, 41. [3]ACW 57:734. [4]Heb 10:1. [5]Acts 2:4. [6]FC 83:42.

16:13-17 FEAST OF BOOTHS

[16]"Three times a year all your males shall appear before the Lord your God at the place which he will choose: at the feast of unleavened bread, at the feast of weeks, and at the feast of booths. They shall not appear before the Lord empty-handed."

Overview: To be empty-handed before the Lord is to be without a meritorious life (Paterius).

16:16 They Shall Not Appear Empty-handed

Bringing in the Sheaves. Paterius: He appears empty-handed in the sight of the Lord who brings none of the fruits of his labor with him. One man seethes with desire to increase his power; another pants with longing to gather praise. But because the dying man leaves all these things behind, he appears before the Lord empty-handed, for he brings nothing with him when he appears before the judge. Thus the law admonishes us to good effect when it says, "You will not appear empty-handed in the sight of the Lord." For the man who does not plan for the reward of a meritorious life by acting well appears empty-handed in the sight of the Lord. The psalmist says of the just, "coming they will come rejoicing, carrying their sheaves."[1] They who come to the judge's court carrying sheaves are the ones who display in themselves good works by which they merit life. Exposition of the Old and New Testament, Deuteronomy 6.[2]

---

[1] Ps 126:6. [2] PL 79:776, citing Gregory the Great Moral Interpretation of Job 7.29.38, which Paterius has rearranged.

16:18-20 JUDGES

[18]"You shall appoint judges and officers in all your towns which the Lord your God gives you, according to your tribes; and they shall judge the people with righteous judgment. [19]You shall not pervert justice; you shall not show partiality; and you shall not take a bribe, for a bribe blinds the eyes of the wise and subverts the cause of the righteous. [20]Justice, and only justice, you shall follow, that you may live and inherit the land which the Lord your God gives you."

Overview: An unjust profit is always balanced by a just loss (Caesarius of Arles). We may not pervert justice with our own view of the truth (Jerome).

16:19 A Bribe Blinds the Wise

The Justice of Judges. Caesarius of Arles: Those who hear cases should decide them justly and not accept bribes at the expense of the innocent, "for gifts blind the hearts of the wise and change the words of the just." Otherwise, while they are acquiring money, they may lose their soul. No one obtains unjust profit without a just loss. Where the gain is, there is the loss: a gain in the money coffer but a loss in the conscience. SERMONS 13.2.[1]

16:20 Follow Only Justice

JUSTICE AND TRUTH. JEROME: In another place:

"You shall follow justly after that which is just," lest we turn from justice, by asserting our own view of truth, recalling the experience of Saul and Agag.[2] AGAINST THE PELAGIANS 2.3.[3]

---

[1]FC 31:76. [2]1 Sam 15:9. [3]FC 53:297.

16:21 — 17:7 PAGAN WORSHIP

[2]*"If there is found among you, within any of your towns which the LORD your God gives you, a man or woman who does what is evil in the sight of the LORD your God, in transgressing his covenant,* [3]*and has gone and served other gods and worshiped them, or the sun or the moon or any of the host of heaven, which I have forbidden, . . .* [6]*on the evidence of two witnesses or of three witnesses he . . . shall be put to death; a person shall not be put to death on the evidence of one witness."*

OVERVIEW: The two witnesses at the Lord's resurrection fulfilled the law (TERTULLIAN).

17:3 The Sun, Moon or Heaven

See ORIGEN ON DEUTERONOMY 4:19.

17:6 Evidence of Two Witnesses

TWO WITNESSES AT THE RESURRECTION. TERTULLIAN: "Two angels, however, appeared there."[1] For just so many honorary companions were required by the Word of God, which usually prescribes "two witnesses." Moreover, the women, returning from the sepulcher and from this vision of the angels were foreseen by Isaiah, when he says, "Come, you women, who return from the vision";[2] that is, "come" to report the resurrection of the Lord. AGAINST MARCION 4.43.2.[3]

---

[1]Lk 24:4. [2]Is 27:11 LXX. [3]ANF 3:422.

17:8-13 JUDGES

[8]*"If any case arises requiring decision between one kind of homicide and another, one kind of legal right and another, or one kind of assault and another, . . .* [10]*you shall do according to what*

they declare to you from that place which the Lord will choose; and you shall be careful to do according to all that they direct you; [11]*according to the instructions which they give you, and according to the decision which they pronounce to you, you shall do; you shall not turn aside from the verdict which they declare to you, either to the right hand or to the left."*

Overview: We need to walk the middle way (Augustine).

17:11 Not Turning Aside

The Path Between Pride and Sloth.
Augustine: Just as a person has to pick his way between fire and water so as to be neither burned nor drowned, so we should steer our way between the pinnacle of pride and the whirlpool of sloth, as it is written, "turning nei- ther to the right nor to the left." For there are some who, through fear of being carried up to the heights on the right, slip and are drowned on the left. Others . . . fear to be sucked in by the soft ease of sloth on the left and are ruined and destroyed by the ostentation of boasting on the other side, and [they] vanish into smoke and ashes. Letter 48.[1]

[1]FC 12:232-33.

17:14-20 THE KING

[14]*"When you come to the land which the Lord your God gives you, and you possess it and dwell in it, and then say, 'I will set a king over me, like all the nations that are round about me';* [15]*you may indeed set as king over you him whom the Lord your God will choose. . . .*

[18]*"And when he sits on the throne of his kingdom, he shall write for himself in a book a copy of this law, . . .* [20]*that his heart may not be lifted up above his brethren, and that he may not turn aside from the commandment, either to the right hand or to the left; so that he may con- tinue long in his kingdom, he and his children, in Israel."*

Overview: The foundation of faith is Jesus Christ, built into a precious temple (Basil).

17:20 Following the Commandment

Walk the King's Highway. Basil the Great: You are a wayfarer, like to him who prayed, "Direct my steps."[1] "Give heed to your- self" that you may swerve not from the path, that you decline neither to the right nor the left. Keep to the king's highway. The architect should lay the firm foundation of faith which is Jesus Christ and let the builder look to his materials: not wood, nor hay nor stubble but gold, silver, precious stones.[2] Homily on the Words "Give Heed to Yourself."[3]

[1]Ps 119:133. [2]1 Cor 3:11-12. [3]FC 9:437.

18:1-22 PRIESTS AND PROPHETS

[15]"The Lord your God will raise up for you a prophet like me from among you. . . . [17]And the Lord said to me, . . . [20]'But the prophet who presumes to speak a word in my name which I have not commanded him to speak, or who speaks in the name of other gods, that same prophet shall die.'"

Overview: A prophet would come to mediate between God and humanity and to establish a new covenant (Origen). The Samaritan woman called Jesus a prophet (Augustine). The false prophet claims a word of wisdom but does not speak the Lord's word (Origen).

18:15 The Lord Will Raise a Prophet

Israel Did Not Find the Prophet Like Moses. Origen: It is written in Deuteronomy, "[The Lord] your God will raise up a prophet like me for you from your brothers. You shall hear him; and it shall be that every soul which will not hear that prophet shall be destroyed from his people."[1] Therefore some prophet was specially expected who would be similar to Moses in some respect, to mediate between God and humanity, and who would receive the covenant from God and give the new covenant to those who became disciples. And the people of Israel knew so far as each of the prophets was concerned that no one of them was the [special] one announced by Moses..Commentary on the Gospel of John 6.90.[2]

Christ Like Moses in the Flesh. Augus-

tine: "Like me," says Moses. This means according to the form of the flesh, not to the eminence of majesty. Therefore we find the Lord Jesus called a prophet. Accordingly that woman[3] is no longer greatly in error when she says, "I see that you are a prophet."[4] She begins to call her husband, to exclude the adulterer. "I see that you are a prophet." And she begins to ask about a thing that constantly disturbs her. Tractate on the Gospel of John 15.23.1.[5]

18:20 The Prophet Who Presumes to Speak

Beware of False Prophets. Origen: We can be prepared to find some prophet even of impiety—and perhaps not just one but several—who will tell us of a word of the Lord, which the Lord has not at all commanded, or a "word of wisdom"[6] which has nothing whatever to do with wisdom. His purpose is to slay us by the word of his mouth. Exhortation to Martyrdom 8.[7]

---

[1]Acts 3:22-23; Lev 23:29. [2]FC 80:193-94. [3]That is, the Samaritan woman of Jn 4:7-30. [4]Jn 4:19. [5]FC 79:92-93*. [6]1 Cor 12:8. [7]ACW 19:148.

19:1-13 CITIES OF REFUGE

[4]"This is the provision for the manslayer, who by fleeing there may save his life. If any one kills his neighbor unintentionally without having been at enmity with him in time past—[5]as

when a man goes into the forest with his neighbor to cut wood, and his hand swings the axe to cut down a tree, and the head slips from the handle and strikes his neighbor so that he dies—he may flee to one of these cities and save his life."

Overview: We need to be cautious when correcting the faults of another (Gregory the Great). Sin can be committed in ignorance (Jerome).

19:5 Unintentional Killing

Restraint in Correcting Others. Gregory the Great: Now we go into a wood with a friend as often as we turn our attention to the sins of subjects, and guilelessly we hew wood when we cut away the faults of sinners with loving intention. But the axe flies from the hand when reproof oversteps itself and degenerates into hardship. The iron flies from the handle when the words of reproof are excessively harsh and the friend is struck and killed. Thus a contumelious utterance kills the spirit of love in the hearer. Pastoral Care 2.10.[1]

Ignorance Can Be Sinful. Jerome: The very words of Scripture[2] indicate that even ignorance is a sin. This is why Job offers holocausts for his sons, lest perchance they may have sinned unwittingly in thought.[3] And if a man is killed by the iron of an axe that flies off the handle when a man is hewing wood, the wood hewer is ordered to flee to a city of refuge and remain in that place until the death of the high priest.[4] That is to say, [he remains there] until he is redeemed by the blood of the Savior, either in the house of baptism or by repentance, which supplies the efficacy of the grace of baptism through the ineffable mercy of the Savior. [The Savior] does not wish anybody to perish, nor does he find his delight in the death of sinners, but [he would] rather that they be converted from their way and live.[5] Against the Pelagians 1.33.[6]

---

[1]ACW 11:86*. [2]The speaker is Atticus, who is a Catholic arguing against a Pelagian. [3]Job 1:5. [4]Josh 20:6. [5]Ezek 18:23. [6]FC 53:279.

19:14 REMOVAL OF LANDMARKS

[14]*"In the inheritance which you will hold in the land that the Lord your God gives you to possess, you shall not remove your neighbor's landmark, which the men of old have set."*

Overview: Keep boundaries intact. To covet a woman is a serious wrong (Ambrose).

19:14 Not Removing Landmarks

Guard Boundaries. Ambrose: And since we have taken an example drawn from agriculture, enjoin them to keep the laws about borders intact and to guard the ancestral boundaries which the law protects. The good will of a neighbor is often more important than the love of a brother. For a brother is often far away, but a neighbor, close at hand, is a witness to the whole of one's life and a judge of one's dealings. LETTER 36 (2).30.[1]

PASSIONS ARE THE AUTHOR OF GUILT.
AMBROSE: But on the contrary, if your eye has looked upon a woman to covet her, you have opened a wound, you have driven a weapon into your body. Your very members become tools of

sin.[2] If you look upon the property of orphans and drive them from the dwellings of their fathers,[3] you are changing the landmarks that your forefathers set. Your members are tools of iniquity. And so the passions are the author of guilt and not the flesh, for the flesh is the servant of the will. JACOB AND THE HAPPY LIFE 1.3.10.[4]

---

[1]CSEL 82 2:19. [2]Mt 5:28. [3]1 Kings 21:4. [4]FC 65:126.

19:15-21 FALSE WITNESSES

[15]*"A single witness shall not prevail against a man for any crime or for any wrong in connection with any offense that he has committed; only on the evidence of two witnesses, or of three witnesses, shall a charge be sustained."*

OVERVIEW: There were not only two or three but many witnesses to Christ's resurrection (CYRIL OF JERUSALEM). The three witnesses are the persons of the Trinity. Sometimes the testimony of only one witness is preferable (AUGUSTINE). The Word of God was conceived by Mary with the Trinity as witness (MAXIMUS OF TURIN).

19:15 Two or Three Witnesses

WITNESSES TO CHRIST'S RESURRECTION.
CYRIL OF JERUSALEM: [Christ] did then truly rise, and after he had risen, he was seen again by his disciples. And the twelve disciples were witnesses of his resurrection, testifying not with words meant to please but contending for the truth of the resurrection even unto torture and death. Further, "on the word of two or three witnesses every word may be confirmed," according to Scripture. There are twelve witnesses to the resurrection of Christ, and do you still disbelieve in the resurrection? CATECHETICAL LEC-

TURE 4.12.[1]

THE TRINITY MYSTERIOUSLY REVEALED.
AUGUSTINE: Therefore if a people composed of a great multitude was found a false witness, how must it be understood, "In the mouth of two or three witnesses every word shall stand," except that in this way. The Trinity, in which is unending stability of truth, was revealed through a mystery. Do you want to have a good case? Have two or three witnesses, the Father and the Son and the Holy Spirit. TRACTATE ON THE GOSPEL OF JOHN 36.10.1.[2]

ONE WITNESS SPEAKS THE TRUTH. AUGUSTINE: As a matter of fact, a single witness generally speaks the truth, while a mob may tell lies. And the world, in its conversion to Christianity, believed one apostle preaching the gospel rather than the mistaken multitude who persecuted him. AGAINST FAUSTUS, A MANICHAEAN 16.13.[3]

---

[1]FC 61:125. [2]FC 88:92. [3]NPNF 1 4:223.

The Trinity Attests to Christ's Birth.
Maximus of Turin: At the birth of the Savior,
then, there was fulfilled that divine sentence
which says, "Every word shall stand with two or
three witnesses." For see, the Word of God is
born with the Trinity as witness. For indeed, in
the womb of holy Mary—when the Holy Spirit
comes upon her, when the Most High overshad-
ows her, when Christ is begotten—there is
implied a confession of faith in him. Sermon
61b.3.[4]

---

[4]ACW 50:252.

20:1-9 COURAGE IN WAR

[1]"When you go forth to war against your enemies, and see horses and chariots and an army
larger than your own, you shall not be afraid of them; for the Lord your God is with you, who
brought you up out of the land of Egypt. . . . [5]Then the officers shall speak to the people, saying,
'What man is there that has built a new house and has not dedicated it? Let him go back to his
house, lest he die in the battle and another man dedicate it. [6]And what man is there that has
planted a vineyard and has not enjoyed its fruit? Let him go back to his house, lest he die in the
battle and another man enjoy its fruit. [7]And what man is there that has betrothed a wife and
has not taken her? Let him go back to his house, lest he die in the battle and another man take
her.'"

Overview: The law mercifully spares some
young men from military service (Clement of
Alexandria).

20:5 One Who Has Built a New House

The Law Is Merciful. Clement of Alexandria: Again, the law in its humanity says that if
a man has built a new house but has not yet
moved in, or laid out a new vineyard but has not
yet enjoyed the fruit, or become betrothed to a
girl but has not yet married her, he is to be
excused military service. This makes military
sense, since we would be unenthusiastic in our
military service if we were being pulled in the
direction of the things we longed for. People
expose themselves to danger without a second
thought only if they are free in relation to natural impulses. It is also humane, in the calculation
that the outcome of war is uncertain and it is
unjust for such a man not to benefit from his
own labors or for someone else who has taken
no trouble to possess the property of those who
have put in the work. Stromateis 2.18.82.1-3.[1]

---

[1]FC 85:213.

[20:10-18 CITIES OF THE ENEMY]

20:19-20 TREES OF A BESIEGED CITY

[19]*"When you besiege a city for a long time, making war against it in order to take it, you shall not destroy its trees by wielding an axe against them; for you may eat of them, but you shall not cut them down. Are the trees in the field men that they should be besieged by you?* [20]*Only the trees which you know are not trees for food you may destroy and cut down that you may build siegeworks against the city that makes war with you, until it falls."*

OVERVIEW: The law spares trees and crops from the ravages of war (CLEMENT OF ALEXANDRIA).

20:19 When You Besiege a City

MERCY EVEN IN CONQUEST. CLEMENT OF ALEXANDRIA: The Logos in his goodness, richly equipped with love of humankind, teaches that it is not right to cut down cultivated trees, still less to cut crops for purposes of vandalism before harvest, and even less still to destroy, root and branch, cultivated fruit, whether of the land or of the soul. It does not even allow the razing of enemy land. Yes, and farmers find their profit from the law. It enjoins them to take care of their young trees right to their third year, pruning them to prevent them being oppressed by excessive weight and being weakened through shortage of a nourishment spread too thinly. It enjoins them to trench and dig around them to prevent parasites from inhibiting their growth. It does not allow the harvesting of immature fruit from immature trees. After three years, the first fruits are to be consecrated to God after the tree has reached maturity. STROMATEIS 2.18.95.1-3.[1]

---

[1]FC 85:220-21.

[21:1-9 EXPIATION OF UNTRACED MURDER]

21:10-17 MARRIAGE WITH A FEMALE CAPTIVE

[10]*"When you go forth to war against your enemies, and the LORD your God gives them into your hands, and you take them captive,* [11]*and see among the captives a beautiful woman, and you have desire for her and would take her for yourself as wife,* [12]*then you shall bring her home to your house, and she shall shave her head and pare her nails.* [13]*And she shall put off her captive's garb, and shall remain in your house and bewail her father and her mother a full month; after that you may go in to her, and be her husband, and she shall be your wife.* [14]*Then, if you*

have no delight in her, you shall let her go where she will; but you shall not sell her for money, you shall not treat her as a slave, since you have humiliated her."

OVERVIEW: The beautiful woman of the enemy is the spoils of pagan learning, from which all that is worthless must be cut away (ORIGEN). The law teaches a young man to exercise restraint, even toward a captive woman (CLEMENT OF ALEXANDRIA).

21:10-11 When You Go to War

THE SPOILS OF PAGAN LEARNING. ORIGEN: But nevertheless I also intellectually have "gone out to war against my enemies, and I saw there" in the plunder "a woman with a beautiful figure." Whatever we find said well and reasonably among our philosophical enemies, or we read anything said among them wisely and knowingly, we must cleanse it. We must remove and cut off all that is dead and worthless. It is as if one were trimming the hairs of the head and the nails of the woman taken from the spoils of the enemy. Only then would

you take her as a wife. HOMILIES ON LEVITICUS 7.6.7.[1]

21:13 She Shall Mourn Her Parents

ACTING WITH RESTRAINT. CLEMENT OF ALEXANDRIA: The [Deuteronomic] law wishes males to have responsible sexual relations with their marriage partners, solely for the generation of children. This is clear when a bachelor is prevented from enjoying immediate sexual relations with a woman prisoner of war. If he once falls in love with her, he must let her cut her hair short and mourn for thirty days. If even so his desire has not faded away, then he may father children by her. The fixed period of time enables the overpowering impulse to be scrutinized and to turn into a more rational appetency. STROMATEIS 3.11.71.4.[2]

---

[1]FC 83:150.   [2]FC 85:300.

21:15-17 RIGHTS OF THE FIRSTBORN

[15]*"If a man has two wives, the one loved and the other disliked, and they have borne him children, both the loved and the disliked, and if the first-born son is hers that is disliked,* [16]*then on the day when he assigns his possessions as an inheritance to his sons, he may not treat the son of the loved as the first-born in preference to the son of the disliked, who is the first-born,* [17]*but he shall acknowledge the first-born, the son of the disliked, by giving him a double portion of all that he has, for he is the first issue of his strength; the right of the first-born is his."*

OVERVIEW: The two wives are not two souls but two forms of the one soul. The true firstborn son is the offspring of holiness (AMBROSE).

21:15 Two Wives, One Loved and One Disliked

THE QUALITIES OF ONE SOUL. AMBROSE: Since

that discourse[1] took up an example from Deuteronomy for its assertion, where it is connected with "the man who had two wives, one hateful, the other lovable," it is not unreasonable for you to be concerned, lest someone should perhaps think that the passage advocated that the man had two souls. This is not at all possible.

Truly, you yourself are not unaware that sometimes when Scripture speaks allegorically, one thing refers to the form of the synagogue, another to the church. One thing refers to the soul, another to the mystery of the Word and another to different forms and qualities of souls which the spiritually discerning person recognizes. In the following chapter of the law I judge that not two souls but different qualities of one soul were meant. For there is the form of the lovable soul, which delights in pleasures, flees from labor, shuns compunction and rejects the judgment of God. It is lovable in this way: it seems sweet and agreeable at the time. This form of the soul does not affect the mind but diverts it. But that other form of the soul is rather sadder. It is perfected by zeal for God, just as the severe wife is unwilling to allow her spouse to go to harlots. She does not endure it. She simply does not allow it. This form of the soul does not indulge the body in any way; she yields to no pleasures or delights. She rejects shameful secrets; she pursues harsh labors and grave dangers. LETTER 14 (33).1-2.[2]

21:17 *Acknowledging the Firstborn*

THE TRUE ELDEST SON. AMBROSE: So the digression we made from one law to another was not pointless, so that we teach that the firstborn is not of that lovable wife, that is, the son of the wife who is indulgent and devoted to pleasure, although the verses before us express this thought. The words of Scripture say, "He shall not propose the son of his lovable wife as the firstborn when he knows that the son of his hateful wife is the firstborn." Rather, he who is the holy offspring of a holy mother is genuinely the firstborn; true sons do not stray from their true mother though sinners do. Therefore, he is not the true firstborn who is not the son of the true mother, but like a firstborn he is helped by richers and honored lest he be in need. But the firstborn receives "a double portion of all that he has" in order that he may be rich, [just as] in Genesis you find that each patriarch received a gift of two cloaks from their brother Joseph when they were sent back to their father. [This signified] that their brother Joseph, who their father believed to be dead, was found. LETTER 14(33).6.[3]

---

[1]Ambrose's previous letter to Irenaeus, a lay person of Milan. In it Ambrose discusses the liberation of the soul from its enemies, and the forms of right living for the soul. [2]CSEL 82 1:107-8. [3]CSEL 82 1:110-11.

[21:18-21 THE INCORRIGIBLE SON]

21:22-23 CORPSE OF A CRIMINAL

[22]"And if a man has committed a crime punishable by death and he is put to death, and you hang him on a tree, [23]his body shall not remain all night upon the tree, but you shall bury him the same day, for a hanged man is accursed by God; you shall not defile your land which the LORD your God gives you for an inheritance."

OVERVIEW: In the Deuteronomic law it is prefigured that Christ would become a curse for us by suffering death on a cross (ATHANASIUS).

21:23 Accursed by God

CHRIST HAD TO DIE ON A CROSS. ATHANASIUS: If any of our own people also inquire, not from love of debate but from love of learning, why he suffered death in no other way except on the cross, let him also be told that no other way than this was good for us and that it was well that the Lord suffered this for our sakes. For if he himself came to bear the curse laid upon us, how else could he have "become a curse"[1] unless he received the death set for a curse? And that is the cross. For this is exactly what is written: "Cursed is he that hangs on a tree." ON THE INCARNATION 25.[2]

---

[1]Gal 3:13. [2]LCC 3:79.

22:1-4 CARE FOR LOST ANIMALS

[1]"You shall not see your brother's ox or his sheep go astray, and withhold your help[p] from them; you shall take them back to your brother. [2]And if he is not near you, or if you do not know him, you shall bring it home to your house, and it shall be with you until your brother seeks it; then you shall restore it to him. [3]And so you shall do with his ass; so you shall do with his garment; so you shall do with any lost thing of your brother's, which he loses and you find; you may not withhold your help. [4]You shall not see your brother's ass or his ox fallen down by the way, and withhold your help[p] from them; you shall help him to lift them up again."

p *Heb* hide yourself

OVERVIEW: Scripture bids us return the property not only of a brother but also of an enemy (GREGORY THAUMATURGUS). Something found is to be treated as a trust (CLEMENT OF ALEXANDRIA). If we ought to help animals, how much more should we help fellow believers in need? (CAESARIUS OF ARLES).

22:1-4 Animals Gone Astray

RETURNING AN ENEMY'S CATTLE. GREGORY THAUMATURGUS: So says Deuteronomy. But in

311

Exodus, even if someone finds what belongs to his enemy, not just his brother, it says, "Turn and take them back to their owner's house."[1] CANONICAL EPISTLE 4.[2]

NATURAL FELLOWSHIP AND TRUST. CLEMENT OF ALEXANDRIA: Scripture teaches us by means of natural fellowship to treat the object found as a trust and not to hold hatred of an enemy. STROMATEIS 2.18.87.3.[3]

HELP OFFERED TO ONE IN NEED. CAESARIUS

OF ARLES: You are commanded to pull out the ass or the ox which is lying in the mud. Do you then see a Christian like yourself, who was redeemed by the blood of Christ, lying in the sewer of drunkenness and wallowing in the mud of dissipation, and remain silent? Do you pass by and not stretch forth the hand of mercy? Do you merely shout at him or rebuke him or instill fright in him? SERMON 225.4.[4]

---

[1]Ex 23:4. [2]FC 98:149. [3]FC 85:216. [4]FC 66:154.

22:5-12 VARIOUS PRECEPTS

[5]"A woman shall not wear anything that pertains to a man, nor shall a man put on a woman's garment; for whoever does these things is an abomination to the LORD your God.

[6]"If you chance to come upon a bird's nest, in any tree or on the ground, with young ones or eggs and the mother sitting upon the young or upon the eggs, you shall not take the mother with the young; [7]you shall let the mother go, but the young you may take to yourself; that it may go well with you, and that you may live long.

[8]"When you build a new house, you shall make a parapet for your roof, that you may not bring the guilt of blood upon your house, if any one fall from it.

[9]"You shall not sow your vineyard with two kinds of seed, lest the whole yield be forfeited to the sanctuary,[q] the crop which you have sown and the yield of the vineyard. [10]You shall not plow with an ox and an ass together. [11]You shall not wear a mingled stuff, wool and linen together.

[12]"You shall make yourself tassels on the four corners of your cloak with which you cover yourself."

q *Heb* become holy

OVERVIEW: Men and women should be distinguished in their dress as they are in other traits (AMBROSE). The parapet of a house prevents people from falling (ORIGEN). The pure and the impure should not be mixed in the cultivation of the Logos (CLEMENT OF ALEXANDRIA). One cannot reap grain and thorns from the same soul

(GREGORY OF NYSSA). The preacher must discriminate among his hearers (PATERIUS).

22:5 Appropriate Garments

MEN AND WOMEN HAVE DIFFERENT STRENGTHS. AMBROSE: If you consider it truly, there is an incongruity that nature itself abhors. For why, man, do you not want to appear to be what you were born as? Why do you put on a strange guise? Why do you ape a woman? Or why do you, woman, ape a man? Nature arrays each sex with its own garments. Men and women have different customs, different complexions, gestures and gaits, different sorts of strength, different voices. LETTER 15 (69).2.[1]

22:8 A Parapet for a Roof

PROTECT THE LIVES OF OTHERS. ORIGEN: When you build a house, you do not quit before building the protective parapet of the house. It is this parapet that prevents one who has ascended onto the house from falling. So it is with the house of the Word. Consequently those who fall because of unfinished buildings fall only from houses which lack the parapet. Those architects and builders bear the blame for such slaughters and falls. COMMENTARY ON THE GOSPEL OF JOHN 6.7.[2]

22:10 Not Plowing with an Ox and an Ass Together

AGAINST RACIAL JUDGMENTS. CLEMENT OF ALEXANDRIA: There it is perhaps guessing at the disparity between the animals. It is at the same time showing clearly that we must not wrong any of those from other races by bringing them under the same yoke when we have nothing

against them apart from their foreignness, for which they are not responsible, which is not an immoral trait and does not spring from one. It is my view that this is an allegory, meaning that we should not share the cultivation of the Logos on equal terms between pure and impure, faithful and faithless, as the ox is accounted a clean animal and the donkey unclean. STROMATEIS 2.18.94.4-5.[3]

EVIL AND VIRTUE. GREGORY OF NYSSA: What does Scripture mean by these riddles? That it is not right for evil and virtue to grow together in the same soul. Nor is it right, dividing one's life between opposites, to reap thorns and grain from the same soul. Nor is it right for the bride of Christ to commit adultery with the enemies of Christ or to bear light in the womb and beget darkness. ON THE CHRISTIAN MODE OF LIFE.[4]

PREACHING TO THE WISE AND TO FOOLS. PATERIUS: Man is forbidden to plow with an ox and an ass at the same time. This is as if to say you should not bring together fools and the wise to hear your teaching. Otherwise you will cause the one who cannot fulfill your words to stand in the way of the one who can. EXPOSITION OF THE OLD AND NEW TESTAMENT, DEUTERONOMY 10.[5]

---

[1]CSEL 82 1:112. [2]FC 80:169-70*. [3]FC 85:220. [4]FC 58:138. [5]PL 79:778, citing Gregory the Great *Moral Interpretation of Job* 1.16.23.

[22:13—23:1 CRIMES AGAINST MARRIAGE]

23:2-9 MEMBERSHIP IN THE COMMUNITY

[7]*"You shall not abhor an Edomite, for he is your brother; you shall not abhor an Egyptian, because you were a sojourner in his land. [8]The children of the third generation that are born to them may enter the assembly of the LORD."*

OVERVIEW: We are not to think of strangers as enemies (CLEMENT OF ALEXANDRIA). It is wicked to demand interest of one in need (AMBROSE).

23:7 Do Not Abhor an Egyptian

EGYPTIANS ARE GENTILES. CLEMENT OF ALEXANDRIA: At any rate [Scripture] says openly, "You shall not loathe Egyptians, since you lived as strangers in Egypt." By Egyptian it means "Gentile," in fact anyone from anywhere in the world. It is further forbidden to think of enemies as enemies, even if they are presently besieging your walls in the effort to capture your city, until you have sent them an envoy to invite them to peace.[1] STROMATEIS 2.18.88.2-3.[2]

---

[1]Deut 20:10. [2]FC 85:216-17.

[23:10-14 CLEANLINESS IN THE CAMP]

23:15-25 VARIOUS LAWS

[19]*"You shall not lend upon interest to your brother, interest on money, interest on victuals, interest on anything that is lent for interest. [20]To a foreigner you may lend upon interest, but to your brother you shall not lend upon interest; that the LORD your God may bless you in all that you undertake in the land which you are entering to take possession of it.*

[21]*"When you make a vow to the LORD your God, you shall not be slack to pay it; for the LORD your God will surely require it of you, and it would be sin in you. [22]But if you refrain from vowing, it shall be no sin in you. [23]You shall be careful to perform what has passed your lips, for you have voluntarily vowed to the LORD your God what you have promised with your mouth.*

[24]*"When you go into your neighbor's vineyard, you may eat your fill of grapes, as many as you wish, but you shall not put any in your vessel. [25]When you go into your neighbor's standing grain, you may pluck the ears with your hand, but you shall not put a sickle to your neighbor's standing grain."*

OVERVIEW: A vow is a request for a benefit from God (AMBROSE). The law permits us to satisfy our hunger in another's field (AUGUSTINE).

23:19 Do Not Lend on Interest

AGAINST USURY. AMBROSE: [Scripture] orders money to be returned without usury. It is a mark of kindly feeling to help one who has nothing. It is a sign of a hard nature to extort more than one has given. If one has need of your assistance because he has not enough of his own wherewith to repay a debt, is it not a wicked thing to demand under the guise of kindly feeling a larger sum from him who has not the means to pay off a lesser amount? DUTIES OF THE CLERGY 3.3.20.[1]

23:21 When You Make a Vow

DEFINITION OF A VOW. AMBROSE: A vow is a request for a benefit from God with a promise to give something in return. Hence, when you have obtained what you sought, it would be an ungrateful act to delay what you have promised. CAIN AND ABEL 1.7.25.[2]

23:24 Into a Neighbor's Vineyard

SERVANTS OF GOD MAY EAT IN ANOTHER'S FIELD. AUGUSTINE: Let all the servants of God grant [the monks] permission to enter their fields whenever they wish and to depart when well fed and satisfied. This is according to the law given to the people of Israel that no one should arrest a thief in his fields unless he wished to take something away with him. Rather, the owner of the field should permit him who had touched nothing but what he had eaten to depart free and unpunished. ON THE WORK OF MONKS 23.28.[3]

---

[1]NPNF 2 10:70. [2]FC 42:383-84. [3]FC 16:373.

24:1-5 MARRIAGE LAWS

[1]*"When a man takes a wife and marries her, if then she finds no favor in his eyes because he has found some indecency in her, and he writes her a bill of divorce and puts it in her hand and sends her out of his house, and she departs out of his house,* [2]*and if she goes and becomes another man's wife,* [3]*and the latter husband dislikes her and writes her a bill of divorce and puts it in her hand and sends her out of his house, or if the latter husband dies, who took her to be his wife,* [4]*then her former husband, who sent her away, may not take her again to be his wife, after she has been defiled; for that is an abomination before the LORD, and you shall not bring guilt upon the land which the LORD your God gives you for an inheritance."*

OVERVIEW: The law requires a man to proceed slowly if he wants to divorce his wife (AUGUSTINE).

24:1 A Bill of Divorce

DO NOT RUSH INTO DIVORCE. AUGUSTINE: The Lord explains the intention of the law, which required a bill of divorce in every case where a wife was put away. The precept not to put away a wife is the opposite of saying that a man may put away his wife if he pleases, which is not what the law says. On the contrary, to prevent the wife from being put away, the law required this intermediate step, that the eagerness for separation might be checked by the writing of this bill and the man might have time

to think of the evil of putting away his wife. AGAINST FAUSTUS, A MANICHAEAN 19.26.[1]

---

[1]NPNF 1 4:249-50.

24:6—25:4 JUSTICE, EQUITY AND CHARITY

[6]*"No man shall take a mill or an upper millstone in pledge; for he would be taking a life in pledge. . . .*

[10]*"When you make your neighbor a loan of any sort, you shall not go into his house to fetch his pledge.* [11]*You shall stand outside, and the man to whom you make the loan shall bring the pledge out to you.* [12]*And if he is a poor man, you shall not sleep in his pledge;* [13]*when the sun goes down, you shall restore to him the pledge that he may sleep in his cloak and bless you; and it shall be righteousness to you before the LORD your God. . . .*

[19]*"When you reap your harvest in your field, and have forgotten a sheaf in the field, you shall not go back to get it; it shall be for the sojourner, the fatherless, and the widow; that the LORD your God may bless you in all the work of your hands.* [20]*When you beat your olive trees, you shall not go over the boughs again; it shall be for the sojourner, the fatherless, and the widow.* [21]*When you gather the grapes of your vineyard, you shall not glean it afterward; it shall be for the sojourner, the fatherless, and the widow.* [22]*You shall remember that you were a slave in the land of Egypt; therefore I command you to do this."*

OVERVIEW: When sinners confess their sins, they give a sort of pledge, and they match fear and hope. To preach to a sinner is to keep in balance. The sun of justice should not set in our hearts before we have accepted another person's confession of sin (PATERIUS). The charity of the Old Law must be exceeded by that of the New (PSEUDO-BASIL).

24:6 Millstones as a Pledge

KEEPING HOPE AND FEAR IN BALANCE. PATERIUS: To take (*accipere*) means "to take away." Thus those birds that are eager to seize other

birds are called hawks (*accipiter*).[1] Paul says, "For you bear it, if anyone consumes you, if anyone takes you."[2] The same would be true if he said, if anyone seizes you.

The sinner's confession is like the pledge of a debtor. For the pledge is received from the debtor when the sinner makes his confession of sin. The upper and lower millstones[3] in this confession are hope and fear. Hope draws us up to the heights. Fear keeps the heart low. But upper and lower millstones must be joined together;

---

[1]A false etymology; *accipiter* means "swift-flying."   [2]2 Cor 11:20.
[3]Thus the Vulgate at Deut 24:6.

one without the other is useless. Thus in the sinner's confession, hope and fear should always be joined, because the sinner hopes in vain for mercy if he does not also fear justice. In vain did he fear justice if he does not also trust in mercy. Hence merely an upper millstone or a lower millstone alone may not be taken as a pledge.

One who preaches to a sinner should compose his sermon with such balance that he does not take away fear by offering hope alone or leave the sinner only in fear by taking away hope. For the upper or lower millstone is taken away if the preacher's tongue separates either fear from hope for hope from fear in the sinner's heart. EXPOSITION OF THE OLD AND NEW TESTAMENT, DEUTERONOMY 16.[4]

24:13 Restoring a Pledge

WHEN A BROTHER SINS AGAINST US. PATERIUS: Our brother becomes our debtor when our neighbor is shown to have committed some sin against us. For we call sins debts. Thus the sinful servant is told, "I have forgiven you your whole debt."[5] And each day in the Lord's Prayer we pray, "Forgive us our debts as we forgive our debtors."[6] We receive a pledge from our debtor when we receive a confession of sin from him who is known to have sinned against us. His confession bids us to forgive the sin he has committed against us. If he confesses the sin he has committed and seeks pardon, he has already given a pledge for his debt. It is no wonder that we are bidden to return the pledge before sunset. Before the sun of justice sets in us because our hearts are grieved, we ought to accept his confession of sin. For it was he who made his confession of guilt to us. He has remembered that he has sinned against us. Let him soon feel forgiveness for his sin from us. EXPOSITION OF THE OLD AND NEW TESTAMENT, DEUTERONOMY 17.[7]

24:19 Not Getting the Sheaf

CHARITY TO THE POOR. PSEUDO-BASIL: [Of old,] it was wicked and unlawful to gather the sheaves left after the harvest, or to glean the vines after the vintage or to gather up the olives that remain after the trees were picked, because these things were to be left for the poor. Now if this was commanded those who were under the law, what shall we say of those who are in Christ? To them the Lord says, "Unless your justice abounds more than that of the scribes and Pharisees, you shall not enter into the kingdom of heaven."[8] ON MERCY AND JUSTICE.[9]

---

[4]PL 79:780, citing Gregory the Great *Moral Interpretation of Job* 33.12.24. [5]Mt 18:32. [6]Mt 6:12. [7]PL 79:781, citing Gregory the Great *Moral Interpretation of Job* 16.5.6. [8]Mt 5:20. [9]FC 9:510-11.

25:5-10 LEVIRATE MARRIAGE

[5]"If brothers dwell together, and one of them dies and has no son, the wife of the dead shall not be married outside the family to a stranger; her husband's brother shall go in to her, and take her as his wife, and perform the duty of a husband's brother to her. . . . [7]And if the man does not wish to take his brother's wife, . . . [9]then his brother's wife shall go up to him in the presence of the elders, and pull his sandal off his foot, and spit in his face; and she shall answer and say, 'So shall it be done to the man who does not build up his brother's house.'"

OVERVIEW: The levirate law explains the two fathers of Joseph whom Scripture names. In the Old Covenant, obedience, not desire, compelled women to marry (AUGUSTINE).

25:5 If One Dies and Has No Son

HOW JOSEPH HAD TWO FATHERS. AUGUSTINE: In the third book,[1] then, when I was solving the question of how it was possible for Joseph to have two fathers,[2] I indeed said that "he was begotten by one and adopted by the other." But I should have mentioned too the kind of adoption, for what I said sounds as if another living father had adopted him. The law, however, also adopted the children of the deceased by ordering that "a brother marry the wife" of his childless, deceased brother and "raise up seed" by the same woman "for his deceased brother." In this way the explanation of this matter of the two fathers of one man is indeed made clearer. RECONSIDERATIONS 2.33.2.[3]

25:9 Not Building Up a Brother's House

WOMEN OF THE OLD COVENANT DESIRED OFFSPRING. AUGUSTINE: The role of holy women was different in the times of the prophets. Obedience, not concupiscence, impelled women to marry for the propagation of the people of God, among whom the forerunners of Christ were sent in advance. For this people, by the things that happened to them as a type, whether they recognized these types or not, were indeed prophetic of Christ, from whom Christ was to take flesh. Hence, in order that this race might be multiplied, the man who did not raise up seed in Israel was held accursed by sentence of the law. That is why holy women were animated by the pious desire of offspring rather than by desire. We may rightly believe that they would not have sought the marriage union if children could have been obtained in any other way. ON THE GOOD OF WIDOWHOOD 7.10.[4]

---

[1]Of his *Against Faustus, a Manichaean.* [2]Mt 1:16; Lk 3:23. [3]FC 60:133. [4]FC 16:288-89.

[25:11-19 VARIOUS PRECEPTS]

[26:1-11 THANKSGIVING FOR THE HARVEST]

[26:12-15 PRAYER WITH THE TITHES]

26:16-19 THE COVENANT

⁵"And you shall make response before the Lᴏʀᴅ your God, 'A wandering Aramean was my father; and he went down into Egypt and sojourned there, few in number; and there he became a nation, great, mighty, and populous. ⁶And the Egyptians treated us harshly, and afflicted us, and laid upon us hard bondage. ⁷Then we cried to the Lᴏʀᴅ the God of our fathers, and the Lᴏʀᴅ heard our voice, and saw our affliction, our toil, and our oppression; ⁸and the Lᴏʀᴅ brought us out of Egypt with a mighty hand and an outstretched arm, with great terror, with signs and wonders; ⁹and he brought us into this place and gave us this land, a land flowing with milk and honey.' . . .

¹⁷"You have declared this day concerning the Lᴏʀᴅ that he is your God, and that you will walk in his ways, and keep his statutes and his commandments and his ordinances, and will obey his voice; ¹⁸and the Lᴏʀᴅ has declared this day concerning you that you are a people for his own possession, as he has promised you, and that you are to keep all his commandments."

Overview: Even one person who serves God is on equal terms with the whole people (Cʟᴇᴍᴇɴᴛ ᴏғ Aʟᴇxᴀɴᴅʀɪᴀ).

26:9 A Land with Milk and Honey

See ᴄᴏᴍᴍᴇɴᴛs ᴏɴ Exᴏᴅᴜs 3:8.

26:18 A People for God's Possession

Hᴀɴᴅs, Hᴇᴀʀᴛ, Mᴏᴜᴛʜ. Cʟᴇᴍᴇɴᴛ ᴏғ Aʟᴇx-ᴀɴᴅʀɪᴀ: These are evidently symbolic—hands, of action; heart, of deliberation; mouth, of speech. There is an excellent text on the subject of the penitent: "You have chosen God today to be your God, and the Lord has chosen you today to be his people." God makes his own the person who is eager to serve truth and reality and comes as a suppliant. Even if he is only one in number, he is honored on equal terms with the whole people. He is a part of the people. He becomes the complement of the people once he is reestablished out of his previous position, and the whole in fact takes its name from the part. Sᴛʀᴏᴍᴀᴛᴇɪs 2.19.98.1-2.[1]

¹FC 85:222.

27:1-13 CEREMONIES

⁴"And when you have passed over the Jordan, you shall set up these stones, concerning which I command you this day, on Mount Ebal, and you shall plaster them with plaster. ⁵And there you shall build an altar to the Lᴏʀᴅ your God, an altar of stones; you shall lift up no iron tool upon them."

Overview: The stones of the altar were to be natural and free of artifice (Gregory of Nazianzus).

27:5 An Altar of Stones

What Is Consecrated to God. Gregory of Nazianzus: It was once counted a glory for the altar that no axe had been lifted upon it, no stonecutter's tool seen or heard. The higher meaning was that whatever was consecrated to God should be natural and free from artifice. Oration 18.10.[1]

---

[1]FC 22:126.

27:14-26 THE TWELVE CURSES

[15]" 'Cursed be the man who makes a graven or molten image, an abomination to the Lord, a thing made by the hands of a craftsman, and sets it up in secret.' And all the people shall answer and say, 'Amen.'

[16]" 'Cursed be he who dishonors his father or his mother.' And all the people shall say, 'Amen.'

[17]" 'Cursed be he who removes his neighbor's landmark.' And all the people shall say, 'Amen.'

[18]" 'Cursed be he who misleads a blind man on the road.' And all the people shall say, 'Amen.'

[19]" 'Cursed be he who perverts the justice due to the sojourner, the fatherless, and the widow.' And all the people shall say, 'Amen.'

[20]" 'Cursed be he who lies with his father's wife, because he has uncovered her who is his father's.'[w] And all the people shall say, 'Amen.'

[21]" 'Cursed be he who lies with any kind of beast.' And all the people shall say, 'Amen.'

[22]" 'Cursed be he who lies with his sister, whether the daughter of his father or the daughter of his mother.' And all the people shall say, 'Amen.'

[23]" 'Cursed be he who lies with his mother-in-law.' And all the people shall say, 'Amen.'

[24]" 'Cursed be he who slays his neighbor in secret.' And all the people shall say, 'Amen.'

[25]" 'Cursed be he who takes a bribe to slay an innocent person.' And all the people shall say, 'Amen.'

[26]" 'Cursed be he who does not confirm the words of this law by doing them.' And all the people shall say, 'Amen.' "

w Heb uncovered his father's skirt

Overview: Those who lead the blind astray, as heretics do, are accursed (Irenaeus). The law curses those who observe it negligently (Basil).

27:17 Curse for Removing a Landmark

See comments on Deuteronomy 19:14.

27:18 *Curse for Misleading the Blind*

GNOSTICS LEAD THE BLIND ASTRAY. IRE-NAEUS: This [that is, the behavior of the Gnostics] is not the behavior of those who heal and give life but rather of those who aggravate disease and increase ignorance. The law shows itself much truer than such people when it says that whoever leads a blind man astray from the way is accursed. The apostles were sent to find those who were lost and to bring sight to those who did not see and healing to the sick. They did not speak to them in accordance with their previous opinions but by a revelation of the truth. For no one would be acting rightly if one told the blind who were already beginning to fall over the precipice to continue in their dangerous way as if it were a sound one and as if they would come through all right. AGAINST HERESIES 3.5.2.[1]

27:26 *Curse for Not Following the Law*

PENALTIES. BASIL THE GREAT: Moses was the writer of a great part of the law. Did he not add to it a threat against the transgressor or the negligent? He presents a general malediction upon all violators. This is seen in his introduction to the announcement of this most frightful penalty: "Cursed be every man that abides not in all that is written in the book of this law"; and elsewhere, "Cursed be he that does the work of the Lord negligently."[2] If he is accursed who does the work of the Lord negligently, what does he deserve who does not follow the law at all? CONCERNING BAPTISM 5.[3]

---

[1]LCC 1:376-77. [2]Jer 48:10. [3]FC 9:403*.

28:1-6 BLESSINGS FOR OBEDIENCE

[1]"And if you obey the voice of the LORD your God, . . . [5]blessed shall be your basket and your kneading-trough. [6]Blessed shall you be when you come in, and blessed shall you be when you go out."

OVERVIEW: For the soul to be prosperous, it must be cultivated and enriched with heavenly waters (BASIL).

28:5 *Blessed Shall Be Your Basket*

PROSPERITY OF SOUL. BASIL THE GREAT: The prosperity of a city is dependent upon the supply of goods for sale in the market. We say that a country is prosperous which produces much fruit. So also there is a certain prosperity of the soul when it has been filled with works of every kind. It is necessary first for it to be laboriously cultivated and then to be enriched by the plentiful streams of heavenly waters, so as to bear fruit thirtyfold, sixtyfold and a hundredfold[1] and to obtain the blessing which says, "Blessed shall be your barns and blessed your stores." EXEGETIC HOMILIES 14.5.[2]

---

[1]Mt 13:23. [2]FC 46:220.

28:7-14 VICTORY AND PROSPERITY

[12]"The LORD will open to you his good treasury the heavens, to give the rain of your land in its season and to bless all the work of your hands; and you shall lend to many nations, but you shall not borrow. [13]And the LORD will make you the head, and not the tail; and you shall tend upward only, and not downward; if you obey the commandments of the LORD your God, which I command you this day, being careful to do them, [14]and if you do not turn aside from any of the words which I command you this day, to the right hand or to the left, to go after other gods to serve them."

OVERVIEW: The rain is the word of God that falls in the soul and makes it fruitful (AMBROSE).

28:12 The Lord Will Open the Heavens

RAIN RECEIVED IN THE WORDS OF SCRIP-TURE. AMBROSE: The good God reveals an understanding of this gift to his saints and gives it "from his good treasury," as the sacred law attests, when it says, "The Lord swore to your fathers to give to you" and to open "his good treasury." From this heavenly treasury he gives rain to his earth "to bless all the works of your hands." The rain is this: "the utterance" of the law, which falls like dew upon the soul that is fecund and fertile with good works, so that it may possess the moisture of grace. LETTER 11 (29).4.[1]

---

[1]CSEL 82 1:80-81.

[28:15-19 CURSES FOR DISOBEDIENCE]

28:20-35 SICKNESS AND DEFEAT; DESPOILMENT

[15]"But if you will not obey the voice of the LORD your God or be careful to do all his commandments and his statutes which I command you this day, . . . [23]the heavens over your head shall be brass, and the earth under you shall be iron. . . .

[29]"You shall grope at noonday, as the blind grope in darkness, and you shall not prosper in your ways; and you shall be only oppressed and robbed continually, and there shall be no one to help you."

OVERVIEW: The heavens are like brass when they yield no rain (BASIL). The earth is like iron when it receives no seeds (AMBROSE). The soul without discernment is like a blind person (EPHREM).

28:23 The Heavens Shall Be Brass

BRASS MEANS DROUGHT. BASIL THE GREAT: What is meant by "a heaven of brass"? Absolute dryness and lack of aerial waters through which the earth produces its fruits. EXEGETIC HOMILIES 3.8.[1]

HEAVEN OF BRASS, EARTH OF IRON. AMBROSE: By "brass heaven" Scripture means that the heavens are shut up and deny their benefit to the earth. And the earth is iron when it rejects crops and refuses to receive. It is as if in hostile hardness the seed is cast upon the earth, which should be a fruitful field, but it is hard and hostile. The earth ought to nourish the seeds as if in the bosom of a gentle mother. But when does iron bear fruit? When does copper let loose showers? LETTER 44 (68).2.[2]

28:29 Groping at Noonday

ERROR AND BLINDNESS. EPHREM THE SYRIAN: At times when we were in error, mired in the pride of our mind as if with our feet in the mud, we did not perceive our error because our soul was unable to see itself. Although we would look [into the mirror] each day, we would "grope around" in the dark "like blind men." Our inner mind did not possess that which is necessary for discernment. LETTER TO PUBLIUS 11.[3]

---

[1]FC 46:50. [2]CSEL 82 2:43. [3]FC 91:348*.

[28:36-46 EXILE; FRUITLESS LABORS]

28:47-68 INVASION AND SIEGE; PLAGUES; EXILE

[64]"And the LORD will scatter you among all peoples, from one end of the earth to the other; and there you shall serve other gods, of wood and stone, which neither you nor your fathers have known. [65]And among these nations you shall find no ease, and there shall be no rest for the sole of your foot; but the LORD will give you there a trembling heart, and failing eyes, and a languishing soul; [66]your life shall hang in doubt before you; night and day you shall be in dread, and have no assurance of your life."

OVERVIEW: Moses foretold that Christ would hang on the cross (ATHANASIUS).

28:66 Life Hanging in Doubt

CHRIST'S DEATH FORETOLD. ATHANASIUS: Perhaps you have heard of the prophecy of Christ's death. You ask to learn [from Moses] what is set forth concerning the cross. Not even this is passed over. It is displayed by the holy men with great plainness. For first Moses predicts it, and that even with a loud voice, when he says, "You shall see your Life hanging before

your eyes and shall not believe." ON THE INCARNATION 35.[1]

---

[1]LCC 3:88.

[29:1-9 PAST FAVORS RECALLED]

[29:10-15 ALL ISRAEL BOUND TO THE COVENANT]

29:16-29 WARNING AGAINST IDOLATRY; PUNISHMENT FOR INFIDELITY

[5]*"I have led you forty years in the wilderness; your clothes have not worn out upon you, and your sandals have not worn off your feet;* [6]*you have not eaten bread, and you have not drunk wine or strong drink; that you may know that I am the* LORD *your God. . . .*

[18]*"Beware lest there be among you a man or woman or family or tribe, whose heart turns away this day from the* LORD *our God to go and serve the gods of those nations. . . .* [20]*The* LORD *would not pardon him, ...* [22]*and the generation to come, your children who rise up after you, and the foreigner who comes from a far land, would say, when they see the afflictions of that land and the sicknesses with which the* LORD *has made it sick—*[23]*the whole land brimstone and salt, and a burnt-out waste, unsown, and growing nothing, where no grass can sprout, an overthrow like that of Sodom and Gomorrah."*

OVERVIEW: When God is said to act like a man, it must be for our instruction (ORIGEN).

29:5 Clothes Not Worn Out

See COMMENTS ON DEUTERONOMY 8:4.

29:23 The Lord's Wrath

SCRIPTURE USES ANTHROPOMORPHISMS.

ORIGEN: He pretends then that he does not see your future so that he may preserve your self-determination by not foretelling or foreknowing whether you will repent or not. So he says to the prophet, "Speak, perhaps they will repent." You will find numerous other passages where Scripture talks about God "taking on the manners of" man. If you hear of the anger of God and his wrath, do not suppose that anger and wrath are passions of God. The purposes of using this way of speaking are for converting and educating the infant, since we also use a fearful expression with children, not from an actual state of mind but because of a purpose to cause fear. HOMI- LIES ON JEREMIAH 18.6.7.[1]

---

[1]FC 97:200-201.

[30:1-10 MERCY FOR THE REPENTANT]

30:11-14 GOD'S COMMAND CLEAR

[11]"For this commandment which I command you this day is not too hard for you, neither is it far off. [12]It is not in heaven, that you should say, 'Who will go up for us to heaven, and bring it to us, that we may hear it and do it?' [13]Neither is it beyond the sea, that you should say, 'Who will go over the sea for us, and bring it to us, that we may hear it and do it?' [14]But the word is very near you; it is in your mouth and in your heart, so that you can do it."

OVERVIEW: Bombast is an offense against God (CLEMENT OF ALEXANDRIA). All people participate in Christ insofar as he is Word—that is, Reason. To pray for the coming of God's kingdom is to pray that it will be established within ourselves (ORIGEN).

30:14 God's Word in Your Mouth and Heart

THREE INSTRUMENTS. CLEMENT OF ALEXANDRIA: "Anyone who tries to act high-handedly annoys God,"[1] says Scripture. For bombast is a spiritual vice. Scripture tells us to repent from it as from the other vices by turning from disharmony and by linking ourselves to a change for the better through the three instruments of mouth, heart and hands. STROMATEIS 2.19.97.3.[2]

PARTICIPATION IN CHRIST AS WORD. ORIGEN: But consider if perhaps all people participate in him insofar as he is Word. This is why the apos- tle teaches us that he is sought within the seekers by those who choose to find him. He says, "Do not say in your heart, 'Who shall ascend into heaven?' that is, to bring Christ down; or, 'Who shall descend into the deep?' that is, to bring Christ up again from the dead. But what does the Scripture say? The Word is near you, even in your mouth, and in your heart."[3] This is as though Christ and the Word which is sought are the same. COMMENTARY ON THE GOSPEL OF JOHN 1.269.[4]

THE KINGDOM IS WITHIN YOU. ORIGEN: But what does Scripture say? The Word is very near you, in your mouth and in your heart. And to these the Savior also kindly points out the matters pertaining to the kingdom of God, that they may not seek it outside themselves or say, "Behold here or behold there."[5] For he says to them, "The kingdom of God is within

---

[1]Num 15:30. [2]FC 85:222. [3]Rom 10:6-8. [4]FC 80:89. [5]Lk 17:21.

you."[6] COMMENTARY ON THE GOSPEL OF JOHN 19.77.[7]

WE PRAY FOR THE KINGDOM IN OURSELVES. ORIGEN: The "kingdom of God," according to the word of our Lord and Savior, "comes not with observation"; and "neither shall they say: Behold here, or behold there"—but "the kingdom of God is within us"[8] (for "the Word is very nigh unto" us, "in our mouth and in our heart"). So it is clear that he who prays for the coming of the kingdom of God rightly prays that the kingdom of God might be established and bear fruit and be perfected in himself. ON PRAYER 25.1.[9]

---

[6]Lk 17:21. [7]FC 89:185. [8]Lk 17:21. [9]ACW 19:84-85.

30:15-20 THE CHOICE BEFORE ISRAEL

[15]"See, I have set before you this day life and good, death and evil. . . . [19]I call heaven and earth to witness against you this day, that I have set before you life and death, blessing and curse; therefore choose life, that you and your descendants may live, [20]loving the LORD your God, obeying his voice, and cleaving to him; for that means life to you and length of days, that you may dwell in the land which the LORD swore to your fathers, to Abraham, to Isaac, and to Jacob, to give them."

OVERVIEW: Life and death, good and evil, are to be balanced within ourselves (BASIL). Life is the enjoyment of breath and of all goods (AMBROSE). By his grace God has left us free to choose between heaven and hell. We are called to choose the narrow way, the way of life (CAESARIUS OF ARLES). What people grasp and cleave to, they have for eternity (SALVIAN).

30:15 Life and Good, Death and Evil

INTERIOR BALANCE. BASIL THE GREAT: There is a certain balance constructed in the interior of each of us by our Creator, on which it is possible to judge the nature of things. "I have set before you life and death, good and evil," two natures contrary to each other. Balance them against each other in your own tribunal. HOMILY ON PSALM 61.4.[1]

THE NATURE OF LIFE AND DEATH. AMBROSE: Let us ponder the nature of life and of death. Life is the enjoyment of the gift of breath, death the deprivation of it. Further, this gift of breath is considered by most people as a good. And so life is this, the enjoyment of goods, but death is the divestiture of them. And Scripture says, "Behold, I have set before your face life and death, good and evil," for it calls life good and death evil and attributes to each its proper deserts. DEATH AS A GOOD 1.2.[2]

30:19 Life and Death, Blessing and Curse

FREE TO MAKE A CHOICE. CAESARIUS OF ARLES: As he himself said . . . "Behold before you are fire and water, death and life. Choose

---

[1]FC 46:347. [2]FC 65:70.

life, that you may live." Everything we mentioned above, that is, good and evil, is contained in these two. For heaven and hell, Christ and the devil, height and depth are proposed to us in them. Through his grace God has put it into the power of each one to choose and to stretch out his hand to whatever he wishes. Sermon 149.1.[3]

Make the Right Choice. Caesarius of Arles: Behold, man, you have before you "water and fire, life and death, good and evil," heaven and hell, the legitimate king and a cruel tyrant, the false sweetness of the world and the true blessedness of paradise. Power is given to you through the grace of Christ: "Stretch forth your hand to whichever you choose." "Choose life, that you may live"; leave the broad way on the left which drags you to death and cling to the narrow path on the right which happily leads you to life. Do not allow the wideness of that road on the left to keep you or give you pleasure. Sermon 151.5.[4]

What You Grasp You Have Forever. Salvian the Presbyter: For since, as it is written, man is confronted equally with life and death and stretches out his hand toward what he wants, it is necessary that whatever a man grasps with his hands in time he must possess forever in eternity. What here he cleaves to in affection, he must in the future cleave to forever, with his will and mind wholly fixed upon it. Four Books of Timothy to the Church 1.1.7.[5]

---

[3]FC 47:320. [4]FC 47:329-30. [5]FC 3:271.

[31:1-6 THE LORD'S LEADERSHIP]

[31:7-8 CALL OF JOSHUA]

[31:9-13 THE READING OF THE LAW]

[31:14-15 COMMISSION OF JOSHUA]

[31:16-22 A COMMAND TO MOSES]

[31:23 COMMISSION OF JOSHUA]

[31:24-29 THE LAW PLACED IN THE ARK]

31:30 — 32:43 THE SONG OF MOSES

[3]"The LORD your God himself will go over before you; he will destroy these nations before you, so that you shall dispossess them; and Joshua will go over at your head, as the LORD has spoken. [4]And the LORD will do to them as he did to Sihon and Og, the kings of the Amorites, and to their land, when he destroyed them. . . . [6]He will not fail you or forsake you." . . .

[30]Then Moses spoke the words of this song until they were finished, in the ears of all the assembly of Israel:

32 [1]"Give ear, O heavens, and I will speak;
    and let the earth hear the words of my mouth.
[2]May my teaching drop as the rain,
    my speech distil as the dew,
as the gentle rain upon the tender grass,
    and as the showers upon the herb.
[3]For I will proclaim the name of the LORD.
    Ascribe greatness to our God!

[4]"The Rock, his work is perfect;
    for all his ways are justice.
A God of faithfulness and without iniquity,
    just and right is he.
[5]They have dealt corruptly with him,
    they are no longer his children because of their blemish;
    they are a perverse and crooked generation.
[6]Do you thus requite the LORD,
    you foolish and senseless people?
Is not he your father, who created you,
    who made you and established you?
[7]Remember the days of old,
    consider the years of many generations;
ask your father, and he will show you;
    your elders, and they will tell you.
[8]When the Most High gave to the nations their inheritance,
    when he separated the sons of men,
he fixed the bounds of the peoples
    according to the number of the sons of God.[d]
[9]For the LORD's portion is his people,

Jacob his allotted heritage.

¹⁰"He found him in a desert land,
   and in the howling waste of the wilderness;
he encircled him, he cared for him,
   he kept him as the apple of his eye.
¹¹Like an eagle that stirs up its nest,
   that flutters over its young,
spreading out its wings, catching them,
   bearing them on its pinions,
¹²the LORD alone did lead him,
   and there was no foreign god with him.
¹³He made him ride on the high places of the earth,
   and he ate the produce of the field;
and he made him suck honey out of the rock,
   and oil out of the flinty rock.
¹⁴Curds from the herd, and milk from the flock,
   with fat of lambs and rams,
   herds of Bashan and goats,
with the finest of the wheat—
   and of the blood of the grape you drank wine.

¹⁵"But Jeshurun waxed fat, and kicked;
   you waxed fat, you grew thick, you became sleek;
then he forsook God who made him,
   and scoffed at the Rock of his salvation. . . .

¹⁹"The LORD saw it, and spurned them,
   because of the provocation of his sons and his daughters.
²⁰And he said, 'I will hide my face from them,
   I will see what their end will be,
for they are a perverse generation,
   children in whom is no faithfulness.
²¹They have stirred me to jealousy with what is no god;
   they have provoked me with their idols.
So I will stir them to jealousy with those who are no people;
   I will provoke them with a foolish nation. . . .

²³"'And I will heap evils on them; . . .

^{25}In the open the sword shall bereave,
  and in the chambers shall be terror,
destroying both young man and virgin,
  the sucking child with the man of gray hairs.' . . .

^{32}"For their vine comes from the vine of Sodom,
  and from the fields of Gomorrah;
their grapes are grapes of poison,
  their clusters are bitter;
^{33}their wine is the poison of serpents,
  and the cruel venom of asps.

^{34}"Is not this laid up in store with me,
  sealed up in my treasuries?
^{35}Vengeance is mine, and recompense,*
  for the time when their foot shall slip;
for the day of their calamity is at hand,
  and their doom comes swiftly. . . .

^{39}" 'See now that I, even I, am he,
  and there is no god beside me;
I kill and I make alive;
  I wound and I heal;
  and there is none that can deliver out of my hand.
^{40}For I lift up my hand to heaven,
  and swear, As I live for ever,
^{41}if I whet my glittering sword,^{f}
  and my hand takes hold on judgment,
I will take vengeance on my adversaries,
  and will requite those who hate me.
^{42}I will make my arrows drunk with blood,
  and my sword shall devour flesh—
with the blood of the slain and the captives,
  from the long-haired heads of the enemy.' "

d *Compare Gk: Heb* Israel   *LXX On the day of vengeance, I shall repay; Vg. Vengeance is mine, I shall repay   f *Heb* the lightning of my sword

Overview: God keeps promises (Augustine). The Fathers reflected at length on the Song of Moses, as a kind of last will and testament (Nicetas of Remesiana). Moses addressed both clergy and laity, not heaven and earth as if physical realities (Paterius). The rain, spiritually understood, falls generously upon the saints (Origen). The rain is the Word of God. Only the just receive it.

The dry and hard places need to be watered with the Scriptures and the Fathers (CAESARIUS OF ARLES). The Lord is faithful and true, unlike a shadow or an image. In redemption the Savior is said to have acquired what was already his own (ORIGEN). Moses called us to "ask our fathers" rather than to rely on private judgment alone (JOHN CASSIAN). The angels of the nations could not prevent their apostasy (PSEUDO-DIONYSIUS). Scripture depicts an educator of children (CLEMENT OF ALEXANDRIA). The eagle retains only the strong among its young (AMBROSE). The Lord guards and protects us. The Lord spread out his arms for us on the cross (JEROME). The Lord's protection is gentle and kind (PATERIUS). The true saints are also faithful in times of tranquility (CHRYSOSTOM). Nowhere in Scripture does honey or oil flow from a rock (PATERIUS). The Jews were ruined by the ease that they enjoyed (CHRYSOSTOM). When God turns his face away, evils pile up. When God appears to be angry, it is for our good (CLEMENT OF ALEXANDRIA). God utterly destroyed the land of the Sodomites (ORIGEN). Vengeance belongs to God. We are to pray for those who harm us (AMBROSE). If God can give us life, he can restore it too (APHRAHAT). In God's order, affliction precedes grace (BASIL). Evil and good cannot coexist within us (GREGORY OF NYSSA). God is both angry and gentle with the same people. Like a surgeon, God may cut in order to heal. When God strikes us down, we come to understand the inadequacy of our own justice (AUGUSTINE). The One besides whom there is no God is the Trinity (HILARY OF POITIERS). The sword of God slays those who think carnally (PATERIUS).

31:6 Not Fail or Forsake You

GOD KEEPS PROMISES. AUGUSTINE: Pay attention to what comes next: "Without love, a measure of money is sufficient for present needs, because he himself said, 'I will not forsake you; I will not desert you.'"[1] "You were afraid of all kinds of evils, against which you were saving

money; count me as your guarantor." That's what God says to you. God—not a man, not your equal or you yourself—says to you: "I will not forsake you; I will not desert you." If a person made such a promise, you would trust him. God makes it, and you hesitate? He made the promise, put it in writing, made out the bond; you needn't worry at all. SERMONS 177.11.[2]

31:30 Moses Spoke the Words of This Song

MOSES' SONG IS HIS TESTAMENT. NICETAS OF REMESIANA: Moses again, when about to depart from this life, sang a fear-inspiring canticle in Deuteronomy. He left the song as a sort of testament to the people of Israel, to teach them the kind of funeral they should expect, if ever they abandoned God. LITURGICAL SINGING 3.[3]

32:1 Give Ear, O Heavens

WORDS ADDRESSED TO RATIONAL CREATURES. PATERIUS: By heavens he means the order of the clergy and by earth the people subject to them. For "Listen, O heavens, and I shall speak" was addressed not to insensible but to rational creation. EXPOSITION OF THE OLD AND NEW TESTAMENT, DEUTERONOMY 19.[4]

32:2 Teaching Drops as Rain

THE RAIN IS MOSES' SPEECH. ORIGEN: Therefore let us seek in the Scriptures what is "the rain" which is given only to the saints and concerning which "it is commanded to the clouds that they do not pour their rain"[5] upon the unjust. Therefore Moses and the Lawgiver himself teach us what this rain is. For he himself says in Deuteronomy, "Consider, O heaven, and I will speak, and let the earth hear the words from my mouth; let my speech be awaited like rain." Are these words my

---

[1]Heb 13:5; Deut 31:6, 8; Josh 1:5. [2]*WSA* 3 5:287-88. [3]FC 7:68. [4]PL 79:781, citing Gregory the Great *Moral Interpretation of Job* 2.31.51. [5]Is 5:6.

speech? Do we pervert violently the meaning of divine law by arguments of rhetoric? Is it not Moses who says that it is "rain" of which he speaks? He says, "Let my speech be awaited like rain and my words descend as dew, as a storm upon the grass and as snow upon the hay." Homilies on Leviticus 16.2.3.[6]

See also Ambrose on Deuteronomy 28:12.

Only the Just Receive God's Word. Caesarius of Arles: Behold the nature of the rain which is given only to the just and denied to sinners. Therefore the rain is the Word of God. Only the just are prepared to receive it. Lovers of the world, however, who are proud, dissolute or avaricious are unwilling to receive the rain of God's Word even if it is forced upon them. Why is this? Because they are unwilling to hunger or thirst after justice. Those who are saturated with the filth of dissipation do not deserve to be refreshed with the rain of God's Word. Sermon 105.2.[7]

Water God's Garden. Caesarius of Arles: All of us wish to have refreshing waters in our gardens. If there are no waters in them, we draw them from the sea with great effort in order to provide vegetables for our bodies. If so how much more solicitous should we be for the Lord's garden, that is, the church of God, that the dry places be watered and the hard places softened by the rivers of sacred Scripture and the spiritual streams or fountains of the ancient Fathers, so that afterwards what is harmful may be uprooted and what is useful planted? Sermon 1.15.[8]

32:4 A God of Faithfulness

The Lord Is Faithful and True. Origen: But he who is on the white horse is called "faithful,"[9] not so much because he trusts as because he is trustworthy, that is, he is worthy of being trusted. According to Moses, the Lord is faithful and true. For he is also true in contradistinction to a shadow and a type and an image, since the

Word that powers from heaven is true. For the Word on earth is not like the Word in heaven, inasmuch as he has become flesh and is expressed by means of a shadow and types and images. Commentary on the Gospel of John 2.49.[10]

32:6 Your Father, Who Created You

Did Christ Acquire Us? Origen: But if the Lord himself is Creator of all things, we must consider in what manner he is said "to have acquired" what is without doubt his own. It is said also in another song in Deuteronomy: "Is not he himself your God who made you and created you and acquired you?" For each one appears to acquire that which was not his own. Indeed, on this basis the heretics also say of the Savior that he "acquired" those who were not his; for with the price which was paid he purchased men whom the Creator had made. And it is certain, they say, that everyone buys that which is not his own; indeed, the apostle says, "You have been bought with a price."[11] Homilies on Exodus 6.9.[12]

32:7 Ask Your Father

Respect the Teachings of the Elders. John Cassian: Who then would be so presumptuous and blind as to dare to trust in his own judgment and discretion when the vessel of election[13] testifies that he needed to confer with his fellow apostles? From this it is clearly proven that the Lord shows the way of perfection to no one who has the means of being educated but who disdains the teaching and the instruction of the elders and who considers as insignificant that saying which ought to be diligently observed: "Ask your father, and he will declare it to you, your elders, and they will tell you." Conference 2.15.3.[14]

---

[6]FC 83:264. [7]FC 47:119-20. [8]FC 31:18. [9]Rev 19:11. [10]FC 80:107. [11]1 Cor 7:23. [12]FC 71:295. [13]Acts 9:15, Paul. [14]ACW 57:99.

32:8 *The Bounds of the Peoples*

THE WORD GAVE PHILOSOPHY TO THE GREEKS. CLEMENT OF ALEXANDRIA: This is he who bestows on the Greeks also their philosophy through the inferior angels. For by an ancient and divine ordinance angels are assigned to the different nations. But to be the Lord's portion is the glory of believers. STROMATEIS 7.2.6.4.[15]

THE NATIONS WENT TO IDOLATRY. PSEUDO-DIONYSIUS: Someone might ask why it was that only the Hebrew people were lifted up to the divine enlightenment. The answer to this is that the angels have done their work of guardianship and that it is no fault of theirs if other nations wandered off into the cult of false gods.[16] Indeed, it was on their own initiative that these others abandoned the good uplifting toward the divine. CELESTIAL HIERARCHY 9.3.[17]

32:10 *God Encircled His Own*

SCRIPTURE DEPICTS A TEACHER. CLEMENT OF ALEXANDRIA: As far as I can see, Scripture is undoubtedly presenting a picture of the educator of children and describing the guidance he imparts. CHRIST THE EDUCATOR 1.7.56.[18]

32:11 *Like an Eagle*

THE EAGLE FOSTERS TRUE OFFSPRING. AMBROSE: He supported them like the eagle, which was accustomed to examine its progeny, so as to keep and to bring up those whom it observed to possess the qualities of a true offspring and the gift of an undamaged constitution and to reject those in whom it detected weakness of a degenerate origin even at that tender age. THE PRAYER OF JOB AND DAVID 4.5.21.[19]

THE LORD PROTECTS US. JEROME: Like an eagle, the Lord spreads his wings over us, his nestlings. There the Lord is compared with the eagle guarding its young. The simile therefore is appropriate that God protects us as a father and as a hen guarding her chicks lest they be snatched away by a hawk. Nevertheless a different interpretation is also permissible. "With his pinions he will cover you":[20] he will be lifted up on the cross; he will stretch forth his hands to shelter us. "And under his wings you shall take refuge."[21] HOMILIES ON THE PSALMS 20.[22]

JEROME: The song in Deuteronomy says that he bore the people of Israel upon his shoulders and like the eagle guarded them. This same versicle may be interpreted also of the Savior because on the cross he gave us the shelter of his wings. "Under his wings you shall take refuge."[23] "All the day long I stretched out my hand to a people unbelieving and contradicting."[24] The hands of the Lord lifted up to heaven were not begging for help but were sheltering us, his miserable creatures. HOMILY 68.[25]

LIKE A MOTHER BIRD. PATERIUS: The Lord protects us, his little ones. He nourishes us and restores us—not in a heavy and burdensome way but with gentle and kind protection. He shows his mercies toward us, as if extending his wings over us as a bird does. EXPOSITION OF THE OLD AND NEW TESTAMENT, DEUTERONOMY 20.[26]

32:13 *Honey and Oil Out of the Rock*

THE LITERAL SENSE IS NOT HISTORICAL. PATERIUS: Nothing like this is ever found in Scripture in the literal sense, even if one reviews the whole body of the Old Testament. People never sucked honey or oil from a rock. But since, according to Paul, the rock was Christ,[27] they did suck honey from a rock, because they beheld the

---

[15]LCC 2:96. [16]The Fathers often took Deut 32:8 to show that God had assigned a guardian angel to each Gentile nation. [17]PDCW 171. [18]FC 23:51. [19]FC 65:405. [20]Ps 91:4. [21]Ps 91:4. [22]FC 48:157. [23]Ps 91:4. [24]Rom 10:21. [25]FC 57:83. [26]PL 79:781, citing Gregory the Great *Moral Interpretation of Job* 32.5.7. [27]1 Cor 10:4.

deeds and miracles of that same Redeemer of ours. They did suck oil from a solid rock, because after his resurrection they deserved to be anointed with the outpouring of the Holy Spirit. Thus the Lord gave them honey in the solid rock when he, still subject to death, showed his disciples the sweetness of his miracles. And the solid rock poured forth oil, because after his resurrection, when he became impassible, he founded the house of holy anointing by the outpouring of the Spirit. The prophet says of this oil, "The yoke will fall from before the oil."[28] We were held under the yoke of demonic domination, but we have been anointed with the oil of the Holy Spirit. And because the grace of liberty has anointed us, the yoke of demonic domination has fallen. Exposition of the Old and New Testament, Deuteronomy 21.[29]

32:15 Becoming Fat and Kicking

Faithful in Good Times. Chrysostom: One must not so much admire those saints who in the height of sorrow were so pious and lovers of wisdom as those who, even when the turbulence subsided and tranquility ensued, remained in the same goodness and earnestness. Homilies on Repentance and Almsgiving 4.8.[30]

Abundance Can Ruin Us. Chrysostom: For we have continuous need for a curb to keep us walking straight on the path, since even the Jews wandered from the path and drew down upon themselves the anger of heaven. When they enjoyed considerable ease and had become free after their harsh bondage in Egypt, they should have given greater thanks and been more eager to offer their praise to the Master. They should have been better disposed toward him who had bestowed such benefits upon them. But they did quite the opposite and were ruined by the ease which was theirs in abundance. On this account the Holy Scripture accuses them and says, "Jacob ate his fill; the darling became fat and frisky." Baptismal Instructions 5.16.[31]

The Free Child Sought Slavery. Chrysostom: "They ate" and drank "and kicked." When fed with their manna, they ought not to have asked for luxury, seeing they had known the evils which proceed from it. And they acted precisely as if a free child, when sent to school, should ask to be reckoned with the slaves and to wait on them. So did these people also in seeking Egypt. While receiving all needful sustenance, such as becomes a free person, and already sitting at his father's table, he still has a longing for the ill-savored and noisy one of the servants. Homilies on Colossians 4.[32]

32:20 I Will Hide My Face

When God Turns Away. Clement of Alexandria: There is peace and joy in the hearts of those upon whom the face of the Lord looks. But for those from whom he turns away there is an accumulation of evils. He does not desire to look upon evil, because he is good. But if he deliberately looks toward evil, then wickedness takes root, because of humankind's infidelity. Christ the Educator 1.8.70.[33]

32:23 I Will Heap Evils on Them

God Appears to Be Angry. Clement of Alexandria: The Divinity is not angry, as some suppose, but when he makes so many threats he is only making an appeal and showing humankind the things that are to be accomplished. Such a procedure is surely good, for it instills fear to keep us away from sin. Christ the Educator 1.8.68.[34]

32:32 From the Vine of Sodom

God Destroyed the Land of Sinners. Origen: It was the work of the good God,

---

[28]Is 10:27 Vulgate; RSV has "from your neck." [29]PL 79:781-82, citing Gregory the Great, HOG 26.3-4. [30]FC 96.46. [31]ACW 31:86-87. [32]NPNF 1 13:278*. [33]FC 23:62-63. [34]FC 23:61.

indeed, to destroy the land of the Sodomites and to dry up all its remaining moisture, so that there might no longer be a vineyard of the Sodomites, or a vine branch of Gomorrah, or grapes of gall, or a cluster of bitterness, or wine, the wrath of dragons and the incurable wrath of asps. COMMENTARY ON THE GOSPEL OF JOHN 20.28.[35]

32:35 Vengeance Is Mine

VENGEANCE AND THE GOSPEL. AMBROSE: Since God said in the Old Testament, "Vengeance is mine, I shall repay," he says in the Gospel that we should pray for those who harm us, in order that he who promised vengeance might not seek revenge against them. For [God] wants to forgive by your will, which is fitting according to his promise. But if you seek revenge, you have it, since the unjust man is punished more by his thoughts than by judicial severity. LETTER 14 EXTRA COLL. (63).84.[36]

32:39 No God Beside Me

THESE WORDS APPLY TO GOD AS TRINITY. HILARY OF POITIERS: In order that the godlessness of the heretics may not perhaps apply the meaning of these words to the unbegotten God the Father, the sense itself of the words and the authority of the apostle come to our aid. He, as we have already explained, interprets this whole passage as pertaining to the person of the only-begotten God. ON THE TRINITY 5.36.[37]

GOD MAKES ALIVE WHAT IS DEAD. APHRAHAT: We are sure that he causes to die. We see it. Just so also is it sure and worthy of belief that he makes alive. And from all that I have explained to you, receive and believe that in the day of the resurrection your body shall arise in its entirety, and you shall receive from our Lord the reward of your faith. And in all that you have believed, you shall rejoice and be made glad. DEMONSTRATIONS 9.25.[38]

AFFLICTION AND GRACE. BASIL THE GREAT: He himself permits the suffering which he again restores. The One who strikes is the One who heals. The afflictions precede in order that the graces may be lasting. Only then do we exert ourselves exceedingly for the preservation of what has been given. HOMILY ON PSALM 29.4.[39]

EVIL MUST DIE. GREGORY OF NYSSA: It is not possible for the good to exist in me unless it is made to live through the death of my enemy. As long as we keep grasping opposites with each of our hands, it is impossible for there to be participation in both elements in the same being. For if we are holding evil, we lose the power to take hold of virtue. ON PERFECTION.[40]

GOD'S ANGER AND PITY. AUGUSTINE: He is God, so he also takes pity. He gets angry, and he takes pity. He gets angry and strikes; he takes pity and heals. He gets angry and does to death; he takes pity and brings to life. In one person he does this. It's not that he does some people to death and brings others to life, but in the same people he is both angry and gentle. He is angry with errors; he is gentle with bad habits put right. "I will strike and I will heal: I will kill and I will make alive." One and the same Saul, afterward Paul, he both laid low and raised up. He laid low an unbeliever; he raised up a believer. He laid low a persecutor; he raised up a preacher. SERMON 24.7.[41]

GOD AS PHYSICIAN. AUGUSTINE: [Paul's conversion] fulfilled in him what was written in the prophet, "I will strike, and I will heal." What God strikes, you see, is that in people which lifts up itself against God. The surgeon isn't being heartless when he lances the tumor, when he cuts or burns out the suppurating sore. He's causing pain; he certainly is, but in order to

---

[35]FC 89:212. [36]CSEL 82 3:280. [37]FC 25:165. [38]NPNF 2 13:383. [39]FC 46:219*. [40]FC 58:100. [41]WSA 3 2:77.

restore health. It's a horrid business; but if it wasn't, it wouldn't be any use. SERMON 77.3.[42]

GOD STRUCK PAUL AND HEALED HIM.
AUGUSTINE: So the apostle was petrified, knocked down and laid low, raised up and patched up. The words, you see, were realized in him: "It is I that will strike and I that will heal." You see, it doesn't say, "I will heal, and I will strike," but "I will strike, and I will heal." I will strike you and give myself to you. Thus being laid low, he was horrified at his own justice, in which he was certainly without reproach, praiseworthy, great, even glorious among the Jews. He reckoned it was waste, he thought it was loss, he counted it dung, "that he might be

found in him, not having his own justice, which is from the law; but that which is through the faith of Christ, which is," he says, "from God."[43] SERMON 169.10.[44]

32:42 My Sword Devours Flesh

THE LAST JUDGMENT. PATERIUS: The sword of God consumes flesh, because at the last judgment his sentence slays those who think carnally. EXPOSITION OF THE OLD AND NEW TESTAMENT, DEUTERONOMY 25.[45]

---

[42]WSA 3 3:318. [43]Phil 3:9. [44]WSA 3 5:228. [45]PL 79:783, citing Gregory the Great *Moral Interpretation of Job* 18.13.20.

[32:44-47 FINAL APPEAL]

32:48-52 MOSES TO VIEW CANAAN

[48]*And the* LORD *said to Moses that very day,* [49]*"Ascend this mountain of the Abarim, Mount Nebo, which is in the land of Moab, opposite Jericho; and view the land of Canaan, which I give to the people of Israel for a possession;* [50]*and die on the mountain which you ascend, and be gathered to your people, as Aaron your brother died in Mount Hor and was gathered to his people;* [51]*because you broke faith with me in the midst of the people of Israel at the waters of Meri-bath-kadesh, in the wilderness of Zin; because you did not revere me as holy in the midst of the people of Israel.* [52]*For you shall see the land before you; but you shall not go there, into the land which I give to the people of Israel."*

OVERVIEW: Moses joyfully ascended the mountain where he was to die (ATHANASIUS). Moses' death put an end to his doubting. Moses' punishment was for a single sin (AUGUSTINE).

32:48-49 Ascend This Mountain

MOSES' COURAGE. ATHANASIUS: The great

Moses, who previously had hidden himself from Pharaoh and had withdrawn into Midian for fear of him when he received the commandment "Return into Egypt,"[1] did not fear to do so. And again, when he was bidden to go up into the mountain Abarim and die, he delayed not

---

[1]Ex 3:10.

through cowardice but even joyfully proceeded there. DEFENSE OF HIS FLIGHT 18.[2]

32:50 *Die on the Mountain*

MOSES LEARNED TO CEASE DOUBTING.
AUGUSTINE: Let's take a look at this text too: "Climb the mountain and die." The bodily death of Moses stood for the death of his doubting, but on the mountain. What marvelous mysteries! When this has been definitely explained and understood, how much sweeter it is to the taste than manna! Doubting was born at the rock, died on the mountain. SERMON 352.5.[3]

32:51 *Because You Broke Faith*

MOSES WAS PUNISHED FOR ONE SIN. AUGUSTINE: [Moses] touched the rock with his rod with doubt and thus distinguished this miracle from the rest, in which he had not doubted. He thus offended, thus deserved to hear that he should die without entering into the land of promise. For being disturbed by the murmurs of an unbelieving people, he did not hold fast that confidence which he ought to have held. EXPLANATION OF THE PSALMS 106.26.[4]

---

[2]NPNF 2 4:261.   [3]WSA 3 10:143.   [4]NPNF 1 8.530.

33:1-29 BLESSING UPON THE TRIBES

[1]*This is the blessing with which Moses the man of God blessed the children of Israel before his death.*
[2]*He said,*
"The Lord came . . .
with flaming fire at his right hand.
[3]*"Yea, he loved his people;[k]*
all those consecrated to him were in his[x] hand;
so they followed[j] in thy steps,
receiving direction from thee. . . .

[6]*"Let Reuben live, and not die,*
nor let his men be few." . . .

[8]*And of Levi he said,*
"Give to Levi[m] thy Thummim,
and thy Urim to thy godly one,
whom thou didst test at Massah,
with whom thou didst strive at the waters of Meribah;
[9]*who said of his father and mother,*
'I regard them not';

he disowned his brothers,
>   and ignored his children.
> For they observed thy word,
>   and kept thy covenant. . . .

¹³And of Joseph he said,
>   "Blessed by the LORD be his land, . . .
¹⁷His firstling bull has majesty,
>   and his horns are the horns of a wild ox;
> with them he shall push the peoples,
>   all of them, to the ends of the earth;
> such are the ten thousands of Ephraim,
>   and such are the thousands of Manasseh."

²²And of Dan he said,
>   "Dan is a lion's whelp,
>   that leaps forth from Bashan."

²³And of Naphtali he said,
>   "O Naphtali, satisfied with favor,
>   and full of the blessing of the LORD,
>   possess the lake and the south."

²⁴And of Asher he said,
>   "Blessed above sons be Asher;
>   let him be the favorite of his brothers,
>   and let him dip his foot in oil.
²⁵Your bars shall be iron and bronze;
>   and as your days, so shall your strength be."

k *Gk: Heb* peoples   x *Heb* thy   j *The meaning of the Hebrew word is uncertain*   m *Gk: Heb lacks* Give to Levi

---

OVERVIEW: God's left and right hands mean the reprobate and the elect (PATERIUS). Moses absolved Reuben of his sin (APHRAHAT). A holy person loves carnal relatives in holy ways (PATERIUS). Jews and Gentiles together comprise the fullness of the church. The church anoints all with spiritual oil (AMBROSE). Iron and bronze mean virtue and perseverance (PATERIUS).

33:2 With Flaming Fire

GOD'S RIGHT HAND. PATERIUS: What does God's left hand mean, except the reprobate, who are to be placed at God's left hand? The elect are called God's right hand. For at God's right hand there is a fiery law, because by no means do the elect hear the heavenly commands with cold hearts but flame up at these commands like torches of inner love. The word comes to their ears, and their minds burn with the flame of inner sweetness. EXPOSITION OF THE OLD AND NEW TESTAMENT, DEUTERONOMY 26.[1]

33:6 Let Reuben Live

MOSES ABSOLVES REUBEN. APHRAHAT: Moses wished by his priestly power to absolve Reuben from his transgression and sin, in that he had lain with Bilhah, his father's concubine, so that when his brothers should rise, he might not be cut off from their number. So he said in the beginning of his blessing, "Reuben shall live and not die and shall be in the number." DEMONSTRATION 8.8.[2]

33:9 I Regard Them Not

A HOLY PERSON LOVES CARNAL RELATIVES IN A HOLY WAY. PATERIUS: That man desires to know God more closely who, out of love for piety, does not want to know those he knew according to the flesh. Divine knowledge suffers a grave loss if it is shared with fleshly knowledge. Each one ought to stand apart from his relatives and neighbors if he wishes to be joined more truly to the Father of all. Those he manfully neglects for the sake of God he loves more firmly, to the extent that he ignores the passing attachment of carnal relationship. In the world of time, indeed, we should be more helpful to those we are related to more closely than to others, since this flame grows into a fire when fuel is supplied. But the fire first burns where it is kindled. We ought to acknowledge the bond of earthly relationship but ignore it when it blocks the journey of the mind. This happens when the faithful soul, on fire with devotion to God, does not despise what is joined to it below, rightly orders these relations within itself and transcends them by its love of what is highest. So we ought to see to it by resourceful concern lest such love should make its entry for the sake of the flesh and turns the heart's progress away from the right path. It could

weaken the power of higher love and press the rising mind down by loading a weight on it. Thus one ought to sympathize with his relatives' needs in such a way that, through compassion, he does not allow the effect of his decision to be blocked. The emotions of the mind should fill the heart but not turn it away from its spiritual vocation. For holy men do not love their carnal relatives by failing to give them what they need, but by love of spiritual things they conquer that love in themselves, insofar as they temper it with the reins of discretion. Through this love, at least in a small measure, they will not stray from the right path. Cows are figures that suggest these men to us.[3] As the cows move to the high place before God's ark, they walk with eagerness and a determined pace, while their calves have been left in the stable. For Scripture has it, "walking on and lowing, giving forth bellows from within, and yet not turning their steps away from the path, they have set out."[4] EXPOSITION OF THE OLD AND NEW TESTAMENT, DEUTERONOMY 27.[5]

33:17 Ephraim and Manasseh

THE FULLNESS OF THE CHURCH. AMBROSE: "The ten thousands of Ephraim and the thousands of Manasseh," that is, let him rule over both the Jews and the Gentiles and acquire the fullness of the church for himself from both peoples. THE PATRIARCHS 11.56.[6]

33:22 Dan Is a Lion's Whelp

THE TRIBE OF DAN AND THE ANTICHRIST. AMBROSE: Moses blessed this tribe, saying, "Dan is a lion's whelp, and he shall flee away from Bashan," that is, from confusion. For this reason we ought rather to interpret according to

---

[1]PL 79:783, citing Gregory the Great, *HOG* 30.5. [2]NPNF 2 13:377. [3]Paterius (or rather Gregory, whom he is quoting) has in mind the two cows that the Philistines used to pull the cart with the ark of the covenant back to Israel; see 1 Sam 6:10-12 for the details. [4]1 Sam 6:12. [5]PL 79:783, citing Gregory the Great *Moral Interpretation of Job* 7.30.41-42. [6]FC 65:272.

the Greek, from which our translation comes, that Dan himself became a serpent sitting in the way. Dan expounds judgment, and therefore that tribe has entered into a severe danger of judgment, for the serpent, the antichrist, has slipped into it to injure it with his poisons as it runs. The Patriarchs 7.34.[7]

33:24 Let Him Dip His Foot in Oil

ANOINTING WITH OIL. AMBROSE: With this oil the church anoints the necks of its children so that they might take up the yoke of Christ. With this oil it anointed the martyrs so that it might wash them clean of worldly filth. With this oil it anointed the confessors so that they might not cease to labor nor succumb to fatigue and so that they might not be overcome by the commotion of this world. For that reason it anointed them, so that spiritual oil might refresh them. LETTER I EXTRA COLL. (41).20.[8]

33:25 Bars of Iron and Bronze

THE EVANGELIST'S VOCATION. PATERIUS: Moses says this with regard to the holy church. Shoe[9] in Holy Scripture means the office of preaching, as is written, "Feet have been shod in preparation for the gospel of peace."[10] Since iron means virtue and bronze means perseverance, a man's shoes are said to be iron and bronze when his preaching is strengthened with incisiveness and persistence. With iron he penetrates opposing evils, and with bronze he preserves the good he had patiently proposed. EXPOSITION OF THE OLD AND NEW TESTAMENT, DEUTERONOMY 28.[11]

---

[7]FC 65:261. [8]CSEL 82 3:156. [9]So the Vulgate; the RSV has "bars." [10]Eph 6:15. [11]PL 79:784, citing Gregory the Great *Moral Interpretation of Job* 34.9.19.

34:1-12 DEATH AND BURIAL OF MOSES

[4]*And the LORD said to him, "This is the land of which I swore to Abraham, to Isaac, and to Jacob, 'I will give it to your descendants.' I have let you see it with your eyes, but you shall not go over there."* [5]*So Moses the servant of the LORD died there in the land of Moab, according to the word of the LORD,* [6]*and he buried him in the valley in the land of Moab opposite Beth-peor; but no man knows the place of his burial to this day.* [7]*Moses was a hundred and twenty years old when he died; his eye was not dim, nor his natural force abated.* [8]*And the people of Israel wept for Moses in the plains of Moab thirty days; then the days of weeping and mourning for Moses were ended.*

[9]*And Joshua the son of Nun was full of the spirit of wisdom, for Moses had laid his hands upon him; so the people of Israel obeyed him, and did as the LORD had commanded Moses.*

OVERVIEW: Moses was not forgiven until his death was imminent (PAULUS OROSIUS). Moses' beauty remained unchanged, even in death (GREGORY OF NYSSA). Moses did not grow sick but died at God's word (AMBROSE). Neither his enemies nor his people know the place of Moses' tomb (APHRAHAT). God alone is the witness to Moses' burial place (PAULINUS). The laying on of hands signifies the conferral of power (CYRIL OF JERUSALEM).

34:4 Seeing the Land

MOSES FORGIVEN. PAULUS OROSIUS: And yet only before his death was [Moses] forgiven; and this was the man who, because of this guilt, was ordered to die lest he enter the Promised Land. DEFENSE AGAINST THE PELAGIANS 28.[1]

34:5 Moses Died in Moab

MOSES' DEATH WAS SUBLIME. GREGORY OF NYSSA: Moses' death is recorded to have been even more sublime than his life. He died on a mountain peak and left behind neither trace nor memorial of his earthly burden in life. The impress of beauty was not altered by time but remained unchangeable in the changeable nature. INSCRIPTIONS OF THE PSALMS 1.56.[2]

MOSES DIED BY GOD'S WORD. AMBROSE: We do not read of [Moses], as we do of others, that he fell sick and died. We read that "he died by the word of God"—for God does not grow weak or undergo diminution or addition. Hence Scripture added, "No man has known of his sepulcher until this present day"—by which we are to understand that he was taken up into heaven rather than buried, for death may be called a separation of the soul from the body. He died therefore as the Scripture states: "by the word of God"—not "in accordance with the word"—so as to make known that this was not an announcement of his death but was more in the nature of a gracious gift to one who was translated rather than left here and whose sepulcher was known to no one. CAIN AND ABEL 1.2.8.[3]

34:6 No One Knows the Place of His Burial

WHY THE PLACE IS UNKNOWN. APHRAHAT: Two godly benefits did his Lord accomplish for Moses in not making known his tomb to the children of Israel. He rejoiced that his adversaries should not know it and cast forth his bones from his tomb; and in the second place, that the children of his people should not know it and make his tomb a place of worship, for he was accounted as God in the eyes of the children of his people. DEMONSTRATION 8.9.[4]

ONLY MOSES' GRAVE IS UNKNOWN. PAULINUS: God had granted the gift of being buried in secret ground to only one of his friends, for it was right that so great a distinction should be appropriate only for that body which had shone from the close presence and conversation of God. Thus when Moses had performed his duties as man, he could take joy in having God alone as witness of his grave. POEMS 15.213.[5]

See also AMBROSE ON EXODUS 32:32.

34:9 Moses Had Laid His Hands on Joshua

THE LAYING ON OF HANDS. CYRIL OF JERUSALEM: It is written, "Now Joshua, the son of Nun, was filled with the Spirit of wisdom, since Moses had laid his hands upon him." Note the same ceremonial everywhere, both in the Old and the New Testament. In Moses' day the Spirit was given by the imposition of hands; and Peter imparted the Spirit by the imposition of hands. Upon you also, who are to be baptized, the grace will come. CATECHETICAL LECTURE 16.26.[6]

---

[1]FC 99:154-55. [2]GNTIP 102-3. [3]FC 42:364. [4]NPNF 2 13:378. [5]ACW 40:90. [6]FC 64:92.

Early Christian Writers and the Documents Cited

The following table lists all the early Christian documents cited in this volume by their authors (where known) and English titles, providing Latin equivalents of the titles for those desiring to locate the original sources. See the bibliography for publishers and electronic database information.

Ambrose
Cain and Abel *(De Cain et Abel)*
Concerning Repentance *(De paenitentia)*
Concerning Virgins *(De virginibus)*
Death as a Good *(De bono mortis)*
Duties of the Clergy *(De officiis ministrorum)*
Flight from the World *(De fuga saeculi)*
Isaac, or the Soul *(De Isaac vel anima)*
Jacob and the Happy Life *(De Jacob et vita beata)*
Joseph *(De Joseph)*
Letters *(Epistulae)*
On His Brother, Satyrus *(De excessu fratris Satyri)*
On Paradise *(De paradiso)*
On the Christian Faith *(De fide, libri quinque)*
On the Holy Spirit *(De Spiritu Sancto)*
On the Mysteries *(De mysteriis)*
The Patriarchs *(De patriarchis)*
Prayer of Job and David *(De interpellatione Job et David)*
Six Days of Creation *(Hexaemeron)*

Aphrahat
Demonstrations *(Demonstrationes)*

Athanasius
Defense of His Flight *(Apologia de fuga sua)*
Festal Letters *(Epistulae festales)*
On the Incarnation *(De incarnatione verbi)*

Augustine
Against Faustus, a Manichean *(Contra Faustum)*
Against Two Letters of the Pelagians *(Contra duas epistulas pelagianorum)*
City of God *(De civitate Dei)*
Confessions *(Confessionum)*
Explanation of the Psalms *(Ennarationes in Psalmos)*
A Handbook on Faith, Hope and Love *(Enchiridion de fide, spe et caritate)*
Letters *(Epistulae)*
On Baptism *(De baptismo)*
On Christian Teaching *(De doctrina christiana)*
On Eighty-three Varied Questions *(De diversis quaestionibus octoginta tribus)*

On Faith and the Creed (*De fide et symbolo*)
On Faith and Works (*De fide et operibus*)
On Genesis, Against the Manicheans (*De genesi contra manichaeos*)
On Grace and Free Will (*De gratia et libero arbitrio*)
On Lying (*Contra mendacium* and *De Mendacio*)
On Marriage and Concupiscence (*De nuptiis et concupiscentia*)
On the Catholic and the Manichaean Ways of Life (*De moribus ecclesiae catholicae et de moribus manichaeorum*)
On the Good of Marriage (*De bono coniugali*)
On the Good of Widowhood (*De bono viduitatis*)
On the Grace of Christ and Original Sin (*De gratia christi et de peccato originali*)
On the Lord's Sermon on the Mount (*De sermone Domini in monte*)
On the Merits and Forgiveness of Sin and on Infant Baptism (*De peccatorum meritis et remissione et de baptismo parvulorum*)
On the Nature of the Good (*De natura boni*)
On the Perfection of Human Righteousness (*De perfectione justitiae hominis*)
On the Spirit and the Letter (*De spiritu et littera*)
On the Work of Monks (*De opere monachorum*)
Questions on Exodus (*Quaestionum in heptateuchum libri septem*)
Questions on Leviticus (*Quaestionum in heptateuchum libri septem*)
Questions on the Heptateuch (*Quaestionum in heptateuchum libri septem*)
Reconsiderations (*Retractationum libri duo*)
Sermons (*Sermones*)
Tractate on the Gospel of John (*In Johannis euangelium tractatus*)
The Trinity (*De Trinitate*)

Basil (= Basil the Great)
Concerning Baptism (*De baptismo libri duo*)
Exegetic Homilies (*Homiliae in hexaemeron*)
Homilies on the Psalms (*Homiliae super Psalmos*)
Homily (*Homiliae*)
Homily on the Words "Give Heed to Yourself" (*Homiliae in illud: Attende tibi ipsi*)
Letters (*Epistulae*)
On the Spirit (*De Spiritu Sancto*)
Preface on the Judgment of God (*Prologus 7 [De judicio Dei]*)

Bede
Commentary on 1 Peter (*In epistulam septem catholicas*)
Commentary on the Acts of the Apostles (*Expositio actuum apostolorum*)
Homilies on the Gospel (*Homiliarum evangelii*)
On the Tabernacle (*De tabernaculo et euasis eius ac vestibus sacerdotem libri iii*)

Caesarius of Arles
Sermon (*Sermones*)

Cassiodorus
Exposition of the Psalms (*Expositio Psalmorum*)

Clement of Alexandria
Christ the Educator (*Paedagogus*)
Stromateis (*Stromata*)

Clement of Rome
Letter to the Corinthians (*Epistula i ad Corinthios*)

Constitutions of the Holy Apostles (*Constitutiones apostolorum*)

Cyprian
Exhortation to Martyrdom (*Ad Fortunatum [De exhortatione martyrii]*)
The Good of Patience (*De bono patientiae*)
Letter (*Epistulae*)
The Unity of the Catholic Church (*De ecclesiae catholicae unitate*)

Cyril of Alexandria
Homilies on the Gospel of Luke (*Commentarii in Lucam*)
Letter (*Epistulae*)

Cyril of Jerusalem
Catechetical Lecture (*Catecheses ad illuminandos 1-18*)
Catechetical Lecture (*Mystagogiae*)

Didache
Teaching of the Twelve Apostles (*Didache xii apostolorum*)

Ephrem the Syrian
Commentary on Exodus (*In Exodum*)
Commentary on Tatian's Diatessaron (*In Tatiani Diatessaron*)
Homily on Our Lord (*Sermo de Domino nostro*)
Hymns on Paradise (*Hymni de paradiso*)
Letter to Publius (*Epistula ad Publium*)

Eusebius
Ecclesiastical History (*Historia ecclesiastica*)
Proof of the Gospel (*Demonstratio evangelica*)

Evagrius
Chapters on Prayer (*De oratione*)

Fulgentius of Ruspe
Letters (*Epistulae, et varia*)
To Peter on the Faith (*De fide ad Petrum seu de regula fidei*)

Gregory of Nazianzus
Letter 101 (*Epistulae theologicae*)
Letters (*Epistulae*)
On His Father (*Funebris oratio in patrem [orat. 18]*)
On St. Basil (*Funebris oratio in laudem Basilii Magni Caesareae in Cappadocia episcopi [orat. 43]*)
Oration 2, In Defense of His Flight to Pontus (*Apologetica [orat. 2]*)
Oration 40 (*In sanctum baptisma*)
Oration 42 (*Supremum vale*)
Oration 45 (*In sanctum pascha*)
Theological Oration 2 (Oration 28, cf. LCC 3) (*De theologia*)
Theological Oration 4 (Oration 30, cf. LCC 3) (*De filio*)

Gregory of Nyssa
Against Eunomius (*Contra Eunomium* and *Refutatio confessionis Eunomii*)
The Life of Gregory the Wonderworker (*De vita Gregorii Thaumaturgi*)
Life of Moses (*De vita Mosis*)
On Not Three Gods (*Ad Ablabium quod non sint tres dei*)
On Perfection (*De perfectione Christiana ad Olympium monachum*)
On the Baptism of Christ (*In diem luminum [*vulgo *In baptismum Christi oratio]*)

On the Christian Mode of Life (*De instituto Christiano*)
On the Faith (*Ad Simplicium de fide*)
On the Inscriptions of the Psalms (*In inscriptiones Psalmorum*)
On the Soul and Resurrection (*Dialogus de anima et resurrectione*)
On Virginity (*De virginitate*)

Gregory Thaumaturgus
Canonical Epistle (*Epistula canonica*)

Gregory the Great
Homily (*Homiliarum xl in evangelica*)
Letter (*Registrum epistularum*)
Moral Interpretation of Job (*Moralia in Job*)
Pastoral Care (*Regula pastoralis*)

Hilary
On the Trinity (*De Trinitate*)

Irenaeus
Against Heresies (*Adversus haereses*)

Isaac of Nineveh
Discourse (*Homilia*)

Isidore of Seville
Questions on the Old Testament (*Mysticorum expositiones sacramentorum seu quaestiones in vetus testamentum*)

Jerome
Against Helvidius (*Adversus Helvidium de Mariae virginitate perpetua*)
Against Jovinianus (*Adversus Jovinianum*)
Against the Pelagians (*Dialogi contra Pelagianos libri iii*)
Homilies on the Psalms (*Tractatus in librum psalmorum*)
Homily 68, 72 (*Tractatuum in Psalmos series altera*)
Homily 75, 76 (*Tractatus in Marci evangelium*)
Homily 90 (*Sermo de quadragesima*)
Homily 91 (*De exodo, in vigilia Paschae*)
Letter (*Epistulae*)

John Cassian
Conference (*Collationes*)

John Chrysostom
Baptismal Instructions (*Catechesis ad illuminandos*)
Discourses Against Judaizing Christians (*Adversus Judaeos [orationes 1-8]*)
Homilies Concerning the Statues (*Ad populam Antiochenum homiliae [de statuis]*)
Homilies on 1 Corinthians (*In epistulam i ad Corinthios [homiliae 1-44]*)
Homilies on 2 Corinthians (*In epistulam ii ad Corinthios [homiliae 1-30]*)
Homilies on Acts (*In Acta apostolorum [homiliae 1-55]*)
Homilies on Colossians (*In epistulam ad Colossenses [homiliae 1-12]*)
Homilies on Hebrews (*In epistulam ad Hebraeos argumentum et homiliae*)
Homilies on Genesis (*In Genesim [homiliae 1-67]*)
Homilies on Repentance and Almsgiving (*De paenitentia*)
Homilies on the Gospel of John (*In Joannem [homiliae 1-88]*)
Homilies on the Gospel of Matthew (*In Matthaeum [homiliae 1-90]*)
Homily 6 (*De incomprehensibili dei natura [Contra Anomaeos]*)
Homily to Those Who Had Not Attended the Assembly (*In illud: Si esurierit inimicus*)

Letter to the Fallen Theodore (*Ad Theodorum*)
On the Priesthood (*De sacerdotio*)

John of Damascus
On Divine Images (*Orationes de imaginibus tres*)
Orthodox Faith (*Expositio fidei*)

Justin Martyr
Dialogue with Trypho (*Dialogus cum Tryphone*)

Lactantius
Epitome of the Divine Institutes (*Epitome divinarum institutionum*)

Leo the Great
Sermon (*Tractatus septem et nonaginta*)

Marius Victorinus
Against Arius (*Adversus Arium*)

Martin of Braga
On the Pascha (*De pascha*)

Maximus of Turin
Sermon (*Collectio sermonum antiqua*)

Methodius
Banquet of the Ten Virgins (*Convivium decem virginum*)

Nicetas of Remesiana
Liturgical Singing (*De psalmodiae bono [de utilitate hymnorum]*)

Novatian
Jewish Foods (*De cibis judaicis*)
The Trinity (*De Trinitate*)

Origen
Against Celsus (*Contra Celsum*)
Commentary on the Gospel of John (*Commentarii in evangelium Joannis*)
Commentary on the Gospel of Matthew (*Commentarium in evangelium Matthaei*)
Commentary on the Song of Songs (*Libri x in Canticum canticorum [fragmenta]*)
Exhortation to Martyrdom (*Exhortatio ad martyrium*)
Fragment on the Gospel of Luke (*Fragmenta in Lucam [in catenis]*)
Homilies on Exodus (*Homiliae in Exodum*)
Homilies on Genesis (*Homiliae in Genesim [fragmenta]*)
Homilies on Jeremiah (*In Jeremiam [homiliae 12-20]*)
Homilies on Leviticus (*Homiliae in Leviticum*)
Homilies on Numbers (*In Numeros homiliae*)
Homilies on the Gospel of Luke (*Homiliae in Lucam*)
On First Principles (*De principiis*)
On Prayer (*De oratione*)

Pacian of Barcelona
Letters

Paterius
Exposition of the Old and New Testament (*Liber de expositione veteris ac novi testamenti*)

Paulinus of Nola
Poems (*Carmina*)

Paulus Orosius
Defense Against the Pelagians (*Liber apologeticus contra Pelagianos*)
Seven Books of History Against the Pagans (*Historiarum adversum paganos, libri vii*)

Peter Chrysologos
Sermons (*Sermones*)

Procopius of Gaza
Catena on the Octateuch (*Catena in Octateuchum*)

Prudentius
The Divinity of Christ (*Liber Apotheosis*)
Hymns for Everyday (*Liber Cathemerinon*)

Pseudo-Athanasius
Fourth Oration Against the Arians (*Oratio quarta contra Arianos*)

Pseudo-Basil
On Mercy and Justice (*Homilia de misericordia et judicio*)

Pseudo-Dionysius
Celestial Hierarchy (*De caelesti hierarchia*)

Pseudo-Macarius
Homily (*Homiliae spirituales 50*)

Salvian the Presbyter
Four Books of Timothy to the Church (*Ad ecclesiam sive adversus avaritiam*)
The Governance of God (*De gubernatione Dei*)

Symeon the New Theologian
Discourse (*Catecheses*)

Tertullian
Against Marcion (*Adversus Marcionem*)
Answer to the Jews (*Adversus Judaeos*)
On Baptism (*De baptismo*)
On Idolatry (*De idolatria*)
On Purity (*De pudicitia*)
On the Flesh of Christ (*De carne Christi*)
On the Resurrection of the Flesh (*De resurrectione mortuorum*)

Theodoret of Cyr
Dialogue (*Eranistes*)
Questions on Exodus (*Quaestiones in Octateuchum*)
Questions on Numbers (*Quaestiones in Octateuchum*)

Vincent of Lérins
Commonitories (*Commonitorium*)

Timeline of Patristic Authors

Location / Period	British Isles	Gaul	Spain, Portugal	Italy	Africa
2nd century		Irenaeus of Lyons, c. 135-c. 202 (Greek)		Clement of Rome, fl. c. 92-101 (Greek)	
				Justin Martyr (Ephesus, Rome), c. 100/110-165 (Greek)	
				Valentinus the Gnostic, fl. c. 140, (Greek)	
				Marcion, fl. 144 (Greek)	
3rd century					Clement of Alexandria, c. 150-215 (Latin)
				Callistus of Rome, regn. 217-222 (Latin)	Tertullian of Carthage, c. 155/160-225/250 (Latin)
				Minucius Felix of Rome, fl. c. 218-235 (Latin)	Origen (Alexandria, Caesaria of Palestine), 185-254 (Greek)
				Novatian of Rome, fl. 235-258 (Latin)	Cyprian of Carthage, fl. 248-258 (Latin)
				Marius Victorinus (Rome), fl. 355-362 (Latin)	Dionysius of Alexandria, d. 264 (Latin)
4th century		Lactantius, c. 260-330 (Latin)			
					Arius (Alexandria), fl. c. 320 (Greek)
					Alexander of Alexandria, fl. 312-328 (Greek)
					Pachomius (Egypt), c. 292-347 (Coptic/Greek?)
				Eusebius of Vercelli, fl. c. 360 (Latin)	Athanasius of Alexandria, c. 295-373; fl. 325-373 (Greek)
		Hilary of Poitiers, c. 315-367 (Latin)	Potamius of Lisbon, fl. c. 350-360 (Latin)	Lucifer of Cagliari (Sardinia), fl. 370 (Latin)	Macarius of Egypt, c. 300-c. 390 (Greek)
			Gregory of Elvira, fl. 359-385 (Latin)	Faustinus (Rome), fl. 380 (Latin)	Didymus (the Blind) of Alexandria, 313-398 (Greek)
				Filastrius of Brescia, fl. 380 (Latin)	
			Prudentius, c. 348-c. 410 (Latin)	Ambrosiaster (Italy?), fl. c. 366-384 (Latin)	
				Gaudentius of Brescia, fl. 395 (Latin)	
				Ambrose of Milan, c. 333-397; fl. 374-397 (Latin)	
				Rufinus of Aquileia, c. 345-411 (Latin)	Augustine of Hippo, 354-430 (Latin)

Greece	Asia Minor	Syria	Mesopotamia, Persia	Palestine	Location Unknown
	Polycarp of Smyrna, c. 69-155 (Greek)	Ignatius of Antioch, 35- d. 107/112 (Greek)			
Athenagoras, fl. 176-180 (Greek)		Theophilus of Antioch, c. late 2nd cent. (Greek)			
				Hippolytus (Palestine?), fl. 222-245 (Greek)	
	Gregory Thaumaturgus (Neocaesarea), fl. c. 248-264 (Greek)				
	Methodius of Olympus (Lycia), d. c. 311 (Greek)		Aphrahat c. 270-350 (Syriac)	Eusebius of Caesarea (Palestine), c. 260/263-340 (Greek)	Commodian, c. 3rd or 5th cent. (Latin)
Epiphanius of Salamis (Cyprus), c. 315-403 (Greek)		Eusebius of Emesa, c. 300-c. 359 (Greek)		Acacius of Caesarea (Palestine), d. c. 366 (Greek)	
	Basil the Great, b. c. 330; fl. 357-379 (Greek)	Ephrem the Syrian, c. 306-373 (Syriac)		Cyril of Jerusalem, c. 315-386 (Greek)	
	Macrina the Younger, c. 327-379 (Greek)				
	Apollinaris of Laodicea, 310-c. 392 (Greek)				
John Chrysostom (Antioch, Constantinople), 344/354-407 (Greek)	Gregory of Nazianzus, b. 329/330; fl. 372-389 (Greek)				
	Gregory of Nyssa, c. 335-394 (Greek)				
	Evagrius of Pontus, c. 345-399 (Greek)	Nemesius of Emesa (Syria), fl. late 4th cent. (Greek)		Diodore of Tarsus, d. c. 394 (Greek)	
	Theodore of Mopsuestia, c. 350-428 (Greek)			Jerome (Rome, Antioch, Bethlehem), c. 347-420 (Latin)	

Timeline of Patristic Authors

Location Period	British Isles	Gaul	Spain, Portugal	Italy	Africa
5th century	Fastidius, c. 4th-5th cent. (Latin)	John Cassian (Palestine, Egypt, Constantinople, Rome, Marseilles), 360-432 (Latin)		Chromatius (Aquileia), fl. 400 (Latin)	Cyril of Alexandria, 375-444 (Greek)
		Sulpicius Severus, c. 360-c. 420 (Latin)		Pelagius (Britain, Rome), c. 354 c. 420 (Greek)	Quodvultdeus (Carthage), fl. 430 (Latin)
		Vincent of Lérins, d. 435 (Latin)		Maximus of Turin, d. 408/423 (Latin)	Palladius of Helenopolis, c. 363/364-c. 431 (Greek)
		Valerian of Cimiez, fl. c. 422-439 (Latin)		Paulinus of Nola, 355-431 (Latin)	Ammonius of Alexandria, 5th cent. (Greek)
		Eucherius of Lyons, fl. 420-449 (Latin)		Peter Chrysologus (Ravenna), c. 380-450 (Latin)	
		Hilary of Arles, c. 401-449 (Latin)		Leo the Great (Rome), regn. 440-461 (Latin)	
		Salvian the Presbyter of Marseilles, c. 400-c. 480 (Latin)			
6th century		Caesarius of Arles, c. 470-543 (Latin)	Paschasius of Dumium (Portugal), c. 515-c. 580 (Latin)	Benedict of Nursia, c. 480-547 (Latin)	
				Cassiodorus (Calabria), c. 485-c. 540 (Latin)	
					Fulgentius of Ruspe, c. 467-532 (Latin)
			Leander of Seville, c. 545-c. 600 (Latin)	Gregory the Great, c. 540-604 (Latin)	
			Isidore of Seville, c. 560-636 (Latin)		
7th century			Braulio of Saragossa, c. 585-651 (Latin)		
8th century	Bede the Venerable, c. 672/673-735 (Latin)				

Greece	Asia Minor	Syria	Mesopotamia, Persia	Palestine	Location Unknown
Nestorius (Constantinople), c. 381-c. 451 (Greek)	Basil of Seleucia, fl. 444-468 (Greek)	Severian of Gabala, fl. c. 400 (Greek)		Hesychius of Jerusalem, fl. 412-450 (Greek)	
		Theodoret of Cyr, c. 393-466 (Greek)			
	Diadochus of Photice, c. 400-474 (Greek)				
Gennadius of Constantinople, d. 471 (Greek)					
		Philoxenus of Mabbug, c. 440-523 (Syriac)			
			Jacob of Sarug, c. 450-c. 520 (Syriac)		
				Procopius of Gaza (Palestine), c. 465-530 (Greek)	
		Severus of Antioch, fl. 488-538 (Greek)			
	Mark the Hermit (Tarsus), c. 6th cent. (Greek)			Dorotheus of Gaza, fl. c. 525-540 (Greek)	Pseudo-Dionysius the Areopagite, fl. c. 500 (Greek)
	Oecumenius (Isauria), 6th cent. (Greek)			Cyril of Scythopolis, c. 525-d. after 557 (Greek)	(Pseudo-)Constantius, before 7th cent. ? (Greek)
Maximus the Confessor (Constantinople), c. 580-662 (Greek)					Andreas, c. 7th cent. (Greek)
		Sahdona, fl. 635-640 (Syriac)			
		John of Damascus, c. 650-750 (Greek)	Isaac of Nineveh, d. c. 700 (Syriac)		
			John the Elder, 8th cent. (Syriac)		

Biographical Sketches & Short Descriptions of Select Anonymous Works

This listing is cumulative, including all the authors and works cited in this series to date.

Acacius of Caesarea (d. c. 365). Pro-Arian bishop of Caesarea in Palestine, disciple and biographer of Eusebius of Caesarea, the historian. He was a man of great learning and authored a treatise on Ecclesiastes.

Alexander of Alexandria (fl. 312-328). Bishop of Alexandria and predecessor of Athanasius, upon whom he asserted considerable theological influence during the rise of Arianism. Alexander excommunicated Arius, whom he had appointed to the parish of Baucalis, in 319. His teaching regarding the eternal generation and divine substantial union of the Son with the Father was eventually confirmed at the Council of Nicea (325).

Ambrose of Milan (c. 333-397; fl. 374-397). Bishop of Milan and teacher of Augustine who defended the divinity of the Holy Spirit and the perpetual virginity of Mary.

Ambrosiaster (fl. c. 366-384). Name given by Erasmus to the author of a work once thought to have been composed by Ambrose.

Ammonius (c. fifth century). An Aristotelian commentator and teacher in Alexandria, where he was born and of whose school he became head. Also an exegete of Plato, he enjoyed fame among his contemporaries and successors, although modern critics accuse him of pedantry and banality.

Andreas (c. seventh century). Monk who collected commentary from earlier writers to form a catena on various biblical books.

Aphrahat (c. 270-350 fl. 337-345). "The Persian Sage" and first major Syriac writer whose work survives. He is also known by his Greek name Aphraates.

Apollinaris of Laodicea (310-c. 392). Bishop of Laodicea who was attacked by Gregory of Nazianzus, Gregory of Nyssa and Theodore for denying that Christ had a human mind.

Apostolic Constitutions (c. 381-394). Also known as *Constitutions of the Holy Apostles* and thought to be the work of the Arian bishop Julian of Neapolis. The work is divided into eight books, and is primarily a collection of and expansion on previous works such as the *Didache* (c. 140) and the *Apostolic Traditions*. Book 8 ends with eighty-five canons from various sources and is elsewhere known as the *Apostolic Canons*.

Arius (fl. c. 320). Heretic condemned at the Council of Nicaea (325) for refusing to accept that the Son was not a creature but was God by nature like the Father.

Athanasius of Alexandria (c. 295-373; fl. 325-373). Bishop of Alexandria from 328, though often in exile. He wrote his classic polemics against the Arians while most of the eastern bishops were against him.

Athenagoras (fl. 176-180). Early Christian philosopher and apologist from Athens, whose only authenticated writing, *A Plea Regarding Christians*, is addressed to the emperors Marcus Aurelius and Commodius, and defends Christians from the common accusations of atheism, incest and cannibalism.

Augustine of Hippo (354-430). Bishop of Hippo and a voluminous writer on philosophical, exegetical, theological and ecclesiological topics. He formulated the Western doctrines of predestination and original sin in his writings against the Pelagians.

Babai the Great (d. 628). Syriac monk who founded a monastery and school in his region of Beth Zabday and later served as third superior at the Great Convent of Mount Izla during a period of crisis in the Nestorian church.

Basil the Great (b. c. 330; fl. 357-379). One of the Cappadocian fathers, bishop of Caesarea and champion of the teaching on the Trinity propounded at Nicaea in 325. He was a great administrator and founded a monastic rule.

Basil of Seleucia (fl. 444-468). Bishop of Seleucia in Isauria and ecclesiastical writer. He took part in the Synod of Constantinople in 448 for the condemnation of the Eutychian errors and the deposition of their great champion, Dioscurus of Alexandria.

Basilides (fl. second century). Alexandrian heretic of the early second century who is said to have believed that souls migrate from body to body and that we do not sin if we lie to protect the body from martyrdom.

Bede the Venerable (c. 672/673-735). Born in Northumbria, at the age of seven he was put under the care of the Benedictine monks of Saints Peter and Paul at Jarrow and given a broad classical education in the monastic tradition. Considered one of the most learned men of his age, he is the author of *An Ecclesiastical History of the English People*.

Benedict of Nursia (c. 480-547). Considered the most important figure in the history of Western monasticism. Benedict founded many monasteries, the most notable found at Monte-cassino, but his lasting influence lay in his fa-

mous Rule. The Rule outlines the theological and inspirational foundation of the monastic ideal while also legislating the shape and organization of the coenobitic life.

Book of Steps (c. 400). Written by an anonymous Syriac author, this work consists of thirty homilies or discourses and which specifically deal with the more advanced stages of growth in the spiritual life.

Braulio of Saragossa (c. 585-651). Bishop of Saragossa 631-651 and noted writer of the Visigothic renaissance. His *Life* of St. Aemilianus is his crowning literary achievement.

Caesarius of Arles (c. 470-543). Bishop of Arles renowned for his attention to his pastoral duties. Among his surviving works the most important is a collection of some 238 sermons that display an ability to preach Christian doctrine to a variety of audiences.

Callistus of Rome (d. 222). Pope (217-222) who excommunicated Sabellius for heresy. It is very probable that he suffered martyrdom.

Cassian, John (360-432). Author of a compilation of ascetic sayings highly influential in the development of Western monasticism.

Cassiodorus (c. 485-c. 540). Founder of Western monasticism whose writings include valuable histories and less valuable commentaries.

Chromatius (fl. 400). Friend of Rufinus and Jerome and author of tracts and sermons.

Clement of Alexandria (c. 150-215). A highly educated Christian convert from paganism, head of the catechetical school in Alexandria and pioneer of Christian scholarship. His major works, *Protrepticus*, *Paedagogus* and the *Stromata*, bring Christian doctrine face to face with the ideas and achievements of his time.

Clement of Rome (fl. c. 92-101). Pope whose *Epistle to the Corinthians* is one of the most important documents of subapostolic times.

Commodian (c. third or fifth century). Poet of unknown origin (possibly Syrian?) whose two surviving works focus on the Apocalypse and Christian apologetics.

Constitutions of the Holy Apostles. *See Apostolic*

Constitutions.

Cyprian of Carthage (fl. 248-258). Martyred bishop of Carthage who maintained that those baptized by schismatics and heretics had no share in the blessings of the church.

Cyril of Alexandria (375-444; fl. 412-444). Patriarch of Alexandria whose strong espousal of the unity of Christ led to the condemnation of Nestorius in 431.

Cyril of Jerusalem (c. 315-386; fl. c. 348). Bishop of Jerusalem after 350 and author of *Catechetical Homilies*.

Cyril of Scythopolis (b. c. 525, d. after 557). Palestinian monk and author of biographies of famous Palestinian monks. Because of him we have precise knowledge of monastic life in the fifth and sixth centuries and a description of the Origenist crisis and its suppression in the mid-sixth century.

Diadochus of Photice (c. 400-474). Antimonophysite bishop of Epirus Vetus whose work *Discourse on the Ascension of Our Lord Jesus Christ* exerted influence in both the East and West through its Chalcedonian Christology. He is also the subject of the mystical *Vision of St. Diadochus Bishop of Photice in Epirus*.

Didache (c. 140). Of unknown authorship, this text intertwines Jewish ethics with Christian liturgical practice to form a whole discourse on the "way of life." It exerted an enormous amount of influence in the patristic period and was especially used in the training of catechumen.

Didymus the Blind (c. 313-398). Alexandrian exegete who was much influenced by Origen and admired by Jerome.

Diodore of Tarsus (d. c. 394). Bishop of Tarsus and Antiochene theologian. He authored a great scope of exegetical, doctrinal and apologetic works, which come to us mostly in fragments because of his condemnation as the predecessor of Nestorianism. Diodore was a teacher of John Chrysostom and Theodore of Mopsuestia.

Dionysius of Alexandria (d. c. 264). Bishop of Alexandria and student of Origen. Dionysius actively engaged in the theological disputes of his day, opposed Sabellianism, defended himself against accusations of tritheism and wrote the earliest extant Christian refutation of Epicureanism. His writings have survived mainly in extracts preserved by other early Christian authors.

Dionysius the Areopagite. The name long given to the author of four mystical writings, probably from the late fifth century, which were the foundation of the apophatic school of mysticism in their denial that anything can be truly predicated of God.

Dorotheus of Gaza (fl. c. 525-540). Member of Abbot Seridos's monastery and later leader of a monastery where he wrote *Spiritual Instructions*. He also wrote a work on traditions of Palestinian monasticism.

Epiphanius of Salamis (c. 315-403). Bishop of Salamis in Cyprus, author of a refutation of eighty heresies (the *Panarion*) and instrumental in the condemnation of Origen.

Epiphanius the Latin. Author of the late fifth-century or early sixth century Latin text *Interpretation of the Gospels*. He was possibly a bishop of Benevento or Seville.

Ephrem the Syrian (b. c. 306; fl. 363-373). Syrian writer of commentaries and devotional hymns which are sometimes regarded as the greatest specimens of Christian poetry prior to Dante.

Eucherius of Lyons (fl. 420-449). Bishop of Lyons c. 435-449. Born into an aristocratic family, he, along with his wife and sons, joined the monastery at Lérins soon after its founding.

Eunomius (d. 393). Bishop of Cyzicyus who was attacked by Basil and Gregory of Nyssa for maintaining that the Father and the Son were of different natures, one ingenerate, one generate.

Eusebius of Caesarea (c. 260/263-340). Bishop of Caesarea, partisan of the Emperor Constantine and first historian of the Christian church. He argued that the truth of the gospel had been foreshadowed in pagan writings but had to defend his own doctrine against suspicion of Arian sympathies.

Eusebius of Emesa (c. 300-c. 359). Bishop of

Emesa from c. 339. A biblical exegete and writer on doctrinal subjects, he displays some semi-Arian tendencies of his mentor Eusebius of Caesarea.

Eusebius of Vercelli (fl. c. 360). Bishop of Vercelli who supported the trinitarian teaching of Nicaea (325) when it was being undermined by compromise in the West.

Euthymius (377-473). A native of Melitene and influential monk. He was educated by Bishop Otreius of Melitene, who ordained him priest and placed him in charge of all the monasteries in his diocese. When the Council of Chalcedon (451) condemned the errors of Eutyches, it was greatly due to the authority of Euthymius that most of the Eastern recluses accepted its decrees. The empress Eudoxia returned to Chalcedonian orthodoxy through his efforts.

Evagrius of Pontus (c. 345-399). Disciple and teacher of ascetic life who astutely absorbed and creatively transmitted the spirituality of Egyptian and Palestinian monasticism of the late fourth century. Although Origenist elements of his writings were formally condemned by the Fifth Ecumenical Council (Constantinople II, A.D. 553), his literary corpus continued to influence the tradition of the church.

Fastidius (c. fourth-fifth centuries). British author of *On the Christian Life*. He is believed to have written some works attributed to Pelagius.

Faustinus (fl. 380). A priest in Rome and supporter of Lucifer and author of a treatise on the Trinity.

Filastrius (fl. 380). Bishop of Brescia and author of a compilation against all heresies.

Fulgentius of Ruspe (c. 467-532). Bishop of Ruspe and author of many orthodox sermons and tracts under the influence of Augustine.

Gaudentius of Brescia (fl. 395). Successor of Filastrius as bishop of Brescia and author of numerous tracts.

Gennadius of Constantinople (d. 471). Patriarch of Constantinople, author of numerous commentaries and an opponent of the Christology of Cyril of Alexandria.

Gnostics. Name now given generally to followers of Basilides, Marcion, Valentinus, Mani and others. The characteristic belief is that matter is a prison made for the spirit by an evil or ignorant creator, and that redemption depends on fate, not on free will.

Gregory of Elvira (fl. 359-385). Bishop of Elvira who wrote allegorical treatises in the style of Origen and defended the Nicene faith against the Arians.

Gregory of Nazianzus (b. 329/330; fl. 372-389). Bishop of Nazianzus and friend of Basil and Gregory of Nyssa. He is famous for maintaining the humanity of Christ as well as the orthodox doctrine of the Trinity.

Gregory of Nyssa (c. 335-394). Bishop of Nyssa and brother of Basil, he is famous for maintaining the equality in unity of the Father, Son and Holy Spirit.

Gregory Thaumaturgus (fl. c. 248-264). Bishop of Neocaesarea and a disciple of Origen. There are at least five legendary *Lives* that recount the events and miracles which led to his being called "the wonder worker." His most important work was the *Address of Thanks to Origen*, which is a rhetorically structured panegyric to Origen and an outline of his teaching.

Gregory the Great (c. 540-604). Pope from 590, the fourth and last of the Latin "Doctors of the Church." He was a prolific author and a powerful unifying force within the Latin Church, initiating the liturgical reform that brought about the Gregorian Sacramentary and Gregorian chant.

Hesychius of Jerusalem (fl. 412-450). Presbyter and exegete, thought to have commented on the whole of Scripture.

Hilary of Arles (c. 401-449). Archbishop of Arles and leader of the Semi-Pelagian party. Hilary incurred the wrath of Pope Leo I when he removed a bishop from his see and appointed a new bishop. Leo demoted Arles from a metropolitan see to a bishopric to assert papal power over the church in Gaul.

Hilary of Poitiers (c. 315-367). Bishop of Poitiers and called the "Athanasius of the West" because of his defense (against the Arians) of the common nature of Father and Son.

Hippolytus (fl. 222-245). Recent scholarship places Hippolytus in a Palestinian context, personally familiar with Origen. Though he is known mostly for *The Refutation of All Heresies*, he was primarily a commentator on Scripture (especially the Old Testament) and other sacred texts.

Ignatius of Antioch (c. 35-107/112). Bishop of Antioch who wrote several letters to local churches while being taken from Antioch to Rome to be martyred. In the letters, which warn against heresy, he stresses orthodox Christology, the centrality of the Eucharist and unique role of the bishop in preserving the unity of the church.

Irenaeus of Lyon (c. 135-c. 202). Bishop of Lyons who published the most famous and influential refutation of Gnostic thought.

Isaac of Nineveh (d. c. 700). Also known as Isaac the Syrian or Isaac Syrus, this monastic writer served for a short while as bishop of Nineveh before retiring to live a secluded monastic life. His writings on ascetic subjects survive in the form of numerous homilies.

Isho'dad of Merv (fl. c. 850). Nestorian commentator of the ninth century. He wrote especially on James, 1 Peter and 1 John.

Isidore of Seville (d. 636). Youngest of a family of monks and clerics, including sister Florentina and brothers Leander and Fulgentius. He was an erudite author of comprehensive scale in matters both religious and sacred, including his encyclopedic *Etymologies*.

Jacob of Nisibis (d. 338). Bishop of Nisibis. He was present at the council of Nicaea in 325 and took an active part in the opposition to Arius.

Jacob of Sarug (c. 450-c. 520). Syriac ecclesiastical writer. Jacob received his education at Edessa. At the end of his life he was ordained bishop of Sarug. His principal writing was a long series of metrical homilies, earning him the title "The Flute of the Holy Spirit." His theolog-

ical views are not certain, but it seems that he expressed a moderate monophysite position.

Jerome (c. 347-420). Gifted exegete and exponent of a classical Latin style, now best known as the translator of the Latin Vulgate. He defended the perpetual virginity of Mary, attacked Origen and Pelagius and supported extreme ascetic practices.

John Chrysostom (344/354-407; fl. 386-407). Bishop of Constantinople who was famous for his orthodoxy, his eloquence and his attacks on Christian laxity in high places.

John of Damascus (c. 650-750). Arab monastic and theologian whose writings enjoyed great influence in both the Eastern and Western Churches. His most famous writing was the *Orthodox Faith*.

John the Elder (c. eighth century) A Syriac author who belonged to monastic circles of the Church of the East and lived in the region of Mount Qardu (north Iraq). His most important writings are twenty-two homilies and a collection of fifty-one short letters in which he describes the mystical life as an anticipatory experience of the resurrection life, the fruit of the sacraments of baptism and the Eucharist.

Josephus, Flavius (c. 37-c. 101). Jewish historian from a distinguished priestly family. Acquainted with the Essenes and Sadducees, he himself became a Pharisee. He joined the great Jewish revolt that broke out in 66 and was chosen by the Sanhedrin at Jerusalem to be commander-in-chief in Galilee. Showing great shrewdness to ingratiate himself with Vespasian by foretelling his elevation and that of his son Titus to the imperial dignity, Josephus was restored his liberty after 69 when Vespasian become emperor.

Justin Martyr (c. 100/110-165, fl. c. 148-161). Palestinian philosopher who was converted to Christianity, "the only sure and worthy philosophy." He traveled to Rome where he wrote several apologies against both pagans and Jews, combining Greek philosophy and Christian theology; he was eventually martyred.

Lactantius (c. 260-c. 330). An eloquent writer known to us through Jerome. He is acknowledged more for his technical writing skills than for his theological thought.

Leander (c. 545-c. 600). Latin ecclesiastical writer, of whose works only two survive. He was instrumental is spreading Christianity among the Visigoths, gaining significant historical influence in Spain in his time.

Leo the Great (regn. 440-461). Bishop of Rome whose *Tome to Flavian* helped to strike a balance between Nestorian and Cyrilline positions at the Council of Chalcedon in 451.

Letter of Barnabas (c. 130). An allegorical and typological interpretation of the Old Testament with a decidedly anti-Jewish tone. It was included with other New Testament works as a "Catholic epistle" at least until Eusebius of Caesarea (c. 260/263-340) questioned its authenticity.

Letter to Diognetus (c. third century). A refutation of paganism and an exposition of the Christian life and faith. The author of this letter is unknown, and the exact identity of its recipient, Diognetus, continues to elude patristic scholars.

Lucifer (d. 370/371). Bishop of Cagliari and vigorous supporter of Athanasius and the Nicene Creed. He and his followers entered into schism after refusing to acknowledge less orthodox bishops appointed by the emperor Constantius.

Luculentius (fifth century). Unknown author of a group of short commentaries on the New Testament, especially Pauline passages. His exegesis is mainly literal and relies mostly on earlier authors such as Jerome and Augustine. The content of his writing may place it in the fifth century.

Macarius of Egypt (c. 300-c. 390). One of the Desert Fathers. Accused of supporting Athanasius, Macarius was exiled c. 374 to an island in the Nile by Lucius, the Arian successor of Athanasius. Macarius continued his teaching of monastic theology until his death.

Macrina the Younger (c. 327-379). The elder sister of Basil the Great and Gregory of Nyssa, she is known as "the Younger" to distinguish her from her paternal grandmother. She had a powerful influence on her younger brothers, especially on Gregory, who called her his teacher and relates her teaching in *On the Soul and the Resurrection*.

Manichaeans. A religious movement that originated circa 241 in Persia under the leadership of Mani but was apparently of complex Christian origin. It is said to have denied free will and the universal sovereignty of God, teaching that kingdoms of light and darkness are coeternal and that the redeemed are particles of a spiritual man of light held captive in the darkness of matter (*see* Gnostics).

Marcion (fl. 144). Heretic of the mid-second century who rejected the Old Testament and much of the New Testament, claiming that the Father of Jesus Christ was other than the Creator God (*see* Gnostics).

Marius Victorinus (b. c. 280/285; fl. c. 355-363). Grammarian who translated works of Platonists and, after his late conversion (c. 355), used them against the Arians.

Mark the Hermit (c. sixth century). Monk who lived near Tarsus and produced works on ascetic practices as well as christological issues.

Martin of Braga (fl. c. 568-579). Anti-Arian metropolitan of Braga on the Iberian peninsula. He was highly educated and presided over the provincial council of Braga in 572.

Maximus of Turin (d. 408/423). Bishop of Turin who died during the reigns of Honorius and Theodosius the Younger (408-423). Over one hundred of his sermons survive.

Maximus the Confessor (c. 580-662). Greek theologian and ascetic writer. Fleeing the Arab invasion of Jerusalem in 614, he took refuge in Constantinople and later Africa. He died near the Black Sea after imprisonment and severe suffering. His thought centered on the humanity of Christ.

Methodius of Olympus (d. 311). Bishop of Olympus who celebrated virginity in a *Sympo-*

sium partly modeled on Plato's dialogue of that name.

Minucius Felix of Rome (second or third century). Christian apologist who flourished between 160 and 300 (the exact dates are not known). His *Octavius* agrees at numerous points with the *Apologeticum* of Tertullian. His birthplace is believed to be in Africa.

Montanist Oracles. Montanism was an apocalyptic and strictly ascetic movement begun in the latter half of the second century by a certain Montanus in Phrygia, who, along with certain of his followers, uttered oracles they claimed were inspired by the Holy Spirit. Little of the authentic oracles remains and most of what is known of Montanism comes from the authors who wrote against the movement. Montanism was formally condemned as a heresy before by Asiatic synods.

Nemesius of Emesa (fl. late fourth century). Bishop of Emesa in Syria whose most important work, Of the Nature of Man, draws on several theological and philosophical sources and is the first exposition of a Christian anthropology.

Nestorius (c. 381-c. 451). Patriarch of Constantinople 428-431 and credited with the foundation of the heresy which says that the divine and human natures were associated, rather than truly united, in the incarnation of Christ.

Nicetas of Remesiana (fl. second half of fourth century). Bishop of Remesiana in Serbia, whose works affirm the consubstantiality of the Son and the deity of the Holy Spirit.

Novatian of Rome (fl. 235-258). Roman theologian, otherwise orthodox, who formed a schismatic church after failing to become pope. His treatise on the Trinity states the classic western doctrine.

Oecumenius (sixth century). Called the Rhetor or the Philosopher, Oecumenius wrote the earliest extant Greek commentary on Revelation. Scholia by Oecumenius on some of John Chrysostom's commentaries on the Pauline Epistles are still extant.

Origen of Alexandria (b. 185; fl. c. 200-254). Influential exegete and systematic theologian.

He was condemned (perhaps unfairly) for maintaining the preexistence of souls while denying the resurrection of the body, the literal truth of Scripture and the equality of the Father and the Son in the Trinity.

Pachomius (c. 292-347). Founder of cenobitic monasticism. A gifted group leader and author of a set of rules, he was defended after his death by Athanasius of Alexandria.

Pacian of Barcelona (c. fourth century). Bishop of Barcelona whose writings polemicize against popular pagan festivals as well as Novatian schismatics.

Palladius of Helenopolis (c. 363/364-c. 431). Bishop of Helenopolis (400-417) and then Aspuna in Galatia. A disciple of Evagrius of Pontus and admirer of Origen, Palladius became a zealous adherent of John Chrysostom and shared his troubles in 403. His *Dialogus de vita S. Johannis* is essentially a work of edification, stressing the spiritual value of the life of the desert, where he spent a number of years a monk.

Paschasius of Dumium (c. 515-c. 580). Translator of sentences of the Desert Fathers from Greek into Latin while a monk in Dumium.

Paterius (c. sixth-seventh century). Disciple of Gregory the Great who is primarily responsible for the transmission of Gregory's works to many later medieval authors.

Paulinus of Nola (355-431). Roman Senator and distinguished Latin poet whose frequent encounters with Ambrose of Milan (c. 333-397) led to his eventual conversion and baptism in 389. He eventually renounced his wealth and influential position and took up his pen to write poetry in service of Christ. He also wrote many letters to, among others, Augustine, Jerome and Rufinus.

Paulus Orosius (b. c. 380). An outspoken critic of Pelagius mentored by Augustine. His *Seven Books of History Against the Pagans* was perhaps the first history of Christianity.

Pelagius (c. 354-c. 420). Christian teacher whose followers were condemned in 418 and 431 for maintaining that a Christian could be perfect and that salvation depended on free will.

Peter of Alexandria (d. c. 311). Bishop of Alexandria. He marked (and very probably initiated) the reaction at Alexandria against extreme doctrines of Origen. During the persecution of Christians in Alexandria, Peter was arrested and beheaded by Roman officials. Eusebius of Caesarea described him as "a model bishop, remarkable for his virtuous life and his ardent study of the Scriptures."

Peter Chrysologus (c. 380-450). Latin archbishop of Ravenna whose teachings included arguments for the supremacy of the papacy and the relationship between grace and Christian living.

Philoxenus of Mabbug (c. 440-523). Bishop of Mabbug (Hierapolis) and a leading thinker in the early Syrian Orthodox Church. His extensive writings in Syriac include a set of thirteen *Discourses on the Christian Life*, several works on the incarnation and a number of exegetical works.

Poemen (c. fifth century) One-seventh of the sayings in the *Sayings of the Desert Fathers* are attributed to Poemen, which is Greek for shepherd. Poemen was a common title among early Egyptian desert ascetics, and it is unknown whether all of the sayings come from one person.

Polycarp of Smyrna (c. 69-155). Bishop of Smyrna who vigorously fought heretics such as the Marcionites and Valentinians. He was the leading Christian figure in Roman Asia in the middle of the second century.

Potamius of Lisbon (fl. c. 350-360). Bishop of Lisbon who joined the Arian party in 357, but later returned to the Catholic faith (c. 359?). His works from both periods are concerned with the larger Trinitarian debates of his time.

Procopius of Gaza (c. 465-c. 530). A Christian Sophist educated in Alexandria. He wrote numerous theological works and commentaries on Scripture (particularly the Hebrew Bible), the latter marked by the allegorical exegesis for which the Alexandrian school was known.

Prudentius (c. 348-c. 410). Latin poet and hymn-writer who devoted his later life to Christian writing. He wrote didactic poems on the theology of the incarnation, against the heretic Marcion and against the resurgence of paganism.

Pseudo-Dionysius the Areopagite (fl. c. 500). Author who assumed the name of Dionysius the Areopagite mentioned in Acts 17:34, and who composed the works known as the *Corpus Areopagiticym* (or *Dinysiacum*), although the author's true identity remains a mystery.

Pseudo-Macarius (fl. c. 390). An imaginative writer and ascetic from Mesopotamia to eastern Asia Minor with keen insight into human nature and clear articulation of the theology of the Trinity. His work includes some one hundred discourses and homilies.

Quodvultdeus (fl. 430). Carthaginian deacon and friend of Augustine who endeavored to show at length how the New Testament fulfilled the Old Testament.

Rufinus of Aquileia (c. 345-411). Orthodox Christian thinker and historian who nonetheless translated Origen and defended him against the strictures of Jerome and Epiphanius.

Sabellius (fl. 200). Allegedly the author of the heresy which maintains that the Father and Son are a single person. The patripassian variant of this heresy states that the Father suffered on the cross.

Sahdona (fl. 635-640). Known in Greek as Martyrius, this Syriac author was bishop of Beth Garmai for a short time. His most important work is the deeply scriptural *Book of Perfection* which ranks as one of the masterpieces of Syriac monastic literature.

Salvian the Presbyter of Marseilles (c. 400-c. 480). An important author for the history of his own time. He saw the fall of Roman civilization to the barbarians as a consequence of the reprehensible conduct of Roman Christians.

Second Letter of Clement (c. 150). The so-called *Second Letter of Clement* is the earliest surviving Christian sermon probably written by a Corinthian author, though some scholars have assigned it to a Roman or Alexandrian author.

Severian of Gabala (fl. c. 400). A contemporary

of John Chrysostom, he was highly regarded preacher in Constantinople, particularly at the imperial court, and ultimately sided with Chrysostom's accusers. His sermons are dominated by antiheretical concerns.

Severus of Antioch (fl. 488-538). A monophysite theologian, consecrated bishop of Antioch in 522. Severus believed that Christ's human nature was an annex to his divine nature and argued that if Christ were both divine and human, he would necessarily have been two persons.

Shepherd of **Hermas** (second century). Divided into five *Visions,* twelve *Mandates* and ten *Similitudes,* this Christian apocalypse was written by a former slave and named for the form of the second angel said to have granted him his visions. This work was highly esteemed for its moral value and was used as a textbook for catechumens in the early church.

Sulpicius Severus (c. 360-c. 420). An ecclesiastical writer born of noble parents. Devoting himself to monastic retirement, he became a personal friend and enthusiastic disciple of St. Martin of Tours. His ordination to the priesthood is vouched for by Gennadius, but no details of his priestly activity have reached us.

Symeon the New Theologian (c. 949-1022). Compassionate spiritual leader known for his strict rule. He believed that the divine light could be perceived and received through the practice of mental prayer.

Tertullian of Carthage (c. 155/160-225/250; fl. c. 197-222). Brilliant Carthaginian apologist and polemicist who laid the foundations of Christology and trinitarian orthodoxy in the West, though he himself was estranged from the main church by its laxity.

Theodore of Heraclea (d. c. 355). An anti-Nicene bishop of Thrace. He was part of a team seeking reconciliation between Eastern and Western Christianity. In 343 he was excommunicated at the council of Sardica. His writings focus on a literal interpretation of Scripture.

Theodore of Mopsuestia (c. 350-428). Bishop of Mopsuestia, founder of the Antiochene, or literalistic, school of exegesis. A great man in his day, he was later condemned as a precursor of Nestorius.

Theodoret of Cyr (c. 393-466). Bishop of Cyr (Cyrrhus), he was an opponent of Cyril, whose doctrine of Christ's person was finally vindicated in 451 at the Council of Chalcedon.

Theophilus of Antioch (late second century). Bishop of Antioch. His only surviving work is *Ad Autholycum,* where we find the first Christian commentary on Genesis and the first use of the term *Trinity.* Theophilus's apologetic literary heritage had influence on Irenaeus and possibly Tertullian.

Theophylact of Ohrid (c. 1050-c. 1108). Byzantine archbishop of Ohrid (or Achrida) in what is now Bulgaria. Drawing on earlier works, he wrote commentaries on several Old Testament books and all of the New Testament except for Revelation.

Valentinus (fl. c. 140). Alexandrian heretic of the mid-second century who taught that the material world was created by the transgression of God's Wisdom, or Sophia (*see* Gnostics).

Valerian of Cimiez (fl. c. 422-439). Bishop of Cimiez. He participated in the councils of Riez (439) and Vaison (422) with a view to strengthening church discipline. He supported Hilary of Arles in quarrels with Pope Leo I.

Victorius of Petovium (d. c. 304). Latin biblical exegete. With multiple works attributed to him, his sole surviving work is the *Commentary on the Apocalypse* and perhaps some fragments from *Commentary on Matthew.* Victorinus expressed strong millenarianism in his writing, though his was less materialistic than the millenarianism of Papias or Irenaeus. In his allegorical approach he could be called a spiritual disciple of Origen. Victorinus died during the first year of Diocletian's persecution, probably in 304.

Vincent of Lérins (d. 435). Monk who has exerted considerable influence through his writings on orthodox dogmatic theological method, as contrasted with the theological methodologies of the heresies.

BIBLIOGRAPHY

This bibliography refers readers to original language sources and supplies Thesaurus Linguae Graecae (=TLG) or Cetedoc Clavis (=Cl.) numbers where available.

Ambrose of Milan. "De bono mortis." Pages 3-261 in *Sancti Ambrosii opera*. Edited by K. Schenkl. Corpus Scriptorum Ecclesiasticorum Latinorum, vol. 32, pt. 1. Vienna, Austria: Hoelder-Pichler-
Tempsky, 1897. Cl. 0129.

———. "De Cain et Abel." Pages 3-261 in *Sancti Ambrosii opera*. Edited by K. Schenkl. Corpus Scriptorum Ecclesiasticorum Latinorum, vol. 32, pt. 1. Vienna, Austria: Hoelder-Pichler-Tempsky,
1897. Cl. 0125.

———. "De excessu fratris Satyri." Pages 3-261 in *Sancti Ambrosii opera*. Edited by K. Schenkl. Corpus
Scriptorum Ecclesiasticorum Latinorum, vol. 32, pt. 1. Vienna, Austria: Hoelder-Pichler-
Tempsky, 1897. Cl. 0157.

———. "De fide, libri quinque." Pages 3-307 in *Sancti Ambrosii opera*. Edited by O. Faller. Corpus
Scriptorum Ecclesiasticorum Latinorum, vol. 78. Vienna, Austria: Hoelder-Pichler-Tempsky,
1955. Cl. 0150.

———. "De fuga saeculi." Pages 163-207 in *Sancti Ambrosii opera*. Edited by K. Schenkl. Corpus Scriptorum Ecclesiasticorum Latinorum, vol. 32, pt. 2. Vienna, Austria: F. Tempsky; Leipzig, Germany:
G. Freytag, 1897. Cl. 0133.

———. "De interpellatione Job et David." Pages 211-96 in *Sancti Ambrosii opera*. Edited by K. Schenkl.
Corpus Scriptorum Ecclesiasticorum Latinorum, vol. 32, pt. 2. Vienna, Austria: Hoelder-Pichler-
Tempsky, 1897. Cl. 0134.

———. "De Isaac vel anima." Pages 641-760 in *Sancti Ambrosii opera*. Edited by K. Schenkl. Corpus
Scriptorum Ecclesiasticorum Latinorum, vol. 32, pt. 2. Vienna, Austria: Hoelder-Prichler-
Tempsky, 1897. Cl. 0128.

———. "De Jacob et vita beata." Pages 3-70 in *Sancti Ambrosii opera*. Edited by K. Schenkl. Corpus
Scriptorum Ecclesiasticorum Latinorum, vol. 32, pt. 2. Vienna, Austria: F. Tempsky; Leipzig, Germany: G. Freytag. Cl. 0130.

———. "De Joseph." Pages 73-122 in *Sancti Ambrosii opera*. Edited by K. Schenkl. Corpus Scriptorum
Ecclesiasticorum Latinorum, vol. 32, pt. 2. Vienna, Austria: Hoelder-Pichler-Tempsky, 1897. Cl.
0131.

———. "De mysteriis." Pages 89-116 in *Sancti Ambrosii opera*. Edited by O. Faller. Corpus Scriptorum
Ecclesiasticorum Latinorum, vol. 73. Vienna, Austria: Hoelder-Pichler-Tempsky, 1955. Cl. 0155.

———. "De officiis ministrorum." 2 vols. Edited by M. Testard. Collection des universités de France.

Paris: Belles Lettres, 1984, 1992. Cl. 0144.

———. "De paenitentia." Pages 340-97 in *Sancti Ambrosii opera*. Edited by O. Faller. Corpus Scriptorum Ecclesiasticorum Latinorum, vol. 73. Vienna, Austria: Hoelder-Pichler-Tempsky, 1955. Cl. 0156.

———. "De paradiso." Pages 263-336 in *Sancti Ambrosii opera*. Edited by K. Schenkl. Corpus Scriptorum Ecclesiasticorum Latinorum, vol. 32, pt. 2. Vienna, Austria: F. Tempsky; Leipzig; Germany: G. Freytag, 1897. Cl. 0124.

———. "De spiritu sancto." Pages 7-222 in *Sancti Ambrosii opera*. Edited by O. Faller. Corpus Scriptionorum Ecclesiasticorum Latinorum, vol. 73. Vienna, Austria: Hoelder-Pichler-Tempsky, 1955. Cl. 0151.

———. "De virginibus." Pages 100-204 in *Sancti Ambrosii: De Virginibus*. Edited by O. Faller. Florilegium patristicum, vol. 31. Bonn: Hanstein, 1933. Cl. 0145.

———. *Epistulae*. Edited by O. Faller and M. Zelzer. Corpus Scriptorum Ecclesiasticorum Latinorum, vol. 82, pts 2, 3. Vienna, Austria: Hoelder-Pichler-Tempsky, 1955. Cl. 0160.

———. "Hexaemeron." Pages 3-261 in *Sancti Ambrosii opera*. Edited by O. Faller. Corpus Scriptorum Ecclesiasticorum Latinorum, vol. 32, pt. 1. Vienna, Austria: Hoelder-Pichler-Tempsky, 1897. Cl. 0123.

Aphrahat. *Demonstrationes*. Edited by R. Graffin. Patrologia syriaca, vol. 1. Paris: Firming-Didot et socii, 1910.

Athanasius. "Apologia de fuga sua." Pages 133-67 in *Athanase d'Alexandrie. Apologie à l'empereur Constance. Apologie pour sa fuite*. Edited by J.-M. Szymusiak. Sources chrétiennes, vol. 56. Paris: Cerf, 1958. TLG 2035.012.

———. "De incarnatione verbi." Pages 258-468 in *Sur l'incarnation du verbe*. Edited by C. Kannengiesser. Sources chrétiennes, vol. 199. Paris: Cerf, 1973. TLG 2035.002.

———. *Epistulae festales*. Edited by A. Mai. *Sancti Athanasii Epistulae Festales Syriace et Latine*. Nova Patrum Bibliotheca, vol. 6, part 1. Rome: 1853 [Syriac].

Augustine of Hippo. *Confessionum*. Edited by Lucas Verheijen. Corpus Christianorum, Series Latina, vol. 27. Turnhout, Belgium: Typographi Brepols Editores Pontificii, 1955. Cl. 0251.

———. "Contra duas epistulas Pelagianorum." Pages 423-570. Edited by C. F. Vrba and J. Zycha. Corpus Scriptorum Ecclesiasticorum Latinorum, vol. 60. Vienna, Austria: F. Tempsky, 1913. Cl. 0346.

———. "Contra Faustum." Pages 251-797 in *Sancti Aureli Augustini opera*. Edited by J. Zycha. Corpus Scriptorum Ecclesiasticorum Latinorum, vol. 25. Vienna, Austria: F. Tempsky, 1891. Cl. 0321.

———. "Contra mendacium." Pages 469-528 in *Sancti Aureli Augustini opera*. Edited by J. Zycha. Corpus Scriptorum Ecclesiasticorum Latinorum, vol. 41. Vienna, Austria: F. Tempsky, 1900. Cl. 0304.

———. "De baptismo." Pages 145-375 in *Sancti Aureli Augustini opera*. Edited by M. Petschenig. Corpus Scriptorum Ecclesiasticorum Latinorum, vol. 51. Vienna, Austria: F. Tempsky, 1908. Cl 0332.

———. "De bono coniugali." Pages 187-230 in *Sancti Aureli Augustini opera*. Edited by J. Zycha. Corpus Scriptorum Ecclesiasticorum Latinorum, vol. 41. Vienna, Austria: F. Tempsky, 1900. Cl. 0299.

———. "De bono viduitatis." Pages 305-43 in *Sancti Aureli Augustini opera*. Edited by J. Zycha. Corpus Scriptorum Ecclesiasticorum Latinorum, vol. 41. Vienna, Austria: F. Tempsky, 1900. Cl. 0301.

———. *De civitate Dei*. Edited by B. Dombart and A. Kalb. Corpus Christianorum, Series Latina, vols. 47, 48. Turnhout, Belgium: Typographi Brepols Editores Pontificii, 1955. Cl. 0313.

———. "De diversis quaestionibus octoginta tribus." Pages 11-249 in *Aurelii Augustini opera*. Edited by A. Mutzenbecher. Corpus Christianorum, Series Latina, vol. 44A. Turnhout, Belgium: Typographi Brepols Editores Pontificii, 1975. Cl. 0289.

———. "De doctrina christiana." Pages 1-167 in *Aurelii Augustini opera*. Edited by J. Martin. Corpus Christianorum, Series Latina, vol. 32. Turnhout, Belgium: Typographi Brepols Editores Pontificii, 1962. Cl. 0263.

———. "De fide et operibus." Pages 35-97 in *Sancti Aureli Augustini opera*. Edited by J. Zycha. Corpus Scriptorum Ecclesiasticorum Latinorum, vol. 41. Vienna, Austria: Hoelder-Pichler-Tempsky, 1900. Cl. 0294.

———. "De fide et symbolo." Pages 3-32 in *Sancti Aureli Augustini opera*. Edited by J. Zycha. Corpus Scriptorum Ecclesiasticorum Latinorum, vol. 41. Vienna, Austria: F. Tempsky, 1900. Cl. 0293.

———. "De Genesi contra Manichaeos." Pages 173-220 in *Opera omnia*. Edited by J.-P. Migne. Patrologiae Cursus Completus, Series Latina, vol. 34. Paris: Migne, 1845. Cl. 0294.

———. "De gratia Christi et de peccato originali." Pages 125-206 in *Sancti Aureli Augustini opera*. Edited by C. F. Vrba and J. Zycha. Corpus Scriptorum Ecclesiasticorum Latinorum, vol. 42. Vienna, Austria: F. Tempsky, 1902. Cl. 0349.

———. "De gratia et libero arbitrio." Pages 881-912 in *Opera omnia*. Edited by J.-P. Migne. Patrologiae Cursus Completus, Series Latina, vol. 44. Paris: Migne, 1845. Cl. 0352.

———. "De mendacio." Pages 413-66 in *Sancti Aureli Augustini opera*. Edited by J. Zycha. Corpus Scriptorum Ecclesiasticorum Latinorum, vol. 41. Vienna, Austria: F. Tempsky, 1900. Cl. 0303.

———. "De moribus ecclesiae catholicae et de moribus Manichaeorum." Cols. 1309-78 in *Opera omnia*. Edited by J.-P. Migne. Patrologiae Cursus Completus, Series Latina, vol. 32. Paris: Migne, 1845. Cl. 0261.

———. "De natura boni." Pages 855-89 in *Sancti Aureli Augustini opera*. Edited by J. Zycha. Corpus Scriptorum Ecclesiasticorum Latinorum, vol. 25. Vienna, Austria: F. Tempsky, 1892. Cl. 0323.

———. "De nuptiis et concupiscentia." Pages 211-319 in *Sancti Aureli Augustini opera*. Edited by C. F. Vrba and J. Zycha. Corpus Scriptorum Ecclesiasticorum Latinorum, vol. 42. Vienna, Austria: F. Tempsky, 1902. Cl. 0350.

———. "De opere monachorum." Pages 531-95 in *Sancti Aureli Augustini opera*. Edited by J. Zycha. Corpus Scriptorum Ecclesiasticorum Latinorum, vol. 41. Vienna, Austria: F. Tempsky, 1900. Cl. 0305.

———. "De peccatorum meritis et remissione et de baptismo parvulorum." Pages 3-151 in *Sancti Aureli Augustini opera*. Edited by C. F. Vrba and J. Zycha. Corpus Scriptorum Ecclesiasticorum Latinorum, vol. 60. Vienna, Austria: F. Tempsky, 1913. Cl. 0342.

———. "De perfectione justitiae hominis." Pages 3-48 in *Sancti Aureli Augustini opera*. Edited by C. F. Vrba and J. Zycha. Corpus Scriptorum Ecclesiasticorum Latinorum, vol. 42. Vienna, Austria: F. Tempsky, 1902. Cl. 0347.

———. "De sermone Domini in monte." Pages 1-188 in *Sancti Aureli Augustini opera 7.2*. Edited by A. Mutzenbecher. Corpus Christianorum, Series Latina, vol. 35. Turnhout, Belgium: Typographi Brepols Editores Pontificii, 1967. Cl. 0274.

———. "De spiritu et littera." Pages 155-229 in *Sancti Aureli Augustini opera*. Edited by C. F. Vrba and J. Zycha. Corpus Scriptorum Ecclesiasticorum Latinorum, vol. 60. Vienna, Austria: F. Tempsky, 1913. Cl. 0343.

———. *De Trinitate*. Edited by W. J. Mountain. Corpus Christianorum, Series Latina, vols. 50, 50A. Turnhout, Belgium: Typographi Brepols Editores Pontificii, 1968. Cl. 0329.

———. *Enarrationes in Psalmos*. Edited by E. Dekkers and J. Fraipont. Corpus Christianorum, Series Latina, vols. 38, 39, 40. Turnhout, Belgium: Typographi Brepols Editores Pontificii, 1956. Cl. 0283.

———. "Enchiridion de fide, spe et caritate." Pages 49-114 in *Aurelii Augustini opera*. Edited by E. Evans.

Corpus Christianorum, Series Latina, vol. 46. Turnhout, Belgium: Typographi Brepols Editores Pontificii, 1969. Cl. 0295.

———. "Epistulae." In *Sancti Aureli Augustini opera*. Edited by A. Goldbacher. Corpus Scriptorum Ecclesiasticorum Latinorum, vols. 34, pt. 1; 34, pt. 2; 44; 57; 58. Vienna, Austria: F. Tempsky, 1895-1898. Cl. 0262.

———. *In Johannis euangelium tractatus*. Edited by R. Willems. Corpus Christianorum, Series Latina, vol. 36. Turnhout, Belgium: Typographi Brepols Editores Pontificii, 1954. Cl. 0278.

———. "Quaestionum in Heptateuchum libri septem." Pages 1-377 in *Aurelii Augustini opera*. Edited by J. Fraipont. Corpus Christianorum, Series Latina, vol. 33. Turnhout, Belgium: Typographi Brepols Editores Pontificii, 1958. Cl. 0270.

———. "Retractationum libri duo." Pages 5-143 in *Aurelii Augustini opera*. Edited by A. Mutzenbecher. Corpus Christianorum, Series Latina, vol. 57. Turnhout, Belgium: Typographi Brepols Editores Pontificii, 1984. Cl. 0250.

———. *Sermones*. Edited by J.-P. Migne. Patrologiae Cursus Completus, Series Latina, vols. 38, 39. Paris: Migne, 1845,1846. Cl. 0284.

———. *Sermones*. In *Sancti Augustini Sermones post Maurinos reperti*. Edited by G. Morin. Miscellanea Agostiana, vol. 1. Rome: Tipgafia poliglotta vaticana, 1930. Cl. 0284.

———. *Sermones*. Pages 154-350 in *Sermon pour la Pache*. Edited by S. Poque. Sources chrétiennes, vol. 116. Paris: Cerf, 1966. Cl. 0284.

Basil the Great (of Caesarea). "De baptismo libri duo." Cols. 1513-628 in *Opera omnia*. Patrologiae Cursus Completus, Series Graeca, vol. 31. Edited by J.-P. Migne. Paris: Migne, 1885. TLG 2040.052.

———. "De spiritu sancto." Pages 250-530 in *Basile de Césarée. Sur le Saint-Esprit*, 2nd ed. Edited by B. Pruche. Sources chrétiennes, vol. 17. Paris: Cerf, 1968. TLG 2040.003.

———. "Epistulae." Pages 2:101-218, 3:1-229 in *Saint Basile. Lettres*, vols. 2, 3. Edited by Y. Courtonne. Paris: Les Belles Lettres, 1961, 1966. TLG 2040.004.

———, [Pseudo-]. "Homilia de misericordia et judicio." Cols. 1705-714 in *Opera omnia*. Patrologiae Cursus Completus, Series Graeca, vol. 31. Edited by J.-P. Migne. Paris: Migne, 1885. TLG 2040.069.

———. "Homiliae in hexaemeron." Pages 86-522 in *Basile de Césarée. Homélies sur l'hexaéméron*, 2nd ed. Edited by S. Giet. Sources chrétiennes, vol. 26. Paris: Cerf, 1968. TLG 2040.001.

———. "Homiliae in illud: Attende tibi ipsi." Pages 23-37 *in L'homélie de Basile de Césarée sur le mot 'observe-toi toi-même'*. Edited by S.Y. Rudberg. Stockholm: Almqvist & Wiksell, 1962. TLG 2040.006.

———. "Homiliae super Psalmos." Pages 209-494 in *Opera omnia*. Patrologiae Cursus Completus, Series Graeca, vol. 29. Edited by J.-P. Migne. Paris: Migne, 1886. TLG 2040.018.

———. "Prologus 7 [De judicio Dei]." Cols. 653-676 in *Opera omnia*. Patrologiae Cursus Completus, Series Graeca, vol. 31. Edited by J.-P. Migne. Paris: Migne, 1885. TLG 2040.043.

Bede. "De tabernaculo et euasis eius ac vestibus sacerdotem libri iii." Pages 5-139 in *Bedae Venerabilis opera*. Edited by D. Hurst. Corpus Christianorum, Series Latina, vol. 119A. Turnhout, Belgium: Typographi Brepols Editores Pontificii, 1969. Cl. 1345.

———. "Expositio actuum apostolorum." Pages 3-99 in *Bedae Venerabilis opera*. Edited by D. Hurst. Corpus Christianorum, Series Latina, vol. 121. Turnhout, Belgium: Typographi Brepols Editores Pontificii, 1953. Cl. 1357.

———. "Homiliarum evangelii." Pages 1-378 in *Bedae Venerabilis opera*. Edited by D. Hurst. Corpus Christianorum, Series Latina, vol. 122. Turnhout, Belgium: Typographi Brepols Editores Pontificii, 1956. Cl. 1367.

———. "In epistulam septem catholicas." Pages 181-342 in *Bedae Venerabilis opera*. Edited by D. Hurst. Corpus Christianorum, Series Latina, vol. 121. Turnhout, Belgium: Typographi Brepols Editores Pontificii, 1953. Cl. 1362.

Caesarius of Arles. *Sermones*. Edited by G. Morin. Corpus Christianorum, Series Latina, vols. 103, 104. Turnhout, Belgium: Typograpi Brepols Editores Pontificii, 1953. Cl. 1008.

Cassian, John. *Collationes*. Edited by M. Petscheig. Corpus Scritorum Ecclesiasticorum Latinorum, vol. 13. Vienna, Austria: F. Tempsky, 1886. Cl. 0512.

Cassiodorus. *Expositio Psalmorum*. Edited M. Adriaen. Corpus Christianorum, Series Latina, vols. 97, 98. Turnhout, Belgium: Typographi Brepols Editores Pontificii, 1958. Cl. 0900.

Clement of Alexandria. "Paedagogus." Pages 1:108-294, 2:10-242, 3:12-190 in *Le pédagogue [par] Clément d'Alexandrie*. 3 vols. Edited by M. Harl, H. Marrou, C. Matray and C. Mondésert. Sources chrétiennes, vols. 70, 108, 158. Paris: Cerf, 1960, 1965, 1970. TLG 0555.002.

———. "Stromata." Pages 2:3-518 3:3-102 in *Clemens Alexandrinus*, vol. 2, 3rd ed., and vol. 3, 2nd ed. Edited by O. Stählin, L. Früchtel and U. Treu. Die griechischen christlichen Schriftsteller, vols. 52(15), 17. Berlin: Akademie-Verlag, 1960, 1970. TLG 0555.004.

Clement of Rome. "Epistula i ad Corinthios." Pages 98-204 in *Clément of Rome: Épître aux Corinthiens*. Edited by A. Jaubert. Sources chrétiennes, vol. 167. Paris: Cerf, 1971. TLG 1271.001.

Constitutions of the Holy Apostles ("Constitutiones apostolorum"). Pages 1:100-338; 2:116-394; 3:18-310 in *Les constitutions apostoliques*. Edited by M. Metzger. Sources chrétiennes, vols. 329, 336. Paris: Cerf, 1985, 1986, 1987. TLG 2894.001.

Cyprian. "Ad fortunatum (de exhortatione martyrii)." Pages 183-216 in *Sancti Cyprian episcopi opera*. Edited by R. Weber. Corpus Christianorum, Series Latina, vol. 3. Turnhout, Belgium: Typographi Brepolis Editores Pontificii, 1972. Cl. 0045.

———. "De bono patientiae." Pages 118-33 in *Sancti Cypriani episcopi epistularium*. Edited by C. Moreschini. Corpus Christianorum, Series Latina, vol. 3A. Turnhout, Belgium: Typographi Brepolis Editores Pontificii, 1976. Cl. 0048.

———. "De ecclesiae catholicae unitate." Pages 249-68 in *Sancti Cyprian episcopi opera*. Edited by R. Weber. Corpus Christianorum, Series Latina, vol. 3. Turnhout, Belgium: Typographi Brepolis Editores Pontificii, 1972. Cl. 0041.

———. *Epistulae*. Edited by G. F. Diercks. Corpus Christianorum, Series Latina, vols. 3B, 3C. Turnhout, Belgium: Typographi Brepols Editores Pontificii, 1994, 1996. Cl. 0050.

Cyril of Alexandria. "Commentarii in Lucam." Cols. 476-949 in *Opera omnia*. Patrologiae Cursus Completus, Series Graeca, vol. 72. Edited by J.-P. Migne. Paris: Migne, 1864. TLG 4090.030.

———. "Epistulae." In *Concilium universale Ephesenum*. Edited by E. Schwartz. Berlin: Walter De Gruyter, 1927. TLG5000.001.

Cyril of Jerusalem. "Catecheses ad illuminandos 1-18." Pages 1:28-320, 2:2-342 in *Cyrilli Hierosolymorum archiepiscopi opera quae supersunt omnia*, 2 vols. Edited by W. C. Reischl and J. Rupp. Munich: Lentner, 1848, 1860. Repr., Hildesheim: Olms, 1967. TLG 2110.003.

———. "Mystagogiae 1-5." In *Cyrille de Jérusalem. Catéchèses mystagogiques*. Edited by A. Piédagnel and P. Paris. Sources chrétiennes, vol. 126. Paris: Cerf, 1966. TLG 2110.002.

Didache. Pages 226-242 in *Instructions des Apôtres*. Edited by J. P. Audet. Paris: Lecoffre, 1958. TLG 1311.001.

Ephrem the Syrian. "In Exodum." Pages 104-34 in *Sancti Ephraem Syri in Genesim et in Exodum commentarii*. Edited by R.-M. Tonneau. Corpus Scriptorum Christianorum Orientalium, vol. 152 (Scriptores Syri 71). Louvain: Imprimerie Orientaliste L. Durbecq, 1955.

———. "Epistula ad Publium." S. Brock, *Le Muséon* 89 (1976), 261-305.

———. "Hymni de paradiso." In *Des Heiligen Ephraem des Syrers Hymnen de paradiso und contra Julianum.* Edited by E. Beck. Corpus Scriptorum Christianorum Orientalium, vol. 174 (Scriptores Syri 78). Louvain: Imprimerie Orientaliste L. Durbecq, 1957.

———. "Sermo de Domino nostro." In *Des Heiligen Ephraem des Syrers Sermo de Domino Nostro.* Edited by E. Beck. Corpus Scriptorum Christianorum Orientalium, vol. 270 (Scriptores Syri 116). Louvain: Imprimerie Orientaliste L. Durbecq, 1966.

———. "In Tatiani Diatessaron." In *Saint Éphrem: Commentaire de l'Evangile Concordant — Text Syriaque, (Ms Chester-Beatty 709), Folios Additionnels.* Edited by L. Leloir. Chester-Beatty Monographs, no. 8, Leuven, Paris, 1990.

Eusebius of Caesarea. "Demonstratio evangelica." Pages 493-96 in *Eusebius Werke, Band 6: Die Demonstratio evangelica.* Edited by I. A. Heikel. Die griechischen christlichen Schriftsteller, vol. 23. Leipzig: Hinrichs, 1913.

———. "Historia ecclesiastica." Pages 1:3-215, 2:4-231, 3:3-120 in *Eusèbe de Césarée. Histoire ecclésiastique*, 3 vols. Edited by G. Bardy. Sources chrétiennes, vols. 31, 41, 55. Paris: Cerf, 1952, 1955, 1958. Cl. 0198k.

Evagrius. "De oratione." Cols. 1165-1200 in *Opera omnia.* Patrologiae Cursus Completus, Series Graeca, vol. 79. Edited by J.-P. Migne. Paris: Migne, 1865.

Fulgentius of Ruspe. "De fide ad Petrum seu de regula fidei." Pages 711-60 in *Opera.* Edited by J. Fraipont. Corpus Christianorum, Series Latina, vol. 91A. Turnhout, Belgium: Typographi Brepols Editores Pontificii, 1968. Cl. 0826.

———. *Epistulae, et Varia.* Edited by J. Fraipont. Corpus Christianorum, Series Latina, vols. 91, 91A. Turnhout, Belgium: Typographi Brepols Editores Pontificii, 1968. Cl. 0817.

Gregory of Nazianzus. "Apologetica [orat. 2]." Cols. 408-513 in *Opera omnia.* Patrologiae Cursus Completus, Series Graeca, vol. 35. Edited by J.-P. Migne. Paris: Migne, 1885. TLG 2022.016.

———. "Contra Julianum imperatorem [orat. 4]." Cols. 532-664 in *Opera omnia.* Patrologiae Cursus Completus, Series Graeca, vol. 35. Edited by J.-P. Migne. Paris: Migne, 1885. TLG 2022.018.

———. "De filio [orat. 30]." Pages 170-216 in *Gregor von Nazianz. Die fünf theologischen Reden.* Edited by J. Barbel. Düsseldorf, Germany: Patmos-Verlag, 1963. TLG 2022.010.

———. "De theologia [orat. 28]." Pages 62-126 in *Gregor von Nazianz. Die fünf theologischen Reden.* Edited by J. Barbel. Düsseldorf, Germany: Patmos-Verlag, 1963. TLG 2022.008.

———. "Epistulae." Pages 1:1-118, 2:1-148 in *Saint Grégoire de Nazianze. Lettres*, 2 vols. Edited by P. Gallay. Paris: Les Belles Lettres, 1964, 1967. TLG 2022.001.

———. "Epistulae theologicae." Pages 36-94 in *Grégoire de Nazianze. Lettres théologiques.* Edited by P. Gallay. Sources chrétiennes, vol. 208. Paris: Cerf, 1974. TLG 2022.002.

———. "Funebris oratio in laudem Basilii Magni Caesareae in Cappadocia episcopi [orat. 43]." Pages 58-230 in *Grégoire de Nazianze. Discours funèbres en l'honneur de son frère Césaire et de Basile de Césarée.* Edited by F. Boulenger. Paris: Picard, 1908. TLG 2022.006.

———. "Funebris oratio in patrem [orat. 18]." Cols. 985-1044 in *Opera omnia.* Patrologiae Cursus Completus, Series Graeca, vol. 35. Edited by J.-P. Migne. Paris: Migne, 1885. TLG 2022.031.

———. "In sanctum baptisma [orat. 40]." Cols. 360-425 in *Opera omnia.* Patrologiae Cursus Completus, Series Graeca, vol. 36. Edited by J.-P. Migne. Paris: Migne, 1886. TLG 2022.048

———. "In sanctum pascha [orat. 45]" Cols. 624-64 in *Opera omnia.* Patrologiae Cursus Completus, Series Graeca, vol. 36. Edited by J.-P. Migne. Paris: Migne, 1886. TLG 2022.052.

———. "Supremum vale [orat. 42]." Cols. 457-92 in *Opera omnia*. Patrologiae Cursus Completus, Series Graeca, vol. 36. Edited by J.-P. Migne. Paris: Migne, 1886. TLG 2022.050.

Gregory of Nyssa. "Ad Ablabium quod non sint tres dei." Pages 37-57 in *Gregorii Nysseni opera*, vol. 3.1. Edited by F. Mueller. Leiden: Brill, 1958. TLG 2017.003.

———. "Ad simplicium de fide." Pages 61-67 in *Gregorii Nysseni opera*, vol. 3.1. Edited by F. Mueller. Leiden: Brill, 1958. TLG 2017.004.

———. "Contra Eunomium." Pages 1.1:3-409, 2.2:3-311 in *Gregorii Nysseni opera*, vols. 1.1 and 2.2. Edited by W. Jaeger. Leiden: Brill, 1960. TLG 2017.030.

———. "De instituto christiano." Pages 40-89 in *Gregorii Nysseni opera*, vol. 8.1. Edited by W. Jaeger. Leiden: Brill, 1963. TLG 2017.024.

———. "De perfectione christiana ad Olympium monachum." Pages 173-214 in *Gregorii Nysseni opera*, vol. 8.1. Edited by W. Jaeger. Leiden: Brill, 1963. TLG 2017.026.

———. "De virginitate." Pages 246-560 in *Grégoire de Nysse. Traité de la virginité*. Edited by M. Aubineau. Sources chrétiennes, vol. 119. Paris: Cerf, 1966. TLG 2017.043.

———. "De vita Gregorii Thaumaturgi." Cols. 893-957 in *Opera omnia*. Patrologiae Cursus Completus. Series Graeca, vol. 46. Edited by J.-P. Migne. Paris: Migne, 1863. TLG 2017.069.

———. "De vita Mosis." Pages 44-326 in *Grégoire de Nysse. La vie de Moïse*, 3rd ed. Edited by J. Daniélou. Sources chrétiennes, vol. 1. Paris: Cerf, 1968. TLG 2017.042.

———. "Dialogus de anima et resurrectione." Cols. 12-160 in *Opera omnia*. Patrologiae Cursus Completus, Series Graeca, vol. 46. Edited by J.-P. Migne. Paris: Migne, 1863. TLG 2017.056.

———. "In diem luminum [*vulgo* In baptismum Christi oratio]." Pages 221-42 in *Gregorii Nysseni opera*, vol. 9.1. Edited by E. Gebhardt. Leiden: Brill, 1967. TLG 2017.014.

———. "In Inscriptiones Psalmorum." Pages 24-175 in *Gregorii Nysseni opera*, vol. 5. Edited by J. McDonough. Leiden: Brill, 1962. TLG 2017.027.

———. "Refutatio confessionis Eunomii." Pages 312-410 in *Gregorii Nysseni opera*, vol. 2.2. Edited by W. Jaeger. Leiden: Brill, 1960. TLG 2017.031.

Gregory Thaumaturgus. "Epistula canonica." Pages 19-30 in *Fonti. Fascicolo ix. Discipline générale antique*, vol. 2. Edited by P. Joannou. Rome: Tipografia Italo-Orientale "S. Nilo," 1963. TLG 2063.005.

Gregory the Great. "Homiliarum xl in evangelica." Cols. 1075-1312 in *Opera omnia*. Edited by J.-P. Migne. Patrologiae Cursus Completus, Series Latina, vol. 76. Paris: Migne, 1857. Cl. 1711.

———. *Moralia in Job*. Edited by D. Norbery. Corpus Christianorum, Series Latina, vol. 143A, 143B. Turnhout, Belgium: Typographi Brepols Editores Pontificii, 1953. Cl. 1708.

———. *Registrum epistularum*. Edited by D. Norbery. Corpus Christianorum, Series Latina, vol. 140, 140A. Turnhout, Belgium: Typographi Brepols Editores Pontificii, 1953. Cl. 1714.

———. *Regula pastoralis*. Edited by F. Rommel and R.W. Clement. Corpus Christianorum, Series Latina, vol. 141. Turnhout, Belgium: Typographi Brepols Editores Pontificii, 1953. Cl. 1712.

Hilary. *De Trinitate*. Edited by P. Smulders. Corpus Christianorum, Series Latina, vols. 62, 62A. Turnhout, Belgium: Typographi Brepols Editores Pontificii, 1979, 1980. Cl. 0433.

Irenaeus. "Adversus haereses [liber 3]." Pages 22-436 in *Irénée de Lyon. Contre les hérésies, livre 3*, vol. 2. Edited by A. Rousseau and L. Doutreleau. Sources chrétiennes, vol. 211. Paris: Cerf, 1974. TLG 1447.002.

Isaac of Nineveh. "Homolia 22." In *Mar Isaacus: De perfectione religiosa*. Edited by P. Bedjan. Paris, 1909.

Isidore of Seville. "Mysticorum expositiones sacramentorum seu quaestiones in vetus testamentum."

Cols. 207-448 in *Opera omnia*. Edited by J.-P. Migne. Patrologiae Cursus Completus, Series Latina, vol. 83. Paris: Migne, 1850.

Jerome. "Adversus Helvidium de Mariae virginitate perpetua." Cols. 193-216 in *Opera omnia*. Edited by J.-P. Migne. Patrologiae Cursus Completus, Series Latina, vol. 23. Paris: Migne, 1845. Cl. 0609.

———. "Adversus Jovinianum." Cols. 221-352 in *Opera omnia*. Edited by J.-P. Migne. Patrologiae Cursus Completus, Series Latina, vol. 23. Paris: Migne, 1845. Cl. 0610.

———. "De exodo, in vigilia paschae." Pages 536-41 in *Opera, Part 2*. Corpus Christianorum, Series Latina, vol. 78. Edited by G. Morin. Turnhout, Belgium: Typographi Brepols Editores Pontificii, 1958. Cl. 0601.

———. "Dialogi contra Pelagianos libri iii." Corpus Christianorum, Series Latina, vol. 80. Edited by C. Moreschini. Turnhout, Belgium: Typograph: Brepols Editores Pontificii. Cl. 0615.

———. *Epistulae, Parts 1-3*. Edited by I. Hilberg. Corpus Scriptorum Ecclesiasticorum Latinorum, vols. 54, 55, 56. Austria: F. Tempsky; Leipzig, Germany: G. F. Freytag, 1910, 1912, 1918. Cl. 0620.

———. "Sermo de quadragesima." Pages 533-35 in *Opera, Part 2*. Edited by G. Morin. Corpus Christianorum, Series Latina, vol. 78. Turnhout, Belgium: Typographi Brepols Editores Pontificii, 1958. Cl. 0600.

———. "Tractatus in librum Psalmorum." Pages 3-352 in *Opera, Part 2*. Edited by G. Morin. Corpus Christianorum, Series Latina, vol. 78. Turnhout, Belgium: Typographi Brepols Editores Pontificii, 1958. Cl. 0592.

———. "Tractatus in Marci Evangelium." Pages 451-500 in *Opera omnia, Part 2*. Corpus Christianorum, Series Latina, vol. 78. Edited by G. Morin. Turnhout, Belgium: Typograph: Brepols Editores Pontificii, 1958. CL. 0594.

———. "Tractatuum in Psalmos series altera." Pages 355-446 in *Opera, Part 2*. Edited by G. Morin. Corpus Christianorum, Series Latina, vol. 78. Turnhout, Belgium: Typographi Brepols Editores Pontificii, 1958. Cl. 0593.

John Chrysostom. "Ad populam Antiochenum homiliae (De statuis)." Cols. 15-222 in *Opera omnia*. Patrologiae Cursus Completus, Series Graeca, vol. 49. Edited by J.-P. Migne. Paris: Migne, 1862. TLG 2062.024.

———. "Ad Theodorum." In *Jean Chrysostome: Á Theodore*. Edited by J. Dumortier. Sources chrétiennes, vol. 117. Paris: Cerf, 1966. TLG 2062.001.

———. "Adversus Judaeos [orationes 1-8]." Cols. 843-942 in *Opera omnia*. Patrologiae Cursus Completus, Series Graeca, vol. 48. Edited by J.-P. Migne. Paris: Migne, 1859. TLG 2062.021.

———. "Catecheses ad illuminandos 1-8 (series tertia)." Pages 108-260 in *Jean Chrysostome. Hait catéchèses baptismales*. 2nd ed. Sources chrétiennes, vol. 50. Paris: Cerf, 1970. TLG 2062.382.

———. "De paenitentia." Cols. 277-350 in *Opera omnia*. Patrologiae Cursus Completus, Series Graeca, vol. 49. Edited by J.-P. Migne. Paris: Migne, 1862. TLG 2062.027.

———. "De incomprehensibili Dei natura (Contra Anomoeos)." Pages 92-322 in *Jean Chrysostome. Sur l'incompréhensibilité de Dieu*. Edited by F. Cavallera, J. Danielou and R. Flaceliere. Sources chrétiennes, vol. 28. Paris: Cerf, 1951. TLG 2062.012.

———. "De sacerdotio (lib. 1-6)." Pages 60-362 in *Jean Chyrsostome. Sur le sacerdoce*. Edited by A.-M Malingrey. Sources chrétiennes, vol. 272. Paris: Cerf, 1980. TLG 2062.085, cf. TLG 2062.119.

———. "In Acta apostolorum [homiliae 1-55]." Cols. 13-384 in *Opera omnia*. Patrologiae Cursus Completus, Series Graeca, vol. 60. Edited by J.-P. Migne. Paris: Migne, 1862. TLG 2062.154.

———. "In epistulam i ad Corinthios [homiliae 1-44]." Cols. 9-382 in *Opera omnia*. Patrologiae Cursus Completus, Series Graeca, vol. 61. Edited by J.-P. Migne. Paris: Migne, 1859. TLG 2062.156.

———. "In epistulam ii ad Corinthios [homiliae 1-30]." Cols. 381-610 in *Opera omnia*. Patrologiae Cursus Completus, Series Graeca, vol. 61. Edited by J.-P. Migne. Paris: Migne, 1859. TLG 2062.157.

———. "In epistulam ad Hebraeos argumentum et homiliae." Cols. 9-236 in *Opera omnia*. Patrologiae Cursus Completus, Series Graeca, vol. 63. Edited by J.-P. Migne. Paris: Migne, 1860. TLG 2062.168.

———. "In epistulam ad Colossenses homiliae." Cols. 299-392 in *Opera omnia*. Patrologiae Cursus Completus, Series Graeca, vol. 62. Edited by J.-P. Migne. Paris: Migne, 1862. TLG 2062.161.

———. "In Genesim homiliae 1-67." Cols. 21-385, 385-580 in *Opera omnia*. Patrologiae Cursus Completus, Series Graeca, vols. 53, 54. Edited by J.-P. Migne. Paris: Migne, 1862. TLG 2062.112.

———. "In illud: Si esurierit inimicus." Cols. 171-86 in *Opera omnia*. Patrologiae Cursus Completus, Series Graeca, vol. 51. Edited by J.-P. Migne. Paris: Migne, 1859. TLG 2062.068.

———. "In Joannem [homiliae 1-88]." Cols. 23-482 in *Opera omnia*. Patrologiae Cursus Completus, Series Graeca, vol. 59. Edited by J.-P. Migne. Paris: Migne, 1859. TLG 2062.153.

———. "In Matthaeum [homiliae 1-90]." Cols. 13-472, 471-794 in Patrologiae Cursus Completus, Series Graeca, vols. 57, 58. Edited by J.-P. Migne. Paris: Migne, 1862. TLG 2062.152.

John of Damascus. "Expositio fidei." Pages 3-239 in *Die Schriften des Johannes von Damaskos*, vol. 2. Edited by B. Kotter. Patristische Texte und Studien, vol. 12. Berlin: De Gruyter, 1973. TLG 2934.004.

———. "Orationes de imaginibus tres." Pages 65-200 in *Die Schriften des Johannes von Damaskos*, vol. 3. Edited by B. Kotter. Patristische Texte und Studien, vol. 17. Berlin: De Gruyter, 1975. TLG 2934.005.

Justin Martyr. "Dialogus cum Tryphone." Pages 90-265 in *Die ältesten Apologeten*. Edited by E.J. Goodspeed. Göttingen: Vandenhoeck & Rupprecht, 1915. TLG 0645.003.

Lactantius. "Epitome divinarum institutionum." Pages 675-761 in *Sancti Lactanti, Opera*. Corpus Scriptorum Ecclesiasticorum Latinorum, vol. 19. Edited by S. Brandt Vienna: Hoelder-Pinchler-Tempsky, 1890. Cl. 0086.

Leo the Great. *Tractatus septem et nonaginta*. Edited by A. Chavasse. Corpus Christianorum, Series Latina, vols. 138, 138A. Turnhout, Belgium: Typographi Brepols Editores Pontificii, 1973. Cl. 1657.

Marius Victorinus. "Aduersus Arium." Pages 54-277 in *Marii Victorini opera*. Corpus Scriptorum Ecclesiasticorum Latinorum, vol. 83, pt. 1. Edited by P. Henry and P. Hadot. Vienna: Hoelder-Pinchler-Tempsky, 1971. Cl. 0095.

Martin of Braga. "De pascha." Pages 259-75 in *Martini episcopi Bracarensis opera omnia*. Edited by C.W. Barlow. New Haven: Yale University Press, 1950.

Maximus of Turin. "Collectio sermonum antiqua." Pages 1-364 in *Maximi episcopi Taurinensis sermones*. Edited by Almut Mutzenbecher. Corpus Christianorum, Series Latina, vol. 23. Turnhout, Belgium: Typographi Brepols Editores Pontificii, 1962. Cl. 0219a.

Methodius. "Convivium decem virginum." Cols. 27-220 in *Opera omnia*. Patrologiae Cursus Completus, Series Graeca, vol. 18. Edited by J.-P. Migne. Paris: Migne, 1857.

Nicetas. "De psalmodiae bono (de utilitate hymnorum)." Edited by C. Turner. *Journal of Theological Studies* 24 (1923): 225-52.

Novatian. "De cibis iudaicis." Pages 89-101 in *Opera*. Edited by G. F. Diercks. Corpus Christianorum, Series Latina, vol. 4. Turnhout, Belgium: Typographi Brepols Editores Pontificii, 1972. Cl. 0068.

———. "De Trinitate." Pages 11-78 in *Opera*. Edited by G. F. Diercks. Corpus Christianorum, Series

Latina, vol. 4. Turnhout, Belgium: Typographi Brepols Editores Pontificii, 1972. Cl. 0071.

Origen. "Commentarii in evangelium Joannis [lib. 1, 2, 4, 5, 6, 10, 13]." Pages 1:56-390, 2:128-580, 3:34-282 in *Origène. Commmentaire sur saint Jean*, 3 vols. Edited by C. Blanc. Sources chrétiennes, vols. 120, 157, 222. Paris: Cerf, 1966, 1970, 1975. TLG 2042.005.

———. "Commentarii in evangelium Joannis [lib. 19, 20, 28, 32]." Pages 298-480 in *Origenes Werke*, vol. 4. Edited by E. Preuschen. Die griechischen christlichen Schriftsteller, vol. 10. Leipzig: Hinrichs, 1903. TLG 2042.079.

———. "Commentarium in evangelium Matthaei [lib. 10-11]." Pages 140-386 in *Origène. Commentaire sur l'évangile selon Matthieu*, vol. 1. Edited by R. Girod. Sources chrétiennes, vol. 162. Paris: Cerf, 1970. TLG 2042.029.

———. "Commentarium in evangelium Matthaei [lib. 10-11]." Pages 69-703 in *Origenes Werke*, vol. 10, pts. 1, 2. Edited by E. Klostermann. Die griechischen christlichen Schriftsteller, vol. 40, pts. 1, 2. Leipzig: Teubner, 1935, 1937. TLG 2042.030.

———. "Contra Celsum." Pages 1:64-476, 2:14-434, 3:14-382, 4:14-352 in *Origène. Contre Celse*, 4 vols. Edited by M. Borret. Sources chrétiennes, vols. 132, 136, 147, 150. Paris: Cerf, 1967, 1968, 1969. TLG 2042.001.

———. "De oratione." Pages 297-403 in *Origenes Werke*, vol. 2. Edited by P. Koestchau. Die griechischen christlichen Schriftsteller, vol. 3. Leipzig: Hinrichs, 1899. TLG 2042.008.

———. "De principiis." Pages 462-560, 668-764 in *Origenes vier Bücher von den Prinzipien*. Edited by H. Görgemanns and H. Karpp. Darmstadt: Wissenschaftliche Buchgesellschaft, 1976. TLG 2042.002.

———. "Exhortatio ad martyrium." Pages 3-47 in *Origenes Werke*, vol. 1. Edited by P. Koetschau. Die griechischen christlichen Schriftsteller, vol. 2. Leipzig: Hinrichs, 1899. TLG 2042.007.

———. "Fragmenta in Lucam [in catenis]." Pages 227-336 in *Origenes Werke*, vol. 9. Edited by M. Rauer. Die griechischen christlichen Schriftsteller, vol. 35. Berlin: Akademie-Verlag, 1930. TLG 2042.017.

———. "Homiliae in Exodum." Pages 217-18, 221-30 in *Origenes Werke*, vol. 6. Edited by W. A. Baehrens. Die griechischen christlichen Schriftsteller, vol. 29. Leipzig: Teubner, 1920. TLG 2042.023.

———. "Homiliae in Genesim [fragmenta]." Pages 23-30 in *Origenes Werke*, vol. 6. Edited by W. A. Baehrens. Die griechischen christlichen Schriftsteller, vol. 29. Leipzig: Teubner, 1920. TLG 2042.022.

———. "Homiliae in Leviticum." Pages 332-34, 395, 402-7, 409-416 in *Origenes Werke*, vol. 6. Edited by W. A. Baehrens. Die griechischen christlichen Schriftsteller, vol. 29. Leipzig: Teubner, 1920. TLG 2042.024.

———. "Homiliae in Lucan." In *Origenes Werke*, vol. 9. 2nd ed. Edited by M. Rauer. Diegriechischen christlichen Schriftsteller, vol 49 (35). Berlin: Akademie-Verlag, 1959. TLG 2042.016.

———. "In Jeremiam [homiliae 12-20]." Pages 85-194 in *Origenes Werke*, vol. 3. Edited by E. Klostermann. Die griechischen christlichen Schriftsteller, vol. 6. Berlin: Akademie-Verlag, 1901. TLG 2042.021.

———. "In Numeros homiliae." Pages 3-285 in *Origenes Werke*, vol. 7. Edited by W. A. Baehrens. Die griechischen christlichen Schriftsteller, vol. 30. Leipzig: Teubner, 1921. Cl. 0198.

———. "Libri x in Canticum canticorum [fragmenta]." Pages 128-32 in *Origenes Werke*, vol. 8. Edited by W. A. Baehrens. Die griechischen christlichen Schriftsteller, vol. 33. Leipzig: Teubner, 1925. TLG 2042.026.

Pacian of Barcelona. "Letters." In *San Paciano. Obras*. Edited by Lisardo Rubio Fernandez. Barcelona: Universidad de Barcelona, 1958.

Paterius. "Liber de expositione Veteris ac Novi Testamenti." Cols. 683-1136 in *Sancti Paterii de diversis libris S. Gregorii Magni Concinnatus*. Patrologiae Cursus Completus, Series Latina 79, Edited by J.–P. Migne. Paris: Migne, 1862.

Paulinus of Nola. "Carmina." Pages 7-329 in *Sancti Paulinus Nolianii. Opera*. Edited by W. Hartel. Corpus Scriptorum Ecclesiasticorum Latinorum, vol. 30. Vienna: Hoelder-Pinchler-Tempsky, 1894. Cl. 0203.

Paulus Orosius. *Historiarum adversum paganos, libri vii*. 3 vols. Edited by H.-P. Arnavd-Lindet. Búde, 1990, 1991. Cl. 0571.

———. "Liber apologeticus contra Pelagianos." Pages 603-64 in *Sancti Paulus orosius. Opera*. Edited by C. Zangemeister. Corpus Scriptorum Ecclesiasticorum Latinorum, vol. 5. Vienna: Hoelder-Pinchler-Tempsky, 1882. Cl. 0572.

Peter Chrysologos. *Sermones*. Edited by A. Olivar. Corpus Christianorum, Series Latina, vols. 24, 24A, 24B. Turnhout, Belgium: Typographi Brepolis Editores Pontificii, 1975, 1981, 1982. Cl. 0227+.

Procopius of Gaza. "Catena in Octateuchum." Cols. 21-1220 in Patrologiae Cursus Completus, Series Graeca, vol. 87.1. Edited by J.-P. Migne. Paris: Migne, 1860. TLG 2598.001.

Prudentius. "Liber apotheosis." Pages 73-115 in *Opera*. Edited by M. P. Cunnigham. Corpus Christianorum, Series Latina, vol. 126. Turnhout, Belgium: Typographi Brepolis Editores Pontificii, 1966. Cl. 1439.

———. "Liber cathemerinon." Pages 3-72 in *Opera*. Edited by M. P. Cunnigham. Corpus Christianorum, Series Latina, vol. 126. Turnhout, Belgium: Typographi Brepolis Editores Pontificii, 1966. Cl. 1438.

Pseudo-Athanasius. "Oratio quarta contra Arianos." Pages 43-87 in *Die pseudoathanasianische 'IVte Rede gegen die Arianer' als 'κατὰ Ἀρειανῶν λόγος' ein Apollinarisgut*. Edited by A. Stegmann. Rottenburg: Bader, 1917. TLG 2035.117.

Pseudo-Clement of Rome. "Recognitiones (Rufinus)." Cols. 1201-1474 in *Opera omnia*. Patrologiae Cursus Completus, Series Graeca, vol. 1. Edited by J.-P. Migne. Paris: Migne, 1886.

Pseudo-Dionysius. "De caelesti hierarchia." Pages 70-225 in *Denys l'Aréopagite. La hiérarchie céleste*. Edited by R. Roques, G. Heil and M. de Gandillac. Sources chréiennes, vol. 58. Paris: Cerf, 1958 Repr. 1970. TLG 2798.001.

Pseudo-Macarius. "Homiliae spirituales 50." Pages 1-322 in *Die 50 geistlichen homilien des Makarios*. Edited by H. Dorries, E. Klostermann and M. Kroeger. Patristische Texte und Studien 4. Berlin: De Gruyter, 1964. TLG 2109.002.

Salvian. "Ad ecclesiam sive adversus avaritiam." *Ouvres*. Edited by G. Lagarrigue. Sources chrétiennes, vol. 220 (t.2). Paris: Cerf, 1975.

———. "De gubernatione Dei." Pages 96-527 in *Ouvres*, vol. 2. Edited by G. LaGarrigue. Sources chrétiennes, vol. 220. Paris: Cerf, 1975. Cl. 0485.

Symeon the New Theologian. *Catecheses, 1-5, 6-22*. Edited by B. Krivochéine and J. Paramelle. Sources chrétiennes, vols. 96, 104. Paris: Cerf, 1963-64.

Tertullian. "Adversus Judaeos." Pages 1339-96 in *Opera*. Edited by E. Kroymann. Corpus Christianorum, Series Latina, vol. 2. Turnhout, Belgium: Typographi Brepols Editores Pontificii, 1954. Cl. 0033 (M).

———. "Adversus Marcionem." Pages 441-726 in *Opera*. Edited by E. Kroymann. Corpus Christianorum, Series Latina, vol. 1. Turnhout, Belgium: Typographi Brepols Editores Pontificii, 1954. Cl. 0014.

————. "De baptismo." Pages 277-95 in *Opera*. Edited by J. G. P. Borleffs. Corpus Christianorum, Series Latina, vol. 1. Turnhout, Belgium: Typographi Brepols Editores Pontificii, 1954. Cl. 0008.

————. "De carne Christi." Pages 817-973 in *Opera*. Edited by E. Kroymann. Corpus Christianorum, Series Latina, vol. 2. Turnhout, Belgium: Typographi Brepols Editores Pontificii, 1954. Cl. 0018.

————. "De idolatria." Pages 1101–24 in *Opera*. Edited by A. Reifferscheid and G. Wissowa. Corpus Christianorum, Series Latina, vol. 2. Turnhout, Belgium: Typographi Brepols Editores Pontificii, 1954. Cl. 0023.

————. "De pudicitia." Pages 1281-330 in *Opera*. Edited by E. Dekkers. Corpus Christianorum, Series Latina, vol. 2. Turnhout, Belgium: Typographi Brepols Editores Pontificii, 1954. Cl. 0030.

————. "De resurrectione mortuorum." Pages 921-1012 in *Opera*. Edited by J. G. PH. Borleffs. Corpus Christianorum, Series Latina, vol. 2. Turnhout, Belgium: Typographi Brepols Editores Pontificii, 1954. Cl. 0019.

Theodoret of Cyr. "Eranistes." Pages 61-266 in *Theodoret of Cyrus. Eranistes*. Edited by G. H. Ettlinger. Oxford: Clarendon Press, 1975. TLG 4089.002.

————. "Quaestiones in Exodum/Numeros." Pages 100-152, 190-226 in *Theodoreti Cyrensis quaestiones in Octateuchum*. Edited by N. Fernández Marcos and A. Sáenz-Badillos. Textos y estudios "Cardenal Cisneros," vol. 17. Madrid: Poliglota Matritense, 1979. TLG 4089.022.

Vincent of Lérins. "Commonitorium." Pages 147-95 in *Foebadius*, et al. Edited by R. Demeulenaere. Corpus Christianorum, Series Latina, vol. 64. Turnhout, Belgium: Typographi Brepols Editores Pontificii, 1985. Cl. 0510.

Authors/Writings Index

Ambrose, xix, 4, 8, 12-14, 20-21, 23, 25, 28, 38, 41, 46, 48, 53, 57, 62, 65, 71, 77, 81-83, 87, 90, 92, 96, 105, 107, 110-11, 117, 121, 131, 137, 141, 143-45, 147, 151, 165, 189-90, 203, 205, 219, 226, 228, 232, 234, 240, 243-45, 249, 251, 256, 259, 272, 278, 282-84, 288-89, 298-99, 305-6, 309-10, 312, 315, 322-23, 326, 333, 335, 339-41

Aphrahat, 15, 335, 339, 341

Apostolic Constitutions. See Constitutions of the Holy Apostles

Athanasius, 63, 68, 112, 311, 323, 336

Augustine, xxi, xxvi-xxvii, xxix, 3-5, 7, 11, 13, 14, 16, 19, 21-25, 27-31, 33, 34-35, 37-39, 41-42, 44-45, 47, 51, 58-60, 63, 65, 67, 69, 72, 76, 80-82, 91, 94-95, 97-98, 101, 103-4, 106-9, 113, 116, 119-20, 135, 138, 141-43, 148-51, 155, 158, 168-69, 173, 179, 187, 189, 194, 203, 216-17, 219, 221, 224, 231, 235, 239, 242, 260, 281, 283-88, 290, 295-96, 303-4, 306, 315, 318, 331, 335-37

Basil the Great, 7, 35, 38, 59, 66, 73, 77, 147, 156, 198,

226, 230, 239, 279, 303, 321, 323, 326, 335

Bede, 58, 63, 72, 84, 96, 99, 105, 121, 124, 128-29, 132, 135-38, 157-59, 161, 164, 170, 175, 177, 179, 194-96, 198, 203, 237, 241

Caesarius of Arles, 1, 12, 14, 25, 30, 52, 63, 74, 80, 87, 90, 98, 101, 105, 118, 143, 154, 178, 186, 200-203, 224-25, 232, 234, 239, 243, 248, 301, 312, 326-27, 332

Cassian, John, 85, 107, 113, 117, 187, 216, 227, 286, 290, 300, 332

Cassiodorus, 1, 22, 26, 36, 43, 55, 71, 73, 86, 110, 141-42, 145, 181, 198, 228, 238, 285

Clement of Alexandria, 7, 11, 23, 40, 79, 89, 116-18, 140, 145, 148, 168, 176-78, 184, 188-89, 193, 197, 223, 287, 289, 297, 307-9, 312-14, 319, 325, 333-34

Clement of Rome, 77, 221, 295

Constitutions of the Holy Apostles, 82, 109

Cyprian, 27, 59, 68-69, 87, 174-75, 224, 228-29, 237

Cyril of Alexandria, xxii, 17, 62, 74, 99, 113, 131, 156, 230

Cyril of Jerusalem, 31, 61, 132, 148-49, 167, 172-73, 195, 218, 251, 281, 291, 306, 341

Didache, 276, 295

Ephrem the Syrian, 5, 10, 12-13, 19, 32, 41, 51, 76, 82, 122, 140-43, 155, 242, 288, 323

Eusebius, xxv, xxix, 12, 20, 35, 96, 103, 222, 246, 248, 273, 280

Evagrius, 14

Fulgentius, 22, 102, 284

Gregory the Great, xxii, 12, 72, 81, 92, 94, 107-8, 114, 122-24, 126, 130-31, 133-34, 143, 156, 159-60, 166, 169, 178, 189, 204, 231, 244, 255, 305

Gregory of Nazianzus, 3, 14, 16, 20, 38, 41, 54, 65, 67, 74, 91, 96-97, 120, 151, 192, 240, 242, 320

Gregory of Nyssa, 14, 76, 102, 150, 157, 220, 251, 283-84, 292, 313, 335, 341

Gregory Thaumaturgus, 311

Hilary of Poitiers, 10, 20, 282, 335

Irenaeus, xviii, xix, 321

Isaac of Nineveh, 124

Isidore of Seville, xxii, 44-46, 48-51, 53, 55, 63

Jerome, xix-xx, xxvi, xxix, 5, 12, 21, 32, 39, 48, 58-59, 61, 65, 69, 73, 80, 84, 90, 106, 110, 141, 144-45, 154, 164-65, 175, 178, 187, 189, 192, 219, 224, 235, 239, 247, 255, 262, 278, 293, 302, 305, 333

John Chrysostom, 5, 7, 23, 34, 59, 65, 69, 75, 81, 87, 92, 94, 105-6, 112, 114, 117-18, 122, 142, 145, 166, 184, 186, 191, 216, 220, 221-22, 226-27, 233, 248, 251, 256, 279, 283, 288, 334

John of Damascus, 14, 66, 126, 154, 182, 184, 278

Justin Martyr, xvii, 86, 92-93, 182, 241, 292

Lactantius, 248

Leo the Great, 133, 178, 248

Macarius, 165

Marius Victorinus, 150

Martin of Braga, 58, 60

Maximus of Turin, 61, 65, 72, 84, 89, 92, 148, 291, 307

Methodius, 4, 55, 125, 165

Nicetas of Remesiana, 331

Novation, 38, 85, 177

Origen, xix, xxi-xxii, xxv-xxx, 2-3, 12, 15, 19, 25, 27, 30-31, 37, 45, 52-53, 55, 60-62, 66, 70, 73, 76, 79, 82, 87-88, 91, 98-99, 102-3, 105, 112, 115, 119, 123-25, 128, 134-35, 141, 152, 156, 165, 168, 174, 177, 190, 192, 197, 203, 206, 217, 220, 224, 229, 236, 245, 250-51, 257, 263-71, 276-78, 280, 282, 291-92, 300, 304, 309, 313, 324-26, 331-32, 334

Pacian of Barcelona, 297

Paterius, xxii, 11, 35, 49, 110, 127-28, 151, 153, 163, 170-72, 180, 189, 210-15, 237, 248-49, 261, 273, 293, 299, 301, 313, 316-17, 331, 333, 336, 338-40

Paulinus, 75, 341

Paulus Orosius, 76, 340

Peter Chrysologus, 13, 39, 72, 82, 86, 121, 149, 259

Procopius of Gaza, xxiii, 252-54, 258, 272

Prudentius, 10

Pseudo-Athanasius, 20

Pseudo-Basil, 116, 317

Pseudo-Clement, 280

Pseudo-Cyril, 213

Pseudo-Dionysius, 29, 333

Pseudo-Macarius, 57, 70

Salvian the Presbyter, 146, 227, 232, 327

Symeon the New Theologian, 224

Tertullian, 19, 23, 25, 70, 83, 92, 112, 119, 130, 180, 183, 185, 200, 245, 251, 302

Theodoret of Cyr, xxiii, 161, 185, 207-9

Vincent of Lérins, 295

Subject Index

Aaron
  anointing of, 173
  blessing of, 174
  complaint of, 220
  genealogy of, 37
  and loaves, 196-97
  as Moses' spokesman, 29
  priesthood of, 41, 220,
    263, 291
  punishment of, 239
  selflessness of, 232
  as type of Christ, 167, 232,
    234
Abib, 70
Abraham, 15, 34, 98, 270-71
abundance. *See* prosperity
adoption, 31
adultery, 106-7, 107
affliction, 34, 335
alcohol, 175,
Alexandrian School, xxvii
allegory, xxiii-xxiv, xxviii
almond, 234
altar, 110, 129
Amalek, 91-93, 249
Amminadab, 205
ancient commentaries, xx-xxiii
angel(s), 32, 244, 333
angel of the Lord, 10-13, 74
animals, 193, 201, 311-12
anthropomorphism, xxx
Antichrist, 55, 339
Antiochene School, xxiii, xxvii
apostles, 195, 196
Aquila, 36
archaeology, xxix
Aristarchus of Samothrace,
  xxiv, xxv, xxvi
Aristophanes of Byzantium,
  xxiv
ark of the covenant, 123, 128,
  135
atonement, 135-36, 144-46
  day of, 135, 257
  Moses and, 144-45
  possibility of, 144
Balaam, 243-49

avarice of, 243
curse of, 243
and the magi, 248, 248-49
prophecy of, 245-46, 247-
  48, 248
and the Spirit, 245
spiritual state of, 251-52
temptation of, 259
Balaam's ass, 244-45
Balak, 243, 245
baptism
  and blessing, 200
  of children, 65
  and Christ, 72
  unto death, 272-73
  and faith, 237
  and grace, 246, 341
  and the law, 182
  prefigured by
    the flood, 182
    the laver, 132, 136
    the Red Sea, 3, 71, 76,
      80, 81, 182
  as purification, 65, 80, 153,
    184
  renewal in, 165
  as sacrament, 33
  sin after, 154, 183
  (mis)understanding of 81
  water and word of, 83-84
beauty, 156
benevolence, 312, 317
Bezalel, 157
birds, 164, 168, 333
bitter herbs, 61
blessing, 106
blindness, 323
blood
  of Christ, 59-60, 60
  plague of. *See* plagues,
    blood
  and salvation, 60, 63, 65,
    132, 223
body, 74
boils. *See* plague, boils
boundaries, 305-6
brass, 323
bread
  and Aaron, 196
  and Christ, 86
  loaves of, 195, 196
  meaning of, 60-61
  the true, 291
  and Word of God, 200
  See also manna
bronze serpent, 241-42
burning bush, 9-17
  and call of Moses, 13

Christ in, 23
God's power in, 10-11
and holy ground, 14
interpretation of, 13
and the mystery of God,
  12
prefiguration of
  crown of thorns, 11-12
  Holy Spirit, 12
  Mary, 14-15
and sandals, 13-14
turning to, 12-13
care, 118
Celsus, 112-13
census, 252
charity. *See* love
chastity, 130, 164
cherubim, 124
Christ (person). *See* Jesus
  Christ
Christ (title), 173
church
  assembly of, 291
  and the elect, 158
  foreshadowing of, 148
  fullness of, 339
  and the Gentiles, 219-20,
    224
  as God's garden, 332
  inviting others to, 118
  and the law, 92-93
  prefigured by
    ark of covenant, 123
    Noah's ark, 69
    Passover, 69
  and pride, 261
  second birth of, 213
  unity of, 68, 69
circumcision, 27, 31-33, 138,
  179, 252
cities of refuge, 112
cloud and fire, 72, 96
colors, 207
commandments, 189, 269
  first commandment, 102
  great commandment, 282-
    84
  See also, ten command-
    ments
compassion, 116
conquest, 308
contemplation, 211
correction, 305
covenant, xviii, 129, 195-96,
  280
covetousness. *See* greed
creation, 57, 66
cross

as an altar, 134
planks of, 239
prefigured by
  Aaron's staff, 234
  bronze serpent, 241,
    241-42
  Moses' staff, 5
sign of, 65, 65-66, 66, 92,
  93
cross-dressing, 313
crucifixion, 133-34, 147
curses, 321
darkness, 74, 148. *See also*
  plagues, darkness
Dathan and Abiram, 228, 230
David, 108
death. *See* plague, death
decalogue. *See* ten commandments
demons, 115, 116
desert. *See* wilderness
desire, 203
despoiling of the Egyptians.
  See Egyptians, despoiling of
destroyer. *See* angel of the Lord
devil, 25, 81, 91-92, 202
Deuteronomy, 276
dietary laws, 176-78, 297-98
disciples, 84, 131
discipleship, 159
divine economy. *See* God,
  economy of
divorce, 315-16
doctrine, 97
doubt, 337
drought, 323
Easter, 58
ecclesia, 172-73. *See also* church
Egypt(ians)
  abomination of, 48-49
  confusion of, 76
  Christ in, 246
  death of, 81-82
  deities of, 49
  despoiling of, 23-24, 25,
    54, 55, 56, 67
  evidence of, 76-77
  faithlessness of, 75
  as Gentiles, 314
  hardening of hearts of, 77
  magicians of 41-43, 47
  paganism of, 140
  as spiritual bondage, 3, 4,
    7, 59, 76, 80, 85
  as the world, 216
Eldad, 218
elders, 217, 332
Eleazar, 240